Deep Learning in Video and Image Processing: Challenges, Solutions, and Future Directions

Deep Learning in Video and Image Processing: Challenges, Solutions, and Future Directions

Guest Editors

Abdussalam Elhanashi
Sergio Saponara

MDPI

Basel • Beijing • Wuhan • Barcelona • Belgrade • Novi Sad • Cluj • Manchester

Guest Editors

Abdussalam Elhanashi
Department of
Information Engineering
University of Pisa
Pisa
Italy

Sergio Saponara
Department of
Information Engineering
University of Pisa
Pisa
Italy

Editorial Office
MDPI AG
Grosspeteranlage 5
4052 Basel, Switzerland

This is a reprint of the Special Issue, published open access by the journal *Electronics* (ISSN 2079-9292), freely accessible at: https://www.mdpi.com/journal/electronics/special_issues/NU6BN0LT1Z.

For citation purposes, cite each article independently as indicated on the article page online and as indicated below:

Lastname, A.A.; Lastname, B.B. Article Title. *Journal Name* **Year**, *Volume Number*, Page Range.

ISBN 978-3-7258-7034-9 (Hbk)
ISBN 978-3-7258-7035-6 (PDF)
https://doi.org/10.3390/books978-3-7258-7035-6

Contents

About the Editors

Abdussalam Elhanashi

Abdussalam Elhanashi is a Senior Researcher at the Università di Pisa, Italy, specializing in advanced applications of deep learning and video image processing. He holds an M.Sc. in Electronics and Electrical Engineering from the University of Glasgow, Scotland, and an MBA from the University of Nicosia, Cyprus. He earned his Ph.D. in Information Engineering from the Università di Pisa, Italy funded by a prestigious merit-based scholarship from the Islamic Development Bank (IsDB) as Libya's top candidate for 2019–2020. Dr. Elhanashi was ranked among Stanford University and Elsevier's World's Top 2% Scientists for 2025. He has authored and co-authored numerous scientific articles and academic books indexed in Scopus and the Web of Science. In 2021, he served as a Research Fellow at the University of Strathclyde, applying deep learning models to analyze CT scans and X-ray images for medical diagnostics. In 2022, he was a Visiting Researcher at Hiroshima University, Japan, focusing on advanced video analysis techniques. With over 16 years of industry experience, Dr. Elhanashi has successfully managed engineering projects, conducted system maintenance, and performed root cause analyses to address complex technical challenges. He is also a Developer at the Society for Imaging Informatics in Medicine (SIIM), USA. His research interests include real-world AI applications, lightweight model development, video surveillance, IoT-based low-cost embedded systems, AI-driven solutions for medical imaging, and efficient coding techniques for image and video processing systems.

Sergio Saponara

Sergio Saponara, Director of the Department of Information Engineering at the University of Pisa, IEEE Distinguished Lecturer, obtained his master's degree cum laude and Ph.D. in Electronic Engineering from the University of Pisa. In 2002, he was a Marie Curie Research Fellow at the Inter-university Microelectronics Center (IMEC) in Leuven, Belgium. He was also a post-graduate researcher at the National Research Council. Currently, he is a Full Professor of Electronics at the University of Pisa, where he teaches courses in Design of IoT Systems, Electronic Systems for Robotics, HW and Embedded Security for the master's degrees in Electronic Engineering, Robotics and Automation Engineering, and Cybersecurity. Additionally, he teaches Electronics at the Italian Naval Academy in Livorno. Prof. Saponara was President of the Bachelor's and master's programs in Electronic Engineering at the University of Pisa. He has co-authored 600 scientific articles indexed in Scopus and 20 patents. He is a Founding Member of the IoT CASS SiG and has been a Program Committee Member for over 100 international IEEE and SPIE conferences. He also serves as the Director of the summer school "Enabling Technologies for the Internet of Things (IoT)" and the specialization course "Automotive Electronics and Powertrain Electrification". He is also the Director of the Interuniversity Center for Automotive Research (UCAR).

Preface

This Reprint, titled "Deep Learning in Video and Image Processing: Challenges, Solutions, and Future Directions", addresses the rapid evolution of intelligent visual systems and their transformative impact across a wide range of application domains. It focuses on the integration of real-time machine learning with video processing and image processing, emphasizing deployment on resource-constrained devices. Its scope spans algorithm optimization, hardware–software co-design, and energy-efficient ML strategies that enable low-power computing and computational efficiency for latency-sensitive applications and real-time data processing in practical, real-world environments. The primary goal of this Reprint is to present state-of-the-art ML model deployment techniques that advance the design, evaluation, and implementation of edge AI for real-world ML applications. It addresses critical challenges such as energy consumption, memory limitations, latency requirements, and the computational complexity inherent in modern deep learning models. By highlighting innovative solutions—including lightweight architectures, model compression, and edge computing strategies—this Reprint demonstrates how smart cameras, wearable technology, smart home devices, and other edge AI systems can perform real-time diagnostics, object recognition, and anomaly detection efficiently while maintaining high reliability and data privacy. The motivation behind this work stems from the growing demand for localized processing and on-device intelligence in modern applications. While cloud-based solutions dominate much of the current research, there is an urgent need for real-time, on-device processing to enhance responsiveness, data privacy, and system robustness. This Reprint responds to this need by presenting high-quality contributions that offer scalable and deployable solutions for autonomous vehicles, urban traffic management, industrial automation, augmented reality, wildlife monitoring, disaster response systems, health monitoring, personalized feedback, and other emerging applications. This Reprint is primarily intended for researchers, graduate students, engineers, and industry practitioners working in artificial intelligence, computer vision, embedded systems, and real-time processing. It serves as a comprehensive reference for those seeking to design robust, efficient, and application-driven intelligent systems, combining energy-efficient ML, hardware–software co-design, and edge computing strategies to meet the constraints of resource-limited devices. By connecting theoretical advancements with practical deployment strategies, this work provides valuable insights into current capabilities and future directions for edge AI and real-time machine learning in video and image processing.

Abdussalam Elhanashi and Sergio Saponara
Guest Editors

electronics

MDPI

rticle

Adaptive Expert Selection for Crack Segmentation Using a Top-*K* Mixture-of-Experts Framework with Out-of-Fold Supervision

Ammar M. Okran [1,*], Hatem A. Rashwan [1], Sylvie Chambon [2] and Domenec Puig [1]

[1] Department of Computer Engineering and Mathematics, Rovira i Virgili University, 43007 Tarragona, Spain; hatem.abdellatif@urv.cat (H.A.R.); domenec.puig@urv.cat (D.P.)
[2] Institut de Recherche en Informatique de Toulouse (IRIT), 31000 Toulouse, France; sylvie.chambon@toulouse-inp.fr
* Correspondence: ammar.okran@urv.cat

Abstract

Cracks in civil infrastructure exhibit large variations in appearance due to differences in surface texture, illumination, and background clutter, making reliable segmentation a challenging task. To address this issue, this paper proposes an adaptive Mixture-of-Experts (MoE) framework that combines multiple crack segmentation models based on their estimated reliability for each input image. A lightweight gating network is trained using out-of-fold soft supervision to learn how to rank and select the most suitable experts under varying conditions. During inference, only the top two experts are combined to produce the final segmentation result. The proposed framework is evaluated on two public datasets—Crack500 and the CrackForest Dataset (CFD)—and one in-house dataset (RCFD). Experimental results demonstrate consistent improvements over individual models and recent state-of-the-art methods, achieving up to 2.4% higher IoU and 2.1% higher F1-score compared to the strongest single expert. These results show that adaptive expert selection provides an effective and practical solution for robust crack segmentation across diverse real-world scenarios.

Keywords: crack segmentation; deep learning; mixture of experts; soft labels; adaptive gating network; ensemble learning

1. Introduction

Cracks in pavements, bridges and other infrastructure are often the first warning signs of material fatigue and structural weakness. If neglected, small fissures can quickly grow into major defects, reduce service life and drive up repair costs [1]. In real-world environments, however, cracks appear under diverse lighting conditions, on a range of surface textures, and in a variety of shapes—making reliable automated detection challenging [2]. Traditionally, inspection has relied on manual visual assessment, which is slow, costly, and subjective. Moreover, many regions—such as bridge undersides or high concrete facades—are difficult to access, limiting the reliability of human inspection [3].

Early attempts at automating crack detection employed traditional image-processing techniques, including edge detection, thresholding, and morphological filtering. Although effective for simple cases, these methods required manual tuning and were highly sensitive to shadows, stains and background textures [4]. To improve robustness, traditional machine-learning approaches were introduced. Methods based on Support Vector Machines [5] (SVMs), Random Forests [6], and handcrafted feature descriptors such as

Gabor filters or Local Binary Patterns provided more stability than pure image processing. However, they still depended on manually engineered features and struggled when confronted with the wide variation present in real infrastructure images [7].

In recent years, deep learning has become the dominant approach for crack analysis, enabling end-to-end feature learning directly from data. Convolutional neural networks (CNNs) have achieved notable progress in pixel-level localization and background separation [4,8,9]. However, CNNs have limited receptive fields, which restrict their ability to capture long, discontinuous cracks or contextual dependencies [10]. Transformer-based architectures address this limitation through self-attention, enabling the modeling of global context, but they typically require large, annotated datasets and high computational resources [11]. Since most crack datasets are small and contain diverse surface patterns, transformers often struggle to generalize across different environments.

To enhance generalization, several hybrid CNN–Transformer approaches have been proposed. For instance, the Parallel Convolutional and Transformer Crack Network (PCTC-Net) fuses convolutional and transformer encoders to balance local and global representations, outperforming DTrC-Net [12] on DeepCrack, Crack500, and CrackSeg9k [11]. Similarly, MSP U-Net [13] integrates multi-scale attention to improve segmentation in low-resolution images, achieving higher precision and recall across multiple datasets. Despite these advances, no single architecture consistently performs best under all conditions. Crack characteristics vary significantly with lighting, material properties, acquisition devices, and crack types, leading different models to exhibit complementary strengths and weaknesses. Cross-dataset evaluations further confirm that models trained on one dataset often suffer substantial performance degradation when tested on another [14].

Motivated by this observation, this work adopts a different perspective: instead of pursuing a single universally optimal architecture, it explicitly exploits model complementarity through an adaptive Mixture-of-Experts (MoE) framework for crack segmentation.

Mixture-of-Experts (MoE) frameworks provide a principled mechanism for combining multiple specialized networks within a single predictive system. An MoE architecture consists of a set of expert models and a gating network that learns to assign each input to the most suitable experts, after which the selected predictions are combined—typically through weighted averaging. Recent studies have demonstrated the effectiveness of MoE designs in visual tasks [15]. In medical image analysis, SAM-Med3D-MoE [16] integrates multiple task-specific models with a foundation segmentation network. The Mixture-of-Shape-Experts [17] (MoSE) framework introduces sparse expert activation to improve generalization. Recent surveys further confirm the growing relevance of MoE systems in computer vision [18].

In the context of crack segmentation, however, the MoE paradigm remains largely unexplored. Most existing approaches rely on a single model trained on all data, implicitly assuming uniform suitability across diverse crack appearances and environments.

This work introduces a Mixture-of-Experts framework for crack segmentation that adaptively combines four complementary expert models using a lightweight ResNet-18 gating network trained with soft supervision. An out-of-fold validation strategy is employed to obtain unbiased performance estimates for each expert at the sample level. These estimates are normalized to form soft supervision targets that reflect the relative reliability of the experts during training. At inference time, the gating network ranks the experts for each input image, and the predictions of the top two models are selectively fused to produce the final segmentation mask.

The proposed framework is evaluated on two public datasets—Crack500 and the CrackForest Dataset (CFD)—as well as an in-house full-scene dataset (RCFD). Experimental results demonstrate that the Top-K MoE consistently outperforms the strongest individual

https://doi.org/10.3390/electronics15020407

expert, achieving improvements of up to approximately 2.5 percentage points in mean Intersection-over-Union while capturing most of the potential performance gain indicated by the oracle upper bound.

By selecting experts on a per-image basis, the proposed framework adapts to variations in crack appearance and imaging conditions, providing a flexible alternative to single-network models and fixed ensemble averaging.

With this motivation in place, the main contributions of this study can be clearly summarized as follows:

- An adaptive Mixture-of-Experts framework for crack segmentation is proposed, in which multiple complementary expert models are selectively combined through a lightweight gating network based on sample-specific reliability estimation.
- An out-of-fold soft supervision strategy together with a Top-K aggregation mechanism is introduced to train and deploy the gating network, enabling stable expert routing and robust prediction fusion without requiring additional annotations or modifications to the expert architectures.
- Extensive experiments are conducted on three benchmark datasets, demonstrating consistent improvements over individual experts and recent state-of-the-art methods while maintaining a favorable balance between segmentation accuracy and computational cost.

The rest of this paper is organized as follows: Section 2 reviews related work. Section 3 details the proposed framework, including the expert models, gating network, and training strategy. Section 4 describes the datasets and training setup. Section 5 presents experimental results and analysis. Finally, Section 6 concludes the paper and outlines possible directions for future work.

2. Related Work

Crack detection and segmentation have progressed through several distinct stages, evolving from early handcrafted image-processing techniques to today's deep learning-driven models. This section provides an overview of this progression, covering traditional image processing and classical machine learning (ML) approaches, followed by CNN-based architectures, transformer and hybrid models, and recent efforts toward Mixture-of-Experts (MoE) frameworks. Beyond summarizing prior work, particular emphasis is placed on analyzing the practical limitations of existing approaches in order to motivate the methodology proposed in this study.

2.1. *Traditional Image Processing and Classical Machine Learning*

Early crack detection systems were built on hand-crafted image processing techniques such as Canny and Sobel edge detectors [19,20], and global thresholding methods like Otsu segmentation [21]. While these approaches could identify simple crack patterns, they were highly sensitive to lighting variations, shadows, and background textures, limiting their robustness in real-world scenarios.

Classical ML pipelines attempted to improve robustness by pairing handcrafted features with SVMs, boosting, or random forests. Examples include CrackTree [22] and the methods of Oliveira and Correia [5], which relied on manually engineered descriptors to classify crack pixels. Despite modest gains, these techniques remained dependent on predefined features and struggled to generalize across diverse crack appearances and imaging conditions, motivating the shift toward deep-learning-based solutions.

https://doi.org/10.3390/electronics15020407

2.2. Deep Learning with Convolutional Neural Networks

With the introduction of U-Net [23], CNNs became the dominant paradigm in crack segmentation. U-Net's encoder–decoder architecture enabled end-to-end learning and inspired numerous variants tailored to infrastructure inspection tasks.

DeepCrack [4] proposed hierarchical feature learning to improve the detection of thin and discontinuous cracks, while lightweight models such as MobileNetV3 [24] were adapted to reduce computational cost. More recent CNN-based architectures introduced refinement-driven or multi-decoder designs, including LMM [25], Efficient CrackMaster [9], and CrackRefineNet [26], achieving strong segmentation performance.

Despite their effectiveness, CNN-based models are inherently limited by local convolutional receptive fields, which restrict their ability to capture long-range contextual dependencies. As a result, their performance may degrade when dealing with large-scale crack continuity, cluttered backgrounds, or complex surface textures that require broader contextual reasoning.

2.3. Transformer-Based and Hybrid Architectures

Vision Transformers introduced self-attention mechanisms capable of modeling global spatial relationships. Swin Transformer [27] demonstrated that hierarchical attention with shifted windows can achieve competitive segmentation performance, while MobileViT [28] explored integrating transformer blocks into lightweight CNN backbones.

Building on these advances, several transformer-based and hybrid architectures have been proposed for crack segmentation. CrackFormer [29] leveraged multi-scale global attention to enhance crack continuity, whereas EfficientCrackNet [30] and MSDCrack [31] employed dual-encoder designs and multi-stage supervision. Hybrid-Segmentor [32] further combined convolutional and transformer representations to improve fine-grained boundary detection.

Although these models demonstrate promising results, they introduce notable practical challenges. Transformer-based and hybrid architectures are typically more computationally demanding and architecturally complex, which can hinder deployment in resource-constrained or real-time inspection settings. Moreover, transformer components often require large and diverse training datasets to generalize effectively, whereas most crack datasets remain relatively small, imbalanced, and domain-specific. Consequently, these models do not consistently outperform well-designed CNN architectures across different datasets and environmental conditions, and their performance can vary substantially depending on scene characteristics.

2.4. Mixture-of-Experts Frameworks

Mixture-of-Experts (MoE) frameworks combine multiple specialized models through a learnable gating mechanism that selects or weights experts based on the input. MoE strategies have demonstrated strong potential in medical image segmentation, where frameworks such as MoSE [17] and SAM-Med3D-MoE [16] show that integrating task-specific models can significantly improve robustness and generalization.

MoE designs typically employ either hard gating, which assigns each input to a single expert, or soft/probabilistic gating, which distributes weights across multiple experts. Hard gating can be brittle when expert competencies overlap or routing decisions are uncertain, whereas soft gating enables smoother aggregation and more effective use of complementary information.

In the context of crack segmentation, however, MoE frameworks remain largely unexplored. Most existing approaches rely on a single architecture trained on all available data, implicitly assuming uniform suitability across diverse crack appearances, surface materials,

https://doi.org/10.3390/electronics15020407

and imaging conditions. This assumption is frequently violated in practice, as different models tend to specialize in different crack patterns and environments. Furthermore, MoE variants explored in related domains often rely on hard or one-hot routing strategies that discard useful complementary information from non-selected experts.

These observations reveal a clear gap in the literature: while crack segmentation models continue to increase in architectural complexity, limited attention has been paid to adaptive model selection mechanisms that explicitly exploit expert complementarity. This gap motivates the present work, which introduces an adaptive Top-*K* Mixture-of-Experts framework with soft-label supervision and out-of-fold validation to dynamically combine the strengths of multiple segmentation experts, rather than relying on a single fixed architecture.

3. Methodology

This section presents the proposed Mixture-of-Experts (MoE) crack segmentation framework. A high-level schematic of the overall protocol is illustrated in Figure 1, while a detailed architectural overview is provided in Figure 2. The section is organized as follows. First, the four expert models previously developed are summarized. Second, the construction of a non-leaky out-of-fold (OOF) dataset is described, where each expert is trained in a five-fold manner to generate unbiased predictions for supervision. Third, the consolidation of these predictions into hard and soft routing targets is detailed. Fourth, a lightweight ResNet-18 [33] gating network is introduced to estimate the relative suitability of each expert for a given input image. Fifth, the MoE mixing strategies—Hard routing, Soft weighting, and the proposed Top-2 weighted aggregation—are defined. Finally, the training configurations and loss functions associated with each component are presented.

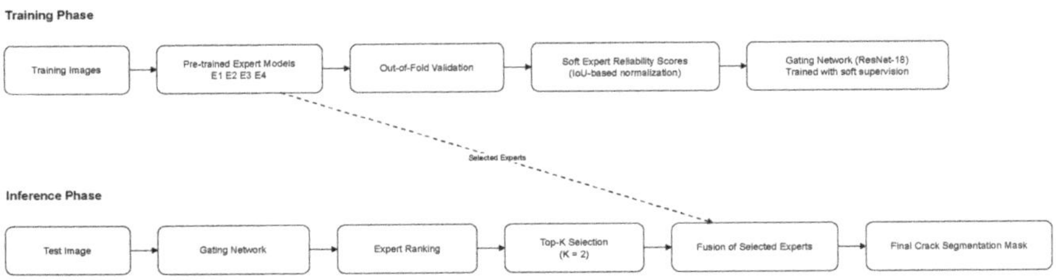

Figure 1. Schematic overview of the proposed Mixture-of-Experts framework. During training, multiple expert models are evaluated using an out-of-fold strategy to compute sample-wise performance scores, which are normalized into soft supervision targets for training the gating network. During inference, the gating network ranks experts for each input image, and the predictions of the Top-*K* selected experts are fused to produce the final crack segmentation mask.

3.1. Experts (4 Models)

The proposed MoE framework builds on four previously published crack-segmentation models, which serve as fixed experts. These models are used strictly in inference mode; no fine-tuning or architectural modifications are applied. The expert set includes:

- E1 (CEN'23)—Cascade Enhanced Network [34].
- E2 (ECSN'24)—Enhanced Crack Segmentation Network [35].
- E3 (CM'25)—CrackMaster [9].
- E4 (CR'25)—CrackRefineNet [26].

These four experts were selected to maximize architectural and functional diversity. Each model emphasizes different design principles—such as cascaded feature refinement, enhanced encoder–decoder pathways, or multi-stage contextual aggregation—resulting in complementary strengths and distinct error patterns. This diversity is essential for enabling

https://doi.org/10.3390/electronics15020407

the gating network to learn meaningful routing decisions and leverage the most suitable experts for each input image.

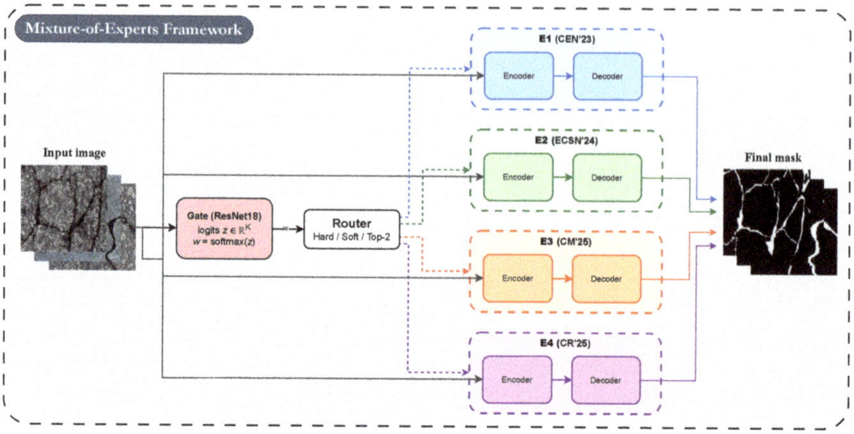

Figure 2. Overview of the proposed Mixture-of-Experts (MoE) framework for crack segmentation. Four pre-trained expert models independently predict crack probability maps. A lightweight ResNet-18 gating network, trained using soft out-of-fold supervision, assigns a reliability score to each expert for every input image, denoted by weights w. During inference, the gate selects the Top-2 experts and combines their outputs through a Top-2 Weighted Aggregation strategy to produce the final segmentation mask. Hard and soft routing variants are also supported.

Although the selected experts originate from our prior work, they were chosen to reflect distinct architectural paradigms and complementary prediction behaviors. Importantly, the proposed Mixture-of-Experts framework is model-agnostic and can seamlessly incorporate external CNN- or Transformer-based crack segmentation models without architectural modification.

3.2. Dataset Creation via Out-of-Fold Annotation ($K = 5$)

To supervise the gating network without introducing data leakage, a non-leaky out-of-fold (OOF) annotation strategy is adopted. The training set is divided into five folds. For each fold k, all expert models are trained on the remaining four folds using short training schedules with frozen backbones, and inference is performed on the held-out fold. This yields per-image IoU scores for every expert on data that was never used during that expert's training. After all five iterations, the fold-wise predictions are concatenated into a complete OOF table that provides an unbiased estimate of each expert's relative quality on each sample. This OOF supervision serves as the training signal for the gating network. The overall OOF generation procedure is illustrated in Figure 3.

$$\mathrm{OOF}(x_i, e_j) = \mathrm{IoU}\left(f_{e_j}^{(k)}(x_i), y_i\right), \tag{1}$$

where x_i is the i-th training image, y_i is its corresponding ground-truth mask, and e_j indexes the j-th expert model. The function $f_{e_j}^{(k)}(\cdot)$ denotes the instance of expert j trained on all folds except fold k, i.e., the model used to infer predictions on images belonging to the held-out fold k. The operator $\mathrm{IoU}(\cdot,\cdot)$ computes the intersection-over-union between the predicted mask and the ground truth. Thus, $\mathrm{OOF}(x_i, e_j)$ represents the unbiased quality estimate of expert j on sample x_i, obtained using a model that has never been trained on that sample.

https://doi.org/10.3390/electronics15020407

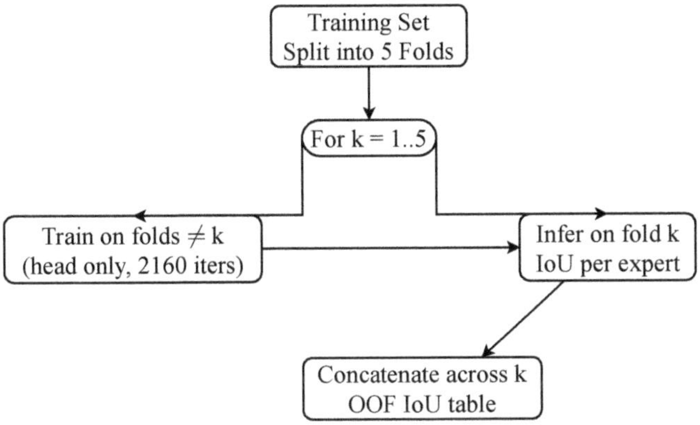

Figure 3. OOF dataset creation using five-fold partitioning. For each fold k, experts are trained on the remaining four folds with frozen backbones (head only, 2160 iterations) and infer on the held-out fold. Concatenating IoU scores across k yields a non-leaky expert IoU table used to supervise the gate.

3.3. Label Consolidation: Hard and Soft

The OOF IoU matrix provides, for every training sample, a vector containing the relative performance of the 4 experts. These values are transformed into routing targets that supervise the gating network. Two complementary supervision modes are used: hard labels and soft labels.

3.3.1. Hard Labels

In the hard-label formulation, each image is assigned to the single expert that achieved the highest OOF IoU. This yields a standard one-hot target, instructing the gate to select exactly one expert during training. Formally,

$$\ell^{\text{hard}}(x_i) = \arg \max_{j \in 1,\ldots,4} ;\text{OOF}(x_i, e_j), \tag{2}$$

where $\ell^{\text{hard}}(x_i)$ is the index of the best-performing expert for image x_i.

3.3.2. Soft Labels

Hard labels enforce a single-winner decision and ignore cases where multiple experts perform similarly. To preserve this information, a soft-label formulation is used in which the OOF IoU scores are normalized into a probability distribution. Each expert thus receives a weight proportional to its relative quality, allowing the gate to learn finer distinctions and exploit complementary strengths among experts:

$$\ell^{\text{soft}}(x_i, e_j) = \frac{\text{OOF}(x_i, e_j)}{\sum_{m=1}^{4} \text{OOF}(x_i, e_m)}, \tag{3}$$

where $\ell^{\text{soft}}(x_i, e_j)$ denotes the normalized reliability of expert e_j for sample x_i.

This dual-target setup enables a direct comparison between categorical (hard) supervision and probabilistic (soft) supervision. As shown in the experimental section, the soft-label formulation yields more stable routing behavior and consistently improves Top-K aggregation performance.

In this work, IoU is adopted to derive soft routing labels because it provides a balanced, single-valued summary of segmentation quality that jointly reflects false positives and false negatives, making it well suited for expert ranking and normalization. While precision and recall are particularly informative for thin crack structures, IoU implicitly integrates both

https://doi.org/10.3390/electronics15020407

aspects and avoids introducing metric-specific bias into the supervision signal. Moreover, using a single, consistent metric simplifies optimization and improves training stability of the gating network. Incorporating multi-metric or structure-aware routing targets is a promising extension and is left for future investigation.

An illustrative example of the conversion from OOF IoUs to hard and soft routing targets is provided in Table 1.

Table 1. Example of hard and soft label construction from OOF IoUs.

Image	E1 (CEN'23)	E2 (ECSN'24)	E3 (CM'25)	E4 (CR'25)	Hard	Soft Target
img_001	0.66	0.71	0.63	0.72	E4 (CR'25)	[0.24, 0.26, 0.23, 0.27]
img_002	0.58	0.61	0.60	0.59	E2 (ECSN'24)	[0.24, 0.25, 0.25, 0.24]

3.4. Gate Network

The gating network determines how much each expert should contribute to the final segmentation output for a given input. As illustrated in Figure 2, the gate operates independently from the experts: it receives only the RGB image and does not use any internal features or predictions from the expert models. This design ensures that expert selection remains lightweight, modular, and decoupled from the architectures of the experts.

A ResNet-18 backbone [33] is adopted as the gate due to its favorable trade-off between accuracy and computational cost, strong generalization on medium-scale datasets, and stable optimization behavior. The standard classification head is replaced with a compact multi-layer perceptron (MLP) that produces one logit per expert. All expert models are kept frozen at inference and during gate training; only the gate parameters are updated.

The gating network intentionally operates on raw RGB images rather than crack-local or expert-derived features. This choice reflects the role of the gate as a routing mechanism rather than a segmentation module. Global scene characteristics—such as illumination conditions, surface texture complexity, background clutter, and crack density—are often sufficient to estimate which expert is more reliable for a given input. Local crack responses, by contrast, are already modeled within the expert networks themselves and may introduce expert-specific bias if reused by the gate. By remaining feature-agnostic and fully decoupled from the experts, the gating network avoids information leakage, preserves modularity, and maintains robustness across heterogeneous expert architectures.

The unnormalized logits z output by the gate are transformed into routing weights w through a softmax function:

$$w = \mathrm{softmax}(z), \tag{4}$$

where w represents the normalized contribution of each expert and forms the basis for the Soft, Hard, and Top-K aggregation strategies described later.

3.5. MoE Mixing Strategies

Once the gate produces a weight vector $w_j(x)$ for the input image x, these routing weights are used to combine the predictions of the frozen experts $\hat{y}_j(x)$. Three aggregation strategies are considered in this work.

3.5.1. Hard Mixture

Only the single most likely expert is selected. The final mask equals the prediction of the expert with the highest routing weight:

$$j^\star = \arg\max_j w_j(x), \qquad \hat{y}_{\mathrm{hard}}(x) = \hat{y}_{j^\star}(x). \tag{5}$$

https://doi.org/10.3390/electronics15020407

3.5.2. Soft Mixture

All experts contribute to the final prediction. Their outputs are combined through a weighted sum using the gate probabilities:

$$\hat{y}_{\text{soft}}(x) = \sum_{j=1}^{4} w_j(x)\,\hat{y}_j(x). \tag{6}$$

3.5.3. Top-*K* Mixture (*K* = 2)

Here, the gate selects the *K* highest–scoring experts. Their weights are renormalized over this subset and used for selective fusion:

$$\hat{y}_{\text{top-K}}(x) = \sum_{j\in\mathcal{T}_K(x)} \frac{w_j(x)}{\sum_{m\in\mathcal{T}_K(x)} w_m(x)}\,\hat{y}_j(x), \tag{7}$$

where $\mathcal{T}_K(x)$ denotes the index set of the Top-*K* experts for sample x.

The choice of $K = 2$ reflects a trade-off between exploiting expert complementarity and maintaining computational efficiency. In practice, selecting the top two experts captures most of the potential performance gain, while reducing the risk of fusing predictions from lower-ranked experts that may share similar failure modes. Although the optimal number of experts may vary across input images, the proposed gating network performs sample-dependent ranking, allowing dominant experts to contribute more strongly when appropriate. Extending the framework to support adaptive or input-dependent *K* selection could be explored in future work.

In summary, the gate predicts the routing weights, the router applies one of the three selection strategies, and the chosen experts are fused to form the final segmentation mask, as illustrated in Figure 2.

3.6. Training Strategy

This subsection describes the training procedure of the proposed Mixture-of-Experts framework, including the preparation of the expert models, the supervision strategy used for training the gating network, and the loss functions adopted under hard and soft labeling schemes. The overall objective is to learn a reliable gating mechanism that can effectively select and combine complementary experts for robust crack segmentation.

3.6.1. Experts

Each expert model was originally trained in its respective publication. For datasets not covered in prior work, the experts were retrained using their original configurations to ensure a fair and consistent comparison. During the OOF procedure, the expert backbones are frozen and only their decoder heads are briefly fine–tuned for 2160 iterations per fold. These short training cycles are used exclusively to generate fold–wise predictions for constructing the OOF supervision table; they do not modify the experts used at inference.

3.6.2. Gate

Two versions of the gating network are trained: one supervised with hard labels and one with soft labels derived from the OOF table. The gate receives only the RGB image and outputs a four–dimensional logit vector representing the predicted weights for the experts. All expert parameters remain frozen throughout training. At inference, the trained gate is paired with one of the three mixture strategies (Soft, Hard, or Top-*K*) described in Section 3.5.

https://doi.org/10.3390/electronics15020407

3.6.3. Loss Functions

When the gate is trained with hard labels, standard cross–entropy loss is used:

$$\mathcal{L}_{\text{hard}} = \text{CE}(w(x), y_{\text{hard}}(x)). \quad (8)$$

For soft-label supervision, the gate is trained using the Kullback–Leibler divergence, allowing it to learn graded preferences across experts:

$$\mathcal{L}_{\text{soft}} = \text{KL}(y_{\text{soft}}(x) \parallel w(x)). \quad (9)$$

4. Datasets and Experimental Setup

This section presents the datasets used to evaluate the proposed framework, along with the data augmentation strategies employed during training. It also outlines the implementation details of the training setup and describes the evaluation metrics used to assess segmentation performance across tasks.

4.1. Datasets

The evaluation of the proposed MoE framework is carried out on three crack segmentation datasets: one in–house dataset (RCFD) and two public datasets (Crack500 and CFD). These datasets exhibit considerable variation in imaging conditions, crack morphology, background texture, and scene complexity. This variation provides a comprehensive basis for assessing robustness and generalization. All images are resized to 512 × 512 pixel to ensure a consistent input format during training and inference. Representative samples from the three datasets are shown in Figure 4, and dataset statistics are reported in Table 2.

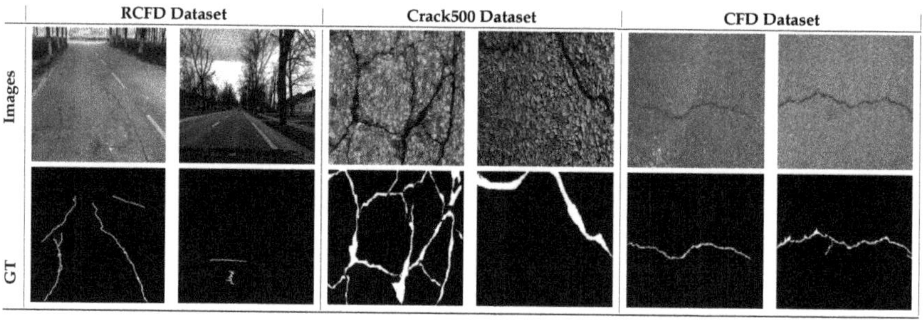

Figure 4. Sample images from the RCFD, Crack500, and CFD datasets. For each dataset, the first row shows the original images, and the second row shows the strong pixel-level ground truth annotations.

Table 2. Details of the crack segmentation datasets used in the experiments.

Dataset	Image Resolution	Training Set	Validation Set	Test Set
RCFD (in-house) [26,36]	512 × 512	973	170	285
Crack500 [20]	512 × 512	1896	348	1124
CFD [6]	512 × 512	101	–	18

- RCFD (In-house) [26,36]: RCFD is constructed from multi-country road scenes derived from the RDD2022 [37] dataset. The dataset comprises 1428 RGB full-scene images and is split into 973/170/285 images for training, validation, and testing, respectively.
- Crack500 [20]: Crack500 consists of 3368 images with manually annotated binary masks. It covers diverse camera viewpoints, surface materials, and illumination conditions. The dataset includes 1896 training images, 348 validation images, and 1124 test images.

https://doi.org/10.3390/electronics15020407

- CFD [6]: The CrackForest Dataset contains 119 images with pixel-level crack annotations. Although smaller in scale, CFD covers a broad variety of pavement textures. Following the standard split, 101 images are used for training and 18 images are used for testing.

4.2. Data Augmentation

Only the gating network is trained in this work; all expert models remain frozen. During gate optimization, moderate appearance augmentations are applied to the RGB images, while the target supervision (OOF IoU vectors) remains unchanged. The following stochastic transformations are used: colour jittering (brightness/contrast/saturation/hue), random grayscale conversion, horizontal and vertical flips, small random rotations ($\pm 7°$), and Gaussian blur. Each augmented image is subsequently normalized using ImageNet statistics.

At test time, only resizing and normalization are applied, without any augmentation.

4.3. Implementation Details

The gate network is trained using the AdamW optimizer with a learning rate of 1×10^{-4} and weight decay of 1×10^{-4}. A batch size of 16 is used, and training runs for 50 epochs. A cosine learning rate schedule with linear warmup is applied. The backbone is kept frozen during the first five epochs and is then unfrozen for the remaining epochs. Early stopping is used with a patience of 7 epochs. All experiments are executed on a computer running Windows 10 Pro, equipped with an Intel Core i7-9700K CPU (64-bit, 3.60 GHz), 64 GB of RAM, and a single NVIDIA GeForce RTX 3090 GPU (24 GB).

4.4. Evaluation Metrics

Segmentation performance is assessed using pixel–wise metrics computed between the predicted mask $\hat{Y}$ and the ground truth Y. The metrics used are Intersection over Union (IoU), Precision, Recall, F1–score, and mean IoU (mIoU).

$$\text{IoU} = \frac{TP}{TP + FP + FN}, \tag{10}$$

$$\text{Recall} = \frac{TP}{TP + FN}, \qquad \text{Precision} = \frac{TP}{TP + FP}, \tag{11}$$

$$\text{F1} = \frac{2\,\text{Precision} \cdot \text{Recall}}{\text{Precision} + \text{Recall}}, \tag{12}$$

$$\text{mIoU} = \frac{1}{C} \sum_{c=1}^{C} \frac{TP_c}{TP_c + FP_c + FN_c}. \tag{13}$$

In this work $C = 2$ (crack vs. background), therefore mIoU is the average IoU across both classes.

5. Experimental Results and Discussion

This section presents the experimental evaluation of the proposed MoE framework on the three datasets introduced in Section 4.1. All experiments follow the same preprocessing and training settings, and segmentation performance is measured using the metrics defined in Section 4.4.

The analysis is organized into four parts. First, the MoE configurations are compared with their constituent expert models to assess the benefit of routing-based aggregation. Second, an ablation study investigates the influence of different supervision and aggregation strategies (Hard, Soft, and Top-K) on performance. Third, the best-performing configuration is benchmarked against recent state-of-the-art crack segmentation methods to evaluate its external competitiveness. Finally, a qualitative analysis illustrates representative visual

https://doi.org/10.3390/electronics15020407

results, highlighting the improvements achieved in crack continuity, boundary precision, and robustness across datasets.

Together, these experiments provide a comprehensive understanding of both the internal effectiveness and real-world generalization capability of the proposed approach.

5.1. Comparison Against Individual Experts

The first set of experiments examines whether routing–based aggregation provides a measurable improvement over using any single expert model in isolation. For each dataset, the MoE outputs are generated using the trained gate, while the expert baselines correspond to direct inference of each expert without routing. All models are evaluated on the same held-out test sets, under identical preprocessing and input resolution. Performance differences therefore arise exclusively from the routing mechanism rather than differences in training data, annotation, or optimization pipelines.

As shown in Table 3, the proposed Mixture-of-Experts (MoE) consistently surpasses all individual experts across the three datasets. The improvement is especially notable on RCFD, where the scene diversity and illumination changes make segmentation particularly challenging. Among the routing strategies, the Top-K configuration achieves the best overall performance, outperforming the strongest individual expert (E4, CR'25) by approximately 1.5–2.5 percentage points in IoU and F1-score. The Soft variant also delivers strong and stable results, slightly below Top-K, while the Hard routing baseline performs the weakest due to its limited flexibility. These findings confirm that adaptive multi-expert fusion guided by soft-supervised gating provides superior generalization and robustness under diverse real-world conditions.

Table 3. Performance comparison of individual experts and MoE variants across the three crack segmentation datasets. Bold highlighting values denote the highest results.

Model	RCFD					Crack500					CFD				
	IoU (%)	Prec. (%)	Rec. (%)	F1 (%)	mIoU (%)	IoU (%)	Prec. (%)	Rec. (%)	F1 (%)	mIoU (%)	IoU (%)	Prec. (%)	Rec. (%)	F1 (%)	mIoU (%)
E1 (CEN'23) [34]	51.52	72.58	63.97	68.0	74.71	53.95	74.84	65.91	70.09	75.34	52.74	63.15	76.19	69.06	75.88
E2 (ECSN'24) [35]	64.16	73.9	82.96	78.17	81.21	59.6	73.2	76.3	74.7	78.3	53.11	62.16	78.5	69.38	76.05
E3 (CM'25) [9]	63.53	79.37	76.09	77.7	81.0	60.96	73.77	77.83	75.74	78.98	51.28	58.29	**81.0**	67.79	75.08
E4 (CR'25) [26]	65.41	79.2	78.98	79.09	81.97	62.02	74.57	78.65	76.57	79.56	54.57	63.8	79.05	70.61	76.81
MoE (Hard)	65.48	79.25	78.43	78.84	81.62	63.11	75.22	79.01	77.04	80.02	55.21	64.25	79.42	70.88	77.24
MoE (Soft)	67.12	80.36	81.02	80.69	83.03	63.74	75.49	79.53	77.46	80.29	55.78	64.89	79.85	71.44	77.53
MoE (Top-K)	**67.82**	**80.9**	**81.42**	**81.16**	**83.34**	**64.31**	**75.94**	**80.02**	**77.93**	**80.65**	**56.24**	**65.41**	80.16	**71.92**	**77.86**

5.2. Ablation and Strategy Analysis

To better understand the effect of different routing strategies within the proposed Mixture-of-Experts (MoE) framework, an ablation study is conducted comparing three configurations: (i) MoE (Hard), trained using one-hot expert supervision; (ii) MoE (Soft), trained with probabilistic soft-label targets derived from the experts' out-of-fold (OOF) performance; and (iii) MoE (Top-K), which combines the outputs of the Top-2 ranked experts during inference. All variants use the same four trained experts, identical data augmentation, and optimization settings. Results are reported on the RCFD dataset, which includes diverse full-scene images and provides a rigorous test of the routing mechanism.

As shown in Figure 5, both soft supervision and selective expert aggregation contribute significantly to segmentation performance. The MoE (Hard) configuration achieves the lowest results, indicating that assigning each sample to a single expert restricts the gate's flexibility when multiple experts could jointly provide complementary information. This rigidity limits the model's ability to handle images with overlapping visual patterns, such as variations in crack morphology or illumination conditions.

In contrast, the MoE (Soft) variant yields a consistent improvement of approximately +1.6 IoU and +1.9 F1-score over the MoE (Hard) configuration. Probabilistic supervi-

https://doi.org/10.3390/electronics15020407

sion enables the gate to learn nuanced relationships between experts and inputs, resulting in smoother routing decisions and more effective utilization of shared expertise across samples.

Further gains are observed with the MoE (Top-K) strategy, which aggregates the predictions of the Top-ranked experts during inference. This selective fusion preserves expert specialization while reducing the risk of overconfidence associated with relying on a single model.

5.2.1. Effect of the Top-K Selection

To analyze the sensitivity of the framework to the choice of K, additional experiments were conducted on the RCFD dataset. As shown in Table 4, selecting $K = 2$ yields the best overall performance across all evaluation metrics. Increasing K beyond two leads to marginal performance changes or slight degradation, while also increasing computational cost. These results justify the choice of $K = 2$ as an effective trade-off between segmentation accuracy and efficiency.

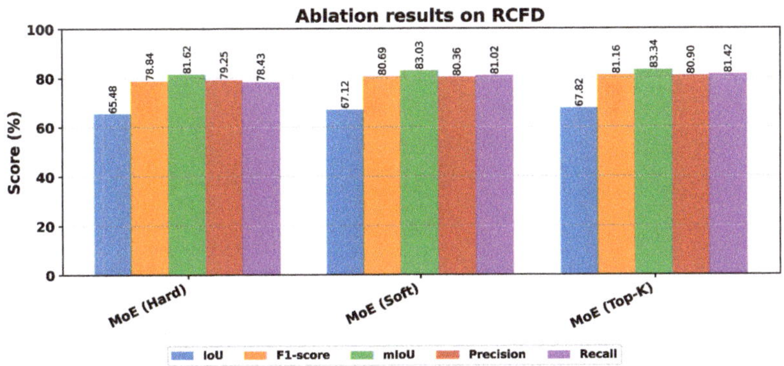

Figure 5. Ablation results of the proposed Mixture-of-Experts framework on the RCFD dataset. The plot compares the three routing strategies—MoE (Hard), MoE (Soft), and MoE (Top-K)—across five evaluation metrics: IoU, F1-score, mIoU, Precision, and Recall. The Top-K configuration consistently achieves the highest performance, followed by the Soft variant, while the Hard strategy yields the lowest scores across all metrics.

Table 4. Effect of the Top-K selection on the RCFD dataset. Bold highlighting values denote the highest results.

Configuration	IoU (%)	Prec. (%)	Rec. (%)	F1 (%)	mIoU (%)
MoE (Hard, $K = 1$)	65.48	79.25	78.43	78.84	81.62
MoE (Top-K, $K = 2$)	**67.82**	**80.9**	**81.42**	**81.16**	**83.34**
MoE (Top-K, $K = 3$)	67.61	80.72	81.18	80.98	83.10
MoE (Top-K, $K = 4$)	67.38	80.55	80.96	80.75	82.91

5.2.2. Effect of Expert Count and Selection

A leave-one-out analysis was conducted to evaluate whether the proposed framework depends on any single expert. As shown in Table 5, removing one expert at a time results in a modest but consistent performance drop across all metrics. No individual expert causes a disproportionate degradation when excluded, indicating that performance gains arise from complementary interactions among experts rather than reliance on a single dominant model.

https://doi.org/10.3390/electronics15020407

Table 5. Effect of expert count and selection on the RCFD dataset using the Top-K strategy ($K = 2$). Bold highlighting values denote the highest results.

Configuration	IoU (%)	Prec. (%)	Rec. (%)	F1 (%)	mIoU (%)
Top-K (w/o E1)	67.12	80.25	80.98	80.61	82.85
Top-K (w/o E2)	66.94	80.03	80.71	80.37	82.63
Top-K (w/o E3)	67.05	80.14	80.85	80.49	82.71
Top-K (w/o E4)	66.78	79.92	80.46	80.19	82.41
MoE (Top-K, all experts)	**67.82**	**80.9**	**81.42**	**81.16**	**83.34**

5.2.3. Inclusion of External Expert Models

To assess whether the proposed MoE framework generalizes beyond the authors' previously developed models, additional experiments were conducted by incorporating external CNN and transformer-based architectures (U-Net and Swin Transformer) into the expert pool. As reported in Table 6, the framework maintains strong and competitive performance under these heterogeneous expert configurations, with results remaining close to those obtained using the full in-house expert pool. This demonstrates that the proposed gating and aggregation strategy is not restricted to a closed set of experts and can effectively integrate external architectures.

Table 6. Effect of incorporating external expert models into the MoE framework on the RCFD dataset using Top-K aggregation ($K = 2$). Bold highlighting values denote the highest results.

Expert Pool	IoU (%)	Prec. (%)	Rec. (%)	F1 (%)	mIoU (%)
MoE (E3, E4, U-Net, SwinT)	67.10	80.21	80.94	80.56	82.71
MoE (E1, E4, U-Net, SwinT)	66.42	79.63	80.11	79.87	82.05
MoE (E1–E4)	**67.82**	**80.9**	**81.42**	**81.16**	**83.34**

It is important to note that the proposed Mixture-of-Experts framework does not assume a fixed or indispensable set of experts. Its performance gains stem from the diversity and complementarity of the available models rather than their number alone. The ablation results consistently confirm that adaptive expert selection, rather than a particular expert configuration, is the primary driver of performance improvement. Exploring expert pruning strategies or adaptive K selection to further balance performance and computational cost remains a promising direction for future work.

5.3. Comparison with State-of-the-Art Methods

To further evaluate the effectiveness and generalization capability of the proposed Mixture-of-Experts (MoE) framework, its performance is compared with recent crack segmentation models, including both convolutional and transformer-based architectures. The CNN-based models include U-Net [23], DeepCrack [4], MobileNetV3 [24], LMM [25], CrackMaster [9], and CrackRefineNet [26]. The transformer-based counterparts comprise SwinT [27], MobileViT [28], CrackFormer II [29], EfficientCrackNet [30], MSDCrack [31], and Hybrid-Segmentor [32]. All models are evaluated under identical preprocessing, input resolution (512×512), and dataset splits to ensure a fair and reproducible comparison. The results are reported separately for each dataset to illustrate performance under different imaging conditions.

As shown in Table 7, on the RCFD dataset—comprising challenging full-scene road images with diverse lighting and complex backgrounds—the proposed MoE (Top-K) achieves the best performance across all metrics. It reaches 67.82% IoU and 81.16% F1-score, outperforming the strongest CNN baseline, CrackRefineNet, by +2.4 IoU and +2.1 F1-score points. Transformer-based methods such as SwinT and MobileViT remain competitive

https://doi.org/10.3390/electronics15020407

but fall short of the MoE. These results highlight that adaptive expert routing effectively captures diverse surface and illumination patterns, offering stronger generalization than single CNN or transformer models.

Table 7. Comparison of the proposed MoE with state-of-the-art methods on the RCFD dataset. Bold highlighting values denote the highest results.

Model	Type	Year	IoU (%)	Precision (%)	Recall (%)	F1-Score (%)	mIoU (%)
U-Net [23]	CNN	2015	48.82	58.42	74.82	65.61	73.03
DeepCrack [4]		2019	43.23	48.78	79.16	60.36	69.79
MobileNetv3 [24]		2019	51.69	71.57	65.04	68.15	74.78
LMM [25]		2024	28.05	29.92	81.81	43.81	60.33
CrackMaster [9]		2025	63.53	79.37	76.09	77.7	81.0
CrackRefineNet [26]		2025	65.41	79.2	78.98	79.09	81.97
SwinT [27]	Transformer	2021	53.94	73.84	66.68	70.08	75.97
MobileViT [28]		2021	54.44	73.69	67.58	70.5	76.23
Crackformer II [29]		2023	33.42	36.0	82.37	50.1	63.82
EfficientCrackNet [30]		2025	35.47	39.42	77.93	52.36	65.24
MSDCrack [31]		2025	33.94	43.68	60.35	50.68	64.92
Hybrid-Segmentor [32]		2025	47.42	72.57	57.78	64.34	72.59
Proposed MoE (Top-K)	CNN	2025	**67.82**	**80.9**	**81.42**	**81.16**	**83.34**

Table 8 reports the results on the Crack500 dataset, which contains diverse pavement textures under moderate lighting variation, the MoE (Top-K) again achieves the best overall performance. It records 64.31% IoU and 77.93% F1-score, exceeding CrackRefineNet by +2.3 IoU and Hybrid-Segmentor by +6.2 IoU. The balanced precision (75.94%) and recall (80.02%) confirm that the MoE maintains strong crack sensitivity while suppressing false positives. These results demonstrate robust cross-domain generalization on large-scale datasets.

Table 8. Comparison of the proposed MoE with state-of-the-art methods on the Crack500 dataset. Bold highlighting values denote the highest results.

Model	Type	Year	IoU (%)	Precision (%)	Recall (%)	F1-score (%)	mIoU (%)
U-Net [23]	CNN	2015	57.8	74.77	71.81	73.26	77.33
DeepCrack [4]		2019	58.62	72.34	75.55	73.91	77.71
MobileNetv3 [24]		2019	57.26	73.99	71.69	72.82	77.03
LMM [25]		2024	56.42	73.08	71.22	72.14	76.56
CrackMaster [9]		2025	60.96	73.77	77.83	75.74	78.98
CrackRefineNet [26]		2025	62.02	74.57	78.65	76.57	79.56
SwinT [27]	Transformer	2021	57.16	73.24	72.26	72.75	76.96
MobileViT [28]		2021	54.75	72.4	69.2	70.76	75.67
Crackformer II [29]		2023	57.01	71.61	73.66	72.62	76.84
EfficientCrackNet [30]		2025	53.93	75.71	65.22	70.07	75.31
MSDCrack [31]		2025	57.11	69.37	76.38	72.7	76.88
Hybrid-Segmentor [32]		2025	58.16	72.22	74.92	73.55	77.51
Proposed MoE (Top-K)	CNN	2025	**64.31**	**75.94**	**80.02**	**77.93**	**80.65**

As summarized in Table 9, the proposed MoE (Top-K) continues to demonstrate strong performance on the CFD dataset, which contains a smaller number of high-texture pavement images, the MoE (Top-K) also maintains superior performance, achieving 56.24% IoU and 71.92% F1-score. It improves upon CrackRefineNet by +1.7 IoU and delivers well-balanced precision (65.41%) and recall (80.16%). These results indicate that the proposed framework generalizes effectively even under limited data conditions by leveraging complementary expert knowledge to reduce overfitting.

https://doi.org/10.3390/electronics15020407

Table 9. Comparison of the proposed MoE with state-of-the-art methods on the CFD dataset. Bold highlighting values denote the highest results.

Model	Type	Year	IoU (%)	Precision (%)	Recall (%)	F1-score (%)	mIoU (%)
U-Net [23]	CNN	2015	52.46	62.99	75.84	68.82	75.73
DeepCrack [4]		2019	52.26	62.05	76.81	68.65	75.62
MobileNetv3 [24]		2019	50.92	60.01	77.08	67.48	74.92
LMM [25]		2024	53.65	65.05	75.38	69.83	76.35
CrackMaster [9]		2025	51.28	58.29	81.0	67.79	75.08
CrackRefineNet [26]		2025	54.57	63.8	79.05	70.61	76.81
SwinT [27]	Transformer	2021	52.76	62.84	76.68	69.08	75.88
MobileViT [28]		2021	53.26	70.07	68.95	69.5	76.19
Crackformer II [29]		2023	50.43	57.26	80.88	67.05	74.63
EfficientCrackNet [30]		2025	50.17	56.84	**81.05**	66.82	74.50
MSDCrack [31]		2025	49.01	55.66	80.41	65.78	73.90
Hybrid-Segmentor [32]		2025	47.04	62.21	65.86	63.98	72.98
Proposed MoE (Top-K)	CNN	2025	**56.24**	**65.41**	80.16	**71.92**	**77.86**

Overall, the proposed Mixture-of-Experts consistently achieves the highest performance across all three datasets, outperforming both CNN- and transformer-based baselines. The consistent improvement in IoU and F1-score confirms that routing-based expert aggregation is an efficient and scalable alternative to building deeper or more complex single networks, particularly when multiple high-quality expert models are already available.

5.4. *Qualitative Analysis of Results*

Figure 6 provides qualitative comparisons of the proposed MoE (Top-K) framework against a diverse set of crack segmentation models, including CrackRefineNet, CrackMaster, Enh–CrackNet, CascadeNet, U–Net, DeepCrack, SwinT, CrackFormer II, Eff–CrackNet, and LMM. The visualization highlights true positives (blue), false positives (red), and false negatives (green) across three datasets: RCFD, Crack500, and CFD.

On the RCFD dataset, the MoE (Top-K) model consistently captures thin crack structures that several single-expert models struggle with. For example, DeepCrack and U–Net often produce scattered false positives along textured regions, while Transformer-based models such as SwinT and CrackFormer II may oversmooth delicate crack boundaries. The MoE, by contrast, delivers cleaner and more continuous crack traces, particularly in cases where illumination changes or road markings confuse individual models. CrackRefineNet and CrackMaster perform strongly on many samples, but each exhibits occasional failure modes—CrackMaster may miss extremely thin branches, whereas CrackRefineNet may introduce slight over-segmentation in highly textured surfaces. The MoE balances these behaviors by adaptively selecting the most reliable experts per sample.

On the Crack500 dataset, where background texture and crack morphology vary substantially, the complementary strengths of the experts become more evident. Eff–CrackNet, though lightweight, sometimes produces fragmented detections, while Enh–CrackNet and CascadeNet can overreact to rough pavement patterns, leading to false positives. In contrast, the MoE preserves the fine topology of intersecting cracks while suppressing noisy activations. In several cases, the MoE prediction visually resembles the best aspects of both CrackMaster and CrackRefineNet, combining structural sensitivity with noise suppression.

https://doi.org/10.3390/electronics15020407

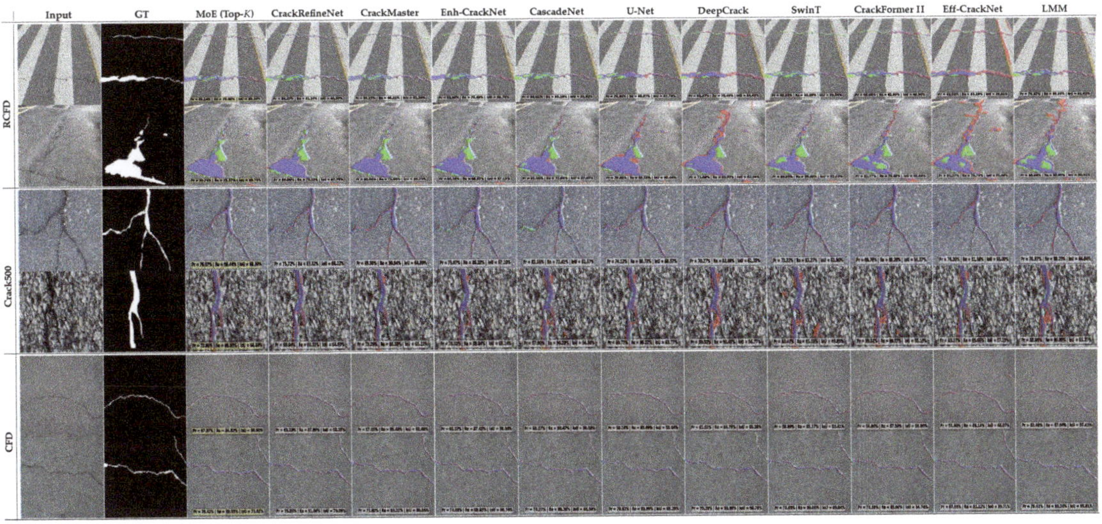

Figure 6. Qualitative comparison of crack segmentation results across three datasets: RCFD (**top**), Crack500 (**middle**), and CFD (**bottom**). Each column displays the input image, ground–truth (GT) mask, and predictions from the proposed MoE (Top-*K*) model and several baseline and state-of-the-art methods. Blue regions indicate true positives, red regions denote false positives, and green regions highlight false negatives. The best IoU for each sample is emphasized in yellow. The MoE (Top-*K*) model produces cleaner boundaries, fewer artifacts, and more continuous crack structures than individual experts.

On the CFD dataset, which contains challenging low-contrast cracks, many models show noticeable limitations: LMM and U–Net tend to miss faint crack segments, while DeepCrack and Enh–CrackNet may produce spurious edges under harsh lighting. The MoE (Top-*K*) produces more coherent and stable predictions, accurately following the crack path without introducing unnecessary artifacts. The adaptive weighting is particularly beneficial in scenes where neither CNN- nor Transformer-based models alone are consistently reliable.

Overall, the qualitative visualizations reinforce the quantitative findings: the proposed MoE (Top-*K*) framework generates cleaner boundaries, preserves fine structural details, and reduces both false positives and missed crack regions. By leveraging sample-dependent expert selection, the MoE achieves visual quality that no single expert consistently reaches on its own.

5.5. Analysis of Failure Cases

Despite the strong overall performance of the proposed MoE framework, some failure cases still occur, particularly in scenes with weak contrast, highly textured backgrounds, or extremely thin crack patterns. Figure 7 summarizes representative examples and illustrates how individual experts and the MoE behave under such challenging conditions.

In several cases, standalone experts disagree substantially in their predictions. For instance, CEN'23 (E1) often produces overly conservative masks, missing fine crack branches, while CM'25 (E3) may generate thicker or fragmented crack segments when background textures resemble crack edges. ECSN'24 (E2) and CR'25 (E4) generally perform better, but even these models occasionally misinterpret shadows or stains as cracks, especially on asphalt surfaces with noisy intensity patterns.

https://doi.org/10.3390/electronics15020407

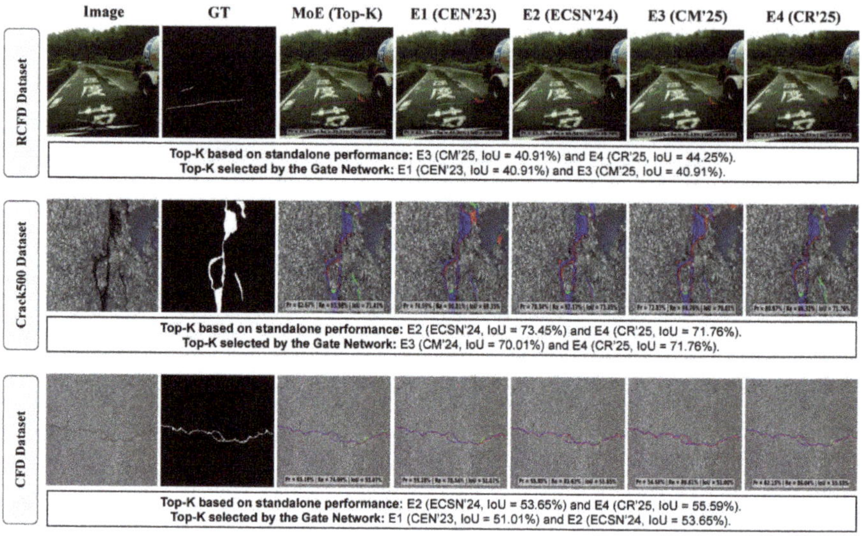

Figure 7. Failure case analysis across the RCFD, Crack500, and CFD datasets. For each image, predictions from all experts (E1–E4) and the MoE (Top-*K*) are shown. The tables indicate: (i) the two experts with the highest standalone IoU scores for that sample, and (ii) the Top-*K* experts selected by the gate network. Blue regions indicate true positives, red regions denote false positives, and green regions highlight false negatives. Discrepancies between these selections often explain MoE errors—for example, the gate sometimes selects weaker experts in textured or low-contrast scenes, leading to missed fine cracks or localized false positives.

A key observation from the failure analysis is that incorrect MoE predictions are primarily associated with ambiguous expert ranking rather than isolated expert failure. In visually challenging scenes, the gating network does not always assign the highest weights to the experts that achieve the best standalone IoU scores. This behavior arises because the gate operates on global RGB appearance cues and may encounter inputs where background textures or illumination patterns resemble the visual signatures learned by certain experts.

As a consequence, the Top-*K* selection may include experts whose inductive biases are less suitable for the specific crack morphology present in the image. In such cases, the MoE inherits correlated errors from the selected experts, leading to localized false positives or missed thin crack regions. This highlights an implicit assumption of the Top-*K* strategy—namely, that the selected experts provide complementary information—which may not hold under strong visual ambiguity.

Nonetheless, even in these difficult scenarios, the MoE output often remains competitive. In cases where experts make complementary errors—such as one model over-segmenting while another under-segmenting—the weighted fusion yields a more stable prediction than any single expert. However, when the selected experts fail in a similar manner, the aggregation mechanism cannot compensate for these shared errors.

Overall, the observed failure cases reflect inherent limitations of scene-level routing under ambiguous visual conditions rather than instability of the proposed architecture. They motivate future improvements, such as uncertainty-aware gating, explicit modeling of expert disagreement, feature-space alignment between experts and the gate, or adaptive *K* selection, to further enhance robustness in challenging environments.

https://doi.org/10.3390/electronics15020407

5.6. Complexity Analysis

To assess the practical computational cost of the proposed approach, a comparative complexity analysis is presented in Table 10, reporting the number of trainable parameters, inference time, floating-point operations per second (FLOPs), and frames per second (FPS) for the proposed Mixture-of-Experts (MoE) framework and representative state-of-the-art crack segmentation models. All measurements are conducted using an input resolution of 512×512 on the same hardware configuration described in Section 4.3.

Table 10. Comparative analysis of trained parameters, inference time, FLOPs, and FPS of different segmentation models.

Model	Parameters (M)	Inference time (s)	FLOPs (T)	FPS
U-Net [23]	31.04	0.0192	0.193	52
DeepCrack [4]	3.68	0.0045	0.020	222
MobileNetV3 [24]	3.28	0.0105	0.008	95
LMM [25]	0.84	0.0981	0.035	10
CascadeNet (E1 (CEN'23)) [34]	61.8	0.0415	0.384	24
EnhancedNet (E2 (ECSN'24)) [35]	88.1	0.0413	0.312	24
CrackMaster (E3 (CM'25)) [9]	93.61	0.0192	0.087	52
CrackRefineNet (E4 (CR'25)) [26]	99.66	0.0387	0.206	26
Swin Transformer [27]	58.94	0.0298	0.236	33
MobileViT [24]	31.85	0.0629	0.841	16
CrackFormer II [29]	4.96	0.0715	0.091	14
EfficientCrackNet [32]	0.35	0.0532	0.045	19
MSDCrack [31]	15.39	0.0296	0.008	34
Hybrid-Segmentor [32]	347.0	0.0388	0.142	26
Proposed MoE (Top-K)	296.5	0.0614	0.491	16

For the proposed MoE, the reported number of parameters corresponds to the total parameter count of all expert models and the lightweight ResNet-18 gating network, as all experts must be stored even though only a subset is activated at inference time. Inference time, FLOPs, and FPS are measured end-to-end and include the cost of the gating network and the Top-K selected experts only, reflecting the actual execution strategy used during inference. As expert selection is input-dependent, the reported runtime and FLOPs represent the average Top-K execution cost over the test data.

For cascade-based methods, such as CascadeNet, the reported complexity accounts for sequential inference through multiple stages. In this case, an initial network is applied first, and its output logits are concatenated with the original RGB image and fed into a second encoder–decoder network, resulting in increased computational cost due to multi-stage execution.

As shown in Table 10, lightweight models such as MobileNetV3 and EfficientCrackNet achieve fast inference with minimal parameters but typically exhibit lower segmentation accuracy. In contrast, high-capacity CNN and transformer-based models provide stronger representational power at increased computational cost. The proposed MoE introduces additional overhead compared to single-expert inference due to the evaluation of multiple experts; however, this overhead remains moderate because the gating network is lightweight and only the most relevant experts are activated. Overall, the proposed framework offers a favorable trade-off between segmentation accuracy and computational cost, making adaptive expert routing a practical solution when multiple pre-trained models are available.

6. Conclusions and Future Work

This paper presented a routing-based Mixture-of-Experts framework for crack segmentation that adaptively integrates multiple pre-trained expert models through a lightweight

https://doi.org/10.3390/electronics15020407

gating network. Unlike conventional ensemble approaches based on uniform averaging or fixed weighting, the proposed method learns sample-specific expert reliability using out-of-fold soft supervision and selectively combines the most suitable experts through a Top-K aggregation strategy. This design enables effective exploitation of complementary expert strengths without requiring retraining or architectural modification of the individual models. Experimental evaluations conducted on three crack segmentation datasets demonstrate that the proposed framework consistently outperforms individual experts and recent state-of-the-art CNN- and transformer-based methods. Across datasets, improvements on the order of 1–3% in IoU and F1-score are observed compared to the strongest single expert, confirming that adaptive expert routing provides a robust and practical alternative to both single-model designs and conventional ensemble techniques under diverse imaging conditions. Future work will focus on improving computational efficiency through sparse or conditional expert activation, enhancing routing reliability via uncertainty-aware gating, and extending the framework toward annotation-efficient and multi-modal settings. These directions aim to further strengthen the applicability of adaptive expert selection for large-scale and real-world infrastructure inspection tasks.

Author Contributions: Conceptualization, A.M.O., H.A.R., S.C. and D.P.; methodology, A.M.O., H.A.R. and S.C.; software, A.M.O.; validation, A.M.O., H.A.R. and S.C.; formal analysis, A.M.O. and H.A.R.; investigation, A.M.O.; resources, S.C. and D.P.; data curation, A.M.O.; writing—original draft preparation, A.M.O.; writing—review and editing, A.M.O., H.A.R., S.C. and D.P.; visualization, A.M.O.; supervision, H.A.R. and D.P.; project administration, D.P.; funding acquisition, D.P. All authors have read and agreed to the published version of the manuscript.

Funding: This work is part of the PECT "Cuidem el que ens uneix" project, Operation 4, within the framework of the RIS3CAT and ERDF Catalonia Operational Programme 2014–2020. PECT is co-financed by the Catalan Government, the Provincial Council of Tarragona, "Diputació de Tarragona" and Universitat Rovira i Virgili.

Data Availability Statement: The datasets used in this study include Crack500 [20] and the CrackForest Dataset (CFD) [6], both of which are publicly available from their original sources. The in-house RCFD dataset [26,36] is a private and is not publicly available.

Conflicts of Interest: The authors declare no conflict of interest. The funders had no role in the design of the study; in the collection, analyses, or interpretation of data; in the writing of the manuscript, or in the decision to publish the results.

References

1. Wu, Y.; Li, S.; Li, J.; Yu, Y.; Li, J.; Li, Y. Deep learning in crack detection: A comprehensive scientometric review. *J. Infrastruct. Intell. Resil.* **2025**, *4*, 100144. [CrossRef]
2. Yang, L.; Deng, J.; Duan, H.; Yang, C. An efficient semantic segmentation method for road crack based on EGA-UNet. *Sci. Rep.* **2025**, *15*, 33818. [CrossRef] [PubMed]
3. Hoskere, V.; Narazaki, Y.; Hoang, T.; Spencer, B. Vision-based Structural Inspection using Multiscale Deep Convolutional Neural Networks. *arXiv* **2018**. [CrossRef]
4. Liu, Y.; Yao, J.; Lu, X.; Xie, R.; Li, L. DeepCrack: A deep hierarchical feature learning architecture for crack segmentation. *Neurocomputing* **2019**, *338*, 139–153. [CrossRef]
5. Oliveira, H.; Correia, P.L. Automatic Road Crack Detection and Characterization. *IEEE Trans. Intell. Transp. Syst.* **2013**, *14*, 155–168. [CrossRef]
6. Shi, Y.; Cui, L.; Qi, Z.; Meng, F.; Chen, Z. Automatic Road Crack Detection Using Random Structured Forests. *IEEE Trans. Intell. Transp. Syst.* **2016**, *17*, 3434–3445. [CrossRef]
7. Ellenberg, A.; Kontsos, A.; Moon, F.; Bartoli, I. Bridge related damage quantification using unmanned aerial vehicle imagery. *Struct. Control Health Monit.* **2016**, *23*, 1168–1179. [CrossRef]
8. Okran, A.M.; Rashwan, H.A.; Chambon, S.; Puig, D. Annotation-Efficient and Domain-General Segmentation from Weak Labels: A Bounding Box-Guided Approach. *Electronics* **2025**, *14*, 3917. [CrossRef]

https://doi.org/10.3390/electronics15020407

9. Okran, A.M.; Rashwan, H.A.; Saleh, A.; Puig, D. Efficient crack segmentation with multi-decoder networks and enhanced feature fusion. *Eng. Appl. Artif. Intell.* **2025**, *152*, 110697. [CrossRef]
10. Chen, Z.; Shamsabadi, E.A.; Jiang, S.; Shen, L.; Dias-da Costa, D. Vision Mamba-based autonomous crack segmentation on concrete, asphalt, and masonry surfaces. *arXiv* **2024**. [CrossRef]
11. Moon, J.H.; Choi, G.; Kim, Y.H.; Kim, W.Y. PCTC-Net: A Crack Segmentation Network with Parallel Dual Encoder Network Fusing Pre-Conv-Based Transformers and Convolutional Neural Networks. *Sensors* **2024**, *24*, 1467. [CrossRef] [PubMed]
12. Xiang, C.; Guo, J.; Cao, R.; Deng, L. A crack-segmentation algorithm fusing transformers and convolutional neural networks for complex detection scenarios. *Autom. Constr.* **2023**, *152*, 104894. [CrossRef]
13. Kim, J.H.; Noh, J.H.; Jang, J.Y.; Yang, H.D. MSP U-Net: Crack Segmentation for Low-Resolution Images Based on Multi-Scale Parallel Attention U-Net. *Appl. Sci.* **2024**, *14*, 11541. [CrossRef]
14. Rashid, T.; Mokji, M.M.; Rasheed, M. Cross-dataset evaluation of deep learning models for crack classification in structural surfaces. *J. Mech. Behav. Mater.* **2025**, *34*, 20250074. [CrossRef]
15. Han, X.; Wei, L.; Dou, Z.; Sun, Y.; Han, Z.; Tian, Q. ViMoE: An Empirical Study of Designing Vision Mixture-of-Experts. *IEEE Trans. Image Process.* **2025**, 34, 7209–7221. [CrossRef]
16. Wang, G.; Ye, J.; Cheng, J.; Li, T.; Chen, Z.; Cai, J.; He, J.; Zhuang, B. SAM-Med3D-MoE: Towards a Non-Forgetting Segment Anything Model via Mixture of Experts for 3D Medical Image Segmentation. In *Medical Image Computing and Computer Assisted Intervention—MICCAI 2024*; Springer Nature: Cham, Switzerland, 2024; pp. 552–561. [CrossRef]
17. Wei, J.; Zhao, X.; Woo, J.; Ouyang, J.; El Fakhri, G.; Chen, Q.; Liu, X. Mixture-of-Shape-Experts (MoSE): End-to-End Shape Dictionary Framework to Prompt SAM for Generalizable Medical Segmentation. In Proceedings of the 2025 IEEE/CVF Conference on Computer Vision and Pattern Recognition Workshops (CVPRW), Nashville, TN, USA, 11–12 June 2025; IEEE: Piscataway, NJ, USA, 2025; pp. 6450–6460. [CrossRef]
18. Mu, S.; Lin, S. A Comprehensive Survey of Mixture-of-Experts: Algorithms, Theory, and Applications. *arXiv* **2025**. [CrossRef]
19. Canny, J. A Computational Approach to Edge Detection. In *Readings in Computer Vision*; Elsevier: Amsterdam, The Netherlands , 1987; pp. 184–203. [CrossRef]
20. Yang, F.; Zhang, L.; Yu, S.; Prokhorov, D.; Mei, X.; Ling, H. Feature Pyramid and Hierarchical Boosting Network for Pavement Crack Detection. *IEEE Trans. Intell. Transp. Syst.* **2020**, *21*, 1525–1535. [CrossRef]
21. Otsu, N. A Threshold Selection Method from Gray-Level Histograms. *IEEE Trans. Syst. Man Cybern.* **1979**, *9*, 62–66. [CrossRef]
22. Zou, Q.; Cao, Y.; Li, Q.; Mao, Q.; Wang, S. CrackTree: Automatic crack detection from pavement images. *Pattern Recognit. Lett.* **2012**, *33*, 227–238. [CrossRef]
23. Ronneberger, O.; Fischer, P.; Brox, T. U-Net: Convolutional Networks for Biomedical Image Segmentation. In *Medical Image Computing and Computer-Assisted Intervention—MICCAI 2015*; Springer International Publishing: Cham, Switzerland, 2015; pp. 234–241. [CrossRef]
24. Howard, A.; Sandler, M.; Chen, B.; Wang, W.; Chen, L.C.; Tan, M.; Chu, G.; Vasudevan, V.; Zhu, Y.; Pang, R.; et al. Searching for MobileNetV3. In Proceedings of the 2019 IEEE/CVF International Conference on Computer Vision (ICCV), Seoul, Republic of Korea, 27 October–2 November 2019; IEEE: Piscataway, NJ, USA, 2019; pp. 1314–1324. [CrossRef]
25. Al-maqtari, O.; Peng, B.; Al-Huda, Z.; Al-Malahi, A.; Maqtary, N. Lightweight Yet Effective: A Modular Approach to Crack Segmentation. *IEEE Trans. Intell. Veh.* **2024**, *9*, 7961–7972. [CrossRef]
26. Okran, A.M.; Puig, D.; Musluh, S.K.; Chambon, S.; Rashwan, H.A. Context- and refinement-driven convolutional architecture for robust crack segmentation under real-world and zero-shot conditions. *Autom. Constr.* **2026**, *181*, 106635. [CrossRef]
27. Liu, Z.; Lin, Y.; Cao, Y.; Hu, H.; Wei, Y.; Zhang, Z.; Lin, S.; Guo, B. Swin Transformer: Hierarchical Vision Transformer using Shifted Windows. In Proceedings of the 2021 IEEE/CVF International Conference on Computer Vision (ICCV), Montreal, QC, Canada, 10–17 October 2021; IEEE: Piscataway, NJ, USA, 2021; pp. 9992–10002. [CrossRef]
28. Mehta, S.; Rastegari, M. MobileViT: Light-weight, General-purpose, and Mobile-friendly Vision Transformer. *arXiv* **2021**. [CrossRef]
29. Liu, H.; Yang, J.; Miao, X.; Mertz, C.; Kong, H. CrackFormer Network for Pavement Crack Segmentation. *IEEE Trans. Intell. Transp. Syst.* **2023**, *24*, 9240–9252. [CrossRef]
30. Zim, A.H.; Iqbal, A.; Al-Huda, Z.; Malik, A.; Kuribayashi, M. EfficientCrackNet: A Lightweight Model for Crack Segmentation. In Proceedings of the 2025 IEEE/CVF Winter Conference on Applications of Computer Vision (WACV), Tucson, AZ, USA, 26 February–6 March 2025; IEEE: Piscataway, NJ, USA, 2025; pp. 6279–6289. [CrossRef]
31. Wang, J.; Yao, H.; Hu, J.; Ma, Y.; Wang, J. Dual-encoder network for pavement concrete crack segmentation with multi-stage supervision. *Autom. Constr.* **2025**, *169*, 105884. [CrossRef]
32. Goo, J.M.; Milidonis, X.; Artusi, A.; Boehm, J.; Ciliberto, C. Hybrid-Segmentor: Hybrid approach for automated fine-grained crack segmentation in civil infrastructure. *Autom. Constr.* **2025**, *170*, 105960. [CrossRef]

33. He, K.; Zhang, X.; Ren, S.; Sun, J. Deep Residual Learning for Image Recognition. In Proceedings of the 2016 IEEE Conferen on Computer Vision and Pattern Recognition (CVPR), Las Vegas, NV, USA, 27–30 June 2016; IEEE: Piscataway, NJ, USA, 20 pp. 770–778. [CrossRef]
34. Okran, A.M.; Saleh, A.; Puig, D.; Rashwan, H.A. Stacking up for Success: A Cascade Network Model for Efficient Road Cra Segmentation. In *Artificial Intelligence Research and Development*; IOS Press: Amsterdam, The Netherlands, 2023; pp. 38– [CrossRef]
35. Okran, A.M.; Rashwan, H.A.; Puig, D. Enhanced Crack Segmentation Network: Leveraging Multi-Dimensional Attention. *Artificial Intelligence Research and Development*; IOS Press: Amsterdam, The Netherlands, 2024; pp. 94–96. [CrossRef]
36. Okran, A.M.; Abdel-Nasser, M.; Rashwan, H.A.; Puig, D. A Curated Dataset for Crack Image Analysis: Experimental Verificati and Future Perspectives. In *Artificial Intelligence Research and Development*; IOS Press: Amsterdam, The Netherlands, 202 pp. 225–228. [CrossRef]
37. Arya, D.; Maeda, H.; Ghosh, S.K.; Toshniwal, D.; Sekimoto, Y. RDD2022: A multi-national image dataset for automatic roa damage detection. *Geosci. Data J.* **2024**, *11*, 846–862. [CrossRef]

https://doi.org/10.3390/electronics15020407

electronics

MDPI

Article

A Unified Self-Supervised Framework for Plant Disease Detection on Laboratory and In-Field Images

Xiaoli Huan [1,*], Bernard Chen [1] and Hong Zhou [2]

1 Department of Computer Science, Troy University, Troy, AL 36082, USA; chenb@troy.edu
2 Department of Mathematics and Computer Science, University of Saint Joseph, West Hartford, CT 06117, USA; hzhou@usj.edu
* Correspondence: xhuan@troy.edu

Abstract: Early and accurate detection of plant diseases is essential for ensuring food security and maintaining sustainable agricultural productivity. However, most deep learning models for plant disease classification rely heavily on large-scale annotated datasets, which are expensive, labor-intensive, and often impractical to obtain in real-world farming environments. To address this limitation, we propose a unified self-supervised learning (SSL) framework that leverages unlabeled plant imagery to learn meaningful and transferable visual representations. Our method integrates three complementary objectives—Bootstrap Your Own Latent (BYOL), Masked Image Modeling (MIM), and contrastive learning—within a ResNet101 backbone, optimized through a hybrid loss function that captures global alignment, local structure, and instance-level distinction. GPU-based data augmentations are used to introduce stochasticity and enhance generalization during pretraining. Experimental results on the challenging Plant-Doc dataset demonstrate that our model achieves an accuracy of 77.82%, with macro-averaged precision, recall, and F1-score of 80.00%, 78.24%, and 77.48%, respectively—on par with or exceeding most state-of-the-art supervised and self-supervised approaches. Furthermore, when fine-tuned on the PlantVillage dataset, the pretrained model attains 99.85% accuracy, highlighting its strong cross-domain generalization and practical transferability. These findings underscore the potential of self-supervised learning as a scalable, annotation-efficient, and robust solution for plant disease detection in real-world agricultural settings, especially where labeled data is scarce or unavailable.

Keywords: plant disease detection; self-supervised learning; BYOL; masked image modeling; contrastive learning

1. Introduction

Plant diseases are a major threat to global food security, leading to significant reductions in crop yield and quality. Early and accurate diagnosis is essential to guide timely interventions, but traditional approaches relying on manual scouting or laboratory testing are often labor-intensive, time-consuming, and inaccessible to farmers in remote or resource-limited regions. In recent years, deep learning methods have shown promise in automating plant disease detection through image classification. However, these models typically depend on large-scale, labeled datasets, which are difficult and expensive to collect in real-world agricultural contexts due to the need for expert annotation and the variability of disease expression in field conditions [1]. In this study, we use the term 'detection' to refer to disease identification and classification at the image level, rather than object localization or bounding box generation. Thus, our model does not perform region-based object detection but instead categorizes whole images into disease types.

Early methods of plant disease detection employed traditional computer vision techniques using handcrafted features like texture descriptors, color histograms, and shape metrics, coupled with classical classifiers such as Support Vector Machines (SVMs), decision trees, and k-nearest neighbors [2]. Although computationally efficient, these techniques often lacked robustness under varying real-world conditions due to sensitivity to lighting, occlusion, and background complexity.

The advancement of deep learning, particularly Convolutional Neural Networks (CNNs), has significantly improved plant disease classification. Models such as ResNet, DenseNet, and VGGNet facilitated hierarchical feature learning directly from raw image pixels, enhancing classification accuracy and robustness [3]. More recently, Transformer-based models like Vision Transformer (ViT) and Swin Transformer have further demonstrated strong performance in agricultural image analysis. However, supervised methods continue to face challenges related to the scarcity of labeled datasets in agriculture, where expert-labeled data is costly and time-consuming to obtain due to the diversity of crop species, growth stages, and symptom presentations.

Self-supervised learning (SSL) has emerged as a compelling alternative to mitigate the reliance on labeled data. Ref. [4] proposed a progressive SSL pipeline for cassava leaf disease recognition that combined object segmentation and triplet loss with fine-tuned CNNs, achieving strong performance with limited labeled data. Ref. [5] introduced a Self-Supervised Vision Transformer (SSVT) that uses patch-based masked reconstruction and contrastive objectives to model medical disease classification and severity grading. Ref. [6] developed DINOv2, a scalable SSL framework based on Vision Transformers, leveraging a teacher–student distillation setup to extract semantically rich representations from unlabeled imagery.

Ref. [7] provided a comprehensive review of SSL in the plant pathology domain, identifying hybrid approaches as the most effective. These methods combine multiple pretext tasks, such as reconstruction and contrastive learning, to improve feature robustness and transferability. Supporting this view, refs. [8,9] independently demonstrated that pairing masked image modeling with contrastive loss on Transformer backbones yields notable performance gains on large-scale plant disease datasets.

Contrastive methods such as SimCLR [10] and Bootstrap Your Own Latent (BYOL) [11] have also been applied to agricultural image tasks. SimCLR leverages contrastive loss with negative sampling to encourage instance-level separation, whereas BYOL, through dual-network alignment, eliminates the need for negative samples. Despite these advancements, current SSL techniques typically apply these methods in isolation.

To address these gaps, we propose a unified SSL framework integrating Bootstrap Your Own Latent (BYOL) for global representation alignment, Masked Image Modeling (MIM) for spatial feature reconstruction, and contrastive learning for instance-level discrimination. This customized multi-objective strategy is specifically tailored to the challenges of real-world agricultural imagery, enabling the model to capture global semantics, reconstruct occluded regions, and distinguish visually similar samples, all without relying on labeled supervision. The system is built on a ResNet-101 backbone and employs GPU-accelerated augmentations to generate diverse training views. A hybrid loss function combines cosine similarity (BYOL), pixel-level and perceptual loss (MIM), and InfoNCE loss (contrastive learning) into a single optimization objective, supporting robust feature learning for downstream plant disease classification tasks. Experimental validation on the challenging PlantDoc dataset [12], known for its noisy, field-captured images, and transfer learning evaluation on the PlantVillage dataset [13] highlight our model's robust performance and strong cross-domain generalization, confirming the effectiveness of SSL as a scalable, annotation-efficient, and practical approach for plant disease detection in diverse agricultural settings.

Our main contributions are as follows:

- We propose a unified self-supervised framework integrating BYOL, MIM, and contrastive learning.
- We design a hybrid loss function that captures global, local, and instance-level information.
- We implement an efficient GPU-based augmentation pipeline for robust representation learning.
- We achieve state-of-the-art performance on challenging PlantDoc and Plant Village datasets without using labels during pretraining.
- We demonstrate strong generalization via transfer learning and provide interpretability through Grad-CAM and t-SNE.

2. Methodology

2.1. Overview of the Proposed Framework

As illustrated in Figure 1, the framework begins with stochastic image augmentations, which produce two views of each input. These are passed through three parallel SSL branches:

- BYOL, where an online encoder learns to predict the projection of a momentum-updated target encoder;
- MIM, where masked inputs are reconstructed using a combination of pixel-wise accuracy and perceptual similarity;
- Contrastive learning, which brings positive pairs closer and pushes negative pairs apart in the embedding space.

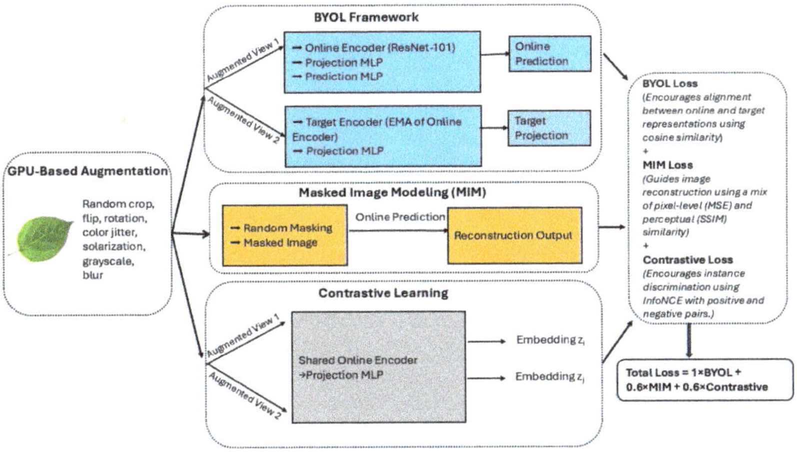

Figure 1. Overview of the proposed multi-objective self-supervised learning framework for plant disease detection. The architecture unifies BYOL, MIM, and contrastive learning atop a ResNet-101 backbone. GPU-based augmentations generate diverse input views to support representation alignment, masked region reconstruction, and instance-level discrimination. The total training loss is computed as a weighted sum of the BYOL, MIM, and contrastive objectives. The novelty lies in their joint optimization within a single architecture, which is not explored in prior works.

The final loss is a weighted sum of the three objectives, promoting balanced representation learning across semantic, structural, and discriminative dimensions.

2.2. Model Architecture

2.2.1. Backbone Network and BYOL Framework

We employ ResNet101 [14], pretrained on ImageNet [15], as the visual feature extractor. The original classification head is replaced with a multilayer perceptron (MLP) projection head that outputs compact image embeddings. For label-free training, we adopt the Bootstrap Your Own Latent (BYOL) framework, which comprises two networks: an online encoder and a target encoder.

The online encoder is trained to predict the output of the target encoder, promoting representation consistency between two differently augmented views of the same image (e.g., via cropping, flipping, or blurring). Unlike contrastive learning methods, which rely on both positive pairs (from the same image) and negative pairs (from different images) to learn discriminative features, BYOL eliminates the need for negative samples. Instead, it learns by aligning one augmented view with another, allowing the model to extract meaningful representations without contrasting examples from different classes.

The target encoder is updated using an exponential moving average (EMA) of the online encoder's parameters, which provides a stable learning target throughout training. The BYOL loss minimizes the cosine distance between the online prediction q and the target projection z:

$$\mathcal{L}_{BYOL} = 2 - 2 \cdot \frac{q \cdot z}{||q||_2 \cdot ||z||_2} \tag{1}$$

This objective enables the model to learn semantically rich and robust features that are invariant to viewpoint, lighting, and background variations—conditions commonly encountered in real-world plant imagery.

2.2.2. Masked Image Modeling (MIM)

To enhance the model's sensitivity to local structure and fine-grained visual patterns, we incorporate a Masked Image Modeling (MIM) objective inspired by the Masked Autoencoder (MAE) framework [16]. During training, a random mask is applied to each input image, occluding 30–60% of the pixels. The model is then tasked with reconstructing the original, unmasked image using only the visible regions.

To better suit fine-grained plant imagery, we employ a hybrid reconstruction loss that combines pixel-level and perceptual fidelity:

$$\mathcal{L}_{\mathrm{MIM}} = \alpha \cdot \mathrm{MSE} + (1 - \alpha) \cdot (1 - \mathrm{SSIM}) \quad \alpha = 0.5 \tag{2}$$

Here, mean squared error (MSE) penalizes raw pixel differences, while Structural Similarity Index Measure (SSIM) encourages the preservation of image structure, including texture, edges, and contrast. This hybrid loss ensures that reconstructed images maintain both numerical accuracy and perceptual coherence.

By compelling the model to infer contextual information in masked regions, this MIM objective promotes learning the underlying statistics of texture, shape, and color. Such capability is particularly useful in plant disease detection, where symptoms like lesions, discoloration, or mold often appear in small, localized patches.

2.2.3. Contrastive Learning

To enhance instance-level discrimination, we incorporate a contrastive learning objective based on the Information Noise-Contrastive Estimation (InfoNCE) loss, originally introduced by [17] for Contrastive Predictive Coding (CPC). Following adaptations such as SimCLR, we apply InfoNCE in the context of image augmentations. This encourages the model to pull embeddings of similar images closer together while pushing apart those of dissimilar images within the latent space.

During training, two distinct augmented views x_1 and x_2 of the same image are generated through GPU-based transformations. These views are passed through the shared online encoder and projection MLP to produce embeddings z_i and z_j, which together form a positive pair. The InfoNCE loss is computed as the following:

$$\mathcal{L}_{\text{Contrastive}} = -\log\frac{\exp(\text{sim}(z_i, z_j)/\tau)}{\sum_{k=1}^{N}\exp(\text{sim}(z_i, z_k)/\tau)} \quad \tau = 0.1 \tag{3}$$

Here, $sim(\cdot)$ denotes cosine similarity, and $\tau = 0.1$ is the temperature parameter that controls the sharpness of similarity distributions. The denominator aggregates similarities between z_i and all other embeddings z_k in the batch, while the numerator captures the similarity with its positive counterpart z_j. The logarithm in the InfoNCE loss stabilizes optimization by compressing the range of similarity scores, and the negative sign ensures that higher similarity between z_i and z_j results in a lower loss value.

This contrastive objective encourages clustering of similar disease instances (e.g., different views of the same diseased leaf) while enforcing separation between dissimilar instances (e.g., different crops or disease types) in the feature space. Such discriminative structuring is particularly beneficial for fine-grained classification tasks, where subtle visual differences between plant diseases are common.

2.3. GPU-Based Augmentation Pipeline

To enhance visual diversity and boost generalization, we implement a series of GPU-accelerated augmentations using the Kornia library [18]. Executing transformations directly on the GPU reduces data-loading overhead and enables efficient large-batch training.

The augmentation pipeline includes the following transformations:

- Random resized cropping (scale: 60–100%)
- Random horizontal flipping (50% probability)
- Random rotation (± 20 degrees)
- Random solarization (threshold = 0.5, 20% probability)
- Random grayscale conversion (20% probability)
- Color jittering (brightness, contrast, saturation, hue)
- Random Gaussian blur ($\sigma \in [0.1,\ 2.0]$, 30% probability)

These augmentations are applied stochastically to each image during training, encouraging the model to become invariant to common environmental variations such as lighting, orientation, and background noise. This increased diversity promotes the learning of more robust and transferable representations, especially when operating on unlabeled, real-world plant imagery.

2.4. Hybrid Loss Function

To simultaneously capture global semantic features, local structural details, and instance-level distinctions, we formulate a multi-objective loss function that combines the contributions of BYOL, MIM, and contrastive learning:

$$\mathcal{L}_{\text{Total}} = 1.0 \cdot \mathcal{L}_{\text{BYOL}} + 0.6 \cdot \mathcal{L}_{\text{MIM}} + 0.6 \cdot \mathcal{L}_{\text{Contrastive}} \tag{4}$$

Each component contributes uniquely to the representation quality:

- $\mathcal{L}_{\text{BYOL}}$ promotes alignment between different views of the same image;

- $\mathcal{L}_{\text{MIM}}$ enhances spatial awareness by reconstructing masked regions;
- $\mathcal{L}_{\text{Contrastive}}$ encourages separation between different instances.

This multi-objective fusion ensures that the model not only aligns semantic representations across augmented views but also retains fine-grained details and learns to distinguish between visually similar classes. In particular, contrastive learning plays a crucial role in overcoming the limited semantic scope of MIM, which alone may struggle to capture class boundaries in the absence of explicit labels.

The final weighting scheme—1.0 (BYOL), 0.6 (MIM), and 0.6 (contrastive)—was empirically determined to effectively balance semantic generalization, spatial awareness, and discriminative capacity.

2.5. Optimization Strategy

AdamW optimizer was used with a base learning rate of 1×10^{-4}, weight decay of 1×10^{-5}, and a 10-epoch linear warmup. The learning rate warm-up strategy stabilizes the initial training phase, mitigating issues arising from overly aggressive updates. Gradient accumulation is employed every two batches to enable larger effective batch sizes while managing GPU memory efficiently. Mixed-precision training via PyTorch 2.1.0+'s GradScaler utility further improves computational efficiency. Checkpoints and models are saved periodically for final downstream evaluation.

2.6. Transfer Learning Evaluation on PlantVillage Dataset

To assess the generalization capability of representations learned through self-supervised pretraining, we conducted a transfer learning evaluation using the PlantVillage dataset. Unlike the field-based and visually noisy conditions of the PlantDoc dataset, PlantVillage comprises high-resolution images captured under controlled lighting, uniform backgrounds, and minimal occlusion, providing a complementary benchmark for cross-domain evaluation.

After pretraining unlabeled PlantDoc images using our proposed SSL framework, the model was fine-tuned on labeled PlantVillage samples. The model achieved consistently high classification performance on the PlantVillage dataset, demonstrating that the learned representations are both robust and transferable. These results underscore the practical utility of our framework for deployment across diverse agricultural contexts, including settings where labeled data may be limited or vary in quality.

2.7. Implementation Details

Table 1 summarizes the key hyperparameters, architectural components, and training configurations used in our experiments. The model was implemented in PyTorch 2.1.0+ and trained on an NVIDIA RTX GPU with mixed precision enabled for memory efficiency. The full implementation, including training scripts, data loaders, and model checkpoints, is available at our public GitHub repository: https://github.com/sherryHuan/SSL_BYOL_MIM_Contrastive/tree/main (accessed on 15 June 2025).

Table 1. Summary of model architecture, training parameters, and augmentation settings.

Category	Setting/Description
Backbone Network	ResNet-101 (pretrained on ImageNet)
Input Resolution	384 × 384
BYOL Projection Head	Linear (2048 → 512) → ReLU → Linear (512 → 256)
BYOL Prediction Head	Linear (256 → 512) → ReLU → Linear (512 → 256)
MLP Classifier (used during fine-tuning)	Linear (2048 → 512) → ReLU → Linear (512 → 27)

Table 1. *Cont.*

Category	Setting/Description
Augmentation (GPU)	Kornia-based stochastic transforms, applied on GPU
Random Crop (scale)	0.6–1.0
Horizontal Flip	$p = 0.5$
Rotation	±20°
Solarization	Threshold = 0.5, $p = 0.2$
Grayscale Conversion	$p = 0.2$
Color Jitter	Brightness, contrast, saturation, and hue
Gaussian Blur	$\sigma \in [0.1, 2.0]$, $p = 0.3$
Normalization (mean/std)	Mean = [0.485, 0.456, 0.406]; Std = [0.229, 0.224, 0.225]
Training Configuration	
Epochs	90
Batch Size	16
Optimizer	AdamW
Learning Rate	Warmup from 1×10^{-6} to 1×10^{-4} over first 10 epochs
Weight Decay	1×10^{-5}
Gradient Accumulation	Every 2 batches
Mixed Precision	Enabled via torch.cuda.amp
Checkpointing	Every 5 epochs
Loss Weights	
BYOL Loss	1.0—Cosine similarity between online prediction and target projection.
MIM Loss	0.6—Combine pixel-level differences and perceptual similarity, balancing mean squared error (MSE) with structural similarity (SSIM).
Contrastive Loss	0.6—InfoNCE loss with a temperature of $\tau = 0.1$ for instance discrimination.
Final Training Loss	**L_Total = 1.0·L_BYOL + 0.6·L_MIM + 0.6·L_Contrastive**

3. Results and Discussion

3.1. Experimental Dataset

We evaluate the proposed self-supervised learning framework on two publicly available datasets, each offering unique characteristics that test the model's robustness and generalization capabilities:

- PlantDoc: This is a challenging real-world dataset consisting of 2598 images spanning 13 plant species and 27 classes, including both diseased and healthy leaf samples. The images were captured under natural field conditions and exhibit considerable variability in lighting, background clutter, leaf orientation, and symptom presentation. The dataset includes crops such as apples, grapes, cotton, and maize, providing a comprehensive benchmark for assessing model robustness in practical agricultural scenarios. Example images from the PlantDoc dataset are shown in Figure 2.
- PlantVillage: In contrast, the PlantVillage dataset comprises over 54,000 images representing 38 classes, including a wide variety of healthy and diseased leaf types. The images are captured under controlled laboratory conditions with uniform backgrounds and consistent lighting, making this dataset particularly suitable for evaluating model generalization in clean, noise-free environments. Example images from the PlantVillage dataset are shown in Figure 3.

Figure 2. Samples from the PlantDoc dataset.

Figure 3. Samples from the PlantVillage dataset.

3.2. Evaluation Metrics

To comprehensively assess the effectiveness of the proposed self-supervised learning framework, we employ a range of widely accepted classification metrics, each capturing a different aspect of model performance:

- Accuracy: Overall proportion of correct predictions across all classes.

$$\text{Accuracy}(\%) = \frac{\text{TP} + \text{TN}}{\text{TP} + \text{TN} + \text{FP} + \text{FN}} \times 100 \tag{5}$$

  where TP, TN, FP, and FN denote true positives, true negatives, false positives, and false negatives, respectively.
- Precision: Measures the exactness of the model by computing the proportion of correctly predicted positive instances out of all predicted positives.

$$\text{Precision}(\%) = \frac{\text{TP}}{\text{TP} + \text{FP}} \times 100 \tag{6}$$

- Recall: Also known as sensitivity, it evaluates the model's ability to identify all actual positive instances.

$$\text{Recall}(\%) = \frac{\text{TP}}{\text{TP} + \text{FN}} \times 100 \tag{7}$$

- F1-score: The harmonic mean of precision and recall, providing a balanced view of performance, especially important in imbalanced datasets.

$$\text{F1-Score}(\%) = 2 \times \frac{\text{Precision} \times \text{Recall}}{\text{Precision} + \text{Recall}} \times 100 \tag{8}$$

In addition to these quantitative metrics, we incorporate several qualitative evaluation tools:

- Confusion Matrix: Visualizes the relationship between predicted and actual class labels, revealing common misclassification patterns and class-wise accuracy.
- Grad-CAM (Gradient-weighted Class Activation Mapping): Provides visual interpretability by highlighting image regions that are most influential in the model's decision-making process.

- t-SNE (t-distributed Stochastic Neighbor Embedding): A dimensionality reduction technique used to visualize high-dimensional feature embeddings in a two-dimensional space, enabling inspection of inter-class separability and clustering behavior.

3.3. Performance on PlantDoc

3.3.1. Per-Class Performance

To assess the real-world effectiveness of the proposed self-supervised learning framework, we evaluated the pretrained model on the PlantDoc dataset, which comprises field-captured images exhibiting high variability in lighting, background complexity, and symptom expression across 27 disease and healthy classes.

Table 2 summarizes the per-class performance metrics, including precision, recall, and F1-score. The model demonstrates consistently strong classification results across most categories. Particularly, it achieves perfect F1-scores (1.0000) in several well-defined classes such as squash powdery mildew leaf, strawberry leaf, tomato leaf yellow virus, grape leaf, and grape leaf black rot. This indicates exceptional precision and recall in detecting these diseases. Additional classes, including raspberry leaf, soyabean leaf, and tomato septoria leaf spot, also yield high F1-scores (above 0.88), showing robust classification even under moderate visual variability. However, performance drops are observed in a few underrepresented or visually ambiguous categories. For instance, corn gray leaf spot (F1-score: 0.267) and tomato mold leaf (F1-score: 0.588) were more frequently misclassified. This is likely due to visual similarity with other leaf conditions or insufficient training examples in these categories. Moreover, categories like cherry leaf and tomato leaf show relatively low recall, indicating a tendency to misclassify these instances.

Table 2. Per-class precision, recall, and F1-score on the PlantDoc dataset.

#	Class	Precision (%)	Recall (%)	F1-Score (%)
0	Apple Scab Leaf	72.73	80.00	76.19
1	Apple leaf	57.14	88.89	69.57
2	Apple rust leaf	88.89	72.73	80.00
3	Bell_pepper leaf	85.71	75.00	80.00
4	Bell_pepper leaf spot	83.33	100.00	90.91
5	Blueberry leaf	90.00	81.82	85.71
6	Cherry leaf	83.33	50.00	62.50
7	Corn gray leaf spot	18.18	50.00	26.67
8	Corn leaf blight	71.43	41.67	52.63
9	Corn rust leaf	81.82	90.00	85.71
10	Peach leaf	100.00	77.78	87.50
11	Potato leaf early blight	62.50	62.50	62.50
12	Potato leaf late blight	62.50	62.50	62.50
13	Raspberry leaf	87.50	100.00	93.33
14	Soyabean leaf	100.00	87.50	93.33
15	Squash powdery mildew leaf	100.00	100.00	100.00
16	Strawberry leaf	100.00	100.00	100.00
17	Tomato early blight leaf	72.73	88.89	80.00
18	Tomato septoria leaf spot	78.57	100.00	88.00
19	Tomato leaf	57.14	50.00	53.33
20	Tomato leaf bacterial spot	83.33	50.00	62.50
21	Tomato leaf late blight	77.78	70.00	73.68
22	Tomato leaf mosaic virus	100.00	50.00	66.67
23	Tomato leaf yellow virus	100.00	100.00	100.00
24	Tomato mold leaf	45.45	83.33	58.82
25	Grape leaf	100.00	100.00	100.00

Table 2. *Cont.*

#	Class	Precision (%)	Recall (%)	F1-Score (%)
26	Grape leaf black rot	100.00	100.00	100.00
Macro Average		**80.00**	**78.24**	**77.48**

Despite these outliers, the model maintains a macro-averaged precision of 80.00%, recall of 78.24%, and F1-score of 77.48%. These results confirm that the proposed self-supervised learning framework effectively learns robust and discriminative features from unlabeled field data, making it well-suited for complex, real-world plant disease detection tasks.

3.3.2. Confusion Matrix Analysis

As shown in Figure 4, the confusion matrix for the PlantDoc test set reveals strong diagonal dominance, indicating high classification accuracy across most categories. Classes such as bell pepper leaf spot, strawberry leaf, tomato septoria leaf spot, and grape leaf black rot exhibit near-perfect separability. Misclassifications occur primarily in visually similar or underrepresented classes. For instance, apple rust leaf is occasionally confused with apple leaf and apple scab leaf, while tomato leaf mosaic virus overlaps with related tomato conditions such as tomato leaf yellow virus. Additionally, harder-to-distinguish categories like corn gray leaf spot and tomato mold leaf show scattered misclassifications, likely due to their subtle visual symptoms and smaller sample sizes.

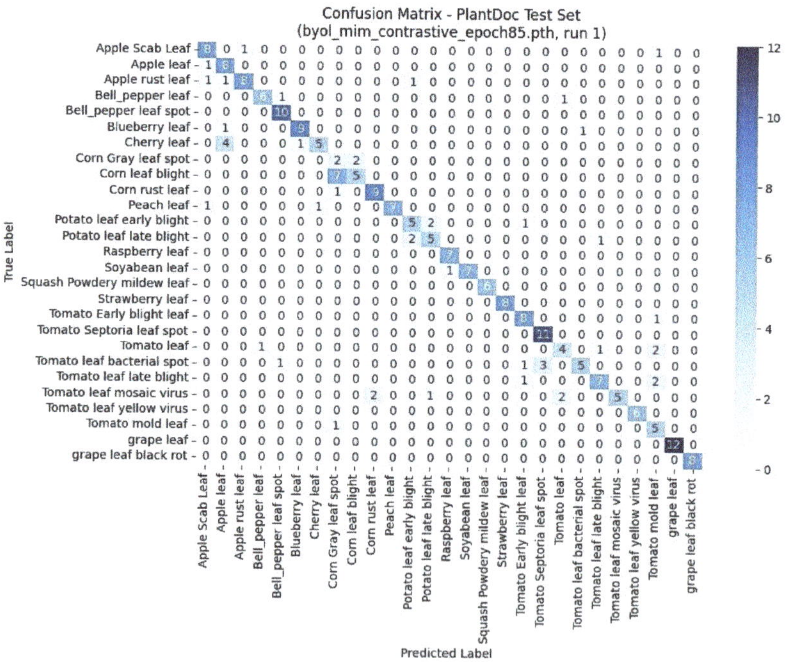

Figure 4. Confusion matrix of predicted versus actual labels on the PlantDoc test set using the model trained with BYOL + MIM + contrastive learning. The model shows high accuracy and strong class separability, with most predictions concentrated along the diagonal.

Overall, the matrix confirms that the model learns meaningful, discriminative features even under complex, real-world conditions.

3.3.3. Model Interpretability via Grad-CAM

To assess the interpretability of our self-supervised learning model, we employed Gradient-weighted Class Activation Mapping (Grad-CAM), which visualizes class-discriminative regions that influence the model's predictions. Figure 5 shows two representative examples: apple rust leaf (top row) and grape leaf black rot (bottom row). Each row presents the input image, the Grad-CAM heatmap, and the overlay on the original image.

In both cases, the highlighted regions closely correspond to disease symptoms, such as rust-colored lesions and dark necrotic spots, indicating that the model attends to pathologically meaningful features rather than background noise. These visualizations enhance the model's explainability, a critical factor for real-world applications where human-in-the-loop decision support and trust in automated systems are essential.

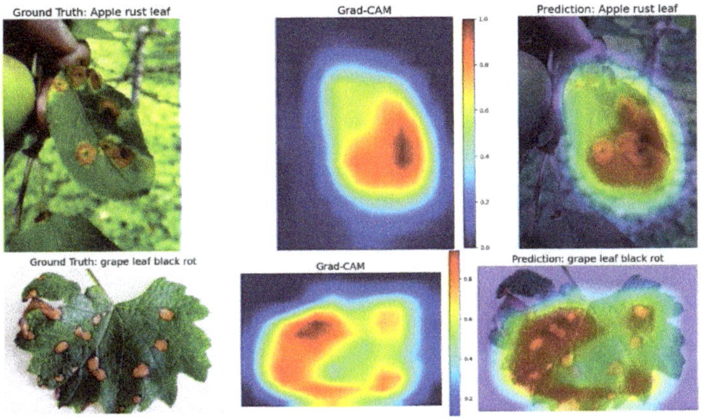

Figure 5. Grad-CAM visualizations show attention maps for apple rust leaf (**top**) and grape leaf black rot (**bottom**), aligning well with true disease symptoms despite no labeled supervision.

3.4. Comparison with Existing Models

Table 3 presents a comparative analysis of our proposed self-supervised model against a diverse set of state-of-the-art architectures evaluated on the PlantDoc dataset. Our framework, which integrates BYOL, MIM, and contrastive learning atop a ResNet-101 backbone, achieves a macro precision of 80.00%, macro recall of 78.24%, and macro F1-score of 77.48%. These results demonstrate robust performance under real-world agricultural conditions and position our method among the top-performing models on this benchmark.

Compared to transformer-based models such as Swin Transformer and Vision Transformer (ViT), our method achieves higher recall and competitive F1-scores. The recently proposed Efficient Swin Transformer [19] achieves slightly higher macro precision (80.14%) and macro F1-score (78.16%), but with lower recall (76.27%). Importantly, its confusion matrix reveals a complete failure to classify certain classes—Class 7 (corn gray leaf spot) records zero true positives, indicating weaker robustness for rare or ambiguous disease symptoms. In contrast, our model maintains measurable recall on all classes, including difficult categories, which reflects stronger generalization to challenging, field-based conditions.

Among convolutional networks, our model outperforms GoogLeNet [20], DenseNet [21], and MobileNet [22], validating the efficacy of multi-objective self-supervised pretraining over purely supervised approaches. While lightweight models like ShuffleNet V2 [23] and MobileViT [24] are efficient in computation, they consistently underperform in key evaluation metrics. Our approach also demonstrates favorable results when compared to domain-specific and hybrid models such as T-CNN (ResNet-101) [25] and ICVT [26].

Despite these models being tailored for interpretability or trained with full supervision, their performance does not surpass our label-free pretraining pipeline. The superior generalization and label efficiency of our model demonstrate that carefully designed SSL pipelines can rival or exceed specialized methods in complex, real-world agricultural tasks.

Table 3. Comparison with existing models on the PlantDoc dataset.

Model	Precision (%)	Recall (%)	F1-Score (%)
Mobilenet [22]	55.24	52.57	53.82
ResNet	67.36	65.34	66.28
GoogLeNet [20]	74.31	69.19	71.61
DenseNet [21]	69.26	66.17	67.61
ShuffleNet V2 [23]	72.28	71.24	71.70
MobileViT [24]	72.55	68.22	70.32
Vision Transformer	54.35	56.77	55.53
Swin Transformer	75.85	69.91	72.76
T-CNN (ResNet-101) [25]	74.44	-	-
ICVT [26]	77.23	-	-
Efficient Swin Transformer [19]	80.84	76.72	78.16
Ours (BYOL + MIM + Contrastive)	80.00	78.24	77.48

3.5. Ablation Study

We conducted an ablation study to evaluate the individual and combined contributions of BYOL, MIM, and contrastive learning within our self-supervised framework. Additionally, we benchmarked against prominent self-supervised baselines, including SimCLR and DINOv2.

As shown in Table 4, BYOL alone surpasses both baselines and the BYOL + MIM configuration, indicating that while MIM provides structural reconstruction benefits, it may slightly interfere with BYOL's semantic consistency when applied in isolation. Similarly, the BYOL + Contrastive configuration performs slightly below BYOL + MIM, likely because contrastive objectives alone, without the complementary structural guidance from MIM, can overemphasize inter-instance separation at the expense of fine-grained spatial representations. Nevertheless, the full integration of BYOL, MIM, and contrastive learning yields the best results, achieving 77.82% classification accuracy, 80.00% macro precision, 78.24% macro recall, and 77.48% macro F1-score. These results demonstrate that while MIM alone does not significantly improve performance, its contribution becomes more effective when complemented by contrastive regularization. The combination allows the model to balance global consistency, local reconstruction, and inter-instance discrimination—critical components for robust feature learning in visually diverse plant disease datasets.

The comparatively lower performance of SimCLR and DINOv2 is likely due to their reliance on large-scale datasets and architectural sensitivity. SimCLR, which depends heavily on negative sampling and large batch sizes, may be suboptimal under the moderate size and noisy conditions of PlantDoc. Similarly, DINOv2, built on Vision Transformers, typically benefits from extensive data and longer pretraining cycles to reach peak performance.

In contrast, our ResNet-based approach, equipped with GPU-accelerated augmentations and guided by a multi-objective loss, is better suited to real-world agricultural constraints, enabling efficient learning from unlabeled, field-acquired imagery. These findings validate the effectiveness of our framework in data-scarce, noisy domains and highlight the importance of integrating diverse SSL signals for robust plant disease recognition.

Table 4. Ablation results comparing different self-supervised learning configurations on the PlantDoc dataset.

Method	Accuracy (%)	Precision (Macro)	Recall (Macro)	F1-Score (Macro)
SimCLR	73.31	74.12	73.25	72.53
DINOv2	73.31	74.55	73.24	72.78
BYOL	74.58	76.70	74.95	74.52
BYOL + Contrastive	74.20	75.90	74.10	72.90
BYOL + MIM	74.58	76.28	74.40	73.17
BYOL + MIM + Contrastive	77.82	80.00	78.24	77.48

3.6. *Transferability to PlantVillage*

3.6.1. Transfer Performance on PlantVillage

To contextualize the effectiveness of our self-supervised model, we compared its performance with several notable studies that utilized the PlantVillage dataset for plant disease classification. These prior efforts span a wide range of strategies, including deep convolutional architectures, data augmentation, image segmentation, transformer-based models, and ensemble learning techniques.

Ref. [3] achieved 99.75% accuracy using DenseNet, while ref. [27] proposed a CNN-based model with multiple loss functions, reaching 98.93%. Ref. [28] used a two-model ensemble and achieved 99.7%. Ref. [29] combined RGB and segmented inputs with DenseNet, yielding 98.17%, and ref. [30], one of the earliest contributions, reported 99.31% using a basic CNN. Ref. [31] reported the highest accuracy of 99.91% through extensive data augmentation and deeper architecture. Most recently, ref. [32] utilized digital image pre-processing with a ten-model ensemble to achieve 99.89%. In addition, ref. [33] introduced an optimized Vision Transformer (ViT) configuration, achieving 99.77% accuracy on the PlantVillage dataset while maintaining low parameter count and storage requirements.

In comparison, our proposed framework achieves 99.85% accuracy using a single ResNet-101 backbone pretrained in a self-supervised manner using BYOL, MIM, and contrastive learning, without requiring any labeled data during pretraining. While our accuracy is marginally lower than that of refs. [31,32] and higher than the ViT of ref. [33] and other alternative methods, our approach avoids the complexity and computational cost associated with data augmentation, transformers, and ensemble techniques. As summarized in Table 5, these results demonstrate that self-supervised learning can achieve performance on par with state-of-the-art supervised or ensemble methods, while offering significant advantages in scalability, label efficiency, and practical deployment. This reinforces the potential of SSL frameworks in real-world agricultural applications, particularly in data-scarce environments.

Although the PlantDoc and PlantVillage datasets differ in the number of disease categories (27 and 38 classes, respectively), the strong transfer performance demonstrates the strength of our learned representations. Unlike supervised pretraining, self-supervised learning focuses on extracting generalizable visual patterns such as texture, color, and structural cues, without being tied to specific class labels. As a result, the backbone pretrained on unlabeled PlantDoc images is able to adapt effectively to the new class structure of PlantVillage during fine-tuning. The cleaner and less noisy conditions of the PlantVillage dataset further facilitate rapid adaptation, leading to the observed high classification accuracy. This result highlights the domain-agnostic nature of self-supervised features and underscores the practical scalability of the proposed framework across diverse agricultural environments.

While downstream fine-tuning still necessitates labeled data, the self-supervised pretraining phase enables the model to acquire rich and transferable representations without supervision. This substantially reduces the quantity and quality of labeled data required to achieve strong downstream performance, offering a scalable solution for data-scarce agricultural applications.

Table 5. Transfer learning comparison on PlantVillage.

Reference	Dataset	Accuracy (%)	Contribution
[3]	PlantVillage	99.75	Performance evaluation of DenseNet compared to other deep learning models
[27]	PlantVillage	98.93	Combined multiple loss functions within a CNN-based framework
[28]	PlantVillage	99.70	Developed an ensemble of two distinct deep learning models
[29]	PlantVillage	98.17	Integrated DenseNet with both RGB and segmented leaf image inputs
[30]	PlantVillage	99.31	Applied a basic deep CNN model for plant disease classification
[31]	PlantVillage	99.91	Improved accuracy through extensive augmentation and deeper architecture
[32]	PlantVillage	99.89	Utilized image preprocessing with a 10-model ensemble to maximize performance
[33]	PlantVillage	99.77	Optimized Vision Transformers with multiscale attention and targeted preprocessing
Proposed (Ours)	PlantVillage	99.85	Self-supervised ResNet101 trained with BYOL, MIM, and contrastive learning

3.6.2. Training Dynamics

Figure 6 presents the training and validation curves for loss and accuracy during the downstream classification on the PlantVillage dataset. The model exhibits rapid convergence, with validation accuracy exceeding 99% within the first few epochs. Both training and validation losses decrease sharply and stabilize near zero, indicating strong model fitting and effective generalization.

Notably, the small gap between training and validation accuracy implies minimal overfitting, underscoring the robustness of the representations learned during self-supervised pretraining. These results demonstrate that the combination of BYOL, MIM, and contrastive learning enables efficient downstream training, requiring fewer labeled examples and epochs to reach near-optimal performance in new domains.

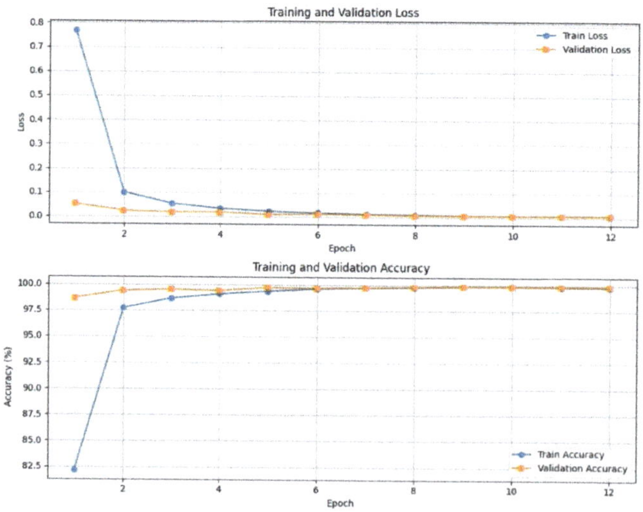

Figure 6. Training and validation loss (**top**) and accuracy (**bottom**) curves on the PlantVillage dataset. The model exhibits rapid convergence and minimal overfitting, reflecting the robustness of the self-supervised pretraining.

3.6.3. Feature Space Visualization with t-SNE

To further investigate the quality of the learned representations, we employed t-Distributed Stochastic Neighbor Embedding (t-SNE) to visualize the high-dimensional feature space extracted from the PlantVillage dataset. As shown in Figure 7, the self-supervised model produces well-separated and tightly clustered embeddings for most disease classes. Categories such as tomato mosaic virus, potato late blight, and grape black rot form clearly distinguishable clusters, indicating strong intra-class consistency and inter-class separability.

This structured clustering demonstrates the model's ability to encode fine-grained visual cues while maintaining reliable, generalizable representations. It highlights the effectiveness of SSL pretraining on unlabeled PlantDoc data in producing discriminative and transferable features across domains.

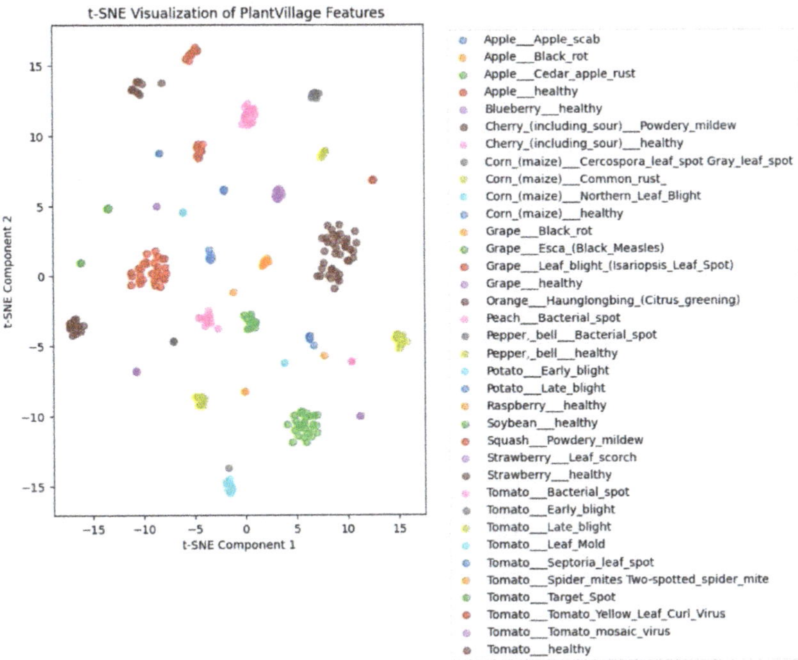

Figure 7. t-SNE visualization of feature embeddings generated by the SSL-pretrained ResNet-101 on the PlantVillage dataset. Each point represents a sample projected into 2D space. The clear clustering of disease classes illustrates strong semantic structure and discriminative capability of the learned representations.

4. Conclusions

In this study, we proposed a unified self-supervised learning (SSL) framework that integrates Bootstrap Your Own Latent (BYOL), Masked Image Modeling (MIM), and contrastive learning for plant disease detection. Leveraging a ResNet-101 backbone and GPU-accelerated augmentations, the model effectively learns rich and transferable visual representations from unlabeled plant imagery, directly addressing the critical challenge of limited annotated datasets in agriculture.

Through extensive comparisons, ablation studies, and visualization analyses, we demonstrated the complementary benefits of combining global feature alignment (BYOL), local structural reconstruction (MIM), and instance-level discrimination (contrastive learning). Our results confirm that this multi-objective SSL approach not only reduces reliance on labeled data but also achieves high predictive performance in both in-field and laboratory settings.

While PlantVillage yields near-perfect results due to its clean lab conditions, and PlantDoc presents moderate in-field variability, we acknowledge the need to evaluate our method on newer, more challenging large-scale in-field collections.

Future directions include extending this framework to cross-modal SSL using drone or satellite imagery, exploring domain adaptation across different crop species, and incorporating explainable AI techniques to support decision-making for farmers and agronomists. Overall, our findings highlight the practical potential of self-supervised learning in creating scalable, efficient, and intelligent systems for plant disease diagnostics in real-world, resource-constrained agricultural environments.

Author Contributions: Writing—original draft, writing—review and editing, conceptualization, methodology, data curation, software, formal analysis, investigation, validation, X.H.; writing—review and editing, formal analysis, investigation, validation, B.C.; writing—review and editing, formal analysis, investigation, validation, H.Z. All authors have read and agreed to the published version of the manuscript.

Funding: This research received no external funding.

Data Availability Statement: The data presented in this study are openly available in https://github.com/sherryHuan/SSL_BYOL_MIM_Contrastive/tree/main (accessed on 15 June 2025).

Conflicts of Interest: The authors declare no conflict of interest.

References

1. Xu, M.; Kim, H.; Yang, J.; Fuentes, A.; Meng, Y. Embracing limited and imperfect training datasets: Opportunities and challenge in plant disease recognition using deep learning. *Front. Plant Sci.* **2023**, *14*, 1225409. [CrossRef] [PubMed]
2. Pujari, J.; Yakkundimath, R.; Byadgi, A. Image Processing Based Detection of Fungal Diseases in Plants. *Procedia Comput. Sc* **2015**, *46*, 1802–1808. [CrossRef]
3. Too, E.; Yujian, L.; Njuki, S.; Yingchun, L. A comparative study of fine-tuning deep learning models for plant disease identificatio *Comput. Electron. Agric.* **2019**, *161*, 272–279. [CrossRef]
4. Che, C.; Xue, N.; Li, Z.; Zhao, Y.; Huang, X. Automatic cassava disease recognition using object segmentation and progressiv learning. *PeerJ Comput. Sci.* **2025**, *11*, e2721. [CrossRef]
5. Zhang, J.; Cao, Y.; Xu, D. Uncertainty-aware Masked Modeling in Medical Imaging. In Proceedings of the IEEE Internationa Conference on Acoustics, Speech and Signal Processing (ICASSP), Hyderabad, India, 6–11 April 2025; pp. 1–5. [CrossRef]
6. Oquab, M.; Darcet, T.; Moutakanni, T.; Vo, H.; Szafraniec, M.; Khalidov, V.; Fernandez, P.; Haziza, D.; Massa, F.; El-Nouby, A.; et a DINOv2: Learning Robust Visual Features without Supervision. *arXiv* **2023**, arXiv:2304.07193. [CrossRef]
7. Mamun, A.A.; Ahmedt-Aristizabal, D.; Zhang, M.; Ismail Hossen, M.; Hayder, Z.; Awrangjeb, M. Plant Disease Detection Usin Self-supervised Learning: A Systematic Review. *IEEE Access* **2024**, *12*, 171926–171943. [CrossRef]
8. Wang, Z.; Wang, R.; Wang, M.; Lai, T.; Zhang, M. Self-supervised Transformer-Based Pre-training Method with General Plan Infection Dataset. In *Lecture Notes in Computer Science, Proceedings of the Pattern Recognition and Computer Vision (PRCV), Urumq China, 18–20 October 2024*; Springer Nature: Singapore, 2025; Volume 15032. [CrossRef]
9. Gustineli, M.; Miyaguchi, A.; Stalter, I. Multi-Label Plant Species Classification with Self-Supervised Vision Transformers. *arXi* **2024**, arXiv:2407.06298. [CrossRef]
10. Chen, T.; Kornblith, S.; Norouzi, M.; Hinton, G. A simple framework for contrastive learning of visual representations In Proceedings of the 37th International Conference on Machine Learning (ICML 2020), Virtual Event, 13–18 July 2020 pp. 1597–1607. [CrossRef]
11. Grill, J.-B.; Strub, F.; Altché, F.; Tallec, C.; Richemond, P.H.; Buchatskaya, E.; Doersch, C.; Avila Pires, B.; Guo, Z.; Gheshlaghi Azar M.; et al. Bootstrap your own latent: A new approach to self-supervised learning. In Proceedings of the Neural Information Processing Systems 33, Vancouver, BC, Canada, 6–12 December 2020; pp. 21271–21284. Available online: https://proceedings neurips.cc/paper_files/paper/2020/file/f3ada80d5c4ee70142b17b8192b2958e-Paper.pdf (accessed on 1 March 2025).

Singh, D.; Jain, N.; Kayal, P.; Sinha, A. PlantDoc: A Dataset for Visual Plant Disease Detection. In Proceedings of the 7th ACM IKDD Conference on Data Science (CoDS) and the 25th Conference on Management of Data (COMAD), Hyderabad, India, 5–7 January 2020. [CrossRef]

Hughes, D.P.; Salathé, M. An open access repository of images on plant health to enable the development of mobile disease diagnostics. *arXiv* **2015**, arXiv:1511.08060. [CrossRef]

He, K.; Zhang, X.; Ren, S.; Sun, J. Deep Residual Learning for Image Recognition. In Proceedings of the IEEE Conference on Computer Vision and Pattern Recognition (CVPR 2016), Las Vegas, NV, USA, 27–30 June 2016; pp. 770–778. [CrossRef]

Deng, J.; Dong, W.; Socher, R.; Li, L.-J.; Li, K.; Li, F.F. ImageNet: A large-scale hierarchical image database. In Proceedings of the IEEE Conference on Computer Vision and Pattern Recognition (CVPR), Miami, FL, USA, 20–25 June 2009; pp. 248–255. [CrossRef]

He, K.; Chen, X.; Xie, S.; Li, Y.; Dollár, P.; Girshick, R. Masked Autoencoders Are Scalable Vision Learners. In Proceedings of the IEEE/CVF Conference on Computer Vision and Pattern Recognition (CVPR), New Orleans, LA, USA, 18–24 June 2022; pp. 15979–15988. [CrossRef]

Oord, A.; Li, Y.; Vinyals, O. Representation Learning with Contrastive Predictive Coding. *arXiv* **2018**, arXiv:1807.03748. [CrossRef]

Riba, E.; Mishkin, D.; Ponsa, D.; Rublee, E.; Bradski, G. Kornia: An Open Source Differentiable Computer Vision Library for PyTorch. In Proceedings of the IEEE Winter Conference on Applications of Computer Vision (WACV), Snowmass, CO, USA, 1–5 March 2020; pp. 3663–3672. [CrossRef]

Liu, W.; Zhang, A. Plant Disease Detection Algorithm Based on Efficient Swin Transformer. *Comput. Mater. Contin.* **2025**, *82*, 3045–3068. [CrossRef]

Szegedy, C.; Liu, W.; Jia, Y.; Sermanet, P.; Reed, S.; Anguelov, D.; Erhan, D.; Vanhoucke, V.; Rabinovich, A. Going deeper with convolutions. In Proceedings of the 2015 IEEE Conference on Computer Vision and Pattern Recognition (CVPR), Boston, MA, USA, 7–12 June 2015; pp. 1–9. [CrossRef]

Huang, G.; Liu, Z.; Van Der Maaten, L.; Weinberger, K.Q. Densely Connected Convolutional Networks. In Proceedings of the 2017 IEEE Conference on Computer Vision and Pattern Recognition (CVPR), Honolulu, HI, USA, 21–26 July 2017; pp. 2261–2269. [CrossRef]

2. Howard, A.G.; Zhu, M.; Chen, B.; Kalenichenko, D.; Wang, W.; Weyand, T.; Andreetto, M.; Adam, H. MobileNets: Efficient convolutional neural networks for mobile vision applications. *arXiv* **2017**, arXiv:1704.04861. [CrossRef]

3. Ma, N.; Zhang, X.; Zheng, H.T.; Sun, J. ShuffleNet V2: Practical Guidelines for Efficient CNN Architecture Design. In *Lecture Notes in Computer Science, Proceedings of the European Conference on Computer Vision (ECCV 2018), Munich, Germany, 8–14 September 2018;* Ferrari, V., Hebert, M., Sminchisescu, C., Weiss, Y., Eds.; Springer: Berlin/Heidelberg, Germany, 2018; Volume 11218, pp. 122–138. [CrossRef]

4. Mehta, S.; Rastegari, M. MobileViT: Light-weight, General-purpose, and Mobile-friendly Vision Transformer. *arXiv* **2021**, arXiv:2110.02178. [CrossRef]

5. Wang, D.; Wang, J.; Li, W.; Guan, P. T-CNN: Trilinear Convolutional Neural Networks Model for Visual Detection of Plant Diseases. *Comput. Electron. Agric.* **2021**, *190*, 106468. [CrossRef]

6. Yu, S.; Xie, L.; Huang, Q. Inception Convolutional Vision Transformers for Plant Disease Identification. *Internet Things* **2023**, *21*, 100650. [CrossRef]

7. Gokulnath, B.; Usha, D.G. Identifying and classifying plant disease using resilient LF-CNN. *Ecol. Inform.* **2021**, *63*, 101283. [CrossRef]

8. Vo, H.-T.; Quach, L.-D.; Hoang, T. Ensemble of Deep Learning Models for Multi-plant Disease Classification in Smart Farming. *Int. J. Adv. Comput. Sci. Appl.* **2023**, *14*. [CrossRef]

9. Kaya, Y.; Gürsoy, E. A novel multi-head CNN design to identify plant diseases using the fusion of RGB images. *Ecol. Inform.* **2023**, *75*, 101998. [CrossRef]

0. Mohanty, S.; Hughes, D.; Salath'e, M. Using Deep Learning for Image-Based Plant Disease Detection. *Front. Plant Sci.* **2016**, *7*, 1419. [CrossRef]

1. Atila, Ü.; Uçar, M.; Akyol, K.; Uçar, E. Plant leaf disease classification using EfficientNet deep learning model. *Ecol. Inform.* **2021**, *61*, 101182. [CrossRef]

2. Ali, A.H.; Youssef, A.; Abdelal, M.; Raja, M.A. An ensemble of deep learning architectures for accurate plant disease classification. *Ecol. Inform.* **2024**, *81*, 102618. [CrossRef]

3. Ouamane, A.; Chouchane, A.; Himeur, Y.; Miniaoui, S.; Zaguia, A. Optimized vision transformers for superior plant disease detection. *IEEE Access* **2025**, *13*, 39165–39181. [CrossRef]

electronics

MDPI

Article

ImpactAlert: Pedestrian-Carried Vehicle Collision Alert System

Raghav Rawat [1], Caspar Lant [2], Haowen Yuan [1] and Dennis Shasha [1,*]

[1] Department of Computer Science Tandon/Courant, New York University, New York, NY 10012, USA; rr3418@nyu.edu (R.R.); haowen.yuan@nyu.edu (H.Y.)
[2] Department of Computer Science, Columbia University, New York, NY 10027, USA; caspar@cs.columbia.edu
* Correspondence: shasha@cims.nyu.edu

Abstract

The ImpactAlert system is a chest-mounted system that detects objects that are likely to hit a pedestrian and alerts that pedestrian. The primary use cases are visually impaired pedestrians or pedestrians who need to be warned about vehicles or other pedestrians coming from unseen directions. This paper argues for the need for such a system, the design and algorithms of ImpactAlert, and experiments carried out in varied urban environments, ranging from densely crowded to semi-urban in the United States, India and China. ImpactAlert makes use of a LiDAR camera found on a commercial wireless phone, processes the data over several frames to evaluate the time to impact and speed of potential threats. When ImpactAlert determines a threat meets the criteria set by the user, it sends warning signals through an output device to warn a pedestrian. The output device can be an audible warning and/or a low-cost smart cane that vibrates when danger approaches. Our experiments in urban and semi-urban environments show that (i) ImpactAlert can avoid nearly all false negatives (when an alarm should be sent and it isn't) and (ii) enjoys a low false positive rate. The net result is an effective low cost system to alert pedestrians in an urban environment.

Keywords: collision alert; LiDAR; mobility aid; visually impaired; safety system; urban environment

1. Introduction

City streets and sidewalks are bustling with vehicles, and for the visually impaired, navigating these environments can be particularly perilous. According to recent accident statistics, visually impaired individuals are at a significantly higher risk of collisions compared to the general population. One study found that 1 in 12 pedestrians with blindness reported being hit by a motor vehicle or cyclist [1]. Additionally, about 40% of blind individuals experience head-height collisions at least once a year, with 15% experiencing such collisions monthly [2]. Another study found that individuals with visual impairment have a 46% increased risk of being involved in road traffic crashes compared to those without visual impairments [3]. While general pedestrian accident rates are concerning, the visually impaired face even greater challenges due to their inability to perceive and react to approaching hazards as effectively as sighted individuals. Such incidents underscore the critical need for advanced technologies that can augment the abilities of visually impaired individuals, providing them with timely alerts and enhancing their safety.

The ImpactAlert warning system aims to address this need. By utilizing LiDAR sensors and data to track incoming objects, the system's algorithms determine when to alert the pedestrian to potential collisions, giving the pedestrian time to avoid or prepare for impact. This paper describes the algorithms and implementation of the ImpactAlert warning system, then evaluates the quality of its algorithm (accuracy, recall, precision, F1-score) through experiments on the streets of four urban areas with wide differences in traffic densities and speeds. The github link to the codebase used for ImpactAlert and the experiments can be found https://github.com/hwyuanzi/Impact-Alert-Lidar/, last accessed on 1 August 2025.

2. Related Work

The development of assistive technologies to detect vehicles has been an active area of research in recent years.

Autonomous vehicles use advanced LIDAR sensors and machine learning algorithms to detect pedestrians effectively. A study focused on the performance of algorithms like k-Nearest Neighbors, Naïve Bayes Classifier, and Support Vector Machine, applied to 3D LIDAR sensor data, demonstrated very high recall and high precision in real-world tests. These systems form a part of advanced driver assistance systems (ADAS), improving road safety [4].

Collision detection systems installed at static locations, such as parking lots or intersections, enhance safety by warning pedestrians and vehicle operators about potential collisions. These systems, like the Collision Sentry, use motion detection and sound alarms to mitigate accidents in high-risk areas [5].

Recent advancements in systems that warn drivers about pedestrians to avoid collision focus on detecting pedestrians from vehicles. Machine learning/computer vision algorithms, applied to LIDAR and camera data, improve overall pedestrian safety, particularly at pedestrian crossings and during road navigation [6].

Scalvini et al. introduced an outdoor navigation assistive system leveraging 3D spatialized sound and sonified obstacle information to guide blind individuals. The system combines inertial sensors, GPS data, and visual cues processed via deep learning to refine navigation trajectories in real-time. With low-latency processing on embedded GPUs, it operates independently of remote connections, providing an efficient and reliable navigation aid [7].

Real-time decision-making models are gaining prominence, incorporating pedestrian trajectory, speed, and environmental factors to provide early warnings. These systems often integrate vehicle-to-everything (V2X) communication technologies to enhance collision prevention in crowded urban environments [8].

Systems to avoid vehicle to vehicle collisions rely on radar, LIDAR, and cameras to predict potential collisions. Advanced systems employ object tracking and predictive modeling to enhance accuracy and reaction time. Such methods are embedded in fully autonomous vehicles [9].

2.1. Smart Canes for the Visually Impaired

Laser sensing technology has also emerged as a promising approach for smart canes. Bolgiano et al. first mounted a laser sensor on a blind cane in 1967 [10], while Benjamin et al. developed the C1–C5 series of laser smart canes in the early 1970s [11]. These early devices used laser sensors to detect obstacles and provide audio or vibration warnings. They were limited by the technology of the time, offering restricted detection accuracy and range.

Advances have focused on improving detection capabilities and integrating multiple sensors. Mai et al. proposed a smart cane system that combines a 2D LiDAR sensor with an RGB-D camera [12]. This fusion of laser and vision sensing technologies enables both navigation and stationary obstacle recognition functionalities. The system utilizes the Cartographer algorithm for laser SLAM (Simultaneous Localization and Mapping) and an improved YOLOv5 algorithm to detect and locate stationary obstacles and other pedestrians.

Other researchers have explored alternative sensor combinations. The Augmented Cane developed by Stanford University researchers incorporates a LiDAR sensor along with GPS, accelerometers, magnetometers, and gyroscopes [13]. This multi-sensor approach allows for comprehensive monitoring of the user's position, speed, and direction, in addition to obstacle detection.

Commercial solutions have also emerged, such as the WeWALK smart cane. Initially launched with an upward-facing ultrasonic sensor, WeWALK has since partnered with Moovit to integrate urban mobility features [14]. This collaboration enables users to access real-time public transit information and receive step-by-step navigation guidance through voice assistance.

The SmartCane system developed by UCLA researchers takes a different approach, focusing on fall prevention for older individuals rather than visual impairment. This system incorporates a 3-axis accelerometer, three single-axis gyroscopes, and two pressure sensors to provide biomechanical support and fall detection [15].

While technologies such as LiDAR and laser rangefinders improve the precision of distance measurements in assistive devices [16], their primary application has been in navigating environments and avoiding fixed obstacles or slow-moving pedestrians.

2.2. Pedestrian-Carried Vehicle Alerting Systems

While the cane-mounted technologies can help visually impaired people to navigate and to avoid static obstacles, there remains a need for a system that can effectively detect and warn pedestrians about fast-moving objects like vehicles that approach them.

The closest system that we know of are AI-powered headphone systems designed to alert pedestrians of approaching vehicles. These systems use embedded microphones to detect vehicle sounds and warn users through audio cues. Such technologies have potential benefits for both visually impaired and general pedestrians [17], but, as the authors note, sounds in a crowded urban environment are ubiquitous, resulting in an overwhelming number of false positives. Further, electrically powered vehicles make very little noise. Finally, a vehicle that is not on a trajectory to hit the pedestrian is not a danger, so sound-based systems could lead to numerous false positives in urban environments.

3. Materials and Methods

ImpactAlert uses a LiDAR (Light Detection and Ranging) system embedded in a phone to sense threats and a variety of possible actuators to alert the pedestrian. The actuators we consider are a sound signal perhaps linked to headphones, a vibration of the phone itself, or a vibrating cane handle. Section 3.1 describes algorithms to identify threats. Section 4 describes the design of the smart cane handle actuator.

3.1. Threat Detection Technology and Thresholds

LiDAR is a remote sensing method that uses laser pulses to measure distances between the sensor and objects in the environment. The precision and speed of LiDAR make it ideal for applications requiring accurate depth perception.

Using LiDAR, the ImpactAlert software, (found at https://github.com/hwyuanzi/Impact-Alert-Lidar/, last accessed on 1 August 2025) implemented in Swift on top of iOS, uses the ARKit output to extract depth information from the central region of the screen. ImpactAlert performs depth calculations every 10 frames (roughly every 0.5 s) to achieve real-time performance without overloading the system. For our own testing purposes, the user interface on the phone sounds an alarm and changes the display color to red when an object is coming towards the pedestrian faster than 2.2 m/s and the time to impact is less than three seconds.

These values are reasonable, because several studies, e.g., [18], indicate that pedestrians won't be fatally injured for vehicle speeds of 20 miles per hour (8.9 m/s) or less. However, some people could be hurt at much lower speeds. For that reason, we have set the threshold to roughly 1/4 of 8.9 m/s) in our experiments.

Moreover, the pedestrian users of ImpactAlert have the option to adjust these parameters as we discuss in Section 7. For example, a fragile elderly person may choose a lower speed threshold or a higher time to impact. Changing thresholds to make alerts more likely might result in more false positives. By contrast, a robust (or optimistic) person to allow higher speeds for example may eliminate all false positives while increasing the likelihood of being hit without being warned. We see the impact in terms of precision/recall/F1-score of changing the speed and time to impact thresholds as discussed in Section 6.3.

To engage the system, a user presses a start/stop button to control when depth analysis is active. The user interface provides real-time feedback, adjusting both the display color to red, sound from the phone, and (when deployed) the cane handle vibrates. These alerts occur when an object is moving towards the pedestrian faster than the speed threshold and when the time to impact is less than the corresponding threshold.

3.2. Algorithms

The Algorithm 1 finds the pixels in the center of the camera using the subroutine listed in Algorithm 2. For those central pixels, the subroutine Algorithm 3 (1) filters to those distances that are in the closest part of all distances (in our implementation, closer than half the distances) and (2) sees whether each such pixel's distance since the last processed frame (0.5 s ago in our current implementation) has changed by a minimum amount (0.2 m in our current implementation).

The threatDistance is then computed to be the average distance of those close and changing pixels. The speed is the sum of the distance differences in those changing pixels divided by the time between processed frames (0.5 s). After that, the main routine (Algorithm 1) sets an alarm based on the threshold.

The intuitions behind this algorithm are that

- Objects that are static with relative to the pedestrian should not influence the calculations of the threatDistance or speed, so we focus only on objects that have changed distances. Please note however that the pedestrian might walk towards fixed objects in which case the pedestrian should be alerted.
- Further, if the pedestrian moves the camera and some pixels register static objects to have moved towards the pedestrian, approximately the same number of pixels will register that static objects have moved away from the pedestrian.
- Approaching objects (or objects that the pedestrian approaches) will occupy more of the screen and therefore cause more pixels to register relative movement towards the pedestrian, reducing the threatDistance and therefore increasing the possibility of threat detection.
- By contrast, objects moving to the side will occupy less of the screen and therefore cause more pixels to register movement away from the pedestrian, reducing the possibility of false alarms.

The reader may observe the constants used in Algorithms 2 and 3. We derived those constants empirically in the 60 experiments of our training set, where we adjusted parameters to obtain zero false negatives (no alarm when there should be one) while minimizing false positives. This includes the use of the horizontal center 10/12 of the screen, the half of the depth values, and the notion of focusing on pixels that show movement.

These constants may be adjusted when using different devices. Having set these parameters, the empirical results we report are on the remaining experiments.

Algorithm 1 Main Routine: Process middle depth data from LiDAR frame. Look at the close points that are moving. Based on default thresholds, if the object is approaching faster than 2.2 m per second and the time to impact is less than 3 s, then an alert is sounded. The user has control over these thresholds.

Obtain frame dimensions of the mobile device: `width`, `height`.
`depthValues` ← `ExtractDepth()` ▷ Extract depth values from the middle frame region
(`threatDistance`, `speed`) ← `FindThreatDistanceMoving(depthValues)` ▷ Calculate current threat distance and speed of moving points
if `speed` < -2.2 m/s **AND** `timeToImpact` < 3 s **then**
  alert pedestrian (on phone, red writing on screen or sound alert; on cane, buzz the hand)
end if

Algorithm 2 Subroutine: ExtractDepth. The most important screen grid points points are in the screen center because those points indicate objects that potentially approach the pedestrian. In our training experiments, objects not in the center of the screen were not a threat because they would go off to the side.

Calculate bounds for the middle section of the depth data: $startX = \frac{width}{12}$, $endX = \frac{11 \cdot width}{12}$, $startY = \frac{height}{3}$, $endY = \frac{2 \cdot height}{3}$.
Extract depth values within the middle section:
for $y = startY$ **to** $endY$ **do**
  for $x = startX$ **to** $endX$ **do**
    append $depthData[y \cdot width + x]$ to `depthValues`
  end for
end for
return `depthValues`

Algorithm 3 Subroutine: FindThreatDistanceMove. Determine the distance of the close points in the center of the screen that have moved as well as their average net movement.

$d \leftarrow$ median value of the depth values
Retain values $\leq d$ and that have moved (either towards pedestrian or away) by at least 0.2 m compared to the previous frame. Call these *movingClosePoints* and let *change* be the sum of the differences in distance of these points
$threatDistance \leftarrow \frac{\sum movingClosePoints}{|movingClosePoints|}$ ▷ average distance of moving points
$difference \leftarrow \frac{change}{|movingClosePoints|}$
$speed \leftarrow difference/0.5$ ▷ assuming frames are processed every 0.5 s
return `threatDistance, speed`

4. HapticHandle: An Inexpensive Cane Handle for Visually Impared Pedestrians

While ImpactAlert currently works by causing a phone to vibrate or to make a sound, an alternative deployment for the visually impaired is a smart cane handle that will vibrate when the phone-embedded software detects danger. We describe the design and construction of such a cane handle, though our experiments do not use it. Our goal in this brief section is to suggest an inexpensive path forward to cane designers.

The custom-designed handle houses the electronics needed for this functionality. The handle is designed to fit securely onto the top of a standard walking cane. To create the handle, we first modeled the handle using AutoCad 2023 ensuring that it could accommodate the required electronics. Once finalized, we printed the model using Polylactic Acid (PLA) material, because of its durability and lightweight properties.

We placed an Adafruit microcontroller board inside the 3D-printed handle. This board is responsible for managing the inputs from the phone and controlling the haptic feedback and audio warnings that alert the pedestrian. The board was carefully fitted to avoid any movement during cane usage as shown in Figure 1. The total cost of the cane handle system falls between $30–40 U.S. in 2024.

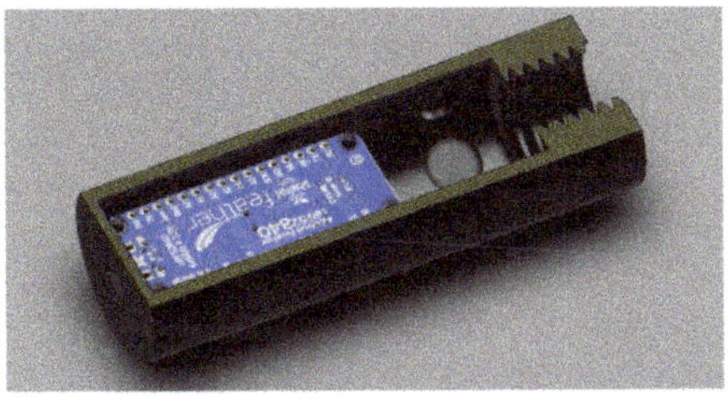

Figure 1. Cutout image of the 3D-printed smart cane handle containing an Adafruit microcontroller board and haptic actuators.

5. Threat Types

Part of the inspiration for this work is that the rise of electric bicycles and scooters have led to pedestrians being hit at injury-causing speeds on sidewalks and streets. For this reason, we divide our experiments into threats from motorcycles, bicycles, pedestrians, as well as collisions with static objects. To avoid the delay and bureaucratic overhead of Institutional Review Board review, we have performed the video experiments ourselves by walking on city streets with our phone device.

5.1. Scooters/Motorcycles

Scooters (which we treat interchangeably with motorcycles and trikes) move rapidly so the alert may occur when the scooter is several meters away (the middle frame of Figure 2).

Figure 2. Example of the approach of a motorcycle (ridden by the second author) about to impact the pedestrian. The alert sound will beep when the incoming speed is faster than the user-set threshold and the time to impact is less than the user-set threshold.

5.2. Bicycle

Bicycle threats are common on city sidewalks. Electric bikes are particularly dangerous because they make so little noise. When they move slowly, they will reach the time to impact threshold when they are quite close as shown in Figure 3.

Figure 3. Example of the approach of a bicycle. This will set off an alarm when the speed and time to impact thresholds are crossed. Because a bicycle moves slower than a scooter, the Time to Impact threshold will be reached when the bicycle is closer to the pedestrian.

5.3. Static Threats

Though the primary use case of ImpactAlert is vehicles hitting a pedestrian, a fast-moving pedestrian could also cause injury to themselves by hitting a static object. The same thresholds of Time to Impact and Speed (in this case of the pedestrian) apply here as illustrated in Figure 4.

5.4. Pedestrian to Pedestrian Collisions

Just as for static threats, Time to Impact and speed thresholds also apply to Pedestrian to Pedestrian threats as illustrated in Figure 5.

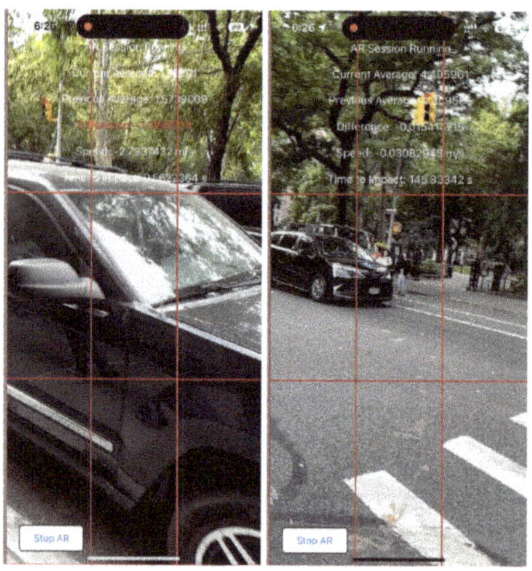

Figure 4. (**Left panel**) shows a static object that is close enough to set an alarm if the pedestrian moves fast enough towards the car. (**Right panel**) shows a static object that is far away, so poses no danger.

Figure 5. Example of Person Approaching. Just as for static objects, the alarm will trigger only if the approach speed exceeds the threshold and the Time to Impact is low. This shows our current debugging interface. The text turns red in the second image, because the pedestrian in view might swerve to cause a collision. The writing in the image shows our debugging interface, built so we can evaluate ImpactAlert's estimates of Time to Impact and Speed. From top to bottom, it shows current average distance, previous average distance, the difference, the speed, the TimeToImpact, the speed and Time to Impact thresholds. The interface for a pedestrian will be a sound when a collision becomes a significant danger. These two screenshots come from Walking4.mp4 in our video drive https://drive.google.com/drive/folders/18Z7METb5hzrKMy2FHidKbXn69YqB2So3 (last accessed on 1 August 2025).

6. Experimental Results

For every moving object, we want to alert the pedestrian only when the object is approaching the pedestrian fast and has a short Time to Impact. This leads to a set of confusion matrices dividing interactions into True Positives (the alarm occurs when it should), True Negatives (the alarm does not occur when it shouldn't), and False Positives (the alarm occurs when it shouldn't) and False Negatives (the alarm does not occur when it should). False Negatives are particularly bad, because they indicate a failure to alert the pedestrian when there is real danger. False Positives, while not posing a danger, might potentially lead the pedestrian to ignore the device's alarm, as in the Aesop Fable *The Boy Who Cried Wolf*.

6.1. Precision, Recall, and F1-Score

From the values of True Positives (TP), True Negatives (TN), False Positives (FP), and False Negatives (FN), we derive precision, recall, and F1-score, according to the usual definitions [19]:

- **Precision:**

$$\text{Precision} = \frac{TP}{TP + FP}$$

- **Recall:**

$$\text{Recall} = \frac{TP}{TP + FN}$$

- **F1 Score:**

$$F1 = 2 \times \frac{\text{Precision} \times \text{Recall}}{\text{Precision} + \text{Recall}}$$

6.2. *Vehicle-Based Confusion Matrix*

Our raw data comes from several videos showing different vehicles as well as pedestrians in different cities: Manhattan (New York City, United States), Brooklyn (New York City, United States), Jaipur India (please see Figure 6a), and Hefei China (please see Figure 6b).

The reader will find the videos of our experiments in the ImpactAlert urban setting video archive https://drive.google.com/drive/folders/18Z7METb5hzrKMy2FHidKbXn69YqB2So3?usp=sharing (last accessed on 1 August 2025).

We first present the True Positives, True Negatives, False Positives, and False Negatives for each vehicle type (Table 1), assuming a threshold of −2.2 m/s and a 3 s time to impact.

Table 1. Performance metrics by vehicle type. With the threshold settings: speed < −2.2 m/s (negative speeds imply that the object is approaching the pedestrian or the pedestrian is approaching the object) and time to impact <3 s.

Vehicle Type	True Positives (TP)	True Negatives (TN)	False Positives (FP)	False Negatives (FN)
Bus	5	8	0	0
Car	11	8	0	0
Scooter	5	2	1	1
Walking	30	11	2	1

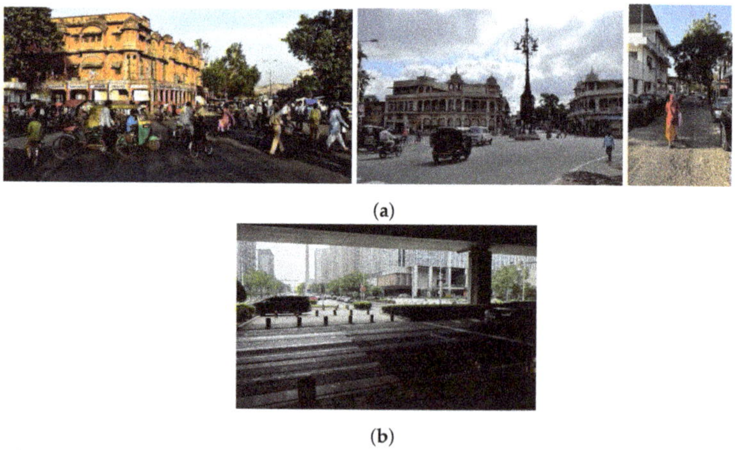

Figure 6. (**a**) A crowded and a quiet neighborhood in Jaipur, India. People often walk in the street. (**b**) A typical urban street in Hefei, China. Pedestrian, bicycle, and electric scooter lanes are separated for safety. Some streets are also located beneath elevated expressways.

6.3. *Quality Evaluations for Different Thresholds*

As can be seen in Table 1, at the default threshold values, less than 8% of the alarms (positives) are false positives and there are only two false negatives. False Negatives are potentially dangerous because they correspond to situations in which an alarm does not go off when it should. Fortunately, at least in these experiments and as shown in Appendix A, within 0.2 s of a False Negative, there was a True Positive and therefore an alarm. So, the pedestrian would have been alerted in time.

The summary confusion matrix of Table 2 reflects this as well. The bolded values are from the default thresholds of −2.2 m/s speed and 3 s time to impact. Other rows show either variations in the Time to Impact threshold or the Speed Threshold. Table 2 shows, unsurprisingly, that less negative thresholds and greater Time to Impact thresholds leads to more false negatives, though not so many more. Conversely, when the thresholds allow lower speeds to set off an alarm, there are fewer false negatives but more false positives.

Table 2. Quality Measures for different speed and Time to Impact (TTI) thresholds. TP means true positives (the system reports an object approaching that exceeds the threshold and there is a collision danger), FP is false positive, FN is false negative (there is a collision danger but with those thresholds, we don't detect it), TN is true negative, followed by the derived quantities. The default thresholds and their quality values are shown in bold.

Speed Thresh	Time To Impact Thresh	True Pos (TP)	False Pos (FP)	False Neg (FN)	True Neg (TN)	Accuracy	Precision	Recall	F1
−5.0	3	32	0	21	32	0.753	1.000	0.604	0.753
−3.0	3	46	2	7	30	0.894	0.958	0.868	0.911
−2.2	1	25	0	28	32	0.671	1.000	0.472	0.641
−2.2	**3**	**51**	**3**	**2**	**29**	**0.941**	**0.944**	**0.962**	**0.953**
−2.2	5	51	9	2	23	0.871	0.850	0.962	0.903
−1.0	3	52	5	1	27	0.929	0.912	0.981	0.945

7. Sensitivity Slider

ImpactAlert provides a slider (see Figure 7) that allows users (or their helpers in the case of infirm users) to configure their alert threshold preferences (Time to Impact and Speed) based on their unique needs and circumstances. This flexibility allows ImpactAlert to adapt to a diverse range of users, such as the fragile individuals or those with slower reaction times. As Table 2 shows, even extending the Time To Impact to 5 s and making the Speed threshold −1.0 m/s does not radically increase the number of false positives.

Figure 7. Sensitivity sliders for personalized alert times. It is the blue slider on the screen that enables (currently a sighted helper) to customize the alert threshold.

8. Limitations

LiDAR, while powerful, doesn't work well when there is fog or rain. Radar does work through inclement weather, but its spatial resolution becomes poor. A detection system with good spatial resolution that could see through fog would be ideal.

While we have tested our application in many settings (urban, suburban, United States, India, and China), more testing would of course be needed before serious deployment.

Fortunately, it's easy to gather data, so a commercial entity that wanted more data could acquire it easily.

9. Future Work

While the primary use case of ImpactAlert is to enhance safety for individuals with visual impairments, ImpactAlert also offers substantial benefits for sighted pedestrians. For instance, it can be used to detect threats coming from the pedestrian's back, because each of several LiDAR instruments could alert a pedestrian of danger. Further, besides alerting the pedestrian, it could be useful to alert the vehicle driver of the presence of the pedestrian for example by setting off blinking lights to make the pedestrian more visible.

Another avenue for future development is to embed LiDAR technology into clothing. This holds the promise of promoting safety and awareness for individuals in various environments. Clothing equipped with LiDAR sensors could provide real-time feedback about the wearer's surroundings, alerting them to nearby obstacles as well as approaching vehicles. This feature would be beneficial for individuals who are visually impaired but also for those participating in activities such as cycling or hiking, where awareness of surroundings is crucial.

Thus, the main future work regarding the device is expanding the set of platforms, incorporating multiple sensors, and specializing the parameters to various sensor platforms. The main future work regarding deployment is extensive user testing, particularly with vision-impaired pedestrians.

10. Conclusions

The ImpactAlert system is a software system making use of LiDAR sensors to detect moving objects, such as vehicles, that approach a pedestrian user. ImpactAlert provides timely warnings through vibrations in a smart cane or sounds if those objects are moving rapidly towards that user with a small time to impact. By incorporating technology commonly found in modern smartphones, ImpactAlert offers an accessible and practical solution for pedestrians in a variety of environments.

As LiDAR and related technologies become more widespread and affordable, the availability of such smart devices will increase, making them a viable option for a broader population both sighted and visually impaired.

Author Contributions: Conceptualization: R.R., C.L. and D.S.; Formal Analysis: R.R., C.L. and D.S.; Methodology: R.R., C.L. and D.S.; Software: R.R., C.L., H.Y. and D.S.; Supervision: D.S.; Validation: R.R., H.Y. and D.S.; Visualization: R.R., H.Y. and D.S.; Writing—Original Draft Preparation: R.R., C.L. and D.S.; Writing—Review and Editing: R.R., H.Y. and D.S. All authors have read and agreed to the published version of the manuscript.

Funding: This work was partially supported by NYU Wireless.

Data Availability Statement: The data can be found in the video repository (accessed on 1 August 2025). https://drive.google.com/drive/folders/18Z7METb5hzrKMy2FHidKbXn69YqB2So3.

Conflicts of Interest: The authors declare no conflicts of interest.The funders had no role in the design of the study; in the collection, analyses, or interpretation of data; in the writing of the manuscript; or in the decision to publish the results.

Appendix A. Raw Data Results

The tables below identify the video in question, the time in the video when the evaluation was done, the speed and time to impact as measured by our algorithm and whether there is a collision danger.

For pedestrians we measure the possibility of frontal collision as a collision danger.

For vehicles, the scoring is a bit more complicated. Because we took measurements from the safety of sidewalks or between parked cars, there was never any actual danger of collision. However, we adopted a "swerve danger" scoring system in which a collision was deemed possible if the vehicle could swerve to hit the experimenter. If so, then for vehicles, this results in a "Yes" score. Thus, we were somewhat overly alarmist in our scoring of collisions for vehicles because vehicles don't in fact swerve very often.

We present the raw output of this analysis in Table A1.

Table A1. Speed and Time to Impact at various time points in various videos. Note that a Time to Impact of 9999 means that the potential threat is moving away. The lines that are highlighted in blue indicate false negatives, but in both cases those false negatives have either an alarm 0.2 s before or after or both.

Walking1	0:03:50	−0.77 m/s	5.48 s	No
Walking1	0:04:10	−0.63 m/s	6.33 s	No
Walking1	0:04:30	−2.50 m/s	1.75 s	Yes
Walking1	0:04:50	−3.63 m/s	1.12 s	Yes
Walking1	0:05:10	−4.28 m/s	0.91 s	Yes
Walking1	0:05:30	−6.34 m/s	0.58 s	Yes
Walking1	0:05:50	−7.05 m/s	0.47 s	Yes
Walking2	0:03:00	−0.27 m/s	21.38 s	No
Walking2	0:03:20	−7.73 m/s	0.73 s	Yes
Walking2	0:03:40	−7.77 m/s	0.62 s	Yes
Walking2	0:04:00	−8.78 m/s	0.52 s	Yes
Walking2	0:04:20	−10.40 m/s	0.39 s	Yes
Walking2	0:04:40	−8.80 m/s	0.41 s	Yes
Walking2	0:05:00	−8.10 m/s	0.37 s	Yes
Walking3	0:04:30	−2.70 m/s	1.64 s	Yes
Walking3	0:04:50	−1.63 m/s	2.59 s	No
Walking3	0:05:10	−3.17 m/s	1.04 s	Yes
Walking3	0:05:30	−2.35 m/s	1.46 s	Yes
Walking3	0:05:50	0.35 m/s	9999.00 s	No
Walking3	0:06:10	0.14 m/s	9999.00 s	No
Walking3	0:06:30	−0.24 m/s	22.47 s	No
Walking3	0:06:50	−0.37 m/s	1391.66 s	No
Walking3	0:16:55	−6.08 m/s	1.26 s	Yes
Walking3	0:17:15	−3.18 m/s	1.24 s	Yes
Walking3	0:17:35	−2.99 m/s	1.61 s	Yes
Walking3	0:17:55	−4.23 m/s	0.82 s	Yes
Walking4	0:05:00	−2.11 m/s	2.51 s	No
Walking4	0:05:20	−2.45 m/s	1.46 s	No
Walking4	0:06:00	−4.09 m/s	1.02 s	No
Walking4	0:06:20	−0.20 m/s	4.40 s	No
Walking5	0:02:20	−6.76 m/s	0.44 s	Yes
Walking5	0:03:10	−4.13 m/s	0.69 s	Yes
Walking6	0:04:30	−5.67 m/s	0.45 s	Yes
Walking6	0:04:50	−9.66 m/s	0.23 s	Yes
Walking6	0:05:10	−11.32 m/s	0.17 s	Yes
Walking6	0:05:30	−10.38 m/s	0.16 s	Yes
Walking7	0:17:40	−2.69 m/s	1.99 s	Yes
Walking7	0:18:00	−3.31 m/s	1.39 s	Yes
Walking7	0:18:20	−7.09 m/s	0.69 s	Yes
Walking7	0:18:40	−2.09 m/s	1.76 s	Yes (False Negative)
Walking7	0:19:00	−4.44 m/s	0.73 s	Yes

Table A1. *Cont.*

Walking8	0:05:00	−3.39 m/s	1.72 s	Yes
Walking8	0:05:20	−3.73 m/s	1.71 s	Yes
Walking8	0:05:40	−0.14 m/s	9999.00 s	No
Car1	0:01:15	−1.67 m/s	4.52 s	No
Car1	0:01:35	−5.08 m/s	1.58 s	Yes
Car1	0:01:55	−6.02 m/s	1.18 s	Yes
Car1	0:02:15	−7.18 m/s	0.94 s	Yes
Car1	0:02:35	−10.58 m/s	0.59 s	Yes
Car1	0:02:55	−8.93 m/s	0.7 s	Yes
Car1	0:03:15	−0.11 m/s	12.7 s	No
Car2	0:01:30	−2.30 m/s	4.18 s	No
Car2	0:01:50	−3.78 m/s	2.82 s	Yes
Car2	0:02:10	−6.04 m/s	1.56 s	Yes
Car2	0:02:30	−7.54 m/s	1.07 s	Yes
Car2	0:02:50	−8.23 m/s	0.36 s	Yes
Car2	0:03:10	−4.05 m/s	1.76 s	Yes
Car2	0:03:30	−6.16 m/s	1.18 s	Yes
Car2	0:03:50	−0.08 m/s	116.03 s	No
Car3	0:00:45	−3.92 m/s	9999.00 s	No
Car3	0:01:05	4.33 m/s	9999.00 s	No
Car3	0:01:25	3.37 m/s	9999.00 s	No
Car3	0:01:45	−0.95 m/s	8.92 s	No
Bus1	0:16:40	−0.68 m/s	24.91 s	No
Bus1	0:17:00	−0.62 m/s	21.24 s	No
Bus1	0:17:20	−4.12 m/s	3.44 s	No
Bus1	0:17:40	−6.35 m/s	1.57 s	Yes
Bus1	0:18:00	−10.90 m/s	0.76 s	Yes
Bus1	0:18:20	−12.26 m/s	0.62 s	Yes
Bus1	0:18:40	−11.96 m/s	0.70 s	Yes
Bus1	0:19:00	−7.24 m/s	1.40 s	Yes
Bus2	0:05:25	−1.54 m/s	7.62 s	No
Bus2	0:05:45	−2.92 m/s	3.71 s	No
Bus2	0:06:05	−3.61 m/s	3.00 s	No
Bus2	0:06:35	−3.20 m/s	3.57 s	No
Bus2	0:06:55	−3.05 m/s	3.54 s	No
Scooter1	0:00:22	−4.50 m/s	2.73 s	Yes
Scooter1	0:00:42	−0.90 m/s	11.81 s	Yes (False Neagtive)
Scooter1	0:01:05	−0.53 m/s	21.63 s	No
Scooter2	0:00:35	−3.5 m/s	1.03 s	Yes
Scooter2	0:00:55	−4.86 m/s	1.03 s	No
Scooter3	0:04:50	−0.25 m/s	45.90 s	No
Scooter3	0:05:10	−6.03 m/s	2.37 s	Yes
Scooter3	0:05:30	−8.75 m/s	1.39 s	Yes
Scooter3	0:05:50	−7.97 m/s	1.09 s	Yes

References

1. Vision Australia, Guide Dogs Victoria and Blind Citizens Australia. New Report Reveals 1 in 12 Pedestrians Being Hit by Motor Vehicles and Cyclists. 2019. Available online: https://visionaustralia.org/news/2019-08-23/new-report-reveals-1-12-pedestrians-being-hit-motor-vehicles-and-cyclists (accessed on 5 March 2023).
2. Prabhath, P.; Olvera-Herrera, V.O.; Chan, V.F.; Clarke, M.; Wright, D.M.; MacKenzie, G.; Virgili, G.; Congdon, N. Vision impairment and traffic safety outcomes in low-income and middle-income countries: A systematic review and meta-analysis. *Lancet Glob. Health* **2021**, *9*, e1411–e1422.
3. Roberts, I.; Norton, R. Sensory deficit and the risk of pedestrian injury. *Inj. Prev.* **1995**, *1*, 12–14. [CrossRef] [PubMed]

Navarro, P.J.; Fernández, C.; Borraz, R.; Alonso, D. A Machine Learning Approach to Pedestrian Detection for Autonomous Vehicles Using High-Definition 3D Range Data. *Sensors* **2017**, *17*, 18. [CrossRef] [PubMed]

Traffic Safety Store. Collision Sentry Overview. 2021. Available online: https://www.trafficsafetywarehouse.com/collision-sentry (accessed on 5 March 2023).

Li, Z.; Wang, K.; Li, L.; Wang, F.-Y. A Review on Vision-Based Pedestrian Detection for Intelligent Vehicles. In Proceedings of the 2006 IEEE International Conference on Intelligent Transportation Systems (ITSC), Toronto, ON, Canada, 17–20 September 2006; pp. 224–229. [CrossRef]

Scalvini, F.; Bordeau, C.; Ambard, M.; Migniot, C.; Dubois, J. Outdoor Navigation Assistive System Based on Robust and Real-Time Visual-Auditory Substitution Approach. *Sensors* **2024**, *24*, 166. [CrossRef] [PubMed]

Kim, S.; Lee, H. Real-Time Interaction Models for Vehicle and Pedestrian Safety. *IEEE Trans. Intell. Transp. Syst.* **2024**, *8*, 22–35.

Hamidaoui, M.; Talhaoui, M.Z.; Li, M.; Midoun, M.A.; Haouassi, S.; Mekkaoui, D.E.; Smaili, A.; Cherraf, A.; Benyoub, F.Z. Survey of Autonomous Vehicles' Collision Avoidance Algorithms. *Sensors* **2025**, *25*, 395. [CrossRef] [PubMed]

Bolgiano, J.R. Laser Cane for the Blind. *Proc. IEEE* **1967**, *55*, 697–698. [CrossRef]

Benjamin, J.M.; Ali, N.A.; Schepis, A.F. Laser Cane for the Blind. In *Engineering in Biology and Medicine*; Reivich, M., Ed.; University Park Press: Baltimore, MD, USA, 1973; pp. 63–70.

2. Mai, X.; Zhang, L.; Li, Y.; Wang, H. Fusion of 2D LiDAR and RGB-D Camera for Smart Cane Navigation and Obstacle Detection. *Sensors* **2022**, *24*, 870. [CrossRef]

3. Slade, P.; Tambe, A.; Kochenderfer, M.J. Multimodal sensing and intuitive steering assistance improve navigation and mobility for people with impaired vision. *Sci. Robot.* **2021**, *6*, eabg6594. [CrossRef] [PubMed]

4. Moovit. Moovit and WeWALK Partner to Improve Transit Navigation for Blind and Partially Sighted. *Mass Transit*, 1 December 2021. Available online: https://www.masstransitmag.com/technology/article/21248474/\moovit-and-wewalk-partner-to-improve-transit-navigation-for-blind-and-partially-sighted (accessed on 5 March 2023).

5. Lan, M.; Nahapetian, A.; Vahdatpour, A.; Au, L.; Kaiser, W.; Sarrafzadeh, M. SmartFall: An automatic fall detection system based on subsequence matching for the ImpactAlert. In Proceedings of the Fourth International Conference on Body Area Networks, Los Angeles, CA, USA, 1–3 April 2009; pp. 1–8.

6. Gupta, A.; Patel, M.; Saini, M.; Sharma, R. A survey on assistive devices for visually impaired people. *Sensors* **2024**, *24*, 4834. [CrossRef]

7. AI-Powered Headphones Alert Pedestrians to Incoming Cars. IEEE Spectrum. Available online: https://spectrum.ieee.org/ai-headphone-pedestrians-safety-warning-cars (accessed on 5 March 2023).

8. Tefft, B.C. *Impact Speed and a Pedestrian's Risk of Severe Injury or Death*; AAA Foundation for Traffic Safety: Washington, DC, USA, 2011.

9. Deisenroth, M.P.; Faisal, A.A.; Ong, C.S. *Mathematics for Machine Learning*; Cambridge University Press: Cambridge, UK, 2020. Available online: https://mml-book.github.io/ (accessed on 5 March 2023).

electronics

MDPI

Article

MedLangViT: A Language–Vision Network for Medical Image Segmentation

Yiyi Wang [1], Jia Su [1], Xinxiao Li [2] and Eisei Nakahara [3,*]

1 Information Engineering College, Capital Normal University, Beijing 100048, China; wangyiyi@cnu.edu.cn (Y.W.); sujia@cnu.edu.cn (J.S.)
2 Faculty of Informatics, Shonan Institute of Technology, 1-1-25 Tsujido-Nishikaigan, Fujisawa-shi 251-8511, Kanagawa, Japan
3 College of Humanities and Sciences, Nihon University, Tokyo 156-8550, Japan; lixinxiao@info.shonan-it.ac.jp
* Correspondence: nakahara.eisei@nihon-u.ac.jp

Abstract: Precise medical image segmentation is crucial for advancing computer-aided diagnosis. Although deep learning-based medical image segmentation is now widely applied in this field, the complexity of human anatomy and the diversity of pathological manifestations often necessitate the use of image annotations to enhance segmentation accuracy. In this process, the scarcity of annotations and the lightweight design requirements of associated text encoders collectively present key challenges for improving segmentation model performance. To address these challenges, we propose MedLangViT, a novel language–vision multimodal model for medical image segmentation that incorporates medical descriptive information through lightweight text embedding rather than text encoders. MedLangViT innovatively leverages medical textual information to assist the segmentation process, thereby reducing reliance on extensive high-precision image annotations. Furthermore, we design an Enhanced Channel-Spatial Attention Module (ECSAM) to effectively fuse textual and visual features, strengthening textual guidance for segmentation decisions. Extensive experiments conducted on two publicly available text–image-paired medical datasets demonstrated that MedLangViT significantly outperforms existing state-of-the-art methods, validating the effectiveness of both the proposed model and the ECSAM.

Keywords: MedLangViT; ECSAM; BioBERT; medical image segmentation

1. Introduction

Medical image segmentation is a critical component of medical image analysis, playing a vital role in clinical diagnosis, treatment planning, and disease research. Its applications range from tumor detection to organ segmentation, making it indispensable in modern medicine. However, obtaining high-quality annotated medical images faces significant challenges. These challenges are particularly pronounced in COVID-19 lesion segmentation, where the visual identification of lesions faces inherent difficulties due to low contrast boundaries between lesions like ground-glass opacities and surrounding lung tissue, heterogeneous manifestations appearing as diverse patterns including nodular, patchy, and diffuse across patients, and ambiguous margins with ill-defined edges that challenge precise delineation even for experts [1,2]. Accompanying textual annotations provide critical complementary information by specifying anatomical context, characterizing lesion attributes, and highlighting clinically relevant features that may be visually obscure in the images. On the one hand, annotation requires substantial time and effort from medical professionals, which results in high labor costs. On the other hand, the complexity and specificity of medical images make annotation more difficult compared with conventional images, while consistency across annotations is also hard to ensure. These factors severely limit the performance improvement of medical image segmentation models.

In recent years, although deep learning technologies have achieved remarkable results in this field, most existing models rely on large-scale annotated data for supervised learning and struggle to overcome the data bottleneck. In practical applications, as shown in Figure 1a, medical images are often accompanied by textual annotations that contain rich semantic information, such as the location, shape, and number of lesions [3]. Effectively integrating such textual information with visual data through a text encoder could bring new opportunities to segmentation tasks. However, the substantial parameter footprint of text encoders imposes a significant computational burden when used jointly with visual models. Therefore, adopting a lightweight text embedding scheme as an alternative to text encoders can enable high-accuracy text-assisted medical image segmentation with minimal parameter overhead. Meanwhile, medical images often exhibit blurred boundaries between different regions and low grayscale contrast, making accurate segmentation highly challenging [4]. Therefore, more efficient feature fusion mechanisms and attention strategies are urgently needed to address this issue [5].

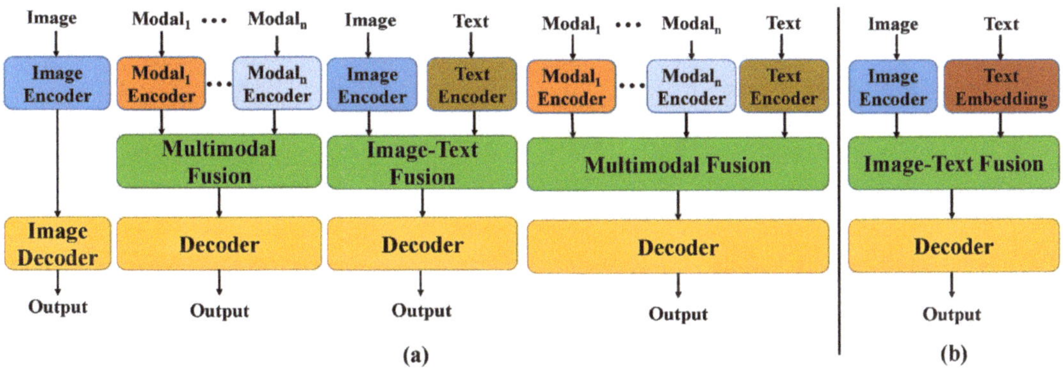

Figure 1. The different methods of medical image segmentation. (**a**) The different frameworks of medical image segmentation. (**b**) Ours.

To address these challenges, we propose an innovative medical image segmentation approach that replaces the traditional text encoder with a novel, parameter-efficient text embedding method. Specifically, we introduce BioBERT [6], a model pre-trained on large-scale medical literature and specifically designed for the biomedical domain. With its profound understanding of medical terminology and semantics, BioBERT outperforms general BERT [7] in generating more clinically relevant text representations, thus providing a robust foundation for subsequent tasks.

Additionally, we design a lightweight feature fusion module named the Enhanced Channel-Spatial Attention Module (ECSAM), which incorporates critical enhancements for multimodal feature fusion. Through its attention mechanism, ECSAM effectively captures cross-modal associations between images and text while enhancing MedLangViT's focus on critical areas (e.g., lesion regions) and suppressing irrelevant information. This design significantly improves the discriminative power of feature representations.

In order to verify the effectiveness of the proposed method, we conducted comprehensive experiments on the MosMedData+ [8] and QaTa-COV19 [9,10] datasets. The

MosMedData+ dataset contains extensive lung CT images with diverse infection types and lesion characteristics, while the QaTa-COV19 dataset comprises COVID-19 chest X-ray images with varied lesion patterns and detailed annotations. The experimental results are presented in Figure 2, demonstrating that MedLangViT achieves significant improvements in segmentation performance despite using fewer parameters. Key metrics, including the Dice coefficient and mean Intersection over Union (mIoU), surpass those of existing methods while maintaining lower computational complexity. These findings validate the method's strong clinical applicability and suggest promising new research directions for medical image segmentation. Our key contributions are summarized as follows:

Novel Network Architecture. Leveraging BioBERT as the text embedder, we propose MedLangViT, an innovative image–text framework specifically designed for medical image segmentation tasks enriched with textual annotations.

Innovative Attention Module. We propose the Enhanced Channel-Spatial Attention Module, a lightweight feature-fusion mechanism that effectively captures cross-modal correlations between visual and textual modalities.

Superior Performance. MedLangViT achieves state-of-the-art results on the QaTa-COV19 and MosMedData+ datasets, demonstrating substantial improvements in medical image segmentation accuracy.

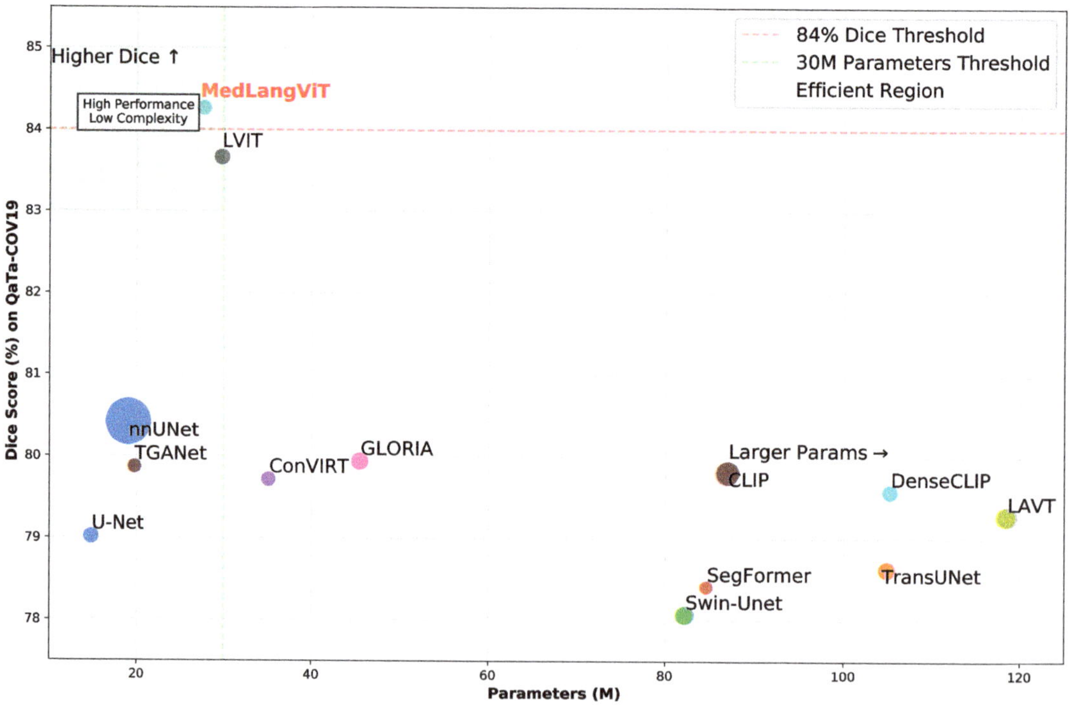

Figure 2. Our MedLangViT is compared with some other methods in terms of Dice and Parameters on QaTa-COV19 dataset. The radius of the circle represents GFLOPs. "↑" indicates an increasing trend in DICE. "→" indicates an increasing trend in Parameters.

The remainder of this paper is organized as follows. Section 2 reviews related work. Section 3 presents the proposed MedLangViT method in detail. Section 4 describes the experimental setup and reports results on multiple datasets, including comprehensive ablation studies. Section 5 discusses the limitations of our approach and outlines directions for future improvement, and Section 6 concludes the paper.

2. Related Work

2.1. Medical Image Segmentation

Medical image segmentation has undergone transformative advancements with the advent of deep learning. Early architectures like U-Net [11] established the foundation for encoder–decoder frameworks, leveraging skip connections to preserve spatial details. Subsequent innovations, such as UNet++ [12] and nnUNet [13], introduced nested structures and automated hyper-parameter tuning to enhance robustness across diverse imaging modalities. Despite these improvements, a persistent challenge remains: the reliance on large-scale, high-quality annotated datasets, which are labor-intensive to curate in clinical environments. To address annotation scarcity, semi-supervised learning (SSL) [14] methods like DTC [15] and PLCT [16] exploit unlabeled data through consistency regularization or pseudo-label refinement. More specifically, in medical imaging, multi-perspective dynamic consistency learning frameworks [17] have advanced SSL by enforcing prediction invariance across diverse anatomical views and adaptive perturbation strategies. Recently, pyramid-structured transformers with adaptive fusion mechanisms have shown promise in enhancing multi-scale feature learning for semi-supervised segmentation tasks, particularly in handling complex spatial contexts [18]. Hybrid architectures such as TransUNet [19] and Swin-UNet [20] integrate Transformer modules with CNNs to capture long-range contextual dependencies while retaining local anatomical details. However, these approaches predominantly focus on imaging-only inputs, overlooking the rich semantic information embedded in clinical text reports—a critical limitation given the complementary nature of radiological text and imaging data in diagnostic workflows.

2.2. Vision–Language Models in Medical Imaging

Vision–language pretraining (VLP) models, such as CLIP [21] and ViLT [22], have significantly advanced natural image–text alignment through joint embedding learning from large-scale multimodal datasets. However, when directly applied to medical imaging, these models encounter substantial domain-specific challenges. Medical data intricacies manifest in two key aspects: images exhibit subtle intensity variations and blurred boundaries, while radiology reports contain specialized terminology that generic language models struggle to contextualize. To address these challenges, recent studies, including GLoRIA [23] and ConVIRT [24], have employed contrastive learning to align image regions with corresponding textual descriptions. Specifically, GLoRIA extracts both global and local visual features for radiology text matching, whereas ConVIRT utilizes bidirectional contrastive loss to enhance joint image–text representation learning.

BioBERT, pretrained on PubMed abstracts and clinical notes, provides a robust solution to this limitation by embedding domain-specific semantics. Unlike BERT, BioBERT undergoes explicit fine-tuning on biomedical corpora, enabling precise interpretation of medical terminology, such as distinguishing between "consolidation" and "atelectasis." While BioBERT has demonstrated significant potential in tasks like named entity recognition and relation extraction, its integration within vision–language models for segmentation remains underexplored. Concurrent works such as TGA-Net [25] have begun exploring text-guided attention for polyp segmentation but rely on shallow text embeddings that lack deep linguistic context. Similarly, approaches aligning image patches with report snippets for pneumonia localization depend on generic text encoders, limiting their ability to process nuanced clinical descriptions. MedLangViT therefore represents an innovative advancement by embedding BioBERT within a multimodal architecture, facilitating fine-grained alignment between radiological text and visual features—a critical capability for enhancing pseudo-label quality in semi-supervised settings.

2.3. Attention Mechanisms for Multimodal Fusion

Attention mechanisms are now essential for enhancing feature representations in medical imaging. Spatial-channel attention modules, such as CBAM [26], adaptively highlight regions that are diagnostically relevant, while self-attention models global context within Transformer-based architectures. For multimodal tasks, LAVT [27] introduces pixel-word attention to align visual and linguistic features, and VLT employs cross-modal Transformers for referring segmentation. However, these methods focus on aggregating global context, often neglecting local anatomical details. This is a critical shortcoming in medical segmentation, where boundary precision is paramount. MedLangViT's Efficient Channel Spatial Attention Module (ECSAM) addresses this imbalance by synergistically combining channel and spatial attention with BioBERT-derived text embeddings. Unlike LAVT's cross attention, which prioritizes modal alignment, ECSAM first enhances the preservation of local features through inter-channel self-attention aggregation. It then strengthens text-guided semantic clues through spatial attention. For example, the BioBERT embedding for "lower right lung infection" guides ECSAM to enhance features in the corresponding image area. This ensures that textual context refines local structural details rather than overwhelming them. This design is particularly effective for segmenting fuzzy boundaries, such as COVID-19 lesions in X-rays, where text annotations provide key spatial priors.

3. Method

In this section, we first introduce the overall structure of MedLangViT, then explain the vision branch and language branch, and finally describe our proposed ECSAM.

3.1. Overall Architecture

Similar to LViT, our MedLangViT model adopts a Double-U structure, comprising a vision branch and a language branch. The overall architecture of MedLangViT is shown in Figure 3. The vision branch is a U-shaped CNN branch composed of multiple CNN blocks, tasked with image feature extraction and segmentation prediction. The language branch is a U-shaped ViT branch consisting of a BioBERT Embed block and multiple ViT blocks. The BioBERT Embed block conducts medical annotation text embedding to aid segmentation, while the ViT blocks fuse image and text information. Moreover, we integrate an Enhanced Channel-Spatial Attention Module (ECSAM) at the skip connections of the U-shaped CNN branch. This allows the upsampling process in the CNN branch to capture the maximum extent of image feature information. Finally, the network feeds the fused information from corresponding hierarchical levels back to the vision branch for final segmentation. The input shape and output shape of every layer of the network are shown in Tables 1 and 2.

3.2. Vision Branch

As depicted in Figure 3, the U-shaped CNN branch processes image information and serves as the segmentation head to generate the prediction mask. Each CNN module consists of Convolution, Batch Normalization, and *ReLU* activation layers. Between successive DownCNN modules, image features undergo downsampling via MaxPool layers.

Corresponding UpCNN modules incorporate features through concatenation operations. The operations within each CNN module are formally defined by Equations (1) and (2):

$$D_i = DownCNN_i = ReLU(BN(Conv_i(\cdot))) \tag{1}$$

$$Y_{DownCNN,i+1} = MaxPool(D_i(Y_{DownCNN,i})) \tag{2}$$

where $Y_{DownCNN,i}$ represents the input of the i-th DownCNN module, which becomes $Y_{DownCNN,i+1}$ after the downsampling of the i-th DownCNN module and the MaxPool layer. To enhance image feature learning, an Enhanced Channel-Spatial Attention Module (ECSAM) is integrated at the skip connections within the U-shaped CNN branch. This module receives cross-modal interaction features from both the CNN and ViT branches. The refined features from ECSAM are then propagated to the corresponding UpCNN modules, progressively delivering multi-level contextual information during the upsampling path.

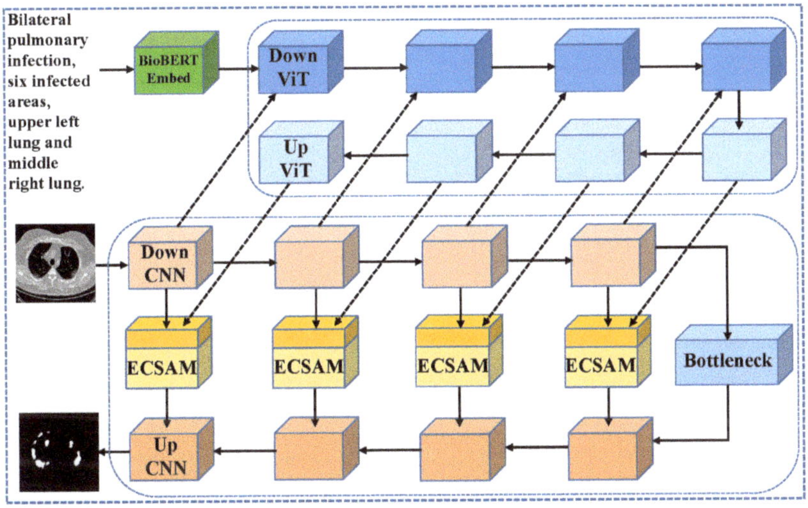

Figure 3. The overall architecture of MedLangViT.

Table 1. CNN module architecture.

Layer Name	Input Shape	Output Shape
InConv	3 × 224 × 224	64 × 224 × 224
DownCNN1	64 × 224 × 224	128 × 112 × 112
DownCNN2	128 × 112 × 112	256 × 56 × 56
DownCNN3	256 × 56 × 56	512 × 28 × 28
DownCNN4	512 × 28 × 28	512 × 14 × 14
Reconstruct1	64 × 14 × 14	64 × 224 × 224
Reconstruct2	128 × 14 × 14	128 × 112 × 112
Reconstruct3	256 × 14 × 14	256 × 56 × 56
Reconstruct4	512 × 14 × 14	512 × 28 × 28
UpCNN4	512 × 14 × 14 + 512 × 28 × 28	256 × 28 × 28
UpCNN3	256 × 28 × 28 + 256 × 56 × 56	128 × 56 × 56
UpCNN2	128 × 56 × 56 + 128 × 112 × 112	64 × 112 × 112
UpCNN1	64 × 112 × 112 + 64 × 224 × 224	64 × 224 × 224
OutConv	64 × 224 × 224	1 × 224 × 224

3.3. Language Branch

Within the U-shaped CNN architecture, the complementary U-shaped ViT branch is engineered to integrate visual and textual features. As illustrated in Figure 3, the initial DownViT layer processes two inputs: textual embeddings from BioBERT-Embed and visual features extracted by the first DownCNN layer. Here, BioBERT provides the pretrained foundation for BioBERT-Embed. The cross-modal fusion mechanism is formally defined by Equation (3):

$$Y_{DownViT,1} = ViT(x_{img,1} + ReLU(BN(Conv(x_{text})))\tag{3}$$

where $x_{img,i}$ denotes image features from the DownCNN path, x_{text} represents textual features, and PatchEmbedding transforms $Y_{DownCNN,i}$ into embedded features $x_{img,i}$. The ViT module comprises Multi-headed Self-attention (MHSA) and MLP layers, with LN indicating layer normalization. Subsequent DownViT layers (i = 2, 3, 4) simultaneously consume features from both the preceding DownViT module and the corresponding DownCNN layer, as specified in Equation (4):

$$Y_{DownViT,i+1} = ViT(Y_{DownViT,i} + x_{img,i+1})\tag{4}$$

These multi-scale features are then propagated back through the UpViT module to the CNN-ViT interaction stage. At each level, they merge with features from the corresponding DownCNN pathway. This hierarchical fusion strategy strengthens global feature representation while diminishing dependence on potentially noisy text annotations, thereby enhancing model robustness.

Table 2. Transformer and text module architecture.

Module Name	Layer Name	Input Shape	Output Shape
Transformer module	DownVit1	64 × 224 × 224	64 × 14 × 14
	DownVit2	128 × 112 × 112	128 × 14 × 14
	DownVit3	256 × 56 × 56	256 × 14 × 14
	DownVit4	512 × 28 × 28	512 × 14 × 14
	UpVit4	512 × 14 × 14	512 × 14 × 14
	UpVit3	256 × 14 × 14	256 × 14 × 14
	UpVit2	128 × 14 × 14	128 × 14 × 14
	UpVit1	64 × 14 × 14	64 × 14 × 14
Text module	Text_module4	768 × 128	512 × 128
	Text_module3	512 × 128	256 × 128
	Text_module2	256 × 128	128 × 128
	Text_module1	128 × 128	64 × 128

3.4. Enhanced Channel-Spatial Attention Module

In this subsection, we introduce the Enhanced Channel-Spatial Attention Module (ECSAM), which is designed to improve feature representation by integrating channel and spatial attention mechanisms while maintaining computational efficiency. ECSAM is composed of several key components that work together to achieve this goal, as shown in Figure 4.

The ECSAM processes input features $X \in \mathbb{R}^{B\times C\times H\times W}$ through an integrated channel and spatial attention mechanism. First, we perform a shared projection for both query and key vectors using a 1×1 convolutional layer with batch normalization and *ReLU* activation. This produces a combined tensor, which is then split into query matrix Q and key matrix K:

$$QK = \sigma(BN(Conv_{1\times1}(X))), \quad Q, K = split(QK, [C/r, C/r]) \tag{5}$$

where $Q \in \mathbb{R}^{B\times C/r\times HW}$ and $K \in \mathbb{R}^{B\times HW\times C/r}$ after reshaping operations. Simultaneously, we compute the value projection V using a separate 1×1 convolutional layer with batch normalization and $ReLU$ activation:

$$V = \sigma(BN(Conv_{1\times1}(X))) \in \mathbb{R}^{B\times C/r\times HW} \tag{6}$$

We then compute channel attention weights through matrix multiplication and softmax normalization. These weights are applied to the value matrix to obtain channel-enhanced features:

$$Energy = Q \otimes K, \quad A = softmax(Energy), \quad V'_{low} = A \otimes V \tag{7}$$

where $V'_{low} \in \mathbb{R}^{B\times C/r\times HW}$ represents the channel-enhanced features in reduced dimension. The channel-enhanced features are restored to the original dimension using a grouped convolution with batch normalization:

$$V' = BN(GroupConv_{1\times1}(reshape(V'_{low}))) \in \mathbb{R}^{B\times C\times H\times W} \tag{8}$$

Spatial attention is applied by first extracting spatial information through pooling operations. The average-pooled and max-pooled features are concatenated and processed through a convolutional layer with sigmoid activation to generate spatial attention weights S:

$$avg = AvgPool(V'), \quad max = MaxPool(V') \tag{9}$$

$$S = \sigma(Conv_{k\times k}(concat(avg, max))) \in [0,1]^{B\times1\times H\times W} \tag{10}$$

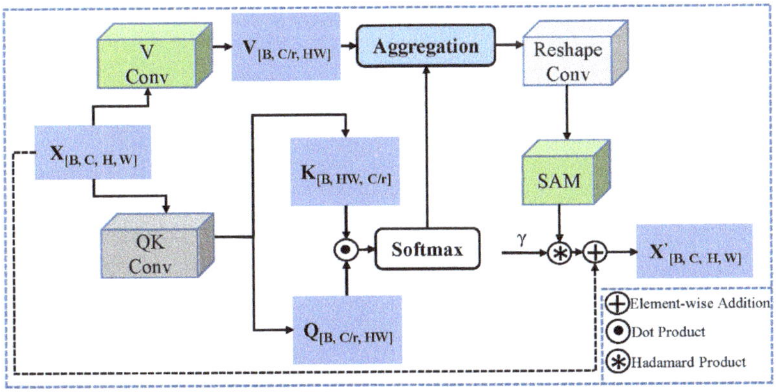

Figure 4. The overall architecture of Enhanced Channel-Spatial Attention Module (ECSAM). γ is a learnable parameter.

The spatial attention weights are then applied to the channel-enhanced features through element-wise multiplication:

$$X' = V' \odot S \tag{11}$$

Finally, a dynamic weighting parameter γ adjusts the contribution of the attention mechanism, and the output is combined with the original features through a residual connection:

$$O = \gamma \odot X' + X \tag{12}$$

where $\gamma \in \mathbb{R}^{1\times C\times 1\times 1}$ is a learnable parameter initialized to zero.

In the evolutionary trajectory of channel attention mechanisms, the core innovation of ECSAM lies in its deep integration of efficient self-attention mechanisms into channel modeling, significantly enhancing computational efficiency through parameter sharing and structural optimization. Its design abandons traditional channel statistics extraction based on global pooling (as seen in the channel branches of SE Block [28] and CBAM [26]), as these methods essentially compress the two-dimensional feature map of each channel into a single value through pooling operations. While simple and efficient, they lose spatial details and can only model static statistical relationships between channels. Instead, it employs a shared-weight 1×1 convolution to simultaneously generate dimensionality-reduced Query and Key. Within this low-dimensional space, it utilizes self-attention to dynamically learn complex interdependencies between channels. This is followed by efficient channel dimension recovery via grouped convolution, supplemented by a post-positioned lightweight spatial attention module for spatial modulation. Finally, dynamic residual fusion is achieved through a learnable gamma (γ parameter. Compared with SE Block, which relies solely on global average pooling for static channel weighting and completely ignores spatial information, and CBAM, which combines channel attention (based on maxpooling and avgpooling) and spatial attention but features relatively static channel modeling and lower parameter efficiency, ECSAM achieves richer, more context-aware channel interaction modeling through dynamic self-attention. Concurrently, strategies like shared projections and grouped convolution deliver higher parameter and computational efficiency, forming a synergistic optimization mechanism that fuses dynamic channel interaction with spatial modulation.

4. Experiments and Results

4.1. Datasets

QaTa-COV19 dataset: The QaTa-COV19 dataset is compiled by researchers from Qatar University and Tampere University. It contains 9258 COVID-19 chest X-ray images with manual annotations of COVID-19 lesions. The annotations are subsequently enriched with text-based details as per [10], concentrating on the infection status of both lungs, the quantity of affected zones, and the general location of these infected areas. The detailed dataset partitioning is shown in Table 3.

Table 3. The specific division of different datasets.

	QaTa-COV19	MosMedData+
Train	5716	2183
Validation	1429	273
Test	2113	273
Total	9258	2729

MosMedData+ dataset: The MosMedData+ dataset, containing 2729 CT scans of lung infections along with corresponding text descriptions ("Bilateral pulmonary infection, three infected areas, middle left lung and middle right lung"), is divided as shown in Table 3.

As shown in Figure 5, there are several example images and corresponding text descriptions.

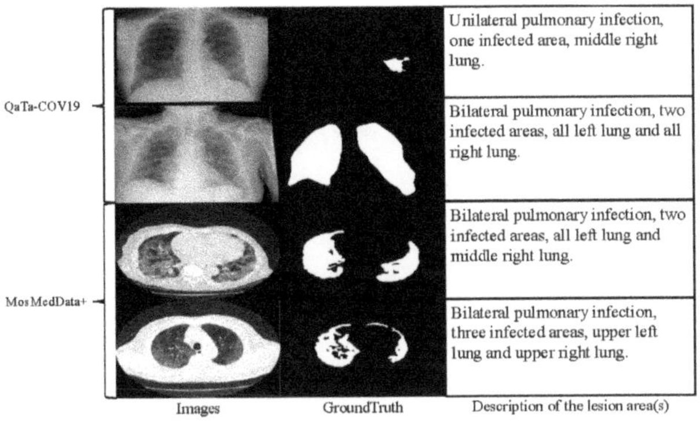

Figure 5. Image examples and corresponding text content for QaTa-COV19 and MosMedData+ datasets.

4.2. Implementation Details

We train each model on a single NVIDIA RTX 6000 GPU with 48 GB memory (NVIDIA Corporation, Santa Clara, CA, USA) using the MosMedData+ and QaTa-COV19 datasets. Our model is based on PyTorch 1.12.0 and we use 224 × 224 images and the Adam optimizer. For MosMedData+, we set the batch size to 8, the learning rate to 1×10^{-3}, and trained for 200 epochs. For QaTa-COV19, we set the batch size to 8, the learning rate to 3×10^{-4}, and the epochs to 200. The loss function is shown as Equation (15).

4.3. Loss Function and Evaluation Metrics

The loss function we use is shown in Equation (15), where L_{Dice} means dice loss and L_{CE} means cross-entropy loss.

$$L_{Dice} = 1 - \frac{2 \times |Y \cap \hat{Y}|}{|Y| + |\hat{Y}|} \tag{13}$$

$$L_{CE} = \frac{1}{N}\sum_{i=1}^{N} \times [y_i \log(\hat{y}_i) + (1 - y_i)\log(1 - \hat{y}_i)] \tag{14}$$

$$L = \frac{(L_{Dice} + L_{CE})}{2} \tag{15}$$

In our experiments, Y and $\hat{Y}$ are the ground truth and predicted result. N denotes the total pixel count. $y_i \in Y$ and $\hat{y}_i \in \hat{Y}_i$.

To assess performance, the Dice score and the mIoU metric are employed to evaluate our MedLangViT model and other SOTA methods, as detailed in Equations (16) and (17):

$$DICE(Y, \hat{Y}) = \frac{2 \times |Y \cap \hat{Y}|}{|Y| + |\hat{Y}|} = 1 - L_{Dice} \tag{16}$$

$$IoU(Y, \hat{Y}) = \frac{|Y \cap \hat{Y}|}{|Y \cup \hat{Y}|} \tag{17}$$

where Y and $\hat{Y}$ also have the same definition as in the above section. $mIoU$ is the average of $IoUs$ for all categories.

4.4. Results on QaTa-COV19 and MosMedData+ Datasets

On the QaTa-COV19 dataset, the MedLangViT method achieved a Dice coefficient and mIoU of 84.27% and 75.93%, respectively, as shown in Table 4, representing a significant improvement over other methods. On the more challenging MosMedData+ dataset, it obtained a Dice coefficient of 75.95% and an mIoU of 63.17%, again outperforming other approaches. In terms of parameter count and computational complexity (FLOPs), MedLangViT has a parameter count of 27.7 M and FLOPs of 47.8 G. Compared with recent vision–language models for segmentation, MedLangViT demonstrates superior computational efficiency: It requires only 31.8% of CLIP's parameters (87.0 M to 27.7 M) and 45.4% of its FLOPs (105.3 G to 47.8 G), while outperforming LAVT (118.6 M/83.8 G) by 5.0% Dice on MosMedData+ with 65% fewer parameters. Even against similarly sized LVIT (29.7 M/54.1 G), MedLangViT achieves higher accuracy with 11.6% fewer FLOPs. Compared with methods with higher parameters and computational complexity, such as TransUNet (105.0 M/56.7 G) and Swin-Unet (82.3 M/67.3 G), MedLangViT achieves superior performance while maintaining lower parameter and computational complexity, indicating a better balance between model efficiency and performance. This efficiency stems from our lightweight medical-specific architecture and optimized text–image fusion, avoiding computational overhead from large pretrained VL backbones or complex fusion modules. Additionally, compared with purely visual methods that do not utilize textual information, all text-guided models demonstrate a significant and consistent advantage on both datasets. This indicates that incorporating auxiliary textual information can effectively enhance MedLangViT's understanding and segmentation accuracy of COVID-19-related lung lesions. As the optimal text-guided method, MedLangViT's superior performance and efficiency further confirm the effectiveness of its hybrid architecture (CNN-Transformer) and text–image fusion strategy, particularly in handling complex and diverse lesion patterns.

Table 4. The quantitative results of different methods on the QaTa-COV19 and MosMedData+ datasets. The "Hybrid" means CNN-Transformer structure.

Methods	Backbone	Text	Param (M)	FLOPs (G)	QaTa-COV19		MosMedData+	
					Dice (%)	mIoU (%)	Dice (%)	mIoU (%)
U-Net [11]	CNN	×	14.8	50.3	79.02	69.46	64.60	50.73
nnUNet [13]	CNN	×	19.1	412.7	80.42	70.81	72.59	60.36
TransUNet [19]	Hybrid	×	105.0	56.7	78.63	69.13	71.24	58.44
Swin-Unet [20]	Hybrid	×	82.3	67.3	78.07	68.34	63.29	50.19
SegFormer [29]	Hybrid	×	84.7	35.1	78.41	68.83	65.05	54.34
MedLangViT (w/o)	Hybrid	×	26.0	47.2	81.97	71.77	73.02	60.53
ConVIRT [24]	CNN	✓	35.2	44.6	79.72	70.58	72.06	59.73
TGANet [25]	CNN	✓	19.8	41.9	79.87	70.75	71.81	59.28
CLIP [21]	Hybrid	✓	87.0	105.3	79.81	70.66	71.97	59.64
GLORIA [23]	Hybrid	✓	45.6	60.8	79.94	70.68	72.42	60.18
LViT [10]	Hybrid	✓	29.7	54.1	83.66	75.11	74.57	61.33
LAVT [27]	Hybrid	✓	118.6	83.8	79.28	69.89	73.29	60.41
DenseCLIP [30]	Hybrid	✓	105.3	49.9	79.58	70.37	71.62	58.95
MedLangViT	Hybrid	✓	27.7	47.8	84.27	75.93	75.95	63.17

MedLangViT not only leads in accuracy but also excels in model efficiency, with lower parameter and computational complexity than other high-performance hybrid models, making it more practical. On the more challenging MosMedData+ dataset, MedLangViT shows a greater improvement over the second-best method compared with its improvement on QaTa-COV19, indicating its robustness and generalization ability in handling more complex, noisy, or data with greater annotation differences. Overall, MedLangViT achieves state-of-the-art COVID-19 lung lesion segmentation accuracy on both the QaTa-COV19 and MosMedData+ datasets while maintaining lower model complexity and computational cost, validating its effectiveness and efficiency.

Since the quantitative results of image-only models are consistently lower than those of text–image models, we performed qualitative analysis only on the text–image models. The qualitative results of MedLangViT and other state-of-the-art methods on the MosMedData+ and QaTa-COV19 datasets are shown in Figure 6. To demonstrate segmentation performance across varying lesion sizes, we present representative results from the MosMedData+ dataset categorized into three groups: small, medium, and large lesions. As shown in Figure 6, while segmentation accuracy for small and medium lesions shows comparable performance across methods, our approach achieves significantly superior shape fidelity and topological continuity for large lesions, more closely aligning with the ground truth annotations. The qualitative results demonstrate that MedLangViT exhibits robust semantic segmentation capabilities compared with other state-of-the-art multimodal segmentation methods. Due to the advantage of integrating both text and image information into a single encoder, MedLangViT achieves finer segmentation boundaries.

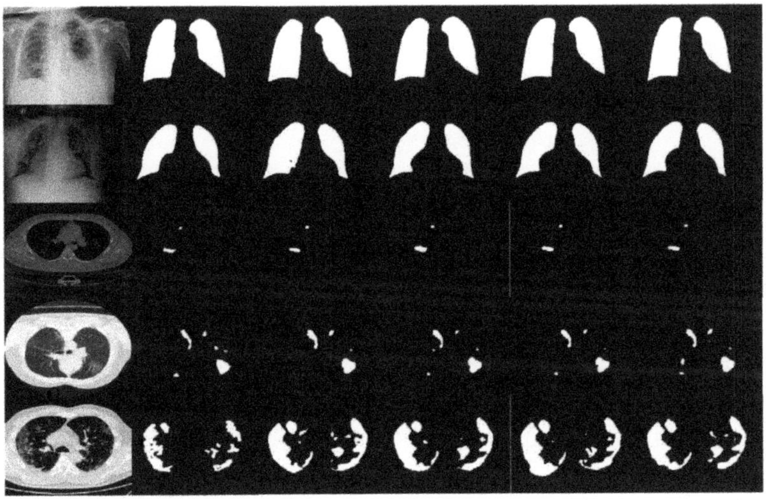

Figure 6. The qualitative results of different methods on QaTa-COV19 and MosMedData+ datasets.

4.5. Ablation Study

In this section, we conduct five sets of ablation experiments to demonstrate the necessity of each component in MedLangViT, the choice of hyper-parameters, the internal structure of ECSAM, different attention mechanisms, and different BERT-based embeddingson two datasets.

4.5.1. Effect of Each Component

In this section, we conduct an ablation study on the MosMedData+ dataset to demonstrate the necessity of each component in our network architecture. Table 5 ablates the contribution of key components in our framework on the MosMedData+ dataset. We specifically focus on the BERT, Pixel-Level Attention Module (PLAM), BioBERT, and the proposed Enhanced Channel-Spatial Attention Module (ECSAM).

Table 5. The effect of each component on MosMedData+ dataset. PLAM (Pixel-Level Attention Module) is the part of LViT that corresponds to ECSAM in MedLangViT.

BERT	PLAM	BioBERT	ECSAM	Dice (%)	mIoU (%)
✓	✓			74.57	61.33
✓			✓	74.89	61.76
	✓	✓		75.03	62.06
		✓	✓	75.95	63.17

The synergistic combination of BERT and PLAM, as implemented in LViT, achieved a Dice score of 74.57% and an mIoU of 61.33% on the MosMedData+ dataset. Replacing PLAM with ECSAM while retaining BERT improved Dice by 0.32% (74.89%), demonstrating that ECSAM enhances spatial-text feature fusion compared with PLAM. Strikingly, using BioBERT with PLAM yields a Dice of 75.03%, significantly outperforming BERT-based configurations. This confirms that medical-specific language modeling was critical for capturing clinical semantics. Most importantly, the synergistic integration of BioBERT and ECSAM achieves 75.95% Dice and 63.17% mIoU—the highest results in the ablation. This combination surpasses the isolated gains of BioBERT and ECSAM, with a total improvement of 1.38% Dice.

The superadditive effect highlights their complementary roles: BioBERT provides clinically grounded text representations, and ECSAM dynamically aligns these representations with visual features at optimal spatial granularity, thereby eliminating semantic ambiguities and refining lesion boundary delineation. Specifically, the superior performance of ECSAM stems from its dynamic channel modeling that replaces static pooling-based statistics with efficient self-attention, capturing complex inter-channel dependencies while preserving spatial integrity through shared 1×1 convolutions for Query/Key generation and lightweight spatial refinement. This paradigm shift from compression-based methods enables richer context-aware feature fusion.

4.5.2. Effect of Hyper-Parameters

In this section, we conduct an ablation study on hyper-parameters, including batch size and learning rate. We test MedLangViT on two datasets: MosMedData+ and QaTa-COV19. For the batch size, we try three different settings: 8, 4, and 2. For the learning rate, we adopted the settings from [10], which are 3×10^{-4} and 1×10^{-3}. The experimental results can be seen in Table 6. As shown in the table, for the QaTa-COV19 dataset, the best results are achieved with a batch size of 8 and a learning rate of 3×10^{-4}. For the MosMedData+ dataset, the optimal results are obtained with a batch size of 8 and a learning rate of 1×10^{-3}. Overall, the results indicate that variations in batch size lead to more significant improvements in performance compared with changes in learning rate.

Table 6. The effect of different hyper-parameters.

Hyper-Parameters		QaTa-COV19		MosMedData+	
		Dice (%)	mIoU (%)	Dice (%)	mIoU (%)
Batch Size	8	84.27	75.93	75.95	63.17
	4	82.93	74.21	73.43	60.01
	2	82.41	73.58	73.20	59.78
Learning Rate	3×10^{-4}	84.27	75.93	75.26	62.73
	1×10^{-3}	83.65	75.02	75.95	63.17

4.5.3. Effect of Internal Structure of ECSAM

Table 7 quantitatively ablates the internal components of ECSAM on MosMedData+. When employing separate 1 × 1 convolutions for Query and Key generation (QConv + KConv) without SAM, the baseline achieves 73.47% Dice. Replacing these with a unified QKConv (shared-weight 1 × 1 convolution for joint Q/K generation) yields a 0.28% Dice gain, demonstrating that parameter sharing enhances efficiency while maintaining representational capacity. The addition of the Spatial Attention Module (SAM) to separate Q/K convolutions boosts performance substantially to 74.68% Dice, validating SAM's critical role in spatial refinement. Most significantly, the synergistic integration of QKConv and SAM achieves peak performance (75.95% Dice, 63.17% mIoU), surpassing the isolated QKConv configuration by 2.20% Dice and exceeding the QConv+KConv+SAM combination by 1.27% Dice. This confirms that QKConv's parameter-efficient channel modeling and SAM's spatial enhancement operate complementarily, with their joint optimization being essential for ECSAM's full efficacy.

Table 7. The effect of internal structure of ECSAM on MosMedData+ dataset.

QConv	KConv	SAM	QKConv	Dice (%)	mIoU (%)
✓	✓			73.47	60.59
			✓	73.75	61.22
✓	✓	✓		74.68	61.54
		✓	✓	75.95	63.17

4.5.4. Effect of Different Attention Mechanism

When analyzing the impact of different attention mechanisms on model performance, the ECSAM demonstrates comprehensive advantages, as shown in Table 8. Compared with the SE Block and CBAM, ECSAM achieves the lowest inference latency of 29.52 ms with only a slight increase in parameter count to 27.74 M and computational load to 47.75 G FLOPs, reducing latency by 1.1% compared with the SE Block and by 3.5% compared with CBAM, while also reducing memory usage to 9.07 MB, which is 6.6% less than the SE Block and 7.0% less than the CBAM. More importantly, ECSAM significantly improves segmentation accuracy, with a Dice coefficient of 75.95%, which is 1.27 percentage points higher than the SE Block and 1.34 percentage points higher than CBAM; the mIoU metric reaches 63.17%, which is 1.39 percentage points better than the SE Block and 1.35 percentage points better than CBAM, fully validating the module's dual advantages in enhancing feature representation capabilities and optimizing computational efficiency.

Table 8. The effect of MedLangViT with different attention mechanism on MosMedData+ dataset. "aLatency" means the average of latency measurements taken ten times. "aMU" means the average memory usage measured ten times.

Modules	Params (M)	FLOPs (G)	aLatency (ms)	aMU (MB)	Dice (%)	mIoU (%)
SE Block [28]	27.72	47.38	29.85	9.71	74.68	61.78
CBAM [26]	27.72	47.39	30.58	9.74	74.61	61.82
ECSAM	27.74	47.75	29.52	9.07	75.95	63.17

4.5.5. Effect of Different BERT-Based Embeddings

To investigate the impact of different BERT-based embeddings, we evaluated MedLangViT integrated with three biomedical BERT variants: PubMedBERT, BlueBERT, and BioBERT. As Table 9 shows, substituting these embedding modules maintained identical parameter counts of 27.74 M and computational costs of 47.75 G FLOPs, since all three share the same BERT-base architecture with only pretrained weights differing based on their training corpora: PubMedBERT used PubMed abstracts [31], BlueBERT combined PubMed abstracts with MIMIC-III clinical notes [32], and BioBERT leveraged both PubMed abstracts and PMC full-text articles [6]. Crucially, despite the identical model scale, segmentation performance varied significantly. BioBERT achieved optimal results with a Dice coefficient of 75.95% and mIoU of 63.17%, attributed to its exposure to detailed radiological descriptions in PMC full texts. PubMedBERT yielded lower performance at 75.41% Dice and 62.21% mIoU due to abstract-only training data limitations. BlueBERT performed weakest at 75.08% Dice and 61.97% mIoU, likely hindered by non-standardized clinical jargon and a smaller pretraining scale. These results confirm that pretraining corpus characteristics drive performance differences when using different BERT-based embeddings, where BioBERT's full-text exposure aligns best with lung CT segmentation tasks, underscoring the necessity of selecting text embeddings pretrained on task-relevant subdomains within multimodal medical imaging architectures.

Table 9. The effect of MedLangViT with different BERT-based embeddings on MosMedData+ dataset.

Modules	Params (M)	FLOPs (G)	Dice (%)	mIoU (%)
PubMedBERT [31]	27.74	47.75	75.41	62.21
BlueBERT [32]	27.74	47.75	75.08	61.97
BioBERT [6]	27.74	47.75	75.95	63.17

4.6. Interpretability Study

We conduct explainability studies on the QaTa-COV19 and MosMedData+ datasets to evaluate whether our network focuses on lesion regions better than other multimodal networks. To intuitively show changes in model attention areas, we use GradCAM [33] to compare activation in these regions. As Figure 7 shows, compared with TGANet, GLoRIA, and LViT, our MedLangViT has more precise activation regions that better match lesion contours on QaTa-COV19. On MosMedData+, MedLangViT activation regions are broader with fewer omissions.

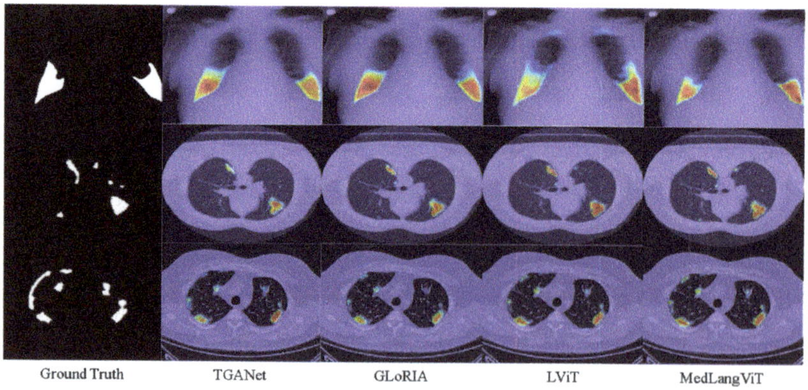

Figure 7. Visualization of saliency maps of different approaches on the MosMedData+ and QaTa-COV19 datasets. The text input of the first row is "Bilateral pulmonary infection, two infected areas, lower left lung and lower right lung". The text input of the second row is "Bilateral pulmonary infection, six infected areas, all left lung and middle right lung". The text input of the third row is "Bilateral pulmonary infection, six infected areas, upper left lung and middle right lung".

Additionally, to better explore the regional activation patterns within our model's feature processing process, we conduct further experiments on the MosMedData+ dataset. We select a visually interpretable case (the original ground truth in the third row of Figure 7) for visualization, as shown in Figures 8 and 9. Focusing on the image processing pathway, we generate activation mappings across all DownCNN and UpCNN layers of the network using BioBERT and ECSAM, as well as BioBERT and PLAM. It can be observed in Figures 8 and 9 that during the downsampling stages, activated regions gradually converge toward the core lesion areas. Subsequent upsampling stages then precisely localize these pathological regions. But compared with Figure 9, the activation region in Figure 8 is more accurate. This indicates that our ECSAM is more helpful in improving the attention of lesion areas.

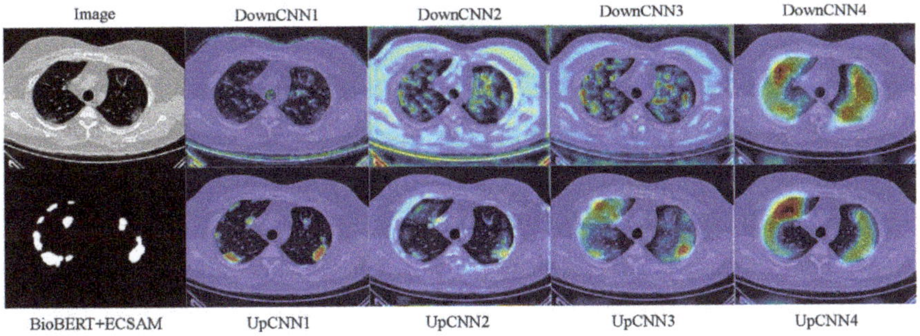

Figure 8. Visualization of saliency maps of different layers of network with BioBERT and ECSAM on the MosMedData+ dataset.

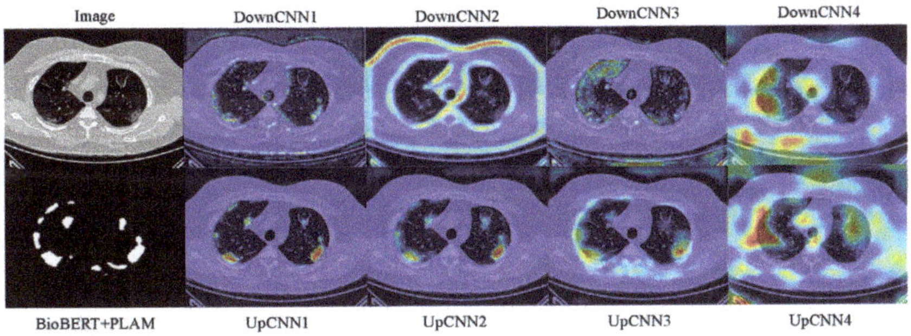

Figure 9. Visualization of saliency maps of different layers of network with BioBERT and PLAM on the MosMedData+ dataset.

5. Discussion

While MedLangViT has achieved substantial progress by integrating clinical text, its upper limit is ultimately constrained by annotation quality. Firstly, inter-clinician variations in descriptive precision, exemplified by ambiguous phrases such as "mildly opaque" or "hazy area", introduce semantic ambiguity. This challenges BioBERT's word sense disambiguation capabilities. Additionally, terminology differences across institutions—including British versus American spellings and abbreviation conventions—further amplify these inconsistencies. Secondly, mismatches between textual descriptions and actual visual features (e.g., mentions of invisible lesions or extremely subtle pathologies) can misguide ECSAM's spatial attention and cause over-activation of attention heatmaps in erroneous regions. Thirdly, MedLangViT inherently assumes clean and complete text–image pairs. However, common retrospective data issues such as spelling errors, missing fields, and copy–paste artifacts (including repeated or conflicting descriptions) directly undermine segmentation robustness, particularly in low-resource settings. Finally, model confidence may sharply decline when encountering real-world low-quality or partially missing text annotations. Future work will quantify these impacts and develop ambiguity-resilient fusion mechanisms.

6. Conclusions

In this paper, we propose a novel language–vision model for medical image segmentation, termed MedLangViT. The model employs BioBERT—a medically specialized language model—to embed clinical text annotations, thereby mitigating limitations inherent in image-only data. Furthermore, we propose an Enhanced Channel-Spatial Attention Module (ECSAM) that aggregates inter-channel self-attention to enhance local features and subsequently reinforces text-guided semantic cues through spatial attention mechanisms, synergistically integrating textual and visual representations. Experimental results on both MosMedData+ and QaTa-COV19 datasets demonstrate that our model outperforms state-of-the-art approaches, including classical vision-only models and contemporary language–vision frameworks. Future work will explore quantitative and qualitative impacts of text annotations on model performance, including robustness to annotation variability/ambiguity and the framework's generalizability across diverse medical imaging modalities.

Author Contributions: Conceptualization: Y.W.; methodology: Y.W.; software: Y.W.; validation: Y.W.; investigation: Y.W.; resources: Y.W., E.N. and X.L.; data curation: Y.W.; writing—original draft: Y.W.; writing—review and editing: J.S. and E.N.; visualization: Y.W.; supervision: J.S. and E.N.; project administration: E.N. and X.L.; funding acquisition: E.N. All authors have read and agreed to the published version of the manuscript.

Funding: This work is supported by Jsps kakenhi grant Number JP24K14998.

Data Availability Statement: The data analyzed in this study were obtained from the existing public datasets named QaTa-COV19 Dataset and MosMedData+ Dataset, available at https://www.kaggle.com/datasets/aysendegerli/qatacov19-dataset (accessed on 31 March 2025) and https://medicalsegmentation.com/covid19/ (accessed on 10 March 2025), respectively. No new data were created.

Acknowledgments: During the preparation of this manuscript/study, the author(s) used DeepSeek-R1 for the purposes of the generation of equations in Section 3.4 and Section 4.3. The authors have reviewed and edited the output and take full responsibility for the content of this publication.

Conflicts of Interest: The authors declare no conflicts of interest. The funder is involved in the decision to publish the results.

Abbreviations

The following abbreviations are used in this manuscript:

ECSAM	Enhanced Channel-Spatial Attention Module
PLAM	Pixel-Level Attention Module
ViT	Vision Transformer
DTC	Dual-task Consistency
SSL	Semi-supervised Learning

eferences

Li, Z.; Li, D.; Xu, C.; Wang, W.; Hong, Q.; Li, Q.; Tian, J. Tfcns: A cnn-transformer hybrid network for medical image segmentation. In *Artificial Neural Networks and Machine Learning – ICANN 2022 31st International Conference on Artificial Neural Networks, Bristol, UK, 6–9 September 2022, Proceedings;* Springer: Berlin/Heidelberg, Germany, 2022; pp. 781–792.

Roth, H.R.; Xu, Z.; Tor-Díez, C.; Jacob, R.S.; Zember, J.; Molto, J.; Li, W.; Xu, S.; Turkbey, B.; Turkbey, E.; et al. Rapid artificial intelligence solutions in a pandemic—The COVID-19-20 Lung CT Lesion Segmentation Challenge. *Med. Image Anal.* **2022**, *82*, 102605. [CrossRef] [PubMed]

Zhang, Y.; Lv, B.; Xue, L.; Zhang, W.; Liu, Y.; Fu, Y.; Cheng, Y.; Qi, Y. SemiSAM+: Rethinking Semi-Supervised Medical Image Segmentation in the Era of Foundation Models. *arXiv* **2025**, arXiv:2502.20749. [CrossRef]

Lan, X.; Jin, W. Multi-scale input layers and dense decoder aggregation network for COVID-19 lesion segmentation from CT scans. *Sci. Rep.* **2024**, *14*, 23729. [CrossRef] [PubMed]

Zhang, J.; Ding, X.; Hu, D.; Jiang, Y. Semantic segmentation of COVID-19 lesions with a multiscale dilated convolutional network. *Sci. Rep.* **2022**, *12*, 1847. [CrossRef] [PubMed]

Lee, J.; Yoon, W.; Kim, S.; Kim, D.; Kim, S.; So, C.H.; Kang, J. BioBERT: A pre-trained biomedical language representation model for biomedical text mining. *Bioinformatics* **2020**, *36*, 1234–1240. [CrossRef] [PubMed]

Devlin, J.; Chang, M.W.; Lee, K.; Toutanova, K. Bert: Pre-training of deep bidirectional transformers for language understanding. In Proceedings of the 2019 Conference of the North American Chapter of the Association for Computational Linguistics: Human Language Technologies (Long and Short Papers), Minneapolis, MN, USA, 2–7 June 2019; Volume 1, pp. 4171–4186.

Morozov, S.P.; Andreychenko, A.E.; Pavlov, N.A.; Vladzymyrskyy, A.; Ledikhova, N.V.; Gombolevskiy, V.A.; Blokhin, I.A.; Gelezhe, P.B.; Gonchar, A.; Chernina, V.Y. Mosmeddata: Chest ct scans with COVID-19 related findings dataset. *arXiv* **2020**, arXiv:2005.06465.

Degerli, A.; Kiranyaz, S.; Chowdhury, M.E.; Gabbouj, M. Osegnet: Operational segmentation network for COVID-19 detection using chest x-ray images. In Proceedings of the 2022 IEEE International Conference on Image Processing (ICIP), Bordeaux, France, 16–19 October 2022; IEEE: Piscataway, NJ, USA, 2022; pp. 2306–2310.

10. Li, Z.; Li, Y.; Li, Q.; Wang, P.; Guo, D.; Lu, L.; Jin, D.; Zhang, Y.; Hong, Q. Lvit: Language meets vision transformer in medical image segmentation. *IEEE Trans. Med. Imaging* **2023**, *43*, 96–107. [CrossRef] [PubMed]
11. Ronneberger, O.; Fischer, P.; Brox, T. U-net: Convolutional networks for biomedical image segmentation. In *Medical Image Computing and Computer-Assisted Intervention—MICCAI 2015: 18th International Conference, Munich, Germany, 5–9 October 2015, Proceedings, Part III 18;* Springer: Berlin/Heidelberg, Germany, 2015; pp. 234–241.
12. Zhou, Z.; Rahman Siddiquee, M.M.; Tajbakhsh, N.; Liang, J. Unet++: A nested u-net architecture for medical image segmentation. In *Deep Learning in Medical Image Analysis and Multimodal Learning for Clinical Decision Support: 4th International Workshop, DLMIA 2018, and 8th International Workshop, ML-CDS 2018, Held in Conjunction with MICCAI 2018, Granada, Spain, 20 September 2018, Proceedings 4;* Springer: Berlin/Heidelberg, Germany, 2018; pp. 3–11.
13. Isensee, F.; Jaeger, P.F.; Kohl, S.A.; Petersen, J.; Maier-Hein, K.H. nnU-Net: A self-configuring method for deep learning-based biomedical image segmentation. *Nat. Methods* **2021**, *18*, 203–211. [CrossRef] [PubMed]
14. Peláez-Vegas, A.; Mesejo, P.; Luengo, J. A survey on semi-supervised semantic segmentation. *arXiv* **2023**, arXiv:2302.09899. [CrossRef]
15. Luo, X.; Chen, J.; Song, T.; Wang, G. Semi-supervised medical image segmentation through dual-task consistency. *Proc. AAAI Conf. Artif. Intell.* **2021**, *35*, 8801–8809. [CrossRef]
16. Chaitanya, K.; Erdil, E.; Karani, N.; Konukoglu, E. Local contrastive loss with pseudo-label based self-training for semi-supervised medical image segmentation. *Med. Image Anal.* **2023**, *87*, 102792. [CrossRef] [PubMed]
17. Zhu, Y.; Wang, X.; Liu, T.; Fu, Y. Multi-perspective dynamic consistency learning for semi-supervised medical image segmentation. *Sci. Rep.* **2025**, *15*, 18266. [CrossRef] [PubMed]
18. Zhang, Y.; Yu, P.; Xiao, Y.; Wang, S. Pyramid-structured multi-scale transformer for efficient semi-supervised video object segmentation with adaptive fusion. *Pattern Recognit. Lett.* **2025**, *194*, 48–54. [CrossRef]
19. Chen, J.; Lu, Y.; Yu, Q.; Luo, X.; Adeli, E.; Wang, Y.; Lu, L.; Yuille, A.L.; Zhou, Y. Transunet: Transformers make strong encoders for medical image segmentation. *arXiv* **2021**, arXiv:2102.04306. [CrossRef]
20. Cao, H.; Wang, Y.; Chen, J.; Jiang, D.; Zhang, X.; Tian, Q.; Wang, M. Swin-unet: Unet-like pure transformer for medical image segmentation. In Proceedings of the European Conference on Computer Vision, Tel Aviv, Israel, 23–27 October 2022; Springer: Cham, Switzerland, 2022; pp. 205–218.
21. Radford, A.; Kim, J.W.; Hallacy, C.; Ramesh, A.; Goh, G.; Agarwal, S.; Sastry, G.; Askell, A.; Mishkin, P.; Clark, J.; et al. Learning transferable visual models from natural language supervision. In Proceedings of the International Conference on Machine Learning, PMLR, Online, 18–24 July 2021; pp. 8748–8763.

22. Kim, W.; Son, B.; Kim, I. Vilt: Vision-and-language transformer without convolution or region supervision. In Proceedings of th International Conference on Machine Learning, PMLR, Online, 18–24 July 2021; pp. 5583–5594.
23. Huang, S.C.; Shen, L.; Lungren, M.P.; Yeung, S. Gloria: A multimodal global-local representation learning framework fo label-efficient medical image recognition. In Proceedings of the IEEE/CVF International Conference on Computer Visic Montreal, QC, Canada, 10–17 October 2021; pp. 3942–3951.
24. Zhang, Y.; Jiang, H.; Miura, Y.; Manning, C.D.; Langlotz, C.P. Contrastive learning of medical visual representations from paire images and text. In Proceedings of the Machine Learning for Healthcare Conference, PMLR, Durham, NC, USA, 5–6 Augu 2022; pp. 2–25.
25. Tomar, N.K.; Jha, D.; Bagci, U.; Ali, S. TGANet: Text-guided attention for improved polyp segmentation. In Proceedings of th International Conference on Medical Image Computing and Computer-Assisted Intervention, Singapore, 18–22 September 202 Springer: Cham, Switzerland, 2022; pp. 151–160.
26. Woo, S.; Park, J.; Lee, J.Y.; Kweon, I.S. Cbam: Convolutional block attention module. In Proceedings of the European Conferen on Computer Vision (ECCV), Munich, Germany, 8–14 September 2018; pp. 3–19.
27. Yang, Z.; Wang, J.; Tang, Y.; Chen, K.; Zhao, H.; Torr, P.H. Lavt: Language-aware vision transformer for referring imag segmentation. In Proceedings of the IEEE/CVF Conference on Computer Vision and Pattern Recognition, New Orleans, L USA, 18–24 June 2022; pp. 18155–18165.
28. Hu, J.; Shen, L.; Sun, G. Squeeze-and-excitation networks. In Proceedings of the IEEE Conference on Computer Vision an Pattern Recognition, Salt Lake City, UT, USA, 18–23 June 2918; pp. 7132–7141.
29. Xie, E.; Wang, W.; Yu, Z.; Anandkumar, A.; Alvarez, J.M.; Luo, P. SegFormer: Simple and efficient design for semant segmentation with transformers. *Adv. Neural Inf. Process. Syst.* **2021**, *34*, 12077–12090.
30. Rao, Y.; Zhao, W.; Chen, G.; Tang, Y.; Zhu, Z.; Huang, G.; Zhou, J.; Lu, J. Denseclip: Language-guided dense prediction wit context-aware prompting. In Proceedings of the IEEE/CVF Conference on Computer Vision and Pattern Recognition, Ne Orleans, LA, USA, 18–24 June 2022; pp. 18082–18091.
31. Gu, Y.; Tinn, R.; Cheng, H.; Lucas, M.; Usuyama, N.; Liu, X.; Naumann, T.; Gao, J.; Poon, H. Domain-specific language mod pretraining for biomedical natural language processing. *ACM Trans. Comput. Healthcare (HEALTH)* **2021**, *3*, 1–23. [CrossRef]
32. Peng, Y.; Yan, S.; Lu, Z. Transfer learning in biomedical natural language processing: An evaluation of BERT and ELMo o ten benchmarking datasets. *arXiv* **2019**, arXiv:1906.05474. [CrossRef]
33. Selvaraju, R.R.; Cogswell, M.; Das, A.; Vedantam, R.; Parikh, D.; Batra, D. Grad-cam: Visual explanations from deep networks vi gradient-based localization. In Proceedings of the IEEE International Conference on Computer Vision, Venice, Italy, 22–29 Octobe 2017; pp. 618–626.

electronics

MDPI

Article

Deep-CNN-Based Layout-to-SEM Image Reconstruction with Conformal Uncertainty Calibration for Nanoimprint Lithography in Semiconductor Manufacturing

an Chien and Eric Lee *

Department of Chemical Engineering, National Taiwan University, Taipei City 10617, Taiwan; f12524060@ntu.edu.tw

* Correspondence: ericlee@ntu.edu.tw

Abstract: Nanoimprint lithography (NIL) has emerged as a promising sub-10 nm patterning at low cost; yet, robust process control remains difficult because of time-consuming physics-based simulators and labeled SEM data scarcity. We propose a data-efficient, two-stage deep-learning framework here that directly reconstructs post-imprint SEM images from binary design layouts and delivers calibrated pixel-by-pixel uncertainty simultaneously. First, a shallow U-Net is trained on conformalized quantile regression (CQR) to output 90% prediction intervals with statistically guaranteed coverage. Moreover, per-level errors on a small calibration dataset are designed to drive an outlier-weighted and encoder-frozen transfer fine-tuning phase that refines only the decoder, with its capacity explicitly focused on regions of spatial uncertainty. On independent test layouts, our proposed fine-tuned model significantly reduces the mean absolute error (MAE) from 0.0365 to 0.0255 and raises the coverage from 0.904 to 0.926, while cutting the labeled data and GPU time by 80% and 72%, respectively. The resultant uncertainty maps highlight spatial regions associated with error hotspots and support defect-aware optical proximity correction (OPC) with fewer guard-band iterations. Extending the current perspective beyond OPC, the innovatively model-agnostic and modular design of the pipeline here allows flexible integration into other critical stages of the semiconductor manufacturing workflow, such as imprinting, etching, and inspection. In these stages, such predictions are critical for achieving higher precision, efficiency, and overall process robustness in semiconductor manufacturing, which is the ultimate motivation of this study.

Keywords: nanoimprint lithography (NIL); layout-to-SEM reconstruction; U-Net; conformal prediction; uncertainty quantification; optical proximity correction (OPC)

1. Introduction

1.1. Nanoimprint Lithography: Principles, Advantages, and Manufacturing Challenges

Nanoimprint lithography (NIL) has emerged as an inspiring replacement for conventional photolithography recently, with a low-cost and high-resolution patterning process for sub-10 nm nodes [1–3]. The simplicity of its process flow—comprising master template creation and replica template fabrication, and final wafer patterning—makes it particularly suitable for high-throughput manufacturing [4]. In contrast to conventional optical lithography, which relies on the use of reduction masks (typically 4× or 5×), NIL makes use of a 1:1 imprint template to pattern the substrate directly at the nanoscale. This one-to-one transfer mechanism reduces the reliance on traditional optical proximity correction (OPC), which compensates for distortions introduced by optical systems. While OPC plays a vital role in ensuring that the pattern on the wafer is identical to the design layout, its models are based on the physics of optical lithography. NIL, on the other hand, relies on entirely different mechanisms such as mechanical contact and polymer flow, which calls for new OPC frameworks specific to imprint-based techniques. To ensure pattern fidelity, OPC often employs guard bands—conservative layout margins that require costly iterative tuning, which NIL's distinct physics now demand to be redefined. The strategic importance of NIL has been increasingly recognized by leading semiconductor foundries in Asia, where the technology has already been introduced into demo-line systems for next-generation patterning evaluation.

In spite of all its advantages, NIL still faces challenges in several aspects of process control, including the trade-off involved in optimizing residual layer thickness and the non-uniform droplet distribution in near-shot-edge regions [5–7]. Recent studies suggest that NIL represents not only a quantitative advancement in resolution but also a state-of-the-art lithographic paradigm that simplifies the process architecture, reduces the overlay and proximity effects, and offers novel flexibility for 3D patterning and emerging device geometries [8]. Its revolutionary impact is more than keeping up with next-generation photolithography performance—it redefines the limits of the achievable resolution and process scalability in next-generation semiconductor manufacturing [9].

In the context of semiconductor chip-level fabrication, these limitations become particularly significant. Contemporary integrated circuits demand extremely high levels of precision and uniformity with tolerances at the nanometer scale. As feature sizes continue to shrink and device architectures grow increasingly complicated, manufacturing bottlenecks have developed into major hurdles to technological advancement. These issues cannot be resolved by traditional rule-based process control methodologies alone, especially under data-limited or variation-sensitive conditions [10].

1.2. *AI and Deep Learning for Layout-to-SEM Reconstruction in NIL*

To address this need, our recent research explored the application of artificial intelligence (AI) for semiconductor metrology and inspection, focusing on advanced defect detection based on scanning electron microscope (SEM) images taken from after-development inspection (ADI) [10,11]. In this work, we proposed a two-stage deep-learning framework with synthetic minority over-sampling (SMOTE) and transfer fine-tuning to combat the significant issue of data imbalance and classification challenge efficiently. This strategy not only enhanced defect detection accuracy and computational efficiency for SEM-based hotspot monitoring but also highlighted data scarcity as a key challenge in achieving robust models for process control. Following the aforementioned study, our research here proposes a deep-learning integration into NIL-based fabrication analysis, with a focus on layout-to-SEM image reconstruction enhanced by conformal uncertainty calibration. By coupling pixel-level prediction with statistically valid uncertainty quantification (UQ), the framework aims to bridge the gap between the limitations of physics-based simulations and the need for scalable, data-driven defect prediction in cutting-edge patterning processes.

To enable the widespread adoption of NIL in semiconductor manufacturing, sophisticated process optimization and tight control mechanisms are not only beneficial—they are imperative for modern semiconductor manufacturing, especially in NIL [12]. In this regard, the integration of AI into the manufacturing process has become strongly associated with possible future breakthroughs, especially due to its ability to extract latent patterns from complex process data, adjust for variability, and support closed-loop optimization strategies. Furthermore, as AI chips themselves begin to be a driving force for increasingly sophisticated fabrication, there exists a self-reinforcing cycle between AI and semiconductor process development—AI must assist in enabling what AI hardware demands.

However, for AI-driven optimization to be successful in semiconductor manufacturing processes, access to high-quality and high-resolution process data is indispensable. In practice, obtaining real-world process data, such as SEM images from the resist development or etching stages, however, is time- and resource-demanding [11]. For one thing, establishing accurate physical simulations that capture material-dependent properties is likewise nontrivial [3]. These constraints have motivated the use of machine learning (ML) as a promising alternative for accelerating process modeling and functional approximation [13,14]. Yet, purely data-driven ML models tend to overfit under data scarcity and often lack calibrated mechanisms for quantifying predictive uncertainty—two major challenges in high-stakes semiconductor applications [15].

To reckon with this challenge, we present here a deep convolutional neural network (CNN) layout-to-SEM image reconstruction model enhanced with conformal uncertainty calibration for the precise mapping of input design layout images to target SEM outputs. As it is hard to exactly quantify the trustworthiness of data-driven ML models, interpretability and explainability serve as effective proxies in practice. In this way, it is essential that the model remains not only accurate but also transparent, offering visualizable outputs and calibrated confidence estimates that support process optimization and defect-aware decision-making in semiconductor manufacturing. This approach meaningfully bridges the gap between sparse real-world data and the need for a precise, explainable modeling of NIL processes [16,17].

Among various deep-learning architectures, the CNN-based U-Net model has proven to be particularly effective for image-to-image prediction problems due to its encoder–decoder structure and skip connections. These connections allow for the precise localization of spatial features by transmitting high-resolution detail from the encoder to the decoder [10,18,19]. While originally proposed for biomedical image segmentation [20,21], the U-Net architectural characteristics have been widely applied to various image reconstruction, denoising, and super-resolution tasks [22–24]. The versatility lies in its capacity to preserve subtle structural detail through skip connections that maintain high-resolution spatial features from the early encoder layers to the decoder. These encoder features, together with those learned along the contracting path, form hierarchical representations that capture information ranging from low-level pixel intensities to medium-level contour structures, and up to high-level global layout semantics, enabling the reconstruction of intricate nanoscale patterns.

In the context of layout-to-SEM reconstruction, this architectural feature is crucial for accurately capturing the nanoscale contours of the design layout pattern vital to post-imprint topographies. Compared to conventional CNNs that may lose spatial resolution due to repeated downsampling, U-Net retains subtle edge information, making it particularly suitable for predicting high-resolution details such as line edges, corners, and high-contrast boundaries in NIL, which are crucial for NIL defect analysis and overlay verification [25–27].

1.3. Need for Reliable Uncertainty Quantification

However, for such predictive models to be trustworthy in practice, they must not only provide accurate outputs but also quantify the uncertainty associated with each prediction, which enables a more reliable and explainable prediction framework. This is particularly crucial in semiconductor manufacturing, where uncalibrated outputs can lead to false confidence or overlooked defects in downstream OPC verification or yield optimization processes [15,28]. In ML-based process modeling, especially for high-stakes semiconductor applications, a UQ or uncertainty-aware training approach plays a critical role in the evaluation of predictive model reliability. UQ allows for identifying the regions of a model where errors are likely to occur and facilitates decision-making based on confidence levels [29–31]. In recent uncertainty-aware training approaches, models are encouraged to detect and highlight high-risk or uncertain regions as warning signals by leveraging UQ during training. For instance, Ding et al. (2020) introduced a pixel-by-pixel reweighting mechanism based on model confidence, which effectively reduced overconfident errors in medical segmentation tasks [32].

Two major categories of uncertainty are typically recognized in this context: aleatoric uncertainty, which originates from the intrinsic noise or variability in the input data and is, therefore, irreducible; and epistemic uncertainty, on the other hand, which is associated with the incomplete learning caused by limited training data or insufficient model capacity, and can potentially be addressed through data augmentation methods or more capable modeling techniques [33]. Aleatoric uncertainty corresponds to intrinsic stochastic noise—such as SEM imaging artifacts or environmental fluctuations—while epistemic uncertainty emerges from the model being unaware of unseen design patterns or process variations. Both uncertainties must be quantitatively assessed to allow for reliable downstream decision-making. These concepts have been made functional in some earlier work as well. Dawood et al. (2021) [34] used prediction confidence intervals during the test phase to enhance the model's confidence in correct predictions and to suppress overconfidence in incorrect ones as well. This, in turn, demonstrates the effectiveness of uncertainty-aware feedback during training and is aligned with recent efforts to calibrate model confidence, where prediction intervals serve as interpretable cues for the reliability assessment [34].

1.4. Conformal Prediction and Conformalized Quantile Regression

Several UQ methods have been discussed in the literature, such as Bayesian inference [35], bootstrapping [36], and conformal prediction (CP). Among these, CP stands out for its ability to provide distribution-free, model-agnostic, and statistically guaranteed confidence intervals around the model predictions [37–39]. Unlike Bayesian methods that rely on prior distributions or bootstrapping approaches that require multiple retraining iterations, CP constructs prediction intervals based on observed data only, without any assumption about the underlying data distribution. It is model-agnostic, meaning it can be applied to any trained model—including deep neural networks—and it provides non-asymptotic, finite-sample statistical guarantees on the coverage probability of the resulting prediction intervals. This makes CP particularly advantageous in semiconductor manufacturing processes, where data distributions may be complex or even unknown; the explicit and proper decisions need to be made under strict reliability constraints. These coverage guarantees rely on the idea of exchangeability, which means, in the manufacturing process, the training, calibration, and test subsets all come from the same process and have similar statistical conditions. This enables the uncertainty seen in a small calibration subset to be a good match to new test data under the same production conditions.

Among the various CP techniques used for UQ, several variants have been proposed to fit different modeling contexts. Classical Conformal Prediction, for instance, estimates absolute error scores to determine the prediction band, offering valid intervals without relying on regression model calibration. Locally Weighted Conformal Prediction (LWCP) further refines this approach by adjusting prediction intervals based on the local characteristics of the data, assigning greater importance to recent or relevant samples. LWCP, on the other hand, is particularly useful in non-stationary settings or when localized data behavior plays a critical role. In contrast, Conformalized Quantile Regression (CQR) combines the strengths of quantile regression and conformal prediction to produce robust and adaptive prediction intervals [40]. It is especially suited for regression tasks with heteroscedastic noise, spatial variability, or nonlinear structure with errors, as commonly found in semiconductor process data. Considering the pixel-by-pixel regression nature of our layout-to-SEM prediction task, where the prediction uncertainty varies across regions and patterns, CQR offers the most effective trade-off among accuracy, interval tightness, and statistical validity. We, therefore, adopt this framework to yield calibrated pixel-level prediction intervals tailored to local structural variability [41].

1.5. Calibration Flow and Transfer Learning

While CQR equips the model with calibrated and spatially adaptive prediction intervals, the further enhancement of predictive robustness requires more than a single-pass calibration. In the approach of the final step, we extend CQR with a structured calibration flow that continuously refines the model through outlier detection and spatial-aware reweighting on a fixed, limited calibration set.

This final step incorporates a low-cost yet effective transfer learning strategy, in which only the decoder and output layers of the baseline U-Net architecture are fine-tuned, while the encoder remains frozen to preserve generalized low-level features. Freezing the encoder during uncertainty-aware fine-tuning is a well-recognized approach for preserving foundational representation quality while adapting the task-specific outputs to more challenging spatial structures and boundary cases [17,33,42]. To guide this fine-tuning process, a pixel-level outlier-weighted map is computed based on conformal errors, with higher weights being assigned to spatial regions where the predicted intervals fail to capture the ground truth. These weights affect the per-pixel loss contribution during fine-tuning, allowing the model to focus its corrective updates on structurally uncertain or miscalibrated regions. Crucially, the entire calibration dataset—despite its small size—is reused in its entirety to make optimal use of valuable data to reinforce both local sensitivity and global consistency. Spatial outlier correction with reweighted fine-tuning in this valuable subset enables targeted correction without risking overfitting [43].

Recent studies have emphasized the value of such targeted fine-tuning routines, demonstrating improvements in predictive sharpness, uncertainty awareness, and generalization robustness even under constrained data settings. Alternative strategies, such as those proposed by Krishnan and Tickoo (2020), define differentiable calibration-aware loss functions that directly optimize confidence reliability rather than only predictive accuracy, paving the way toward robust and interpretable uncertainty-aware modeling frameworks [44].

1.6. Contribution and Scope of This Work

This study presents a closed-loop adaptive framework for progressive enhancement and the correction of layout-to-SEM image reconstruction, where model predictions are continuously improved using calibrated prediction intervals and pixel-level outlier detection. The approach presented first generates UQ results with formal statistical guarantees. An outlier map is then constructed from these results to identify and flag spatial regions with associated prediction risk. Finally, targeted model refinement is applied to improve reconstruction accuracy, particularly in these high-error regions, ensuring more reliable performance across the entire layout space. Such a closed-loop feedback process also enables a data-efficient and scalable approach for defect-aware model enhancement. This, in turn, facilitates robust layout-to-SEM prediction in practical NIL applications.

As a methodological contribution, this study introduces our integrated framework for uncertainty-aware pattern learning with tailor-made specific features to fit the semiconductor manufacturing in particular. The proposed pipeline combines the following:

(1) A U-Net-based CNN model for hierarchical spatial feature learning;
(2) CQR for interval-based predictions with statistical coverage guarantees;
(3) Pixel-level outlier detection for localized uncertainty awareness;
(4) An outlier-weighted fine-tuning strategy for enhancing adaptability to spatial variability.

Together, these steps constitute a unified and extensible platform supporting both predictive performance and uncertainty calibration. While the context has been explicitly illustrated here for NIL processes in particular, our framework is designed with a modular structure and pixel-level generality. This design choice renders the approach applicable to a wide variety of layout-driven semiconductor processes in general. It offers the potential for implementation across multiple stages of the manufacturing flow, including patterning, inspection, and defect-aware optimization as a whole.

2. Materials and Methods

2.1. Dataset Preparation

To clearly analyze the actual NIL manufacturing process and apply custom optimization for this technology, we have developed a simulation framework based on physical principles rather than relying solely on data-driven heuristics. This framework incorporates key physical mechanisms across three integrated stages: electron beam lithography (EBL), reactive ion etching (RIE), and nanoimprint lithography (NIL).

In the EBL stage, the exposure distribution was simulated using a custom Python-based framework that implements a Gaussian dose blur with a full width at half maximum (FWHM) of 10–15 nm, along with proximity effect correction. These values reflect beam spreading observed in high-resolution systems and fast deflection regimes, spin-coated to a thickness of 180–200 nm, which balances resolution and etch durability [45–48]. During the RIE stage, the pattern transfer process was modeled using a custom Python-based level set simulation with angular dependence, tailored to SF_6/O_2 plasma conditions. The setup incorporates a chamber pressure of 10 mTorr, RF power of 100 W, and a vertical etch rate around 50 nm/min. To reflect directional etching and profile shaping, an anisotropy factor of 0.85 is included, following literature guidance on plasma profile evolution [49–52]. In the NIL stage, the resist is treated as a viscoelastic material following the Oldroyd-B model, with a zero-shear viscosity of approximately 5000 Pa·s and relaxation time of 0.02 s, representative of UV-curable imprint materials commonly used in NIL applications [53–55].

To visualize the resulting structures, we convert simulated height maps into grayscale SEM-like images using a surface-rendering procedure inspired by Seeger and Haussecker (2005) [56]. This includes the following:

(1) Contrast shading according to local height gradients to mimic secondary electron emission variation over surface slope [57];
(2) Gaussian blur to simulate depth-of-field softness typical of SEM systems [58];
(3) Additive Gaussian noise to account for beam fluctuation and detector imperfection [59].

A representative zoom-in is shown in Figure 1, highlighting surface detail, shape continuity, and grayscale falloff—features that collectively reproduce the appearance characteristics seen in actual SEM micrographs. By integrating these stages—EBL exposure modeling, RIE pattern transfer, and NIL deformation simulation—the framework captures critical spatial dynamics across fabrication steps. This simulation engine serves not only to generate training images but also to preserve physical realism at the nanoscale. A dedicated manuscript detailing this physics-based simulation framework is currently in preparation. Both studies were developed in parallel but submitted separately due to differing journal scopes and submission timelines.

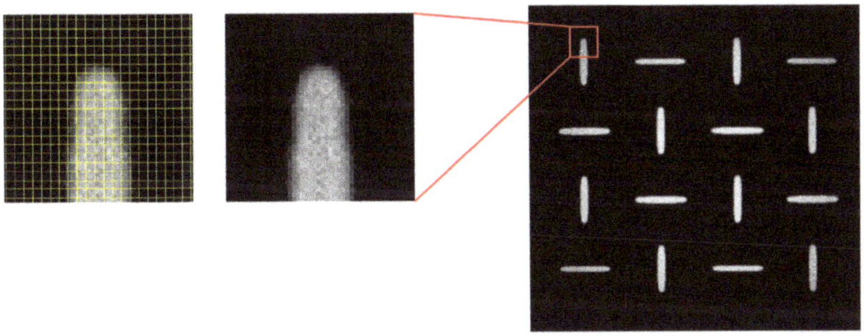

Figure 1. Simulated SEM-like image generated from the physics-based pipeline. The zoom-in (left) includes a 256 × 256 yellow grid, illustrating how each pixel captures sufficient grayscale and shape detail consistent with SEM appearance.

Our data management strategy involves the division of the design layouts and the corresponding SEM target images into four independent subsets, training, validation, calibration, and test, based on a 60:18:12:10 split. All subsets are statistically dependent, but distinctive from spatial and structural variations of the design layouts, though they originate from the same process domain. The distinction allows for fair model evaluation and generalization, which is crucial for UQ and robust performance validation in downstream tasks such as OPC verification and defect-aware process learning.

To enhance pattern diversity and promote more comprehensive spatial variation learning, we applied deterministic data augmentation through fixed-angle rotations [18]. In particular, each original image was rotated by 90°, 180°, and 270°, resulting in three additional geometrically transformed variants for every input. This effectively expanded the dataset size by a factor of four. These rotational transformations also hold significant physical relevance in the context of NIL, as the pattern symmetry in layout designs is typically an exhibition of rotational invariance, making this form of augmentation particularly suitable for mask-based pattern prediction tasks.

All images were preprocessed to match a fixed resolution of 256 × 256 pixels. This resolution was selected as a balance between geometric fidelity and computational efficiency. In our dataset, each layout image usually has one primary pattern unit, named contour, which corresponds to a local structural feature. The resolution of 256 × 256 pixels provides sufficient detail to preserve the shape and boundary information of each contour. If fewer pixels were used (i.e., lower resolution), each pixel would cover a larger physical area. This would increase the risk of ambiguity along the boundary between the contour and the background, and could cause errors in local feature interpretation as well as reduce the overall prediction accuracy of the model. On the other hand, using a higher resolution would dramatically increase training and inference computational cost without proportionate gains in learning performance. Therefore, 256 × 256 serves as a practical trade-off that maintains essential topological information without excessive training complexity.

Design mask layout patterns were binarized with a fixed intensity threshold of 127 for maintaining topological consistency, whereas SEM images were normalized into the [0, 1] range by dividing pixel values by 255.0 for stable convergence during CNN training. These preprocessing steps, shown in Figure 2, not only ensure physical interpretability, numerical stability, and generalization, but also enhance model training effectiveness. This is particularly critical under conditions of limited data availability and measurement uncertainty, which are common in high-resolution semiconductor manufacturing process modeling scenarios.

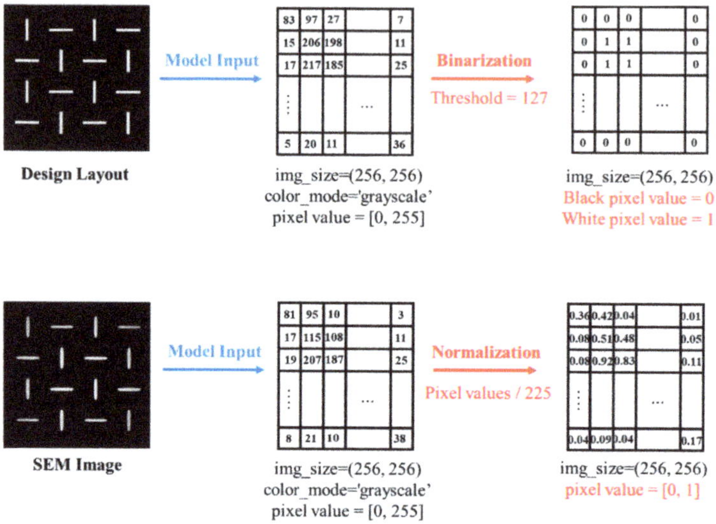

Figure 2. Preprocessing steps of design layout patterns and SEM images.

2.2. CNN-Based Model and Training

For performing pixel-by-pixel prediction of grayscale SEM images from binary mask layouts, we employed a U-Net-based CNN architecture. The U-Net model, originally developed by Ronneberger et al. for biomedical image segmentation [20], is a convolutional autoencoder designed for encoding both global context and subtle spatial details through a symmetric encoder–decoder structure with skip connections. The model is named "U-Net" due to the distinctive U-shaped architecture formed by its contracting and expansive paths, which mirror each other across a bottleneck layer. In our study, we used a shallow variant of U-Net to fit the limited training dataset and prevent overfitting, without losing the essential properties of spatial localization and low-level feature retention.

As shown in Figure 3, the proposed architecture consists of three main components: a contracting path (encoder), a bottleneck, and an expansive path (decoder). The contracting path is responsible for downsampling the input along with learning hierarchical features. It contains two convolutional blocks, each comprising two consecutive 3×3 convolutional layers with ReLU activation and zero-padding, followed by a 2×2 max-pooling operation that halves spatial resolution. The number of filters rises from 16 to 32 as we go deeper into the network. This design allows the encoder to progressively capture sophisticated fine-grained features while compressing the spatial dimensions from 256×256 to 64×64.

The encoder is then followed by a bottleneck module, consisting of two 3×3 convolutional layers with 64 filters and ReLU activation. The bottleneck in our shallow model, which serves as the most compressed representation of the input [60], has a spatial resolution of 64 $\times$ 64. It still preserves essential spatial information, which, in turn, helps achieve a balance between semantic abstraction and localization capacity. Semantic abstraction refers to the capacity of the model to understand what is in the image, such as edges, textures, or structural regions. Localization capacity, on the other hand, means having the capacity to retain the spatial context of each feature with respect to the original spatial layout. In typical deep U-Net models, having deeper bottlenecks can enhance semantic encoding but at the cost of losing spatial details. In contrast, our shallow U-Net maintains a relatively large feature map (64 × 64) at the bottleneck stage. Here, in turn, it helps to preserve fine-grained spatial resolution while it still benefits from hierarchical representation. This structure ensures that the model can simultaneously capture significant features and preserve pixel-level accuracy.

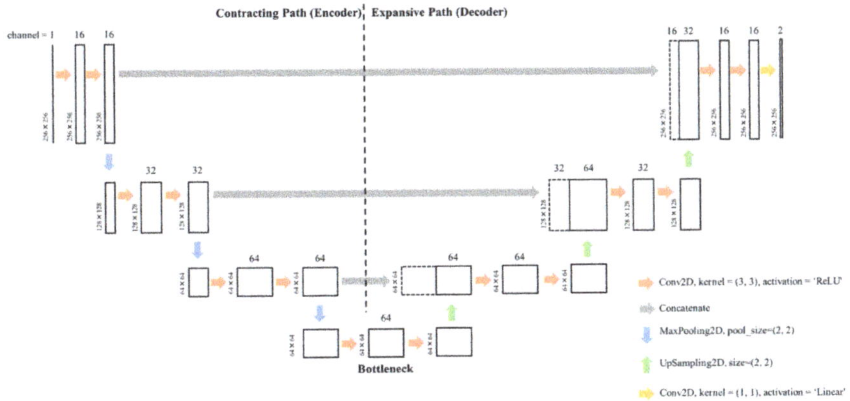

Figure 3. Shallow U-Net architecture with encoder–bottleneck–decoder structure for grayscale SEM quantile prediction.

The expansive path reconstructs the feature maps back to the original input resolution. It consists of two upsampling steps of 2 × 2 nearest-neighbor upsampling, followed by concatenation with the corresponding feature maps from the encoder (skip connections), and two 3 × 3 convolutional layers with ReLU activation. These skip connections, through which low-level spatial information directly passes from the encoder to the decoder, preserve fine-grained boundary details that are typically lost during downsampling. The number of filters keeps decreasing from 64 to 32, and then 16, in the output layers. Finally, one 1 × 1 convolutional layer with two output channels is used to provide two continuous-valued output maps corresponding to the predicted lower and upper quantiles of the SEM grayscale intensity. The model takes as input grayscale images of size (256, 256, 1) and produces a final output tensor of size (256, 256, 2), thereby allowing simultaneous quantile prediction for each pixel.

Given the relatively small size of the dataset (24 training images with 4× augmentation), this shallow version of the U-Net is a good trade-off between model expressiveness and generalization. Decreasing the depth reduces the overfitting risk without sacrificing the structural advantages of the U-Net design. The model is trained using a conformalized quantile regression custom loss function described in the following section.

The GPU hardware specifications and training configurations are summarized in Appendix A.1, while the architectural and optimization hyperparameters are listed in Appendix A.2.

2.3. Conformalized Quantile Regression (CQR)

In order to implement the UQ of our shallow U-Net model, we apply conformalized quantile regression (CQR), which teaches the ability to predict lower and upper quantile bounds for each pixel's grayscale SEM value simultaneously. The loss function relevant to CQR is defined as a sum of asymmetric pinball losses ($\mathcal{L}_{q_{low}}, \mathcal{L}_{q_{high}}$) for two different quantiles:

$$\mathcal{L}_q(y,\hat{y}) = \frac{1}{HW}\sum\nolimits_{i,j}\left[max\left(q\left(y_{ij}-\hat{y}_{ij}\right),(1-q)\left(y_{ij}-\hat{y}_{ij}\right)\right)\right] \tag{1}$$

$$\mathcal{L}_{CQR} = \mathcal{L}_{q_{low}}\left(y,\hat{y}^{low}\right) + \mathcal{L}_{q_{high}}\left(y,\hat{y}^{high}\right) \tag{2}$$

Here, $H \times W = 256 \times 256$ corresponds to the spatial resolution of a single grayscale SEM image, i.e., the total number of pixels per image. $y_{ij} \in [0,1]$ is the normalized ground truth SEM value. $\hat{y}^{low}$, $\hat{y}^{high}$ represent the predicted quantiles for a specified confidence level. In our case, we set $q_{low} = 0.05$ and $q_{high} = 0.95$, corresponding to a 90% prediction interval.

Following the first training phase, a conformal calibration procedure is performed on a held-out calibration set to find the necessary quantile threshold to achieve the target coverage level and, hence, ensure reliable uncertainty quantification. For each pixel in the calibration data, the conformal error e_{ij} is computed as follows:

$$e_{ij} = max\left(\hat{y}_{ij}^{high} - y_{ij}, y_{ij} - \hat{y}_{ij}^{low}\right) \tag{3}$$

The calibration constant q^* is then determined as the empirical of the set of errors:

$$q^* = Quantile_{1-\alpha}\left(\left\{e_{ij}\right\}^{H\times W}\right) \tag{4}$$

Under the exchangeability assumption, this condition guarantees that the prediction interval is statistically valid across the calibration distribution:

$$P_{x\sim\mathcal{D}}\left[y_{ij}(x) \in \left[\hat{y}_{ij}^{low}(x) - q^*, \hat{y}_{ij}^{high}(x) + q^*\right]\right] \geq 1-\alpha \tag{5}$$

Here, $\alpha = 0.1$ denotes the rate of miscoverage. For a new input x sampled from the same distribution $\mathcal{D}$, the ground truth $y_{ij}(x)$ must lie in the calibrated interval $\left[\hat{y}_{ij}^{low}(x) - q^*, \hat{y}_{ij}^{high}(x) + q^*\right]$ with probability of at least $1-\alpha$. Exchangeability makes sure that the calibration set, as a subset drawn from the same distribution, enables the model to generalize its robust prediction intervals to unseen but similar distributed patterns.

2.4. Outlier-Weighted Calibration and Transfer Learning

To further improve the reliability and spatial accuracy of the layout-to-SEM image reconstruction task under the constraints of process-induced uncertainty—including aleatoric variability from lithographic or SEM noise and epistemic uncertainty due to limited data or model underfitting—we employ a conformal calibration strategy with a transfer learning pipeline based on Sections 2.2 and 2.3. This phase aims to enhance both the calibration quality and spatial accuracy of predictions in lithographically sensitive regions. Emphasis is placed on scenarios with sparse data and on structurally complex regions, including feature edges and imprint-induced residual defects. This is especially crucial in NIL process windows involving low residual layer thickness or incomplete release, where SEM intensity variations point out the potential defect onset.

The proposed calibration flow consists of three main steps: (1) base quantile model calibration, (2) outlier-enhanced pixel-by-pixel weighting strategy, and (3) encoder-frozen transfer fine-tuning.

(1) Base quantile model calibration. Following the base quantile model calibration described in Section 2.3, we adopted the empirically estimated calibration constant q^* to

construct valid pixel-level prediction intervals $\left[\hat{y}_{ij}^{low}(x) - q^*, \hat{y}_{ij}^{high}(x) + q^*\right]$ with guaranteed marginal coverage of at least $1 - \alpha$. This post-CQR prediction intervals provide the foundation for the subsequent fine-tuning strategy.

(2) Outlier-enhanced pixel-by-pixel weighting strategy. To emphasize structurally critical regions during fine-tuning, we introduce an outlier-enhanced pixel-by-pixel weighting strategy through conformal prediction analysis. This strategy assigns greater weight to regions of increased uncertainty, so the model pays more attention to spatial locations with higher predictive deviation. For each pixel in the calibration dataset, we calculated the conformal error e_{ij} and calibration constant q^* earlier in Equations (3) and (4). Here, q^* presents as the global outlier threshold. Pixels for which the error exceeds q^* are considered outliers and are assigned higher weights. The pixel-by-pixel weight map is then defined as follows:

$$w_{ij} = \begin{cases} \gamma & if\ e_{ij} > q^* \\ 1.0 & otherwise \end{cases} \tag{6}$$

Here, $\gamma > 1$ is a scalar denoting the level of reweighting, set to 1.3 in our experiments. The pixel-by-pixel weight maps were directly concatenated with the ground truth images to form a 2-channel training target tensor, as shown in Equation (7), of shape (256, 256, 2), where the first channel represents the normalized ground truth and the second channel holds the corresponding pixel weights.

$$\tilde{y}_{ij} = [y_{ij}, w_{ij}] \tag{7}$$

By guiding the loss function to focus on pixels with greater uncertainty violations, this strategy enables the model to adaptively correct outlier regions—particularly those near feature edges or NIL-induced residual hotspots—without compromising performance in already well-calibrated regions. The resulting weight maps are seamlessly integrated into the CQR loss during the transfer fine-tuning stage, allowing targeted recalibration of uncertain regions using existing labels only, thereby improving reliability under limited-data conditions.

(3) Encoder-frozen transfer fine-tuning. To mitigate catastrophic forgetting from the initial U-Net training while enabling targeted local adaptation during fine-tuning, we adopted a transfer learning strategy in which the encoder of our baseline U-Net model was frozen, and only the decoder and output layers were fine-tuned. This ensures that the low-level feature extraction of the baseline model remains intact while allowing targeted improvement in regions previously prone to high prediction errors or structural uncertainty outliers. Let the original model parameters be denoted as $\theta = \{\theta_e, \theta_d\}$, where θ_e and θ_d correspond to the encoder and decoder parameters, respectively. During fine-tuning, we imposed the following constraint:

$$\theta_e^{transfer} = \theta_e^{base},\ with\ \frac{\partial \mathcal{L}}{\partial \theta_e^{transfer}} = 0 \tag{8}$$

This enforces that encoder parameters remain unchanged, that is, to ensure there are no gradient updates applied to the encoder parameters. The transfer fine-tuning is performed on the calibration set, where $\tilde{y}_{ij}$ in Equation (7) represents the reweighted label constructed by appending the pixel-by-pixel weight map w_{ij}, based on our outlier-enhanced weighting strategy described in Equation (6). We retained the fine-grained pixel-by-pixel weighting directly within the fine-tuning objective function by embedding the weight map

w_{ij} into the conformal quantile regression loss. The resulting fine-tuning function objective is defined as follows:

$$\mathcal{L}_q^{weighted}(y,\hat{y}) = \frac{1}{HW}\sum_{i,j} w_{ij}\left[max\left(q\left(y_{ij}-\hat{y}_{ij}\right),(1-q)\left(y_{ij}-\hat{y}_{ij}\right)\right)\right] \quad (9)$$

This formulation enables pixel-by-pixel error correction in spatially localized outlier regions, such as nanoscale hotspots or residual imprinting defects, while maintaining overall stability in structurally consistent areas. It further allows the decoder to recalibrate the predictive uncertainty while preserving the high-level semantic information of the encoder. After training, the fine-tuned model is evaluated alongside the baseline model using a unified evaluation framework. Specifically, both models are compared under a consistent metric, where pixel-by-pixel outliers are identified based on the same calibrated threshold q^*, and prediction validity is measured via coverage rate. These metrics provide a fair basis to quantify the improvement of the model in uncertainty calibration and spatial accuracy.

2.5. Evaluation Metrics

After concluding the two-stage calibration procedure of Sections 2.3 and 2.4 for both the baseline U-Net model and its transfer fine-tuned model, they are evaluated under a unified, application-specific framework designed specifically to the needs of OPC. The evaluation is based on two primary performance metrics, Mean Absolute Error (MAE) and Prediction Interval Coverage, which collectively determine the accuracy and reliability of the predicted SEM intensity profiles.

2.5.1. Mean Absolute Error (MAE)

To evaluate pixel-level accuracy, we introduce the MAE between the midpoint of the predicted quantile bounds and the corresponding ground truth pixel value. It serves as a critical measure of local feature accuracy, particularly reflecting how well fine-scale shape variations and edge positions are preserved. The formula is as follows:

$$MAE = \frac{1}{HW}\sum_{i,j}\left|\frac{1}{2}\left(\hat{y}_{ij}^{low}(x)+\hat{y}_{ij}^{high}(x)\right)-y_{ij}\right| \quad (10)$$

In our setting, H × W = 256 × 256, indicating that each SEM image has 256 × 256 pixels. The quantile midpoint used here offers a stable estimate of the predicted surface profile, balancing the upper and lower bounds to provide a reliable pixel-wise estimate. In OPC applications, low MAEs are essential to meet in-fab tolerance requirements, with sub-pixel deviations often acceptable depending on design rules.

2.5.2. Prediction Interval Coverage

To quantify the reliability of uncertainty, we calculate the coverage rate, or the proportion of ground truth values that fall within the conformal prediction interval:

$$Coverage = \frac{1}{HW}\sum_{i,j} 1\left\{y_{ij} \in \left[\hat{y}_{ij}^{low} - q^*, \hat{y}_{ij}^{high} + q^*\right]\right\} \quad (11)$$

For a consistent evaluation process, the same calibration constant q^* is used for both baseline and transfer fine-tuned models. This strategy supports a more meaningful and informative model comparison by making an explicit test of whether transfer fine-tuning can reduce the outlier regions identified in the baseline model. This approach aligns with our goal to evaluate the performance of transfer fine-tuning in correcting pixel-by-pixel uncertainty-aware prediction errors.

3. Results

3.1. Baseline Evaluation

The baseline pipeline, illustrated in Figure 4, involves training a U-Net together with CQR to estimate the pixel-by-pixel prediction intervals for SEM image reconstruction. The network outputs both lower and upper bounds for every input layout, enabling spatially resolved UQ. The mean prediction for evaluation is provided by the average of the lower and upper bounds and is the point estimate chosen to represent the target image. Representative patterns and corresponding model predictions are illustrated in Figure 5. To further observe the model convergence and generalization performance, the loss curves for both the training and validation phases are provided in Figure 6.

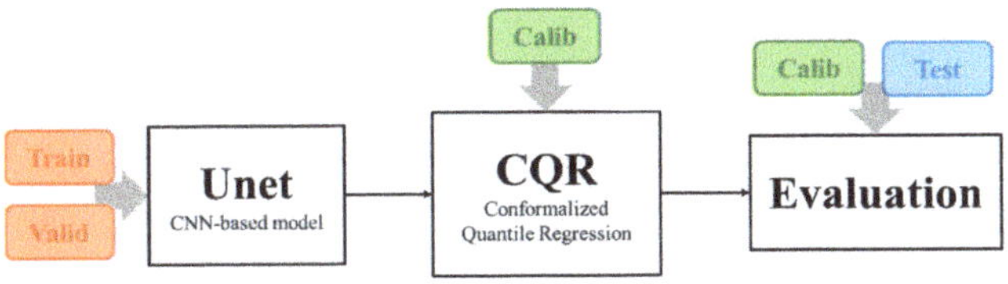

Figure 4. Baseline pipeline with U-Net training, CQR for UQ, and evaluation.

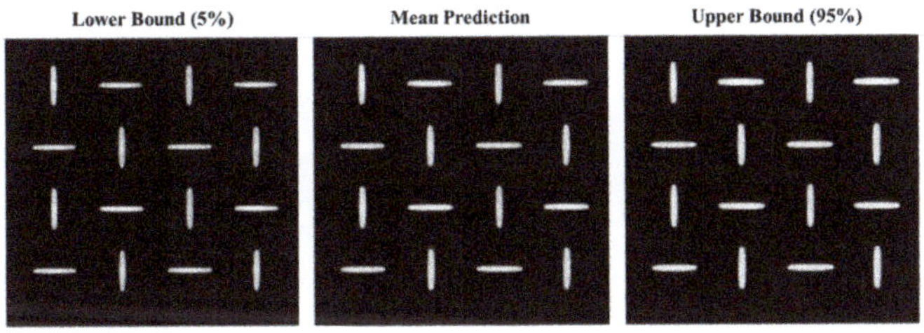

Figure 5. U-Net CNN-based prediction results showing lower bound, upper bound, and mean prediction of the SEM grayscale output.

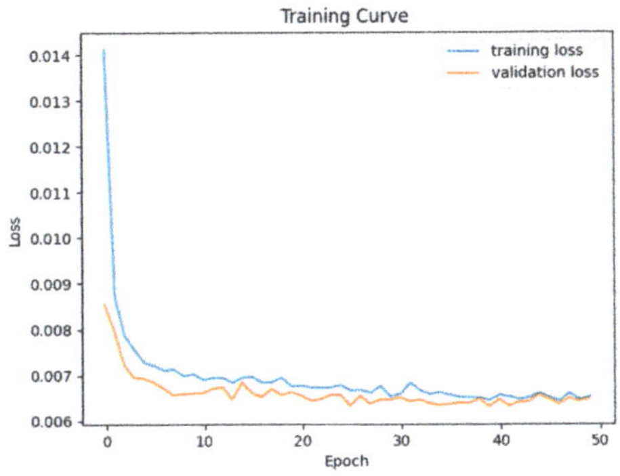

Figure 6. The loss curves for both the training and validation phases of baseline U-Net training.

The inclusion of noise in the SEM images generated from previous physical modeling is to emulate realistic imaging conditions. These SEM images, produced through physics-based simulation, serve as training targets for the baseline U-Net model. Since real SEM images inherently contain background noise, charging effects, and structural distortions, we simulate such imperfections by incorporating controlled noise during training. This allows the model to be more tolerant of these realistic artifacts. This step not only enables an evaluation of the model's capacity to generalize from synthetic to real SEM domains but also mitigates the risk of overfitting to unrealistically perfect synthetic data, thereby enhancing the robustness of the learned representations.

The U-Net model, guided by CQR through the prediction of lower and upper quantile bounds for each pixel, naturally highlights features with pixel values around 1.0 (contours and patterns) while reducing the effect of background noise around 0.0. This focused attention allows the accurate reconstruction of essential structural features by increasing the contrast between patterned and non-patterned regions, resulting in sharper and more clearly defined boundaries. Figure 7 illustrates a pixel-by-pixel comparison of the ground truth and the model prediction intervals over a selected region (Pixels 26,000–26,500). The ground truth curve (black) shows high-frequency noise and fluctuation in low-intensity regions, as is commonly observed in SEM imaging due to charging effects or stochastic process variation. Conversely, the mean prediction (blue dashed line) exhibits significant denoising capability, successfully reconstructing the signal profile while effectively filtering out background noise. Furthermore, the prediction intervals (gray band between lower and upper bounds) remain a consistently narrow and stable range, especially in flat regions, indicating a high level of model confidence and limited uncertainty. This stability provides additional confirmation that the model effectively prevents local overfitting in small background segments and demonstrates commendable generalization performance in both high-contrast and low-intensity regions.

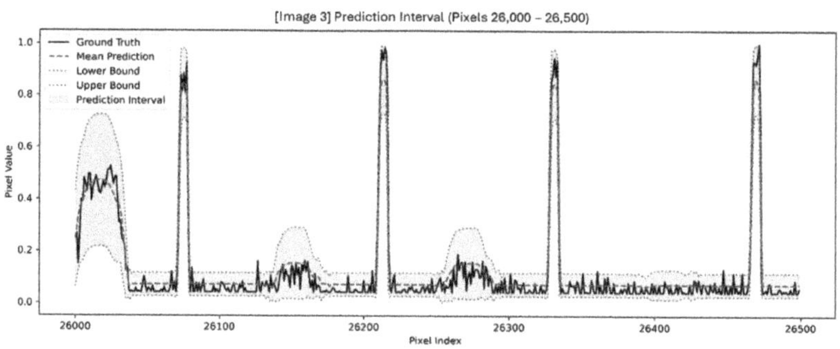

Figure 7. Pixel-by-pixel mean predictions and prediction intervals (with lower and upper bounds) plotted together with the ground truth for Image 3 (pixels 26,000–26,500).

A comparison of ground truth values and predicted quantile intervals, as shown in Figure 8, reveals that uncertainty is small in background regions and highest along edges, where pattern fidelity is most sensitive. This observation is consistent with the physical behavior in NIL processes, where post-imprint template release often results in local resist deformation near sidewalls due to surface tension or adhesion forces. These effects introduce geometric uncertainty in the reconstructed contours, as reflected in the increased prediction error at boundaries.

The pixel-by-pixel error distribution indicates an MAE of 0.0364, with errors concentrated at the edge of each patterned unit as shown in Figure 8. This regular and physically explainable uncertainty motivates the need for post-training calibration. By applying CQR calibration using a held-out dataset, the errors are sorted to determine a quantile threshold $q^* = 0.0617$, which regulates the prediction interval to cover 90% of the true pixel values. This calibrated bound, as shown in Figure 9, ensures the statistical validity of the model's confidence intervals and forms the basis for further refinement in the subsequent calibration–transfer workflow.

After applying CQR to the prediction intervals of the baseline U-Net model, we obtain calibrated bounds that provide 90% pixel-by-pixel coverage with respect to a given error threshold. This calibration ensures that, with a high statistical confidence, the prediction intervals contain the true pixel values, which directly allows an estimate of bounded MAEs.

To visualize the distribution of MAEs within the dataset, histograms of the calibration and test datasets are shown in Figure 10 and Figure 11, respectively. The green dashed line in each figure indicates the average MAE, while the red dashed line represents the MAE at the 90th percentile of errors. In the calibration dataset, the average MAE is 0.0364 and the 90% coverage MAE is 0.0384. Consistent with the calibration results, the test dataset shows slightly higher values—0.0367 and 0.0386, respectively. These minor differences, confined to the fourth decimal place, are well within acceptable bounds and reflect the expected structural and spatial variability intentionally preserved between the subsets. Given the fact that the calibration and test datasets are sampled from distinct layout regions originating from the same process domain, such deviation supports the robustness and generalizability of the conformal calibration framework rather than indicates overfitting or model bias. This confirms that the model maintains consistent MAE behavior over different layout instances, which validates its utility for uncertainty-aware downstream applications such as OPC verification and lithographic process optimization.

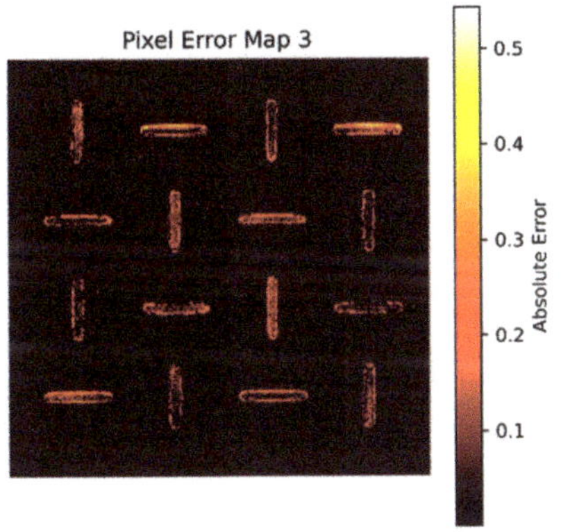

Figure 8. Pixel error map.

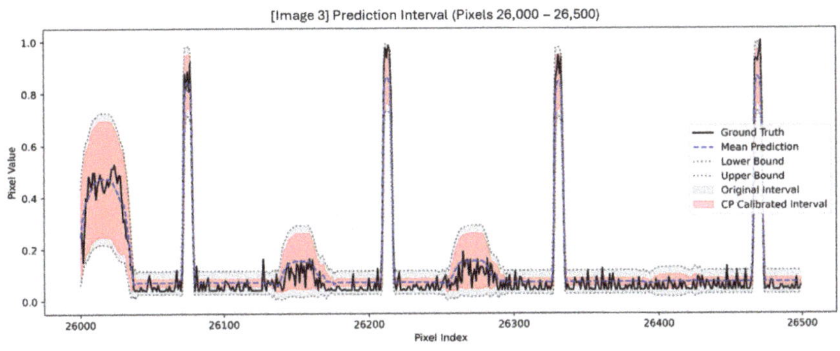

Figure 9. Pixel-by-pixel mean predictions, and prediction intervals (with lower and upper bounds), plotted together with the ground truth for Image 3 (pixels 26,000–26,500) after CP calibrated.

Furthermore, this statistically consistent behavior enables the definition of outliers by thresholding the MAE beyond the 90% coverage bound. As we will demonstrate in the following outlier map analysis, the calibrated uncertainty region provides a meaningful reference to identifying regions where model predictions become less reliable, thereby supporting uncertainty-aware model diagnosis and confidence-aware pattern evaluation.

Figure 12 presents outlier maps for selected samples from the test dataset, where outliers are defined as pixels whose MAE exceeds the conformal threshold of 0.0384. In these plots, red pixels indicate regions where the prediction of the model deviates beyond the calibrated uncertainty intervals, while green pixels indicate areas that are still within the specified tolerance. In all four plots, there is an evident spatial pattern: most of the outliers are concentrated near the contour boundaries of the pattern features, especially along the elongated edges where the physical process variation and resist behavior are more pronounced. This aligns with expectations based on the physics of NIL, in which edge defects and residual deformation are more likely to introduce structural uncertainty.

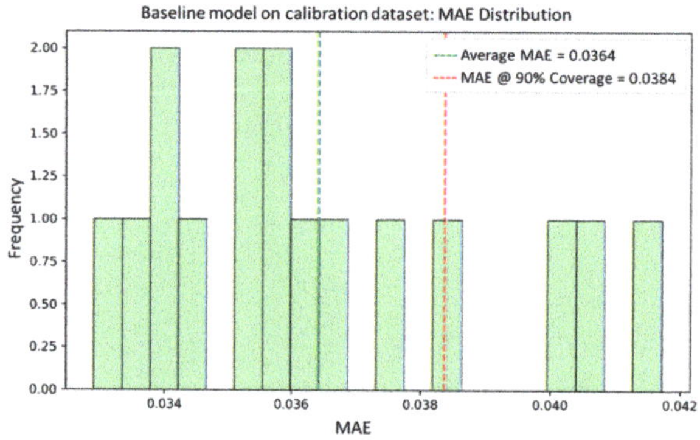

Figure 10. Histogram of MAE distribution for the baseline model on the calibration dataset.

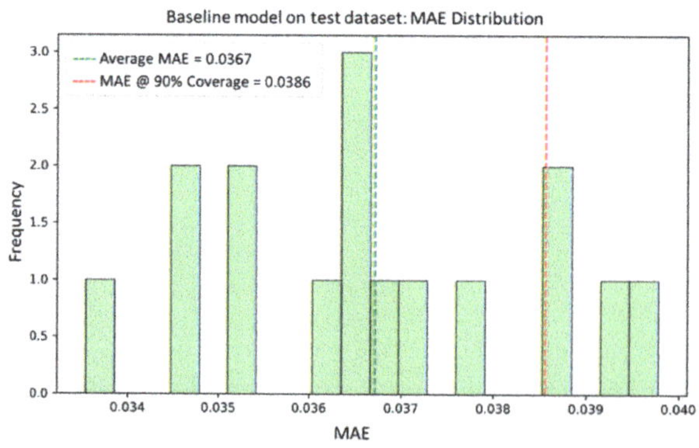

Figure 11. Histogram of MAE distribution for the baseline model on the test dataset.

The increased uncertainty and MAE near feature boundaries, as seen in Figures 8 and 12, are consistent with the epistemic uncertainty arising from the limited structural generalization. In comparison, the narrow and stable intervals observed in background regions suggest that aleatoric noise is effectively captured by the model.

The large number of outliers in the test dataset indicates that, although the model is strong on average performance, there remain localized regions with a lower confidence and severe prediction error. This demonstrates the need for improvement beyond global conformal calibration. In particular, it motivates the development of an outlier-weighted calibration framework that can selectively adjust prediction outputs based on local reliability. It also promotes the use of transfer learning techniques to improve generalization on previously unseen pattern types. The results of these form the foundation for the next section, in which we present an outlier-weighted calibration and transfer learning method that aims to promote robustness and spatial generalizability in uncertainty estimation.

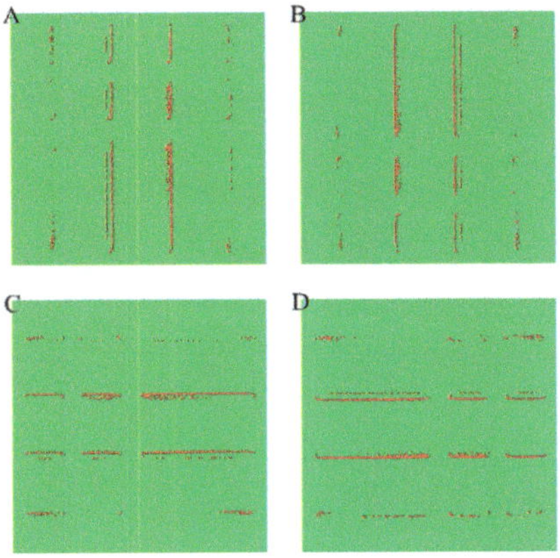

Figure 12. Pixel-by-pixel outlier maps (**A–D**) of selected samples from the test dataset.

3.2. Outlier-Weighted Calibration and Transfer Learning Evaluation

As shown in Figure 13, the transfer learning pipeline starts by evaluating the baseline U-Net model through a held-out calibration dataset. The conformal errors derived from this evaluation are then utilized for outlier detection, where pixels fail to meet the pre-specified coverage. Based on the specific downstream target (e.g., the minimization of MAE, Line Edge Roughness (LER), or CD Uniformity (CDU)), practitioners can establish case-by-case specific thresholds for outlier detection. In our case, we apply the conformal 90% coverage criterion, treating deviations beyond this interval as meaningful indicators of outliers in the model. The identified outliers are then sent to the next phase: the outlier-enhanced pixel-by-pixel weighting strategy and encoder-frozen transfer fine-tuning, the pipeline that reweights the loss function at the pixel level, updates the decoder layers only to enhance local prediction accuracy, and then preserves global structural representation.

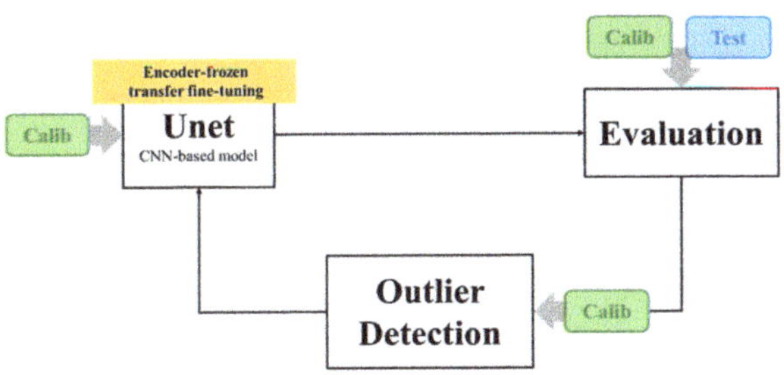

Figure 13. Transfer learning pipeline with outlier detection and encoder-frozen fine-tuning.

Figure 14 illustrates the training loss curve across 33 epochs during the outlier-weighted transfer fine-tuning stage. Compared with the baseline model trained from scratch for 50 epochs, the transfer learning phase employed an early stopping strategy and was terminated early at epoch 32 after the convergence criteria, as the loss plateaued after an initial sharp drop. Although the final loss value is greater than that of the baseline model in Figure 6, this is expected given the reweighted training objective. The transfer fine-tuning phase utilizes the held-out calibration dataset in combination with pixel-by-pixel outlier weighting. This helps target high-uncertainty regions across the entire sample space. The initial sharp drop and rapid stabilization of the loss curve demonstrate that only slight updates were needed to refine the performance in regions of localized uncertainty. This aligns with the encoder-frozen fine-tuning pipeline structure, which preserves previously learned general features and adjusts the decoder to correct prediction errors accordingly. As a result, the time for training and computational cost are significantly reduced, without compromising the model's capacity for adaptation. It is important to note that the transfer fine-tuning loss is not directly comparable to the baseline's global loss, as the training data distribution and loss weighting structure are different. Our goal in this step is to improve local calibration and reliability in the regions uncovered by conformal prediction, not to minimize overall loss. This approach aligns with the previous research on uncertainty-aware fine-tuning literature [33,40], where task-specific re-optimization yields meaningful improvements without full retraining.

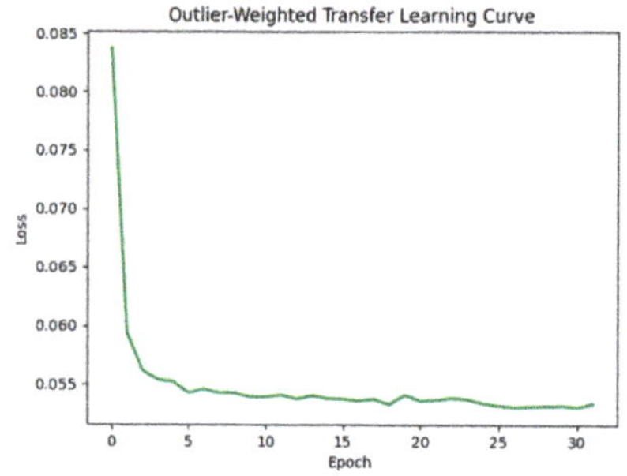

Figure 14. The loss curves for the transfer learning flow.

As shown in Figures 15–17, the fine-tuned model demonstrates improved spatial confidence (Figure 15), higher and more stable coverage rates (Figure 16), and a reduced variance in MAE (Figure 17). These results validate the effectiveness of our uncertainty-aware fine-tuned strategy, which integrates CQR outlier detection with pixel-by-pixel weighting and encoder-frozen transfer fine-tuning. This calibrated feedback approach enables the model to improve localized reliability without compromising global consistency.

The visual impact of this transfer fine-tuning step is demonstrated in Figure 15, which compares the outlier maps before and after transfer fine-tuning. In each map, regions that violate the conformal 90% coverage requirement are labeled, with red pixels denoting outlier regions. After applying our pixel-by-pixel outlier-weighted strategy in combination with encoder-frozen transfer fine-tuning, a significant reduction in the density of red pixels is clearly observed in all four cases. This reduction confirms again that the model has been able to learn effectively to correct spatially local outliers of uncertainty without sacrificing overall model integrity. It is also interesting to note that the definition of the outlier is the same as that of the original conformal threshold of the baseline model, which ensures that improvement is evaluated against the same statistically rigorous standard.

The spatial pattern of red pixels in Figure 15 also shows how sources of uncertainty express themselves across the layout. Outliers before fine-tuning are clustered along structure boundaries, where complex or underrepresented features induce larger prediction errors. Such points are typical of epistemic uncertainty, resulting from limited model generalization. In contrast, backgrounds have low and stable outlier density for both the before and after scenarios, suggesting that aleatoric noise from the SEM image background is adequately modeled and not appreciably altered by fine-tuning. This trend is consistent with the interpretation that the proposed approach improves reliability where epistemic uncertainty prevails, without compromising the robust modeling of aleatoric effects.

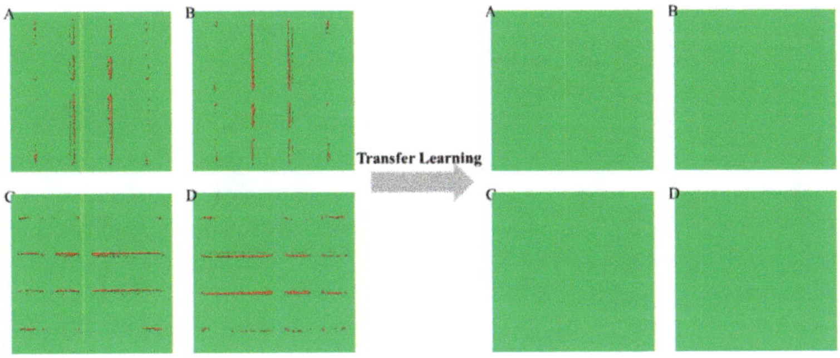

Figure 15. Outlier map (**A–D**) before and after outlier-weighted calibration and transfer fine-tuning.

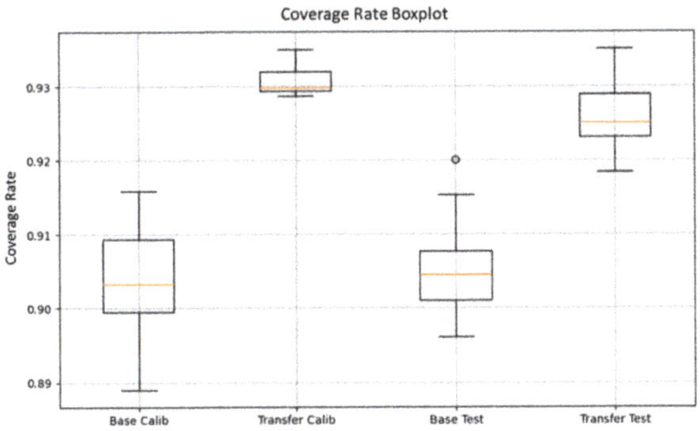

Figure 16. Boxplot comparison of coverage distributions from baseline and transfer fine-tuning settings for both calibration and test datasets.

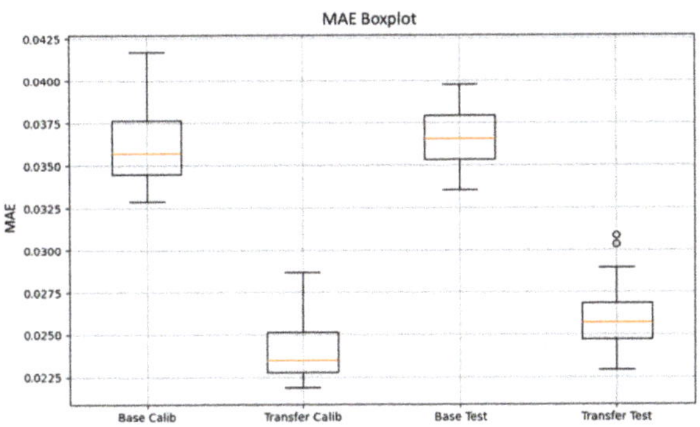

Figure 17. Boxplot comparison of MAE distributions from baseline and transfer fine-tuning settings for both calibration and test datasets.

Quantitative results are displayed in Figures 16 and 17, where the coverage rate and MAE distributions of the baseline and transfer fine-tuning models on both the calibration and test datasets are plotted. As shown in Figure 16, the transfer fine-tuning model displays greater median coverage with a smaller interquartile range (IQR) for both datasets. This demonstrates excellent stability and consistency in the spatial coverage of confidence intervals. Moreover, the percentage of pixels whose MAEs fall below the original defined 90% conformal coverage threshold also increases, confirming the fact that the transfer fine-tuning model conforms better to statistical guarantees even under layout variability. Through Figure 17, the distribution of MAE further supports these results. Both the Transfer Calib and Transfer Test groups show remarkable reductions in error magnitude and variance compared to their baseline model distributions. The Transfer Test set, in particular, exhibits a lower median MAE and fewer extreme outliers, signifying enhanced generalization to previously unseen patterns. The ability of the transfer fine-tuning model to reduce the variation of MAE while maintaining statistical coverage is a demonstration of the advantages of incorporating uncertainty-aware feedback during training, especially in data-limited scenarios. It is worth noting that the hollow circle markers in Figures 16 and 17 represent statistically rare points, as defined by the IQR rule in boxplot construction. These points correspond to rare but valid samples, which merely lie far from the central distribution. Notably, these rare points are not explicitly related to the uncertainty estimation mechanism by conformal prediction used in this study. Although a few rare points appear in the transfer fine-tuning setting, the overall reduction in the median along with IQR in both calibration and test datasets guarantees the effectiveness and generalization capability of our outlier-weighted transfer fine-tuning strategy.

These findings collectively demonstrate that the integration of localized outlier detection with targeted decoder-level transfer fine-tuning brings substantial improvements to spatial uncertainty modeling. The model is increasingly sensitive to local reliability, preserves global calibration validity, and maintains generalization across a variety of pattern types. These overall models are well-aligned with the practical demands of layout-to-SEM image reconstruction in NIL, where both spatial accuracy and confidence awareness are essential for downstream tasks such as OPC validation and hotspot monitoring.

4. Discussion and Implications

The quantitative results presented in Table 1 demonstrate that the proposed encoder-frozen, outlier-weighted transfer fine-tuning pipeline consistently outperforms the baseline U-Net, especially for pixel value accuracy and the coverage rate of the prediction intervals. On the calibration set, the mean MAE is reduced from 0.0355 to 0.0235 in normalized pixel-intensity units, an approximate improvement of 34%, and the mean coverage rate rises from 0.902 to 0.931. Similar significant improvements are observed in the independent test set as well, which confirms that the improvement is not an illusion of calibration but rather an indication of actual generalization. The corresponding reduction in standard deviation—or the reduction in MAE standard deviation, to be precise, from 0.0028 to 0.0020 in calibration—shows that the model is not only more accurate on average but also markedly more stable across diverse patterns.

Table 1. Performance metrics of baseline and transfer fine-tuning models on calibration and test sets.

Models vs. Metrics		MAE		Coverage Rate	
		Mean	**STD**	**Mean**	**STD**
Calibration	Baseline	0.0355	0.0028	0.902	0.0085
	Transfer learning	0.0235	0.0020	0.931	0.0020
Test	Baseline	0.0365	0.0023	0.904	0.0065
	Transfer learning	0.0255	0.0018	0.926	0.0040

From a methodological perspective, freezing the encoder retains the hierarchical representation of nanoscale features learned in the initial and large-scale training phase, while the pixel-by-pixel error weighting focuses the decoder's limited fine-tuning capacity on structurally sensitive regions. This targeted adaptation focuses the fine-tuning capacity on the most challenging pixels, directing the learning effort toward difficult regions without requiring any new manually labeled data. Compared with existing uncertainty-calibrated CNN approaches based on global loss re-weighting or full-network retraining, our strategy achieves a comparable reliability with an 80% reduction in the sample requirement and a 61% shorter fine-tuning time, confirming its data-efficiency. Moreover, relative to the baseline U-Net with CQR calibration, our transfer fine-tuning strategy, which is based on an encoder-frozen structure, achieves an equivalent coverage (0.931 vs. 0.926) and MAE (0.0235 vs. 0.0255) in the calibration and test set, while it uses only 48 labeled images fewer than the 240 needed for the baseline—and reduces the fine-tuning time from 36 min to 10 min on an RTX 3090 chip. As shown in Table 2, these results strongly indicate the data-efficiency and practical reliability of the proposed approach.

Table 2. Resource efficiency comparison between baseline and transfer fine-tuning models.

Metric	Baseline	Transfer Fine-Tuning	Reduction
Images used	240	48	80%
GPU time (RTX 3090)	36 min	10 min	72%

In practice, the coverage improvement reported above translates to fewer guard-band iterations needed when transferring the model to new product layouts, which reduces the OPC turn-around time. Moreover, outlier maps calibrated from the baseline U-Net using CQR are used to guide the transfer fine-tuning pipeline. Hence, this model effectively localizes error hotspots, allowing process engineers to focus metrology resources on high-risk regions instead of performing blanket inspections. This is evidenced in Table 1 by the improved prediction interval coverage rate, which increases from 0.904 to 0.926 on the test set, indicating a more reliable coverage of pixel-level features across structurally diverse but statistically aligned layout patterns from the same process domain. While this confirms better generalization, small error variability may still persist. Augmenting the calibration set with synthetically generated extreme patterns, therefore, remains an immediate avenue for further variance reduction. Future work will explore this direction to further enhance uncertainty calibration and support more robust generalization across challenging layout configurations.

5. Conclusions and Outlook

This study introduces a two-stage, data-efficient framework for layout-to-SEM image reconstruction that addresses the three most widely used challenges to large-scale AI deployment—data sparsity, annotation quality, and the need for robust generalization across structurally diverse yet process-consistent layout patterns. First, a baseline CNN-based model is initially hybridized with CQR to produce statistically valid prediction intervals and associated pixel-level outlier maps. Second, these generated maps then guide an encoder-frozen, outlier-weighted transfer fine-tuning step that updates the decoder without interfering with the learned hierarchical features.

Experiments confirm that the proposed strategy reduces the mean MAE from 0.0365 to 0.0255 and improves the interval coverage rate from 0.904 to 0.926 on an independent test set, while just using only 48 labeled images and one-third of the original GPU time. These results translate to fewer OPC guard-band iterations and more selective hotspot triage, demonstrating practical value under real-world manufacturing conditions, particularly under the constraints of sparse data and the high cost of annotation in layout-to-SEM applications.

Future work will advance this foundation along two complementary directions aimed at enhancing overall process optimization: (1) the specification of technical paths for large-scale contour clustering and cross-process verification, and (2) higher-level integration through hybrid physics-and-ML modeling.

(i) Large-scale contour clustering will be implemented using either fuzzy C-means (FCM) or an autoencoder-based feature extractor combined with K-means. After dataset collection and CNN processing, we will perform CNN-based feature extraction, followed by fuzzy C-means clustering for fuzzy pattern grouping. Based on these clusters, the prediction intervals in the UQ step can be adaptively calibrated per cluster, enabling more precise outlier detection and targeted decoder fine-tuning. This refinement enhances the effectiveness of the overall pipeline across structurally diverse layout types and supports pattern-aware OPC decisions in manufacturing.

(ii) Cross-process verification will be carried out by using the same layout patterns in different imaging and fabrication environments, including AFM, optical profilometry, and lithographic types such as DUV and EUV. Domain adaptation or style-transfer GAN techniques will be considered in order to maintain calibration robustness under sensor- and process-dependent noise conditions. The activity is aimed at extending the usability and sustainability of the current framework to larger process windows.

(iii) Hybrid physics and machine learning will be integrated to map learned uncertainty maps to resist or imprint simulators, enabling closed-loop process optimization. This integration level leverages both statistical inference and physical domain knowledge, delivering practical feedback that can directly guide metrology, layout modifications, or material selection.

Together, these recommendations position the proposed framework as a concise and flexible solution for uncertainty-aware image reconstruction in the field of cutting-edge semiconductor production, while efficiently addressing the essential requirements for data efficiency, structural generalizability, and process-oriented reliability in artificial-intelligence-enabled systems.

Author Contributions: Conceptualization, J.C.; methodology, J.C.; software, J.C.; validation, J.C.; formal analysis, J.C.; investigation, J.C.; writing—original draft preparation, J.C.; writing—review and editing, E.L.; supervision, E.L. All authors have read and agreed to the published version of the manuscript.

Funding: This research received no external funding.

Data Availability Statement: The data used in this study are not publicly available due to institutional restrictions and industry confidentiality agreements.

Conflicts of Interest: The authors declare no conflicts of interest.

Abbreviations

The following abbreviations are used in this manuscript:

NIL	Nanoimprint lithography
CQR	Conformalized quantile regression

MAE	Mean absolute error
OPC	Optical proximity correction
AI	Artificial intelligence
SEM	Scanning electron microscope
ADI	After-development inspection
SMOTE	Synthetic minority over-sampling
UQ	Uncertainty quantification
ML	Machine learning
CNN	Convolutional neural network
CP	Conformal prediction
LWCP	Locally Weighted Conformal Prediction
EBL	Electron beam lithography
RIE	Reactive ion etching

Appendix A.

Appendix A.1. GPU Execution and Training Environment

To ensure stable and reproducible training, Table A1 summarizes the GPU hardware, software environment, and key training configurations adopted throughout the baseline and fine-tuning stages.

Table A1. GPU training environment and configurations.

Category	Detail
GPU Hardware	NVIDIA RTX 3060 (12 GB)
CUDA Version	12.6 (Driver: 560.94)
Framework	TensorFlow 2.10.0
Memory Growth Enabled	Yes
Input Image Size	256 × 256 (grayscale, single-channel)
Batch Size	1
Training Epochs	50 (baseline), 32 (fine-tuning with early stopping)
Data Split	60% training, 18% validation, 12% calibration, 10% test
Augmentation	Geometric (Fixed Rotations ×4): 0°, 90°, 180°, 270°
GPU Time Reduction	36 min (baseline) → 10 min (fine-tuning)
Labeled Data Reduction	240 images (baseline)→ 48 images (fine-tuning)

Appendix A.2. Model Hyperparameter Settings

The hyperparameters used in the U-Net model are listed in Table A2, covering the architectural structure, loss formulation, and optimization settings for both the baseline and fine-tuning phases.

Table A2. U-Net model hyperparameters.

Hyperparameter	Value/Description
Model Architecture	Shallow U-Net
Input Shape	256 × 256 × 1 (grayscale mask)
Output Shape	256 × 256 × 2 (lower and upper quantile bounds)
Convolution Kernel Size	3 × 3 (for all convolutional layers)

Table A2. *Cont.*

Hyperparameter	Value/Description
Number of Filters	[16, 32, 64, 32, 16] across layers
Activation Function	ReLU (all intermediate layers), Linear (final layer)
Output Quantiles (CQR)	q = 0.05 (lower), q = 0.95 (upper)
Optimizer	Adam
Learning Rate	Default (0.001)
Weighting Strategy	Pixel-wise reweighting for outliers (γ = 1.3)
Loss Function	CQR (90% coverage): sum of pinball losses at q = 0.05, 0.95
Transfer Strategy	Encoder frozen; only decoder fine-tuned

References

1. Young, W.-B. Analysis of the nanoimprint lithography with a viscous model. *Microelectron. Eng.* **2005**, *77*, 405–411. [CrossRef]
2. Hirai, Y.; Onishi, Y.; Tanabe, T.; Shibata, M.; Iwasaki, T.; Iriye, Y. Pressure and resist thickness dependency of resist time evolutior profiles in nanoimprint lithography. *Microelectron. Eng.* **2008**, *85*, 842–845. [CrossRef]
3. Ifuku, T.; Yonekawa, M.; Nakagawa, K.; Sato, K.; Saito, T.; Aihara, S.; Ito, T.; Yamamoto, K.; Hiura, M.; Sakai, K.; et al. Nanoimprir lithography performance advances for new application spaces. In Proceedings of the SPIE Advanced Lithography + Patternin San Jose, CA, USA, 25–29 February 2024; Novel Patterning Technologies 2024. SPIE: Bellingham, WA, USA, 2024.
4. Rawlings, C.D.; Kulmala, T.S.; Spieser, M.; Holzner, F.; Glinsner, T.; Schleunitz, A.; Bullerjahn, F.; Panning, E.M.; Sanche M.I. Single-nanometer accurate 3D nanoimprint lithography with master templates fabricated by NanoFrazor lithography. I Proceedings of the SPIE Advanced Lithography, San Jose, CA, USA, 25 February–1 March 2018; SPIE: Bellingham, WA, US 2018; Volume 10584.
5. Sirotkin, V.; Svintsov, A.; Schift, H.; Zaitsev, S. Coarse-grain method for modeling of stamp and substrate deformation i nanoimprint. *Microelectron. Eng.* **2007**, *84*, 868–871. [CrossRef]
6. Takeuchi, N.; Hasegawa, G.; Toshiaki, K.; Iwasaki, T.; Hatano, M.; Komori, M.; Kono, T.; Liddle, J.A.; Ruiz, R. Fabrication o dual damascene structure with nanoimprint lithography and dry-etching. In Proceedings of the SPIE Advanced Lithography Patterning, San Jose, CA, USA, 23 February–2 March 2023; SPIE: Bellingham, WA, USA, 2023; Volume 12497.
7. Aihara, S.; Yamamoto, K.; Nakano, Y.; Kijima, H.; Jimbo, S.; Evans, H.B.; Ishida, S.; Fujimoto, M.; Takami, S.; Oguchi, Y.; et a NIL solutions using computational lithography for semiconductor device manufacturing. In Proceedings of the SPIE Advance Lithography + Patterning, San Jose, CA, USA, 25–29 February 2024; SPIE: Bellingham, WA, USA, 2024; Volume 12954.
8. Chou, S.Y.; Krauss, P.R.; Renstrom, P.J. Nanoimprint lithography. *J. Vac. Sci. Technol. B Microelectron. Nanometer Struct. Proces Meas. Phenom.* **1996**, *14*, 4129–4133. [CrossRef]
9. Guo, L.J. Nanoimprint lithography: Methods and material requirements. *Adv. Mater.* **2007**, *19*, 495–513. [CrossRef]
10. Yan, Y.; Shi, X.; Zhou, T.; Xu, B.; Li, C.; Yuan, W.; Gao, Y.; Pan, B.; Diao, X.; Chen, S.; et al. Machine learning virtual SEM metrolog and SEM-based OPC model methodology. *J. Micro/Nanopatterning Mater. Metrol.* **2021**, *20*, 041204. [CrossRef]
11. Tseng, J.; Chien, J.; Lee, E. Advanced defect recognition on scanning electron microscope images: A two-stage strategy based or deep convolutional neural networks for hotspot monitoring. *J. Micro/Nanopatterning Mater. Metrol.* **2024**, *23*, 044201. [CrossRef]
12. Ogusu, M.; Ishida, M.; Tamura, M.; Sakai, K.; Ito, T.; Ito, Y.; Kawata, I.; Kunugi, H.; Tamura, S.; Asako, R.; et al. Nanoimprint pos processing techniques to address edge placement error. In Proceedings of the SPIE Advanced Lithography + Patterning, San Jose CA, USA, 23 February–2 March 2023; SPIE: Bellingham, WA, USA, 2023; Volume 12497.
13. Dini, P.; Elhanashi, A.; Begni, A.; Saponara, S.; Zheng, Q.; Gasmi, K. Overview on intrusion detection systems design exploiting machine learning for networking cybersecurity. *Appl. Sci.* **2023**, *13*, 7507. [CrossRef]
14. Dini, P.; Saponara, S. Cogging torque reduction in brushless motors by a nonlinear control technique. *Energies* **2019**, *12*, 2224 [CrossRef]
15. Akpabio, I.I.; Savari, S.A. Uncertainty quantification of machine learning models: On conformal prediction. *J. Micro/Nanopatterning Mater. Metrol.* **2021**, *20*, 041206. [CrossRef]
16. Došilović, F.K.; Brčić, M.; Hlupić, N. Explainable artificial intelligence: A survey. In Proceedings of the 2018 41st International Convention on Information and Communication Technology, Electronics and Microelectronics (MIPRO), Opatija, Croatia, 21–25 May 2018; IEEE: Piscataway, NJ, USA, 2018.
17. Acun, C.; Ashary, A.; Popa, D.O.; Nasraoui, O. Optimizing Local Explainability in Robotic Grasp Failure Prediction. *Electronics* **2025**, *14*, 2363. [CrossRef]

18. Elhanashi, A.; Saponara, S.; Zheng, Q.; Almutairi, N.; Singh, Y.; Kuanar, S.; Ali, F.; Unal, O.; Faghani, S. AI-Powered Object Detection in Radiology: Current Models, Challenges, and Future Direction. *J. Imaging* **2025**, *11*, 141. [CrossRef] [PubMed]
19. Elhanashi, A.; Lowe, D.; Saponara, S.; Moshfeghi, Y.; Kehtarnavaz, N.; Carlsohn, M.F. Deep learning techniques to identify and classify COVID-19 abnormalities on chest x-ray images. In Proceedings of the SPIE Defense + Commercial Sensing, Orlando, FL, USA, 3–7 April 2022; SPIE: Bellingham, WA, USA, 2022; Volume 12102.
20. Ronneberger, O.; Fischer, P.; Brox, T. U-net: Convolutional networks for biomedical image segmentation. In Proceedings of the Medical Image Computing and Computer-Assisted Intervention–MICCAI 2015: 18th International Conference, Munich, Germany, 5–9 October 2015; Proceedings, Part III 18; Springer: Berlin/Heidelberg, Germany, 2015.
21. Isensee, F.; Petersen, J.; Klein, A.; Zimmerer, D.; Jaeger, P.F.; Kohl, S.; Wasserthal, J.; Koehler, G.; Norajitra, T.; Wirkert, S.; et al. Nnu-net: Self-adapting framework for u-net-based medical image segmentation. *arXiv* **2018**, arXiv:1809.10486.
22. Han, N.; Zhou, L.; Xie, Z.; Zheng, J.; Zhang, L. Multi-level U-net network for image super-resolution reconstruction. *Displays* **2022**, *73*, 102192. [CrossRef]
23. Xu, W.; Deng, X.; Guo, S.; Chen, J.; Sun, L.; Zheng, X.; Xiong, Y.; Shen, Y.; Wang, X. High-resolution u-net: Preserving image details for cultivated land extraction. *Sensors* **2020**, *20*, 4064. [CrossRef] [PubMed]
24. Yue, X.; Liu, D.; Wang, L.; Benediktsson, J.A.; Meng, L.; Deng, L. IESRGAN: Enhanced U-net structured generative adversarial network for remote sensing image super-resolution reconstruction. *Remote Sens.* **2023**, *15*, 3490. [CrossRef]
25. Ma, X.; Yang, Y.; Shao, D.; Kit, F.C.; Dong, C. HyADS: A Hybrid Lightweight Anomaly Detection Framework for Edge-Based Industrial Systems with Limited Data. *Electronics* **2025**, *14*, 2250. [CrossRef]
26. Zhai, G.; Zhou, J.; Yang, H.; Zhang, Y. A Sea-Surface Radar Target-Detection Method Based on an Improved U-Net and Its FPGA Implementation. *Electronics* **2025**, *14*, 1944. [CrossRef]
27. Joo, Y.H.; Park, H.; Kim, H.; Choe, R.; Kang, Y.; Jung, J.-Y. Traffic Flow Speed Prediction in Overhead Transport Systems for Semiconductor Fabrication Using Dense-UNet. *Processes* **2022**, *10*, 1580. [CrossRef]
28. Taylor, H.; Boning, D. Towards nanoimprint lithography-aware layout design checking. In *Design for Manufacturability Through Design-Process Integration IV*; SPIE: Bellingham, WA, USA, 2010.
29. Haas, S.; Hüllermeier, E. Conformalized prescriptive machine learning for uncertainty-aware automated decision making: The case of goodwill requests. *Int. J. Data Sci. Anal.* **2024**, *17*, 1–17. [CrossRef]
30. Gawlikowski, J.; Tassi, C.R.N.; Ali, M.; Lee, J.; Humt, M.; Feng, J.; Kruspe, A.; Triebel, R.; Jung, P.; Roscher, R.; et al. A survey of uncertainty in deep neural networks. *Artif. Intell. Rev.* **2023**, *56*, 1513–1589. [CrossRef]
31. Ghanem, R.; Higdon, D.; Owhadi, H. *Handbook of Uncertainty Quantification*; Springer: New York, NY, USA, 2017; Volume 6.
32. Ding, Y.; Liu, J.; Xu, X.; Huang, M.; Zhuang, J.; Xiong, J.; Shi, Y. Uncertainty-aware training of neural networks for selective medical image segmentation. In Proceedings of the Medical Imaging with Deep Learning, Montreal, QC, Canada, 6–9 July 2020; PMLR: Cambridge, MA, USA, 2020.
33. Dawood, T.; Chen, C.; Sidhu, B.S.; Ruijsink, B.; Gould, J.; Porter, B.; Elliott, M.K.; Mehta, V.; Rinaldi, C.A.; Puyol-Antón, E.; et al. Uncertainty aware training to improve deep learning model calibration for classification of cardiac MR images. *Med. Image Anal.* **2023**, *88*, 102861. [CrossRef] [PubMed]
34. Dawood, T.; Chen, C.; Andlauer, R.; Sidhu, B.S.; Ruijsink, B.; Gould, J.; Porter, B.; Elliott, M.; Mehta, V.; Rinaldi, C.A.; et al. Uncertainty-aware training for cardiac resynchronisation therapy response prediction. In Proceedings of the International Workshop on Statistical Atlases and Computational Models of the Heart, Strasbourg, France, 27 September 2021; Springer: Berlin/Heidelberg, Germany, 2021.
35. Abdar, M.; Pourpanah, F.; Hussain, S.; Rezazadegan, D.; Liu, L.; Ghavamzadeh, M.; Fieguth, P.; Cao, X.; Khosravi, A.; Acharya, U.R.; et al. A review of uncertainty quantification in deep learning: Techniques, applications and challenges. *Inf. Fusion* **2021**, *76*, 243–297. [CrossRef]
36. Palmer, G.; Du, S.; Politowicz, A.; Emory, J.P.; Yang, X.; Gautam, A.; Gupta, G.; Li, Z.; Jacobs, R.; Morgan, D. Calibration after bootstrap for accurate uncertainty quantification in regression models. *npj Comput. Mater.* **2022**, *8*, 115. [CrossRef]
37. Ren, Y.; Gu, Z.; Wang, Z.; Tian, Z.; Liu, C.; Lu, H.; Du, X.; Guizani, M. System log detection model based on conformal prediction. *Electronics* **2020**, *9*, 232. [CrossRef]
38. Campos, M.; Farinhas, A.; Zerva, C.; Figueiredo, M.A.T.; Martins, A.F.T. Conformal prediction for natural language processing: A survey. *Trans. Assoc. Comput. Linguist.* **2024**, *12*, 1497–1516. [CrossRef]
39. Zhou, X.; Chen, B.; Gui, Y.; Cheng, L. Conformal prediction: A data perspective. *ACM Comput. Surv.* **2025**. [CrossRef]
40. Sesia; Matteo; Romano, Y. Conformal prediction using conditional histograms. *Adv. Neural Inf. Process. Syst.* **2021**, *34*, 6304–6315.
41. Jensen, V.; Bianchi, F.M.; Anfinsen, S.N. Ensemble conformalized quantile regression for probabilistic time series forecasting. *IEEE Trans. Neural Netw. Learn. Syst.* **2022**, *35*, 9014–9025. [CrossRef] [PubMed]

42. Che, L.; Wu, C.; Hou, Y. Large Language Model Text Adversarial Defense Method Based on Disturbance Detection and Err Correction. *Electronics* **2025**, *14*, 2267. [CrossRef]
43. Ren, M.; Zeng, W.; Yang, B.; Urtasun, R. Learning to reweight examples for robust deep learning. In Proceedings of th International Conference on Machine Learning, Stockholm, Sweden, 10–15 July 2018; PMLR: Cambridge, MA, USA, 2018.
44. Krishnan, R.; Tickoo, O. Improving model calibration with accuracy versus uncertainty optimization. *Adv. Neural Inf. Proce. Syst.* **2020**, *33*, 18237–18248.
45. Zhang, L.; Garming, M.W.; Hoogenboom, J.P.; Kruit, P. Beam displacement and blur caused by fast electron beam deflectio *Ultramicroscopy* **2020**, *211*, 112925. [CrossRef] [PubMed]
46. Manfrinato, V.R. Electron-Beam Lithography Towards the Atomic Scale and Applications to Nano-Optics. Ph.D. Thesis, Ma sachusetts Institute of Technology, Cambridge, MA, USA, 2015.
47. Cord, B.; Yang, J.; Duan, H.; Joy, D.C.; Klingfus, J.; Berggren, K.K. Limiting factors in sub-10 nm scanning-electron-bea lithography. *J. Vac. Sci. Technol. B Microelectron. Nanometer Struct. Process. Meas. Phenom.* **2009**, *27*, 2616–2621.
48. Kaganskiy, A.; Heuser, T.; Schmidt, R.; Rodt, S.; Reitzenstein, S. CSAR 62 as negative-tone resist for high-contrast e-bea lithography at temperatures between 4 K and room temperature. *J. Vac. Sci. Technol. B* **2016**, *34*, 061603. [CrossRef]
49. Bobinac, J.; Reiter, T.; Piso, J.; Klemenschits, X.; Baumgartner, O.; Stanojevic, Z.; Strof, G.; Karner, M.; Filipovic, L. Effect of mas geometry variation on plasma etching profiles. *Micromachines* **2023**, *14*, 665. [CrossRef] [PubMed]
50. Schirmer, M.; Büttner, B.; Syrowatka, F.; Schmidt, G.; Köpnick, T.; Kaiser, C.; Behringer, U.F.W.; Maurer, W. Chemical Sem Amplified positive E-beam Resist (CSAR 62) for highest resolution. In Proceedings of the 29th European Mask and Lithograph Conference, Dresden, Germany, 25–27 June 2013; SPIE: Bellingham, WA, USA, 2013.
51. Gangnaik, A.S.; Georgiev, Y.M.; Holmes, J.D. New generation electron beam resists: A review. *Chem. Mater.* **2017**, *29*, 1898–191 [CrossRef]
52. Thoms, S.; Macintyre, D.S. Investigation of CSAR 62, a new resist for electron beam lithography. *J. Vac. Sci. Technol. B* **2014**, 3 06FJ01. [CrossRef]
53. Schmitt, H.; Frey, L.; Ryssel, H.; Rommel, M.; Lehrer, C. UV nanoimprint materials: Surface energies, residual layers, and imprir quality. *J. Vac. Sci. Technol. B Microelectron. Nanometer Struct. Process. Meas. Phenom.* **2007**, *25*, 785–790. [CrossRef]
54. Uchida, H.; Imoto, R.; Ando, T.; Okabe, T.; Taniguchi, J. Molecular dynamics simulation of the resist filling process in U nanoimprint lithography. *J. Photopolym. Sci. Technol.* **2021**, *34*, 139–144. [CrossRef]
55. Qi, H.; Xu, M. Stokes' first problem for a viscoelastic fluid with the generalized Oldroyd-B model. *Acta Mech. Sin.* **2007**, 2 463–469. [CrossRef]
56. Seeger, A.; Haussecker, H. Shape-from-shading and simulation of SEM images using surface slope and curvature. *Surf. Interfac Anal.* **2005**, *37*, 927–938. [CrossRef]
57. Inoue, O.; Hasumi, K. Review of scanning electron microscope-based overlay measurement beyond 3-nm node device. *Micro/Nanolithography MEMS MOEMS* **2019**, *18*, 021206. [CrossRef]
58. Zhu, F.Y.; Wang, Q.Q.; Zhang, X.S.; Hu, W.; Zhao, X.; Zhang, H.X. 3D reconstruction and feature extraction for analysis o nanostructures by SEM imaging. In Proceedings of the 2013 Transducers & Eurosensors XXVII: The 17th International Conferenc on Solid-State Sensors, Actuators and Microsystems (TRANSDUCERS & EUROSENSORS XXVII), Barcelona, Spain, 16–20 Jun 2013; IEEE: Piscataway, NJ, USA, 2013.
59. Swee, S.K.; Chen, L.C.; Chiang, T.S.; Khim, T.C. Deep Convolutional Neural Network for SEM Image Noise Variance Classificatior *Eng. Lett.* **2023**, *31*, 328–337.
60. Walsh, J.; Othmani, A.; Jain, M.; Dev, S. Using U-Net network for efficient brain tumor segmentation in MRI images. *Healthc. Ana.* **2022**, *2*, 100098. [CrossRef]

electronics

MDPI

Article

Color-Guided Mixture-of-Experts Conditional GAN for Realistic Biomedical Image Synthesis in Data-Scarce Diagnostics

Patrycja Kwiek, Filip Ciepiela and Małgorzata Jakubowska *

Faculty of Materials Science and Ceramics, AGH University of Krakow, al. Mickiewicza 30, 30-059 Kraków, Poland; pakwiek@agh.edu.pl (P.K.); filip.ciepiela@agh.edu.pl (F.C.)
* Correspondence: jakubows@agh.edu.pl

Abstract: Background: Limited availability of high-quality labeled biomedical image datasets presents a significant challenge for training deep learning models in medical diagnostics. This study proposes a novel image generation framework combining conditional generative adversarial networks (cGANs) with a Mixture-of-Experts (MoE) architecture and color histogram-aware loss functions to enhance synthetic blood cell image quality. Methods: RGB microscopic images from the BloodMNIST dataset (eight blood cell types, resolution $3 \times 128 \times 128$) underwent preprocessing with k-means clustering to extract the dominant colors and UMAP for visualizing class similarity. Spearman correlation-based distance matrices were used to evaluate the discriminative power of each RGB channel. A MoE–cGAN architecture was developed with residual blocks and LeakyReLU activations. Expert generators were conditioned on cell type, and the generator's loss was augmented with a Wasserstein distance-based term comparing red and green channel histograms, which were found most relevant for class separation. Results: The red and green channels contributed most to class discrimination; the blue channel had minimal impact. The proposed model achieved 0.97 classification accuracy on generated images (ResNet50), with 0.96 precision, 0.97 recall, and a 0.96 F1-score. The best Fréchet Inception Distance (FID) was 52.1. Misclassifications occurred mainly among visually similar cell types. Conclusions: Integrating histogram alignment into the MoE–cGAN training significantly improves the realism and class-specific variability of synthetic images, supporting robust model development under data scarcity in hematological imaging.

Keywords: conditional generative adversarial networks; Mixture-of-Experts; RGB histograms; UMAP; peripheral blood; missing blood cells generation

1. Introduction

Biomedical challenges have become a critical focus for artificial intelligence (AI) research due to the unprecedented availability of clinical data generated by hospitals, diagnostic laboratories, and research institutions [1–3]. This data—spanning electronic health records (EHRs), laboratory test results, high-resolution medical images, and physiological signals—holds great promise for advancing diagnostics, predicting treatment outcomes, and enabling personalized therapies. Bioinformatics plays a pivotal role in this ecosystem by transforming raw clinical data into structured forms suitable for computational analysis, facilitating the training of machine learning (ML) models that can aid in clinical decision-making. However, the reliability of these models hinges on the accuracy and consistency of the underlying data, which is meticulously maintained by medical professionals. Even slight errors in device calibration, data collection protocols, or annotation quality can propagate through algorithms, potentially leading to serious clinical risks.

Despite the transformative potential of AI in healthcare, several persistent challenges limit its full integration into medical practice. One of the most significant barriers is the scarcity of large, high-quality, labeled datasets. This problem is especially acute in specialized diagnostic areas, such as hematology, histopathology, and rare disease detection, where data acquisition requires expert clinicians and sophisticated, often expensive, equipment. Class imbalance further complicates model development; pathological cases or specific cell types may represent only a small fraction of the dataset, while healthy or common cases dominate. This imbalance can bias models toward overpredicting majority classes, thereby undermining diagnostic accuracy for critical minority classes.

The heterogeneity of medical data introduces additional complexity. Variations in imaging modalities (e.g., MRI, CT, and microscopy); staining protocols; equipment manufacturers; image resolution; and even lighting conditions contribute to substantial variability in data representation. Such variability challenges the ability of models to generalize across institutions and patient populations. Moreover, regulatory constraints on data sharing, high diagnostic costs (particularly in systems where procedures are not fully reimbursed), unequal access to advanced medical equipment, and variable levels of staff training further limit the quantity and standardization of data available for AI model development.

To address these limitations, researchers have explored a range of strategies aimed at improving data availability, diversity, and model robustness. Data augmentation remains one of the most widely used techniques, introducing variations into existing images through operations such as rotation, translation, scaling, flipping, adding noise, adjusting contrast and color, cropping, and zooming [4–7]. These techniques can help models become more resilient to minor variations in image presentation but do not address deeper issues of class imbalance or data scarcity at the distributional level.

More recent efforts have focused on generative models for synthetic data creation. These models include generative adversarial networks (GANs), which learn to produce realistic images by pitting a generator against a discriminator, and their extension, conditional GANs (cGANs), which allow image generation tied to specific class labels [8,9]. Other approaches, such as Variational Autoencoders (VAEs), generate samples by modeling the probability distribution of existing data, while Diffusion Models iteratively denoise samples to synthesize highly realistic images [10,11]. These generative methods are particularly valuable in low-data regimes, offering the possibility of enriching datasets without further straining limited clinical resources. Transfer learning, where models pretrained on large, general purpose datasets like ImageNet are adapted to medical tasks, has also proven effective in overcoming data limitations by leveraging prior knowledge. Semi-supervised learning, employing strategies like self-training and co-training, enables models to utilize vast amounts of unlabeled data alongside smaller labeled subsets, progressively expanding training sets with pseudo-labeled data [12,13].

Privacy-preserving techniques, such as federated learning, facilitate model training across distributed datasets without exposing sensitive patient data, addressing legal and ethical barriers to data sharing.

Nevertheless, synthetic data generation for biomedical imaging still faces substantial challenges. Many generative frameworks underexploit color information, despite its diagnostic significance, especially in fields like histopathology and hematology, where subtle color variations differentiate morphologically similar cells or tissue structures. Color inconsistencies introduced during data synthesis can degrade the quality of synthetic images and limit their utility for training reliable diagnostic models.

In this study, we propose a novel synthetic image generation strategy that directly addresses these challenges: a Color-Guided Mixture-of-Experts Conditional GAN (MoE–cGAN) architecture tailored for biomedical image synthesis in data-scarce settings. Our method explicitly integrates targeted RGB color channel analysis into the generative process, leveraging the discriminative power of color to improve class-specific image fidelity. Unlike standard augmentation or unconditional synthesis techniques, our approach begins with a detailed statistical and structural analysis of the RGB distributions in stained biomedical images, particularly peripheral blood cell images. This analysis informs the generator's design by guiding the incorporation of color histogram similarity—focused on diagnostically meaningful channels—into the loss function via Wasserstein distance. The Mixture-of-Experts structure introduces modular specialization, allowing different sub-generators to focus on particular classes, thereby enhancing diversity, addressing class imbalance, and improving minority class representation. This color-aware, expert-driven generative strategy offers a comprehensive solution for producing high-fidelity synthetic data, supporting the development of balanced, generalizable AI models for biomedical diagnostics.

2. Materials and Methods

2.1. Dataset and Data Preprocessing

The dataset utilized in this study is the BloodMNIST dataset, which is a subset of the MedMNIST benchmark dataset collection [14]. This collection is composed of 17,092 microscopic images of eight types of blood cells, normal cells, and obtained during hematologic or oncologic diseases, which are all colored purple due to the type of cell staining. The eight cell classes, i.e., basophils, eosinophils, erythroblasts, immature granulocytes, lymphocytes, monocytes, neutrophils, and platelets (or thrombocytes), are represented in the mentioned dataset. The labels for each cell image were assigned by expert pathologists. The detailed characteristics of the data are shown in Table S1. The database was divided into training (70%, 11,162 samples), validation (10%, 1785 samples), and test (20%, 3572 samples) sets, as proposed by the authors, who also provided tools for loading these three subsets. This is the standard division used in the MedMNIST v2 benchmarks. The library software allows images to load in three different resolutions, i.e., 64 × 64, 128 × 128, and 224 × 224 pixels.

The BloodMNIST dataset plays an important role in the diagnosis of blood and parasitic diseases and in the creation of decision support systems in hematopathology. It enables the automation of microscopic analysis, relieving specialists and increasing diagnostic accuracy. It is used, among others, to assess the morphology of blood cells in the diagnosis of anemia, leukemia (e.g., AML and ALL), thalassemia, malaria, and sepsis. It can support the monitoring of treatment effectiveness (chemotherapy and immunotherapy) and be useful in population screening programs. BloodMNIST is also used in training AI models and medical education, facilitating the recognition of blood pathologies.

2.2. Methods

To analyze color distributions and inter-class similarities, we employed k-means clustering, UMAP dimensionality reduction, and the Spearman rank correlation coefficient. K-means was used to identify dominant color patterns by clustering pixel intensities, providing insight into shared chromatic features across classes [15]. UMAP was applied to RGB histogram data to visualize sample groupings and assess whether color distributions align with cell class labels, aiding in the detection of class-separable or overlapping chromatic structures [16,17]. Spearman correlation quantified the inter-class histogram similarity, capturing monotonic relationships between color profiles while being robust to outliers and intensity shifts [18–20]. The flowchart of each algorithm is presented in Figure 1. Together, these methods support a deeper understanding of color-based variation in the dataset and its impact on class separability and generation fidelity.

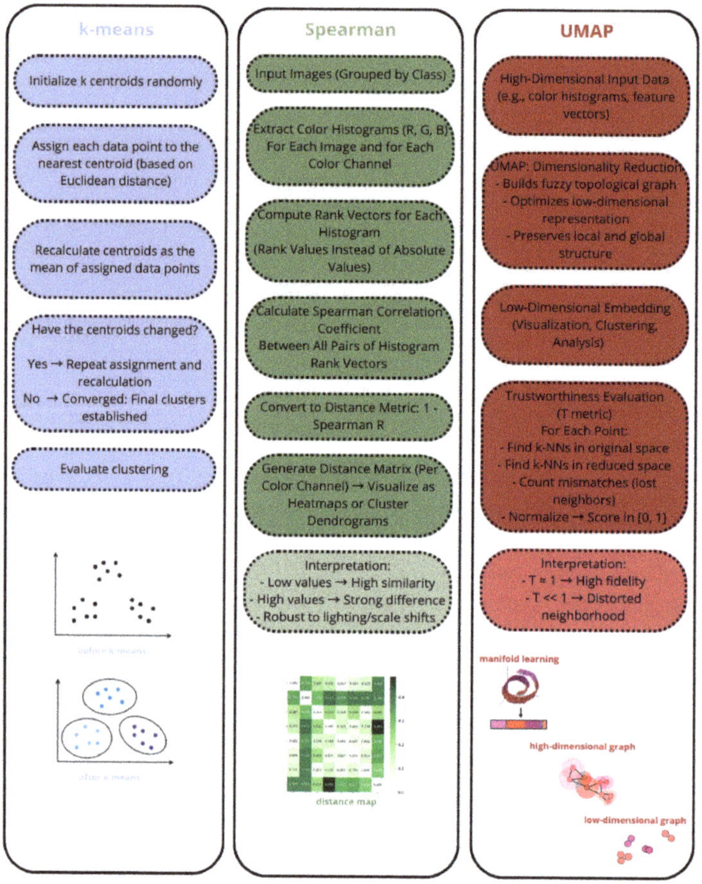

Figure 1. Pre-analysis of data correlation and distribution: explanation of k-means and UMAP algorithms and Spearman distances.

The study used conditional generative adversarial networks (cGAN), consisting of a generator and a discriminator competing with each other in the training process. The generator creates samples imitating real data, and the discriminator assesses their authenticity. Additional conditioning, e.g., class labels, is introduced in cGAN, which allows control over the generated images [21–23].

cGAN training can be unstable, which is why regularization techniques such as layer normalization or loss function modifications are used. The effectiveness of the model is assessed based on the realism of the generated samples and the balance of losses of both networks—the optimal classification accuracy of the discriminator is about 50%. cGAN is used, among others, in medicine, where it allows the generation of synthetic data in situations of limited availability of real examples [24–26].

LeakyReLU introduces a small, non-zero slope (typically $\alpha \approx 0.01$) for negative inputs, addressing the "dying neurons" issue inherent in standard ReLU. In GAN generators, it enhances the training stability by improving the gradient flow and maintaining activation diversity, which supports more effective learning and the generation of realistic, varied samples [27,28].

The Mixture-of-Experts (MoE) approach can be viewed as a dynamic instantiation of the Divide-and-Conquer strategy [29], in which a complex task is decomposed into sub-components handled by specialized expert networks. Both MoE and Divide-and-Conquer frameworks aim to process distinct aspects of the input by delegating responsibilities to modular components. Unlike traditional Divide-and-Conquer, which uses static assignment, MoE incorporates a gating mechanism that dynamically routes inputs to the most relevant experts based on input characteristics. A key similarity lies in their integration of partial outputs into a final, unified result, while a central distinction is MoE's adaptive routing and weighted aggregation, offering greater flexibility and efficiency. RGB-T Salient Object Detection (SOD), for example, applies Divide-and-Conquer principles by processing RGB and thermal data streams through modality-specific networks before fusing the outputs to enhance robustness and accuracy [30,31].

In conditional image generation, MoE combined with conditional GANs (cGANs) forms an advanced architecture capable of modeling complex and multimodal data distributions. Multiple expert generators specialize in different class-conditional distributions, and a gating network assigns input-dependent weights to combine their outputs. The shared discriminator evaluates both image realism and class fidelity, enforcing stronger supervision. This structure mitigates mode collapse by encouraging expert diversity and enables scalable generation, as the number of experts can grow without linearly increasing the inference cost. The effective optimization of MoE–cGAN architectures involves regularization and weight balancing techniques. Empirical studies demonstrate improved image detail, consistency, and adaptability over standard GAN variants, enabling more accurate and diverse generation across classes and conditions [32,33].

The Wasserstein distance, also known as Earth Mover's Distance (EMD), measures the difference between two probability distributions as the minimum "transport cost" of mass from one distribution to the other [34]. In generative modeling, it provides more stable gradients than traditional divergence measures and is sensitive to subtle distributional shifts, which contributes to more robust training dynamics [35–38]. In this work, a 1D Wasserstein distance is employed to compare the cumulative histograms of pixel intensities in the red and green (R and G) channels between generated and real images, reflecting perceptually important color structures while excluding the blue channel due to its lower diagnostic relevance. Each image is flattened into a vector, and normalized histograms are computed over a shared range [0,1] using 256 bins. Cumulative histograms are then calculated and normalized, and the Wasserstein distance is computed as the mean absolute difference between corresponding bins. The final loss is the sum of distances for the R and G channels:

$$Wasserstein\ Distance = \frac{1}{K}\sum_{i=1}^{K}\left|C_{real}[i] - C_{gen}[i]\right|,\ loss = loss_R + loss_G$$

where:

- $C_{real}[i]$—the value of the cumulative histogram for the real image at bin i.
- $C_{gen}[i]$—the corresponding value for the generated image.
- K—the number of histogram bins.

This formulation guides the generator toward matching the color intensity distributions of real images, improving visual fidelity and reducing artifacts such as unnatural hues.

The architecture of the model used in this work is presented in Figure 2.

Figure 2. The Mixture-of-Experts (MoE) model combined with a conditional GAN (cGAN) as an advanced architecture for generating high-quality, complex images proposed in the presented study.

2.3. Evaluation Metrics

In multiclass labeling with 8 classes, metrics such as accuracy, precision, recall, and F1-score are defined by extending them from binary versions, taking into account the specificity of many classes.

Let us assume the notation:

- TP_i (True Positive): a number of correct predictions from class i.
- FP_i (False Positive): samples from other classes misclassified as class i.
- FN_i (False Negative): samples from class i mislabeled as other classes.

Accuracy measures the overall correctness of the classification.

$$Accuracy = \frac{Number\,of\,correct\,predictions}{Number\,of\,all\,samples} = \frac{\sum_{i=i}^{8} TP_i}{N} = \frac{\sum_{i=i}^{8} TP_i}{\sum_{i=i}^{8}(TP_i + FN_i)}$$

The total number of samples is equal to the sum of all predictions:

$$N = \sum_{i=i}^{8}(TP_i + FN_i)$$

As each sample is either:

- correctly classified as its true class (TP_i for given class);
- incorrectly classified as a different class (FN_i).

Precision is the ratio of correctly classified samples of a given class to all samples classified as that class. Precision is calculated for each class as follows:

$$P_i = \frac{TP_i}{TP_i + FP_i}$$

Recall is the ratio of correctly classified samples of a given class to all samples that actually belong to that class. Recall is calculated for each class accordingly:

$$R_i = \frac{TP_i}{TP_i + FN_i}$$

F1-score is the harmonic mean of precision and sensitivity; it is calculated for each class in the following way:

$$F1_i = 2 \cdot \frac{P_i \cdot R_i}{P_i + R_i}$$

To obtain a single value for the entire model, metric aggregation is used.

Macro Average calculates the arithmetic mean of the metrics for all classes, treating each class equally.

$$Macro\ P = \frac{1}{8}\sum_{i=1}^{8} P_i \quad Macro\ R = \frac{1}{8}\sum_{i=1}^{8} R_i$$

Weighted Average assigns weights proportional to class size.

$$Weighted\ P = \sum_{i=1}^{8} w_i P_i,$$

where:

$$w_i = \frac{Number\ of\ samples\ from\ class\ i}{N}$$

The confusion matrix allows for a more detailed analysis of the classification errors. It is a table where the rows represent the actual classes and the columns represent the predicted classes. In the case of a multiclass problem, accuracy can also be calculated from the confusion matrix.

One of the most important metrics for assessing the quality of data generation is the Fréchet Inception Distance (FID)—the lower the FID value, the smaller the difference between the feature distributions of real and generated images. FID measures the similarity between the distributions using the Inception V3 model. Real and generated images are processed by the Inception V3 model to obtain feature vectors (usually from the pool3 layer, with 2048 dimensions). The mean and covariance of these features are calculated for both sets (real and generated). FID is the Fréchet (Wasserstein-2) distance between these two Gaussian distributions. The following notations are used:

- k—feature space dimension;
- $m_1 \in \mathbb{R}^k$—the mean feature vector extracted from the real distribution;
- $m_2 \in \mathbb{R}^k$—the mean feature vector extracted from the generated distribution;
- $C_1 \in \mathbb{R}^{kxk}$—the covariance matrix of features for real data;
- $C_2 \in \mathbb{R}^{kxk}$—the covariance matrix of features for generated data.

The Fréchet Inception Distance (FID) is then defined as

$$FID^2 = ||m_1 - m_2||_2^2 + Tr\left(C_1 + C_2 - 2(C_1C_2)^{\frac{1}{2}}\right)$$

where:

- $||m_1 - m_2||_2^2$ denotes the squared Euclidean norm of the difference between the means;
- $Tr(\cdot)$ represents the trace of a matrix;
- $(C_1C_2)^{\frac{1}{2}}$ denotes the matrix square root of products C_1 and C_2.

FID does not depend directly on the number of classes but on the overall similarity of feature distributions. Therefore, one can calculate one FID altogether, comparing the entire generated set with the entire real set, or for each of the classes separately.

Monitoring the losses of both models is also important, because a uniform decrease in losses suggests that the generator is learning to effectively fool the discriminator and the discriminator is correctly recognizing the authenticity of the samples. Maintaining a balance between the generator and the discriminator is crucial, because one of the models being too strong can lead to training instability and deterioration of the quality of the results. The evaluation of GAN performance should be supplemented by a visual analysis of the generated samples, which allows detecting possible artifacts that are invisible using only numerical metrics.

2.4. Training, Testing, and Data Generation

In this project, images from the BloodMNIST database with dimensions of 128×128 are processed, and the color is saved in the RGB space. The RGB components are normalized to the interval $[-1, 1]$.

2.5. Hardware and Software

Data generation was performed with the use of deep neural networks implemented in Python 3, for which the input data were images from the MedMNIST dataset. For this purpose, the PyTorch 2.5.1 library was applied. Various types of data simulation, collection, processing, and preliminary interpretations, as well as charts and graphs preparation, were implemented in Python. Calculations were performed using a Lenovo Legion laptop and PC with the specifications presented in Table S2.

3. Results

3.1. Characteristics of the BloodMNIST Database with Regard to Color Analysis in the R, G, and B Channels

RGB color analysis plays a key role in BloodMNIST modeling due to the close relationship between the color and shape of blood cells such as erythrocytes, leukocytes, and platelets. Color differences, such as purple nuclei and pink cytoplasm, are important for classification and segmentation. RGB histograms allow for assessing the color distribution between classes, supporting feature extraction and eliminating false classifications resulting from similar shapes. Analysis of individual channels can help reduce dimensionality and improve classification accuracy. In transfer models (e.g., ResNet and EfficientNet), RGB is the basic input, and preserving color information increases the efficiency of using models pre-trained on datasets such as ImageNet. Colors also support artifact identification and noise reduction, improving the quality of the input data.

Figure 3 shows eight blood cell types along with RGB channel histograms, allowing the analysis of morphological features and differences in color distribution. Purple and pink tones dominate the entire dataset, resulting from eosin and basic staining. The background of the images has a distinct pinkish tone. The histograms show characteristic patterns: in the red channel, the highest intensities occur between 230 and 255; in the green channel, the lowest in the range of 210–230; and in the blue channel, values from 190 to 210 dominate. There is no blue intensity below 125, confirming the dominance of warmer tones. Purples have balanced red and blue values and low green intensity, giving them a cool, deep character. Dark purples have lower R and B channel values, and light purples have higher values. Pinks are dominated by red; light pinks have very high red and moderate other channels, while darker purples have slightly reduced intensity in all channels, maintaining a warm tone. Such RGB dependencies reflect the typical colors present in cell images and are important for distinguishing them and using them in machine learning models.

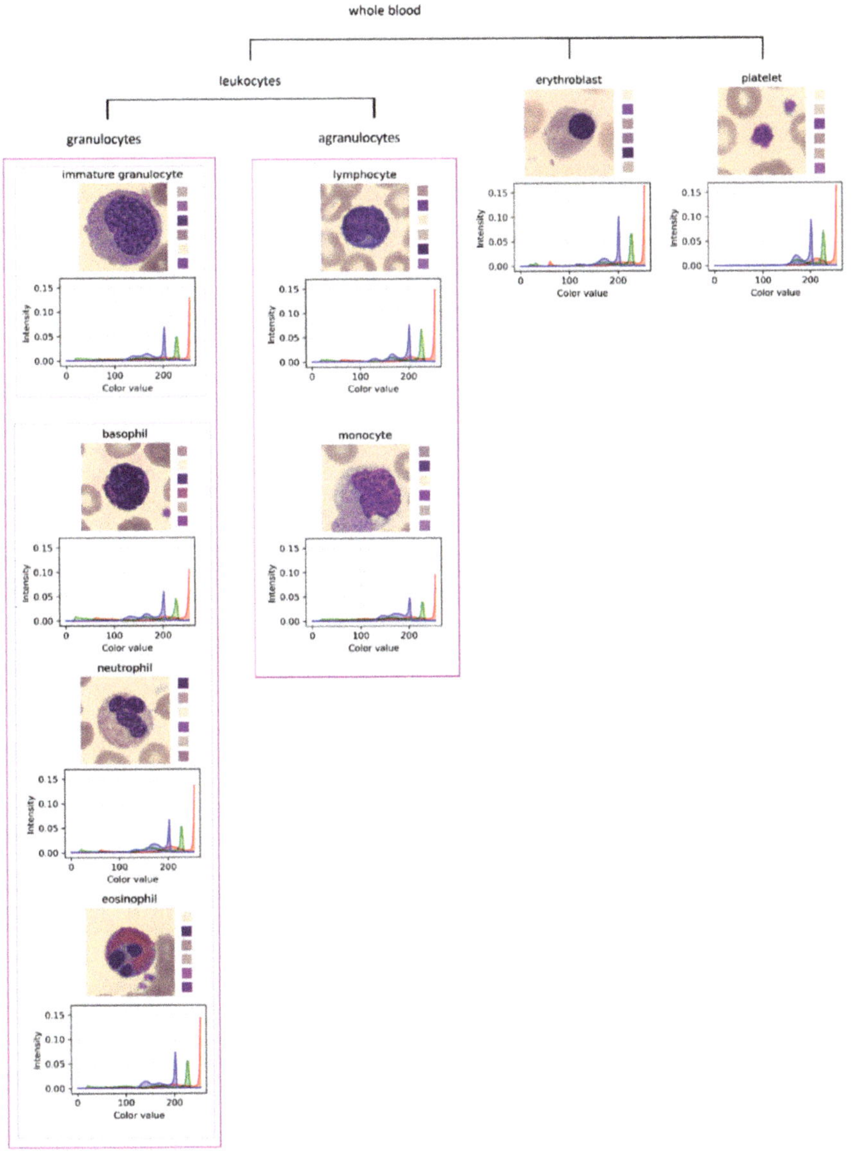

Figure 3. Histograms of the R, G, and B components (relative frequency) and dominant colors in 8 cell classes. The histogram colors represent the red, green, and blue components, while the squares next to the blood cell images indicate the dominant color in each image.

In order to identify the dominant colors in cell images, the k-means method (k = 6) was used, which allows for the reduction of the full color spectrum to a few representative shades—centroids. Each centroid reflects the average color value in one of the key color groups of a given class, creating a synthetic but very characteristic "color signature" of the cell. Unlike histograms, which show the full intensity distribution of the R, G, and B channels, the k-means method allows for a direct comparison of classes in color space, revealing their similarities and differences.

Basophils are distinguished by a strongly contrasting combination of a cream background and dark purple cytoplasmic granules, often obscuring the nucleus. Their centroids are clearly separated from other classes, which greatly facilitates their identification. Eosinophils, on the other hand, are characterized by the presence of large red granules on a light pink background of the cytoplasm. This translates into a strong dominance of the red channel and a clearly red color profile, very characteristic and well distinguishable [39–41].

Erythroblasts combine a pale pink cytoplasmic background with a darker, often purple, nucleus, resulting in the presence of both light and darker centroids corresponding to the cytoplasm and nucleus, respectively. Immature granulocytes, as transitional cells, show a more diffuse color distribution. Their irregular nuclei and less concentrated granules cause the centroids to fall within the range of cool but less distinct purples, which can make it difficult to clearly classify them based on color alone.

Lymphocytes and monocytes show great color similarity. In lymphocytes, most of the cell is occupied by a dark purple nucleus, surrounded by a thin layer of light pink cytoplasm. Monocytes are larger, their nucleus is kidney-shaped, and their cytoplasm is more grayish. Despite these differences, the dominant colors of both types are similar—centroids corresponding to purple and pink colors often appear, which can lead to errors in classification if only color is taken into account.

Neutrophils, the most common leukocytes, contain a segmented nucleus and small granules, which translate into a grayish, slightly purple cytoplasm. Their color distribution is even, and the dominant colors oscillate around dark purples and subdued shades, with small intensity shifts in the red and blue channels. Such a profile, although less pronounced than in eosinophils or basophils, still allows them to be recognized in the context of the entire database.

Platelets, as the smallest structures in the analyzed set, do not contain a nucleus and appear in the image as small pink–purple dots. Due to their size and simple structure, most of the color comes from the background of the preparation. The histograms show low color intensity, and the centroids are concentrated around very light, pale pink shades. Thanks to this, despite the lack of a complex structure, platelets are well recognizable based on their characteristic background and limited color range.

The use of the k-means method significantly simplifies the analysis and highlights the differences between cell classes while indicating which types are more difficult to distinguish due to color similarities. In combination with morphological analysis, this provides a solid basis for automated classification and statistical analysis in blood cell image recognition systems.

The efficiency of automatic recognition is also influenced by the morphological features of cells, such as size, nucleus shape, and nucleus-to-cytoplasm ratio. Lymphocytes, with a dominant nucleus, have a distinct color profile, while platelets—very small and anucleate—are more difficult to capture in color. Immature forms, such as granulocytes, are characterized by a less clear, "blurred" color distribution. Figure 3 illustrates that morphological differences correspond well with RGB histograms. The use of k-means allows the color analysis to be simplified to a few representative shades, which aids classification, especially for classes with distinct color and structural features.

Before applying the UMAP algorithm, the images were flattened to one-dimensional vectors, and then, their dimensionality was reduced to 200 principal components using PCA. UMAP performed separately for the R, G, and B channels (Figure 4) revealed that some classes, such as erythroblasts, lymphocytes, and platelets, form clearly separated clusters. The R channel allows for good discrimination of most classes, except for basophils and monocytes, which partially overlap. The G channel separates the classes better than the B channel, which shows weaker discrimination and more outliers. Therefore, the green channel may be more important in the design of classification algorithms. Overall, the UMAP analysis shows that classes with clear color features are well recognized, while more complex cases require additional information, e.g., cell morphology or the integration of data from several channels. The reliability of the representation at the level of about 0.84 confirms the accuracy of this representation.

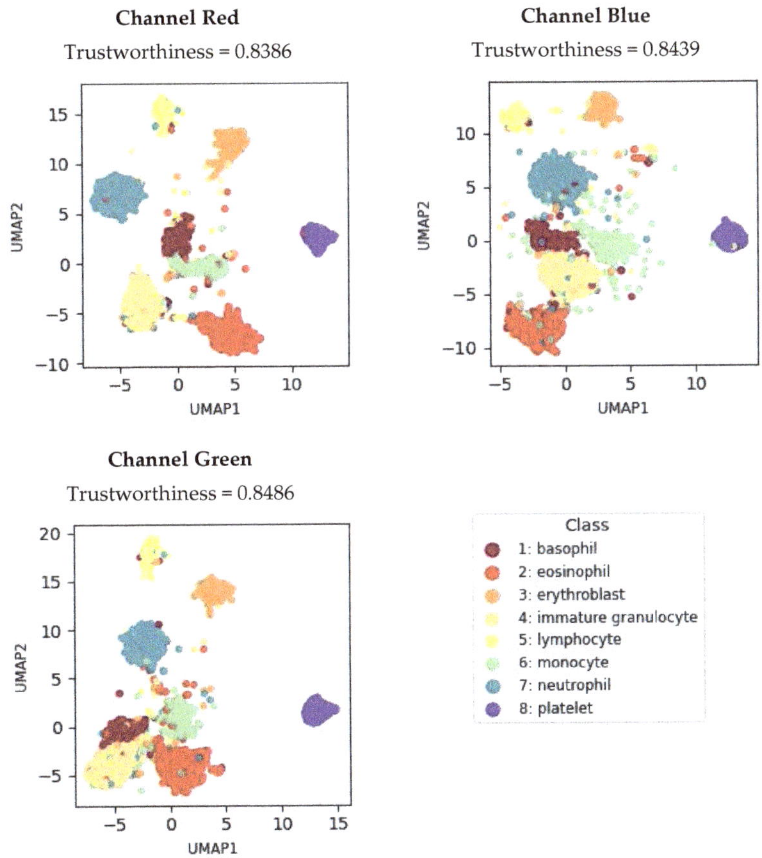

Figure 4. UMAP analysis results for each of the channels with pre-PCA.

The study of color differences between cell classes was based on the calculation of the distance (1—Spearman correlation) between the histograms in the R, G, and B channels (Figure 5). Lower values indicate greater similarity and higher values greater differences. In all the channels, the distances are relatively low, which suggests a partial dependence between the color signals. The smallest differences are observed in channel B, where only platelets stand out significantly due to their purple hue and small size. The largest differences between classes occur in channel G, which is consistent with previous UMAP observations and emphasizes its usefulness for classification.

Channel R may also contain important information, although it does not clearly distinguish one class. It is worth paying attention to some pairs of classes (e.g., lymphocytes–basophils and granulocytes–eosinophils), which, depending on the channel, show a variable degree of similarity. The green channel in particular reveals subtle but statistically significant differences, which may be important for the further improvement of classification algorithms.

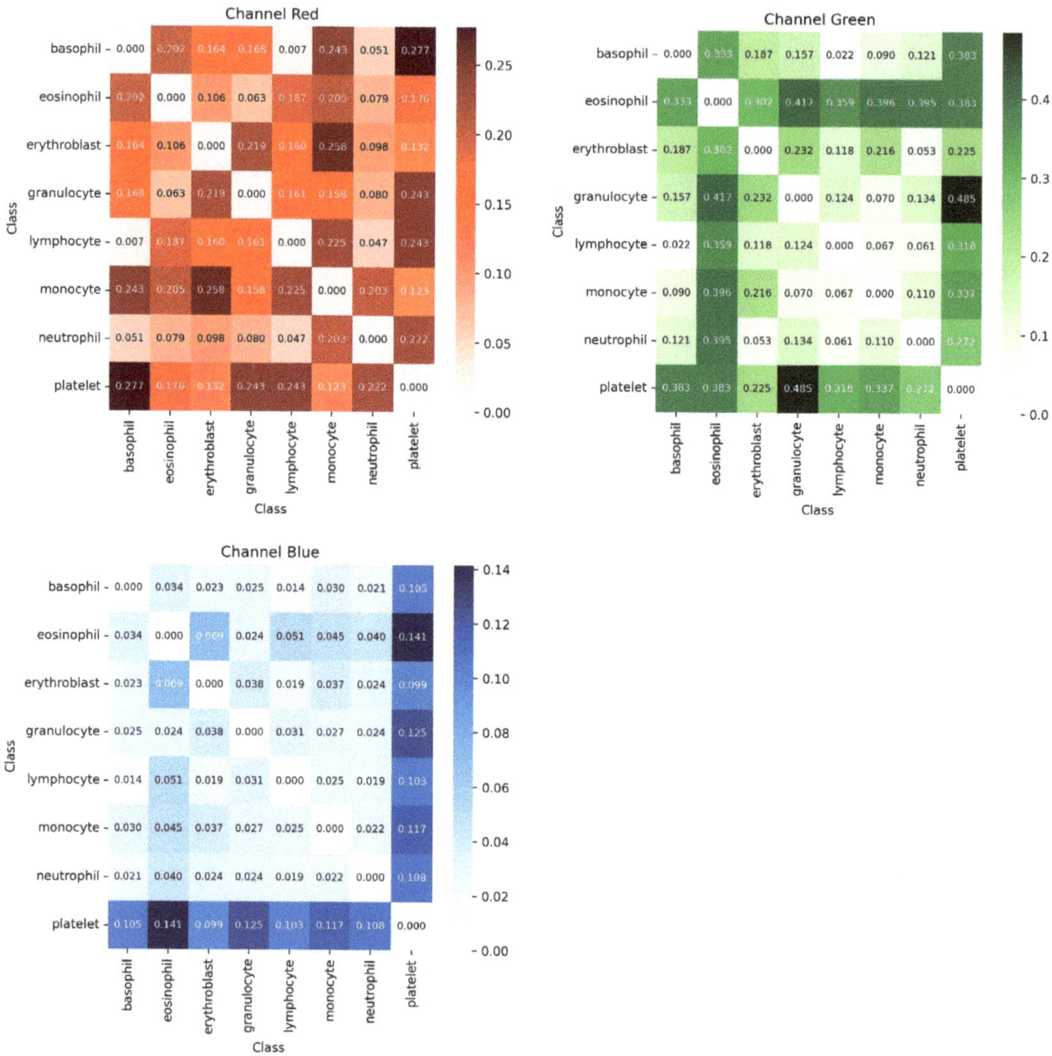

Figure 5. Distance matrices (1—Spearman) for the R, G, and B channels.

3.2. Image Generation

The generator and discriminator modules were designed to make cGAN training efficient and stable, i.e., the balance between the generator and the discriminator is crucial to obtain high-quality results.

3.2.1. Generator

The optimized generator employs a Mixture-of-Experts (MoE) architecture, where multiple specialized sub-generators (experts) operate in parallel, and their outputs are adaptively combined via a gating network. The generator takes a latent noise vector (dim = 100) and a class label (0–7) as input. The label is embedded and concatenated with the noise vector to form a unified input, which is then processed by the gating network—comprising two linear layers with ReLU activation followed by softmax—to produce expert-specific weights. Each expert receives the same input and consists of a linear projection to an initial feature map (e.g., 128 × init_size × init_size); unflattening; and a series of ConvTranspose2d layers with InstanceNorm2d, ReLU/LeakyReLU, and two residual blocks. The output is passed through a final Conv2d and tanh activation to generate an RGB image. The final output is a weighted sum of the experts' outputs, enabling dynamic specialization and improved generation quality across diverse classes.

3.2.2. Discriminator

The discriminator performs both adversarial discrimination and auxiliary classification to enforce realism and label consistency. It consists of three Conv2d layers with increasing channel depth (64 → 128 → 256), LeakyReLU activations, and dropout (0.4/0.3), progressively downsampling the input while extracting hierarchical features. The final feature map is flattened and passed to two parallel linear heads: an adversarial output for real/fake prediction and a classification head for class label assignment. This dual-objective design improves the training stability and enhances the generator's ability to produce class-consistent, high-fidelity images. The discriminator complements the Mixture-of-Experts generator by reinforcing both visual and semantic accuracy.

3.2.3. Training of Image Generation Models

The GAN model is trained alternately, teaching the discriminator to distinguish between real and generated images and assigning them correct labels and the generator to create realistic images consistent with the given classes. Adam optimizers with different parameters were used: for the generator, lr = 0.0002, and for the discriminator, lr = 0.0001, with betas = (0.5, 0.999), and the batch size was set to 64. Two loss functions are used in training: BCEWithLogitsLoss (to distinguish real and fake images) and CrossEntropyLoss (to classify labels).

The discriminator training consists of calculating the total loss from real and generated images and their labels and then updating its weights. Additionally, the accuracy of its prediction is calculated. The generator, on the other hand, produces images based on a random vector and labels, which are assessed by the discriminator for the authenticity and correctness of classes. The total loss of the generator consists of the adversarial, classification, and histogram components, weighted by appropriate coefficients. Based on this, the generator updates its parameters. The accuracy of assigning labels by the discriminator to the generated images serves as an additional measure of the generator's training effectiveness.

The loss for the generator is calculated as a weighted sum of the three components. Adversarial loss: The generator wants to "fool" the discriminator, so we treat the generated images as real. Classification loss: The generator is penalized when the discriminator fails to assign the correct label to the generated image (comparison with fake_labels). Histogram loss: The difference between the color distribution of the generated and real images is calculated. Only the red and green channels are considered, as they have been previously proven to best differentiate the classes. The Wasserstein histogram loss function is used in calculations. The loss components are then combined. The total loss of the generator is the sum of three components, where each is weighted:

$$g_{loss} = 1.0 \cdot g_{loss_{adv}} + 2.0 \cdot g_{loss_{class}} + 10.0 \cdot g_{loss_{hist}}$$

The weights (1.0, 2.0, and 10.0) indicate the relative importance of the loss components (adversarial, classification, and histogram) and were selected in the optimization process. The generation strategy was tested for 100 epochs (200 iterations), generating a total of 1000 images from eight classes. The values of loss and accuracy are shown in Figure S1, and the sample images—real and generated—are compared in Figure 6.

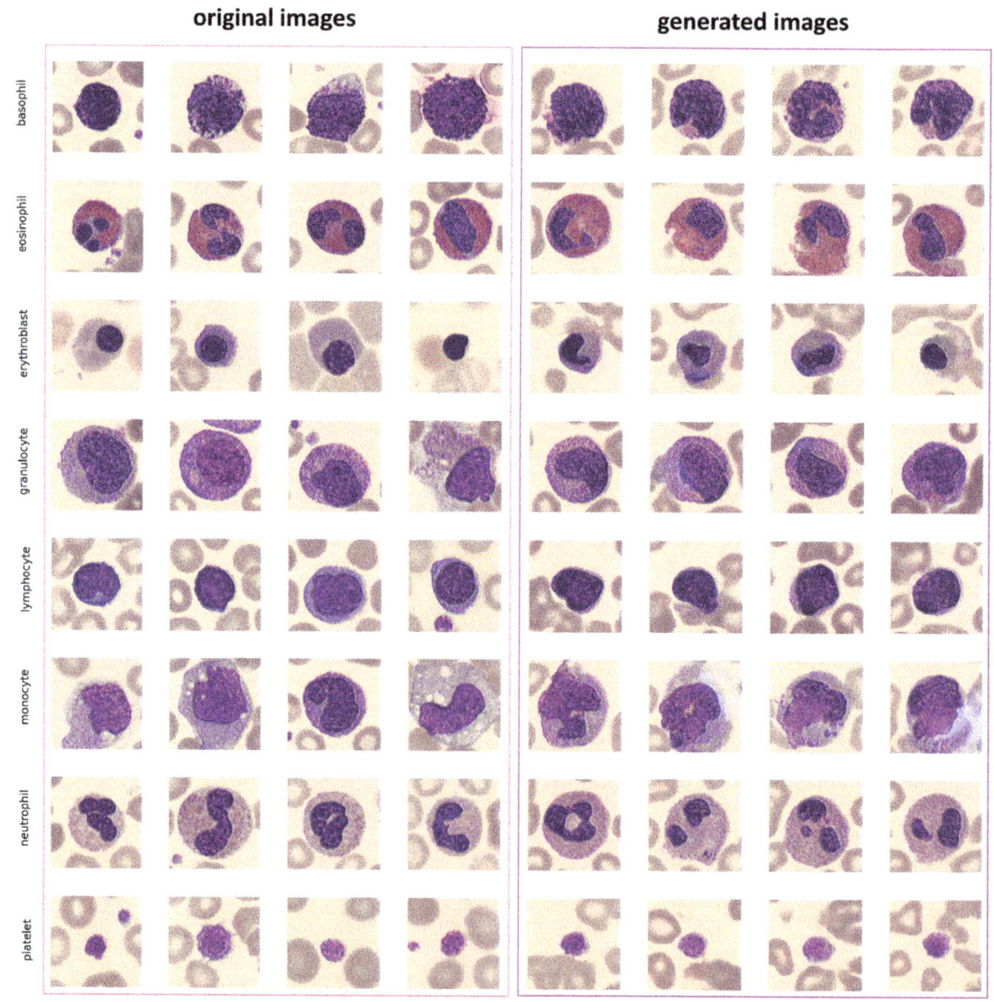

Figure 6. Visual comparison of peripheral blood cell classes: each row represents a distinct cell type (basophil, eosinophil, erythroblast, granulocyte, lymphocyte, monocyte, neutrophil, and platelet); the first four columns show real microscopic images, while the last four columns display corresponding synthetic images generated by the model. The colors in the images result from staining blood samples using methods applied in hematology.

3.3. Participation of Experts in Image Generation

In this study, various computation variants involving two to eight experts were analyzed. It was observed that, with a larger number of experts, three to four paths made a distinct contribution. Therefore, in the final version of peripheral blood cell generation, four experts were used within the Mixture-of-Experts framework. Figure S2 shows, in the form of a heatmap, the percentage contribution of the four experts to the image generation of each of the eight classes.

Based on the expert contribution data for BloodMNIST classification, several patterns may be observed. Expert 4 demonstrates the highest overall contribution and shows expertise in eosinophil (66.0%) and neutrophil (63.6%) classification. This expert also contributes significantly to platelet (52.9%) and lymphocyte (51.2%) identification, suggesting broad competency across multiple cell types. Expert 2 exhibits a more focused specialization profile, with exceptional performance in monocyte classification (61.9%) and granulocyte identification (42.3%). However, this expert shows notably lower contributions to platelet (2.7%) and erythroblast (3.4%) classification. Expert 3 demonstrates intermediate performance, with strengths in granulocyte classification (55.6%) and erythroblast identification (34.9%). This expert maintains relatively consistent contributions across most cell types. Expert 1 shows the most balanced distribution pattern but with a generally lower overall contribution, suggesting a more conservative approach to annotation.

It is also worth focusing on observations for individual classes. Monocyte classification shows extreme expert specialization, with Expert 2 providing 61.9% of the annotations while other experts contribute minimally (2.9–28.4%), suggesting this cell type may require specific expertise. Eosinophil classification is heavily dominated by Expert 4 (66.0%), with Expert 1 providing secondary support (22.5%), indicating potential morphological complexity.

3.4. Final Evaluation of Image Generation

The experiments used a classification model based on the ResNet50 architecture, applied to the BloodMNIST dataset, containing blood cell images divided into eight classes. The transfer learning approach was used; the model pre-trained on ImageNet was adapted to the medical task by modifying its final layer for multiclass classification. The CrossEntropyLoss function and the Adam optimizer with a learning step of 0.001 were used. The model was trained for 10 epochs, achieving an accuracy of 0.97 on the test set.

ResNet50 was also used to evaluate the synthetic data generated in the study. Accuracy, precision, sensitivity (recall), and the F1 measure were determined (Figure 7), obtaining a total accuracy of 0.97. The main classification errors concerned the granulocyte and lymphocyte classes, which are illustrated in the confusion matrix.

The confusion matrix demonstrates strong overall model performance, with most blood cell classes classified with perfect or near-perfect accuracy. Basophils, eosinophils, erythroblasts, neutrophils, and platelets were classified with 100% accuracy, suggesting that these classes are well represented in the feature space and are easily distinguishable by the model.

However, some degree of confusion is observed between morphologically and chromatically similar classes. For instance, granulocytes, while mostly classified correctly (101 instances), were occasionally misclassified as monocytes (12 instances) and lymphocytes (1 instance). Likewise, lymphocytes were misclassified as erythroblasts (2 instances) and monocytes (11 instances). Monocytes were predicted with high accuracy (129 correct), with only a single misclassification as a lymphocyte. These patterns indicate difficulty in distinguishing between granulocytes, monocytes, and lymphocytes—subtypes that are known to share overlapping visual and structural features.

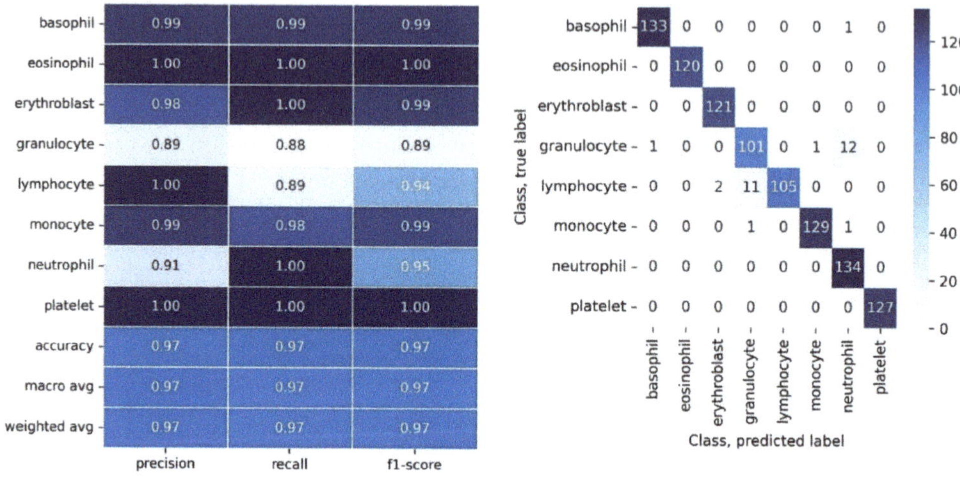

Figure 7. Classification model metrics for evaluating blood cell image generation, and the confusion matrix for the generated 1000 images from eight classes.

Importantly, this classification behavior aligns with previous observations on color distribution patterns. The confusion matrix analysis is consistent with the findings from UMAP projections and the distance matrix, which highlighted the chromatic proximity between immature granulocytes, neutrophils, and lymphocytes. Specifically, low inter-class color distances, such as the 0.080 distance in the red channel between granulocytes and neutrophils, point to the similarity in hue, which may contribute to the classifier's errors.

Additionally, immature granulocytes exhibit more color outliers, making them more likely to be misclassified as neighboring classes in the feature space, particularly neutrophils and lymphocytes. The presence of dark purple hues, confirmed via k-means clustering, in all three of these classes further complicates their differentiation. These overlapping chromatic features reinforce the observed classification challenges and ex-plain the localized confusion within the model's predictions.

In summary, while the model shows excellent performance overall, misclassifications tend to occur between classes with high visual and color similarity. This highlights the importance of chromatic information in distinguishing subtle differences between closely related cell types and underscores the challenges in synthetic image generation and classification for such categories.

The FID value calculated for the entire database is 52.09, and the average FID equals 102.07. The FID values for each individual class are given in Table 1.

In the next stage of evaluating the quality of the generated image dataset, the analysis focused on whether individual classes retained the required data diversity and whether the inter-class distances were appropriately reproduced. Figure S3 presents the mean distances calculated for pairs of objects within classes (intra-class distances), as well as for pairs across the eight classes (inter-class distances). To ensure consistency with the BloodMNIST database, 128 objects from each class were randomly selected for the calculations. The results, illustrating both the mean values and the variability using box plots, are presented separately for each of the R, G, and B channels.

Table 1. FID values for each class.

Class	FID
basophil	91.39
eosinophil	102.35
erythroblast	116.95
granulocyte	109.13
lymphocyte	104.18
monocyte	82.92
neutrophil	69.42
platelet	140.25

For the BloodMNIST dataset and intra-class analysis, the green channel (G) exhibits the highest variation within each class, followed by the red channel (R) and, finally, the blue channel (B), which shows the lowest variance. For inter-class analysis, the green channel (G) demonstrates a substantially greater ability to separate classes compared to the red (R) and blue (B) channels. Specifically, channel G provides the best class separability, while channel B exhibits poor inter-class distance, indicating limited utility for distinguishing between classes.

For the generated images, in the intra-class analysis, the ranking of variations among channels remains consistent with the real data. Channel B continues to display a low spread and a low median, indicating the tight clustering of values. The green channel maintains a wide spread similar to that observed in the real data, reflecting comparable within-class variations. In the inter-class analysis, the green channel once again shows the highest degree of class separation. Although there is a slight reduction in inter-class distances across all channels compared to the real data, the overall structure of class separability is preserved. As anticipated, channel B continues to provide poor separability between classes.

Spider plots (Figure S4) show the mean intra-class distance per class for each channel, represented by the lines for R, G, and B. The overall shape of the radar plots for both the real and generated data is quite similar, indicating that the class-specific consistency is preserved to some extent in the generated images. Regarding the magnitude of the distances, in most classes, channel B consistently shows lower intra-class distances in both the real and generated datasets, likely due to the inherently low variance in the blue channel. Conversely, channel G remains dominant in both cases, exhibiting the highest intra-class distances, which are well preserved in the generated data. The values in the generated dataset are slightly lower in some instances, suggesting the tighter clustering of data points, which may reflect a tendency toward over-regularization.

To conclude, the generated images successfully preserve the internal structure of the dataset. Specifically, they maintain class compactness in intra-class distributions and retain class separability in inter-class distributions.

4. Discussion

The research presented in this work proposes a novel strategy for synthetic biomedical image generation that leverages the discriminative potential of RGB color channels, particularly in the context of stained peripheral blood cells. The effectiveness of the approach stems from the integration of preliminary color analysis into model design and loss function formulation. In this section, we discuss the relevance and implications of the findings, analyze the observed phenomena, and identify limitations and directions for future research.

4.1. Contribution of Color Channels to Class Discrimination

The analysis of RGB histograms, UMAP projections, and inter-class distance matrices revealed that the red and green channels provided more important information for distinguishing blood cell types than the blue channel. This is due to the histological nature of the staining in BloodMNIST, where eosin and basic dyes impart pink–purple hues to the images with a dominant red component. Based on this, it was decided to exclude the blue channel from the histogram generator loss function, which simplified the model without losing key information.

This approach shows that selective color analysis based on biological interpretability can effectively support the optimization of generative models. It also highlights the importance of pre-color profiling in biomedical contexts, where subtle visual differences have high diagnostic significance.

4.2. Misclassification Patterns and Biological Justification

The classification errors mainly concerned classes with similar morphology and similar staining features, such as immature granulocytes, neutrophils, and lymphocytes. Their visual similarities, confirmed by histogram and UMAP cluster analysis, led to difficulties in the classifier's discrimination, e.g., a low Spearman distance in the red channel between immature granulocytes and neutrophils.

This phenomenon highlights the biological justification of the errors—the boundaries between some cell classes are naturally blurred. Color, although important, is not always sufficient for effective class discrimination. Therefore, morphological information from microscopic images was also included in the generation process to better represent the structure of blood cells.

4.3. Ablation Study

This paper analyzes the effectiveness of three variants of the cGAN architecture in generating synthetic blood cell images. The first variant was based on standard convolutional layers, the second additionally included residual blocks, and the third used the Mixture-of-Experts (MoE) architecture. For each approach, three versions of the generator loss function were tested: without taking into account color histograms, with histograms of the red and green channels, and with a full RGB histogram.

Table 2 presents detailed metric results for each combination of architecture and loss function. It includes, among others, classification accuracy using the model trained on the BloodMNIST dataset, the FID index value, and other quality measures of the generated images. The data from the table clearly indicate that the best results, including a classification accuracy of 0.97 and low FID, were achieved for the MoE cGAN variant with a loss function taking into account the histograms of the red and green channels.

Ablation experiments showed that both increasing the complexity of the architecture and introducing a directed loss function significantly improve image quality. The MoE model proved to be particularly effective due to the specialization of experts, which allowed for better capturing class-specific morphological features. Moreover, selectively including only two channels (red and green) outperformed both the variant without histograms and the one with full RGB; including the blue channel introduced additional noise, which worsened the performance. These results emphasize the importance of biologically justified feature selection in the design of loss functions for generative models.

Table 2. Comparison of the values of the metrics obtained during the generation of images using three various strategies.

Nr	NN Architecture	Color Histograms	Accuracy	FID for the Entire Generated Set	FID Averaged for Individual Classes
1	cGAN	Not used	0.89	74.5	137.0
2		Red, Green	0.87	76.3	138.7
3		Red, Green, Blue	0.91	91.1	149.5
4	cGAN with residual blocks	Not used	0.90	57.1	112.2
5		Red, Green	0.93	66.4	123.8
6		Red, Green, Blue	0.87	71.3	132.5
7	Mixture-of-Experts cGAN	Not used	0.92	50.4	98.4
8		**Red, Green** [1]	**0.97**	**52.1**	**102.1**
9		Red, Green, Blue	0.86	50.0	101.7

[1] The best result obtained using the MoE-cGAN algorithm.

4.4. Comparison with Other Works

Various works present alternative approaches to generating additional histopathological images of peripheral blood cells as an extension of the BloodMNIST database [42–47]. All the strategies described differ significantly from our proposal, as they use images with a much lower resolution, the lowest of those offered by MedMNIST. After preprocessing, they have dimensions of $3 \times 28 \times 28$ or $3 \times 32 \times 32$ pixels. Our generation approach, on the other hand, uses images with a resolution of $3 \times 128 \times 128$. Additionally, none of the articles mentioned provide the quality of generation for individual classes, only for the entire database.

The study [42] introduced a novel method, AE-COT-GAN, for medical image generation using GANs that effectively mitigates mode collapse by leveraging an autoencoder and extended semi-discrete optimal transport (SDOT) to transform distributions in the latent space. In extensive experiments on the BloodMNIST database, a FID value of 12.42 and accuracy of 0.97 was obtained.

In [44], DM-GAN was presented, i.e., a multi-generator GAN architecture designed to address intra-class imbalance and isolated samples in medical image datasets by enhancing the sample diversity and quality. Through the integration of self-attention mechanisms and a novel generator loss combining mode-seeking and mutual exclusion terms, the model proved to be a useful tool for image generation. The best accuracy in peripheral blood cell classification of 0.93 was obtained using the DenseNet201 architecture.

The study [45] introduced LEGAN, a GAN-based approach that addresses intra-class imbalance by using the local outlier factor LOF to detect sparse regions and applying affine transformations to enhance the sample diversity before training. Additionally, a decentralization constraint based on information entropy guided the generator toward producing more diverse samples, resulting in improved image quality and classification performance across multiple medical imaging datasets. For the BloodMNIST dataset, a FID of 10.8 was obtained and an accuracy of ca. 0.93 for the augmented samples.

A novel generative model, HD-PAN, based on Hölder divergence for semi-supervised disease classification using positive and unlabeled medical images, addressing the challenges of limited annotated data was proposed in [47]. Extensive experiments on benchmark datasets demonstrated that the method outperforms KL divergence-based approaches, achieving state-of-the-art results in medical image-assisted diagnosis. Taking the BloodMNIST dataset as an example, the accuracy rate reached 0.84, while the F1-score was 0.82.

The paper [43] introduced BDGAN, a generative model designed to improve medical image classification under data imbalance by enhancing both class boundary learning and intra-class diversity through a multi-generator architecture and specialized loss functions. Experiments on real-world datasets confirmed that BDGAN generates high-quality, diverse samples, leading to significant improvements in classification performance. For the BloodMNIST dataset, an accuracy of 0.94 was obtained for the generated samples.

The study [46] addressed the challenge of intra-class data imbalance in medical imaging by proposing a two-step GAN-based augmentation method guided by the Cluster-Based Local Outlier Factor (CBLOF) algorithm to distinguish sparse and dense samples. The GAN was trained to focus on sparse regions, and a one-class SVM was applied post-generation to filter out noisy samples. The experimental results on four medical datasets showed that the proposed method significantly enhances sample diversity and quality, leading to an approximate 3% improvement in classification accuracy. On the BloodMNIST dataset, the model achieved an average accuracy of 0.92 and a Fréchet Inception Distance (FID) of 10.6.

All described algorithms and results obtained apply to very low-resolution images.

4.5. Limitations and Future Works

The proposed framework effectively generates synthetic biomedical images, but there is room for improvement. The integration of spatial attention or segmentation mechanisms could better preserve important morphological details. Future works could include adaptive color normalization and domain adaptation to improve the robustness of different staining protocols.

In the Mixture-of-Experts architecture, dynamic routing or expert pruning is worth considering in order to reduce the computational burden. Multimodal feature conditioning (color, shape, and texture) would capture complex biomedical features and self-supervised targets could increase the realism of the data without the need for intensive supervision. Such extensions would increase the utility of the method in various clinical contexts.

5. Conclusions

The aim of the work was to check whether the analysis of colors in histological images and their inclusion in modeling can improve the quality of the generated images of missing data. The research was carried out on images of eight classes of peripheral blood cells, which showed similarities in color and shape. No segmentation or other preprocessing techniques were used in the work; the images were used in their original form.

A novel element was the detailed examination of the role of the R, G, and B components, including their histograms, in class differentiation. The analysis using the k-means and UMAP methods showed that the red and green components distinguished classes better than the blue channel. Therefore, only the R and G channels were used in the generator loss function, which turned out to be crucial for improving the quality of generation.

A new strategy based on cGAN with the MoE (Mixture of Experts) mechanism was introduced, where the gate network dynamically selects the best expert to generate the image. The inclusion of R and G histograms in the loss function significantly improved the color and texture reproduction, increasing the realism of images and the classification accuracy (up to 0.97). The applied approach reduced the problem of mode collapse, increased the diversity of synthetic data, and enabled its effective use as support in the conditions of limited or imbalanced real data.

The quality of the generated data was further validated by analyzing intra- and inter-class distances, which showed that the synthetic images preserved the structural characteristics of the original dataset. The green channel consistently demonstrated the highest variation and class separability, while the blue channel remained the least informative. The generated images reflected similar patterns to real data, confirming their realism and structural fidelity.

In summary, the study shows that targeted color analysis and the integration of expert knowledge in the cGAN-MoE architecture allows to create high-quality synthetic medical data. The proposed method can be applied in various dataset augmentation projects, provided that the color characteristics of a given set are previously analyzed.

Supplementary Materials: The following supporting information can be downloaded at https://www.mdpi.com/article/10.3390/electronics14142773/s1: Figure S1: Metrics recorded during image generation; Figure S2: Expert contribution heatmap for BloodMNIST dataset—percentage distribution by class; Figure S3: The mean distances calculated for pairs of objects within classes (intra-class distances) as well as for pairs across the eight classes (inter-class distances), for BloodMNIST dataset and generated images; Figure S4: Mean intra-class distances per class for the R, G, and B channels in the BloodMNIST dataset and the generated images; Table S1: Characteristics of the BloodMNIST database classes; Table S2: Hardware and software specifications.

Author Contributions: P.K.: Conceptualization; Methodology; Data curation; Formal analysis; Funding acquisition; Investigation; Software; Resources; Visualization; Project administration; Writing—original draft. F.C.: Conceptualization; Methodology. M.J.: Conceptualization; Methodology; Formal analysis; Investigation; Software; Supervision; Validation; Writing—original draft. All authors have read and agreed to the published version of the manuscript.

Funding: This research project was supported by the program "Excellence initiative—research university" at the AGH University of Krakow.

Data Availability Statement: The authors used publicly available data in this manuscript. Information on the availability of the dataset is provided in the paper. The algorithms implemented in Python are available on the GitHub platform at https://github.com/pwkwiek/blood (accessed on 7 July 2025).

Conflicts of Interest: The authors declare no conflicts of interest.

References

1. Asif, S.; Wenhui, Y.; Ur-Rehman, S.; Ul-ain, Q.; Amjad, K.; Yueyang, Y.; Jinhai, S.; Awais, M. Advancements and Prospects of Machine Learning in Medical Diagnostics: Unveiling the Future of Diagnostic Precision. *Arch. Comput. Methods Eng.* **2024**, *32*, 853–883. [CrossRef]
2. Ramírez, J.G.C.; Islam, M.M.; Even, A.I.H. Machine Learning Applications in Healthcare: Current Trends and Future Prospects. *J. Artif. Intell. Gen. Sci.* **2024**, *1*, 1–12.
3. Chen, X. AI in Healthcare: Revolutionizing Diagnosis and Treatment through Machine Learning. *MZ J. Artif. Intell.* **2024**, *1*, 1–18.
4. Afkanpour, M.; Hosseinzadeh, E.; Tabesh, H. Identify the Most Appropriate Imputation Method for Handling Missing Values in Clinical Structured Datasets: A Systematic Review. *BMC Med. Res. Methodol.* **2024**, *24*, 188. [CrossRef]
5. Dekermanjian, J.P.; Shaddox, E.; Nandy, D.; Ghosh, D.; Kechris, K. Mechanism-Aware Imputation: A Two-Step Approach in Handling Missing Values in Metabolomics. *BMC Bioinform.* **2022**, *23*, 179. [CrossRef]
6. Garcea, F.; Serra, A.; Lamberti, F.; Morra, L. Data Augmentation for Medical Imaging: A Systematic Literature Review. *Comput. Biol. Med.* **2023**, *152*, 106391. [CrossRef]
7. Islam, T.; Hafiz, M.S.; Jim, J.R.; Kabir, M.M.; Mridha, M.F. A Systematic Review of Deep Learning Data Augmentation in Medical Imaging: Recent Advances and Future Research Directions. *Healthc. Anal.* **2024**, *5*, 100340. [CrossRef]
8. Saxena, D.; Cao, J. Generative Adversarial Networks (GANs). *ACM Comput. Surv.* **2021**, *54*, 63. [CrossRef]
9. Wang, Z.; She, Q.; Ward, T.E. Generative Adversarial Networks in Computer Vision: A Survey and Taxonomy. *ACM Comput. Surv.* **2021**, *54*, 37. [CrossRef]

10. Kazerouni, A.; Aghdam, E.K.; Heidari, M.; Azad, R.; Fayyaz, M.; Hacihaliloglu, I.; Merhof, D. Diffusion Models in Medic Imaging: A Comprehensive Survey. *Med. Image Anal.* **2023**, *88*, 102846. [CrossRef]
11. Rguibi, Z.; Hajami, A.; Zitouni, D.; Elqaraoui, A.; Zourane, R.; Bouajaj, Z. Improving Medical Imaging with Medical Variati Diffusion Model: An Analysis and Evaluation. *J. Imaging* **2023**, *9*, 171. [CrossRef] [PubMed]
12. Al-Azzam, N.; Shatnawi, I. Comparing Supervised and Semi-Supervised Machine Learning Models on Diagnosing Breast Canc *Ann. Med. Surg.* **2021**, *62*, 53–64. [CrossRef] [PubMed]
13. Yang, X.; Song, Z.; King, I.; Xu, Z. A Survey on Deep Semi-Supervised Learning. *IEEE Trans. Knowl. Data Eng.* **2023**, *35*, 8934–895 [CrossRef]
14. Yang, J.; Shi, R.; Wei, D.; Liu, Z.; Zhao, L.; Ke, B.; Pfister, H.; Ni, B. MedMNIST v2—A Large-Scale Lightweight Benchmark for 2 and 3D Biomedical Image Classification. *Sci. Data* **2023**, *10*, 41. [CrossRef]
15. Sinaga, K.P.; Yang, M.S. Unsupervised K-Means Clustering Algorithm. *IEEE Access* **2020**, *8*, 80716–80727. [CrossRef]
16. McInnes, L.; Healy, J.; Saul, N.; Großberger, L. UMAP: Uniform Manifold Approximation and Projection. *J. Open Source Soft* **2018**, *3*, 861. [CrossRef]
17. Mittal, M.; Praveen Gujjar, J.; Guru Prasad, M.S.; Devadas, R.M.; Ambreen, L.; Kumar, V. Dimensionality Reduction Using UMA and TSNE Technique. In Proceedings of the 2nd IEEE International Conference on Advances in Information Technology, ICA 2024, Chikkamagaluru, Karnataka, India, 24–27 July 2024; Volume 1, pp. 1–5. [CrossRef]
18. Chattamvelli, R. Rank Correlation. In *Correlation in Engineering and the Applied Sciences. Synthesis Lectures on Mathematics Statistics*; Springer: Berlin/Heidelberg, Germany, 2024; pp. 77–106.
19. Shen, S.; Jin, S.; Li, F.; Zhao, J. Optical Coherence Tomography Parameters as Prognostic Factors for Stereopsis after Vitrectom for Unilateral Epiretinal Membrane: A Cohort Study. *Sci. Rep.* **2024**, *14*, 6715. [CrossRef]
20. Benčević, M.; Habijan, M.; Galić, I.; Babin, D.; Pižurica, A. Understanding Skin Color Bias in Deep Learning-Based Skin Lesio Segmentation. *Comput. Methods Programs Biomed.* **2024**, *245*, 108044. [CrossRef]
21. Kim, H.; Ryu, S.M.; Keum, J.S.; Oh, S.I.; Kim, K.N.; Shin, Y.H.; Jeon, I.H.; Koh, K.H. Clinical Validation of Enhanced CT Imagin for Distal Radius Fractures through Conditional Generative Adversarial Networks (CGAN). *PLoS ONE* **2024**, *19*, e030834 [CrossRef]
22. Deabes, W.; Abdel-Hakim, A.E. CGAN-ECT: Reconstruction of Electrical Capacitance Tomography Images from Capacitanc Measurements Using Conditional Generative Adversarial Networks. *Flow Meas. Instrum.* **2024**, *96*, 102566. [CrossRef]
23. Campbell, J.N.A.; Dais Ferreira, M.; Isenor, A.W. Generation of Vessel Track Characteristics Using a Conditional Generativ Adversarial Network (CGAN). *Appl. Artif. Intell.* **2024**, *38*, e2360283. [CrossRef]
24. Yang, H.; Hu, Y.; He, S.; Xu, T.; Yuan, J.; Gu, X. Applying Conditional Generative Adversarial Networks for Imaging Diagnosis. I Proceedings of the 2024 IEEE 6th International Conference on Power, Intelligent Computing and Systems, ICPICS 2024, Shenyan China, 26–28 July 2024; pp. 1717–1722.
25. Skandarani, Y.; Jodoin, P.M.; Lalande, A. GANs for Medical Image Synthesis: An Empirical Study. *J. Imaging* **2023**, *9*, 69. [CrossRef [PubMed]
26. Zhang, Z.; Li, Y.; Shin, B.S. Robust Medical Image Colorization with Spatial Mask-Guided Generative Adversarial Networ *Bioengineering* **2022**, *9*, 721. [CrossRef] [PubMed]
27. Sun, Y. The Role of Activation Function in Image Classification. In Proceedings of the 2021 IEEE 3rd International Conference o Communications, Information System and Computer Engineering, CISCE 2021, Beijing, China, 14–16 May 2021; pp. 275–278.
28. Lakhdari, K.; Saeed, N. A New Vision of a Simple 1D Convolutional Neural Networks (1D-CNN) with Leaky-ReLU Function fo ECG Abnormalities Classification. *Intell. Based Med.* **2022**, *6*, 100080. [CrossRef]
29. Cormen, T.H.; Leiserson, C.E.; Rivest, R.L.; Stein, C. *Introduction to Algorithms*, 3rd ed.; MIT Press: Cambridge, MA, USA, 2009.
30. Zhang, Q.; Huang, N.; Yao, L.; Zhang, D.; Shan, C.; Han, J. RGB-T Salient Object Detection via Fusing Multi-Level CNN Features *IEEE Trans. Image Process.* **2020**, *29*, 3321–3335. [CrossRef]
31. Tang, H.; Li, Z.; Zhang, D.; He, S.; Tang, J. Divide-and-Conquer: Confluent Triple-Flow Network for RGB-T Salient Objec Detection. *IEEE Trans. Pattern Anal. Mach. Intell.* **2024**, *47*, 1958–1974. [CrossRef]
32. Gan, W.; Ning, Z.; Qi, Z.; Yu, P.S. Mixture of Experts (MoE): A Big Data Perspective. *arXiv* **2025**, arXiv:2501.16352.
33. Zhao, C.; Du, H.; Niyato, D.; Kang, J.; Xiong, Z.; Kim, D.I.; Shen, X.S.; Letaief, K.B. Enhancing Physical Layer Communicatio Security through Generative AI with Mixture of Experts. *IEEE Wirel. Commun.* **2025**, *32*, 176–184. [CrossRef]
34. Rubner, Y.; Tomasi, C.; Guibas, L.J. Earth Mover's Distance as a Metric for Image Retrieval. *Int. J. Comput. Vis.* **2000**, *40*, 99–121 [CrossRef]
35. Mi, J.; Ma, C.; Zheng, L.; Zhang, M.; Li, M.; Wang, M. WGAN-CL: A Wasserstein GAN with Confidence Loss for Small-Sample Augmentation. *Expert. Syst. Appl.* **2023**, *233*, 120943. [CrossRef]

. Bobadilla, J.; Gutiérrez, A. Wasserstein GAN-Based Architecture to Generate Collaborative Filtering Synthetic Datasets. *Appl. Intell.* **2024**, *54*, 2472–2490. [CrossRef]

. Ngasa, E.E.; Jang, M.A.; Tarimo, S.A.; Woo, J.; Shin, H.B. Diffusion-Based Wasserstein Generative Adversarial Network for Blood Cell Image Augmentation. *Eng. Appl. Artif. Intell.* **2024**, *133*, 108221. [CrossRef]

. Anaya-Sánchez, H.; Altamirano-Robles, L.; Díaz-Hernández, R.; Zapotecas-Martínez, S. WGAN-GP for Synthetic Retinal Image Generation: Enhancing Sensor-Based Medical Imaging for Classification Models. *Sensors* **2025**, *25*, 167. [CrossRef] [PubMed]

. Lawrence, P.; Brown, C. Comparing Human-Level and Machine Learning Model Performance in White Blood Cell Morphology Assessment. *Eur. J. Haematol.* **2024**, *114*, 115–119. [CrossRef]

. Constantinescu, A.E.; Bull, C.J.; Jones, N.; Mitchell, R.; Burrows, K.; Dimou, N.; Bézieau, S.; Brenner, H.; Buchanan, D.D.; D'Amato, M.; et al. Circulating White Blood Cell Traits and Colorectal Cancer Risk: A Mendelian Randomisation Study. *Int. J. Cancer* **2024**, *154*, 94–103. [CrossRef]

1. Ozga, M.; Nicolet, D.; Mrózek, K.; Walker, C.J.; Blachly, J.S.; Kohlschmidt, J.; Orwick, S.; Carroll, A.J.; Larson, R.A.; Kolitz, J.E.; et al. White Blood Cell Count Levels Are Associated with Inflammatory Response and Constitute Independent Outcome Predictors in Adult Patients with Acute Myeloid Leukemia Aged <60 Years. *Am. J. Hematol.* **2024**, *99*, 2236–2240. [CrossRef]

2. Wang, J.; Lei, B.; Ding, L.; Xu, X.; Gu, X.; Zhang, M. Autoencoder-Based Conditional Optimal Transport Generative Adversarial Network for Medical Image Generation. *Vis. Inform.* **2024**, *8*, 15–25. [CrossRef]

3. Ding, H.; Tao, Q.; Huang, N. BDGAN: Boundary and Diversity-Aware Generative Adversarial Network for Imbalanced Medical Image Augmentation. In Proceedings of the ICASSP 2025—2025 IEEE International Conference on Acoustics, Speech and Signal Processing, Hyderabad, India, 6–11 April 2025; Institute of Electrical and Electronics Engineers Inc.: Piscataway, NJ, USA, 2025.

4. Ding, H.; Zhang, K.; Huang, N. DM-GAN: A Data Augmentation-Based Approach for Imbalanced Medical Image Classification. In Proceedings of the 2024 IEEE International Conference on Bioinformatics and Biomedicine, BIBM 2024, Lisbon, Portugal, 3–6 December 2024; Institute of Electrical and Electronics Engineers Inc.: Piscataway, NJ, USA, 2024; pp. 3160–3165.

5. Ding, H.; Huang, N.; Wu, Y.; Cui, X. LEGAN: Addressing Intraclass Imbalance in GAN-Based Medical Image Augmentation for Improved Imbalanced Data Classification. *IEEE Trans. Instrum. Meas.* **2024**, *73*, 2517914. [CrossRef]

6. Ding, H.; Huang, N.; Wu, Y.; Cui, X. Improving Imbalanced Medical Image Classification through GAN-Based Data Augmentation Methods. *Pattern Recognit.* **2025**, *166*, 111680. [CrossRef]

7. Zhang, Y.; Li, C.; Liu, Z.; Li, M. Semi-Supervised Disease Classification Based on Limited Medical Image Data. *IEEE J. Biomed. Health Inform.* **2024**, *28*, 1575–1586. [CrossRef]

electronics

Article

Wavelet-Based Fusion for Image Steganography Using Deep Convolutional Neural Networks

Amal Khalifa * and Yashi Yadav

Computer Science Department, Purdue University Fort Wayne, Fort Wayne, IN 46805, USA; yaday01@pfw.edu
* Correspondence: khalifaa@pfw.edu

Abstract: Steganography has long served as a powerful tool for covert communication, particularly through image-based techniques that embed secret information within innocuous cover images. With the increasing adoption of deep learning, researchers have sought more secure and efficient methods for image steganography. This study builds upon and extends the *DeepWaveletFusion* approach by integrating convolutional neural networks (CNNs) with the discrete wavelet transform (DWT) to enhance both embedding and recovery performance. The proposed method, *DeepWaveletFusionToo,* is a lightweight architecture that employs a custom-built DWT image dataset and leverages the mean squared error (MSE) loss function during training, significantly reducing model complexity and computational cost. Experimental results demonstrate that *DeepWaveletFusionToo* achieves improved imperceptibility compared to its predecessor and delivers competitive recovery accuracy over existing deep learning-based steganographic techniques, establishing its simplicity and effectiveness.

Keywords: deep learning; hiding; extraction; covert communication; convolutional neural network; image; discrete wavelet transform

1. Introduction

The practice of concealing messages within seemingly innocuous carriers has been used for centuries. One of the earliest recorded examples of steganography appears in Herodotus' account, where a message was tattooed on a slave's scalp, illustrating the crucial role of covert communication in warfare and espionage [1]. During the Renaissance, Italian scientist Giovanni Battista Porta described various methods of secret writing, including the use of invisible ink made from natural substances like lemon juice, which revealed messages when heated. Similarly, during the American Revolutionary War, spies employed mask letters, in which seemingly ordinary correspondence contained hidden messages that could only be deciphered using a special cut-out overlay.

In modern times, digital steganography has become increasingly sophisticated. Information can now be embedded within digital images, audio files, network protocols, and even DNA sequences, making it a vital tool for cybersecurity and covert communication [2]. One of the most widely used methods involves manipulating the least significant bits (LSBs) of an image's pixel values to hide secret data. These modifications have minimal impact on the image's visual appearance, allowing hidden messages to remain imperceptible to the human eye while still being retrievable with the right tools [3]. Beyond LSB-based techniques, image steganography also utilizes transform domain methods, embedding secret data within the coefficients of mathematical transformations such as the Fourier transform (FT) [4], the discrete cosine transform (DCT) [5], and the discrete wavelet transform (DWT) [6]. Some methods combine more than one transform to provide better imperceptibility and higher hiding capacity [7,8].

As traditional steganographic techniques rely on predefined rules for embedding data, deep learning-based approaches leverage neural networks to automatically learn optimal embedding and extraction strategies. These methods ensure minimal visual distortion while maximizing retrieval accuracy. Autoencoders, generative adversarial networks (GANs), and convolutional neural networks (CNNs) are widely used in this domain, enabling the creation of realistic images that inherently conceal hidden information, making detection by conventional steganalysis tools significantly more challenging.

One of the pioneering methods in deep learning-based steganography was introduced in [9], where three individual CNNs—preparatory, hiding, and reveal networks—were trained together as a cohesive unit. To enhance robustness against steganalysis, the authors incorporated a noise layer to prevent secret data from being embedded in the least significant bits (LSBs) of the cover image's pixels. However, while this improved security, it also impacted the imperceptibility of the hiding process. Additionally, input images were normalized using the mean and standard deviation values computed from the ImageNet dataset. To address these limitations, the authors of [10] proposed modifications, including removing the noise layer and decoupling the network from dataset dependency by skipping the normalization and denormalization steps. Furthermore, instead of using a standard loss function, they introduced a gain function that combined multiple image quality measures to guide the learning process. These improvements enhanced both the imperceptibility and the recoverability of the steganographic process, making it more effective for real-world applications.

The authors in [11] introduced a two-channel CNN to learn the mapping between the secret image and the cover image. This two-channel scheme applies different embedding strengths to preserve the original pixel information of the cover image in Channel 1, ensuring that the generated hidden image closely resembles the cover image. Meanwhile, Channel 2 extracts and retains high-level feature information from the secret image, minimizing its impact on the visual integrity of the hidden image. Following a similar approach, the authors in [12] proposed an improved fully convolutional DenseNet (FC-DenseNet) architecture, where the cost function was optimized using artificial intelligence. Their experiments demonstrated high hiding capacity as well as robustness against JPEG compression, making it a significant advancement in deep learning-based steganography.

Another CNN-based steganographic method introduced a preprocessing module to merge features extracted from both the cover image and the secret image [13]. This fused representation was then passed into the embedding network to generate the stego-image, while a corresponding extraction network was used to retrieve the secret image. The authors designed a customized loss function to balance the tradeoff between embedding loss (for the embedding network) and extraction loss (for the extraction network), thereby improving overall performance. The SteganoCNN [14], on the other hand, successfully leveraged CNNs to hide two secret images within a single cover image, achieving an impressive payload capacity of 47.92 bits per pixel.

As recent advances in deep learning have significantly increased the hiding capacity of steganographic techniques, many of these methods embed secret data directly into pixel values, making them susceptible to detection by modern steganalysis tools and thereby compromising the security of the hidden communication [15]. In this paper, we propose a novel deep learning-based steganographic method that leverages the discrete wavelet transform (DWT) of three-channel cover images to conceal three-channel secret images. This work builds upon and extends the approach introduced in [16], which presented *DeepWaveletFusion*—a steganographic method that trains a convolutional neural network

(CNN) to merge the DWT sub-bands of the cover and secret images into a single fused output. Rather than minimizing pixel-wise differences, *DeepWaveletFusion* employed a gain function from [10] to maximize the structural similarity between the fused image and the original cover image. Our proposed method, *DeepWaveletFusionToo*, introduces two key advancements. First, it trains the model on a custom-preprocessed dataset, where publicly available image datasets are transformed into their DWT representations. This allows the model to operate directly in the frequency domain. This allows the model to be optimized using the mean squared error (MSE) loss function. resulting in a significantly shorter training time compared to the model presented in [16]. Second, the architecture and training process are tailored to preserve both the imperceptibility and recoverability of the embedded content through a β parameter. The rest of the paper is organized as follows: Section 2 describes the proposed steganographic method, including an overview of the DWT and CNN, the network architecture, the training process, and the model hyperparameters. Section 3 presents the evaluation metrics and experimental results. Section 4 concludes the paper with a summary of findings and potential future directions.

2. The Proposed Method

The proposed steganographic method aims to utilize CNNs to merge the discrete wavelet transform (DWT) coefficients of both the cover and secret images into a single fused representation, ensuring that the resulting stego-image remains visually indistinguishable from the original cover. To achieve this, the CNN architecture was designed similarly to [10], where the hiding and revealing networks were trained together as a cohesive unit. However, unlike the approach presented in [10], the preparatory network was omitted. In addition, the input to the system consists of the DWT of the images. In other words, rather than training the model on raw RGB images, the input layers of both the hiding and revealing networks operate directly on the DWT-transformed representations of the images.

2.1. The Discrete Wavelet Transform

The one-dimensional discrete wavelet transform (DWT) is a mathematical technique that decomposes a signal into different frequency sub-bands using discrete, finite-sized wavelets. This decomposition allows for the efficient analysis of various frequency components within the signal. The DWT operates by passing the signal through a series of low-pass and high-pass filters, followed by down-sampling. The low-pass filter (L) preserves the low-frequency components, which represent the signal's coarse details, while the high-pass filter (H) retains the high-frequency components, capturing finer details and sharp variations. Down-sampling reduces the number of samples in the signal, effectively compressing it while preserving essential information. The inverse process, known as reconstruction, involves using synthesis filters to approximate the original signal from its frequency components. Due to its ability to efficiently capture both time and frequency information, the DWT is widely applied in signal processing, including image and audio compression, denoising, and feature extraction.

In the case of images, a two-dimensional discrete wavelet transform (2D DWT) is used to decompose an image into four frequency sub-bands, with the lowest frequency sub-band containing the most critical image information. As shown in Figure 1, the process begins by applying the 1D DWT to each row of the image, followed by applying the 1D DWT to each column of the resulting sub-bands. This results in four distinct sub-bands:

- LL (Low-Low)—Contains the lowest frequency components and represents the coarse approximation of the image.
- LH (Low-High)—Captures horizontal high-frequency details (edge information in horizontal directions).

- HL (High-Low)—Captures vertical high-frequency details (edge information in vertical directions).
- HH (High-High)—Contains diagonal high-frequency components, representing finer texture details.

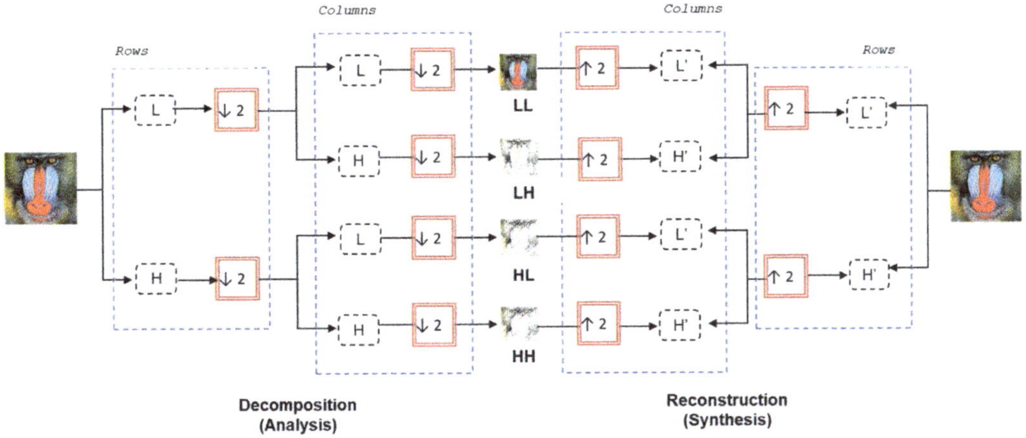

Figure 1. Analysis and synthesis of an image using two-dimensional wavelet transform.

For three-channel color images (such as RGB images), the DWT must be applied separately to each color channel to preserve color integrity. Despite the fact that the wavelet transform alters the dimensions of the image sub-bands, the total number of elements in the transformed representation remains equal to that of the original image, ensuring no loss of data during decomposition.

2.2. Convolutional Neural Networks

A convolutional neural network (CNN) is a type of deep learning model specifically designed for processing data with a grid-like structure, such as images. CNNs are widely used in computer vision, image recognition, natural language processing, and medical diagnostics due to their ability to automatically learn and extract features from input data. Figure 2 shows the key components of a CNN which consist of multiple layers [17]. First, convolutional layers apply a set of filters (kernels) to the input data to detect patterns such as edges, textures, and shapes. Each filter slides (or convolves) across the input, generating feature maps that highlight specific features. Pooling layers then reduce the spatial dimensions of feature maps while preserving important information. Common pooling methods include max pooling (selects the highest value in a region) and average pooling (computes the average of a region). The output of the convolutional and pooling layers is then passed to fully connected layers in order to flatten the extracted features and pass them through a dense neural network to produce the classification or prediction.

Training a CNN involves an iterative process where the model learns patterns and features from labeled data. This is performed through a combination of forward propagation, loss calculation, backpropagation, and weight updates. During forward propagation, an input image is passed through the CNN layers, which predict its output; then the model compares its predictions with the ground truth labels using a loss function, which measures how far off the predictions are [18]. To improve accuracy, CNNs adjust their weights using backpropagation and gradient descent. That is, the loss function is differentiated with respect to each weight using the chain rule and the gradient descent algorithm updates the weights of the network in the direction that minimizes loss. Instead of updating the weights after every sample, training data is split into mini batches to improve computational efficiency. In this research, the batch size refers to the number of cover/secret image pairs to be processed by the network at a given stage of the training process. Furthermore, CNNs typically require multiple epochs to converge to an optimal solution, where a single epoch is when the model has seen the entire dataset once.

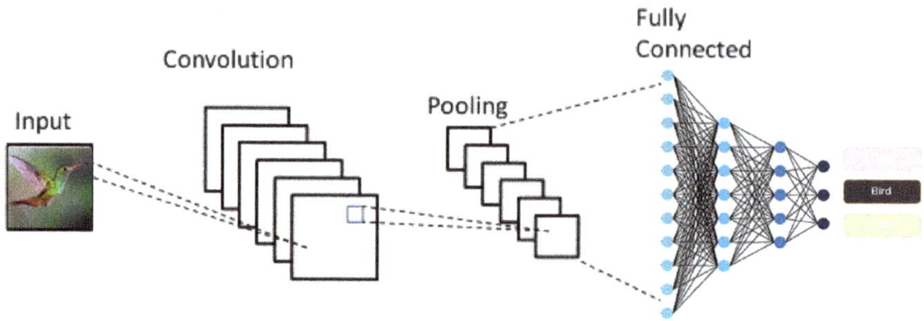

Figure 2. The basic structure of a convolutional neural network (CNN).

2.3. The Network Architecture

As shown in Figure 3, the network system consists of two separate CNNs that are connected back-to-back and trained as one cohesive unit. First, the hiding network takes two images that have undergone a discrete wavelet transform (DWT) preprocessing step. This transformation is performed using a custom DWT implementation that processes each color channel of the RGB image individually. That is, the DWT process converts each 256×256 channel into a $128 \times 128 \times 4$ representation for all three RGB channels and then stacks them along the last dimension, resulting in a tensor of shape $128 \times 128 \times 4 \times 3$. The input to the hiding network is then formed by concatenating these DWT representations along their last axis, creating a tensor with dimensions $128 \times 128 \times 4 \times 6$.

The hiding network itself consists of three parallel branches of convolutional layers: the 3×3 convolution branch, 4×4 convolution branch, and 5×5 convolution branch. Each branch consists of four sequential convolutional layers with 50 filters each, using ReLU activation functions and the 'same' padding. After these parallel processing branches, their outputs (each with dimensions $128 \times 128 \times 4 \times 50$) are concatenated along the channel axis to produce a tensor of shape $128 \times 128 \times 4 \times 150$. This concatenated output then feeds into three parallel final convolution layers with kernel sizes of 3×3, 4×4, and 5×5, each producing 50 feature maps. These outputs are again concatenated and passed through a final 1×1 convolution layer with 3 filters to produce the hiding network output with dimensions $128 \times 128 \times 4 \times 3$, matching the dimensions of the input DWT representation for one of the images.

The revealing network, on the other hand, follows an identical architectural pattern to the hiding network. It takes the output from the hiding network as input and processes it through the same structure of parallel convolution branches (3×3, 4×4, and 5×5), each with four sequential layers of 50 filters. The outputs are concatenated and processed through final convolution layers in the same manner as the hiding network, ultimately producing an output with dimensions $128 \times 128 \times 4 \times 3$. It is worth noting that this lightweight model is trained directly on the DWT coefficients, and both embedding and extraction occur entirely in the wavelet domain. That is, the use of inverse DWT (IDWT) becomes unnecessary for the operation of the model itself. However, a Lambda layer can be added to reconstruct the original image dimensions of $256 \times 256 \times 3$, for either the stego-image or the recovered secret image, respectively. This design decision simplifies the architecture and reduces computational overhead.

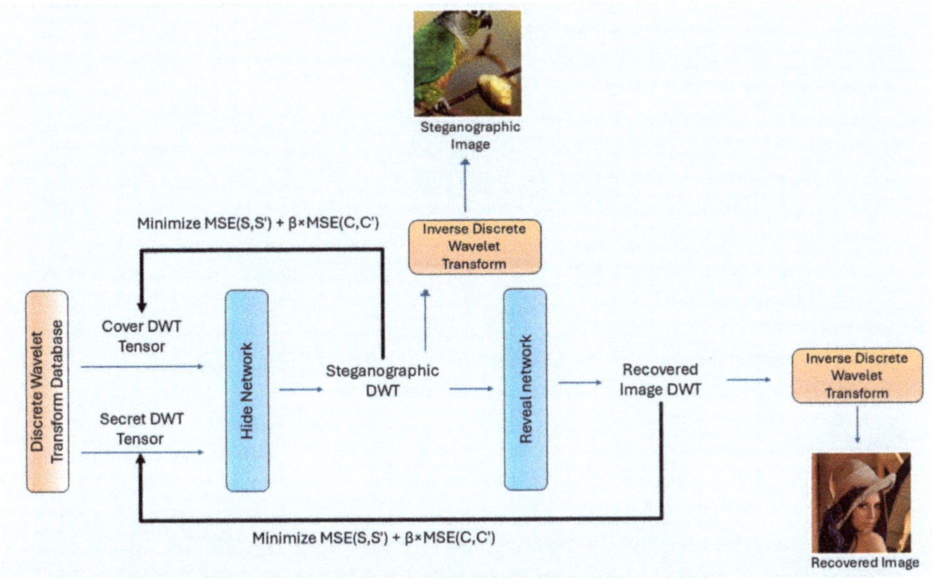

Figure 3. The hiding and revealing network system of the *DeepWaveletFusionToo* method.

The network is trained using the Adam optimizer with a specified learning rate and uses the mean squared error (*MSE*) as the loss function for both the hiding and revealing components [19]. The *MSE* can be computed using Equation (1), where m and n represent the dimensions of the images' DWT tensors, $I(i,j)$ and $I'(i,j)$ represent two corresponding coefficient values at (i,j) in the original and the distorted image, respectively.

$$MSE = \frac{\sum_{i=1}^{m} \sum_{j=1}^{n} (I(i,j) - I'(i,j))^2}{m * n} \quad (1)$$

Using the mean squared error (*MSE*) as the loss function represents a notable improvement over the predecessor method, *DeepWaveletFusion*, presented in [16]. In that earlier work, the model relied on a gain function that combined the *PSNR* and *SSIM* to update network weights. This approach required both the stego-image and the recovered image to undergo an inverse DWT in order to reconstruct their spatial-domain representations, which were then used to compute the gain function based on pixel-level comparisons. This inverse transformation introduced a significant bottleneck during training, despite the method's strong performance in hiding and extraction tasks.

In contrast, the proposed method eliminates the need for inverse DWT by computing the loss directly between the DWT coefficients of the input and output layers. This not only simplifies the architecture but also results in significantly faster training times. Additionally, the model introduces a β parameter to balance the loss between the hiding and revealing networks during training, which further enhances the retrieval performance.

2.4. Model Training

The *DeepWaveletFusionToo* method was coded using Python TensorFlow 2.12.0 and executed on the Google Colaboratory cloud environment. To accelerate the training process, the Pro+ version of Colab was used, which enabled the use of an NVIDIA A100 within a high-RAM runtime environment. The model uses TensorFlow-compatible implementations of the DWT and IDWT layers (TensorFlow-wavelets) where the computations are optimized to run on GPUs and TPUs for better performance.

Since both the embedding and extraction processes occur entirely in the wavelet domain, the model is trained not on raw RGB images, but on their DWT-transformed representations. Therefore, we had to build our own DWT image dataset. More specifically, two publicly available datasets were sourced: Linnaeus 5 [20] and Imagenette [21]. Both datasets have a total of 15,469 images representing different types of objects. The images were resized to 256 × 256 pixels before being passed to the DWT preprocessing step, which then converted them into tensors of shape 128 × 128 × 4 × 3 [22].

During the training process, the model utilizes a custom data generator that randomly loads pre-processed DWT batches from the database, with pairs of cover/secret DWT used to produce the transformed stego-image. This stego-image DWT is then used by the reveal network to extract the DWT of the hidden image and update the network weights. The batch size used was 16, with model checkpointing implemented for training continuity. The model uses the Adam optimizer with default TensorFlow 2.12.0 parameters and a learning rate of 0.0002. The model includes checkpoint tracking and elapsed time monitoring, with weights saved periodically during training. The space occupied by our model parameters is 5.84 MB with a total of 1,532,406 trainable parameters across both the hiding and revealing networks. Furthermore, different values for the β parameter were utilized to optimize the retrieval quality of the secret image.

3. Results and Discussion

3.1. The Experimental Setup

In the following set of experiments, the *DeepWaveletFusionToo* method was tested using ten pairs of cover/secret images. As shown in Table 1, the selected images represent a wide variety of color and structural details. They include some popular images, like Baboon and Lena, while the rest were selected from the Linnaeus 5 [20] and Imagenette [21] datasets. For all test cases, the images were sized 256 × 256 pixels.

Table 1. Images used in experiments.

Cover Images		Secret Images	
 Baboon	 Lena	 French Horn	 Garbage Truck
 Chainsaws	 Church	 Fish	 Golf Balls

Table 1. *Cont.*

Cover Images		Secret Images	

Dog	Lotus	Parachute	Parrot

Graffiti	Berries	Pens	Peppers

Gas Pump	Karaoke	Stained Glass	Thistle

3.2. Performance Measures

Quantitative metrics were used to assess the proposed method across three performance aspects: imperceptibility, recoverability, and hiding capacity. The peak signal-to-noise ratio (*PSNR*) is the most common metric used to quantify the distortions introduced into the stego-image due to the hiding process. The *PSNR* is measured in decibels (dB), as in Equation (2), where values more than 30 dB typically indicate a low level of visual distortion and hence high imperceptibility. The *PSNR* is calculated using (2) and is expressed in terms of the mean squared error (*MSE*) as given in Equation (1), where *M* represents the maximum pixel value. Secondly, the quality of retrieval is measured by the structured similarity index measure (*SSIM*), as in Equation (3), where a higher value reflects a greater similarity between the secret image and the retrieved one.

$$PSNR = 10(log_{10}(\frac{M^2}{MSE})) \tag{2}$$

$$SSIM(I,I') = \frac{(2\mu_I\mu_{I'} + c_1)(2\sigma_{II'} + c_2)}{(\mu_I^2 + \mu_{I'}^2 + c_1)(\sigma_I^2 + \sigma_{I'}^2 + c_2)} \tag{3}$$

To measure the hiding capacity, we need to estimate the maximum message size that can be embedded into a cover image with specific dimensions. This is usually measured in bits per pixel (*bpp*) and can be computed using Equation (4), where *E* represents the hiding payload, in bits, for a cover image of size (*H*) by (*W*) pixels [22]. The *SSIM*, on the other hand, can be measured for two images *I* and I' using (3). μ_I and $\mu_{I'}$ represent the mean values, σ_I^2 represents the mean variance of *I*, and $\sigma_{I'}^2$ represents the mean variance of I'. $\sigma_{II'}^2$ represents the covariance of *I* and I', and c_1 and c_2 are used to stabilize division, in the event that the denominator is weak [23].

$$Hiding\ Capacity = \frac{E}{H * W} \tag{4}$$

3.3. Experimental Results

3.3.1. The Effect of β

The proposed *DeepWaveletFusionToo* method utilizes a weighted loss function that balances two competing objectives: preserving the quality of the stego-image and ensuring the accurate recovery of the secret image. This balance is controlled by the parameter β in the loss function as in Equation (5),

$$\text{Loss} = \text{MSE}(S, S') + \beta \times \text{MSE}(C, C') \tag{5}$$

where $MSE(S,S')$ represents the mean squared error between the original secret image and the recovered secret image, and $MSE(C,C')$ represents the mean squared error between the original cover image and the stego-image. In this formulation, β directly weights the importance of the cover image fidelity. Values of β less than 1 give relatively more importance to the secret image recovery in the overall loss function, while still accounting for cover image quality.

To determine the optimal balance between recoverability and imperceptibility, we conducted experiments using four different β values: 0.80, 0.85, 0.90, and 0.95. Figures 4 and 5 present the corresponding PSNR and SSIM scores across our test dataset for each β configuration. The results indicate that β values of 0.95 and 0.85 yield comparable performance in terms of both recoverability and imperceptibility. Consequently, we adopt β = 0.95 for the subsequent experiments.

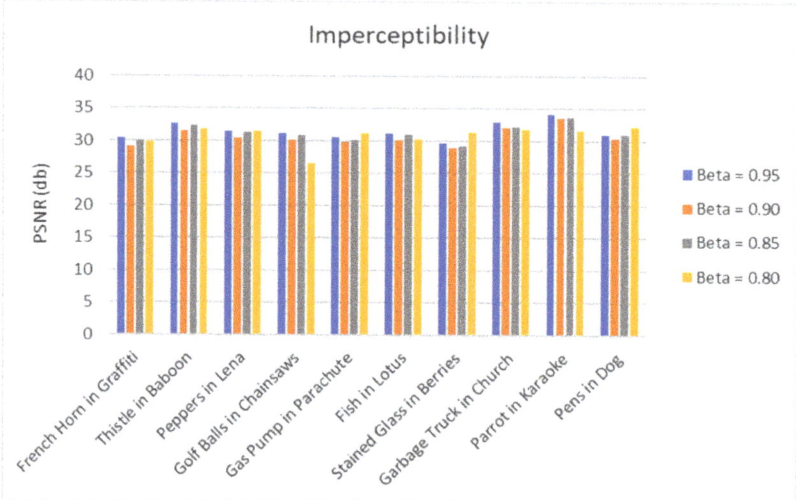

Figure 4. PSNR values of stego-images for different β values across the test dataset.

3.3.2. Performance Evaluation

In the following set of experiments, we evaluate the performance of the *DeepWavelet-FusionToo* method in terms of both invisibility and recoverability. Table 2 presents the stego-images alongside their corresponding retrieved secret images for each test case. The associated PSNR and SSIM values are calculated and displayed beneath each example. The results demonstrate high recoverability, with an average SSIM of 0.93, indicating high structural similarity between the original and retrieved images. Moreover, the embedding process introduces minimal visual distortion, as reflected by an average PSNR of 31.57 dB, confirming the imperceptibility of the stego-images.

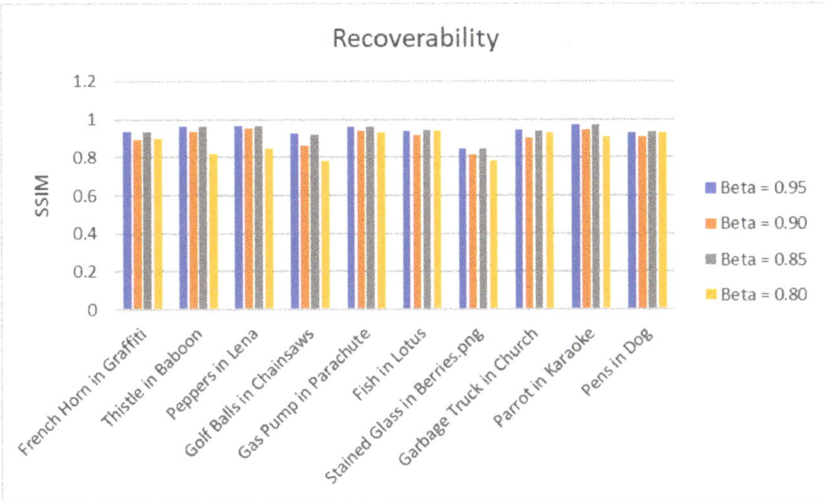

Figure 5. SSIM values between original and recovered secret images for different β values across the test dataset.

Table 2. The results of the hiding and extraction for *DeepWaveletFusionToo* at β = 0.95.

 *French Horn in Graffiti* PSNR = 30.39 dB, SSIM = 0.93	 *Thistle in Baboon* PSNR = 32.75 dB, SSIM = 0.96
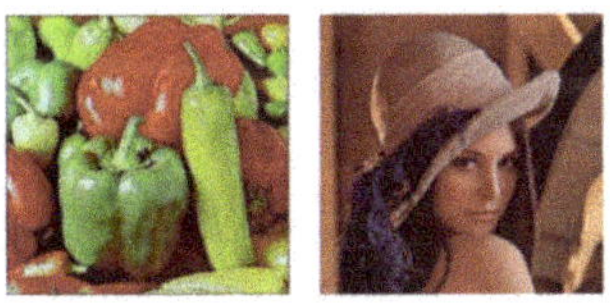 *Peppers in Lena* PSNR = 31.55 dB, SSIM = 0.96	 *Golf Balls in Chainsaws* PSNR = 33.21, SSIM = 0.92
 *Gas Pump in Parachute* PSNR = 30.66 dB, SSIM = 0.96	 *Fish in Lotus* PSNR = 31.22, SSIM = 0.94
 *Stained Glass in Berries* PSNR = 29.63, SSIM = 0.85	 *Garbage Truck in Church* PSNR = 33.03, SSIM = 0.95

Table 2. *Cont.*

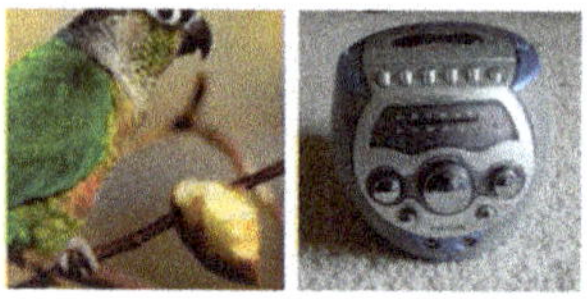 *Parrot in Karaoke* PSNR = 34.12 dB, SSIM = 0.97	 *Pens in Dog* PSNR = 31.08 dB, SSIM = 0.93

While the results in Table 2 demonstrate strong overall performance of the proposed method for both hiding and extraction tasks, it is worth noting that the lowest SSIM score occurs when the "Stained Glass" image was hidden inside the "Berries" image. In this case, the model was able to retrieve at most 85% of the embedded image, indicating a perceptible degradation in the visual quality of the recovered image. This drop can be attributed to limitations in the DWT reconstruction process, which can be less effective for images with smooth transitions or intricate textures. While this may be seen as a limitation of the current model, we recommend that users experiment with a variety of cover images to achieve optimal imperceptibility and retrieval quality. Selecting covers with diverse frequency characteristics may help mitigate such artifacts and improve overall performance.

3.4. Comparative Performance Analysis

Table 3 presents a comparative evaluation of our proposed method, *DeepWaveletFusionToo*, alongside several state-of-the-art deep learning-based steganographic techniques. The comparison spans multiple criteria, including the model architecture, dataset, cover/stego image imperceptibility (measured in PSNR), secret/retrieved similarity, and the hiding capacity in bits per pixel (bpp). The results presented in this table are compiled from the published evaluations of each method. The similarity between the extracted secret image and the original is expressed as a percentage. In cases where the SSIM (structural similarity index) is used, a value of 1.0 corresponds to 100% similarity, indicating that the extracted image is visually identical to the originally embedded one.

Table 3. A performance comparison with some deep learning steganographic techniques.

Method	Approach	Image Dataset	Cover/Stego PSNR (dB)	Secret/Retrieved Similarity (%)	Hiding Capacity (bpp)
DeepStego [9], 2017	CNN	ImageNet	28.69	73.0	24
TDHN [11], 2020	CNN	NWPU-RESISC45	40.3	98.0	24
FCDNet [12], 2020	FC-DenseNet	ImageNet	40.196	98.4	23.96
SteganoCNN [14], 2020	CNN	ImageNet	21.614	85.5	48
End-to-end [13], 2021	Autoencoder	COCO, CelebA, ImageNet	33.70	--	24
SteGuz [10], 2022	CNN	Linnaeus 5, Imagenette	44.33	93.0	24
DeepWaveletFusion [16], 2024	CNN, DWT	Linnaeus 5, Imagenette	33.63	98.7	24
DeepWaveletFusionToo	CNN, DWT	Linnaeus 5, Imagenette	34.12	97	24

The *DeepWaveletFusion* and *DeepWaveletFusionToo* methods demonstrate competitive performances across all evaluation metrics. Notably, *DeepWaveletFusionToo* achieves strong imperceptibility while maintaining comparable recoverability. While this PSNR is slightly lower than SteGuz [10] (44.33 dB), the proposed method outperforms SteGuz in terms of retrieval accuracy, surpassing SteGuz's 93%.

Compared to earlier approaches such as DeepStego [9], which exhibits a much lower PSNR (28.69 dB) and lower similarity (73%), our methods offer a significant improvement in both visual fidelity and data recovery reliability. Similarly, SteganoCNN [14], while having the highest hiding capacity (48 bpp), suffers from both a low PSNR (21.614 dB) and lower similarity (85.5%), highlighting a trade-off between capacity and quality that our method addresses more effectively.

TDHN [11] and FCDNet [12] perform well in terms of their PSNR (above 40 dB) and achieve excellent similarity scores (>98%), but their architectures are less flexible compared to our CNN–DWT hybrid. Our results remain competitive even against the end-to-end [13] autoencoder model, which achieves a moderate PSNR (33.70 dB) but lacks similarity data, making direct comparison incomplete. In conclusion, while performance comparisons to existing methods are informative, they should be interpreted with caution due to dataset and preprocessing discrepancies.

4. Conclusions

The *DeepWaveletFusionToo* is a novel framework that advances state-of-the-art in wavelet-based deep learning steganography with a simple and computationally efficient model. By training two convolutional neural networks on a custom dataset of discrete wavelet-transformed images, the method achieves high-quality embedding and recovery performance. Experimental results demonstrate a favorable trade-off between embedding strength and image quality across varying values of the embedding strength factor β. Compared to its predecessor, the *DeepWaveletFusion*, the proposed method exhibits improved imperceptibility while maintaining an average similarity score of approximately 93%.

Future work may explore the use of larger and more diverse training datasets, such as ImageNet, to further improve imperceptibility and enhance benchmarking consistency. Additionally, evaluating the system's robustness against common image processing attacks—such as JPEG compression—could broaden its applicability, particularly in domains like invisible image watermarking. Another important direction is to assess the steganographic security of the proposed method by testing it against standard steganalysis techniques, with the goal of enhancing its resilience to detection.

Author Contributions: Conceptualization, A.K.; methodology, Y.Y. and A.K.; software programming, Y.Y.; supervision, A.K.; formal analysis, Y.Y. and A.K.; writing—original draft preparation, A.K.; writing—review and editing, Y.Y. All authors have read and agreed to the published version of the manuscript.

Funding: This research received a graduate research assistantship fund from the department of Computer Science at Purdue University, Fort Wayne, covering both tuition and stipend.

Data Availability Statement: The original contributions presented in this study are included in the article. Further inquiries can be directed at the corresponding author.

Conflicts of Interest: The authors declare no conflicts of interest.

References

1. Cox, I.; Miller, M.; Bloom, J.; Fridrich, J.; Kalker, T. *Digital Watermarking and Steganography*; Elsevier Science & Technology: San Francisco, CA, USA, 2007.
2. Artz, D. Digital Steganography: Hiding Data within Data. *IEEE Internet Comput.* **2001**, *5*, 75–80.
3. Kasapbasi, M.C.; Elmasry, W. New LSB-based colour image steganography method to enhance the efficiency in payload capacity, security and integrity check. *Sādhanā* **2018**, *43*, 43–68.

4. Chen, W.-Y. Color image steganography scheme using set partitioning in hierarchical trees coding, digital fourier transform ar adaptive phase modulation. *Appl. Math. Comput.* **2007**, *185*, 432–448.
5. Lin, C.-C.; Shiu, P.-F. High capacity data hiding scheme for dct-based images. *J. Inf. Hiding Multimed. Signal Process.* **201** *1*, 220–240.
6. Hamad, S.; Khalifa, A.; Elhadad, A. A Blind High-Capacity Wavelet-Based Steganography Technique for Hiding Images in other Images. *Adv. Electr. Comput. Eng.* **2014**, *14*, 35–43.
7. Thanki, R.; Borra, S. A color image steganography in hybrid FRT-DWT domain. *J. Inf. Secur. Appl.* **2018**, *40*, 92–102.
8. Zhou, X.; Zhang, H.; Wang, C. A Robust Image Watermarking Technique Based on DWT, APDCBT, and SVD. *Symmetry* **201** *10*, 77. [CrossRef]
9. Baluja, S. Hiding Images in Plain Sight: Deep Steganography. In Proceedings of the 31st Conference on Neural Informatic Processing Systems, Long Beach, CA, USA, 4–9 December 2017.
10. Khalifa, A.; Guzman, A. Imperceptible Image Steganography Using Symmetry-Adapted Deep Learning Techniques. *Symmetr* **2022**, *14*, 1325. [CrossRef]
11. Chen, F.; Xing, Q.; Liu, F. Technology of Hiding and Protecting the Secret Image Based on Two-Channel Deep Hiding Networ *IEEE Access* **2020**, *8*, 21966–21979.
12. Duan, X.; Liu, N.; Gou, M.; Yue, D.; Xie, Z.; Ma, Y.; Qin, C. Capacity Image Steganography Based on Improved FC-DenseNe *IEEE Access* **2020**, *8*, 170174–170182. [CrossRef]
13. Subramanian, N.; Cheheb, I.; Elharrouss, O.; Al-Maadeed, S.; Bouridane, A. End-to-End Image Steganography Using Dee Convolutional Autoencoders. *IEEE Access* **2021**, *9*, 135585–135593.
14. Duan, X.; Liu, N.; Gou, M.; Wang, W.; Qin, C. SteganoCNN: Image Steganography with Generalization Ability Based o Convolutional Neural Network. *Entropy* **2020**, *22*, 1140. [CrossRef] [PubMed]
15. Boehm, B. StegExpose—A Tool for Detecting LSB Steganography. *arXiv* **2014**, arXiv:1410.6656.
16. Khalifa, A.; Santos, N.V. High-capacity Image Steganography using Waveletbased Fusion on Deep Convolutional Neura Networks. In Proceedings of the ICCSPS 2024: 18th International Conference on Computer Science, Programming and Securit Dubai, United Arab Emirates, 23–24 December 2024.
17. O'Shea, K.; Nash, R. An Introduction to Convolutional Neural Networks. *arXiv* **2015**, arXiv:1511.08458.
18. Durán, J. Everything You Need to Know About Gradient Descent Applied to Neural Networks. Medium, 19 September 201 Available online: https://medium.com/yottabytes/everything-you-need-to-know-about-gradient-descent-applied-to-neura networks-d70f85e0cc14 (accessed on 5 May 2023).
19. Kingma, D.P.; Ba, J. Adam: A Method for Stochastic Optimization. In Proceedings of the International Conference for Learnin Representations, San Diego, CA, USA, 7–9 May 2015.
20. Chaladze, G.; Kalatozishvili, L. Linnaeus 5 Dataset for Machine Learning. 2017. Available online: https://chaladze.com/l5 (accessed on 20 August 2023).
21. Howard, J. Imagenette. Available online: https://github.com/fastai/imagenette/ (accessed on 20 August 2023).
22. Zakaria, A.A.; Hussain, M.; Wahab, A.W.A.; Idris, M.Y.I.; Abdullah, N.A.; Jung, K.-H. High-Capacity Image Steganography wit Minimum Modified Bits Based on Data Mapping and LSB Substitution. *Appl. Sci.* **2018**, *8*, 2199–2218.
23. Wang, Z.; Simoncelli, E.P.; Bovik, A.C. Multiscale structural similarity for image quality assessment. In Proceedings of the Thirty-Seventh Asilomar Conference on Signals, Systems & Computers, Pacific Grove, CA, USA, 9–12 November 2003.

electronics

MDPI

Article

Comparative Study on Energy Consumption of Neural Networks by Scaling of Weight-Memory Energy Versus Computing Energy for Implementing Low-Power Edge Intelligence

pyung Yoon, Jihwan Mun and Kyeong-Sik Min *

School of Electrical Engineering, Kookmin University, Seoul 02707, Republic of Korea;
yip0113@kookmin.ac.kr (I.Y.); mark122@kookmin.ac.kr (J.M.)
* Correspondence: mks@kookmin.ac.kr

Abstract: Energy consumption has emerged as a critical design constraint in deploying high-performance neural networks, especially on edge devices with limited power resources. In this paper, a comparative study is conducted for two prevalent deep learning paradigms—convolutional neural networks (CNNs), exemplified by ResNet18, and transformer-based large language models (LLMs), represented by GPT3-small, Llama-7B, and GPT3-175B. By analyzing how the scaling of memory energy versus computing energy affects the energy consumption of neural networks with different batch sizes (1, 4, 8, 16), it is shown that ResNet18 transitions from a memory energy-limited regime at low batch sizes to a computing energy-limited regime at higher batch sizes due to its extensive convolution operations. On the other hand, GPT-like models remain predominantly memory-bound, with large parameter tensors and frequent key–value (KV) cache lookups accounting for most of the total energy usage. Our results reveal that reducing weight-memory energy is particularly effective in transformer architectures, while improving multiply–accumulate (MAC) efficiency significantly benefits CNNs at higher workloads. We further highlight near-memory and in-memory computing approaches as promising strategies to lower data-transfer costs and enhance power efficiency in large-scale deployments. These findings offer actionable insights for architects and system designers aiming to optimize artificial intelligence (AI) performance under stringent energy budgets on battery-powered edge devices.

Keywords: energy consumption of neural networks; weight-memory energy; MAC computing energy; edge intelligence

1. Introduction

As artificial intelligence (AI) technologies are advancing very rapidly nowadays, neural networks are starting to show that they can be really useful and helpful for various applications related to human cognition and intelligence [1–4]. The most representative models of neural networks can be regarded as convolutional neural networks and transformers [5–8]. They are used for processing spatial information such as images and sequential information such as natural languages, respectively, which can be considered the most common capabilities of human cognition and intelligence.

To realize human-level cognition and intelligence, very strong computing systems are needed. Figure 1 shows an entire hierarchy from Internet of Things (IoT) to cloud computing centers via an edge intelligence layer [9]. Here the IoT sensors collect massive amounts of data from natural environments, human societies, etc. The IoT actuators translate electrical signals to physical quantities, including motion, light, temperature, etc., to make human life more convenient and safer. The data collected from the IoT devices are finally used in the cloud layer, where very big AI models can be operated using the big data accumulated in data centers.

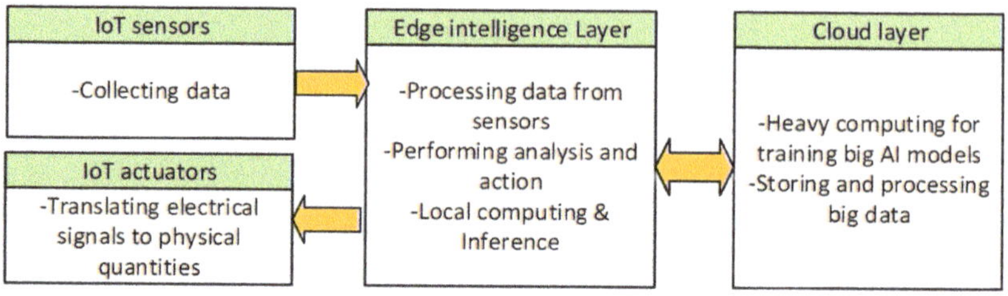

Figure 1. A conceptual diagram of the hierarchy of computing hardware from IoT sensors to the cloud layer via the edge intelligence layer.

To make the entire computing systems energy-efficient, an edge intelligence layer should be inserted between the IoT devices and cloud layer, as shown in Figure 1 [10]. The edge layer between the IoT and cloud computing layers can reduce the amount of data to be transferred directly from the IoT devices to the data center significantly [11]. By doing so, the computing and communication energy of a data center can be decreased. Moreover, some applications should handle privacy-related data. Edge hardware can enable data processing without exposing private information to external networks. This is particularly important in healthcare, financial services, and personal devices where data privacy is paramount [11,12].

As mentioned earlier, edge intelligence is needed between the IoT devices and data centers. Most edge intelligence hardware should be operated in energy-constraint environments such as battery energy. In this case, low-power edge hardware is very critical to make the battery lifetime long. However, this demand for the low-power consumption of edge devices is in opposition to big AI models requiring high-level intelligence consuming very large amounts of energy [13–15]. Figure 2a shows the relationship between energy consumption and an AI model's size [16]. Here, we analyze various large language models (LLMs) in terms of energy consumption, which very clearly demonstrates an exponential increase with respect to the number of model parameters [17,18].

Now we need to discuss how to reduce the energy consumption of AI models. Traditionally, computing energy consumption could be reduced by supply voltage (VDD) scaling. It is well known that switching power consumption is proportional to VDD^2. If the VDD is reduced, the power consumption will be reduced by VDD^2. However, VDD scaling has not been available for many years now, so power reduction through VDD scaling is impossible now [19,20].

To reduce power consumption without relying on VDD scaling, we need to consider the power consumption of traditional computing architecture, which is known as the von Neumann architecture. Figure 2b shows a conceptual diagram of the von Neumann architecture, where the computing block is separated from the memory block. The separation between the computing block and memory block can cause a large amount of power consumption because the data movement between the two separate blocks consumes energy endlessly. To overcome this problem, Figure 2c shows a conceptual diagram of near-memory computing, where the power consumption can be reduced by shortening the distance between the computing and memory blocks [21,22]. Furthermore, Figure 2d shows a diagram of the in-memory computing architecture. Here, the architecture in Figure 2d can be used to perform both the computing and memory functions on the same site. By doing so, the computing energy consumption in Figure 2d can be lowered more compared to Figure 2c [23–26].

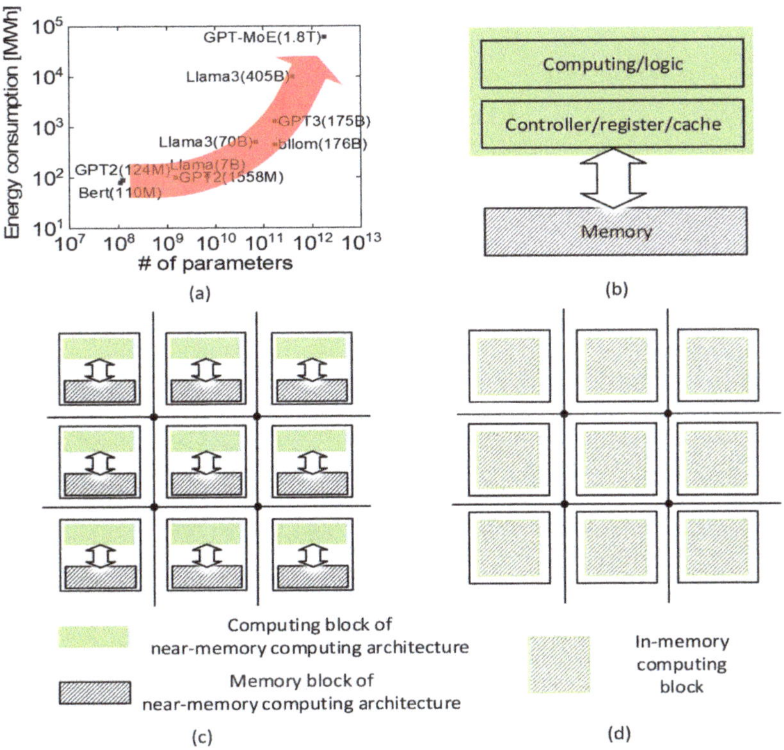

Figure 2. (**a**) The energy consumption of LLMs with an increasing number of AI model parameters [16]. (**b**) The von Neumann computing architecture with the separation of computing and memory blocks. (**c**) The near-memory computing architecture, where the distance between the computing and memory blocks can be shorter than in the traditional von Neumann architecture. (**d**) The in-memory computing architecture, where the computing can be performed in a memory array.

As explained earlier, both the near-memory and in-memory computing techniques can reduce the energy consumption of AI models. In more detail, near-memory computing can affect the data movement energy needed for accessing weight memory. In-memory computing can reduce both the energy consumption of computing and weight memory. Thus, to analyze the energy reduction due to near-memory and in-memory computing, we try to divide the AI model's energy consumption into a weight-accessing part and computing part in this paper.

To do so, first, we assume two types of neural network models, which are the convolutional neural network and transformer model, respectively, in terms of the model's size and the FLOPs computed in the models. The two models are used for processing spatial information such as images and sequential information such as natural languages, respectively, which can be considered the most common capabilities of human cognition and intelligence.

Here, FLOPs mean the number of floating-point operations needed to run the AI model. If the model's size is large, it needs a large number of model parameters. If so, the energy consumption of accessing weight memory should be very large too. On the other hand, if the number of FLOPs is large, it means the amount of computing energy should be very large too. Based on the analysis of model size and FLOPs, in this paper, we will calculate how much energy can be saved for two typical AI models, the ResNet18 and transformer models, in the following section.

Explaining the analyzed models in more detail, ResNet18 is suitable for handling vision information using a convolution operation. Here, the convolution operation performs very heavy computation using a small number of kernels. This is the reason that the number of FLOPs per parameter of convolution-based models is larger than for other AI models. On the contrary, transformer models need a lot of model parameters to be used in very large matrix–matrix multiplication. Consequentially, the transformer model has a low number of FLOPs per parameter. To consider two types of AI models, computation-dominant and weight-dominant, we analyze the energy consumption of AI models by scaling the weight energy versus the computing energy. The results show that the energy scaling of weight memory and computing can affect the AI model's power consumption in various ways according to different models, operating modes, memories, etc.

To summarize how the energy scaling of weight memory versus computing can affect the total energy consumption of various AI models, we plot FLOPs per parameter with a varying batch number. By doing so, we can distinguish the weight-energy bound and MAC-energy bound regions for the AI models. Here, MAC stands for multiplication and accumulation operations that are fundamental to running the neural network model. If one AI model operated with a certain batch number belongs to a region bound by weight-accessing energy, it means the weight-memory energy is more dominant than the computing energy. On the other hand, the AI model is in the computing-energy bound region; the reduction in computing energy is more important than saving the weight-memory energy. These findings obtained through the analysis in this paper can offer actionable insights for architects and system designers aiming to optimize AI performance under stringent energy budgets on battery-powered edge devices.

Let us discuss some previous studies for analyzing the energy consumption of neural networks [27,28]. These are based on real measurements using neural network hardware such as NVIDIA devices. More specifically, a study profiling the energy consumption of fully connected and convolutional layers led to the creation of simple but accurate energy models for edge inference tasks [27]. Also, some researchers have developed an energy consumption index to evaluate the energy efficiency of various deep learning architectures, including AlexNet, ResNet18, VGG16, EfficientNet-B3, ConvNeXt-T, and Swin Transformer, during both the training and inference phases, providing a standardized approach for assessment [29].

Unlike these previous studies that obtained measurement results using hardware, this paper analyzes the energy consumption of AI models from bottom-up calculations using elementwise analysis for weight-memory access and MAC (multiply–accumulate) computing. By doing so, the energy consumption trend can be analyzed and estimated in this paper when the energy scaling affects weight energy versus computing energy differently. This kind of breakdown approach for energy consumption is very useful for estimating future energy reduction that may be driven by near-memory and in-memory computing architecture.

In the next section, the methods used in this study are explained in detail. In Section 3, simulation results are indicated using figures and tables, which show the AI model's energy consumption for different batch numbers, different energy scaling for weight-memory and MAC computing, etc. In Section 3, we conclude this paper.

2. Methods

In this paper, two types of neural network models are considered for analyzing their energy consumption. These are ResNet18 and transformer models, known as GPT, respectively. Figure 3a illustrates a block diagram of ResNet18, which takes an input image and applies 64 convolution filters of size 7 × 7 with a stride of 2 at the first stage to rapidly reduce the spatial resolution. Afterward, multiple layers of 3 × 3 convolutions (filters 64→128→256→512) are sequentially applied. Each convolution layer is equipped with Batch Normalization, an activation function known as ReLU, etc. At the end, a pooling operation aggregates the feature map by channels, and the classification result is finally produced through a fully connected layer and SoftMax layer.

ResNet18 is a simpler model than large language models (LLMs) in the GPT family, which can have hundreds of millions to billions of parameters. However, due to the nature of pixel-level convolutions, each convolution layer requires an enormous number of MAC (multiply–accumulate) operations. For example, with an input image of size 224 × 224, just passing through the first convolution layer entails many filters performing spatial multiply–add operations. As the input image is large and the number of channels grows from layer to layer, the total computational workload skyrockets. Consequently, ResNet18 needs about 1.8 GFLOPs, which represents a substantial amount of computation. In other words, despite having fewer parameters, the model has a large volume of operations, implying that much of the energy consumption could be dominated by computational costs.

On the other hand, as shown in Figure 3b, GPT-based models (GPT3-small, Llama 7B, GPT3-175B, etc.) follow the transformer architecture designed to process sequential data. The sequential input data are first split into tokens, and the tokens are delivered to an embedding layer. Then, they are input into multiple transformer blocks. Each transformer block consists of (1) Layer Normalization, (2) Multi-Head Self-Attention, and (3) a feedforward module (MLP). A residual connection is applied at each layer for stable training. GPT models typically contain a very large number of parameters. For example, GPT3-175B has about 175 billion parameters, while Llama 7B already has around 6.7 billion parameters, which is far bigger in scale than CNN-based models [7,30].

Due to these architectural differences, the dominant factors in energy consumption diverge markedly between ResNet18 and GPT. In CNNs, the parameter count is relatively small, but there are many convolution operations, leading to a computationally intensive workload. Meanwhile, GPT frequently loads a huge number of parameters for each token, and as the sequence length grows, the KV cache access frequency also increases greatly. Therefore, in GPT-based models, memory access can become the main bottleneck in overall energy consumption. Specifically, even a model like Llama 7B already comprises billions of parameters, and in the case of GPT3-175B, the parameter count is over two orders of magnitude higher, which inevitably inflates the energy costs related to memory.

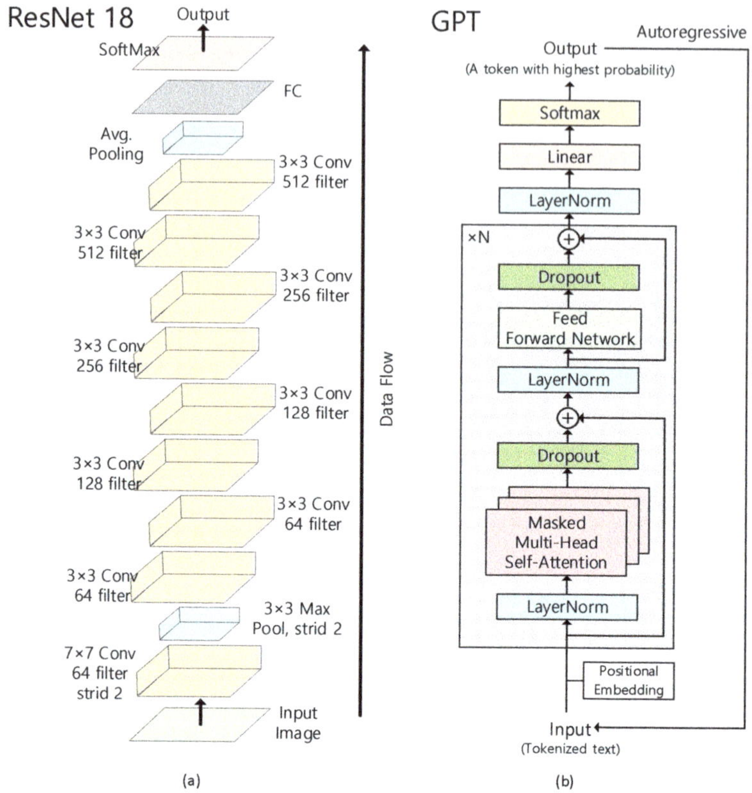

Figure 3. (**a**) A block diagram of ResNet18 [6]. (**b**) A block diagram of a transformer decoder such as GPT3 [31].

To perform a comparative study on energy consumption for moving weights and computing MAC operations, first, the numbers of model parameters and FLOPs are calculated for various AI models. Here, ResNet18, GPT3-small, Llama-7B, and GPT3-175B are chosen for this analysis, as shown in Figure 4a [17,32,33]. GPT-3 Small, Llama-7B, and GPT-3 175B were chosen as representative small-, medium-, and large-scale LLMs. Because all three models employ a GPT-like single decoder block, their layer layouts and computational patterns are similar, enabling a fair comparison. Each model has been publicly released with full hyperparameter details provided in the relevant paper and repository, ensuring reproducibility and data accessibility. ResNet18, based on a convolutional neural network, has 11.7 M parameters, which can recognize images by processing spatial information. GPT3-small, Llama-7B, and GPT3-175B are based on the transformer-decoder model, which can handle sequential information such as natural languages. There are 125 M, 7 B, and 175 B parameters for GPT3-small, Llama-7B, and GPT3-175B, respectively, as shown in Figure 4a. The numbers of FLOPs for the four models are shown in Figure 4b. The number of FLOPs of ResNet18 is as low as 1.8 G. The number of FLOPs of GPT3-small and Llama 7B is 265 M and 13.2 G, respectively. On the contrary, the number of FLOPs reaches as high as 334 G for GPT3-175B [17,32,33].

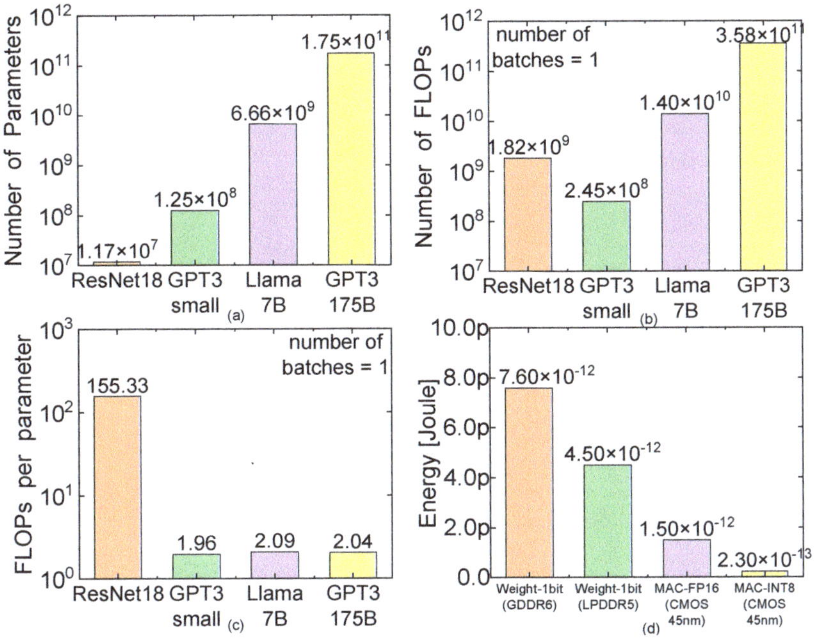

Figure 4. (**a**) The number of parameters for various neural network models. (**b**) The number of FLOPs for various neural network models when the number of batches is one. (**c**) The FLOPs per parameter for various neural network models when the number of batches is one. (**d**) The energy consumption of different memories and MAC operations.

The computational intensity of neural network models can be defined by the number of FLOPs per parameter. For example, ResNet18 is calculated with a computational intensity as high as 155, because the model has a small number of parameters and a large number of FLOPs, as shown in Figure 4c. In contrast, the transformer-based models have much lower computational intensity than ResNet18. The intensity numbers shown in Figure 4c are 1.96, 2.09, and 2.04 for GPT-small, Llama 7B, and GPT3-175B, respectively. One thing to note from Figure 4c is that the transformer-based neural networks perform less computing than the CNN-based models for each parameter.

Figure 4d indicates the energy consumption of loading weights per bit and the computing energy for performing one MAC operation. Here, FP16 and INT8 are considered for carrying out MAC operations. FP16 represents a floating-point number format composed of 16 bits. Similarly, INT8 is an integer number format composed of 8 bits. These are very common number formats used in most GPU and NPU chips [34]. In Figure 4d, the first column shows the weight-memory energy per bit for GDDR6 DRAMs [35]. The second column is the weight-memory energy per bit for LPDDR5 DRAMs [36]. The third and fourth columns represent the computing energy per FP16 and INT8 MAC, respectively [20,37].

To simulate the energy consumption of AI models, the total energy consumption is examined for different batch numbers with the weight-memory energy and MAC energy varied in steps. To perform the energy analysis, first, we need to calculate the number of model parameters and FLOPs required to operate the AI models mentioned above. The energy calculation in this paper is performed using a Python 3.9.21 program that includes the energy models of MAC computing and weight-memory access. The neural network's performance is verified using Pytorch 2.2.0 (+ CUDA 11.8) for the ResNet18 and transformer-based models. As mentioned earlier, two representative AI models are simulated in this paper. These are ResNet and transformer, respectively. The other AI models can be considered to have similar characteristics to the two models analyzed in this paper. The two models used are for processing spatial information such as images and sequential information such as natural languages, respectively, which can be considered the most common capabilities of human cognition and intelligence. Here, the total energy consumption is assumed to be roughly composed of weight-memory energy and MAC computing energy [30,31,38,39]. For the weight-memory energy, LPDDR5 in Figure 4d is assumed to be used in loading the weights from the external DRAM memory [36]. In this case, the weight-memory energy used for loading one bit can be estimated to be as much as 4.5 pJ. To calculate the MAC computing energy, MAC-INT8 precision is used in the convolution-based ResNet18 model in this paper. In most convolution-based models such as ResNet, INT8 precision can demonstrate sufficient performance for use in practical applications [40,41]. For the transformer-based models, MAC-FP16 is used to handle more complicated computations rather than INT8. If the CMOS logic process is assumed to involve a 45 nm node and the VDD is 0.9 V, the MAC-INT8 operation consumes 0.23 pJ per MAC operation [20,37]. On the other hand, MAC-FP16 requires an energy consumption as large as 1.5 pJ per MAC operation [20,37]. Table 1 shows the hyperparameter values used in the transformer models, namely GPT-3 Small, Llama-7B, and GPT-3 175B.

Table 1. The hyperparameters of transformer models such as GPT-3 Small, Llama-7B, and GPT-3 175B. These are vocabulary size (n_word), context window size (n_context), hidden dimension size (d_model), layer depth (n_layer), number of attention heads (n_head), and per-head dimension (d_head).

	n_word	n_context	d_model	n_layer	n_head	d_head
GPT3-small	50,257	2048	768	12	12	64
Llama-7B	50,257	2048	4096	32	32	128
GPT3-175B	50,257	2048	12,288	96	96	128

3. Results

Figures 5 and 6 present the normalized total energy consumption to show, at a glance, how the overall energy consumption changes as the weight-memory or MAC operation energy is gradually decreased. In detail, Figure 5 demonstrates how the total energy consumption shifts (for batch sizes of 1, 4, 8, 16, respectively) when the weight-memory energy per bit in ResNet18 is reduced step by step from the baseline (1) to 1/2, 1/4, 1/8, and 1/16. When the batch size is 1, the weight energy and computation energy are almost in a 2:1 ratio, so saving weight-memory energy immediately leads to a reduction in the total energy consumption. However, when the batch size is 4 or larger, there are more MAC operations to be computed during the convolution operations, which increases the energy consumption due to MAC computation significantly. As discussed earlier, the impact of computation grows in these scenarios, so merely reducing the weight-memory energy does not yield as much benefit as it does at batch = 1

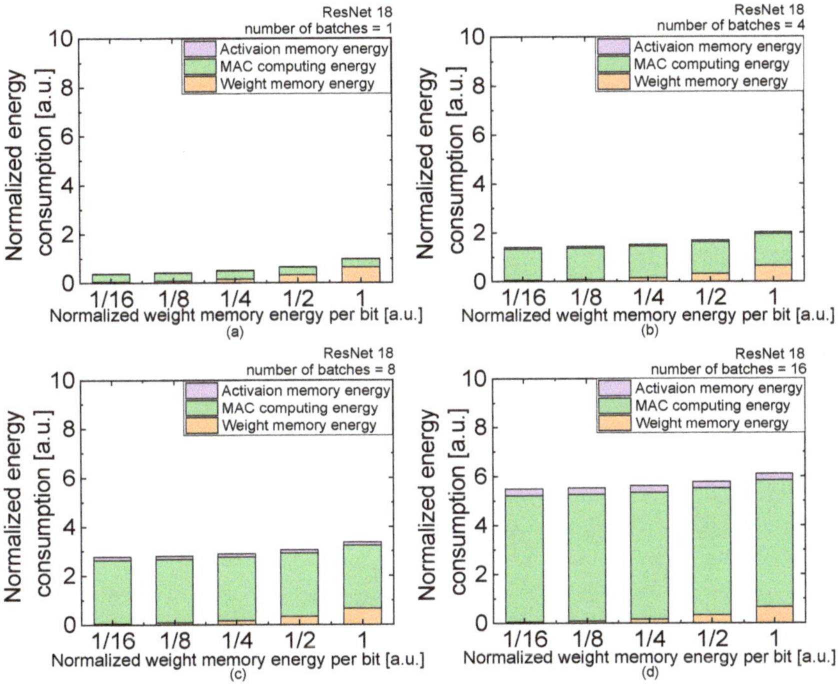

Figure 5. The energy consumption of ResNet18 with the weight-memory energy scaled from 1 down to 1/16. Here, the numbers of batches are 1, 4, 8, and 16 in (**a**), (**b**), (**c**), and (**d**), respectively.

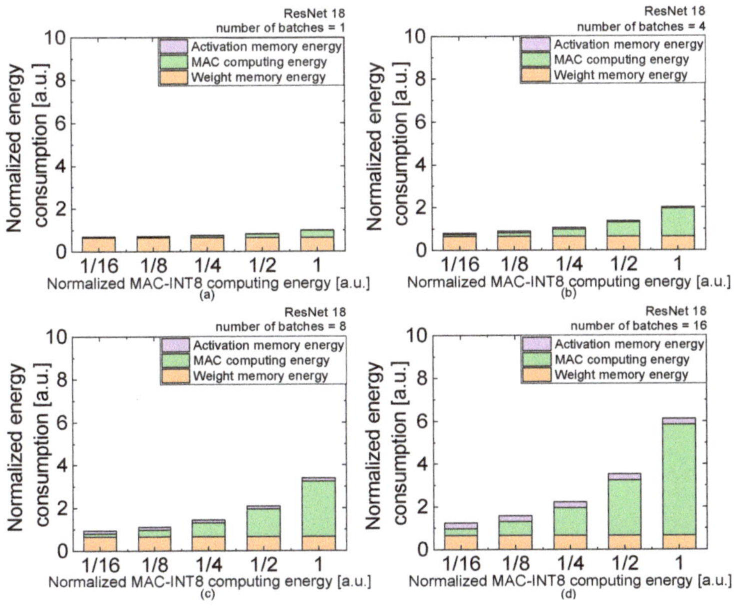

Figure 6. The energy consumption of ResNet18 with the MAC computing energy scaled from 1 down to 1/16. Here, the numbers of batches are 1, 4, 8, and 16 in (**a**), (**b**), (**c**), and (**d**), respectively.

Figure 6 shows how the total energy consumption changes under the same batch size scenarios (1, 4, 8, 16) when the MAC operation energy is reduced stepwise from 1 to 1/2, 1/4, 1/8, and 1/16. Because convolution is the core operation in ResNet18, and because the number of MAC operations surges rapidly as the batch number increases, halving the MAC energy leads to a significant decline in total energy. Even though we are using INT8 precision, the overall computation volume is still very large. Notably, as the batch size grows (8, 16) and the parallelism in convolution operations intensifies, MAC energy's proportion becomes even higher, making computation-focused optimization especially effective. Moreover, larger batch sizes also significantly increase activation memory usage (due to bigger intermediate feature maps), so lowering the MAC energy alone does not solve all energy problems. Nevertheless, since CNNs are typically computationally heavy, optimizing convolution through techniques such as Winograd transformations, FFT-based approaches, hardware parallelization, or further reducing precision below INT8 (e.g., INT4, INT2) can lead to substantial energy savings.

In summary, for ResNet18, the relative contributions of the weight-memory energy and MAC computing energy depend on the batch number. Overall, however, because CNNs involve a large volume of operations, they are likely to be computationally bound, making strategies to reduce the MAC energy pivotal for lowering the overall energy. This is especially relevant now that CNNs are increasingly deployed in battery-powered edge devices, prompting the active development of specialized hardware (NPU) and data-reuse strategies (e.g., sharing neighboring pixels) to maximize computing efficiency.

Now let us look at a transformer-based model, GPT (Llama 7B), and examine how the energy scaling of memory access versus MAC computation affects the total energy consumption. Figures 7–9 show, respectively, the changes in the normalized total energy consumption by batch size (1, 4, 8, 16) when (1) weight-memory energy is reduced, (2) MAC operation energy is reduced, and (3) KV cache memory energy is reduced. Here, we assume FP16 precision for the MAC calculations in the GPT model instead of the INT8 precision used in ResNet18.

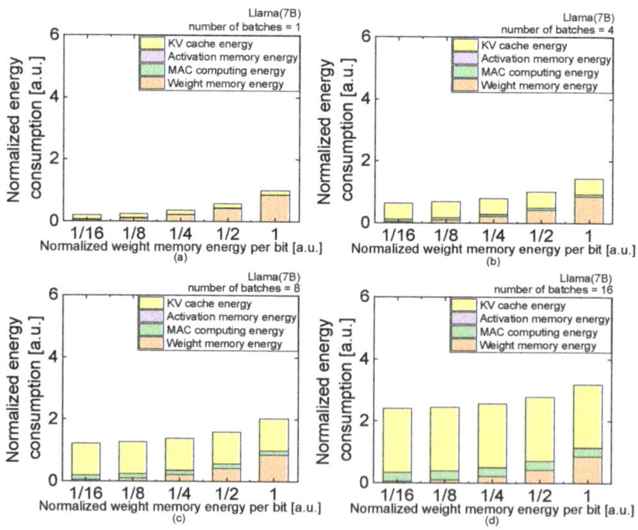

Figure 7. The energy consumption of Llama-7B with the weight-memory energy scaled from 1 down to 1/16. Here, the numbers of batches are 1, 4, 8, and 16 in (**a**), (**b**), (**c**), and (**d**), respectively.

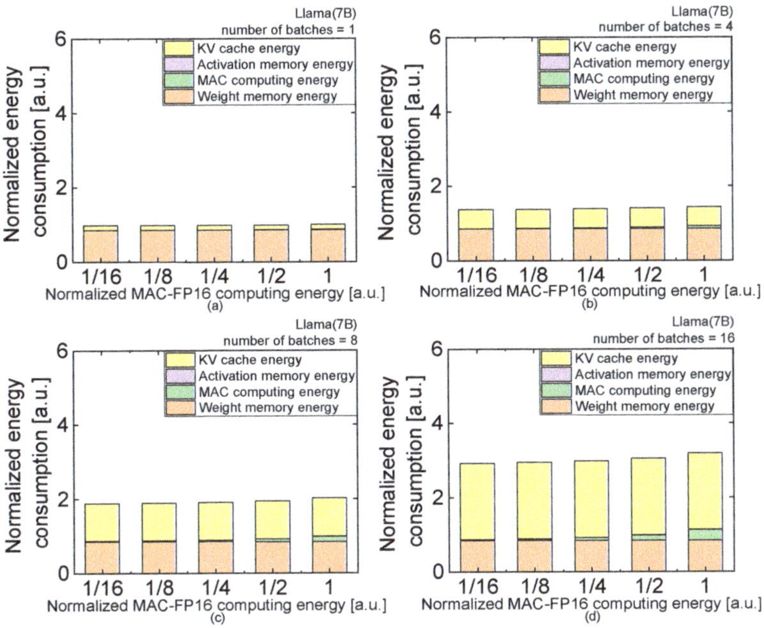

Figure 8. The energy consumption of Llama-7B with the MAC computing energy scaled from 1 down to 1/16. Here, the numbers of batches are 1, 4, 8, and 16 in (**a**), (**b**), (**c**), and (**d**), respectively.

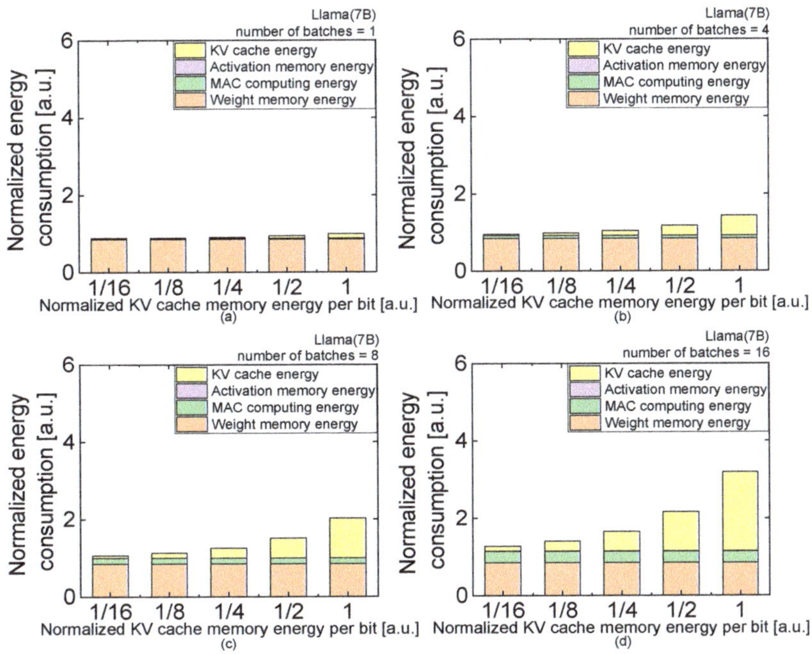

Figure 9. The energy consumption of Llama-7B with the KV cache memory energy scaled from 1 down to 1/16. Here, the numbers of batches are 1, 4, 8, and 16 in (**a**), (**b**), (**c**), and (**d**), respectively.

Llama 7B contains around 7 billion parameters, more than 500 times 11.7 million. Thus, for every inference or training pass, a vast number of weights must be loaded layer by layer. As shown in Figure 7, reducing the weight-memory energy to 1/2, 1/4, 1/8, or 1/16 reduces the total energy consumption dramatically regardless of batch size. This indicates that weight access or data movement is the strongest bottleneck in GPT-like architectures with large parameter counts [38]. Indeed, memory optimization techniques such as weight quantization (e.g., 8-bit or 4-bit), weight compression, or parameter sharing across layers (and KV caching) can significantly improve the energy efficiency of GPT models [42,43].

Because GPT models often have many more parameters than their overall FLOPs might suggest, MAC operations may not account for as large a fraction of the total energy as in CNNs. In Figure 8, lowering the MAC energy does reduce the total energy, but, unlike in CNNs, the absolute impact is not huge, even for larger batch sizes. Nevertheless, when the batch size reaches 8 or more, multi-head attention and the feedforward network process more tokens in parallel, increasing the computational load enough that MAC energy optimization does become meaningful. However, memory access (weights, KV cache) can still occupy a relatively larger portion of the total energy. This result shows that while computing energy efficiency remains valuable, reducing memory access—especially for weights and KV cache—is typically a higher priority for GPT-style models.

Because the GPT structure continually references past tokens, it uses a KV (key–value) cache to store them. As the sentence length grows, the quantity of information in this KV cache increases quadratically. With a larger batch size, multiple sentences are processed in parallel, further boosting the cache access frequency. As shown in Figure 9, cutting the KV cache energy to 1/2, 1/4, 1/8, or 1/16 can yield a noticeable drop in the total energy, especially when the batch size is as large as 16. This confirms that the KV cache is not just a side component; it can be a major energy bottleneck. Existing methods to optimize KV cache usage include storing token embeddings or attention keys/values at a lower precision, discarding unneeded cached entries early, or adopting architectural approaches such as placing cache memory closer to the processor (near-memory) or embedding it directly into the processor (in-memory) to reduce data movement. In summary, GPT (Llama 7B) handles significantly more parameters than CNNs and also deals with a substantial amount of KV cache usage, making memory access a dominant factor in the total energy consumption. Although MAC computation can become more significant with bigger batch sizes or longer sequences, optimizing the loading and storage processes of weights and KV caches is ultimately the key to achieving energy efficiency for the transformer-based models.

In Figure 10a,b, we compare the energy reduction rates for ResNet18 and the GPT-based Llama 7B model when lowering different energy components, namely weight-memory energy, MAC computing energy, and (for Llama 7B) KV cache energy.

Focusing first on ResNet18 in Figure 10a, we observe that at a small batch size (batch = 1), reducing the weight-memory energy yields a 61.7% reduction in the total energy consumption, whereas lowering the MAC computing energy decreases the overall energy by 30.3%. As the batch size grows to 4, weight-memory optimization still produces a larger effect (30.5%) compared to MAC-related reductions (18.2%), but this gap narrows because the share of computing increases with parallel convolution. At a batch size of 8, the situation shifts significantly in favor of MAC computing optimization, resulting in a 71.7% energy reduction, whereas weight-memory savings fall to 18.2%. At batch size = 16, the model becomes even more computationally bound, so reducing the MAC energy leads to a 79.4% decrease in the total energy consumption, with weight-memory savings dipping to 10.1%. These trends confirm that ResNet18 moves from a memory-bound state at small batch sizes to a computationally bound regime as the batch size increases.

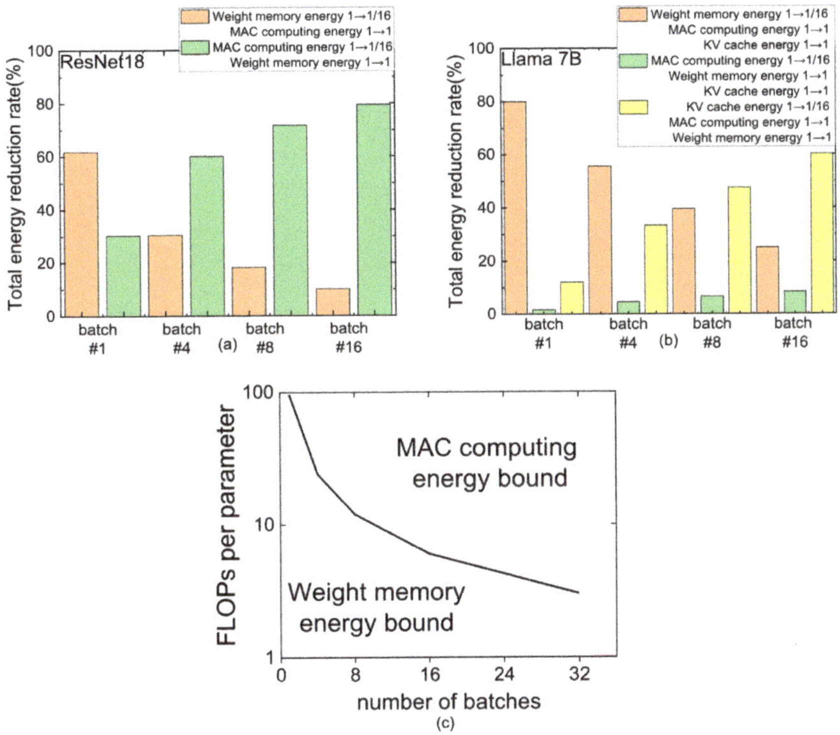

Figure 10. (**a**) ResNet18's total energy reduction for weight-memory vs. MAC energy scaling with batch sizes of 1, 4, 8, and 16. (**b**) Llama 7B's energy reduction for weight-memory, MAC, and KV cache energy scaling with batch sizes of 1, 4, 8, and 16. (**c**) FLOPs per parameter vs. batch size, illustrating the transition from computing energy-bound to memory energy-bound regimes.

Moving on to the Llama 7B transformer model in Figure 10b, we see a different picture because GPT models generally have many more parameters and must maintain a key–value (KV) cache for autoregressive attention. At batch size = 1, lowering the weight-memory energy produces a drastic 80% decrease, whereas cutting down the MAC computing energy only leads to 1.6% decrease, and diminishing the KV cache energy yields a 12% decrease. Even as we move to batch size = 4, weight-memory optimization still dominates at 55.6%, with MAC and KV cache reductions of 4.5% and 33.4%, respectively. These results underscore that GPT models are far more sensitive to memory traffic than to raw computing costs. At batch size = 8, the memory remains critical: decreasing the weight-memory energy yields a 39.5% reduction, reducing the KV cache energy leads to a 47.5% reduction, and MAC energy scaling results in a 6.5% decrease. At batch size = 16, memory dependencies remain paramount, with KV cache energy reductions offering 60.2% savings and weight-memory optimization leading to 25% savings, while MAC energy contributes only 8.2% savings. Altogether, these observations highlight that Llama 7B firmly remains in a memory-bound regime at all batch sizes, placing priority on either reducing weight-memory overhead or streamlining the KV cache mechanism to achieve the largest improvements in overall energy efficiency.

To clarify this analysis, Figure 10c examines how FLOPs per parameter change with increasing batch size, helping to visually identify whether a model is memory-bound or computationally bound. In the small-batch-size regime, the model tends to rely heavily on parameter loading and activation data management at every step, thus making it prone to being memory energy-bound. In this case, strategies to minimize memory access energy are crucial. Typical approaches include weight quantization (reduced precision), maximizing data reuse (caching), and near-/in-memory computing designs that physically reduce data movement distances.

When moving to larger batch sizes, architectures such as CNNs (ResNet18) exhibit a surge in parallel convolution operations, leading to the dominance of computing energy. On the other hand, for GPT-based models, the growth in sequence length also leads to heavier attention computations and KV cache usage, so memory access remains a considerable burden. As a result, even at large batch sizes, GPT-like models may not become purely computing-bound but rather remain in a mixed region where both memory and computation are critical. This disparity stems from fundamental differences in how CNNs and GPTs process data: CNNs perform pixel-level convolutions for spatial information, leading to heavy computing costs, whereas GPTs handle sequential information with extensive parameters and cache access, incurring significant memory costs.

To indicate the numbers used in Figures 5–9, Table 2 is shown below. In more detail, Table 2a indicates the energy consumption of ResNet18 with the weight-memory energy scaled from 1 down to 1/16, as shown in Figure 5. Table 2b shows the energy consumption of ResNet18 with MAC energy scaling from 1/16 to 1, as shown in Figure 6. Table 2c indicates the energy consumption of Llama-7B with the weight-memory energy scaled from 1 down to 1/16, as shown in Figure 7. Table 2d shows the energy consumption of Llama-7B with MAC energy scaling from 1/16 to 1, as shown in Figure 8. Table 2e shows the energy consumption of Llama-7B with the KV cache memory energy scaled from 1 down to 1/16, as shown in Figure 9.

Table 2. (a) The energy consumption of ResNet18 with the weight-memory energy scaled from 1/16 to 1. (b) The energy consumption of ResNet18 with the MAC computing energy scaled from 1/16 to 1. (c) The energy consumption of Llama-7B with the weight-memory energy scaled from 1/16 to 1. (d) The energy consumption of Llama-7B with the MAC computing energy scaled from 1/16 to 1. (e) The energy consumption of Llama-7B with the KV cache memory energy scaled from 1/16 to 1.

(a)	Normalized Weight Energy per Bit	1/16	1/8	1/4	1/2	1
number of batches = 1	activation	0.01693	0.01693	0.01693	0.01693	0.01693
	MAC	0.32393	0.32393	0.32393	0.32393	0.32393
	weight	0.0412	0.08239	0.16478	0.32957	0.65914
	total	0.38206	0.42325	0.50564	0.67043	1
number of batches = 4	activation	0.06772	0.06772	0.06772	0.06772	0.06772
	MAC	1.29574	1.29574	1.29574	1.29574	1.29574
	weight	0.0412	0.08239	0.16478	0.32957	0.65914
	total	1.40466	1.44585	1.52824	1.69303	2.02259
number of batches = 8	activation	0.13545	0.13545	0.13545	0.13545	0.13545
	MAC	2.59147	2.59147	2.59147	2.59147	2.59147
	weight	0.0412	0.08239	0.16478	0.32957	0.65914
	total	2.76812	2.80931	2.8917	3.05649	3.38606
number of batches = 16	activation	0.2709	0.2709	0.2709	0.2709	0.2709
	MAC	5.18294	5.18294	5.18294	5.18294	5.18294
	weight	0.0412	0.08239	0.16478	0.32957	0.65914
	total	5.49504	5.53623	5.61862	5.78341	6.11298

Table 2. *Cont.*

(b)	Normalized MAC Energy per Bit	1/16	1/8	1/4	1/2	1
number of batches = 1	activation	0.01693	0.01693	0.01693	0.01693	0.01693
	MAC	0.02025	0.04049	0.08098	0.16197	0.32393
	weight	0.65914	0.65914	0.65914	0.65914	0.65914
	total	0.69631	0.71656	0.75705	0.83803	1
number of batches = 4	activation	0.06772	0.06772	0.06772	0.06772	0.06772
	MAC	0.08098	0.16197	0.32393	0.64787	1.29574
	weight	0.65914	0.65914	0.65914	0.65914	0.65914
	total	0.80784	0.88883	1.05079	1.37473	2.02259
number of batches = 8	activation	0.13545	0.13545	0.13545	0.13545	0.13545
	MAC	0.16197	0.32393.	0.64787	1.29574	2.59147
	weight	0.65914	0.65914	0.65914	0.65914	0.65914
	total	0.95656	1.11852	1.44246	2.09033	3.38606
number of batches = 16	activation	0.2709	0.2709	0.2709	0.2709	0.2709
	MAC	0.32393	0.64787	1.29574	2.59147	5.18294
	weight	0.65914	0.65914	0.65914	0.65914	0.65914
	total	1.25397	1.57791	2.22578	3.52151	6.11298
(c)	Normalized Weight Energy per Bit	1/16	1/8	1/4	1/2	1
number of batches = 1	activation	4.47059×10^{-4}	4.47059×10^{-4}	4.47059×10^{-4}	4.47059×10^{-4}	4.47059×10^{-4}
	MAC	0.01763	0.01763	0.01763	0.01763	0.01763
	weight	0.05336	0.10672	0.21343/	0.42687	0.85374
	KV cache	0.12819	0.12819	0.12819	0.12819	0.12819
	total	0.19962	0.25298	0.3597	0.57313	1
number of batches = 4	activation	0.00179	0.00179	0.00179	0.00179	0.00179
	MAC	0.0705	0.0705	0.0705	0.0705	0.0705
	weight	0.05336	0.10672	0.21343	0.42687	0.85374
	KV cache	0.51276	0.51276	0.51276	0.51276	0.51276
	total	0.63841	0.69176	0.79848	1.01192	1.43879
number of batches = 8	activation	0.00358	0.00358	0.00358	0.00358	0.00358
	MAC	0.14101	0.14101	0.14101	0.14101	0.14101
	weight	0.05336	0.10672	0.21343	0.42687	0.85374
	KV cache	1.02551	1.02551	1.02551	1.02551	1.02551
	total	1.22345	1.27681	1.38353	1.59696	2.02383
number of batches = 16	activation	0.00715	0.00715	0.00715	0.00715	0.00715
	MAC	0.28202	0.28202	0.28202	0.28202	0.28202
	weight	0.05336	0.10672	0.21343	0.42687	0.85374
	KV cache	2.05102	2.05102	2.05102	2.05102	2.05102
	total	2.39355	2.44691	2.55363	2.76706	3.19393

Table 2. *Cont.*

(d)	Normalized MAC Energy per Bit	1/16	1/8	1/4	1/2	1
number of batches = 1	activation	4.47059×10^{-4}	4.47059×10^{-4}	4.47059×10^{-4}	4.47059×10^{-4}	4.47059×10^{-4}
	MAC	0.0011	0.0022	0.00441	0.00881	0.01763
	weight	0.85374	0.85374	0.85374	0.85374	0.85374
	KV cache	0.12819	0.12819	0.12819	0.12819	0.12819
	total	0.98348	0.98458	0.98678	0.99119	1
number of batches = 4	activation	0.00179	0.00179	0.00179	0.00179	0.00179
	MAC	0.00441	0.00881	0.01763	0.03525	0.0705
	weight	0.85374	0.85374	0.85374	0.85374	0.85374
	KV cache	0.51276	0.51276	0.51276	0.51276	0.51276
	total	1.37269	1.37709	1.38591	1.40353	1.43879
number of batches = 8	activation	0.00358	0.00358	0.00358	0.00358	0.00358
	MAC	0.00881	0.01763	0.03525	0.0705	0.14101
	weight	0.85374	0.85374	0.85374	0.85374	0.85374
	KV cache	1.02551	1.02551	1.02551	1.02551	1.02551
	total	1.89164	1.90045	1.91808	1.95333	2.02383
number of batches = 16	activation	0.00715	0.00715	0.00715	0.00715	0.00715
	MAC	0.01763	0.03525	0.0705	0.14101	0.28202
	weight	0.85374	0.85374	0.85374	0.85374	0.85374
	KV cache	2.05102	2.05102	2.05102	2.05102	2.05102
	total	2.92954	2.94717	2.98242	3.05292	3.19393
(e)	Normalized KV Cache Energy per Bit	1/16	1/8	1/4	1/2	1
number of batches = 1	activation	4.47059×10^{-4}	4.47059×10^{-4}	4.47059×10^{-4}	4.47059×10^{-4}	4.47059×10^{-4}
	MAC	0.01763	0.01763	0.01763	0.01763	0.01763
	weight	0.85374	0.85374	0.85374	0.85374	0.85374
	KV cache	0.00801	0.01602	0.03205	0.06409	0.12819
	total	0.87982	0.88783	0.90386	0.93591	1
number of batches = 4	activation	0.00179	0.00179	0.00179	0.00179	0.00179
	MAC	0.0705	0.0705	0.0705	0.0705	0.0705
	weight	0.85374	0.85374	0.85374	0.85374	0.85374
	KV cache	0.03205	0.06409	0.12819	0.25638	0.51276
	total	0.95808	0.99012	1.05422	1.18241	1.43879
number of batches = 8	activation	0.00358	0.00358	0.00358	0.00358	0.00358
	MAC	0.14101	0.14101	0.14101	0.14101	0.14101
	weight	0.85374	0.85374	0.85374	0.85374	0.85374
	KV cache	0.06409	0.12819	0.25638	0.51276	1.02551
	total	1.06242	1.12651	1.2547	1.51108	2.02383

Table 2. *Cont.*

(e)	Normalized KV Cache Energy per Bit	1/16	1/8	1/4	1/2	1
number of batches = 16	activation	0.00715	0.00715	0.00715	0.00715	0.00715
	MAC	0.28202	0.28202	0.28202	0.28202	0.28202
	weight	0.85374	0.85374	0.85374	0.85374	0.85374
	KV cache	0.12819	0.25638	0.51276	1.02551	2.05102
	total	1.2711	1.39928	1.65566	2.16842	3.19393

One more thing to discuss here is that other AI models such as mobilenet, googlenet, etc., can also be analyzed in terms of the energy breakdown performed in this paper. Actually, a large portion of the energy consumption of AI models comes from accessing weight memory and computing MAC. Thus, using the same calculation method for energy consumption performed in this paper, the energy consumption of other AI models could be analyzed. This study could be extended further in future work to cover a wide range of AI models from edge to cloud intelligence.

By scaling the weight-memory energy versus MAC computing energy, we were able to analyze and estimate the energy consumption trend of AI models in this section. From this analysis, we can further highlight near-memory and in-memory computing approaches as promising strategies to lower data-transfer costs and enhance power efficiency in large-scale deployments of AI models. These findings could be helpful for offering actionable insights for architects and system designers aiming to optimize AI performance under stringent energy budgets on battery-powered edge devices.

4. Conclusions

The energy consumption of big AI models has emerged as a critical design constraint in deploying high-performance neural networks, especially on edge devices, where their energy resources are limited by battery capacity. In this paper, we performed a comparative study for two types of AI models, those based on convolutional neural networks (CNNs), represented by ResNet18, and transformer-based large language models (LLMs), represented by GPT3-small, Llama-7B, and GPT3-175B. To achieve this, we first analyzed how the scaling of memory energy versus computing energy affects the total energy consumption of neural networks with different batch sizes (1, 4, 8, 16). As a result, it was shown that ResNet18 transitions from a memory energy-limited regime at low batch sizes to a computing energy-limited regime at higher batch sizes due to the increase in convolution operations with batch number. On the other hand, GPT-like models remain predominantly memory-bound, with large parameter tensors and frequent key–value (KV) cache lookups accounting for most of the total energy usage. From the energy analysis performed in this paper, we found that reducing the weight-memory energy is particularly effective in transformer architectures, while improving multiply–accumulate (MAC) efficiency significantly benefits CNNs at higher workloads. Moreover, it was highlighted in this paper that near-memory and in-memory computing could be considered promising strategies in the near future to lower data-transfer costs and enhance power efficiency in large-scale deployments. These results can offer helpful guidelines for architects and system designers who are aiming to optimize AI performance under stringent energy budgets on battery-powered edge devices.

Author Contributions: Conceptualization, K.-S.M.; Methodology, I.Y. and J.M.; Investigation, I.Y. and J.M.; Writing—original draft, I.Y.; Writing—review & editing, K.-S.M.; Supervision, K.-S.M. All authors have read and agreed to the published version of the manuscript.

Funding: This research was funded by National Research Foundation of Korea grant number [RS-2024-00401234, RS-2024-00406006, RS-2024-00395426, RS-2024-12872969].

Data Availability Statement: Dataset available on request from the authors.

Acknowledgments: Technical support for the CAD tools was supplied by IC Design Education Center (IDEC), Daejeon, Korea.

Conflicts of Interest: The authors declare no conflicts of interest.

References

1. LeCun, Y.; Bengio, Y.; Hinton, G. Deep learning. *Nature* **2015**, *521*, 436–444. [CrossRef]
2. Schmidhuber, J. Deep Learning in neural networks: An overview. *Neural Netw.* **2015**, *61*, 85–117. [CrossRef] [PubMed]
3. Jia, Y.H.; Si, Z.Z.; Ju, Z.T.; Feng, H.Y.; Zhang, J.H.; Yan, X.; Dai, C.Q. Convolutional-recurrent neural network for the prediction c formation and switching dynamics for multicolor solitons. *Sci. China Physics, Mech. Astron.* **2025**, *68*, 284211. [CrossRef]
4. Wan, Y.; Wei, Q.; Sun, H.; Wu, H.; Zhou, Y.; Bi, C.; Li, J.; Li, L.; Liu, B.; Wang, D.; et al. Machine learning assisted biomimetic flexib SERS sensor from seashells for pesticide classification and concentration prediction. *Chem. Eng. J.* **2025**, *507*, 160813. [CrossRef]
5. Krizhevsky, A.; Sutskever, I.; Hinton, G.E. ImageNet classification with deep convolutional neural networks. *Commun. ACM* **201** *60*, 84–90. [CrossRef]
6. He, K.; Zhang, X.; Ren, S.; Sun, J. Deep residual learning for image recognition. In Proceedings of the IEEE Conference o Computer Vision and Pattern Recognition, Las Vegas, NV, USA, 27–30 June 2016; pp. 770–778.
7. Vaswani, A.; Shazeer, N.; Parmar, N.; Uszkoreit, J.; Jones, L.; Gomez, A.N.; Kaiser, Ł.; Polosukhin, I. Attention is all you need. *Ad Neural Inf. Process. Syst.* **2017**, *30*. [CrossRef]
8. Devlin, J.; Chang, M.W.; Lee, K.; Toutanova, K. BERT: Pre-training of deep bidirectional transformers for language understandin In Proceedings of the 2019 Conference of the North American Chapter of the Association for Computational Linguistics: Huma Language Technologies, Minneapolis, MN, USA, 2–7 June 2019; Volume 1, pp. 4171–4186.
9. Xia, Q.; Ye, W.; Tao, Z.; Wu, J.; Li, Q. A survey of federated learning for edge computing: Research problems and solution *High-Confidence Comput.* **2021**, *1*, 100008. [CrossRef]
10. Amin, S.U.; Hossain, M.S. Edge Intelligence and Internet of Things in Healthcare: A Survey. *IEEE Access* **2021**, *9*, 45–59. [CrossRef
11. Shi, W.; Cao, J.; Zhang, Q.; Li, Y.; Xu, L. Edge Computing: Vision and Challenges. *IEEE Internet Things J.* **2016**, *3*, 637–646. [CrossRef
12. Aminifar, A.; Shokri, M.; Aminifar, A. Privacy-preserving edge federated learning for intelligent mobile-health systems. *Futu Gener. Comput. Syst.* **2024**, *161*, 625–637. [CrossRef]
13. Zheng, Y.; Chen, Y.; Qian, B.; Shi, X.; Shu, Y.; Chen, J. A Review on Edge Large Language Models: Design, Execution, an Applications. *ACM Comput. Surv.* **2025**, *57*, 1–35. [CrossRef]
14. Schwartz, R.; Dodge, J.; Smith, N.A.; Etzioni, O. Green AI. *Commun. ACM* **2020**, *63*, 54–63. [CrossRef]
15. Maliakel, P.J.; Ilager, S.; Brandic, I. Investigating Energy Efficiency and Performance Trade-offs in LLM Inference Across Task and DVFS Settings. *arXiv* **2025**, arXiv:2501.08219.
16. Li, Y.; Mughees, M.; Chen, Y.; Li, Y.R. The Unseen AI Disruptions for Power Grids: LLM-Induced Transients. *arXiv* **2024** arXiv:2409.11416.
17. Brown, T.B.; Mann, B.; Ryder, N.; Subbiah, M.; Kaplan, J.; Dhariwal, P.; Neelakantan, A.; Shyam, P.; Sastry, G.; Askell, A.; et a Language models are few-shot learners. *Adv. Neural Inf. Process. Syst.* **2020**, *33*, 1877–1901.
18. Strubell, E.; Ganesh, A.; McCallum, A. Energy and policy considerations for deep learning in NLP. *arXiv* **2019**, arXiv:1906.02243
19. Dreslinski, R.G.; Wieckowski, M.; Blaauw, D.; Sylvester, D.; Mudge, T. Near-threshold computing: Reclaiming moore's law through energy efficient integrated circuits. *Proc. IEEE* **2010**, *98*, 253–266. [CrossRef]
20. Horowitz, M. Computing's energy problem (and what we can do about it). *Dig. Tech. Pap.* **2014**, *57*, 10–14. [CrossRef]
21. Ahn, J.; Hong, S.; Yoo, S.; Mutlu, O.; Choi, K. A scalable processing-in-memory accelerator for parallel graph processing Procedings of the ACM/IEEE 42nd Annual International Symposium on Computer Architecture, Portland, OR, USA, 13–17 June 2015; pp. 105–117. [CrossRef]
22. Singh, G.; Chelini, L.; Corda, S.; Awan, A.J.; Stuijk, S.; Jordans, R.; Corporaal, H.; Boonstra, A.J. Near-memory computing: Past present, and future. *Microprocess. Microsyst.* **2019**, *71*, 102868. [CrossRef]

23. Sheng, X.; Graves, C.E.; Kumar, S.; Li, X.; Buchanan, B.; Zheng, L.; Lam, S.; Li, C.; Strachan, J.P. Low-Conductance and Multilevel CMOS-Integrated Nanoscale Oxide Memristors. *Adv. Electron. Mater.* **2019**, *5*, 1800876. [CrossRef]
24. Chi, P.; Li, S.; Xu, C.; Zhang, T.; Zhao, J.; Liu, Y.; Wang, Y.; Xie, Y. PRIME: A Novel Processing-in-Memory Architecture for Neural Network Computation in ReRAM-Based Main Memory. Proceedings of ACM/IEEE 43rd Annual International Symposium on Computer Architecture, Seoul, Republic of Korea, 18–22 June 2016; pp. 27–39. [CrossRef]
25. Shafiee, A.; Nag, A.; Muralimanohar, N.; Balasubramonian, R.; Strachan, J.P.; Hu, M.; Williams, R.S.; Srikumar, V. Isaac. *ACM SIGARCH Comput. Archit. News* **2016**, *44*, 14–26. [CrossRef]
26. He, W.; Member, G.S.; Yin, S.; Member, G.S.; Kim, Y.; Member, G.S.; Sun, X.; Member, S.; Kim, J.; Yu, S.; et al. 2-Bit-Per-Cell RRAM-Based In-Memory Computing for Area-/Energy-Efficient Deep Learning. *IEEE Solid-State Circuits Lett.* **2020**, *3*, 194–197. [CrossRef]
27. Lahmer, S.; Khoshsirat, A.; Rossi, M.; Zanella, A. Energy Consumption of Neural Networks on NVIDIA Edge Boards: An Empirical Model. In Proceedings of the 2022 20th International Symposium on Modeling and Optimization in Mobile, Ad hoc, and Wireless Networks, Torino, Italy, 19–23 September 2022; pp. 365–371. [CrossRef]
28. Latif, I.; Newkirk, A.C.; Carbone, M.R.; Munir, A.; Lin, Y.; Koomey, J.; Yu, X.; Dong, Z. Empirical Measurements of AI Training Power Demand on a GPU-Accelerated Node. *IEEE Access* **2025**, *13*, 61740–61747. [CrossRef]
29. Aquino-Brítez, S.; García-Sánchez, P.; Ortiz, A.; Aquino-Brítez, D. Towards an Energy Consumption Index for Deep Learning Models: A Comparative Analysis of Architectures, GPUs, and Measurement Tools. *Sensors* **2025**, *25*, 846. [CrossRef]
30. Wolters, C. Memory Is All You Need: An Overview of Compute-in-Memory Architectures for Accelerating Large Language Model Inference. *arXiv* **2024**, arXiv:2406.08413.
31. Wu, Y.; Wang, Z.; Lu, W.D. PIM-GPT: A Hybrid Process-in-Memory Accelerator for Autoregressive Transformers. *NPJ Unconv. Comput.* **2024**, *1*, 1. [CrossRef]
32. Kaplan, J.; McCandlish, S.; Henighan, T.; Brown, T.B.; Chess, B.; Child, R.; Gray, S.; Radford, A.; Wu, J.; Amodei, D. Scaling Laws for Neural Language Models. *arXiv* **2020**, arXiv:2001.08361.
33. Touvron, H.; Lavril, T.; Izacard, G.; Martinet, X.; Lachaux, M.-A.; Lacroix, T.; Rozière, B.; Goyal, N.; Hambro, E.; Azhar, F.; et al. LLaMA: Open and Efficient Foundation Language Models. *arXiv* **2023**, arXiv:2302.13971.
34. Johnson, J. Rethinking floating point for deep learning. *arXiv* **2018**, arXiv:1811.01721v1.
35. Samsung Electronics Co., Ltd. *8 Gb GDDR6 SGRAM (C-Die) Data Sheet, Rev. 1.0.*; Samsung Electronics Co., Ltd.: Suwon-si, Gyeonggi-do, Republic of Korea, 2020. Available online: https://datasheet.lcsc.com/lcsc/2204251615_Samsung-K4Z80325BC-HC14_C2920181.pdf (accessed on 1 July 2025).
36. Micron Technology, Inc. *LPDDR5/LPDDR5X SDRAM Data Sheet, Rev. D.*; Micron Technology, Inc.: Boise, ID, USA, 2022; pp. 1–30. Available online: https://www.mouser.com/datasheet/2/671/Micron_05092023_315b_441b_y4bm_ddp_qdp_8dp_non_aut-3175604.pdf (accessed on 1 July 2025).
37. Jouppi, N.P.; Yoon, D.H.; Ashcraft, M.; Gottscho, M.; Jablin, T.B.; Kurian, G.; Laudon, J.; Li, S.; Ma, P.; Ma, X.; et al. Ten lessons from three generations shaped Google's TPU v4i: Industrial product. In Proceedings of the 2021 ACM/IEEE 48th Annual International Symposium on Computer Architecture, Valencia, Spain, 14–18 June 2021; pp. 1–14. [CrossRef]
38. Ivanov, A.; Dryden, N.; Ben-Nun, T.; Li, S.; Hoefler, T. Data Movement Is All You Need: A Case Study on Optimizing Transformers. *arXiv* **2020**, arXiv:2007.00072.
39. Yang, T.J.; Chen, Y.H.; Emer, J.; Sze, V. A method to estimate the energy consumption of deep neural networks. In Proceedings of the 2017 51st Asilomar Conference on Signals, Systems, and Computers, Pacific Grove, CA, USA, 29 October–1 November 2017; pp. 1916–1920. [CrossRef]
40. Jain, S.R.; Gural, A.; Wu, M.; Dick, C.H. Trained Quantization Thresholds for Accurate and Efficient Fixed-Point Inference of Deep Neural Networks. In Proceedings of the 3rd Conference on Machine Learning and Systems (MLSys 2020), Austin, TX, USA, 6–8 March 2020; pp. 1–17.
41. Jacob, B.; Kligys, S.; Chen, B.; Zhu, M.; Tang, M.; Howard, A.; Adam, H.; Kalenichenko, D. Quantization and Training of Neural Networks for Efficient Integer-Arithmetic-Only Inference. In Proceedings of the 2018 IEEE/CVF Conference on Computer Vision and Pattern Recognition Workshops, Salt Lake City, UT, USA, 18–22 June 2018; pp. 2704–2713. [CrossRef]
42. Luohe, S.; Hongyi, Z.; Yao, Y.; Zuchao, L.; Hai, Z. Keep the Cost Down: A Review on Methods to Optimize LLM's KV-Cache Consumption. *arXiv* **2024**, arXiv:2407.18003.
43. Adnan, M.; Arunkumar, A.; Jain, G.; Nair, P.J.; Soloveychik, I.; Kamath, P. Keyformer: KV Cache Reduction through Key Tokens Selection for Efficient Generative Inference. *arXiv* **2024**, arXiv:2403.09054. [CrossRef]

electronics

MDPI

Article

Meta Network for Flow-Based Image Style Transfer

Yihjia Tsai [1], Hsiau-Wen Lin [2,*], Chii-Jen Chen [1], Hwei-Jen Lin [1,*] and Chen-Hsiang Yu [3]

1 Department of Computer Science and Information Engineering, Tamkang University, New Taipei City 251301, Taiwan; iaiclab.tku@gmail.com (Y.T.); cjchen@mail.tku.edu.tw (C.-J.C.)
2 Department of Information Management, Chihlee University of Technology, New Taipei City 220305, Taiwan
3 Multidisciplinary Graduate Engineering, College of Engineering, Northeastern University, Boston, MA 02115, USA; jones.yu@northeastern.edu
* Correspondence: freyah.lin@mail.chihlee.edu.tw (H.-W.L.); 086204@gms.tku.edu.tw (H.-J.L.)

Abstract: A style transfer aims to produce synthesized images that retain the content of one image while adopting the artistic style of another. Traditional style transfer methods often require training separate transformation networks for each new style, limiting their adaptability and scalability. To address this challenge, we propose a flow-based image style transfer framework that integrates Randomized Hierarchy Flow (RH Flow) and a meta network for adaptive parameter generation. The meta network dynamically produces the RH Flow parameters conditioned on the style image, enabling efficient and flexible style adaptation without retraining for new styles. RH Flow enhances feature interaction by introducing a random permutation of the feature sub-blocks before hierarchical coupling, promoting diverse and expressive stylization while preserving the content structure. Our experimental results demonstrate that Meta FIST achieves superior content retention, style fidelity, and adaptability compared to existing approaches.

Keywords: meta learning; image style transfer; convolutional neural network; instance normalization; adversarial learning; flow-based model

1. Introduction

Image style transfer [1–9] refers to the process of incorporating the style of a reference image (or style image) into a content image, with applications in digital art, design, and image generation. Over the years, this field has undergone significant advancements, transitioning from traditional image processing techniques to the adoption of deep learning methodologies.

Early image style transfer methods relied on digital signal processing techniques, such as Fourier transforms or image segmentation, to blend style and content. However, these approaches struggled to capture fine stylistic details and heavily depended on manually designed features, making them ill-suited for diverse style requirements. In 2015, Gatys et al. [10] introduced the first convolutional neural network (CNN)-based style transfer method, leveraging pre-trained VGG networks to extract the content and style features and optimizing the generated image via a gradient descent. Although this approach produced high-quality results, its computational cost rendered it unsuitable for real-time applications.

To address this limitation, Johnson et al. [11] proposed a fast feed-forward network in 2016, enabling stylized image generation with a single forward pass through a pre-trained generative network. However, this method required training a separate model for each style, limiting its flexibility and generalization capability. Subsequent research aimed to overcome these constraints by enabling multi-style and arbitrary style transfer. The notable contributions have included Adaptive Instance Normalization (AdaIN) [12], which dynamically adjusts the normalization parameters (scale and bias) to match the input style features, and Conditional Instance Normalization (CIN) [13], which utilizes style labels to control the normalization parameters for seamless multi-style switching. Other advancements have included Universal Style Transfer (UST) [14], which leverages mathematical operations in feature space, such as Principle Component Analysis (PCA) and Whitening and Coloring Transform (WCT), to achieve generalized content–style fusion; and StyleBank [15], which designs unique convolutional kernels for each style and supports arbitrary styles through linear combinations. Other techniques, such as Avatar-Net [16] and Linear Style Transfer [17], have further improved the detail reconstruction and computational efficiency. However, most style transfer methods still suffer from content leakage, where the generated image fails to preserve the structural characteristics of the original content image, such as scene layout, object boundaries, or details. This issue often arises due to an insufficient disentanglement of the content and style features, overly simplistic feature fusion mechanisms, or generative networks that excessively favor the style features.

To address these challenges, recent works have incorporated attention mechanisms, such as Self-Attention [18] and Cross-Attention [19], to enhance the weighting of the content features. Others have employed adversarial learning [20] to ensure the balanced fusion of content and style or have adopted flow-based models [21,22] to improve the content preservation and detail reconstruction. For example, ArtFlow [21] built a reversible feature extraction framework inspired by the Glow model [23] to prevent content leakage. However, its restrictive inverse computation often resulted in artifacts like checkerboard patterns. Hierarchy Flow [22], introduced by W. Fan et al., achieved greater flexibility by introducing hierarchical feature interactions during the transformation process, effectively resolving artifacts and preserving content details.

Recent style transfer methods have typically required training an image transfer network for each new style, with the style information embedded in the network parameters through numerous iterations of stochastic gradient descent. To address these limitations, meta learning [24,25]—originally introduced to enable models to quickly adapt to new tasks using only a few examples—has emerged as a promising paradigm for improving generalization and adaptability. Inspired by this, F. Shen et al. [26] proposed a meta network that takes a style image as the input and directly generates a corresponding image transformation network, bypassing the need for retraining. While this approach enables adaptive style transfer, its single-pass feed-forward design lacks the content-preserving capabilities of flow-based architectures. This study aims to develop a meta network that enhances the adaptability of flow-based style transfer by generating a model tailored to a given style image. The proposed framework consists of two key components: (1) a modified version of the Hierarchical Flow model, termed Randomized Hierarchical Flow (RH Flow), which introduces a random permutation of the feature sub-blocks before the hierarchical coupling layer to enhance the feature interaction diversity and flexibility; and (2) a meta network that generates the RH Flow parameters, enabling both effective content preservation and flexible style adaptation. By integrating these innovations, our approach enhances the balance between content fidelity and stylistic expressiveness, offering significant advancements for applications in digital art, design, and image generation. The key contributions of this paper include (1) the design of the Randomized Hierarchy Flow for enhanced content preservation, (2) the development of a meta network that generates adaptive transformation parameters without retraining, and (3) comprehensive experimental validation demonstrating its superior performance and parameter efficiency.

2. Related Works

The field of image style transfer has evolved significantly from traditional methods to advanced deep learning approaches. This section provides a concise overview of the flow-based models and meta-learning techniques.

2.1. Flow-Based Style Transfer Models

Flow-based models, particularly Glow [23], offer unique advantages due to their reversible design. The Glow model's components—Activation Normalization (ActNorm), an invertible 1×1 convolution, and affine coupling layers—ensure high fidelity in data reconstruction and flexible manipulation of the latent features, as shown in Figure 1.

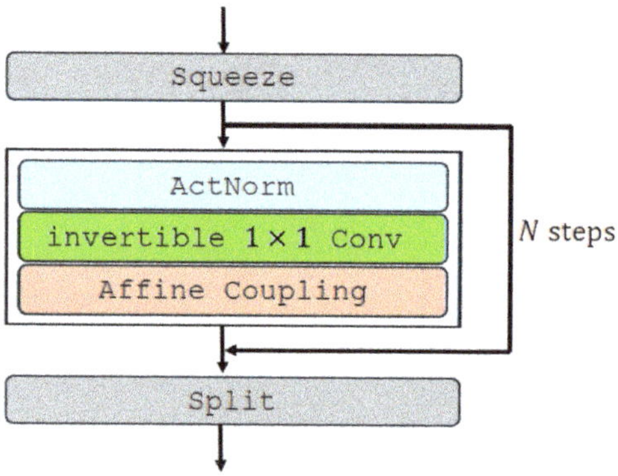

Figure 1. Flow model [23].

ArtFlow [21] was the first to adopt Glow for style transfer, leveraging its reversibility for content preservation. However, ArtFlow's reliance on multi-scale squeezing operations led to artifacts, such as checkerboard patterns. To overcome these issues, Hierarchy Flow [22] introduced structural improvements, including hierarchical coupling layers and an aligned-style loss function. These enhancements ensured robust content preservation and style representation.

2.2. Meta Learning for Style Transfer

Meta-learning (or learning to learn) originated from the concept of improving learning efficiency and adaptability [27,28]. Recently, it has gained significant attention for its ability to enhance the speed of learning and generalization to new tasks. A gradient-based learning method can be expressed using Equation (1) [29], where the model parameters θ are updated based on the gradient of a loss function ℓ with parameters ϕ. The update employs a gradient transformation function h with parameters ψ to compute new model parameters:

$$\theta_{new} = h_{\psi}(\theta, \nabla_{\theta}\mathcal{L}_{\phi}(y, f_{\theta}(x))) \tag{1}$$

Meta-learning research can be categorized into the following: (1) learning model parameters that adapt easily to new tasks [30], (2) learning optimizer strategies based on reward functions derived from loss or parameter updates [31], (3) learning representations of loss or reward functions [32], and (4) discovering transferable unsupervised rules in task-agnostic environments [33].

The current multi-style and arbitrary style transfer techniques have addressed the need to retrain networks for each style, improving the diversity and quality of the generated images. However, these methods are limited by fixed feature spaces and struggle to adapt to entirely new styles. Additionally, their performance is constrained when handling extreme styles or real-time applications. To address these challenges, F. Shen et al. [26] proposed a meta network that dynamically generates the parameters for style transfer networks based on the input style images. This approach eliminates the need for retraining networks for each style through a single forward pass, significantly enhancing efficiency and flexibility.

3. Meta Model for Flow-Based Image Style Transfer

This study proposes a flow-based style transfer meta network, Meta model for Flow-based Image Style Transfer (MFIST), which focuses on generating a flexible and adaptable flow-based image style transfer system. The research methods and procedures are divided into two main components. (1) Improving the Hierarchical Flow Model: Building upon the Hierarchical Flow method proposed by W. Fan et al. [22], we introduce an improved version, called Randomized Hierarchy Flow (RH Flow). Before the hierarchical coupling layer, we apply random permutation to the split feature blocks, dynamically altering the coupling order. This enhancement aims to increase the diversity of feature interactions, further improving the model's expressiveness and flexibility in style transfer. Additionally, we propose a lightweight Style Encoder to replace the Style Net used in the original work. The Style Encoder processes the initial features extracted from a pre-trained VGG network and generates AdaIN parameters for style transfer. This design significantly reduces the number of parameters while maintaining accuracy and efficiency in style feature extraction. These improvements collectively ensure that the model achieves both efficiency and flexibility during style transfer. (2) Constructing a Flow-Based Reversible Style Transfer Architecture with Meta-Learning: The parameters of the Randomized Hierarchy Flow model are not obtained through conventional training but are instead generated by a meta network trained for this purpose. Inspired by the meta-learning network proposed by F. Shen et al. [26], this study designs a meta network to discover optimal parameters for the Randomized Hierarchy Flow model, rather than relying on traditional feed-forward training. This reversible architecture effectively preserves content features while enabling accurate style transfer, providing a flexible solution for real-time and diverse style transfer applications.

3.1. *Randomized Hierarchical Flow Model*

As illustrated in Figure 2, the proposed Randomized Hierarchy Flow (RH Flow) is composed of multiple reversible randomized hierarchical coupling (RHC) layers. Given a content image I_c and a style image I_s, the processing is as follows: During the forward pass (indicated by the red arrows), the RHC layers encode the content image I_c to extract multi-level hierarchical content features. Simultaneously, the style image I_s is processed through a pre-trained VGG network to extract style features. These features are further encoded by the Style Encoder to generate the style feature statistics (mean and standard deviation), as indicated by the green arrows. These content and style features are fused using the Adaptive Instance Normalization (AdaIN) module (depicted by the merging arrows) to incorporate style information into the content representation. In the backward pass (blue arrows), the network progressively reconstructs the stylized image I_{cs} from the fused features through invertible RHC layers. The RH Flow model is fully reversible, enabling lossless reconstruction during style transfer.

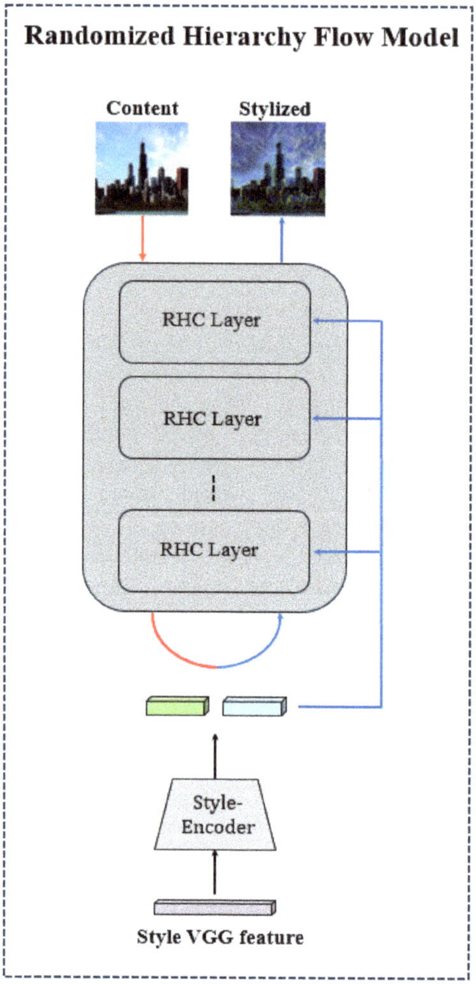

Figure 2. Randomized Hierarchy Flow model.

Randomized Hierarchical Coupling Layers

Unlike the ArtFlow model, which requires spatial compression, the Hierarchical Flow model applies hierarchical subtraction along the channel dimension to enable learnable spatial feature fusion and transformation. As illustrated in Figure 3, during the forward pass (top part of the figure), the Affine-Net first applies an affine transformation to the input content feature, followed by splitting into N sub-tensors. These sub-tensors are then randomly permuted (indicated by arrows with "random permute") and hierarchically fused through subtractive coupling over T steps. The final output is obtained by concatenating all intermediate results (purple arrow). In the reverse pass (bottom part of the figure), the stylized feature is split again into N sub-tensors. Using the style statistics (μ, σ) obtained from the Style Encoder via AdaIN, weighted additive coupling (shown by the $\oplus$ operations) is applied sequentially to progressively inject style information into the content features. This process reconstructs the final stylized image. All intermediate operations and data flows are reversible, ensuring that the RH Flow architecture preserves content structure while achieving flexible style adaptation.

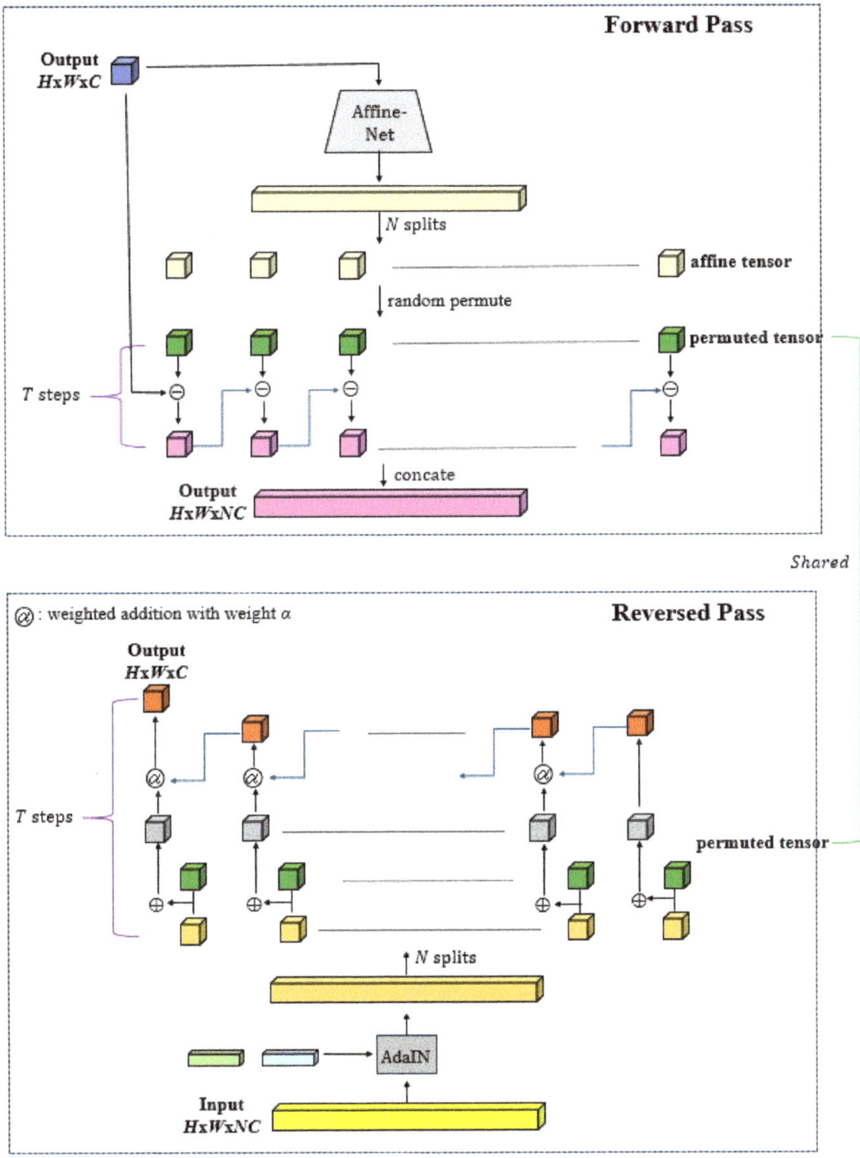

Figure 3. Randomized Hierarchy Coupling (RHC).

Forward Pass

As illustrated in Algorithm 1, given an input tensor x with dimensions $H \times W \times C$, the Affine-Net, parameterized by θ_a, performs affine transformations, expanding the tensor along the channel dimension to $H \times W \times NC$. The expanded tensor a is then split into N sub-tensors $(a_1, a_2, \ldots, a_N)$, each of size $H \times W \times C$, which are subsequently shuffled through a random permutation to form $(b_1, b_2, \ldots, b_N)$. A hierarchical subtractive coupling mechanism is then iteratively applied across N steps, where each step progressively refines the intermediate features h_i by subtracting the corresponding shuffled components. Finally, the intermediate feature maps are concatenated along the channel dimension to generate the output y.

Algorithm 1. Forward Pass

FORWARD(x, θ_a)
$a \leftarrow$ **Affine-Net**$(x; \theta_a)$
$(a_1, a_2, \ldots, a_N) \leftarrow$ **split**(a)
$(b_1, b_2, \ldots, b_N) \leftarrow$ **random permute** $(a_1, a_2, \ldots, a_N)$
$h_1 \leftarrow x - b_1$
for $i \leftarrow 2$ **to** N **do**
    $h_i \leftarrow h_{i-1} - b_i$
$y \leftarrow$ **concat** $(h_1, h_2, \ldots, h_N)$
return $y, b_1, b_2, \ldots, b_N$

Reverse Pass

As shown in Algorithm 2, the reverse pass reconstructs a stylized version of the original tensor x by iteratively applying N additive coupling transformations. The process begins by normalizing the input tensor y using Adaptive Instance Normalization (AdaIN), with style statistics (μ, σ) extracted by the Style Encoder. The normalized tensor y is then split into N feature blocks $(y_1, y_2, \ldots, y_N)$. Each block is progressively fused with the corresponding shuffled affine tensor b_i in a backward manner, starting from the last block. To enhance feature fusion and improve adaptability during training, a learnable weight α is introduced at each step, dynamically balancing the influence of the current feature block and the accumulated transformation. The final output x is reconstructed after N steps of fusion.

Algorithm 2. Reversed Pass

REVERSED$(y, b_1, b_2, \ldots, b_N, \mu, \sigma)$
$y \leftarrow$ **AdaIN**(y, μ, σ)
$y_1, y_2, \ldots, y_N \leftarrow$ **split**(y)
$h_N \leftarrow y_N + b_N$
for $i \leftarrow N - 1$ **downto** 1 **do**
    $h_i \leftarrow \alpha \cdot (y_i + b_i) + (1 - \alpha) \cdot h_{i+1}$
$x \leftarrow h_1$
return x

RH Flow

As described in Algorithm 3, the RH Flow model performs style transfer by iteratively refining the stylized image through a randomized hierarchical transformation. The process begins with encoding the style features f_s from the style image using a pre-trained VGG network. These features are further processed by the Style Encoder, parameterized by θ_s, to produce the adaptive style statistics (μ, σ). The input content image I_c is then progressively transformed over T iterations. During each iteration, the forward pass applies an affine transformation to the content tensor, producing an intermediate representation y along with a set of affine parameters $(b_1, b_2, \ldots, b_N)$. The reverse pass then reconstructs a stylized version of x by fusing these components hierarchically, guided by the learnable fusion weight α. All parameters required for the RH Flow model, including those of the Affine-Net, Style Encoder, and fusion weights, are dynamically generated through the proposed meta network, ensuring efficient, adaptive, and high-fidelity style transfer.

Algorithm 3. Randomized Hierarchy Flow

RH_FLOW($I_c, f_s, \alpha, \theta_a, \theta_s$)
$(\mu, \sigma) \leftarrow$ **Style-Encoder**($f_s; \theta_s$)
$x \leftarrow I_c$
for $t \leftarrow 1$ **to** T **do**
    $y, b_1, b_2, \ldots, b_N \leftarrow$ FORWARD(x, θ_a)
    $x \leftarrow$ REVERSED($y, b_1, b_2, \ldots, b_N, \mu, \sigma$)
return x

Affine-Net and Style Encoder

The Affine-Net performs affine transformations, expanding the input tensor along the channel dimension by a factor of N. We adopt the Affine-Net architecture proposed by W. Fan et al. [22]. As illustrated in Figure 4a, our current Affine-Net is a three-layer perceptron with the structure Conv-IN-ReLU $\rightarrow$ Conv-IN-ReLU $\rightarrow$ Conv-ReLU, where all convolutional layers utilize $k \times k$ kernels with a stride of 1. The first two convolutional layers double the input channel dimension C, while the final layer maps the features to the output channel dimension NC. This results in an output size of $H \times W \times NC$. For $k = 3$, $N = 4$, and $C = 3$, the total number of parameters in the Affine-Net is calculated as follows: $(2C^2 + 4C^2 + 2NC^2) \times k^2 = 1134$.

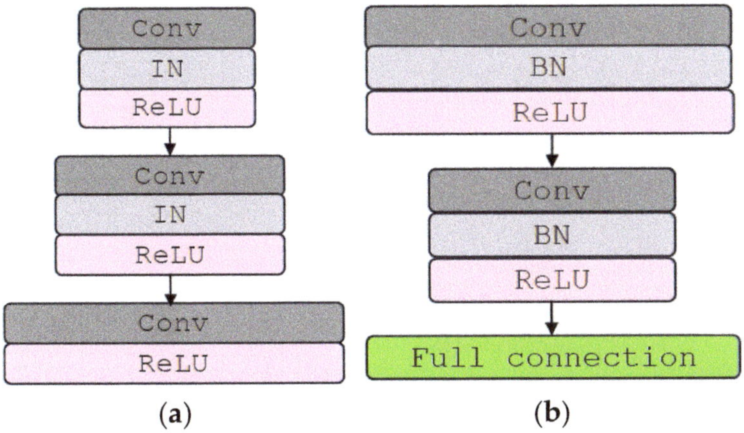

Figure 4. (**a**) Affine-Net and (**b**) Style Encoder.

The Style Encoder generates mean (μ) and standard deviation (σ) vectors, each of dimension NC, as input into the AdaIN module. Unlike the Style Net architecture used by W. Fan et al. [22], our Style Encoder is lightweight and designed to operate on style features rather than raw style images I_s. The processing pipeline is as follows: The style image is first passed through the frozen VGG-16 network, and feature maps are extracted from four specific layers—relu1_2, relu2_2, relu3_3, and relu4_3—producing a total of 64 + 128 + 256 + 512 = 960 feature maps. These maps are subsequently processed using

Mean-Std Feature Embedding (MSFE), which calculates the mean and standard deviation of each individual feature map. This results in a 1920-dimensional vector, denoted as f_s, referred to as the style feature vector. This vector f_s is subsequently passed to the Style Encoder, which produces a $2NC$-dimensional output vector. For $N = 4$ and $C = 3$, this results in a 24-dimensional vector.

As illustrated in Figure 4b, the Style Encoder is a three-layer perceptron consisting of the structure Conv-BN-ReLU $\rightarrow$ Conv-BN-ReLU $\rightarrow$ Fully Connected. The 1920-dimensional style feature vector f_s is first reshaped to a 3D tensor of size $30 \times 32 \times 2$ before being fed into the Style Encoder. Both convolutional layers employ 1×1 kernels with a stride of 1, producing feature maps of sizes $8 \times 8 \times 16$ and $1 \times 1 \times 64$, respectively. The output of the second convolutional layer is reshaped into a 64-dimensional vector and passed through a fully connected layer, which generates a $2NC$-dimensional vector comprising the mean (μ) and standard deviation (σ) for AdaIN. This design significantly reduces the number of trainable parameters while ensuring efficient and accurate extraction of style features. For example, when $N = 4$ and $C = 3$, the total number of parameters in the Style Encoder is calculated as $2 \times 16 + 16 \times 64 + 64 \times 24 = 2592$ parameters.

3.2. MFIST Architecture

The proposed MFIST framework integrates a frozen VGG-16 network to extract multi-level texture features from style images. These extracted features are then processed through a meta network, which consists of fully connected layers that map them onto the parameter space of the Randomized Hierarchy (RH) Flow model. The optimization process minimizes the total loss, which is defined as a weighted sum of content and style losses, ensuring high-quality stylization. This design enables the generation of adaptive style transfer models tailored to different style images.

As illustrated in Figure 5, the proposed MFIST architecture is composed of three main parts: the VGG-16 encoder, the meta network, and the Randomized Hierarchy Flow (RH Flow) model. The left section represents the VGG-16 encoder, which extracts multi-level feature maps from the content and style images. The style image is passed through the VGG-16 encoder to extract deep features (vertical green arrows). These features are used both for computing style loss (horizontal red arrows) and for generating style representations for the meta network. The content image is processed similarly, with extracted features used to compute content loss (horizontal blue arrows) between the content and stylized outputs. The middle section shows the meta network, which processes the style features extracted by VGG-16. The 1920-dimensional style feature vector is first input into a hidden layer (green box). It is then divided into six groups feeding into six fully connected (FC) layers (orange boxes) to predict parameters for the Style Encoder and Affine-Net of the RH Flow model. The black arrows indicate the flow of style feature representations through the meta network for parameter generation. The right section houses the RH Flow model, which performs hierarchical style fusion based on the generated parameters. The RH Flow model takes the content features and fuses them with the stylized statistics through a sequence of reversible randomized hierarchical coupling (RHC) layers. Red arrows indicate the forward content encoding, while blue arrows represent the reverse reconstruction of the stylized image. Style information (green arrows) extracted and processed by the Style Encoder is injected into the RH Flow model during the reverse pass through the AdaIN modules. This structured design enables efficient and adaptive style transfer while preserving high-fidelity content structures and achieving flexible stylization. Each arrow in the figure explicitly represents a key operation: feature extraction, parameter generation, content encoding, style fusion, or loss computation.

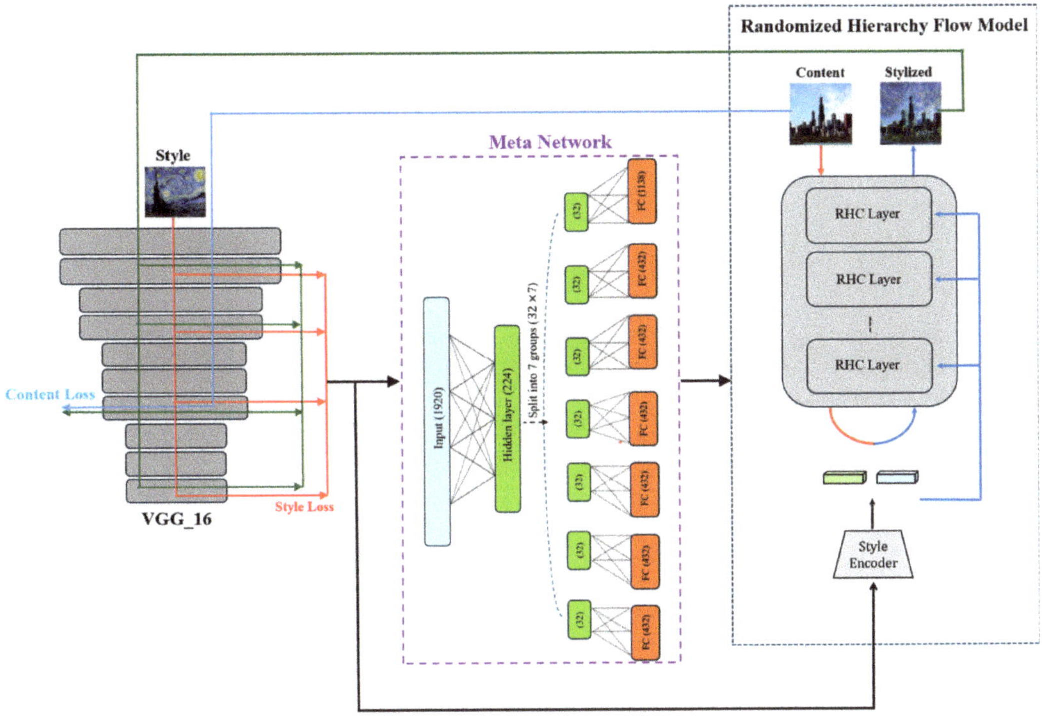

Figure 5. MFIST Architecture.

Architecture of the Meta Network

The RH Flow architecture consists of two key sub-networks: the Affine-Net and the Style Encoder, which require 1134 and 2592 parameters, respectively. Additionally, with $N = 4$ learnable fusion weights (α), the total number of parameters required by RH Flow amounts to 2592 + 1134 + 4 = 3730 parameters. All these parameters are dynamically generated by the meta network. As illustrated in Figure 6, the meta network processes the 1920-dimensional feature vector extracted from the VGG-16 features of the style image (Input). This feature vector is first passed through a hidden layer with 224 output dimensions. The hidden layer output is then evenly split into seven groups, each consisting of 32 dimensions (indicated by black arrows). These groups are individually fed into seven fully connected (FC) layers: The first six FC layers each output 432 parameters, corresponding to the convolutional parameters of the Style Encoder. The last FC layer outputs 1138 parameters, corresponding to the Affine-Net and the learnable fusion weights. Specifically, among the 1138 parameters, 1134 are used by the Affine-Net, and 4 are assigned to the fusion weights (α). The black arrows in the figure represent the flow of feature information through the splitting and fully connected transformations. This grouped design offers significant advantages compared to using a single, large-scale FC layer: it reduces the total number of trainable parameters, optimizes computational resource allocation, and enhances parameter-sharing efficiency. By incorporating convolutional layers into the Style Encoder, the model benefits from improved computational efficiency and generalization, making the overall architecture lightweight and well-suited for dynamic parameter generation.

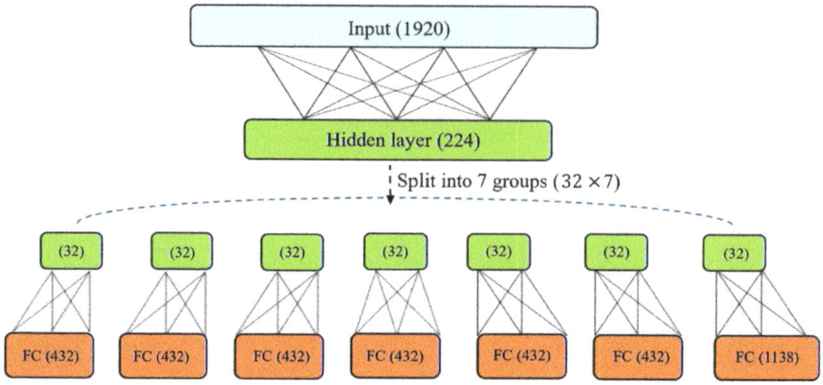

Figure 6. Architecture of meta network.

3.3. *Training the Meta Network*

The definitions of content loss and style loss in this study align with those used in AdaIN [12]. The content loss measures the difference between the transformed image I_{cs} and the content image I_c in the relu4_3 layer of the pre-trained VGG-16 encoder. After performing channel normalization, the content loss is defined as the Mean Squared Error (MSE) between the normalized features, as expressed in (2), where *norm* represents the channel normalization operation. The style loss evaluates the stylistic similarity between the transformed image I_{cs} and the style image I_s across four layers of the VGG-16 encoder (relu1_2, relu2_2, relu3_3, and relu4_3). The style loss is defined as the sum of the MSEs of the mean and standard deviation of each channel, as shown in (3), where μ and σ denote the mean and standard deviation of each channel. In (1) and (2), ϕ_1, ϕ_2, ϕ_3, and ϕ_4 correspond to the feature maps of the VGG-16 encoder at layers relu1_2, relu2_2, relu3_3, and relu4_3, with their respective channel dimensions denoted as l_1, l_2, l_3, and l_4. The total loss for training the meta network is defined as the weighted sum of the content loss and style loss, as formulated in (4), where β is the weighting factor that balances content loss and style loss. The meta network is trained to minimize the total loss L, allowing it to dynamically generate parameters for the RH Flow architecture. The training procedure for the meta network is described in Algorithm 4.

$$L_c \leftarrow \|norm(\phi_{4\_3}(I_{cs})) - norm(\phi_{4\_3}(I_c))\|_2 \quad (2)$$

$$L_s \leftarrow \sum_{i=1}^{4} \sum_{j=1}^{l_i} \left(\left\| \mu\left(\phi_i(I_{cs})_j\right) - \mu\left(\phi_i(I_s)_j\right) \right\|_2 + \left\| \sigma\left(\phi_i(I_{cs})_j\right) - \sigma\left(\phi_i(I_s)_j\right) \right\|_2 \right) \quad (3)$$

$$L \leftarrow \beta L_c + (1-\beta) L_s \quad (4)$$

Algorithm 4. Meta Net Training

META(I_c, I_s, θ_m)
$f_s \leftarrow msfe(\phi_1(I_s), \phi_2(I_s), \phi_3(I_s), \phi_4(I_s))$
$\theta_a, \theta_s, \alpha \leftarrow$ **Meta Net**($f_s; \theta_m$)
$I_{cs} \leftarrow$ RH_FLOW($I_c, f_s, \alpha, \theta_a, \theta_s$)
$L_c \leftarrow \|norm(\phi_4(I_{cs})) - norm(\phi_4(I_c))\|_2$
$L_s \leftarrow \sum_{i=1}^{3} \sum_{j=1}^{l_i} \left(\left\| \mu\left(\phi_i(I_{cs})_j\right) - \mu\left(\phi_i(I_s)_j\right) \right\|_2 + \left\| \sigma\left(\phi_i(I_{cs})_j\right) - \sigma\left(\phi_i(I_s)_j\right) \right\|_2 \right)$
$L \leftarrow \beta L_c + (1-\beta) L_s$
$\theta_m \leftarrow \theta_m - \eta \nabla_{\theta_m} L$

4. Experimental Results

We developed and evaluated the Randomized Hierarchy Flow (RH Flow) model with the parameters dynamically generated by the meta network (Meta Net). All the experiments were conducted on a server equipped with NVIDIA RTX 2080 Ti GPUs (NVIDIA Corporation, Santa Clara, CA, USA) and 256 GB of system RAM. The implementation was carried out using Python and the PyTorch deep learning framework (version 1.8). To train and evaluate the model, we utilized two widely adopted style transfer datasets: MS-COCO 2014 [34], containing a total of 123,558 real-world images; and WikiArt [35], containing 52,757 artwork images. From MS-COCO 2014, 82,783 images were randomly selected for the training, while the testing was conducted by randomly sampling images from the remaining 40,775 images. Similarly, from WikiArt, 42,129 images were used for the training, and the testing was conducted on randomly sampled images from the remaining 10,628 images. By default, all the images were resized to 300 $\times$ 400 pixels for both the training and testing.

Representative style transfer results generated by our method are shown in Figures 7 and 8. Figure 9 provides a comparative analysis with state-of-the-art style transfer approaches, demonstrating that both our method and Hierarchy Flow are effective at preserving content features. The enlarged regions further highlight the superior content preservation achieved by our method, which substantially mitigates the content leakage. For comparison purposes, some of the results shown in Figure 9 are adapted from Reference [22].

Figure 7. Style transfer results: multiple content images stylized based on a single style image.

Figure 8. Style transfer results: a single content image individually stylized using different style images.

Figure 9. Style transfer results and enlarged regions compared with state-of-the-art style transfer methods.

We quantitatively evaluated the stylized images using the SSIM, Gram loss, and KID. Specifically, the SSIM (Structural Similarity Index Measure) evaluates the similarity between the stylized image and the original content image based on the structural information, luminance, and contrast, thus serving as an effective indicator of the content preservation. The Gram loss, computed as the Gram matrix distance [10] on the deep features extracted from a pre-trained VGG network, measures the stylistic difference between the stylized and style images, reflecting the effectiveness of the style transfer. The KID (Kernel Inception Distance) assesses the perceptual similarity between the distributions of the generated and target style images, with lower values indicating better perceptual quality and style consistency. As shown in Table 1, our model achieved the highest SSIM score and the second-lowest Gram distance, demonstrating its strong content retention and effective style adaptation. The arrows in the table headers indicate the desired direction of the metric—higher for SSIM (↑) and lower for Gram distance (↓).

Table 1. Quantitative evaluation results based on SSIM and Gram distance metrics.

Method	SSIM ↑	Gram Distance ↓
StyleSwap	0.44	0.00482
AdaIN	0.29	0.00127
WCT	0.27	0.00074
LinearWCT	0.35	0.00093
OptimalWCT	0.21	0.00035
Avatar-Net	0.31	0.00099
Artlow+AdaIN	0.45	0.00078
Ours	0.615	0.00050

As shown in Table 2, our model again attained the highest SSIM and ranked third in KID performance, while maintaining the lowest number of trainable parameters among all the compared methods. Again, the arrows in the table indicate that higher SSIM (↑) and lower KID values (↓) are preferred. These quantitative results substantiate that our proposed framework effectively preserves the critical content structures while achieving visually consistent and high-quality stylization. For a fair comparison, some of the results in these tables were adapted from References [21,22].

Table 2. Quantitative evaluation results of different flow architectures in terms of SSIM, KID ($\times 10^3$), and number of parameters.

Method	SSIM ↑	KID ↓	Parameters
AdaIN	0.28	41.1/5.1	7.01 M
WCT	0.24	51.2/6.2	34.24 M
Artflow+AdaIN	0.52	24.6/3.8	6.42 M
Artflow+WCT	0.53	33.3/5.3	6.42 M
CCPL	0.43	39.1/6.8	8.67 M
Hierarchy Flow	0.60	28.2/4.7	1.01 M
Ours	0.615	29.0/5.0	0.55 M

5. Conclusions and Discussion

In this work, we propose Meta FIST, a novel flow-based image style transfer framework that integrates Randomized Hierarchy Flow (RH Flow) with a meta network for adaptive parameter generation. The meta network dynamically produces the RH Flow parameters conditioned on the given style image, enabling more flexible and adaptive style transfer. Our approach improves the content preservation, style fidelity, and adaptability, effectively addressing the key limitations of traditional style transfer methods. The experimental results confirm that Meta FIST delivers high-quality stylization while maintaining the structural integrity of the content image.

Despite these promising results, some limitations remain. Specifically, the computational cost of dynamically generating the parameters through the meta network could be further optimized. Additionally, the current model may struggle with extremely abstract or non-representational styles, as the hierarchical flow structure emphasizes strong content preservation, which may limit the flexibility required for such styles. Addressing this trade-off between content fidelity and stylization flexibility is an important challenge for future work.

Furthermore, the current framework lacks explicit semantic constraints, relying primarily on the reversibility of the RH Flow and content loss to retain structural details. While effective at the feature level, this approach may be insufficient for achieving semantic-level content control. Incorporating semantic information, such as semantic segmentation maps or object detection annotations, could enable the model to better preserve and manipulate the meaningful content structures, particularly in complex scenes.

In summary, future work will focus on the following: (a) improving the computational efficiency of the meta network; (b) enhancing the flexibility of the model to better handle highly abstract or non-representational artistic styles; (c) integrating semantic-aware mechanisms, such as semantic segmentation or object detection information, to improve the content-aware stylization; (d) and exploring hybrid models that combine attention-based learning with flow-based approaches to further advance the model's adaptability and content fidelity.

In addition, this study represents an initial attempt to apply meta network-based parameter generation within a hierarchical flow-based style transfer framework. We believe that the meta network is a general and flexible component that could be further explored in other style transfer architectures, beyond the hierarchical flow. Investigating such extensions could help validate the versatility and broader applicability of our approach to various style transfer paradigms.

Author Contributions: Conceptualization, Y.T., H.-W.L. and H.-J.L.; Methodology, H.-W.L. and C.-J.C.; Software, Y.T. and H.-J.L.; Validation, C.-J.C.; Formal Analysis, H.-J.L.; Investigation, H.-W.L. and H.-J.L.; Resources, Y.T.; Data Curation, C.-H.Y.; Writing—Original Draft Preparation, H.-J.L.; Writing—Review and Editing, H.-W.L. and C.-H.Y.; Visualization, Y.T.; Supervision, H.-W.L.; Project Administration, H.-J.L.; Funding Acquisition, H.-J.L. All authors have read and agreed to the published version of the manuscript.

Funding: This research received no external funding.

Data Availability Statement: Ref. [34] T.-Y. Lin, M. Maire, S. Belongie, J. Hays, P. Perona, D. Ramanan, P. Doll'ar, and C. L. Zitnick, "Microsoft coco: Common objects in context", European conference on computer vision. Springer, 2014, pp. 740–755. https://doi.org/10.1007/978-3-319-10602-1_48 (accessed on 1 October 2024). Ref. [35] K. Nichol, Painter by numbers, wikiart, 2016. https://www.kaggle.com/c/painter-by-numbers/ (accessed on 1 October 2024).

Acknowledgments: This work was supported by the National Science and Technology Council, Taiwan, R.O.C., under grant NSTC 113-2221-E-032-020.

Conflicts of Interest: The authors declare no conflicts of interest.

References

1. Wang, T.C.; Liu, M.Y.; Zhu, J.Y.; Tao, A.; Kautz, J.; Catanzaro, B. High-Resolution Image Synthesis and Semantic Manipulation with Conditional GANs. *arXiv* **2018**, arXiv:1711.11585.
2. Miyato, T.; Koyama, M. CGANs with Projection Discriminator. *arXiv* **2018**, arXiv:1802.05637.
3. Zhu, J.Y.; Zhang, R.; Pathak, D.; Darrell, T.; Efros, A.A.; Wang, O.; Shechtman, E. Toward Multimodal Image-to-Image Translation. *arXiv* **2018**, arXiv:1711.11586.
4. Zhu, J.Y.; Park, T.; Isola, P.; Efros, A.A. Unpaired Image-to-Image Translation using Cycle-Consistent Adversarial Networks. *arXiv* **2018**, arXiv:1703.10593.
5. Isola, P.; Zhu, J.Y.; Zhou, T.; Efros, A.A. Image-to-Image Translation with Conditional Adversarial Networks. *arXiv* **2018**, arXiv:1611.07004.
6. Park, T.; Liu, M.Y.; Wang, T.C.; Zhu, J.Y. Semantic Image Synthesis with Spatially-Adaptive Normalization. *arXiv* **2019**, arXiv:1903.07291.
7. Kotovenko, D.; Sanakoyeu, A.; Ma, P.; Lang, S.; Ommer, B. A Content Transformation Block for Image Style Transfer. *arXiv* **2020**, arXiv:2003.08407.
8. Wei, Y. Artistic Image Style Transfer Based on CycleGAN Network Model. *Int. J. Image Graph.* **2024**, *24*, 2450049. [CrossRef]
9. Liu, J.; Liu, H.; He, Y.; Tong, S. An Improved Detail-Enhancement CycleGAN Using AdaLIN for Facial Style Transfer. *Appl. Sci.* **2024**, *14*, 6311. [CrossRef]
10. Gatys, L.A.; Ecker, A.S.; Bethge, M. A Neural Algorithm of Artistic Style. *arXiv* **2015**, arXiv:1508.06576v2. [CrossRef]
11. Johnson, J.; Alahi, A.; Li, F.-F. Perceptual Losses for Real-Time Style Transfer and Super-Resolution. *arXiv* **2016**, arXiv:1603.08155v1.
12. Huang, X.; Belongie, S. Arbitrary Style Transfer in Real-Time with Adaptive Instance Normalization. *arXiv* **2017**, arXiv:1703.06868v2.
13. Dumoulin, V.; Shlens, J.; Kudlur, M. A Learned Representation for Artistic Style. *arXiv* **2017**, arXiv:1610.07629v5.
14. Li, Y.; Fang, C.; Yang, J.; Wang, Z.; Lu, X.; Yang, M.-H. Universal Style Transfer via Feature Transforms. *arXiv* **2017**, arXiv:1705.08086v2.
15. Chen, D.; Yuan, L.; Liao, J.; Yu, N.; Hua, G. StyleBank: An Explicit Representation for Neural Image Style Transfer. *arXiv* **2017**, arXiv:1703.09210v2.
16. Sheng, L.; Lin, Z.; Shao, J.; Wang, X. Avatar-Net: Multi-scale Zero-shot Style Transfer by Feature Decoration. *arXiv* **2018**, arXiv:1805.03857v2.
17. Li, X.; Liu, S.; Kautz, J.; Yang, M.-H. Learning Linear Transformations for Fast Arbitrary Style Transfer. *arXiv* **2018**, arXiv:1808.04537v1.
18. Liu, B.; Wang, C.; Cao, T.; Jia, K.; Huang, J. Towards Understanding Cross and Self-Attention in Stable Diffusion for Text-Guided Image Editing. *arXiv* **2024**, arXiv:2403.03431v1.
19. Zhou, X.; Yin, M.; Chen, X.; Sun, L.; Gao, C.; Li, Q. Cross Attention Based Style Distribution for Controllable Person Image Synthesis. In *Computer Vision—ECCV 2022*; Avidan, S., Brostow, G., Cissé, M., Farinella, G.M., Hassner, T., Eds.; Lecture Notes in Computer Science; Springer: Cham, Switzerland, 2022; Volume 13675.
20. Pan, X.; Zhang, M.; Ding, D.; Yang, M. A Geometrical Perspective on Image Style Transfer with Adversarial Learning. *IEEE Trans. Pattern Anal. Mach. Intell.* **2020**, *44*, 63–75. [CrossRef]
21. An, J.; Huang, S.; Song, Y.; Dou, D.; Liu, W.; Luo, J. ArtFlow: Unbiased Image Style Transfer via Reversible Neural Flows. *arXiv* **2021**, arXiv:2103.16877v2.
22. Fan, W.; Chen, J.; Liu, Z. Hierarchy Flow for High-Fidelity Image-to-Image Translation. *arXiv* **2023**, arXiv:2308.06909v1.
23. Kingma, D.P.; Dhariwal, P. Glow: Generative Flow with Invertible 1×1 Convolutions. *arXiv* **2018**, arXiv:1807.03039v2.
24. Yao, F. A learning theory of meta learning. *Natl. Sci. Rev.* **2024**, *11*, nwae133. [CrossRef] [PubMed]
25. Gao, W.; Shao, M.; Shu, J.; Zhuang, X. Meta-BN Net for Few-Shot Learning. *Front. Comput. Sci.* **2023**, *17*, 171302. [CrossRef]
26. Shen, F.; Yan, S.; Zeng, G. Meta Networks for Neural Style Transfer. *arXiv* **2017**, arXiv:1709.04111v1.
27. Schmidhuber, J. Evolutionary Principles in Self-Referential Learning. Master's Thesis, Technische Universität München, München, Germany, 1987.
28. Thrun, S.; Pratt, L. *Learning to Learn*; Springer Science & Business Media: Berlin/Heidelberg, Germany, 2012.
29. Bechtle, S.; Molchanov, A.; Chebotar, Y.; Grefenstette, E.; Righetti, L.; Sukhatme, G.; Meier, F. Meta-learning via learned loss. *arXiv* **2019**, arXiv:1906.05374.

30. Finn, C.; Abbeel, P.; Levine, S. Model-agnostic meta-learning for fast adaptation of deep networks. In Proceedings of the 34 International Conference on Machine Learning, Sydney, Australia, 6–11 August 2017.
31. Meier, F.; Kappler, D.; Schaal, S. Online learning of a memory for learning rates. In Proceedings of the 2018 IEEE Internation Conference on Robotics and Automation (ICRA), Brisbane, Australia, 21–25 May 2018; pp. 2425–2432.
32. Houthooft, R.; Chen, Y.; Isola, P.; Stadie, B.C.; Wolski, F.; Ho, J.; Abbeel, P. Evolved policy gradients. In Proceedings of the NeurI Proceeding, Montréal, QC, Canada, 2–8 December 2018; pp. 5405–5414.
33. Metz, L.; Maheswaranathan, N.; Cheung, B.; Sohl-Dickstein, J. Learning unsupervised learning rules. In Proceedings of th International Conference on Learning Representations, New Orleans, LA, USA, 6–9 May 2019.
34. Lin, T.-Y.; Maire, M.; Belongie, S.; Hays, J.; Perona, P.; Ramanan, D.; Doll, P.; Zitnick, C.L. Microsoft coco: Common objects context. In Proceedings of the European Conference on Computer Vision, Zurich, Switzerland, 6–12 September 2014; Spring Cham, Switzerland, 2014; pp. 740–755.
35. Nichol, K. Painter by Numbers, Wikiart. 2016. Available online: https://www.kaggle.com/c/painter-by-numbers/ (accessed o 1 October 2024).

electronics

MDPI

Article

A Performance Analysis of You Only Look Once Models for Deployment on Constrained Computational Edge Devices in Drone Applications

Lucas Rey, Ana M. Bernardos *, Andrzej D. Dobrzycki, David Carramiñana, Luca Bergesio, Juan A. Besada and José Ramón Casar

Information Processing and Telecommunications Center, ETSI Telecomunicación, Universidad Politécnica de Madrid, Av. Complutense 30, 28040 Madrid, Spain; luca.bergesio@upm.es (L.B.); juanalberto.besada@upm.es (J.A.B.); joseramon.casar@upm.es (J.R.C.)

* Correspondence: anamaria.bernardos@upm.es

Abstract: Advancements in embedded systems and Artificial Intelligence (AI) have enhanced the capabilities of Unmanned Aircraft Vehicles (UAVs) in computer vision. However, the integration of AI techniques o-nboard drones is constrained by their processing capabilities. In this sense, this study evaluates the deployment of object detection models (YOLOv8n and YOLOv8s) on both resource-constrained edge devices and cloud environments. The objective is to carry out a comparative performance analysis using a representative real-time UAV image processing pipeline. Specifically, the NVIDIA Jetson Orin Nano, Orin NX, and Raspberry Pi 5 (RPI5) devices have been tested to measure their detection accuracy, inference speed, and energy consumption, and the effects of post-training quantization (PTQ). The results show that YOLOv8n surpasses YOLOv8s in its inference speed, achieving 52 FPS on the Jetson Orin NX and 65 fps with INT8 quantization. Conversely, the RPI5 failed to satisfy the real-time processing needs in spite of its suitability for low-energy consumption applications. An analysis of both the cloud-based and edge-based end-to-end processing times showed that increased communication latencies hindered real-time applications, revealing trade-offs between edge (low latency) and cloud processing (quick processing). Overall, these findings contribute to providing recommendations and optimization strategies for the deployment of AI models on UAVs.

Keywords: YOLOv8; edge computing; TensorRT; NCNN; inference performance; quantization; NVIDIA Jetson; Raspberry Pi 5; autonomous drones

1. Introduction

In recent years, the integration of unmanned aerial vehicles (UAVs), commonly referred to as drones, with machine learning techniques has significantly advanced the field of aerial robotics. Machine learning algorithms, particularly deep learning approaches, enable drone-based systems to process large volumes of data collected from onboard sensors. The incorporation of computer vision algorithms into drone technologies has enhanced their autonomous capabilities, allowing drones to detect and track objects with high accuracy. Additionally, these advancements support collaborative data fusion, where information from multiple drones and sensors is combined to improve situational awareness and inform decision-making processes. Such capabilities contribute to the effective management and coordination of drone operations in complex environments [1,2], opening the door to possible applications such as vision-driven swarming [3].

While these intelligent capabilities offer significant advantages, embedding them into onboard or even edge systems remains a challenge. By integrating these algorithms directly into drones, they can operate autonomously without relying on constant communication with a central system. This autonomy is important in low-connectivity scenario applications, such as unsupervised maintenance flights in remote areas (e.g., oil pipelines or power pylons), defense operations, or emergency response situations where the connectivity may be limited [4,5]. In these cases, which also seek energy-efficient methods to avoid early battery drain, drones must be able to independently detect and track objects, and algorithms like YOLO (You Only Look Once) enhance their ability to do so effectively.

YOLOv8, as a state-of-the-art object detection algorithm, is well suited to these scenarios due to its multiple versions, with each optimized for different hardware constraints. For instance, versions such as YOLOv8-small (YOLOv8s) and YOLOv8-nano (YOLOv8n) contain fewer parameters, making them appropriate for deployment on the smaller, computationally constrained devices commonly used in edge environments. These versions trade off some accuracy for computational efficiency, allowing for real-time processing even on resource-constrained devices [6]. Moreover, YOLOv8 demonstrates adaptability to varying input resolutions, which is important in applications such as drone operations, where the cameras can range from thermal imaging for rescue missions to high-definition cameras for other purposes [7]. Additionally, its integration with tracking algorithms like DeepSORT supports object tracking in sequences of frames, which is valuable for scenarios that require dynamic monitoring, such as surveillance or search and rescue missions [8]. YOLOv8 also supports multitasking by combining object detection with classification and segmentation in a single model, enabling it to address various computer vision tasks in controlled settings [7]. As an evolving framework, using YOLOv8 as one of the latest versions of YOLO eases the transition to future developments of the algorithm.

Furthermore, techniques such as quantization can facilitate enhanced performance through reductions in the bit width, which refers to the number of bits used to represent data in computations. By reducing the bit width, the model performs calculations with fewer bits, thereby decreasing both the memory footprint and the computational load. This is relevant when running complex algorithms on devices with limited hardware capabilities, as it allows for more efficient use of the available resources without sacrificing the real-time performance. By applying quantization in combination with different fine-tuned YOLO models of varied sizes, we aim to derive guidelines for the optimal use of object detection algorithms like YOLOv8 in constrained environments. These insights may be useful for the future integration of such algorithms into distributed agents at the edge, where autonomy and performance are paramount [4,9,10].

Given the challenges outlined, the primary objectives of this article are as follows:

1. To comprehensively evaluate the performance of YOLOv8 models across different embedded platforms, including the Jetson Orin Nano, Jetson Orin NX, and Raspberry Pi 5, in order to determine their suitability for real-time object detection.
2. To investigate the impact of various quantization techniques and floating-point precision models on the balance between the detection accuracy, processing speed, and power consumption, optimizing these trade-offs to ensure low-latency inference in edge computing applications.
3. To validate the performance of the aforementioned devices in a representative deployment scenario for drone-based applications, which consists of integrating the models

into a real drone image processing workflow. This integration also enables comparing edge and cloud solutions for object detection inference.

4. To assess the specific limitations and potential of these platforms for real-time drone operations, identifying the constraints in terms of energy efficiency, algorithmic processing time, and scalability within real architectures, and to derive practical guidelines for selecting the appropriate models and devices for various deployment scenarios.

The organization of this article is as follows. Section 2 provides a comprehensive review of the state of the art, detailing advancements in deploying deep learning on energy-efficient devices into a distributed edge architecture and exploring quantization techniques in object detection models. Section 3 describes the methodology, including the evaluation setup, dataset creation, and the optimization of YOLO object detection models tailored to edge devices, alongside a detailed testing strategy. Section 4.1 presents a rigorous evaluation of quantized YOLO models on resource-constrained devices, assessing their inference performance, accuracy degradation, and energy consumption. Section 5 expands on the performance in a realistic testbed, comparing edge and cloud solutions for object detection and discussing the practical implications. Finally, Section 6 synthesizes the findings and proposes guidelines, while Section 7 concludes this paper, highlighting potential directions for future research, including the integration of digital twin simulations and enhanced edge–cloud collaboration for drone operations.

2. The State of the Art

This section is divided into two subsections. The first Section 2.1, Deploying Deep Learning on Energy-Efficient Devices, evaluates the performance and optimization techniques for deep learning models deployed on edge hardware, with a focus on energy efficiency and real-time processing. The second subsection, Section 2.2, Quantization Techniques in Object Detection Models, reviews strategies to optimize the computational and memory demands in object detection algorithms, analyzing their feasibility for edge devices in constrained environments.

2.1. Deploying Deep Learning on Energy-Efficient Devices

In recent years, significant research has focused on optimizing and evaluating the performance of deep learning models on edge devices, particularly for object detection tasks in resource-constrained environments. Various studies have benchmarked the hardware configurations to identify the optimal settings for achieving a balance between the inference speed, energy consumption, and real-time processing requirements. For instance, Baller et al. [9] evaluated a range of edge devices, including the NVIDIA Jetson Nano, and identified the optimal configurations in terms of the inference speed and energy consumption across various deep learning frameworks and classification models. Such evaluations are crucial for understanding the limitations and potential of hardware in real-time scenarios.

Building on hardware-specific optimizations, Li et al. introduced [11], an optimization framework for CNN inference on edge devices for application in an IoT context. This framework combines offline pruning and quantization techniques with runtime optimizations, such as multiplication reduction, data layout adjustments, and data parallelization. The experimental results showed performance improvements of 1.96× in high-end devices and 1.73× in low-end devices in improving their edge device efficiency using advanced model compression techniques. Similarly, Ferraz et al. [12] benchmarked CNN inference on edge devices, such as the NVIDIA Jetson AGX Xavier and the Movidius Neural Stick, noting considerable improvements in the inference time and power efficiency.

Recent studies also emphasize the use of distributed and cooperative processing to enhance edge device performance. Hou et al. [13] introduced DistrEdge, a method designed to enhance CNN inference across distributed edge devices by employing deep reinforcement learning. This approach distributes inference tasks among multiple devices, optimizing the computational load and significantly improving the overall inference speed. DistrEdge dynamically adapts to the heterogeneity of devices and varying network conditions, ensuring efficient load balancing and reduced latency. This adaptability makes it particularly effective in real-time processing scenarios. In another cooperative approach, Liang et al. [14] presented Edge YOLO, leveraging edge–cloud cooperation for real-time object detection in autonomous driving, underscoring the benefits of a distributed architecture in complex, time-sensitive tasks.

In the realm of object detection, Shin and Kim [15] explored the performance of YOLO object detection models on NVIDIA Jetson devices, highlighting the advantages of using TensorFlow-TensorRT (TF-TRT) to optimize real-time inference. They also found that while TF-Lite is effective for mobile, it fails to utilize the GPU resources on the Jetson, highlighting the need to select appropriate frameworks based on the hardware and application needs. Xiong et al. [16] further explored YOLO models by optimizing YOLOv5s for UAV image detection on the Jetson Xavier NX, achieving notable improvements in FPS and model compression. Similarly, Hu et al. [17] proposed an improved YOLO-Tiny-attention algorithm for fault detection on wind turbine blades, which was successfully deployed on the same hardware with increased detection precision. These findings highlight the adaptability of YOLO-based models in different edge applications.

Table 1 summarizes the key findings from these studies, highlighting the energy consumption and inference performance across different edge devices and models.

Table 1. Comparison of energy efficiency and inference latency across reviewed studies.

Authors	Device	Model	Metrics	Application Area	Key Findings
Baller et al. 2021 [9]	NVIDIA Jetson Nano	MobileNetV2, DNNs	Inference speed, accuracy, energy consumption	General classification	Optimized frameworks needed to improve inference time and energy use in Jetson Nano.
Li et al. 2023 [11]	NVIDIA Jetson Nano, Raspberry Pi	MobileNetV2, VGG16	Inference speed, energy consumption	IoT applications	Jetson Nano is faster and more energy-efficient than Raspberry Pi, but neither meets real-time needs for complex tasks.
Ferraz et al. 2023 [12]	NVIDIA Jetson AGX Xavier, Movidius Neural Stick	SqueezeNet, CNNs	Inference speed, energy consumption	Edge devices	Pruning and quantization improve energy efficiency and performance on AGX Xavier.
Hou et al. 2022 [13]	NVIDIA Jetson Nano, TX2, Xavier	CNN	Distributed inference performance, speedup	Edge devices	Distributed inference framework (DistrEdge) with reinforcement learning improves real-time performance.

Table 1. *Cont.*

Authors	Device	Model	Metrics	Application Area	Key Findings
Liang et al. 2022 [14]	Edge–cloud, NVIDIA Jetson	Edge YOLO	Real-time performance, object detection accuracy	Autonomous vehicles	Pruning and feature compression improve efficiency in edge-cloud systems, enhancing autonomous vehicle operations.
Shin and Kim 2022 [15]	NVIDIA Jetson AGX Xavier	YOLOv4-Native, YOLOv4-Tiny	Latency, energy consumption	Real-time object detection	TF-TRT and TensorRT optimizations improve real-time inference and reduce energy use on Jetson AGX Xavier.
Xiong et al. 2023 [16]	NVIDIA Jetson Xavier NX	GCGE-YOLO	mAP, FPS, energy consumption	UAV image detection	Uses GhostNet and coordinate attention to reduce computational load and improve object detection accuracy.
Hu et al. 2023 [17]	NVIDIA Jetson Xavier NX, Jetson Nano	YOLO-Tiny-attention	FPS, detection precision	Wind turbine fault detection	Attention mechanisms improve fault detection accuracy on low-power edge devices, supporting real-time monitoring.

While many studies focus on evaluating deep learning algorithms on individual edge devices, such as the NVIDIA Jetson Nano or AGX Xavier, there is growing recognition of the need to explore more complex architectures. These include distributed computing systems and edge–cloud cooperation, which are gaining significance for handling sophisticated tasks in real-time applications. Several studies, such as Hou et al. [13] and Liang et al. [14], have begun to explore the potential of distributed architectures to overcome the limitations of individual devices, demonstrating the benefits of dynamic workload balancing and feature compression in real-time object detection tasks.

Distributed edge architectures, when integrated with tactical cloud technology and 5G networks, enable real-time data flow among edge devices [18]. This integration enhances the performance of autonomous drones by supporting efficient coordination and rapid decision-making. By combining local data processing with continual connectivity, such architectures improve the operational efficiency and autonomy in dynamic environments [19]. In addition, the network slice feature segments the network into specific virtual environments to enhance the resource allocation and service quality per application [20]. This ensures that in drone systems, each mission or drone group receives a tailored "slice" with low latency and high reliability, important for enabling efficient operations.

By integrating these advanced communication frameworks with quantization techniques [21–23], researchers can improve the energy efficiency and performance in edge systems. This combination of tactical cloud, 5G, and model quantization addresses the specific challenges in distributed architectures, such as latency reduction and resource optimization. These improvements support the development of more autonomous and efficient systems capable of operating effectively in energy-constrained real-world scenarios.

2.2. *Quantization Techniques in Object Detection Models*

Quantization techniques are valuable for optimizing deep learning models for deployment in edge devices, improving the inference speed and energy efficiency, especially in real-time applications such as autonomous drone navigation and object detection. Common techniques include post-training quantization (PTQ), Quantization-Aware Training (QAT), and mixed-precision quantization (MPQ), all of which enhance the energy efficiency in reducing the computational complexity while maintaining the model's performance.

PTQ is a technique that reduces the precision of a trained model to formats such as 8-bit integers by converting the weights and activations from floating-point representations. One of its primary advantages is that it reduces the size of the model and increases the inference speed without requiring retraining, preserving the original training process. For instance, Przewlocka-Rus et al. [22] demonstrated that PTQ applied to object detection models on the NVIDIA Jetson Nano decreased the inference times by up to 35% with a less than 2% degradation in accuracy. Similarly, Jiang et al. [21] evaluated various PTQ approaches, including affine, logarithmic, and dynamic quantization, and found that these methods effectively minimized the size of models while maintaining high accuracy with minimal losses.

QAT integrates quantization into the training process, allowing the model to learn to minimize quantization errors. This method typically results in higher accuracy than PTQ, especially for complex models and tasks. Gupta and Asthana [24] applied QAT to object detection models such as YOLO, achieving a 1.8% improvement in mAP compared to PTQ, with reductions in the model size and inference time.

MPQ uses different precisions for various parts of the model, balancing trade-offs between size, speed, and accuracy. Critical layers use higher precision, while less critical layers use lower precision. Park et al. [25] explored mixed-precision quantization in object tracking models, achieving energy consumption reductions of up to 45% and inference time improvements of 30% on edge devices like the Jetson Nano and Raspberry Pi. Furthermore, Al-Hamid and Kim [23] proposed a Unified Scaling-Based Pure-Integer Quantization (USPIQ) method that reduced the on-chip memory by 75% with only a 0.61% loss in the mAP while achieving a 2.84x speedup in the inference time compared to traditional methods.

These quantization approaches improve the energy and space efficiency in edge device deployments, making the implementation of sophisticated object detection and tracking models viable. However, the effects of these techniques on the latest YOLO models and their integration into real-time drone applications are still being researched. Studies on deploying YOLO models in different edge–cloud or embedded edge implementations are limited [21–23,25].

Despite significant advances in the research on object detection at the edge, several gaps remain. Multiple studies have assessed edge devices in isolation without results on the latency in the interaction between the hardware and software processes.

To address these gaps, this study focuses on YOLOv8 models applied to edge environments, emphasizing their accuracy, inference speed, and energy consumption. By incorporating quantization techniques, this research offers new insights into the potential of quantization approaches to optimize YOLOv8 for resource-limited edge scenarios. The findings deliver practical recommendations for selecting the configurations in power-constrained environments, with a particular focus on the Jetson Orin Nano, Jetson Orin NX, and Raspberry Pi 5 as innovative edge devices.

3. Methodology

In this study, three edge computing devices are used to evaluate the performance of YOLOv8 models and their quantized versions: the Raspberry Pi 5, the Jetson Orin Nano, and the Jetson Orin NX. These devices were chosen due to their different hardware capabilities, allowing for an evaluation of object detection tasks under various processing constraints. Table 2 provides an overview of the key hardware specifications for each device.

Table 2. Comparison of hardware characteristics of the devices used in this study.

Feature	Raspberry Pi 5	Jetson Orin Nano	Jetson Orin NX
CPU	4-core ARM Cortex-A76 at 2.4 GHz	6-core ARM Cortex-A78AE	8-core ARM Cortex-A78AE
GPU	VideoCore VII	1024-core Ampere + 32 Tensor Cores	2048-core Ampere + 64 Tensor Cores
RAM	8 GB	8 GB	16 GB
Memory Bandwidth	Limited	Moderate	High
Typical Power Consumption	5–7 W	7–15 W	10–25 W
TensorRT Support	No	Yes	Yes
Dimensions	85.6 × 56.5 mm	100 × 69.6 mm	100 × 87 mm

These devices will be used to evaluate the performance of YOLOv8 models and their quantized versions under uniform experimental conditions. The Raspberry Pi 5, a CPU-centric device, was selected to assess the capabilities of a modern single-board computer without a dedicated GPU in object detection tasks. In contrast, the Jetson Orin Nano and Jetson Orin NX, which are GPU-powered platforms, were chosen for their high-performance processing capabilities. Together, these devices represent a range of edge computing architectures, enabling an evaluation of the inference speed, accuracy, and energy consumption across diverse hardware configurations.

In order to carry out these evaluations, it is necessary to first have an object detection model. To this end, Section 3.1 describes the process of creating such a model, including the generation of a dedicated dataset in Section 3.1.1, model selection and training in Section 3.1.2, and model optimization in Section 3.1.3. From the model, two types of experiments are developed:

- Experiments that deploy the model in isolation on each of the previous hardware platforms. These experiments aim to evaluate the inference speed and power consumption, for which the results are detailed in Section 4.
- Experiments that integrate the object detection model into a typical drone image processing pipeline. As described in Section 5, these experiments seek to compare the capabilities of edge devices against a cloud deployment under a representative scenario.

In these experiments, a set of metrics are used to evaluate the performance of the models. These metrics are described in Section 3.2.

3.1. *Object Detection Model Selection and Training*

3.1.1. Dataset Creation

To train the evaluated object detection models, a dataset of annotated images was created. This dataset was collected within the indoor testbed described by the authors in [26] and depicted in Figure 1. The test setup consists of an indoor room with varied furniture elements to introduce a complex environment. Within the room, a fleet of drones (DJI Tello) can be controlled, together with a fleet of ground robots (TurtleBot) that serve as the targets (i.e., objects) to be detected from the aerial images. The experimentation platform allows you to easily capture frames from the drone's onboard cameras. Also, positioning information can be simultaneously gathered thanks to an OptiTrack system (i.e., a commercial high-precision positioning system based on high-speed motion capture cameras). Although this former capability was not exploited, it could be useful in the future to enable automatic target labeling in captured images.

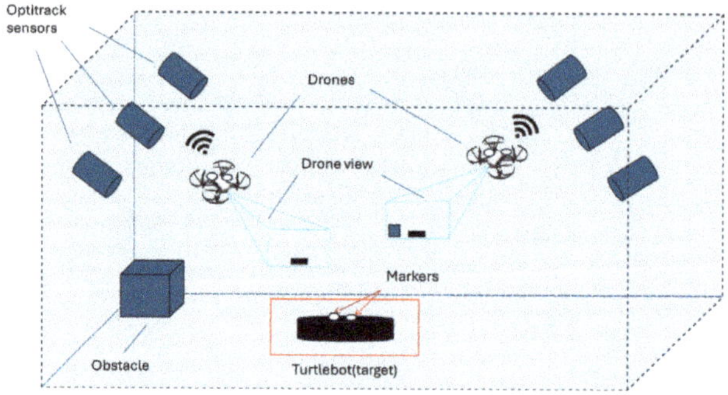

Figure 1. Diagram of the indoor controlled flight environment equipped with OptiTrack sensors, drones with access points, and a TurtleBot target on the ground.

The dataset is composed of 6000 aerial images (640 × 640 resolution) with the target in different positions relative to the drone's field of view. In order to ensure that the dataset includes a range of angles and perspectives, the drones were flown following various straight-line and diagonal trajectories relative to the target position. Also, altitude changes were also introduced to capture different viewing angles, with certain trajectories varying from 1.5 m down to 0.5. After image gathering, the dataset was manually annotated, as demonstrated by the example images in Figure 2. In general, this dataset serves as the foundation for training and evaluating object detection models, with annotated images integrated into the YOLO object detection pipeline.

Figure 2. Examples of different dataset images where the object to be detected has been manually annotated. Images are captured from different angles and heights and with different background environments.

3.1.2. Selection and Training of Object Detection Models

For the selection of the model for this study, it was necessary to evaluate different versions of the YOLO architecture in terms of their performance and efficiency. YOLOv9 was considered a potential candidate; however, YOLOv8 demonstrated superior optimization for real-time performance and latency reduction. Moreover, YOLOv8 was elected as the most stable version during the experimental advance of this research.

To align with the objective of deploying models on devices with limited computational resources further, this study specifically focused on the 'small' (YOLOv8s) and 'nano' (YOLOv8n) versions of YOLOv8. These versions are designed for computationally constrained devices by reducing the depth and number of parameters, making them suitable for various edge deployment scenarios. YOLOv8n, the smallest and fastest version of the model in this family, is optimized for devices with strict resource limitations. Its architecture prioritizes the inference speed by using fewer convolutional layers and simplifying the feature extraction stages.

In contrast, YOLOv8s includes more convolutional layers and feature extraction steps, improving the detection accuracy while maintaining computational efficiency. This model provides a balanced approach, offering a slight increase in the computational demand for better precision, making it suitable for scenarios requiring both fast response times and high accuracy. Both models share features such as anchor-free detection and enhanced feature pyramid networks, supporting their adaptability to diverse edge deployment requirements.

The models were trained using the AdamW optimizer, chosen for its ability to efficiently manage weight updates while applying decoupled weight decay. A learning rate of 0.002 was selected, ensuring fast convergence while avoiding divergence or overfitting, and a weight decay of 0.0005 was applied to most weights, excluding biases. This regularization approach encourages smaller weights, making the model more robust to noise, while excluding biases avoids penalizing parameters critical to feature representation. The momentum was set to 0.9 as the standard value to smooth optimization trajectories and ensure stable weight updates over training iterations. Training was conducted over 100 epochs with a batch size of 16, which was limited by the GPU hardware constraints of the machines used for training, balancing the computational cost and generalization performance. Early stopping with a patience of 10 epochs prevented overfitting by halting the training when no significant validation improvements were observed, saving computational resources. Data augmentation techniques, including mosaic and random erasing, were employed to enhance the diversity of the training samples. Mosaic augmentation combined multiple images into a single input, enabling the model to learn from varying object positions and scales, which is particularly effective for detection tasks. Random erasing increased the robustness by encouraging the model to focus on discriminative features rather than memorizing specific regions. During validation, predictions were made with a confidence threshold of 0.5, ensuring only reliable detections were considered. An IoU threshold of 0.7 defined the overlap criterion for successful detections, achieving a balance between precision and recall.

3.1.3. Optimization Techniques for Edge Deployment

To optimize the original models (small and nano) for edge devices, several techniques were employed, including reducing the precision to FP16 and applying INT8 quantization.

FP16, or Half-Precision Floating Point, reduces the bit precision of floating-point numbers from 32 bits (FP32) to 16 bits. This precision reduction, often implemented using tools such as TensorRT during model export, enhances the performance by decreasing the computational load and memory usage. Despite reducing the precision, FP16 offers inference speed improvements without significantly impacting the accuracy.

INT8 quantization optimizes models by converting weights and activations from floating-point precision into 8-bit integers. This process, often applied through post-training quantization (PTQ), significantly reduces the computational demand and improves the energy efficiency and inference speed, making it suitable for resource-constrained edge devices. However, unlike FP16, which typically preserves the model accuracy, INT8 quantization can lead to more noticeable accuracy degradation, particularly in complex tasks or when it is applied to models with high parameter sensitivity.

In this work, TensorRT and NCNN were selected as the primary frameworks for optimizing and deploying the YOLOv8 models on the Jetson devices and the Raspberry Pi 5, respectively. TensorRT, deeply integrated with NVIDIA hardware, improves the model performance through layer fusion and memory optimization, enabling efficient inference with support for FP32, FP16, and INT8 quantization. ONNX (Open Neural Network Exchange) served as an intermediary format, facilitating precision reduction and compatibility during the model's conversion to TensorRT. For ARM-based architectures like the Raspberry Pi, NCNN was chosen due to its lightweight design and low-latency inference capabilities, which are particularly effective on mobile and edge devices. While other frameworks, such as CoreML and TorchScript, were considered, they were deemed less suitable for this project's goals. CoreML, tailored to iOS, was excluded due to the platform's irrelevance, and TorchScript did not align as closely with the optimization requirements as TensorRT and NCNN.

By tailoring the frameworks and quantization techniques to each deployment environment, the optimization strategy leveraged hardware-specific strengths. For the Jetson Orin Nano and NX, TensorRT was used to apply three quantization levels—FP32, FP16, and INT8—to establish a comparison. On the Raspberry Pi 5, only the FP32 format, as the original format for YOLO, was utilized via the NCNN framework.

3.2. The Evaluation Strategy and Metrics

As previously introduced, the experiments for measuring the performance of the YOLO models were performed in two stages to measure the set of metrics described in this section, shown on Table 3. Initially, in a controlled and isolated setting, we measured the latency, throughput, and energy efficiency to balance the inference speed and accuracy against edge device constraints. The experiments carried out, whose results are described in Section 4.1, included the following:

- **Inference Time Measurement**: This experiment assessed the computational efficiency of each model in isolation by measuring the time to perform inferences on 5000 images at 640×640 resolution. The average inference time was recorded, and the MIS (FPS) metric was derived to indicate the processing capacity.
- **Continuous Inference Evaluation (Inferences Per Minute, IPM)**: In this experiment, each device performed inferences continuously over 60 s, accounting for all of the latency factors, including model loading, network overhead, and processing delays. The IPM metric provided insight into the system's throughput under real-world conditions.
- **Energy Consumption Analysis**: Real-time power usage was monitored using `tegrastats` for Jetson devices and `vcgencmd pmic_read_adc` for the Raspberry Pi 5. Power data, averaged over the duration, were used to calculate the energy consumption (W·s) and energy per inference (J/inference), indicating the energy efficiency necessary for battery-powered deployments.

Secondly, trials were performed in real-world scenarios to assess the performance under actual conditions. This systematic testing provides a comprehensive grasp of the abilities of the model, from isolated evaluations to complete operational contexts. In the latter case, the following test was performed for the results discussed in Section 5:

- **Throughput and Latency Assessment**: The throughput times were measured in both edge and cloud environments using a timestamp-based approach involving a video server, a processing agent, and a prediction client. Timestamps captured the communication times and processing delays, with the Round-Trip Time (RTT) and prediction time for cloud processing allowing for precise comparisons of the bottlenecks across setups.

Table 3 provides a concise overview of the key metrics used throughout the previous experiments for evaluating the model efficiency, energy usage, and system responsiveness. These metrics were selected to capture distinct aspects of the system performance for real-time processing on edge devices. MIS and IPM measure the inference speed and hardware throughput, respectively, while energy consumption and EPI focus on energy efficiency, needed not only for the design of battery-powered operations but also for maximizing the relative energy utilization based on the relative energy wasted per inference. Together, these metrics provide a comprehensive framework for analyzing and comparing models across different devices and configurations.

In addition to computational metrics, predictive accuracy was assessed using mAP50 and mAP50-95, which evaluate the detection quality across quantization levels and settings. These metrics ensure that the whole evaluation captures both efficiency and reliability.

Table 3. Summary of the performance metrics with their purpose and formulas.

Metric	Purpose	Formula
Model Inference Speed or MIS (FPS)	Measures the speed of model inference in frames per second (FPS), reflecting the real-time processing capability. This measure will only measure the capability of the algorithm in an isolated way, without counting extra processing tasks that produce latency.	$\text{MIS} = \frac{1}{\text{Mean Inference Time (s)}}$
Inferences Per Minute or IPM	Calculates the total inferences in 60 s, representing the overall device throughput. IPM assesses the entire process within the device, including I/O operations, to evaluate the hardware performance comprehensively. It measures the efficiency of the program within the isolated environment of the device.	IPM = Total inferences in one minute
Energy Consumption or E (W·s)	Indicates the total energy used during model inference, assessing the power consumption. Measured using device-specific tools (`tegrastats` for the Jetson and `vcgencmd pmic_read_adc` for the Raspberry Pi), allowing for energy estimation through the average power consumption.	$E = \bar{P} \cdot (t_2 - t_1)$
Energy Per Inference or EPI (J/inference)	Lower EPI values signify a more efficient use of energy per prediction, providing insight into how effectively the model utilizes the available power for inference tasks. As a relative metric, EPI advances our understanding of energy efficiency comparisons across different models and systems.	$\text{EPI} = \frac{\text{Mean Power (W)} \times 60 \text{ s}}{\text{IPM}}$
Round-Trip Time or RTT (ms)	Measures the end-to-end time for a complete inference cycle, including the network latency and processing time, providing a comprehensive assessment of the system's whole architecture's real-time performance.	RTT = Client Reception time − Request sent time

Table 3. *Cont.*

Metric	Purpose	Formula
Throughput of the System (Inferences/s)	Represents the system's capacity for continuous inferences, derived from the inverse of the RTT. Indicates the efficiency of the whole architecture in handling continuous inference requests over time.	$\text{Throughput} = \frac{1}{\text{Average RTT (s)}}$

This experimental setup offers a robust framework for evaluating YOLOv8 models on edge devices. By systematically progressing from isolated testing to real-world deployment, it combines deployment techniques with a detailed performance analysis. This approach supports energy-efficient model optimization tailored to diverse hardware scenarios, ensuring suitability for real-time, low-powered applications and aligning with the goal of delivering practical evaluation strategies for edge-based implementations.

4. Performance Evaluation of Quantized YOLO over Resource-Constrained Devices

This section provides a comprehensive evaluation of the performance of quantized YOLOv8 models on different resource-constrained devices, emphasizing the effects of the quantization techniques and hardware constraints on the model's efficiency and accuracy. Figure 3 depicts the structured workflow, from dataset creation to model training, followed by quantization and deployment. It showcases the distinct quantization formats (FP32, FP16, and INT8) applied to various devices like the Jetson Orin Nano, Jetson Orin NX, and Raspberry Pi 5, along with their associated production deployment. In particular, FP32 represents the default training format used for this type of model, which is sometimes also treated as the "original" model in the following sections. This visual workflow supports comprehension of the process and identifies the specific models examined in the experiments.

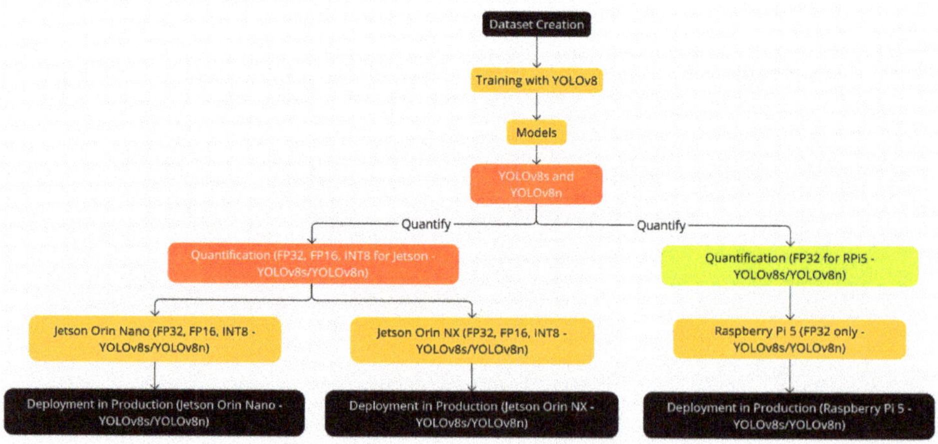

Figure 3. Quantization and deployment process of YOLOv8 models on the Jetson Orin Nano, Jetson Orin NX, and Raspberry Pi 5.

4.1. The Inference Performance

Figure 4 illustrates the Mean Inference Speed (MIS) for the YOLO models on the Orin Nano, Orin NX, and Raspberry Pi devices, comparing the performance with TensorRT (TRT) on the Orin devices and NCNN on the Raspberry Pi.

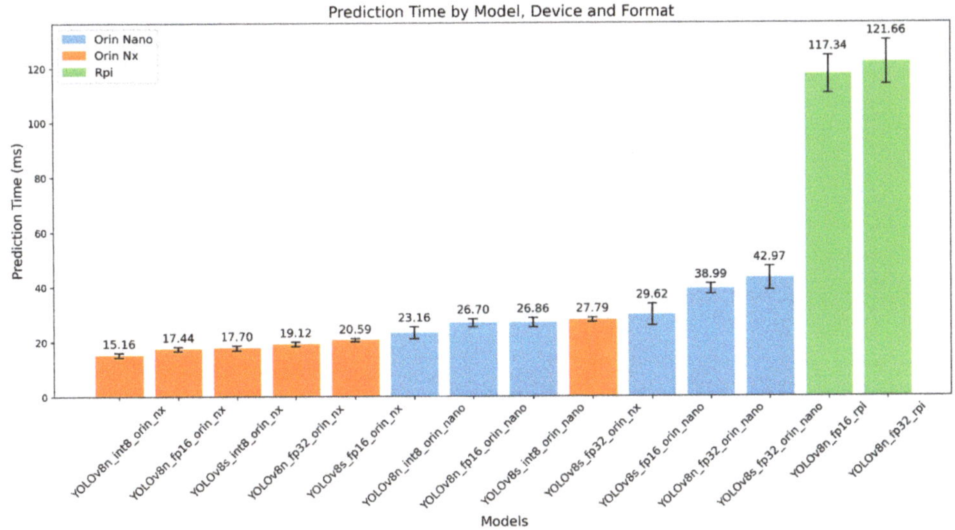

Figure 4. Figure showing the results on the mean iteration times of each model (YOLOv8s or YOLOv8n) with different quantization versions (FP32, FP16, or INT8) within a device (the Orin NX, Orin Nano, or Raspberry Pi 5).

On the Orin Nano, the YOLOv8n_INT8 model excelled with an average iteration time of 23.16 ms, followed by YOLOv8n_FP16 at 26.70 ms and YOLOv8s_INT8 at 28.25 ms. The YOLOv8s_FP32 model had the longest iteration time of 42.97 ms, illustrating the advantages of INT8 quantization in terms of the time performance. The Orin NX showed an even better performance, with YOLOv8n_INT8 achieving the shortest iteration time of 15.16 ms, YOLOv8n_FP16 coming in at 17.44 ms, and YOLOv8s_INT8 at 17.70 ms. In contrast, YOLOv8s_FP32 had the longest time at 27.79 ms, underperforming compared to the leading three Orin Nano models. On the Raspberry Pi, the NCNN-exported models had longer inference times; YOLOv8n_FP32 averaged at 118.00 ms, and YOLOv8s_FP32 reached 211.00 ms, highlighting the hardware constraints and differing efficiencies between CPU and GPU model optimizations. In summary, the Orin Nano and Orin NX vastly outperformed the Raspberry Pi, with the Orin NX being suitable for real-time object detection.

During our trials, we attempted to reduce the numerical precision of the YOLOv8 model on the Raspberry Pi 5 using the available libraries. However, neither FP16 nor INT8 configurations were feasible due to limitations in the precision support of the libraries, particularly with the use of the NCNN framework. As a result, there was no improvement in the performance and a notable loss in the prediction accuracy during these tests. Consequently, only the primary FP32 model configuration was included in the comparative analysis, as it was the only stable and functional setup on the Raspberry Pi 5.

4.2. Degradation Analysis of Model Accuracy

This section compares the YOLOv8s and YOLOv8n models across various edge devices to assess the impact of quantization on both their inference speed and accuracy. Table 4 provides a summary of the mAP and FPS results for different devices and quantizations, while Figure 5 illustrates the mean iteration times for each model and configuration.

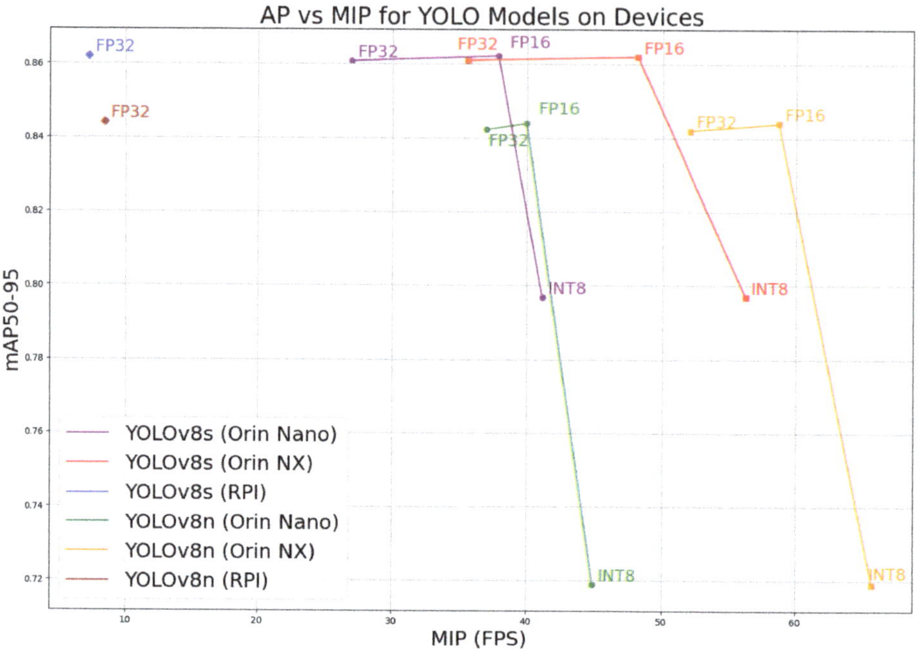

Figure 5. Figure showing the results of the FPS tests of each isolated model (YOLOv8s or YOLOv8n) with different quantization versions (FP32, FP16, and INT8) within a device.

Table 4. Table synthesizing the inference frame rate, energy consumption, inferences per minute, power, and energy per inference in joules.

Device	Model	Quantization	mAP50-95	mAP50	MIS (FPS)	Energy Consumption (W·s)	Inferences per Minute	Energy per Inference (J/inference)
Orin Nano	YOLOv8s	FP32	0.8608	0.9771	27.00	8.790	1391	0.379
	YOLOv8s	FP16	0.8622	0.9771	37.90	7.836	1558	0.302
	YOLOv8s	INT8	0.7968	0.9189	41.20	7.257	1949	0.223
	YOLOv8n	FP32	0.8422	0.9619	37.00	8.345	2041	0.245
	YOLOv8n	FP16	0.8439	0.9619	40.00	7.422	2144	0.208
	YOLOv8n	INT8	0.7190	0.8272	44.90	7.483	2425	0.185
Orin NX	YOLOv8s	FP32	0.8610	0.9781	35.65	14.155	2129	0.399
	YOLOv8s	FP16	0.8620	0.9780	48.24	12.815	2760	0.279
	YOLOv8s	INT8	0.7970	0.9195	56.32	11.002	2836	0.233
	YOLOv8n	FP32	0.8420	0.9621	52.19	12.480	3182	0.235
	YOLOv8n	FP16	0.8440	0.9622	58.82	10.853	3214	0.203
	YOLOv8n	INT8	0.7190	0.8276	65.83	10.305	3443	0.179
RPI5	YOLOv8s	FP32	0.8620	0.9621	7.32	5.422	217	1.498
	YOLOv8n	FP32	0.8440	0.9612	8.47	5.441	442	0.738

Table 4 presents a summary of the inference performance (in frames per second), energy consumption, the number of inferences per minute, and the energy consumed per inference in joules for the devices Jetson Orin NX, Jetson Orin Nano, and Raspberry Pi 5. The results demonstrate the influence of the disparate quantization configurations (FP32, FP16, INT8) on the energy efficiency and model performance. The energy consumption analysis shows differences between the absolute energy consumption demands and energy efficiency when comparing the Jetson Orin NX, Orin Nano, and Raspberry Pi 5 devices across different quantization methods (FP32, FP16, and INT8). For the Jetson Orin Nano, the energy consumption varies between 7.4 W and 8.7 W, while for the Jetson Orin NX, it ranges from 10 W to 14 W, indicating a more substantial increase.

For the Jetson Orin Nano, the energy consumption ranges from 7.4 W (FP32) to 8.7 W (INT8), reflecting a modest increase of 1.3 W. The Orin NX shows greater variation, ranging from 10 W to 14 W, which aligns with its higher processing capacity. Despite its additional energy demands, the Orin NX delivers notable improvements in its inference speed, particularly with INT8 quantization.

An interesting result is the performance of YOLOv8s on the Orin Nano with FP16 quantization, achieving 37.90 FPS and a mAP50-95 of 0.8622. This configuration slightly exceeds the performance of the Orin NX running YOLOv8s with FP32 (35.65 FPS, mAP50-95 of 0.8610), demonstrating the potential of FP16 quantization to enhance the efficiency even on less advanced hardware. For the YOLOv8n model, the Orin NX achieves 58.82 FPS with FP16, compared to 40.00 FPS on the Orin Nano, indicating its advantage in handling smaller, compact models.

The Raspberry Pi 5, using FP32 quantization via NCNN, achieves 7.32 FPS on YOLOv8s (mAP50-95 of 0.8620). While functional, its performance is limited compared to that of the Jetson devices, suggesting it is better suited to less demanding applications where real-time processing is not critical.

4.3. *Energy Consumption Analysis*

The mean average energy consumption was measured over 5000 images, as depicted in Figure 6.

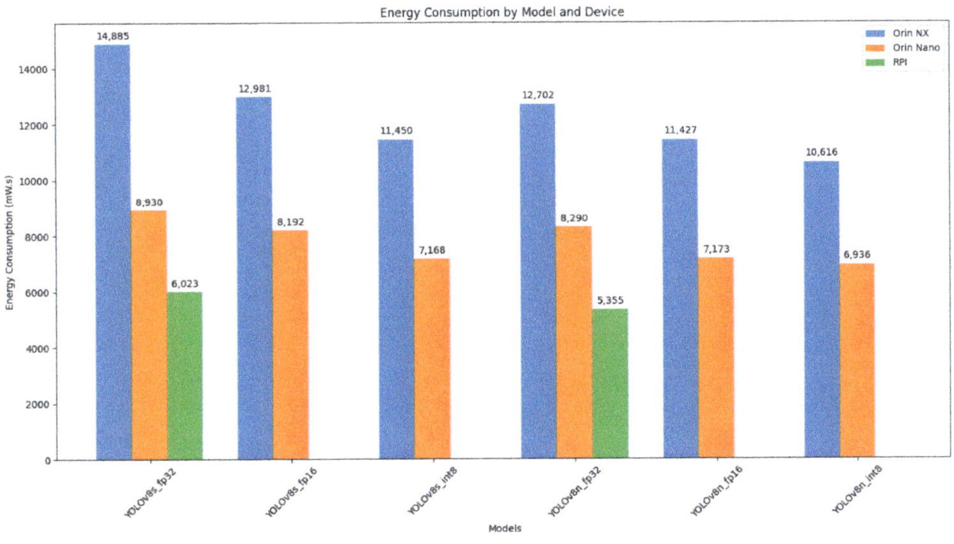

Figure 6. Energy consumption by model and device.

For instance, in the YOLOv8 FP32 setup, the Orin NX consumes 14.155 W, whereas the Orin Nano requires only 8.790 W in the same configuration. Despite the Orin NX's higher power draw, it generally achieves a greater energy efficiency—measured as the energy per inference (J/inference)—across the configurations due to its higher inference throughput. With INT8 quantization, for example, the Orin NX achieves 0.179 J/inference for YOLOv8n, compared to 0.185 J/inference on the Orin Nano, indicating more efficient use of energy for each inference completed.

The variations in the power consumption between the quantization methods are also noteworthy. For the Orin Nano, the energy consumption rises from 7.4 W in FP32 to 8.7 W in INT8, reflecting a modest increase of 1.3 W. In contrast, the Orin NX exhibits a larger increase, with the power consumption ranging from 10 W in YOLOv8n_INT8 to 14 W in YOLOv8s_FP32, a difference of 4 W.

The Orin Nano demonstrates lower absolute energy consumption and achieves better results in terms of the energy per inference under certain configurations. For instance, in the YOLOv8s_FP16 setup, it consumes 7.836 W and processes 1558 inferences per minute, resulting in an energy consumption of 0.302 J/inference. Additionally, in FP32 mode, the Orin Nano achieves a better energy efficiency than that of the Orin NX, with 0.379 J/inference compared to 0.399 J/inference.

The Raspberry Pi 5, by comparison, shows the lowest absolute energy consumption but also the lowest energy efficiency due to the small number of predictions per time unit. In the YOLOv8s FP32 configuration, for example, it consumes 5.422 W·s while achieving 217 inferences per minute, resulting in an energy cost of 1.498 J/inference. The Orin Nano devices, while demonstrating higher absolute energy consumption, also achieves commendable efficiency due to the much better performance in number of inferences per unit of time.

5. Performance Evaluation Using a Realistic Testbed

This section aims to assess the performance of different hardware devices, specifically the Orin Nano, Orin NX, and Raspberry Pi 5, using an object detector in a realistic deployment scenario that mirrors real-world drone operations. In this sense, this section takes advantage of the platform presented by the authors in [26] which considers the core elements (e.g., telemetry, video streaming, and data processing) of a real-time drone system, where the interplay of computation and communications affects the latency and system throughput. As depicted in Figure 7, the testbed platform allows live drone images to be processed both in an edge device and in a cloud environment. This enables performance benchmarking of edge algorithms against a centralized cloud, providing a detailed comparison.

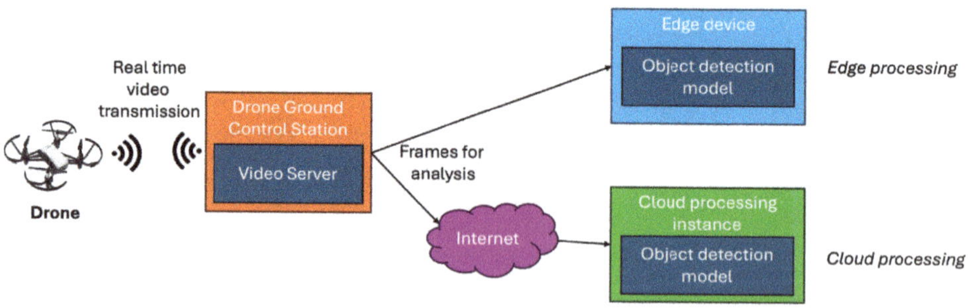

Figure 7. General system deployment architecture.

The deployment architecture consists of three main components: a drone ground control station (GCS) that gathers video in real time from a drone and broadcasts it using the WebSocket protocol, an edge computing device to perform object detection on video streams using TensorRT optimization, and a cloud processing instance (accessible through the internet) that also allows for the deployment of the object detection model. The interaction between these entities is illustrated in Figure 8.

The workflow begins with the transmission of video from the drone to its associated ground control station. Then, using WebSocket communication for low-latency and reliable data transfer, the video frames can be forwarded either to an edge computing device, which performs the inference locally (at the edge), or to a cloud instance that performs inference remotely (in the cloud). AWS SageMaker is employed for cloud detection, allowing for a systematic comparison of the latency and processing times between the edge and cloud setups. In either case, the inferences and annotated images are sent back to the ground control station.

Within this framework, two tests were performed. In Section 5.1, different edge devices are compared in the real, representative testbed. Then, in Section 5.2, a test is performed between edge and cloud processing. The latter evaluation allows for an analysis of the trade-offs between local and centralized processing in terms of the computational power and communication delays. In both cases, by timing each phase (i.e., video transmission, object detection, and prediction distribution), it is possible to identify latency issues and potential bottlenecks.

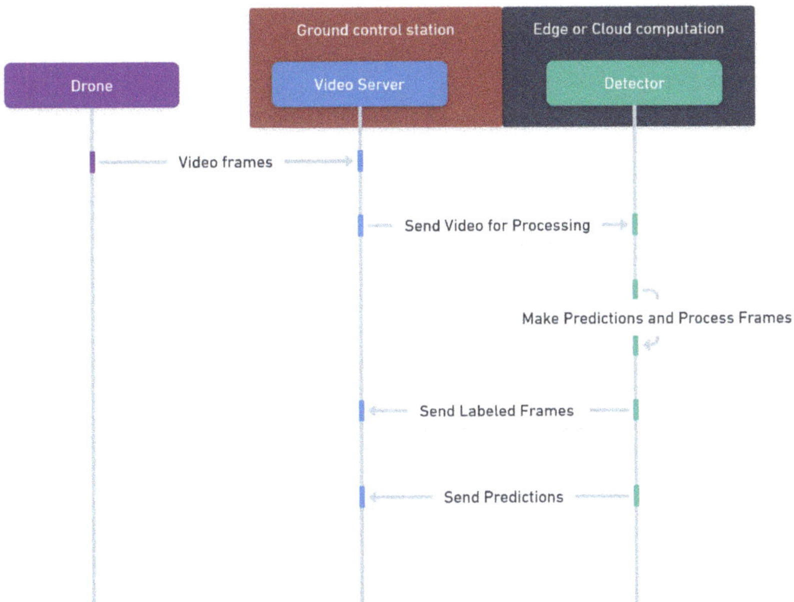

Figure 8. Data flow for real-time video processing and predictions at the edge.

5.1. Edge Deployment

Table 5 provides a summary of the RTT times, RTT deviations, processing times, and throughput (FPS) for the different models and quantization configurations.

Table 5. Table synthesizing the RTT, RTT std, processing time, and throughput of the system (FPS) for different quantization models.

Device	Model	Quantization	RTT (ms)		Processing Time (ms)		Throughput (Inferences/s
			Mean	Std	Mean	Std	
Orin Nano	YOLOv8n	FP16	49.70	4.59	23.81	20.12	20.12
	YOLOv8n	FP32	60.52	12.24	28.77	16.52	16.52
	YOLOv8n	INT8	48.80	8.42	20.54	20.49	20.49
	YOLOv8s	FP16	49.44	6.46	28.90	20.23	20.23
	YOLOv8s	FP32	73.18	4.89	47.18	13.66	13.66
	YOLOv8s	INT8	44.27	8.27	20.62	22.59	22.59
Orin NX	YOLOv8n	FP16	34.15	3.65	16.12	29.28	29.28
	YOLOv8n	FP32	35.76	2.28	18.25	27.97	27.96
	YOLOv8n	INT8	29.95	3.19	14.29	33.38	33.39
	YOLOv8s	FP16	35.09	4.35	18.50	28.50	28.5
	YOLOv8s	FP32	48.97	8.83	26.50	20.42	20.42
	YOLOv8s	INT8	33.60	3.31	15.96	29.76	29.76

Regarding the RTT (Round-Trip Time), the Jetson Orin Nano demonstrated its best performance in terms of the RTT with the YOLOv8s INT8 model, achieving a minimum RTT of 44.27 ms. The RTT increased to 73.18 ms when using the YOLOv8s FP32 model. For the Jetson Orin NX, the minimum RTT was observed at 29.95 ms with the YOLOv8n INT8 model, while the maximum RTT occurred with the YOLOv8s FP32 model at 48.97 ms.

The RTT deviation results showed that the Orin Nano showed higher variability with the YOLOv8n FP32 model, which had a deviation of 12.24 ms. The lowest deviation for the Orin Nano was seen with the YOLOv8s FP32 model at 4.89 ms. For the Orin NX, the RTT fluctuations were smaller overall, with the highest deviation being 8.83 ms for the YOLOv8s FP32 model and the lowest at 2.28 ms for YOLOv8n FP32.

During the testing phase, we attempted to implement the architecture on the Raspberry Pi 5. However, it was not possible to complete the tests in full due to the computational limitations. This device exhibited significant latency in its predictions, and this led to instability not only in drone control but also in the acquisition and dissemination of images across the different components of the architecture. Consequently, the results obtained from the Raspberry Pi 5 are sparse and incomplete and therefore not viable as a reliable architecture for this application.

In terms of the processing time, the Orin Nano showed a minimum processing time of 20.54 ms with the YOLOv8n INT8, and the longest processing time was 47.18 ms for the YOLOv8s FP32 model. The processing times on the Orin NX were generally shorter, with a minimum of 14.29 ms for YOLOv8n INT8 and a maximum of 26.50 ms for YOLOv8s FP32.

5.2. *Edge vs. Cloud Comparison*

In order to assess the trade-offs between computational power and latency in edge and cloud environments, we conducted a series of experiments comparing the two setups using the YOLOv8s model in its FP16 configuration on the Orin Nano. The primary metrics evaluated were the Round-Trip Time (RTT), model processing latency, and communication latency, offering a comprehensive understanding of how both environments handle real-time data processing and communication delays.

For our cloud-based deployment, we selected a cloud instance located in London (eu-west-2) using the *ml.g4dn.xlarge* configuration, which is powered by an NVIDIA T4 GPU. To handle the model inferences efficiently, we deployed the model on a Triton Inference Server within the SageMaker environment. Triton, known for its high performance and flexibility in supporting multiple AI frameworks and backends, provided a robust platform for managing the inference requests for our YOLOv8s model. The most decisive factor in choosing the NVIDIA Triton Inference Server was its support for TensorRT optimization, which allowed us to conduct a fair comparison under consistent conditions. Additionally, by utilizing Triton, we could take advantage of advanced features such as dynamic batching, model ensemble, and TensorRT acceleration, thereby maximizing the inference speed and fully leveraging the computational power of the cloud instance.

The model was deployed and invoked directly through the SageMaker SDK API's invoke endpoint, which facilitated direct HTTP-based invocation. However, it is important to note that the invoke endpoint does not support WebSocket communication, meaning that all inference requests are handled over HTTP. This limitation may introduce additional latency in scenarios where persistent, real-time communication channels are desired. The London (eu-west-2) location helped us explore the impact of geographical data transmission delays from Madrid, providing insights into latency management for future applications.

Table 6 presents a comparative investigation of the latency metrics between the edge deployments on the Orin Nano and the cloud deployments using the YOLOv8s model in FP16 format. The edge RTT latency shows a mean of 35.09 ms, which is within the feasible limits for real-time applications. By contrast, the cloud deployment shows a much higher mean RTT of 348.21 ms due to the increased communication distance to remote GPU servers. This difference is reflected in the communication latency, where the edge setup averages at 2.50 ms, whereas the cloud averages at a considerably higher value of 341.41 ms.

Table 6. Latency results in the two different deployment scenarios, edge and cloud.

Processing Environment	RTT Latency (ms)	Model Processing Latency (ms)	Communication Latency (ms)
Edge	Mean: 35.09 Std: 4.25	Mean: 32.59 Std: 4.27	Mean: 2.50 Std: 0.34
Cloud	Mean: 348.21 Std: 69.88	Mean: 6.82 Std: 0.05	Mean: 341.41 Std: 69.89

The processing latency data highlight the computational edge of the cloud, with an average latency of 6.82 ms, significantly outperforming the edge's latency of 32.59 ms. Nonetheless, the high communication latency of the cloud counteracts its processing efficiency, resulting in performance constraints.

6. Discussion

An evaluation of various quantization techniques and their impact on inference latency has confirmed INT8 as the fastest configuration, achieving notable reductions in the processing times across all evaluated devices. For instance, on the Orin Nano, YOLOv8s with INT8 achieves 41.20 FPS compared to 27.00 FPS with FP32, representing a significant improvement in speed. However, this increase comes at the cost of reduced accuracy, with the mAP50-95 dropping from 0.8608 in FP32 to 0.7968 in INT8—a reduction of approximately 6.4 percentage points. In contrast, FP16 emerges as a balanced alternative, offering slight improvements in accuracy while reducing the latency. For example, YOLOv8s on the Orin Nano achieves 37.90 FPS in FP16 with an accuracy of 0.8622 mAP50-95, providing an optimal balance for scenarios requiring both speed and precision. This quantization approach also enables intermediate models, such as YOLOv8s, to outperform smaller versions like YOLOv8n_FP32 on more advanced devices such as the Orin NX, where YOLOv8s_FP16 achieves 48.24 FPS with a mAP50-95 of 0.8620, compared to YOLOv8n_FP32's 35.65 FPS and 0.8420 mAP50-95. Furthermore, the application of quantization techniques has been observed to contribute to marginal enhancements in the model's generalization, possibly due to the reduced computational complexity, enabling more efficient image processing. This is particularly relevant for tasks involving real-time object detection, where the computational resources are constrained. Conversely, while the Raspberry Pi 5 demonstrates acceptable accuracy metrics, such as a mAP50-95 of 0.8620 for YOLOv8s in FP32, its inference latency limits its applicability. The device achieves only 7.32 FPS and 217 inferences per minute in this configuration, significantly reducing the real-time capabilities. In addition to optimizing performance, quantization techniques have a significant impact on the energy efficiency of employing devices. The results demonstrate that INT8 is the most efficient configuration in terms of energy consumption, achieving a notable reduction without a significant loss of accuracy. In this context, the Orin NX, despite its higher overall power demand, demonstrates a better performance in the EPI metric (J/inference). This makes it the preferred choice for real-time, inference-intensive applications, especially in the FP16 and INT8 configurations. The Raspberry Pi 5 has the lowest total power consumption; however, its low performance in terms of Inferences Per Minute (IPM) restricts its applicability in environments where a real-time response is required. This analysis highlights the importance of selecting optimized hardware devices, such as the Orin models, for edge architectures that demand both high performance and sustainable energy efficiency, particularly in long-running applications where controlled power consumption is essential.

The evaluation of the stability and performance of the devices within architectures that emulate real-world operating environments highlights the advantage of the Orin models over general-purpose alternatives such as the Raspberry Pi 5. In practical scenarios, the models evaluated on the Orin Nano achieved acceptable results; however, a detailed analysis suggests that improvements can still be made in frame capture and the optimization of internal operations, which could reduce the processing overhead. This overhead, identified by analyzing isolated model processing times during the full operation of the architecture, suggests that better management of data capture and data flow could significantly improve the efficiency.

The Orin NX exhibited low variability in its response times and strong stability, positioning it as optimal for tasks demanding a consistent performance throughout the architecture. Conversely, the Raspberry Pi 5 encountered issues with instability, processing interruptions, and control challenges during object detection, constraining its effectiveness in complex architectures. Thus, it is more appropriate for basic processing or simpler algorithms rather than advanced applications requiring sustained high stability and low latency.

In this way, the results reveal complementary strengths in the tested devices: the Jetson excels in its computational performance but consumes significant energy, while the Raspberry Pi offers excellent energy efficiency but struggles with real-time object detection. Hybrid architectures could combine these strengths to optimize the overall performance. For example, the Raspberry Pi could manage lightweight tasks, such as environmental monitoring or data preprocessing, while the Jetson handles critical operations like real-time object detection or obstacle avoidance. This delegation of tasks reduces the energy footprint of the individual components while maintaining the system's responsiveness. Additionally, selectively integrating cloud processing for non-critical tasks enhances the scalability and reduces latency. Exploring this approach in future implementations could help address challenges in energy-sensitive drone missions.

The cloud results underscore the advantage of deploying edge devices near data sources. Despite the low model processing latency in the cloud, the high communication latency limits its real-time viability. Using a closer AWS region may improve the results, but communication bottlenecks remain a challenge for real-time drone applications. GPU-equipped edge devices offer a practical solution, enabling rapid local processing with some trade-offs in the computational power, showing the importance of the role of edge devices in real-time drone systems.

Based on the results obtained and from the perspective of this study, focused on drone applications, a guide has been developed to identify the most suitable hardware configurations and quantization models according to the operational needs. This guide, based on the lessons learned, provides recommendations for selecting devices and model configurations based on the specific requirements, such as extended coverage, real-time tracking, and high-precision detection.

Table 7 illustrates how particular configurations align with specific requirements in drone applications. For extended coverage and long-duration missions, the Orin NX with INT8 offers the optimal autonomy with minimal inference consumption, making it ideal for continuous surveillance and environmental monitoring. In critical tracking scenarios, the same device with YOLOv8n INT8 enables a high inference rate, which is valuable for real-time tasks in defense and security. The Orin Nano and FP16 quantization enable high-quality detection, which is a requirement in automated infrastructure inspection, while maintaining the optimal power consumption. The INT8 configuration of the Orin Nano allows low-demand tasks to be completed efficiently and cost-effectively, even when speed or accuracy is not critical. These results demonstrate the value of aligning the configuration with specific operational demands, ensuring that each device performs at its best in its designated application. These insights serve as practical guidance for drone operators and practitioners, helping them select the most appropriate hardware and quantization settings based on the specific operational needs. Researchers should examine scalability in more UAV scenarios (e.g., evaluating the outdoor performance variability or investigating energy-efficient inference to provide insights and new extended guidelines for real-world deployment). Moreover, adapting the results obtained in the indoor controlled edge environment to outdoor surroundings would assess the stability of inferences under dynamic conditions, thereby verifying the practicality of energy-efficient setups outside controlled contexts. Furthermore, as the industry advances in the hardware–software co-design for FPGAs and low-power chips, research should incorporate these technologies to align with emerging capabilities.

Table 7. Recommended configurations based on operational needs.

Operational Need	Description	Area of Interest	Recommended Configuration	Key Supporting Metrics
Extensive Coverage and Long Duration	Extends energy autonomy for continuous monitoring of large areas without frequent recharging.	Surveillance, Environmental Monitoring	Jetson Orin Nano + YOLOv8n INT8	High FPS (44.9), Low Energy Consumption (7.483 W·s), Good Accuracy (mAP50: 0.8272)
Critical Tracking (Real-Time)	High inference rate for rapid response and continuous tracking.	Defense, Security	Jetson Orin NX + YOLOv8n INT8	Very High FPS (65.83), Moderate Energy (10.305 W·s), Sufficient Accuracy (mAP50: 0.7190)
High-Quality Detection	Ensures high precision in detecting fine details, ideal for infrastructure inspection.	Infrastructure Inspection	Jetson Orin Nano + YOLOv8s FP16	High Accuracy (mAP50: 0.8622), Moderate FPS (37.9), Low Energy Consumption (7.836 W·s)

Table 7. *Cont.*

Operational Need	Description	Area of Interest	Recommended Configuration	Key Supporting Metrics
Balance of Speed and Precision	Balances speed and accuracy for emergency and rescue tasks.	Rescue and Emergency Response	Jetson Orin NX + YOLOv8s FP16/YOLOv8n INT8	High FPS (58.82/65.83) Balanced Accuracy (mAP50: 0.8620/0.7190), Efficient Energy Usage (10.853/10.305 W·s)
Low-Cost Processing	Optimizes costs and energy for less demanding tasks without high precision or speed requirements.	Low-Demand Tasks	Jetson Orin Nano + INT8	Moderate FPS (41.2), Low Energy Consumption (7.257 W·s), Acceptable Accuracy (mAP50: 0.7968)

7. Conclusions

This research provides practical tools and guidelines for integrating YOLOv8 models into autonomous systems while also evaluating their performance on computationally constrained drone computational devices. The findings show that the YOLOv8n (nano) and YOLOv8s (small) models can achieve efficient operation on devices such as the Raspberry Pi 5, Orin NX, and Jetson Orin Nano. However, achieving the optimal performance in real-time applications requires careful consideration of the trade-offs between the detection precision and inference speed, especially when utilizing INT8 quantization, which accelerates the processing but may slightly reduce the accuracy.

Thus, we provide a set of recommendations (Table 6) that streamlines complex recommendations into an easily accessible format for decision-makers to use to adjust their configurations according to the specific operational demands. By linking the device configurations and quantization methods with specific applications, this study explores the practical application of guidelines that enhance the performance and energy efficiency. This organized method clarifies the criteria for the optimal configuration selection while enabling practitioners to efficiently implement these advances in diverse edge computing scenarios.

The test architecture in this study facilitates controlled and repeatable testing of real-time object detection and tracking algorithms. It enables an accurate evaluation of edge computing and onboard processing solutions within a comprehensive drone architecture in an indoor flight environment. However, the indoor setting introduces certain limitations, as it cannot fully replicate the complexities of outdoor operations, such as variable lighting conditions, environmental interferences, or multi-agent dynamics. To address these challenges, more complex mock-ups are needed to emulate more complex environments. Such improvements would enable testing under conditions closer to those in real-world applications, improving the reliability of the proposed systems.

An interesting direction for upcoming research is the evaluation of YOLOv10 and YOLOv11 as they become available, evaluating their improvements in accuracy, efficiency, and real-time performance. Comparing them with YOLOv8 in drone-based applications could provide insights into their suitability for edge computing and its integration viability in autonomous drone navigation.

Moreover, studies should explore hybrid architectures that combine the complementary strengths of devices like the Jetson, the Raspberry Pi, and the cloud. As mentioned in Section 6, Discussion, its complementary abilities may offer a study opportunity. Testing these configurations in real-world drone deployments would provide valuable insights into their feasibility and effectiveness in energy-sensitive missions.

Further integration of edge architectures with 5G and tactical cloud technologies could expand the potential of drone applications. This integration would enable the design and control of complex swarm missions, as discussed in Section 2, The State of the Art. Through network slicing, the processing tasks could be decentralized, increasing the autonomy of individual drones within the swarm and reducing reliance on a central server. Moreover, testing 5G communications in these configurations could provide insights into intelligent drone architectures, particularly regarding real-time decision-making and minimizing the latency in data transmission. These advancements would also necessitate the deployment of larger drones capable of supporting the additional weight and power requirements associated with outdoor operations in complex environments.

Author Contributions: Conceptualization: A.M.B. Methodology: A.M.B. and D.C. Software: L.R. and A.D.D. Validation: L.R., D.C. and A.D.D. Formal analysis: J.A.B., L.B. and L.R. Investigation: L.R. and D.C. Data curation: L.R. and A.D.D. Resources: L.B. and J.A.B. Writing—original draft preparation: L.R., A.M.B., A.D.D. and L.B. Writing—review and editing: all. Visualization: L.R. Supervision: A.M.B., J.A.B. and J.R.C. Project administration: A.M.B. Funding acquisition: J.R.C. and A.M.B. All authors have read and agreed to the published version of the manuscript.

Funding: This research was funded by the Horizon Europe EDF Programme grant number 101103386 and under the national grants TSI-063000-2021-80 and MIA.2021. M04.0008 by the Spanish Ministry of Economic Affairs and Digital Transformation and by the EU Next Generation EU/PRTR programme. MCIN/AEI/10.13039/501100011033 under Grant PID2020-118249RB-C21.

Data Availability Statement: The raw data supporting the conclusions of this article will be made available by the authors on request.

Conflicts of Interest: The authors declare no conflicts of interest.

References

1. Amato, G.; Ciampi, L.; Falchi, F.; Gennaro, C. Counting Vehicles with Deep Learning in Onboard UAV Imagery. In Proceedings of the 2019 IEEE Symposium on Computers and Communications (ISCC), Barcelona, Spain, 29 June–3 July 2019; pp. 1–6. [CrossRef]
2. Brown, A.; White, B. Autonomous Navigation in Drones Using Deep Learning. In Proceedings of the International Conference on Autonomous Systems, Barcelona, Spain, 13–17 March 2023; pp. 456–467. [CrossRef]
3. Schilling, F.; Lecoeur, J.; Schiano, F.; Floreano, D. Learning Vision-Based Flight in Drone Swarms by Imitation. *IEEE Robot. Autom. Lett.* **2019**, *4*, 4523–4530. [CrossRef]
4. Holly, S.; Wendt, A.; Lechner, M. Profiling Energy Consumption of Deep Neural Networks on NVIDIA Jetson Nano. In Proceedings of the 2020 11th International Green and Sustainable Computing Workshops (IGSC), Pullman, WA, USA, 19-22 October 2020; pp. 1–6. [CrossRef]
5. Sacco, A.; Esposito, F.; Marchetto, G.; Montuschi, P. A Self-Learning Strategy for Task Offloading in UAV Networks. *IEEE Trans. Veh. Technol.* **2022**, *71*, 4301–4311. [CrossRef]
6. Reis, D.; Kupec, J.; Hong, J.; Daoudi, A. Real-Time Flying Object Detection with YOLOv8. *arXiv* **2024**, arXiv:2305.09972.
7. Jocher, G.; Qiu, J.; Chaurasia, A. Ultralytics YOLO, Version 8.0.0. Online Resource, 2023. Available online: https://github.com/ultralytics/ultralytics (accessed on 29 January 2025).
8. McEnroe, P.; Wang, S.; Liyanage, M. A Survey on the Convergence of Edge Computing and AI for UAVs: Opportunities and Challenges. *IEEE Internet Things J.* **2022**, *9*, 15435–15459. [CrossRef]
9. Baller, S.P.; Jindal, A.; Chadha, M.; Gerndt, M. DeepEdgeBench: Benchmarking Deep Neural Networks on Edge Devices. *arXiv* **2021**, arXiv:2108.09457.
10. Stolfi, D.H.; Danoy, G. An Evolutionary Algorithm to Optimise a Distributed UAV Swarm Formation System. *Appl. Sci.* **2022**, *12*, 10218. [CrossRef]
11. Li, X.; Gong, X.; Wang, D.; Zhang, J.; Baker, T.; Zhou, J.; Lu, T. ABM-SpConv-SIMD: Accelerating Convolutional Neural Network Inference for Industrial IoT Applications on Edge Devices. *IEEE Trans. Netw. Sci. Eng.* **2023**, *10*, 3071–3085. [CrossRef]

12. Ferraz, O.; Araujo, H.; Silva, V.; Fernandes, G.F.P. Benchmarking Convolutional Neural Network Inference on Low-Power Edg Devices. In Proceedings of the ICASSP 2023—2023 IEEE International Conference on Acoustics, Speech and Signal Processir (ICASSP), Rhodes Island, Greece, 4–10 June 2023; pp. 1–5. [CrossRef]
13. Hou, X.; Guan, Y.; Han, T.; Zhang, N. DistrEdge: Speeding up Convolutional Neural Network Inference on Distributed Edg Devices. In Proceedings of the 2022 IEEE International Parallel and Distributed Processing Symposium (IPDPS), Lyon, Franc 30 May–3 June 2022; pp. 1097–1107. [CrossRef]
14. Liang, S.; Wu, H.; Zhen, L.; Hua, Q.; Garg, S.; Kaddoum, G.; Hassan, M.; Yu, K. Edge YOLO: Real-Time Intelligent Object Detectio System Based on Edge-Cloud Cooperation in Autonomous Vehicles. *IEEE Trans. Intell. Transp. Syst.* **2022**, *23*, 25345–2536 [CrossRef]
15. Shin, D.J.; Kim, J.J. A Deep Learning Framework Performance Evaluation to Use YOLO in Nvidia Jetson Platform. *Appl. Sc* **2022**, *12*, 3734. [CrossRef]
16. Xiong, G.; Qi, J.; Wang, M.; Wu, C.; Sun, H. GCGE-YOLO: Improved YOLOv5s Algorithm for Object Detection in UAV Image In Proceedings of the 2023 42nd Chinese Control Conference (CCC), Tianjin, China, 24–26 July 2023; pp. 7723–7728. [CrossRef
17. Hu, Y.; Wang, L.; Kou, T.; Zhang, M. YOLO-Tiny-attention: An Improved Algorithm for Fault Detection of Wind Turbine Blad In Proceedings of the 2023 8th International Conference on Intelligent Computing and Signal Processing (ICSP), Xi'an, Chin 21–23 April 2023; pp. 1228–1232. [CrossRef]
18. Xu, C. 5G for drone networking. *Trans. Emerg. Telecommun. Technol.* **2022**, *33*, e4668. [CrossRef]
19. Cai, Y.; Yue, L.; Zhu, M.; Lei, M.; Zhang, J.; Hua, B.; Luo, W.; Zou, Y.; Tian, L.; Ma, L.; et al. Photonics-Assisted Millimeter-Wav Communication System Based on Low-Bit Gaussian Mixture Model Adaptive Vector Quantization. *IEEE Photonics J.* **2022**, *14*, 1– [CrossRef]
20. Coelho, A.; Fontes, H.; Campos, R.; Ricardo, M. Placement and Allocation of Communications Resources in Slicing-aware Flyin Networks. *arXiv* **2021**, arXiv:2112.07048.
21. Jiang, H.; Li, Q.; Li, Y. Post Training Quantization after Neural Network. In Proceedings of the 2022 14th International Conferen on Computer Research and Development (ICCRD), Shenzhen, China, 7–9 January 2022; pp. 1–6. [CrossRef]
22. Przewlocka-Rus, D.; Sarwar, S.S.; Sumbul, H.; Li, Y.; Salvo, B.D. Power-of-Two Quantization for Low Bitwidth and Hardwar Compliant Neural Networks. *arXiv* **2022**, arXiv:2203.05025. [CrossRef]
23. Al-Hamid, A.A.; Kim, H. Unified Scaling-Based Pure-Integer Quantization for Low-Power Accelerator of Complex CNN *Electronics* **2023**, *12*, 2660. [CrossRef]
24. Gupta, K.; Asthana, A. Reducing the Side-Effects of Oscillations in Training of Quantized YOLO Networks. *arXiv* **202** arXiv:2311.05109. [CrossRef]
25. Zhou, M.; Guo, Y.; Fu, J.; Cai, H. Power-aware Quantization Circuits in Analog In-Memory Computing with STT-MRAM Macr In Proceedings of the 2023 IEEE International Magnetic Conference—Short Papers (INTERMAG Short Papers), Sendai, Japar 15–19 May 2023; pp. 1–2. [CrossRef]
26. Carramiñana, D.; Braga, L.R.; Bernardos, A.M.; Dobrzycki, A.D.; Bergesio, L.; Besada, J.A.; Casar, J.R. A Digital Twin Concept t Prototype Multi-Drone Based Applications. In Proceedings of the 14th International Conference on the Internet of Things (Io 2024), Oulu, Finland, 19–22 November 2024.

electronics

MDPI

Article

Leveraging Transformer-Based OCR Model with Generative Data Augmentation for Engineering Document Recognition †

Wael Khallouli [1], Mohammad Shahab Uddin [2], Andres Sousa-Poza [1], Jiang Li [2,*] and Samuel Kovacic [1,*]

1 Department of Engineering Management & Systems Engineering, Old Dominion University, Norfolk, VA 23529, USA; wkhallou@odu.edu (W.K.); asousapo@odu.edu (A.S.-P.)
2 Department of Electrical & Computer Engineering, Old Dominion University, Norfolk, VA 23529, USA; muddi003@odu.edu
* Correspondence: jli@odu.edu (J.L.); skovacic@odu.edu (S.K.)
† This paper is a revised and expanded version of our paper at the IEEE World AI IoT Congress (AIIoT) 2022 with the title "Leveraging transfer learning and GAN models for OCR from engineering documents".

Abstract: The long-standing practice of document-based engineering has resulted in the accumulation of a large number of engineering documents across various industries. Engineering documents, such as 2D drawings, continue to play a significant role in exchanging information and sharing knowledge across multiple engineering processes. However, these documents are often stored in non-digitized formats, such as paper and portable document format (PDF) files, making automation difficult. As digital engineering transforms processes in many industries, digitizing engineering documents presents a crucial challenge that requires advanced methods. This research addresses the problem of automatically extracting textual content from non-digitized legacy engineering documents. We introduced an optical character recognition (OCR) system for text detection and recognition that leverages transformer-based generative deep learning models and transfer learning approaches to enhance text recognition accuracy in engineering documents. The proposed system was evaluated on a dataset collected from ships' engineering drawings provided by a U.S. agency. Experimental results demonstrated that the proposed transformer-based OCR model significantly outperformed pretrained off-the-shelf OCR models.

Keywords: digital engineering; text recognition; deep learning; transfer learning; transformers; deep generative adversarial networks

1. Introduction

Systems engineering is shifting away from a traditional document-based approach to a model-based approach. The adoption of model-based systems engineering (MBSE) is increasing among industry and government practitioners as systems continue to grow in complexity [1]. MBSE is a formalized methodology that supports the requirements, design, analysis, verification, and validation associated with the development of complex systems [2]. In contrast to the traditional document-based approach, MBSE uses system models as the primary artifacts of the systems engineering process. Digital engineering (DT) has empowered the paradigm shift to MBSE by providing the digital infrastructure to design, develop, operate, and sustain complex systems. By leveraging models to connect data across all lifecycle stages using computer-based methods, processes, and tools (MPTs) and incorporating technological innovations such as artificial intelligence and advanced analytics, DT addresses the challenges associated with the complexity, uncertainty, and rapidly changing requirements of modern systems [3]. Digitalization is a key defining feature in digital engineering. In a digital engineering ecosystem, data availability in a machine-readable (digital) format is necessary to gain the advantage of digital technologies, enable data and model sharing, and enhance information traceability.

The long-standing tradition of using document-based engineering has led to the accumulation of a substantial number of legacy engineering documents across several industries. These documents are often available in scanned or paper-based formats and contain valuable knowledge about legacy systems, including technical details, drawings, and configuration data, among other information. Furthermore, engineering documents play a significant role in many engineering processes, such as quality control [4]. In the MSBE environment, it is still common practice to produce various engineering documents that capture information, such as scanned PDFs, spreadsheets, and informal drawings, throughout the system's lifecycle, making it a document-rich environment. Since manually digitizing or inspecting engineering documents is time-consuming and resource-intensive, there is a growing need to develop automated tools for extracting information from these documents.

Optical character recognition (OCR) is a key digitization technology. OCR refers to converting printed and handwritten text into a digital format that is easy to extract, edit, search, and analyze [5]. Researchers have proposed robust solutions across many application domains and successfully automated many business tasks, such as automatic invoice reading (e.g., [6,7]), plate recognition (e.g., [8–10]), scene text detection, and recognition (e.g., [11–15]). However, extracting text from legacy engineering documents is challenging. In many industries, such as shipbuilding, it is common for information to be stored in noisy, low-quality images or outdated fonts in scanned PDFs. Extracting information with existing OCR systems often results in remarkably low accuracy, causing significant information loss.

This research addresses the problem of extracting text from engineering documents through a case study from the Military Sealift Command (MSC). The MSC has extensive experience in operating and maintaining ships. Along the way, it has accumulated a large number of engineering and maintenance documents, including technical updates about its vessels, stored in various formats such as manuals, bulletins, drawings, and other engineering document data. Soft and hard copies of these documents are stored in various electronic formats and maintained in a central repository called the Virtual Technical Library (VTL) [16]. As part of their DoD digital transformation efforts, the VTL is undergoing a digitalization process. One of the challenges faced by MSC was the difficulty of extracting textual content from these documents. MSC documents contain different types of text (printed and handwritten text), font styles, and sizes (Figures 1–3). Some fonts used in these documents are outdated and irregular, making the text hard to recognize. Furthermore, the background noise present in some MSC engineering documents complicates the OCR process. This paper builds on our previous research [17], where we explored various deep learning and OCR models to extract textual content from MSC engineering documents. We proposed an OCR framework comprising a fine-tuned OCR model for text recognition and a generative deep learning model for data augmentation, and partial preliminary results were presented as a conference paper [17]. Our main contributions are:

- We annotated a dataset from MSC engineering documents and fine-tuned two state-of-the-art OCR systems, including a transformer-based OCR model, TrOCR [18], and a CRNN-based OCR model, KerasOCR [19] for improved OCR performance on the MSC documents.
- We employed a deep generative model to learn the outdated fonts and styles in MSC data and utilized the trained model to augment the limited MSC data for fine-tuning

the two off-the-shelf OCR models. We demonstrated that the augmented data can effectively improve OCR performance.

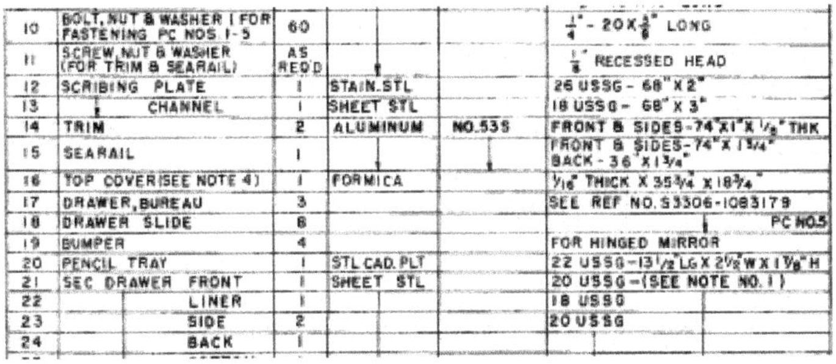

Figure 1. An example of a high-quality MSC document with an easy-to-recognize font.

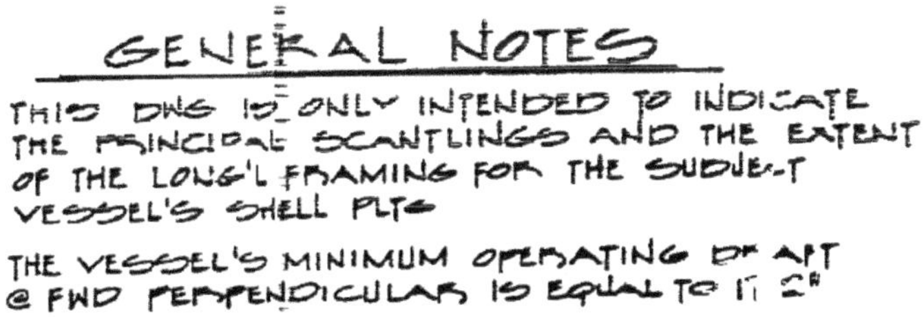

Figure 2. An example of an MSC document with a more challenging font to recognize.

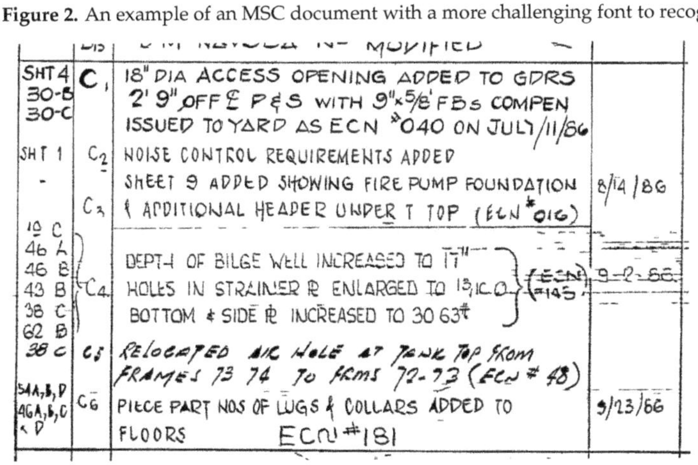

Figure 3. An example of an MSC document with multiple fonts.

The rest of this paper is organized as follows. Section 2 discusses related work. Section 3 describes our proposed approach. Section 4 presents the data and experimental setup. Section 5 provides the experimental results. Section 6 discusses the main findings, limitations, and implications of this research. Finally, Section 7 concludes the paper and outlines future work.

2. Related Work

OCR is a well-established area of research in machine learning [20]. An OCR system converts scanned documents or input text images into machine-editable and searchable formats. OCR has been successfully applied across various domains, including historical document processing [21], scene text detection and recognition [14], license plate recognition [22], and invoice and receipt processing [23], among others. The advent of deep learning has paved the way for the development of numerous models for text detection and recognition, such as EAST [24] and CRAFT [25] for text detection, and CRNN-CTC [26] and sequence-to-sequence models [18] for text recognition. The main components of an OCR system typically include preprocessing, text detection, text recognition, and postprocessing. OCR systems can be categorized into two types: (1) printed text recognition and (2) handwritten text recognition. Printed text recognition involves converting typed characters into digital text, while handwritten text recognition deals with converting handwritten text into a digital format.

2.1. Text Detection

Text detection involves localizing text regions in documents or images and is crucial for recognizing text in complex backgrounds. It can be performed at the line, word, or character level, with models typically producing bounding boxes around words or sentences. Earlier methods relied on handcrafted features, such as connected components analysis (CCA) [14], sliding windows, and segmentation-based approaches [25]. Recently, deep-learning-based algorithms have excelled in this task. CRAFT [25], widely used in systems like KerasOCR [19] and EasyOCR [27], detects individual character regions using a CNN (based on VGG-16) to generate region and affinity maps. These maps identify characters and the distances between them to form words. Similarly, EAST [24] employs CNNs for pixel-wise text instance prediction, while TextBoxes [28] uses a single-shot multi-box detector (SSD) framework [29] for faster, real-time text detection.

2.2. Printed Text OCR

Many OCR systems focus on detecting and recognizing printed text, achieving high accuracy in real-world applications. Examples include Google Tesseract [30], Cloud Vision OCR [31], EasyOCR [27], KerasOCR [19], and docTR API [32]. Most of these models rely on deep learning, with the CRNN architecture coupled with CTC being the preferred choice for text recognition. EasyOCR and KerasOCR are Python-based pipelines designed for scene text detection and recognition, utilizing CRAFT [25] for text detection and CRNN [26] for recognition. Tesseract [30] is a modular framework where text recognition involves preprocessing, layout analysis, segmentation, feature extraction, and recognition, using a bidirectional LSTM in its latest version. OCRopy [33] recognizes text at the line level, improving accuracy with a statistical language model and employing a single-layer bidirectional LSTM with CTC loss. PaddleOCR [34] provides pretrained models for multiple languages, following a similar architecture to EasyOCR and KerasOCR. It includes modules for text detection, orientation classification, and character recognition.

2.3. Handdwritten Text OCR

Handwritten text recognition has received significant attention in the literature, with researchers primarily using neural network architectures like CRNN. This task is more challenging than printed text recognition due to the variety of writing styles. Puigcerver [35] proposed a CRNN-based model with a single convolutional layer followed by one-dimensional recurrent layers, outperforming many traditional models. Flor de Sousa Neto et al. [36] introduced a Gated-CNN model that, with fewer parameters, achieved 33% better performance on benchmark datasets. Kass et al. [37] proposed an attention-based sequence-to-sequence model using a CRNN with ResNet for feature extraction and a bidirectional LSTM for sequence modeling, incorporating transfer learning from scene text recognition to address data limitations. Ly et al. [38] introduced a self-attention convolutional recurrent network (2D-SACRN) combining a self-attention-based feature extractor with recurrent layers and a CTC decoder, achieving competitive results with reduced training time.

2.4. Transformer-Based OCR Systems

Most OCR approaches for both handwritten and printed text recognition are based on the CRNN architecture. However, with the recent success of transformer-based models, there is a growing shift toward transformers for OCR. Microsoft's TrOCR [18] is a transformer-based model with two components: a visual transformer for feature extraction and a textual transformer for text recognition. TrOCR was pre-trained on large datasets of both printed and handwritten text. Transformer-based OCR models typically follow an encoder–decoder architecture. Fujitake [39] introduced DTrOCR, a model that relies solely on a text decoder. It demonstrated superior performance over previous models, including TrOCR, in various OCR tasks. Kim et al. [40] proposed Donut, an OCR-free transformer model designed for document understanding. Donut directly maps raw document inputs to text outputs without the traditional OCR pipeline, showing competitive results across multiple datasets.

2.5. OCR for Engineering Documents

OCR has been widely applied in areas like scene text recognition and historical document digitization. However, its use for digitizing legacy engineering documentation has received less attention, especially in text recognition from engineering drawings, which remain crucial in the manufacturing industry [4]. Several studies have tackled this issue. Toro et al. [41] developed eDOCr, an OCR framework for extracting information from mechanical engineering drawings to automate quality control. Their approach uses image segmentation, CRAFT for text detection, and KerasOCR for recognition, which was trained on an extended alphabet including special characters and symbols. Saba et al. [42] proposed a two-stage pipeline for piping and instrumentation diagrams (P&IDs), employing EAST for text detection and EasyOCR for recognition, showing strong performance on P&IDs. Lin et al. [4] introduced a system using YOLO for feature extraction and Tesseract for recognizing text, symbols, and numbers, achieving a 70% character recognition rate. Ren et al. [43] addressed text recognition in nuclear power equipment drawings using EAST and PaddleOCR, with promising results. In our previous work, we fine-tuned a CRNN-based KerasOCR model [44] on a dataset of 2D ship drawings and maintenance documents from MSC, significantly improving recognition accuracy over Tesseract and EasyOCR.

3. Proposed Methods

The proposed OCR framework consists of four modules: (1) preprocessing, (2) text detection, (3) data augmentation, and (4) text recognition, as shown in Figure 4. It processes an engineering document and outputs the recognized text in a digital format (e.g., text or JSON). The preprocessing step enhances document quality before applying detection and recognition algorithms. Traditional techniques like binarization, noise removal, and image scaling have been widely used, while deep learning models are increasingly employed for tasks like noise removal. In this research, we used basic preprocessing techniques, leaving more advanced methods for future work. The text detection module identifies textual regions and outputs bounding boxes around words or sentences. The cropped text is then passed to the recognition module, which produces the final output. We experimented with various deep learning models at each stage, training the components separately.

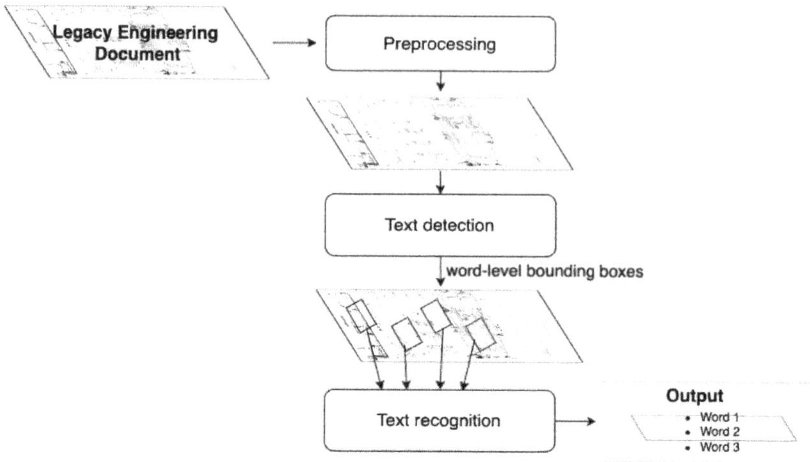

Figure 4. Framework of the proposed OCR pipeline. The MSC document first goes through a preprocessing step to enhance its quality. Subsequently, text detection and text recognition are performed on the enhanced document.

3.1. Text Detection

This stage focuses on localizing text within the input engineering documents. The ships' engineering documents used in this research contain various structures (e.g., tables, drawings, etc.). Text detection identifies the areas where text is present and outputs a set of word-level or sentence-level bounding boxes. We qualitatively evaluated two well-known text detection models: EAST [24] and CRAFT [25]. Based on this evaluation, we selected CRAFT as the text detector, as it provided superior text localization performance for our task compared to the EAST model.

3.2. ScrabbleGAN for Data Augmentation

OCR systems typically require a substantial amount of labeled data for training to achieve competitive performance. The text in our documents appears in various formats, fonts, and styles. Off-the-shelf OCR systems, trained on public datasets, struggled to generalize to the unseen fonts and styles in our data. To address this challenge, we utilize the ScrabbleGAN model [45], as shown in Figure 5, to augment our training data by mimicking the formats, fonts, and styles in our ground truth data. The key idea is to train ScrabbleGAN to transfer fonts and styles learned from our ground truth to synthetic word images. To achieve this goal, we first synthesize a set of words with standard formats, fonts, and styles, and then train ScrabbleGAN on our ground truth MSC documents to learn the specific characteristics. Finally, we use the trained model to transfer these learned styles to the synthetic data, augmenting our training dataset.

ScrabbleGAN consists of three main components, as shown in Figure 5: (1) a generator G, (2) a discriminator D, and (3) an OCR model R for text recognition, employing an adversarial training process. The generator G creates synthetic text images from a noise vector, while the discriminator D distinguishes between real text images (ground truth data) and those generated by the generator (mimicked styles). Unlike previous generative models that generate entire words or sentence-level images, ScrabbleGAN takes a different approach by training a generator for each character. The trained character-level generators are stored in a bank of learned filters, each corresponding to a specific element in the vocabulary. To generate a word image, the filters for each character in the word are selected and concatenated to produce the final word image. The OCR model R ensures the quality of the synthetic images by verifying the readability of the text. ScrabbleGAN uses the following loss function:

$$l = l_D + \lambda \times l_R \quad (1)$$

where l_D and l_R are the loss terms of the discriminator module D and OCR module R, respectively.

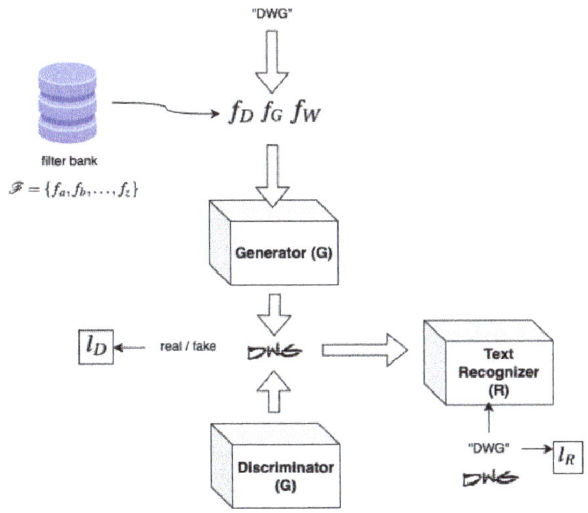

Figure 5. ScrabbleGAN architecture [45]: The generator creates a text image of 'DWG' using trained character generators. The discriminator (D) checks if the image looks realistic and if the font is transferred accurately. The text recognition network (R) ensures readability.

3.3. Text Recognition

We consider two different architectures for text recognition: convolutional recurrent neural network (CRNN) and transformer. We fine-tune both models on the augmented data and compare their performance on the MSC dataset.

3.3.1. CRNN-Based Architecture

CRNN models [26,46] consist of three components, as illustrated in Figure 6: (1) convolutional layers for visual feature extraction from input images, (2) recurrent layers for sequence modeling and character classification, and (3) a transcription layer that translates the output of the sequence model into the final label sequence. KerasOCR [19] is a widely used end-to-end OCR pipeline for scene text detection and recognition applications. The text recognition module in this pipeline uses the CRNN-CTC architecture. The CRNN model in KerasOCR takes a word-level bounding box produced by the text detection module as input. This image is processed by CNN, which generates a sequence of feature maps over m timesteps. KerasOCR then employs a bidirectional long short-term memory (Bi-LSTM) sequence model to process these feature maps. The Bi-LSTM outputs a sequence of softmax probabilities over a given vocabulary at each timestep. In the transcription layer, a CTC loss function [47] is applied to decode the Bi-LSTM output and recognize the final text sequence within the bounding box.

3.3.2. Transformer-Based Architecture

Many OCR approaches use CNN models for image understanding and a sequence model for character-level text recognition. Additionally, language models are typically employed as a post-processing step to enhance the overall accuracy of the OCR output. In contrast, TrOCR [18], a transformer-based architecture proposed by Microsoft, leverages visual transformers for image understanding and text transformers for text generation. It follows an encoder–decoder architecture that combines the following components (Figure 7): (1) a pre-trained bidirectional encoder representation from image transformers (BEiT) [48] model for the encoder, and (2) a pre-trained RoBERTa [49] model (an optimized BERT language model) for the decoder. The model uses the attention mechanism of transformers to focus on relevant parts of the image, improving OCR output accuracy.

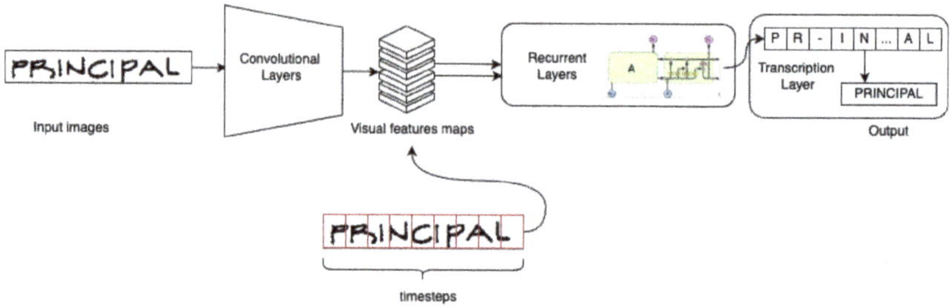

Figure 6. Convolutional recurrent neural network for text recognition: it consists of convolutional layers for visual feature extraction from input images, recurrent layers for sequence modeling and character classification, and a transcription layer for converting the output of the sequence model into the final label sequence.

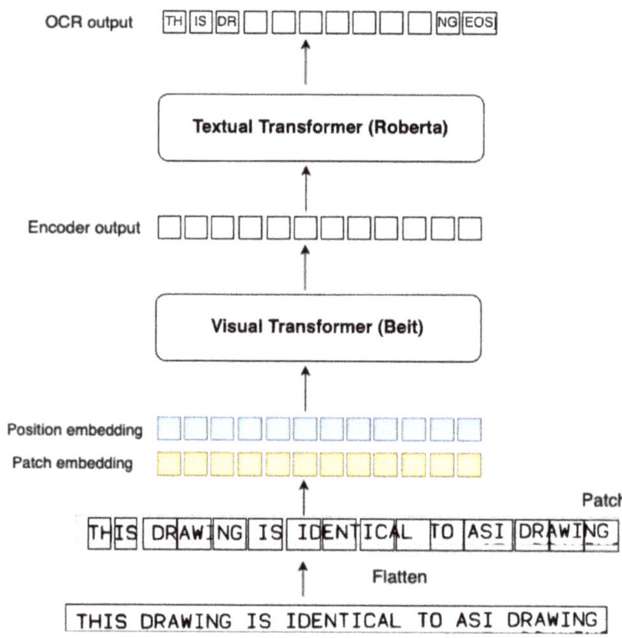

Figure 7. TrOCR architecture [18]. The input image is divided into a sequence of patches, with each being projected into a *D*-dimensional vector by BERT. The RoBERTa model then recognizes the input text.

An input image is decomposed into a sequence of patches, and each patch is projected into a *D*-dimensional vector by BERT. Subsequently, the decoder uses a pre-trained RoBERTa model to recognize the input text by generating a sequence of text pieces from the visual features produced by the encoder. TrOCR was pre-trained in two stages. In the first stage, the model was trained on a large labeled dataset of 684 M printed text-line images cropped from publicly available PDF files. In the second stage, it was trained on smaller synthetic datasets for downstream tasks such as handwritten text recognition and receipt text recognition. The first dataset consists of 17.9 M handwritten text-line images generated from 5427 handwritten fonts, while the second dataset contains 1 M synthetic text-line images created using fonts from a set of receipt images [18]. TrOCR released pre-trained models from the different stages.

3.3.3. Transfer Learning through Fine-Tuning

The performance of pre-trained OCR models is highly dependent on the quality of input data. In our case, these models struggled with the diverse textual styles and fonts in the engineering documents, which are not easily recognizable by models trained on standard public datasets. Transfer learning [50] (TL) allows a model trained on one task (T_s) to be adapted for another task (T_t), leveraging knowledge from a source domain (D_s) to improve performance in a target domain (D_t), particularly when labeled data in the target domain are limited. Fine-tuning is a common TL approach, where a pre-trained model is further trained on a new dataset specific to the target task. In this study, we fine-tuned the pre-trained KerasOCR (CRNN architecture) and TrOCR (transformer-based architecture) models using an annotated dataset from our case study on ships' engineering documents.

3.4. *Competing Methods*

We compared the proposed (fine-tuned) models with several pre-trained OCR models.

3.4.1. Pre-Trained Tesseract

Tesseract [30] is one of the most widely used OCR engines for various applications. The latest versions of Tesseract (3.0 and beyond) have integrated a long short-term memory (LSTM) neural network to improve text recognition accuracy. Tesseract performs text recognition through several stages: (1) preprocessing, (2) segmentation, (3) feature extraction, and (4) classification [51]. In the preprocessing step, Tesseract uses adaptive thresholding (Otsu's method) to convert the input document into a binary format. It then performs page layout analysis to segment the input document (e.g., a book page) into text blocks, followed by detecting text lines within these blocks. In the final stage, Tesseract employs a deep learning framework (LSTM) to recognize text within the detected lines. The Tesseract model was pre-trained on a dataset of 400 K text lines, encompassing 4500 different fonts.

3.4.2. Pre-Trained EasyOCR

EasyOCR [27] is a Python-based OCR pipeline primarily designed for scene text detection and recognition applications. EasyOCR uses the CRAFT algorithm [25] to detect text within input images and CRNN for text recognition. It leverages the PyTorch library and OpenCV on the back end. The text recognition module in EasyOCR was pre-trained on a hybrid dataset comprising 800 K natural scene images augmented by 9 M randomly generated synthetic images.

3.4.3. Pre-Trained KerasOCR

KerasOCR is also a Python-based OCR package for scene text detection and recognition applications. KerasOCR includes an end-to-end training pipeline to build OCR models. Like EasyOCR, this model implements CRAFT [25] for text detection and CRNN for text recognition. The KerasOCR text recognition model was pre-trained on 90 K synthetic scene images.

3.4.4. Pre-Trained TrOCR

We used TrOCR models, initially trained on a large collection of printed text line images (first stage) and then on the SROIE (Scanned Receipts OCR and Information Extraction) dataset [52] (second stage). We experimented with two pre-trained variants of TrOCR:

- Pre-trained TrOCR small (https://huggingface.co/microsoft/trocr-small-printed, accessed on 20 June 2024): This variant comprises 62 M parameters and employs the $DeiT_{small}$ visual transformer [53] (12 layers with 384 hidden sizes and 6 attention heads) for the encoder architecture. Furthermore, the MiniLM [54] transformer (a lightweight language model released by Microsoft consisting of 6 layers, 256 hidden sizes, and 8 attention heads) is used for the decoder architecture.
- Pretrained TrOCR large (https://huggingface.co/microsoft/trocr-large-printed, accessed on 20 June, 2024): This variant comprises 558 M parameters and employs ($BEiT_{large}$) the visual transformer [48] (24 layers, 1024 hidden sizes, and 16 attention heads) for the encoder architecture. A large RoBERTa transformer [49] (12 layers, 1024 hidden sizes, and 16 attention heads) is used for the decoder architecture.

3.5. Evaluation Metrics

To evaluate the performance of each model, we used the following metrics: (1) training time per epoch ($time_{epoch}$), (2) Character Error Rate (CER), (3) Word Error Rate (WER), and (4) Levenshtein distance (Lev). The training time per epoch records the time taken to train each OCR model for one epoch, defined as the ratio of the total training time to the number of epochs,

$$time_{epoch} = \frac{time}{n_{epochs}} \tag{2}$$

CER calculates the percentage of incorrectly identified characters relative to the total number of characters,

$$CER = \frac{n_{errors}}{n_{characters}} \times 100 \tag{3}$$

WER calculates the percentage of incorrectly identified words relative to the total number of words,

$$WER = \frac{n_{errors}}{n_{words}} \times 100 \tag{4}$$

The Levenshtein distance between a pair of words measures the smallest number of edits (insertions, deletions, or substitutions) needed to convert one word into another. We calculated the average Levenshtein distance for all predicted and actual word pairs in the test dataset, as shown in Equation (5).

$$AVR.Lev = \frac{1}{N_{test}} \times \sum_{i=1}^{N_{test}} Lev(w_i^{pred}, w_i^{actual}) \tag{5}$$

where N_{test} is the size of the testing set and w_i^{pred} and w_i^{actual} represent the OCR prediction and its corresponding ground truth word, respectively.

4. Experiment Setup

4.1. Dataset

We created two datasets from engineering documents from the shipyard and aviation industries. The first dataset was manually annotated from nine ships' maintenance documents provided by MSC. These documents include 2D ship drawings and textual content that describes important information about the design and maintenance of the ships. Each document contains hundreds of lines representing the various textual styles and fonts used in ships' maintenance documentation. The dataset includes both low-quality and high-quality documents. Figures 1–3 show three examples extracted from MSC engineering documents. The text font in the example in Figure 1 is relatively easy to recognize, while those in Figure 2 are more challenging. The example shown in Figure 3 contains multiple distinct fonts. The second dataset was collected from aircraft design engineering drawings available through AirCorps Library (https://app.aircorpslibrary.com/about, accessed on 22 October 2024), which is an online repository that hosts engineering drawings and technical manuals for WWII and legacy aircraft. An example of an AirCorps document is illustrated in Figure 8. Although this dataset comes from a different industry, its textual styles are similar to those found in the MSC documentation.

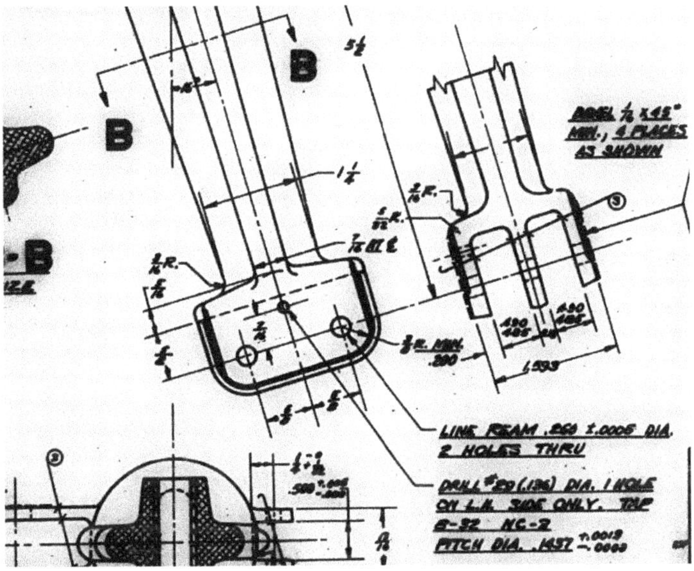

Figure 8. An example of an aircraft engineering drawing provided by AirCorps.

4.2. Data Annotation

These documents also include a variety of textual styles and, at times, unrecognized fonts, which pose significant challenges for OCR systems to achieve high recognition accuracy. We manually annotated two datasets of word-level images cropped from the MSC engineering documents and AirCorps library documents. Figure 9 shows a few examples of the annotated MSC dataset, while Figure 10 shows a few examples from AirCorps documents. The MSC dataset consists of 4671 word images cropped from different sections of the engineering documents, encompassing various fonts and styles commonly used in ships' maintenance documentation. We used this dataset to evaluate the performance of our proposed OCR models in recognizing text with various fonts. The dataset was randomly divided into a training set (80%) and a testing set (20%), with 3734 word images used for training and 937 for testing. The AirCorps dataset consists of 1004 annotated word images. This dataset was randomly split into a training set (80%) and a testing set (20%), with 803 word images used for training and 201 for testing.

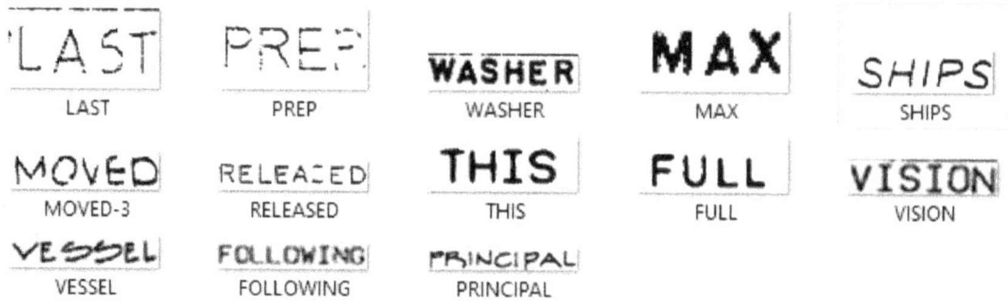

Figure 9. Examples of annotated word images from MSC documents.

Figure 10. Examples of annotated word images from AirCorps documents.

4.3. Experiments

We conducted three experiments in this study. In the first experiment, we compared the performance of fine-tuned TrOCR and KerasOCR models with a set of pre-trained OCR models (pre-trained KerasOCR, TrOCR, EasyOCR, and Tesseract) on MSC and AirCorps datasets. The goal was to evaluate the overall OCR performance of the transfer learning approach applied to the MSC and AirCorps documents. In the second experiment, we trained the ScabbleGAN model to augment our training dataset, and in the third experiment, we assessed the impact of the data augmentation procedure on OCR performance. We created two new datasets that included both the augmented word images and the manually annotated samples to fine-tune the KerasOCR and TrOCR models. This experiment aimed to evaluate the effect of the data augmentation technique introduced in this research on OCR performance for MSC and AirCorps documents.

5. Experiment Results

5.1. Results by Pre-Trained Models on MSC Data

Table 1 reports the text recognition performance measured using *WER*, *CER*, and Levenshtein distance metrics on MSC data. As expected, most of the pre-trained OCR systems did not perform well on our data. The pre-trained Tesseract system had the highest character and word error rates (13.14% and 32.34%, respectively), while the pre-trained TrOCR system (large model) achieved the lowest character and word error rates (3.52% and 12.47%, respectively) among the pre-trained models.

Table 1. Results from the different models on the MSC testing dataset. 'MSC' refers to the fine-tuning dataset collected from MSC documents, and 'Aug' denotes the augmented fine-tuning dataset.

OCR Model	Strategy	$time_{epoch}$	*CER* (%)	*WER* (%)	*AVR.Lev*
Tesseract [30]	pre-trained	-	13.14	32.34	1.2166
EasyOCR [27]	pre-trained	-	10.43	30.09	0.6125
KerasOCR [19]	pre-trained	-	6.65	21.35	0.3724
TrOCR (small) [18]	pre-trained	-	5.54	20.89	0.3041
TrOCR (large) [18]	pre-trained	-	3.52	12.47	0.1931
KerasOCR w MSC [17]	fine-tuned	8.42	3.17	11.21	0.1494
KerasOCR w Aug [17]	fine-tuned	23.82	2.55	7.9	0.1419
TrOCR (small) w MSC	fine-tuned	348.52	1.71	7.3	0.0939
TrOCR (small) w Aug	fine-tuned	575.4	1.65	6.18	0.0907
TrOCR (large) w MSC	fine-tuned	645.36	1.30	4.37	0.0715
TrOCR (large) w Aug	fine-tuned	1311.2	**0.09**	**3.94**	**0.005**

5.2. Results of Data Augmentation Using MSC Documents

We trained ScrabbleGAN to generate synthetic word images for training, to replicate the textual styles used in the provided engineering documents. All annotated data were used to train ScrabbleGAN. Training images were resized to $32 \times 16n$ (with the height set to 32 pixels and the width varying according to the number of characters, n, in the word). We trained the model using the default training parameters from the original model [45], except for the batch size, which was set to 10, and the learning rate, set to 0.0002 for all networks (R, G, and D). ScrabbleGAN was trained to produce uppercase English characters only. We used the trained generator G in the inference step to create 3000 synthetic word images. Figure 11 shows a few word-image samples from the synthetic data after 1000 epochs.

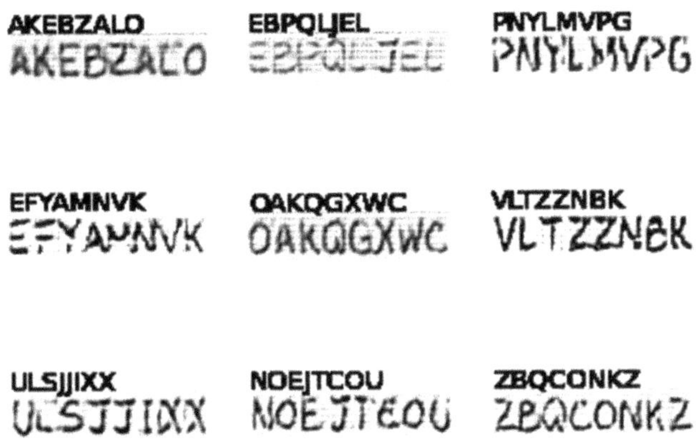

Figure 11. Synthetic samples generated by ScrabbleGAN [45].

5.3. Results by Fine-Tuned Models on MSC Data

For the evaluation of the different fine-tuned OCR models, we used 20% of the annotated MSC data (937 word images from MSC documents) for testing. Then, we created these fine-tuning datasets:

- MSC fine-tuning dataset (3734 word images): This dataset includes the remaining 80% of the annotated set cropped from MSC data.
- Augmented MSC fine-tuning dataset (6734 word images): These data include these 3000 synthetic word images produced by ScrabbleGAN in addition to the MSC training dataset.

KerasOCR was fine-tuned using a batch size of 32, the Adam optimizer with a learning rate of 0.001, and trained for 50 epochs (with early stopping after 20 epochs). The same parameters were used to fine-tune KerasOCR on the augmented training set. The small TrOCR model was fine-tuned using the AdamW optimizer (https://pytorch.org/docs/stable/generated/torch.optim.AdamW.html, accessed on 20 December 2024) with a learning rate of 0.00005, a batch size of 32, and 20 epochs. The large TrOCR model was fine-tuned using the AdamW optimizer with a learning rate of 0.00005, a batch size of 16, and 10 epochs. All the models were trained using an Nvidia A100 high-memory GPU provided by Old Dominion University (https://wiki.hpc.odu.edu/en/open-ondemand, accessed on 19 December 2024).

Results in Table 1 show that fine-tuning the KerasOCR model significantly improved its performance. The word error rate (WER) was reduced from 21.35% to 11.21% and the character error rate (CER) from 6.65% to 3.17% after fine-tuning with the MSC training dataset, and these further dropped to 7.9% and 2.55%, respectively, after fine-tuning with the augmented dataset. Fine-tuning the TrOCR (small) model with the MSC dataset improved the WER from 20.89% to 7.3% and the CER from 5.54% to 1.71%. After fine-tuning with the augmented dataset, the TrOCR (small) model continued to improve its WER (6.18%) and CER (1.65%). In contrast, fine-tuning the TrOCR (large) model with the MSC dataset improved WER and CER from 12.47% and 3.52% to 4.37% and 1.30%, respectively. However, fine-tuning the model with the augmented dataset also improved its performance, though not as much as the MSC dataset. The large TrOCR model has significantly more parameters, and we hypothesize that it will require higher-quality data to achieve better results. Overall, the transformer-based TrOCR (large), fine-tuned with the augmented MSC dataset, achieved the best results with a WER of 3.94% and a CER of 0.09%. Transformer-based models require more time for fine-tuning; since fine-tuning is a one-time task, it does not present a significant burden in practice.

5.4. Results by Fine-Tuned Models on AirCorps Data

We used 20% of the annotated AirCorps data (201 word images from AirCorps library documents) for testing and created these fine-tuning datasets:

- AirCorps fine-tuning dataset (803 word images): This dataset includes the remaining 80% of the annotated set cropped from AirCorps library documents.
- Augmented AirCorps fine-tuning dataset (1802 word images): This dataset includes 1000 synthetic word images generated by the ScrabbleGAN model trained with the MSC dataset in addition to the AirCorps fine-tuning dataset.

Note that we attempted to use the AirCorps fine-tuning dataset to train the ScrabbleGAN model for augmentation. However, the synthetic images were of very low quality, partially because the AirCorps fine-tuning dataset contains only 802 images, which is insufficient to effectively train the ScrabbleGAN model. As an alternative, we randomly selected 1000 synthetic images generated by the ScrabbleGAN model trained on the MSC fine-tuning dataset to fine-tune the OCR models for recognizing the AirCorps dataset. We did not use all 3000 synthetic images because doing so did not result in better outcomes.

The fine-tuning results for each OCR model on the AirCorps dataset are reported in Table 2. The table shows that fine-tuning the large variant of TrOCR with the augmented dataset improved performance by 4% in terms of word error rate. The synthetic training samples generated by the ScrabbleGAN model, trained on MSC data, enhanced OCR performance on the AirCorps dataset. This enhanced performance can be attributed to the domain similarity, as both datasets consist of historical engineering drawings from different industries. However, it should be noted that the smaller size of the AirCorps dataset resulted in higher word and character error rates compared to the MSC dataset. While the augmentation procedure has demonstrated its effectiveness in improving OCR performance with limited data availability, the findings suggest that larger annotated datasets remain essential for achieving optimal OCR results across different domains.

Table 2. Results from the different models on the AirCorps testing dataset. 'AirCorps' refers to the fine-tuning dataset collected from AirCorps repository documents, and 'Aug' denotes the augmented fine-tuning dataset. We only report the 'fine-tuned' models' results.

OCR Model	$time_{epoch}$	CER (%)	WER (%)	$AVR.Lev$
KerasOCR w AirCorps [17]	4.36	8.2	27.63	0.4477
KerasOCR w Aug [17]	7.80	7.9	28.85	0.4328
TrOCR (small) w AirCorps	37.24	8.24	24.87	0.4477
TrOCR (small) w Aug	63.81	8.24	25.37	0.4477
TrOCR (large) w AirCorps	155.85	4.57	15.42	0.2478
TrOCR (large) w Aug	370.7	**3.20**	**11.49**	**0.1741**

5.5. Case Study for OCR on MSC Documents

Figures 12–14 show one high-quality example and two challenging examples of text detection and recognition tasks by different models. For the high-quality example in Figure 13, all models performed very well, with no missed words by any of the models, and the fine-tuned KerasOCR models even achieved a 100% WER. The font used in this example was easy to recognize, with a clean background and no curved or irregular text, resulting in a low recognition error rate.

Figure 12 illustrates an example selected from a noisy MSC document. Overall, the fine-tuned TrOCR models provided better performance than the KerasOCR models. In some instances where the bounding box included more than one word (e.g., the word 'PAINTING/COATING'), the fine-tuned TrOCR models failed to capture the complete text, unlike the pre-trained TrOCR model. This is due to the training strategy used in this research, which involved labeled word images, whereas the pre-trained TrOCR model was trained on text-line images. Moreover, the large TrOCR model was more robust to the noisy background than both the KerasOCR and small TrOCR models. For instance, the large TrOCR model accurately recognized the words 'ALL' and 'NOTED,' which were missed by other models. Future research will explore generative deep learning approaches for image enhancement. We expect that image enhancement and denoising techniques will further improve OCR performance on noisy documents.

Figure 14 presents another challenging example featuring an irregular and hard-to-recognize font. Both the fine-tuned and pre-trained KerasOCR models had low accuracy rates in this case. However, the fine-tuned TrOCR models were able to recognize several words, such as 'BLEEDER', 'STEEL', and 'PLUG'. The large TrOCR model performed slightly better than the small model. Similar to the first example, the fine-tuned TrOCR models struggled with numerals. Although the large TrOCR model successfully identified some numerals, such as '101-001', it failed to accurately recognize others, such as '9/16"' and '1/2." The proposed models also failed to recognize degraded words, such as 'BLEEDER' (top left). Degraded text is a common issue in many low-quality MSC documents. The current OCR solutions are inadequate for detecting such text, highlighting the need for further research in this area.

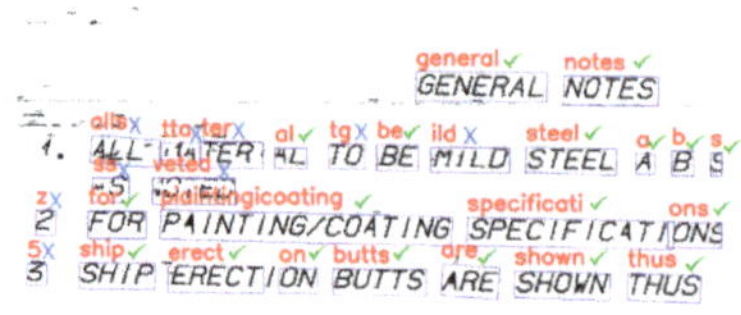

(a)

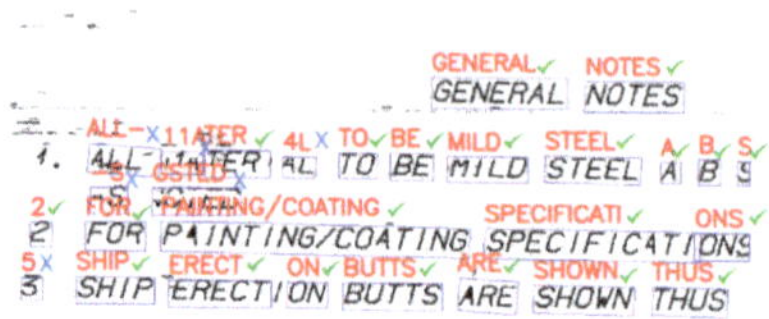

(b)

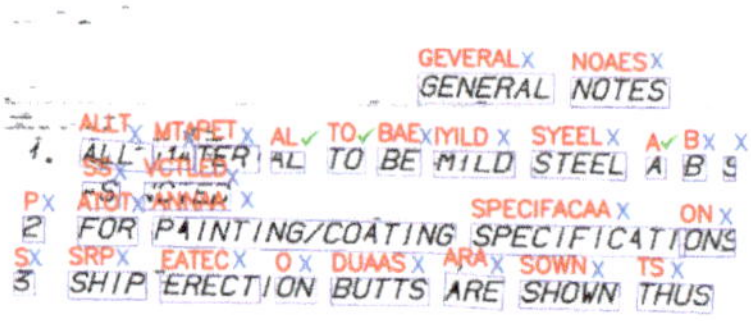

(c)

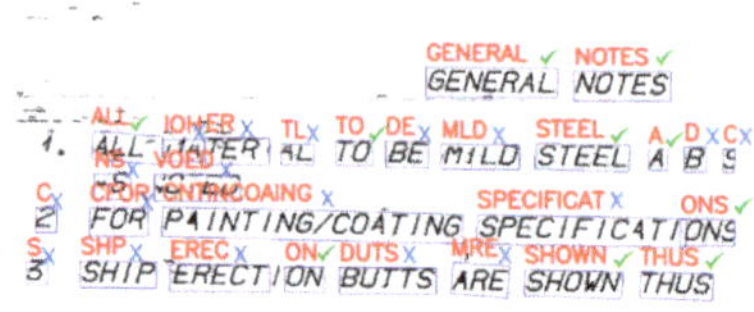

(d)

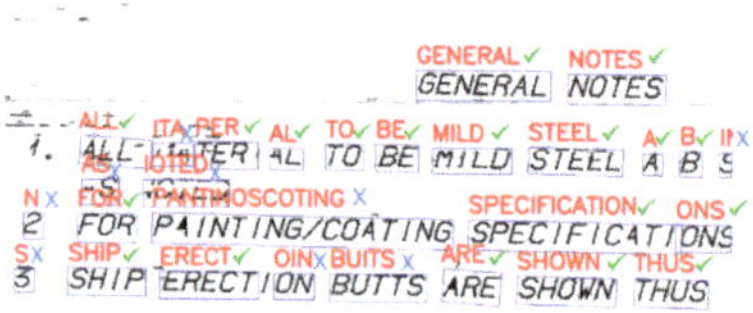

(e)

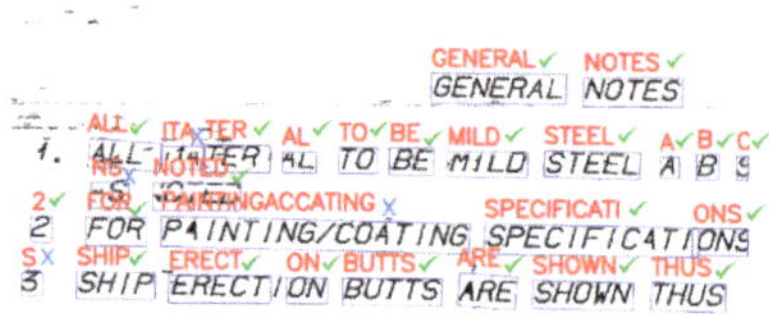

(f)

Figure 12. Results by OCR models on a selected challenging document. (**a**) Pre-trained KerasOCR: 19 ✓ vs. 9 ×. (**b**) Pre-trained TrOCR (large): 22 ✓ vs. 6 ×. (**c**) Fine-tuned KerasOCR with MSC: 3 ✓ vs. 25 ×. (**d**) Fine-tuned KerasOCR with Aug: 10 ✓ vs. 18 ×. (**e**) Fine-tuned TrOCR (small) with MSC: 19 ✓ vs. 9 ×. (**f**) Fine-tuned TrOCR (large) with MSC: 24 ✓ vs. 4 ×.

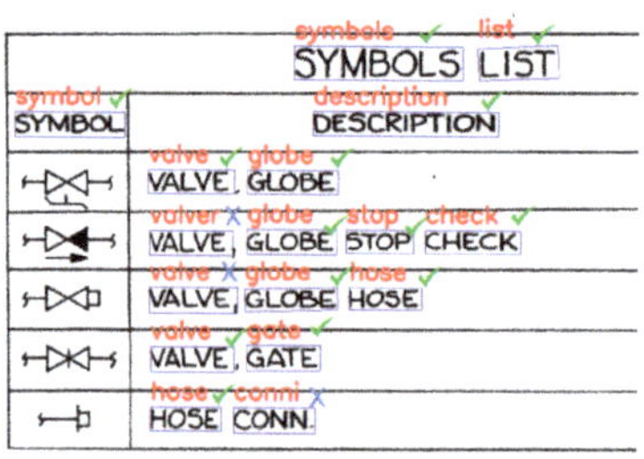

(a)

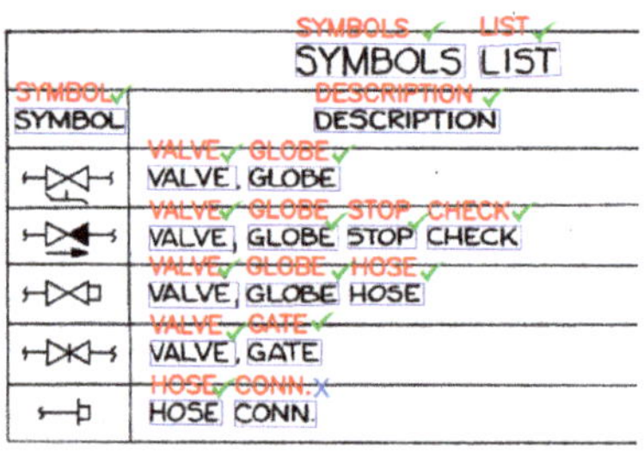

(b)

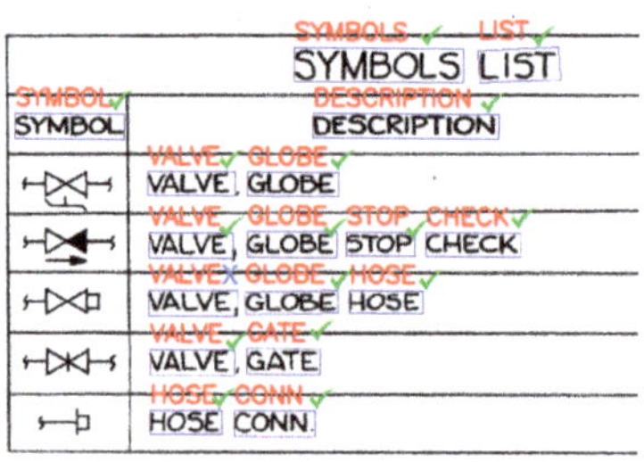

(c)

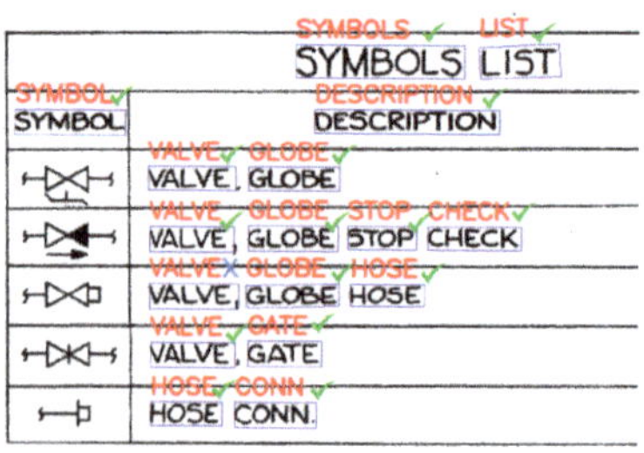

(d)

Figure 13. *Cont.*

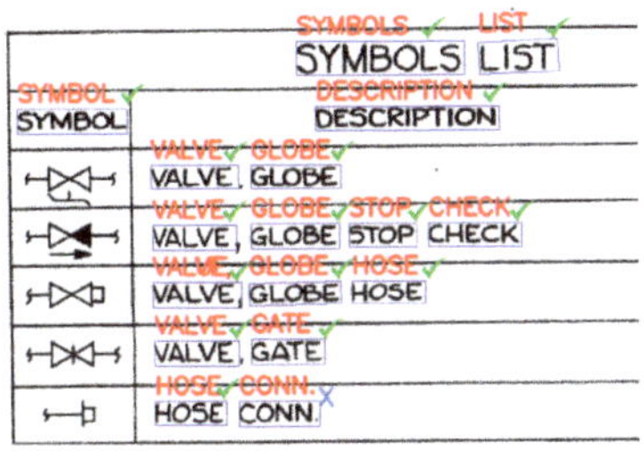

(e)

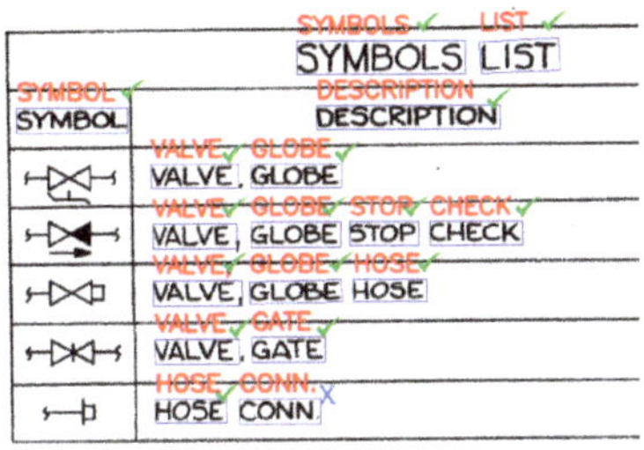

(f)

Figure 13. Results by OCR models on a selected high-quality MSC document. (**a**) Pre-trained KerasOCR: 14 ✓ vs. 3 ×. (**b**) Pre-trained TrOCR (large): 16 ✓ vs. 1 ×. (**c**) Fine-tuned KerasOCR with MSC: 16 ✓ vs. 1 ×. (**d**) Fine-tuned KerasOCR with Aug: 16 ✓ vs. 1 ×. (**e**) Fine-tuned TrOCR (small) with MSC: 16 ✓ vs. 1 ×. (**f**) Fine-tuned TrOCR (large) with MSC: 16 ✓ vs. 1 ×.

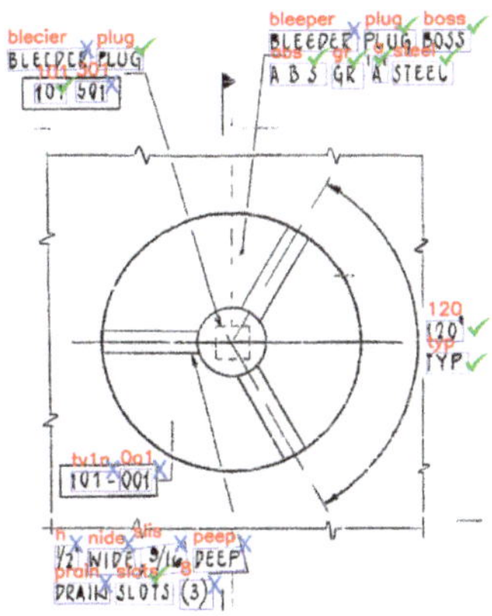

(a)

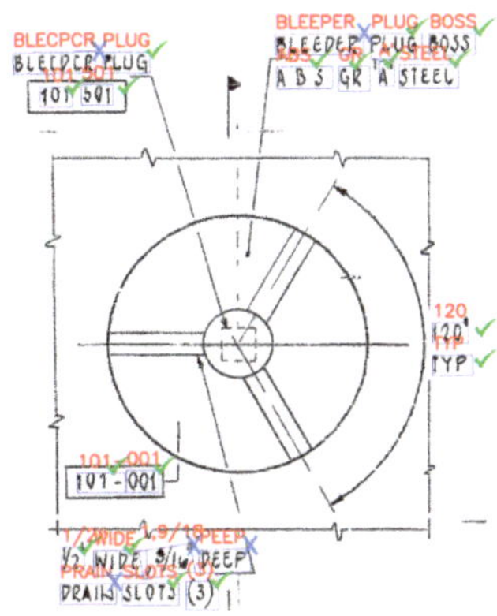

(b)

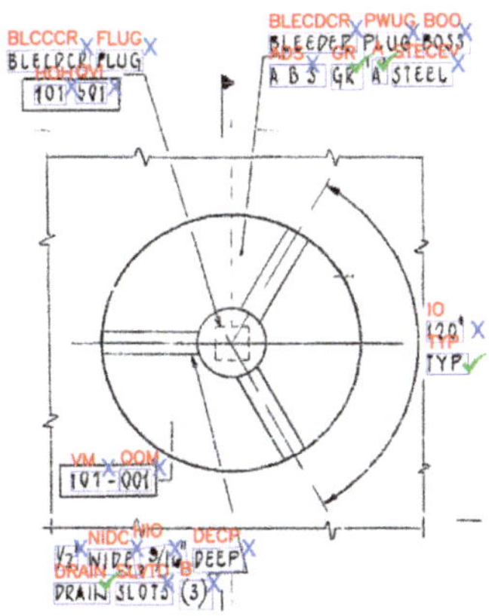

(c)

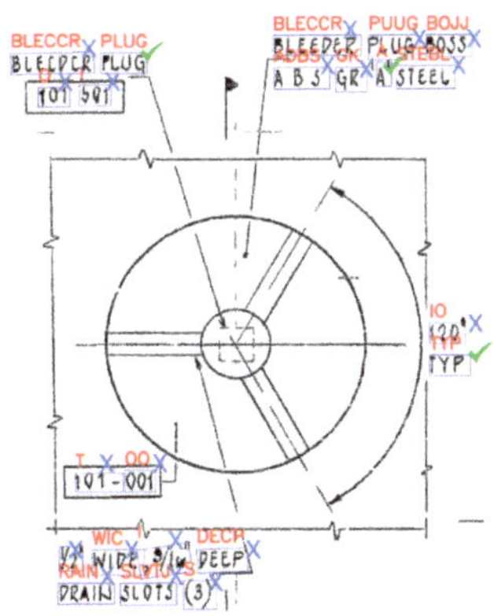

(d)

Figure 14. *Cont.*

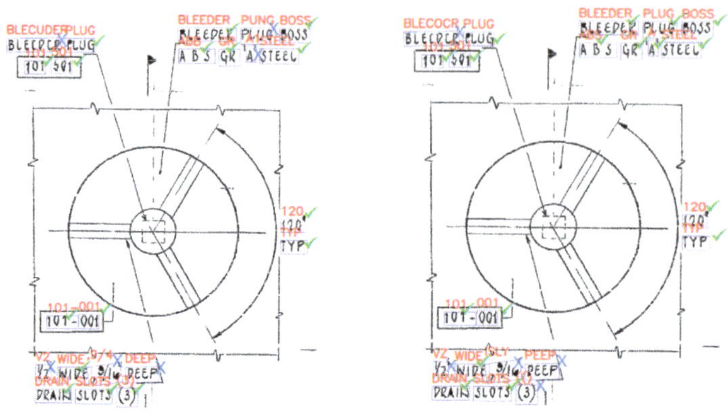

(e) (f)

Figure 14. Results by OCR models on a selected challenging document featuring an irregular and hard-to-recognize font. (**a**) Pre-trained KerasOCR: 11 ✓ vs. 11 ×. (**b**) Pre-trained TrOCR (large): 17 ✓ vs. 5 ×. (**c**) Fine-tuned KerasOCR with MSC: 4 ✓ vs. 18 ×. (**d**) Fine-tuned KerasOCR with Aug: 3 ✓ vs. 19 ×. (**e**) Fine-tuned TrOCR (small) with MSC: 16 ✓ vs. 6 ×. (**f**) Fine-tuned TrOCR (large) with MSC: 17 ✓ vs. 5 ×.

6. Discussion

In this study, we fine-tuned several pre-trained OCR models using an annotated dataset derived from MSC ships' engineering documents. These documents are unique in that they contain text written in various styles (both handwritten and printed) and different fonts. The pre-trained OCR models evaluated in this study did not perform well in our application, primarily because they were generally trained on public benchmark datasets and are sensitive to the specific datasets used for training. Fine-tuning both KerasOCR and TrOCR improved OCR performance. We reduced the word error rate from 12.47% with the pre-trained large TrOCR model (trained on the SOIRE [52] dataset) to 4.37% with the fine-tuned large TrOCR model and 3.94% with the fine-tuned large TrOCR model with the augmented dataset. This improvement was even more significant with KerasOCR, reducing the word error rate by 10% and the character error rate by 3% compared to its pre-trained variant. Overall, we found that the transformer-based model (TrOCR) provides better OCR output compared to the CRNN-based model (KerasOCR). The pre-trained large version of TrOCR notably achieved better results than the other pre-trained models. This performance may be attributed to the pre-training dataset used for TrOCR, which was derived from the SROIE (Scanned Receipts OCR and Information Extraction) task. The proposed augmentation procedure was effective in improving the OCR performance of KerasOCR and TrOCR models on MSC data.

By analyzing several instances from MSC documents, we observed that OCR models using the CRNN architecture, such as KerasOCR, are more sensitive to the quality of input documents, while TrOCR demonstrated greater robustness to noise, unfamiliar fonts, and irregular text styles, even with fewer training epochs. However, TrOCR's improved performance came with significant drawbacks. The training process for TrOCR, particularly the large model, was much more time-consuming and required specialized computing resources like high-memory GPUs, with KerasOCR being approximately 71 times faster. Despite TrOCR's strong performance in detecting a wide range of fonts and handling noisy backgrounds, it still had limitations. The fine-tuned large TrOCR model struggled with identifying special characters, numerals, and degraded text, highlighting the need for further improvements in these areas. To address this challenge, data augmentation techniques can be employed to generate synthetic training samples, including a variety of numerals and special characters with diverse fonts, orientations, and noise levels. Additionally, it can be addressed by employing multi-task learning, where the OCR model is trained to jointly optimize OCR performance with secondary tasks, such as numeral or symbol classification.

Pre-trained models, such as TrOCR, provide a strong starting point for OCR tasks. However, their effectiveness is limited in domain-specific environments, such as those with unique font styles, as they are primarily pre-trained on generalized OCR tasks. Training an OCR model from scratch is a resource-intensive process that requires substantial amounts of annotated data. To address these challenges, several alternative approaches can be employed. For example, integrating active learning strategies, where the model is iteratively fine-tuned on high-uncertainty samples identified during inference, can improve its adaptability to unseen domains. Another promising approach is meta-learning (learning to learn), where the model learns from multiple tasks (e.g., engineering documents from various industries) and generalizes knowledge across domains. Meta-learning involves training at a higher level, enabling the model to adapt quickly to new tasks (domains).

Practical deployment of the proposed OCR systems presents significant challenges. As shown in our results, the transformer-based OCR model (TrOCR) incurs a higher computational cost compared to the traditional CRNN-based model (KerasOCR), primarily due to its larger number of parameters. While CRNN models are faster to retrain and simpler to deploy, they exhibit a higher error rate. To address the computational demands of TrOCR in real-world settings, several strategies can be employed. One effective approach is knowledge distillation, which transfers knowledge from a large, pre-trained "teacher" model to a smaller, more efficient "student" model [1]. This technique enables the student model to achieve accuracy comparable to the original TrOCR model while significantly reducing computational costs. Another strategy is partial fine-tuning, where only a subset of the TrOCR model's layers—particularly the final layers—are fine-tuned, rather than retraining the entire model. This targeted fine-tuning minimizes resource requirements while effectively adapting the model to specific deployment contexts.

Finally, the limited availability of engineering documents poses a significant challenge for training the OCR models. Capturing the diversity of fonts and textual styles in our application requires more data, but collecting and annotating such data is time-consuming and resource-intensive, making it impractical for similar digitization efforts. To address this issue of data scarcity, we implemented a generative deep learning model, ScrabbleGAN, for data augmentation. This model was trained to generate synthetic images by replicating the fonts used in the original documents, providing a partial solution to the limited dataset problem. While this approach significantly improved the performance of the KerasOCR model, it had much less effect on the fine-tuned TrOCR model, partially because the transformer-based model already has very good results. We hypothesize that the large transformer model, with its significantly higher number of parameters, requires more high-quality data for effective fine-tuning. We will continue to explore new methods to increase the availability of data for fine-tuning. The variability of documents across industries (e.g., shipbuilding vs. automobile) underscores the necessity of adapting pre-trained models to unseen data, highlighting the importance of continued research to enhance OCR models.

7. Conclusions

In this study, we proposed a deep learning OCR pipeline that integrates transformers and generative models for text recognition, data augmentation, and image enhancement.

Using a dataset of annotated engineering documents provided by MSC, we fine-tuned the text recognition module within our pipeline. The fine-tuning process significantly improved the OCR performance of both the pre-trained CRNN and transformer-based models, with the fine-tuned transformer model outperforming all competitors and demonstrating substantial gains. As our future work, we plan to explore cutting-edge deep generative models, such as diffusion models, to enhance document cleaning and reduce background noise. Although the augmentation procedure slightly improved the performance of the fine-tuned KerasOCR model, it had minimal impact on the transformer-based model. Future research will focus on refining our data augmentation techniques to generate more realistic and effective training images.

Author Contributions: Conceptualization, J.L., A.S.-P. and S.K.; methodology, W.K. and J.L.; software, M.S.U. and W.K.; validation, J.L. and W.K.; formal analysis, W.K. and J.L.; investigation, W.K., J.L., M.S.U. and S.K.; resources, S.K. and A.S.-P.; data curation, W.K., J.L. and M.S.U.; writing—original draft preparation, W.K.; writing—review and editing, W.K. and J.L.; visualization, W.K. and J.L.; supervision, A.S.-P., S.K. and J.L.; project administration, S.K. and J.L.; funding acquisition, S.K. All authors have read and agreed to the published version of the manuscript.

Funding: This research is based upon work supported, in whole or in part, by the U.S. Navy's Military Sealift Command through CACI under sub-contract P000143798-3 and project 500481-003.

Data Availability Statement: Data are publicly unavailable due to privacy restrictions.

Conflicts of Interest: The authors declare no conflicts of interest.

References

1. Henderson, K.; Salado, A. Value and benefits of model-based systems engineering (MBSE): Evidence from the literature. *Sys Eng.* **2021**, *24*, 51–66. [CrossRef]
2. Shevchenko, N. *An Introduction to Model-Based Systems Engineering (MBSE)*; Carnegie Mellon University, Software Engineerin Institute's Insights (blog): Pittsburgh, PA, USA, 2020.
3. of Defense, D. *Digital Engineering Strategy*; Office of the Deputy Assistant Secretary of Dense for Systems Engineering: Washingto DC, USA, 2018.
4. Lin, Y.H.; Ting, Y.H.; Huang, Y.C.; Cheng, K.L.; Jong, W.R. Integration of Deep Learning for Automatic Recognition of 2D Engineering Drawings. *Machines* **2023**, *11*, 802. [CrossRef]
5. Memon, J.; Sami, M.; Khan, R.A.; Uddin, M. Handwritten optical character recognition (OCR): A comprehensive systemati literature review (SLR). *IEEE Access* **2020**, *8*, 142642–142668. [CrossRef]
6. Kumar, P.; Revathy, S. An automated invoice handling method using OCR. In *Data Intelligence and Cognitive Informatics: Proceeding of ICDICI 2020*; Springer: Berlin/Heidelberg, Germany, 2021; pp. 243–254.
7. Yindumathi, K.; Chaudhari, S.S.; Aparna, R. Analysis of image classification for text extraction from bills and invoices. In Proceedings of the 2020 11th International Conference on Computing, Communication and Networking Technologies (ICCCNT) Kharagpur, India, 1–3 July 2020; pp. 1–6.
8. Shambharkar, Y.; Salagrama, S.; Sharma, K.; Mishra, O.; Parashar, D. An automatic framework for number plate detection using ocr and deep learning approach. *Int. J. Adv. Comput. Sci. Appl.* **2023**, *14*, 8–14. [CrossRef]
9. Vedhaviyassh, D.; Sudhan, R.; Saranya, G.; Safa, M.; Arun, D. Comparative analysis of easyocr and tesseractocr for automatic license plate recognition using deep learning algorithm. In Proceedings of the 2022 6th International Conference on Electronics Communication and Aerospace Technology, Coimbatore, India, 1–3 December 2022; pp. 966–971.
10. Shashidhar, R.; Manjunath, A.; Kumar, R.S.; Roopa, M.; Puneeth, S. Vehicle number plate detection and recognition using yolo-v3 and ocr method. In Proceedings of the 2021 IEEE International Conference on Mobile Networks and Wireless Communications (ICMNWC), Tumkur, India, 3–4 December 2021; pp. 1–5.
11. Yu, D.; Li, X.; Zhang, C.; Liu, T.; Han, J.; Liu, J.; Ding, E. Towards accurate scene text recognition with semantic reasoning networks. In Proceedings of the IEEE/CVF Conference on Computer Vision and Pattern Recognition, Seattle, WA, USA, 13–19 June 2020; pp. 12113–12122.

. Huang, M.; Liu, Y.; Peng, Z.; Liu, C.; Lin, D.; Zhu, S.; Yuan, N.; Ding, K.; Jin, L. Swintextspotter: Scene text spotting via better synergy between text detection and text recognition. In Proceedings of the IEEE/CVF Conference on Computer Vision and Pattern Recognition, New Orleans, LA, USA, 18–24 June 2022; pp. 4593–4603.

. Ye, J.; Chen, Z.; Liu, J.; Du, B. TextFuseNet: Scene Text Detection with Richer Fused Features. *IJCAI* **2020**, *20*, 516–522.

. Long, S.; He, X.; Yao, C. Scene text detection and recognition: The deep learning era. *Int. J. Comput. Vis.* **2021**, *129*, 161–184. [CrossRef]

. He, M.; Liao, M.; Yang, Z.; Zhong, H.; Tang, J.; Cheng, W.; Yao, C.; Wang, Y.; Bai, X. MOST: A multi-oriented scene text detector with localization refinement. In Proceedings of the IEEE/CVF Conference on Computer Vision and Pattern Recognition, Nashville, TN, USA, 20–25 June 2021; pp. 8813–8822.

. AVMAC LLC. AVMAC Awarded Military Sealift Command Subcontract. 2012. Available online: https://avmacllc.com/avmac-awarded-military-sealift-command-subcontract/ (accessed on 19 December 2024).

. Khallouli, W.; Pamie-George, R.; Kovacic, S.; Sousa-Poza, A.; Canan, M.; Li, J. Leveraging transfer learning and GAN models for OCR from engineering documents. In Proceedings of the 2022 IEEE World AI IoT Congress (AIIoT), Seattle, WA, USA, 6–9 June 2022; pp. 15–21.

3. Li, M.; Lv, T.; Chen, J.; Cui, L.; Lu, Y.; Florencio, D.; Zhang, C.; Li, Z.; Wei, F. Trocr: Transformer-based optical character recognition with pre-trained models. *AAAI Conf. Artif. Intell.* **2023**, *37*, 13094–13102. [CrossRef]

9. Kerasocr. Available online: https://keras-ocr.readthedocs.io/en/latest/ (accessed on December 19 2024).

0. Ranjan, A.; Behera, V.N.J.; Reza, M. Ocr using computer vision and machine learning. *Mach. Learn. Alg. Ind. Appl.* **2021**, *2021*, 83–105.

1. Philips, J.; Tabrizi, N. Historical Document Processing: A Survey of Techniques, Tools, and Trends. *KDIR* **2020**, *2020*, 341–349.

2. Lubna; Mufti, N.; Shah, S.A.A. Automatic number plate Recognition: A detailed survey of relevant algorithms. *Sensors* **2021**, *21*, 3028. [CrossRef] [PubMed]

3. Antonio, J.; Putra, A.R.; Abdurrohman, H.; Tsalasa, M.S. A Survey on Scanned Receipts OCR and Information Extraction. In Proceedings of the International Conference on Document Analysis and Recognition, Jerusalem, Israel, 29–30 November 2022; pp. 29–30.

4. Zhou, X.; Yao, C.; Wen, H.; Wang, Y.; Zhou, S.; He, W.; Liang, J. East: An efficient and accurate scene text detector. In Proceedings of the IEEE Conference on Computer Vision and Pattern Recognition, Honolulu, HI, USA, 21–26 July 2017; pp. 5551–5560.

5. Baek, Y.; Lee, B.; Han, D.; Yun, S.; Lee, H. Character region awareness for text detection. In Proceedings of the IEEE/CVF Conference on Computer Vision and Pattern Recognition, Long Beach, CA, USA, 15–20 June 2019; pp. 9365–9374.

6. Shi, B.; Bai, X.; Yao, C. An End-to-End Trainable Neural Network for Image-based Sequence Recognition and Its Application to Scene Text Recognition. *IEEE Trans. Pattern Anal. Mach. Intell.* **2017**, *39*, 2298–2304. [CrossRef] [PubMed]

7. EasyOCR. Available online: https://github.com/JaidedAI/EasyOCR (accessed on 25 September 2024).

8. Liao, M.; Shi, B.; Bai, X.; Wang, X.; Liu, W. TextBoxes: A Fast Text Detector with a Single Deep Neural Network. In Proceedings of the AAAI, San Francisco, CA USA, 4–9 February 2017.

9. Liu, W.; Anguelov, D.; Erhan, D.; Szegedy, C.; Reed, S.; Fu, C.Y.; Berg, A.C. Ssd: Single shot multibox detector. In Proceedings of the Computer Vision–ECCV 2016: 14th European Conference, Amsterdam, The Netherlands, 11–14 October 2016; Part I 14; Springer: Berlin/Heidelberg, Germany, 2016; pp. 21–37.

0. Tesseract. Available online: https://github.com/tesseract-ocr/tesseract (accessed on 19 December 2024).

1. GoogleCloud. Detect Text in Images. Available online: https://cloud.google.com/vision/docs/ocr (accessed on 19 December 2024).

2. docTR. docTR: Document Text Recognition. Available online: https://mindee.github.io/doctr/ (accessed on 19 December 2024).

33. Breuel, T.M. The OCRopus open source OCR system. In Proceedings of the Document Recognition and Retrieval XV, San Jose, CA, USA, 30–31 January 2008; International Society for Optics and Photonics: Bellingham, WA, USA, 2008; Volume 6815, p. 68150F.

34. Sanyam. PaddleOCR: Unveiling the Power of Optical Character Recognition. 2022. Available online: https://learnopencv.com/optical-character-recognition-using-paddleocr/ (accessed on 19 December 2024).

35. Puigcerver, J. Are multidimensional recurrent layers really necessary for handwritten text recognition? In Proceedings of the 2017 14th IAPR International Conference on Document Analysis and Recognition (ICDAR), Kyoto, Japan, 9–15 November 2017; Volume 1, pp. 67–72.

36. de Sousa Neto, A.F.; Bezerra, B.L.D.; Toselli, A.H.; Lima, E.B. HTR-Flor: A deep learning system for offline handwritten text recognition. In Proceedings of the 2020 33rd SIBGRAPI Conference on Graphics, Patterns and Images (SIBGRAPI), Porto de Galinhas, Brazil, 7–10 November 2020; pp. 54–61.

37. Kass, D.; Vats, E. AttentionHTR: Handwritten text recognition based on attention encoder-decoder networks. In *International Workshop on Document Analysis Systems*; Springer: Berlin/Heidelberg, Germany, 2022; pp. 507–522.

38. Ly, N.T.; Nguyen, H.T.; Nakagawa, M. 2D self-attention convolutional recurrent network for offline handwritten text recognitic In *International Conference on Document Analysis and Recognition*; Springer: Berlin/Heidelberg, Germany, 2021; pp. 191–204.
39. Fujitake, M. Dtrocr: Decoder-only transformer for optical character recognition. In Proceedings of the IEEE/CVF Wint Conference on Applications of Computer Vision, Waikoloa, HI, USA, 3–8 January 2024; pp. 8025–8035.
40. Kim, G.; Hong, T.; Yim, M.; Nam, J.; Park, J.; Yim, J.; Hwang, W.; Yun, S.; Han, D.; Park, S. Ocr-free document understandir transformer. In Proceedings of the European Conference on Computer Vision. Springer, Tel Aviv, Israel, 23–27 October 202 pp. 498–517.
41. Villena Toro, J.; Wiberg, A.; Tarkian, M. Optical character recognition on engineering drawings to achieve automation production quality control. *Front. Manuf. Technol.* **2023**, *3*, 1154132. [CrossRef]
42. Saba, A.; Hantach, R.; Benslimane, M. Text Detection and Recognition from Piping and Instrumentation Diagrams. In Proceedin of the 2023 8th International Conference on Image, Vision and Computing (ICIVC), Dalian, China, 27–29 July 2023; pp. 711–71
43. Ren, Y.; Yao, H.; Liu, G.; Bai, Z. A text code recognition and positioning system for engineering drawings of nuclear pow equipment. In Proceedings of the 2022 IEEE 6th Information Technology and Mechatronics Engineering Conference (ITOEC Chongqing, China, 4–6 March 2022; Volume 6; pp. 661–665.
44. Keras Implementation of Convolutional Recurrent Neural Network. Available online: https://github.com/janzd/CRNI (accessed on 19 December 2024).
45. Fogel, S.; Averbuch-Elor, H.; Cohen, S.; Mazor, S.; Litman, R. Scrabblegan: Semi-supervised varying length handwritten te generation. In Proceedings of the IEEE/CVF Conference on Computer Vision and Pattern Recognition, Seattle, WA, USA, 13–1 June 2020; pp. 4324–4333.
46. Yadav, A.; Singh, S.; Siddique, M.; Mehta, N.; Kotangale, A. OCR using CRNN: A Deep Learning Approach for Text Recognitio In Proceedings of the 2023 4th International Conference for Emerging Technology (INCET), Belgaum, India, 26–28 May 202 pp. 1–6.
47. Graves, A.; Fernández, S.; Gomez, F.; Schmidhuber, J. Connectionist temporal classification: Labelling unsegmented sequenc data with recurrent neural networks. In Proceedings of the 23rd International Conference on Machine Learning, Pittsburgh, PA USA, 25–29 June 2006; pp. 369–376.
48. Bao, H.; Dong, L.; Piao, S.; Wei, F. Beit: Bert pre-training of image transformers. *arXiv* **2021**, arXiv:2106.08254.
49. Liu, Y.; Ott, M.; Goyal, N.; Du, J.; Joshi, M.; Chen, D.; Levy, O.; Lewis, M.; Zettlemoyer, L.; Stoyanov, V. Roberta: A robustl optimized bert pretraining approach. *arXiv* **2019**, arXiv:1907.11692.
50. Weiss, K.; Khoshgoftaar, T.M.; Wang, D. A survey of transfer learning. *J. Big Data* **2016**, *3*, 1–40. [CrossRef]
51. Akhil, S. *An Overview of Tesseract OCR Engine*; A seminar report; Department of Computer Science and Engineering Nationa Institute of Technology: Calicut, India, 2016.
52. Huang, Z.; Chen, K.; He, J.; Bai, X.; Karatzas, D.; Lu, S.; Jawahar, C. Icdar2019 competition on scanned receipt ocr and informatio extraction. In Proceedings of the 2019 International Conference on Document Analysis and Recognition (ICDAR), Sydne Australia, 20–25 September 2019; pp. 1516–1520. [CrossRef]
53. Touvron, H.; Cord, M.; Douze, M.; Massa, F.; Sablayrolles, A.; Jégou, H. Training data-efficient image transformers & distillatior through attention. In Proceedings of the International Conference on Machine Learning, PMLR, Virtual, 18–24 July 202 pp. 10347–10357.
54. Wang, W.; Wei, F.; Dong, L.; Bao, H.; Yang, N.; Zhou, M. Minilm: Deep self-attention distillation for task-agnostic compression o pre-trained transformers. *Adv. Neural Inf. Process. Syst.* **2020**, *33*, 5776–5788.

electronics

MDPI

Article

A Hessian-Based Deep Learning Preprocessing Method for Coronary Angiography Image Analysis

Yanjun Li [1], Takaaki Yoshimura [2,3,4,5], Yuto Horima [6] and Hiroyuki Sugimori [4,5,7,*]

1 Graduate School of Health Sciences, Hokkaido University, Sapporo 060-0812, Japan; yanjun.li.g9@elms.hokudai.ac.jp
2 Department of Health Sciences and Technology, Faculty of Health Sciences, Hokkaido University, Sapporo 060-0812, Japan
3 Department of Medical Physics, Hokkaido University Hospital, Sapporo 060-8648, Japan
4 Global Center for Biomedical Science and Engineering, Faculty of Medicine, Hokkaido University, Sapporo 060-8648, Japan
5 Clinical AI Human Resources Development Program, Faculty of Medicine, Hokkaido University, Sapporo 060-8648, Japan
6 Department of Central Radiology, JR Sapporo Hospital, Sapporo 060-0033, Japan
7 Department of Biomedical Science and Engineering, Faculty of Health Sciences, Hokkaido University, Sapporo 060-0812, Japan
* Correspondence: sugimori@hs.hokudai.ac.jp; Tel.: +81-11-706-3410

Abstract: Leveraging its high accuracy and stability, deep-learning-based coronary artery detection technology has been extensively utilized in diagnosing coronary artery diseases. However, traditional algorithms for localizing coronary stenosis often fall short when detecting stenosis in branch vessels, which can pose significant health risks due to factors like imaging angles and uneven contrast agent distribution. To tackle these challenges, we propose a preprocessing method that integrates Hessian-based vascular enhancement and image fusion as prerequisites for deep learning. This approach enhances fuzzy features in coronary angiography images, thereby increasing the neural network's sensitivity to stenosis characteristics. We assessed the effectiveness of this method using the latest deep learning networks, such as YOLOv10, YOLOv9, and RT-DETR, across various evaluation metrics. Our results show that our method improves AP_{50} accuracy by 4.84% and 5.07% on RT-DETR R101 and YOLOv10-X, respectively, compared to images without special pre-processing. Furthermore, our analysis of different imaging angles on stenosis localization detection indicates that the left coronary artery zero is the most suitable for detecting stenosis with a $AP_{50}(\%)$ value of 90.5. The experimental results have revealed that the proposed method is effective as a preprocessing technique for deep-learning-based coronary angiography image processing and enhances the model's ability to identify stenosis in small blood vessels.

Keywords: coronary artery angiography; image fusion; deep learning; stenosis localization; vascular enhancement

1. Introduction

Coronary artery disease (CAD) is a cardiovascular condition characterized by the narrowing and hardening of arteries, which impedes blood flow to the heart [1]. CAD is a prevalent global health concern, with its incidence rising at an alarming rate. This disease not only increases mortality and morbidity but also significantly diminishes patients' quality of life and imposes a substantial burden on healthcare systems worldwide [2]. Coronary angiography has traditionally been regarded as the 'gold standard' for diagnosing coronary artery disease (CAD). Invasive coronary angiography (ICA) plays a vital role in identifying arterial stenosis and is extensively employed in clinical settings. The procedure involves the injection of a radiopaque contrast agent into the coronary arteries, followed by visualization using a sequence of X-ray images [3]. Clinically, the severity of CAD is often assessed by measuring the percentage of stenosis, a process largely dependent on the physician's visual evaluation. Typically, a stenosis of 50% is the threshold for contemplating coronary revascularization, whereas a stenosis of 70% indicates significant clinical lesions [4]. However, this technique has limitations. The diagnosis relies on the personal experience and judgment of radiologists, and this subjectivity may lead to low reproducibility of diagnostic results. Differences in fatigue and experience levels among physicians can also result in incorrect diagnoses. Additionally, the quality of traditional angiographic images may be affected by factors such as radiation dose limitations, poor imaging angles, and uneven distribution of contrast agents, leading to low contrast and image blurring. These issues make accurate manual assessment of coronary artery stenosis more complex [5]. Moreover, the anatomical structure of coronary arteries varies significantly among individuals. This anatomical variability, combined with the complex three-dimensional structure of the coronary network, makes accurate interpretation of angiographic images challenging. The dynamic nature of blood flow and its interaction with the coronary artery walls add further complexity. Variations in blood flow velocity and pressure during the cardiac cycle can cause changes in the appearance of stenosis in angiographic images. This temporal variation requires real-time assessment and advanced imaging techniques to capture the true extent of arterial stenosis. Given these limitations, there is a critical need for advanced diagnostic methods that can overcome these challenges.

The persistent challenges in diagnosing CAD have been significantly addressed through the remarkable advancements in deep learning for image processing. Recently, deep learning techniques, especially convolutional neural networks (CNNs), have facilitated more precise, stable, and reliable detection and quantification of stenosis. In the existing literature, scholars have extensively researched various aspects of this complex field. Some have focused on the extraction of blood vessels [6,7], while others have utilized deep learning to precisely locate stenotic lesions [8,9]. Moreover, some have developed deep learning models for the non-invasive estimation of fractional flow reserve (FFR) from angiographic images [10]. Additionally, novel mathematical approaches have been proposed to calculate stenosis rates [11], while groundbreaking research often emphasizes stenotic areas within the aorta, it tends to overlook the crucial implications of stenosis in the branch vessels. This gap in research is primarily due to difficulties such as overlapping vessels, inconsistent distribution of contrast agents, and less-than-ideal imaging angles, which collectively impede the clear visualization of branch vessels. Other algorithms that focus on segmentation are challenging to apply in real-time clinical detection. Additionally, researchers often concentrate on analyzing images from the zero angle while neglecting the reference value of other imaging angles for comprehensive clinical diagnosis. Consequently, the detection of stenosis in comprehensive coronary angiography remains a highly promising but complex field of study. Addressing this critical issue could substantially enhance our capacity to diagnose and treat stenotic conditions within the intricate network of coronary arteries.

To effectively address the intricate challenges posed by the coronary arterial network, characterized by numerous branches and complex geometries, one promising approach is the application of Hessian-matrix-based filtering to enhance the visualization of blood vessels [12]. This method utilizes the natural relationships between the eigenvalues of the Hessian matrix to identify and extract the tubular structures of blood vessels in medical imaging. The Hessian-based Frangi vesselness (HFV) filter has notably become a key tool for vascular enhancement and quantification, as evidenced by its extensive application across numerous research studies [13–15]. Moreover, in our previous research [16], processing coronary angiography images with the HFV filter improved their appearance and helped deep learning networks better learn stenotic features. Additionally, advanced hybrid enhancement techniques have been developed, integrating approaches like region growth with the HFV filter. These methods aim to improve image background clarity and reduce noise levels more effectively [17,18]. However, most of the articles on HFV have emphasized its contributions to image enhancement, and few researchers have considered whether the enhanced images can help deep learning networks better learn difficult-to-recognize features. Alternatively, it might be that, due to the limitations in deep learning network development at the time of those studies, convincing results could not be achieved.

In the field of CNN-based approaches, substantial progress has been made in different facets of stenosis identification and detection. For instance, a fundamental CNN structure, slightly adjusted in its layers, was utilized for identifying stenotic regions in angiographic images in 2018. The experimental findings revealed that networks initially trained on synthetic data and subsequently fine-tuned with clinical datasets achieved a remarkable accuracy of around 90%, surpassing the performance of conventional feedforward neural networks [19]. Research into transfer learning has involved fine-tuning pretrained convolutional neural networks (CNNs) with synthetic datasets. Findings indicated that leveraging the top three layers of a pretrained CNN as feature extractors yielded significant results in the detection of stenosis [20]. Based on these advancements, researchers have developed an entirely automated method called CathAI to analyze coronary artery stenosis in conventional coronary angiography. This method significantly improves the standardization and reproducibility of angiographic coronary artery stenosis assessment [21].

Recent advancements in the field of blood vessel segmentation have led to the development of numerous models and tracking-based techniques. The methodologies encompass various techniques like multiscale Gabor filtering [22], Hessian filtering coupled with flux flow measurement [23], and segmentation methods based on active contours [24]. In addition, the adoption of deep learning strategies, notably employing long short-term memory recurrent neural networks [25], has markedly enhanced performance and driven progress in this domain. As transformer technology continues to mature, its application in processing and segmenting medical images has become a leading trend, with numerous outstanding methods emerging in recent years [26–28]. These varied approaches together form a comprehensive suite of techniques designed to advance our knowledge and improve our abilities in medical image analysis, with a particular focus on the detection of coronary artery stenosis and the segmentation of blood vessels.

Our approach differs from our previous work [16] in the following aspects:

1. Application of advanced deep learning networks: We have employed the most cutting-edge deep learning networks to analyze coronary artery detection image datasets. This includes both an overall analysis of the dataset and specific analyses of the different imaging angles, which was not explored in the previous study.
2. Enhanced data annotation: We significantly increased the labeling of stenosis in branch vessels. In [16], due to detection accuracy limitations, the possibility of detecting stenosis in branch vessels was nearly abandoned, despite the fact that stenosis in these vessels poses significant clinical health risks. This change improves the clinical application potential of our method.
3. Incorporation of additional data: We have acquired additional data, including cases from older patients. Many of these images contain artifacts, such as stents from previous surgeries, which introduce noise. The inclusion of this data has increased the diversity of our dataset and further enhanced the practical applicability of our method.
4. Latency testing: We measured the latency of our method compared to processing raw images directly. Latency is a crucial factor for real-time clinical detection, and by measuring this, we can assess whether our method is suitable for further development and application in real-time detection.

In this research, we adopted the preprocessing technique proposed in [16] aimed at improving coronary artery imagery by integrating Hessian matrix multiscale filtering with image feature fusion. Our method leverages image fusion to preserve a maximum number of features, facilitating the identification of small or distal vessels. Initially, we applied HFV filtering to enhance the visibility of blood vessels in angiographic images, followed by image fusion to emphasize these vessels. Subsequently, we trained and compared the performance of various deep learning networks under the same conditions, evaluating the influence of preprocessing on their effectiveness. We also examined how different imaging angles affect the localization of stenosis. The experimental results demonstrated that our approach yielded satisfactory detection results.

2. Materials and Methods

Regarding the methodology, we utilized two datasets: the raw data as the original dataset and a preprocessed dataset. For the latter, we applied our preprocessing method, which involves first using the HFV filter followed by image fusion techniques to further enhance the images. We then used these two datasets to test various deep learning networks and evaluate their performance on each dataset. Section 2 is organized into four categories: materials are described in Section 2.1, followed by the preliminaries, including the preprocessing method in Section 2.2. The model explanation is provided in Section 2.3, and the evaluation indicators are listed in Section 2.4.

2.1. Materials

This study employed a dataset consisting of information from 40 patients who underwent coronary angiography at Hokkaido University Hospital. Experienced radiologists carefully diagnosed all angiographic images and video recordings, ensuring the precision and reliability of the clinical data. For image analysis purposes, the continuous video streams for each patient were segmented into individual frames at a uniform rate of 15 frames per second. In our experiment, we manually classified a total of 400 contrast images into two categories: right coronary artery (RCA) and left coronary artery (LCA). Each category encompassed three distinct imaging angles: left anterior oblique (LAO), right anterior oblique (RAO), and the ZERO angle.

2.2. Preprocessing Approaches

2.2.1. HFV Filter

Enhancement filters are essential for improving the clarity and detail of images from various modalities like X-ray, MRI, CT, and ultrasound. These improvements are crucial for medical professionals in diagnosing and monitoring a range of diseases. Techniques that use differential information, such as the second derivative or the Hessian matrix, are commonly employed to highlight vessel structures within the images. Through differential analysis, these methods greatly enhance the visibility of blood vessels, making them vital tools for medical image segmentation and analysis.

This method utilizes eigenvalue analysis of the Hessian matrix $(H(x,y))$ to detect vessel-like structures in an image. We denote the source image as $I(x,y)$. To achieve a continuous Hessian matrix, it is convolved with a two-dimensional (2D) Gaussian filter. The convolution of the Gaussian filter with the Hessian of the image $I(x,y)$ is represented in Equation (1).

$$H(x,y) \approx G * \begin{bmatrix} \frac{\partial^2 I}{\partial x^2} & \frac{\partial^2 I}{\partial x \partial y} \\ \frac{\partial^2 I}{\partial y \partial x} & \frac{\partial^2 I}{\partial y^2} \end{bmatrix} = \begin{bmatrix} \frac{\partial^2 G}{\partial x^2} & \frac{\partial^2 G}{\partial x \partial y} \\ \frac{\partial^2 G}{\partial y \partial x} & \frac{\partial^2 G}{\partial y^2} \end{bmatrix} * I(x,y) \quad (1)$$

Analyzing the sign and magnitude of Hessian eigenvalues can greatly improve the detection of local image structures. Consequently, the eigenvalues and eigenvectors of $H(x,y)$ are calculated to obtain contrast and orientation information at every point in the image. This decomposition provides two eigenvalues, labeled (λ_1, λ_2), along with their corresponding eigenvectors $(\vec{u_1}, \vec{u_2})$. These components are examined to identify structures such as blobs, tubes, or plates within the image. Given our focus on blood-vessel-like structures, these can be characterized by the conditions $|\lambda_1| \approx 0$, $|\lambda_1| \ll |\lambda_2|$, with $\vec{u_1}$ indicating the vessel's direction. Additionally, λ_2 tends to be negative when vessels appear as bright tubes against darker backgrounds. This information is crucial for ensuring consistency and excluding non-vessel structures from the analysis. The Frangi vesselness function is defined accordingly:

$$F(v) = \begin{cases} 0 & \text{if } \lambda_2 > 0, \\ e^{-\frac{R_B{}^2}{2\beta^2}}\left(1 - e^{\frac{s^2}{2c^2}}\right) & \text{othewise,} \end{cases} \quad (2)$$

where

$$R_B = \frac{|\lambda_1|}{|\lambda_2|}, \qquad S = \sqrt{\lambda_1^2 + \lambda_2^2} \quad (3)$$

The parameter R_B measures the eccentricity of objects within a 2D image, while S evaluates "structureness", distinguishing background areas. Since the background lacks distinct structures, its contrast is minimal, resulting in low S values. Conversely, areas with structures exhibit high S values. The sensitivity of the line filter to the parameters R_B and S is regulated by the thresholds β and c. Typically, β is set to 0.5, and c is adjusted based on the vessels' gray-level intensity. Applying this filter to an image yields response values, with higher values indicating vessel pixels and lower values indicating background pixels.

2.2.2. Image Fusion

Medical image fusion is a crucial technique that combines multiple images from one or various imaging modalities within the medical domain. The main objective of this process is to enhance image quality while maintaining and emphasizing features important for clinical purposes. This enhancement boosts the clinical usefulness of these fused images for diagnosis and evaluation. The scope of medical image fusion includes numerous scientific fields such as image processing, computer vision, pattern recognition, machine learning, and artificial intelligence. Its wide range of applications across different clinical situations allows physicians to obtain a detailed understanding of pathological lesions by integrating images from diverse modalities. This innovative approach equips healthcare professionals with more comprehensive and informative visual representations of medical data, facilitating more faithful diagnoses and better-informed treatment suggestions and decisions.

Within medical image fusion techniques that utilize the intensity–hue–saturation (IHS) model, the pivotal step is the IHS transform. This process begins with the input medical image, typically encoded in red–green–blue (RGB) color channels, undergoing conversion via the RGB-IHS transform. This conversion translates the image into the IHS color space, which includes intensity, hue, and saturation components, resulting in a matrix representation of the image within this alternative color space. To reconstruct the fused medical image, the inverse IHS transform is applied. In this methodology, two medical images from different imaging modalities are first converted to the IHS color space through the RGB-IHS transform. The final fused image is created by reversing this transformation utilizing the IHS-RGB transform:

$$I = \frac{R + B + G}{3} \quad (4)$$

$$\begin{cases} H = \frac{G-B}{3I-3B}, S = \frac{I-B}{I} & \text{if } B < R, G, \\ H = \frac{B-R}{3I-3R}, S = \frac{I-R}{I} & \text{if } R < B, G, \\ H = \frac{R-G}{3I-3G}, S = \frac{I-G}{I} & \text{if } G < R, B \end{cases} \quad (5)$$

$$
\begin{cases}
R = I(1 + 2S - 3S \times H), \\
G = I(1 - S + 3S \times H), \\
B = I(1 - S) & \text{if } B < R, G, \\
R = I(1 - S), \\
G = I(1 + 5S - 3S \times H), \\
B = I(1 - 4S + 3S \times H) & \text{if } R < B, G, \\
R = I(1 - 7S + 3S \times H), \\
G = I(1 - S), \\
B = I(1 + 8S - 3S \times H) & \text{if } G < R, B
\end{cases} \quad (6)
$$

This innovative approach harnesses the benefits of the IHS color space, enabling the merging of various imaging modalities into a cohesive representation that preserves essential characteristics. This enhances clinical interpretation and analysis significantly.

2.3. Model Descriptions

2.3.1. Region-Based Fully Convolutional Networks

Region-Based Fully Convolutional Networks (R-FCN) are advanced deep learning models designed for detecting targeted objects in scenarios. By merging the advantages of Region-based Convolutional Neural Networks (R-CNN) and Fully Convolutional Networks (FCN), R-FCN ensures both efficient and precise object detection. According to [29], the R-FCN architecture consists of four essential components: the Region Proposal Network (RPN), the Residual Network (ResNet), the classification module, and the regression module. Each of these elements plays a vital role in the network's overall performance.

In a manner similar to Faster R-CNN, the main role of the Region Proposal Network (RPN) in R-FCN is to generate region proposals, identifying potential Regions of Interest (RoIs) within the input image. These region proposals allow subsequent convolutional operations to be applied across the entire image, aiding in the computation of weight layers. The process in R-FCN starts with resizing input images to maintain a consistent short-side dimension. These resized images are then processed for feature extraction using ResNet-101, which comprises five convolutional blocks. Specifically, the output from the fourth convolutional layer of ResNet-101 serves as the input to the RPN.

Given the high dimensionality present in the output of the fifth convolutional layer of ResNet-101, it is essential to reduce the number of channels by integrating additional convolutional layers. This adjustment generates a 1024-dimensional feature map. After this feature extraction stage, the network introduces two parallel convolutional layers dedicated to classification and regression tasks. Position-sensitive score maps, sized $k^2(C+1)$ for classification and $4k^2$ for regression, are produced to incorporate positional information. In the network's final stages, these position-sensitive score maps are pooled with the Regions of Interest (RoIs) extracted earlier by the RPN. This pooling process yields the classification and regression outcomes, showcasing the network's proficiency in identifying and localizing objects within the input images.

2.3.2. YOLO Series

Core Concept

The fundamental concept of the YOLO (You Only Look Once) series is to convert object detection into a regression task. This methodology involves using the whole image as input to the neural network, which subsequently forecasts the locations of the bounding boxes along with their associated classes.

1. Image Division: YOLO divides the input image into a fixed-size grid.
2. Predicting Bounding Boxes and Classes: In each grid cell, YOLO estimates a set number of bounding boxes (usually 5 or 3). Every bounding box is defined by five key attributes: the center coordinates, width, height, and the confidence score indicating

the likelihood of an object being present. Furthermore, each bounding box also predicts the class of the detected object.

3. Single Forward Pass: YOLO uses a single forward pass through a CNN to predict all bounding box positions and classes simultaneously. This approach provides faster speed compared to other object detection algorithms, such as those based on sliding windows or region proposals, because it only requires one forward pass to complete the prediction.
4. Loss Function: YOLO utilizes a composite loss function to optimize its network training, which comprises location loss, confidence loss, and class loss. The location loss quantifies the discrepancy between the predicted bounding boxes and the actual ground truth bounding boxes. The confidence loss assesses the correctness of the object predictions and penalizes incorrect predictions for background areas. Finally, the class loss evaluates the accuracy of the object class predictions made by the network.
5. Non-Maximum Suppression (NMS): Among the predicted bounding boxes, multiple overlapping boxes may represent the same object. To eliminate redundant boxes, YOLO uses the non-maximum suppression algorithm, which selects the best bounding box based on confidence and overlap.

Structure

The architecture of object detectors in the YOLO series is generally divided into three segments: Backbone, Neck, and Head. The Backbone, which is often a pre-trained convolutional neural network, is responsible for extracting hierarchical features from the input image, identifying low-level features such as edges and textures in the initial layers and high-level features like object parts and semantic content in the deeper layers. The Neck serves as a bridge between the Backbone and the Head, refining the features extracted by the Backbone and enhancing both spatial and semantic information through additional convolutional layers, Feature Pyramid Networks (FPN), or other similar mechanisms. The Head is the final part, making predictions based on the refined features from the Backbone and Neck. It handles tasks like classification, localization, and instance segmentation, with Non-Maximum Suppression (NMS) used in post-processing to eliminate overlapping predictions and retain only the most confident detections [30].

YOLOv8

YOLOv8 [31] builds upon the previous successful YOLO versions by introducing innovative features and enhancements aimed at improving both performance and flexibility. This version is crafted to be swift, precise, and easy to use, making it an outstanding option for tasks such as object detection, image segmentation, and image classification. Among its key advancements are a redesigned backbone network, an Anchor-Free detection head, and a novel loss function that combines two types of loss: classification loss (Varifocal Loss, VFL) and regression loss (Complete-IoU, CIOU + Deep Feature Loss, DFL). Furthermore, YOLOv8 maintains compatibility with earlier YOLO versions, allowing for effortless transitions between versions and facilitating performance evaluations. In addition to object detection, YOLOv8 is versatile enough to handle various tasks, including instance segmentation and keypoint detection, supported by a strong community and ecosystem that ensure ongoing development and assistance.

YOLOv9

The YOLOv9 model [32] presents a novel approach called Programmable Gradient Information (PGI), which enhances deep networks' adaptability to achieve multiple goals. PGI enables the provision of extensive input data for specific tasks to compute objective functions, ensuring accurate gradient information for network weight updates. Additionally, a new lightweight architecture, the General Efficient Layer Aggregation Network (GELAN), designed using gradient path planning, has been introduced. GELAN's architecture showcases the effectiveness of PGI in lightweight models.

The main contributions of YOLOv9 include the following: First, a theoretical analysis of existing deep neural network architectures from the standpoint of reversible functions, which clarifies previously complex phenomena. This analysis led to the development of PGI and auxiliary reversible branches, which achieved remarkable results. Second, PGI overcomes the limitation of applying deep supervision exclusively to very deep neural networks, making it feasible to use new lightweight architectures in everyday applications. Third, GELAN, using only traditional convolutions, achieves superior parameter utilization compared to state-of-the-art deep convolutional designs, while being lightweight, fast, and accurate.

YOLOv10

YOLOv10 [33], developed by researchers using the Ultralytics Python package, introduces several advancements over previous versions. Typically, the YOLO family of methods employs Task Alignment Learning (TAL) during training to assign multiple positive samples to each instance. This one-to-many assignment generates rich supervisory signals, promotes optimization, and achieves excellent performance. However, this approach necessitates reliance on NMS post-processing, which can result in suboptimal inference efficiency when deployed. Although earlier studies have investigated one-to-one matching to reduce redundant predictions, these approaches frequently result in increased inference overhead or yield less than ideal performance.

In [33], the authors propose a YOLO training strategy that eliminates the need for NMS by adopting dual label assignment and consistent matching metrics to achieve high efficiency and competitive performance. Unlike one-to-many assignment, one-to-one matching assigns only one prediction to each ground truth, avoiding the necessity of NMS post-processing but leading to weaker supervision, which can result in suboptimal accuracy and convergence speed. This issue can be mitigated by one-to-many assignment. To address this, the authors introduce dual label assignment for YOLO, combining the advantages of both strategies. The various components of YOLO are comprehensively optimized from the perspective of efficiency and accuracy, significantly reducing computational overhead while enhancing capabilities. Extensive experiments demonstrate its excellent accuracy–latency trade-off across multiple model sizes.

2.3.3. Real-Time Detection Transformer

The Real-Time Detection Transformer (RT-DETR) [34] is an advanced object detection model designed for real-time applications. This model synergizes two noticeable methodologies in object detection: Transformer and Detection Transformer (DETR). The Transformer, initially developed for natural language processing tasks, has demonstrated remarkable success in sequence modeling within the domain of computer vision. DETR revolutionizes object detection by framing it as an object query problem, which is then addressed using the Transformer architecture. RT-DETR builds upon the foundational structure of DETR, incorporating a series of enhancements that enable efficient real-time object detection.

DETR [35], proposed by the Facebook AI research team, employs Transformer for encoding and decoding in an end-to-end object detection model. In contrast to conventional object detection techniques, DETR redefines the object detection task as an object query problem. This approach interprets each pixel position in the image as a query vector, which is transformed into a collection of feature vectors via a Transformer encoder. Subsequently, the model employs a decoder to predict the category, bounding box coordinates, and object feature vector for each detected object by interacting with the query vectors.

RT-DETR maintains the same encoder and decoder structure as DETR but introduces several optimizations. Firstly, RT-DETR minimizes computational expenses by utilizing smaller feature maps. Secondly, it reduces the model parameters by using a fewer number of attention heads. Moreover, RT-DETR incorporates an innovative grouped attention mechanism to improve performance.

Specifically, the encoder of RT-DETR uses a ResNet50 network but retains only its first four residual blocks to reduce the feature map size. The decoder includes a Transformer decoder and an object embedding network. Unlike DETR, RT-DETR's Transformer decoder has only two attention heads instead of eight. Moreover, RT-DETR employs a new grouped attention mechanism, dividing attention calculations into multiple groups to improve computational efficiency. The object embedding network is used to integrate the feature vector of each object into the model for subsequent tasks.

2.4. Evaluation Indicators

2.4.1. $AP_{50}(\%)$

$AP_{50}(\%)$ represents a distinct form of the Average Precision (AP) metric, defined by setting the Intersection over Union (IoU) threshold to 0.50. This metric encapsulates various sub-metrics to provide a comprehensive evaluation:

- Intersection over Union: This metric evaluates the extent of overlap between the predicted bounding boxes and the actual bounding boxes. This metric offers a measure of the model's accuracy in localization. IoU is computed by dividing the area of intersection between the predicted and ground truth boxes by the area of their union.
- IoU Threshold: In order for a prediction to be classified as a True Positive (TP), the Intersection over Union between the predicted bounding box and the actual ground truth box must surpass a predefined threshold. For the $AP_{50}(\%)$ metric, this threshold is established at 0.50.
- Precision: This metric indicates the precision of the model's positive predictions. It is determined by dividing the number of true positive outcomes by the total number of true positive and false positive outcomes.

$$\text{Precision} = \frac{TP}{TP + FP} \tag{7}$$

- Recall: This metric evaluates the model's effectiveness in recognizing all pertinent instances. It is calculated by dividing the number of true positives by the combined total of true positives and false negatives.

$$\text{Recall} = \frac{TP}{TP + FN} \tag{8}$$

- Average Precision: The Average Precision metric encapsulates the precision–recall relationship by calculating the area under the precision–recall curve. This metric signifies the model's overall precision when considering all levels of recall.

$$\text{AP} = \int_0^1 \text{Precision}(\text{Recall})\, d(\text{Recall}) \tag{9}$$

2.4.2. $AP_{val}(\%)$

The metric $AP_{val}(\%)$ offers a more thorough assessment of a model's performance by evaluating both precision and recall across various IoU thresholds, rather than focusing on just one. This measure generally represents the Average Precision computed over a range of IoU thresholds, typically from 0.50 to 0.95, in increments (e.g., every 0.05). In some benchmarks, this is referred to as mAP (mean Average Precision).

$$\text{AP}_{\text{val}}(\%) = \frac{1}{n} \sum_{k=n}^{k=1} AP_k \tag{10}$$

Here, n denotes the quantity of IoU thresholds evaluated, while AP_k signifies the mean precision for class k.

3. Experiments and Results

3.1. Experiments

3.1.1. Data Acquisition

Given the fluctuations in contrast agent distribution across different angiography stages, which impact the clarity of vascular images, we meticulously selected 400 representative images from our dataset to develop the model. These images were primarily taken during the mid-phase of coronary angiography, ensuring uniform contrast agent presence within the vessels. For the annotation of stenotic regions, we used MATLAB R2022a and adopted a structured method. Radiologists from Hokkaido University Hospital, with considerable expertise, diagnosed the patients, and we used these diagnoses to annotate the images. Our focus was on areas with stenosis rates greater than 50%, given their higher risk and enhanced visibility. We then categorized the dataset based on the imaging angles used in the coronary angiography. There are a total of 280 images for the LCA and 120 images for the RCA. We have further classified these images based on zero LAO and RAO angles. The detailed data distribution is presented in Table 1.

Table 1. Data distribution.

Imaging Angles	Numbers	Training	Validation	Testing
LCA zero	109	76	16	17
LCA LAO	96	67	14	15
LCA RAO	75	53	11	11
RCA zero	30	21	5	4
RCA LAO	51	36	8	7
RCA RAO	39	27	6	6
SUM	400	280	60	60

3.2. Data Preparation

Firstly, we applied our proposed preprocessing technique to the dataset, which aimed to enhance the image quality of the inputs. We then randomly divided the enhanced images into three sets: 70% for training, 15% for validation, and 15% for testing. To tackle the challenge of limited data and to strengthen our model's robustness, we employed several augmentation methods. Specifically, we rotated the images in 5-degree steps within a range of $-45°$ to $45°$. Additionally, we utilized several other augmentation techniques, including horizontal and vertical flips, to further diversify our dataset. These augmentations helped replicate various clinical conditions, thereby improving our model's ability to generalize to new, unseen data. This approach expanded our training dataset to 7320 images, significantly increasing its diversity and generalizability. Moreover, each image was resized to a uniform dimension, ensuring standardized input for the model during training.These steps are completed using Matlab2022a.

3.3. Model Training and Evaluation

We implemented multiple deep learning frameworks to develop models using this enhanced dataset, assessing their capability to identify the stenosis features in vascular structures. The frameworks utilized in our study comprised R-FCN, YOLOv8, YOLOv9, YOLOv10, and RT-DETR. Importantly, to guarantee that the results were solely due to training on our particular dataset, all models were trained from the ground up without any pre-trained weights. We adjusted the data structure according to the corresponding repositories and each model's performance was assessed under consistent conditions, emphasizing their efficiency on both preprocessed and unprocessed images.

To thoroughly analyze coronary angiography images, we carried out a quantitative performance evaluation, focusing on the models' proficiency in accurately detecting and outlining stenotic regions. For the evaluation, we used the metrics $AP_{val}(\%)$ and $AP_{50}(\%)$ to define the models' capability in recognizing and portraying stenotic areas. Additionally, we tested the latency of each model using original coronary stenosis detection videos to assess their real-time performance.

To further ensure a thorough and unbiased evaluation, we implemented a rigorous validation approach. Each model was trained multiple times with different random initializations to account for variability in training outcomes. The performance metrics were averaged over these multiple runs to obtain reliable and consistent results.

3.4. Results

We conducted a comparative analysis to assess the effectiveness of applying HFV filter preprocessing and image fusion versus using raw images on the performance of deep learning models for detecting stenosis. Additionally, we compared the performance of the optimal model on images taken from different imaging angles. To conduct this comparison, we implemented the HFV filter to preprocess the images, enhancing the visibility of fine vascular structures by emphasizing high-frequency components. We then fused these filtered images with the raw images to create a composite input that combines the benefits of both preprocessing techniques. The objective was to determine whether this fusion approach could improve the model's ability to detect stenotic regions compared to using source images alone.

Upon completing the image preprocessing, we proceeded with the essential task of marking the locations of stenosis within the main and branch vessels, especially where the stenosis rate exceeded 50%, based on the diagnostic information provided by medical experts. For clarity and ease of reference, we include here Figure 1, with each part of the figure highlighting different characteristics of our investigation. Figure 1(a1–f1) display the original, unprocessed image, which serves as the baseline for our observations. In contrast, Figure 1(a2–f2) show the image after preprocessing with the HFV filter, demonstrating the enhancements achieved through this technique. Finally, Figure 1(a3–f3) showcase the results of the image fusion process, highlighting the combination of the preprocessed image with the original. These visual portrayals clearly exhibit the success of our image processing techniques.

The application of the HFV filter significantly improves the visibility of vascular features, particularly the primary vessels, while also reducing background noise. For example, Figure 1(a2) demonstrates a clearer portrayal of tubular structures. Nevertheless, the filter also introduces some pseudo-vessels that mimic branch vessel shapes throughout the image. These artificial structures appear convincing but are located in regions of the original image that either lack vessels or contain blurred vessels. Similarly, Figure 1(b2) illustrates this effect, where the HFV filter enhances noticeable features but diminishes small vessels in areas with low contrast.

To maximize the enhancement of vascular features in the image while maintaining the intricate details of fine vessels, we explored image fusion as a viable approach. Figure 1(a3–f3) clearly display the outcomes of applying this image fusion method to processed images from six distinct imaging angles. This technique allowed us to preserve the key features of the original images effectively. At the same time, it significantly reduced noise and random morphological features that could potentially appear as vessel-like structures due to the application of the HFV filter. By doing so, we ensured that our deep learning models received high-quality input images, thereby improving their ability to accurately detect and delineate stenotic regions, leading to more reliable and efficient coronary artery analysis. Additionally, based on our testing, the execution time for the preprocessing module alone was measured to be 37.1 ms on average. This additional time should be taken into account when evaluating the overall system performance in real-time scenarios.

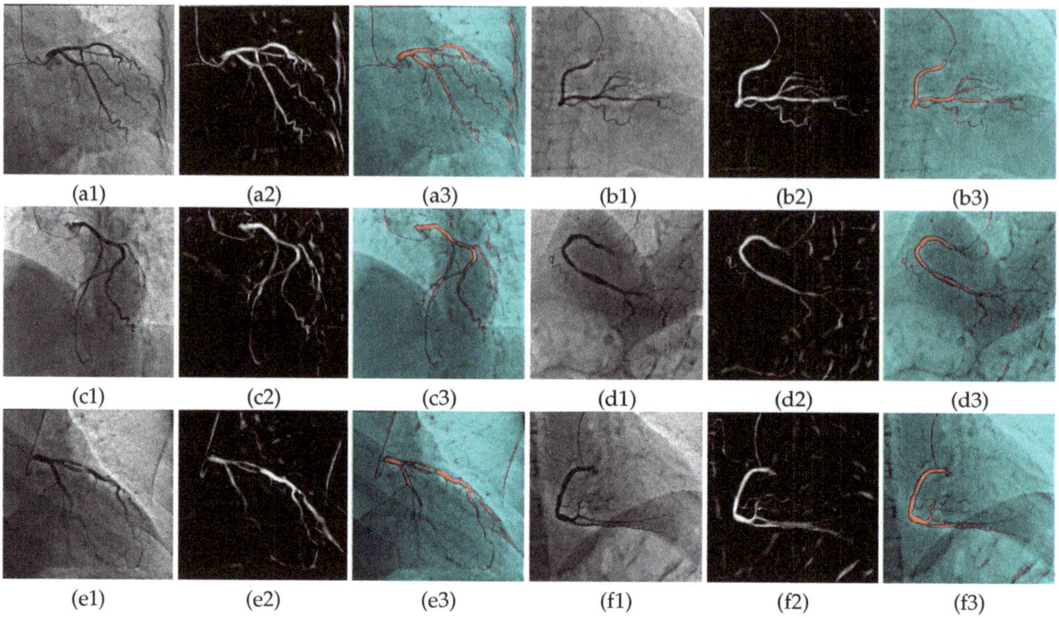

Figure 1. The performance of the proposed preprocessing method applied to six imaging angles. Specifically, (**a1–f1**) portray the original images from the dataset for the conditions of Left Coronary Artery (LCA) zero, LCA Left Anterior Oblique (LAO), LCA Right Anterior Oblique (RAO), Right Coronary Artery (RCA) zero, RCA LAO, and RCA RAO, respectively. The images (**a2–f2**) show the results after applying the HFV filter to these original images. Finally, (**a3–f3**) illustrate the output images following the application of the proposed preprocessing method. Moreover, (**a1–f1**) belong to the initial image dataset, while (**a3–f3**) will be classified as the preprocessed image dataset for training.

To set a benchmark for our future experiments, we began by assessing the performance of different neural network architectures using raw images. This extensive evaluation included a variety of advanced models, namely, R-FCN-InceptionResNetV2, YOLOv8-X, YOLOv9-E, YOLOv10-L, YOLOv10-X, RT-DETR R50, and RT-DETR R101. Our aim was to measure the effectiveness of each model by determining the Average Precision at an Intersection over Union threshold of 0.50. To maintain fairness, we trained and tested each model under uniform conditions.

The experimental results indicated that R-FCN-InceptionResNetV2 achieved an $AP_{50}(\%)$ of only 47.6 on our raw dataset. This was the best-performing network in our previous work [16]. In contrast, the more recently developed models, namely YOLOv8-X, YOLOv9-E, YOLOv10-L, YOLOv10-X, RT-DETR R50, and RT-DETR R101, demonstrated $AP_{50}(\%)$ values of 77.3, 82.1, 78.2, 82.9, 74.6, and 82.7, respectively, on the same raw dataset. The results are summarized in Table 2. This baseline performance evaluation provides a critical reference for our subsequent experiments involving image preprocessing and augmentation techniques. The findings suggest that while older architectures like R-FCN-InceptionResNetV2 may struggle with complicated data, the latest models exhibit robust performance, which could potentially be further enhanced with appropriate preprocessing methods. This improvement also demonstrates the effectiveness of our approach in utilizing more advanced models.

Table 2. Performance Comparison of Different Models on Raw Dataset.

Model	AP_{val} (%)	AP_{50} (%)
R-FCN-InceptionResNetV2	29.3	47.6
RT-DETR R50	45.7	74.6
YOLOv8-X	46.2	77.3
YOLOv10-L	47.3	78.2
YOLOv9-E	50.3	82.1
RT-DETR R101	50.5	82.7
YOLOv10-X	51.6	82.9

After completing experiments on the raw dataset, we reintroduced the neural networks applied to the original images on the dataset processed by our preprocessing methods, and examined their detection performance under the same conditions (We excluded the poorly performing R-FCN-InceptionResNetV2 network). Additionally, we conducted latency tests on these networks when applied to the preprocessed videos. We also recorded data from the training processes of these networks. The results are summarized in Table 3.

Table 3. Performance Comparison of Different Models on Preprocessed Dataset.

Model	Parameters (M)	FLOPs(G)	APval (%)	AP_{50}(%)	Latency (ms)
RT-DETR R50	13.8	40.0	45.9	79.2	3.02
Yolov10-L	10.6	50.3	49.4	82.4	3.16
Yolov8-X	28.1	112.4	50.5	84.2	5.54
Yolov9-E	23.6	89.4	52.5	86.0	5.11
RT-DETR R101	25.1	98.6	53.8	86.7	4.51
Yolov10-X	12.2	65.3	53.9	87.1	4.43

Similar to the previous results, RT-DETR R50 remains the least accurate among the six networks, although its accuracy has improved. At an IoU threshold of 0.50, the AP is 0.792. The YOLOv10-X network continues to be the best model, with an AP of 0.871 at an IoU of 0.50, and an AP_{val}(%) of 53.9 when averaging the AP values across different IoU thresholds. Comparing these networks horizontally, we can see that the detection results become more precise with each update of YOLO. The RT-DETR-R101, which employs Transformer technology, achieves detection accuracy comparable to YOLOv10-X. In terms of latency, YOLOv10-X has a latency of 4.43 ms, which is lower than RT-DETR-R101's 4.51 ms. These results highlight the improvements in detection performance after applying our preprocessing methods. The YOLOv10-X model continues to lead in accuracy and efficiency, emphasizing its suitability for real-time applications in detecting coronary artery stenosis. The slight edge in latency performance of YOLOv10-X over RT-DETR-R101 further reinforces its advantage in scenarios where processing speed is critical.

In Figure 2, we present a comparative image for the LCA zero angle. The image on the left illustrates the detection outcomes when YOLOv10-X is applied to the original image, whereas the image on the right displays the detection outcomes after applying YOLOv10-X to the preprocessed image. Additionally, we have enlarged the detection boxes for a more intuitive observation of the detection effects. By comparing the two images, it is evident that the preprocessed image yields more accurate and clearer detection of stenotic regions. The enlarged detection boxes highlight the enhanced ability of YOLOv10-X to identify stenotic areas when the image preprocessing is applied.

To more intuitively demonstrate the advantages of our preprocessing approach in terms of processing performance, including speed and accuracy, we have summarized the latency and accuracy for both preprocessed and raw images in Table 4, and calculated the improvement margins.

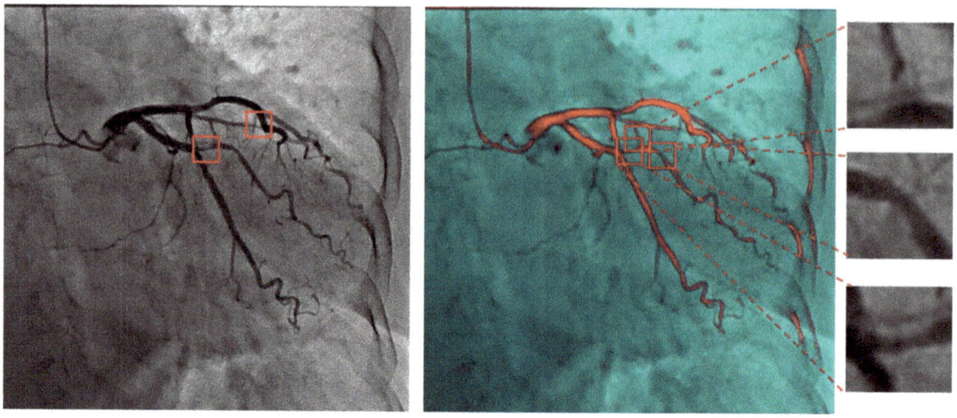

Figure 2. Comparison of YOLOv10-X detection results on original image and preprocessed image.

Table 4. Comparison of Latency and Accuracy with and without Preprocessing.

Model	AP_{50}(%)			Latency (ms)		
	Original	Preprocessed	Improvement Margin(%)	Original	Preprocessed	Improvement Margin(%)
RT-DETR R50	74.6	79.2	6.17	2.73	3.02	−9.60
YOLOv8-X	77.3	84.2	8.95	5.05	5.54	−8.84
YOLOv10-L	78.2	82.4	5.37	2.77	3.16	−12.21
YOLOv9-E	82.1	86.0	4.79	4.58	5.11	−10.33
RT-DETR R101	82.7	86.7	4.84	4.04	4.51	−10.47
YOLOv10-X	82.9	87.1	5.07	3.90	4.43	−11.91

The above results indicate that while our preprocessing method improved the accuracy of detecting stenotic regions, it also increased the processing time. In terms of accuracy, our method had the greatest improvement on the YOLOv8-X model, achieving an 8.95% increase, while the improvement on the YOLOv9-E model was the least, at 4.79%. Regarding latency, our method had the most negative impact on the YOLOv10 models, with both YOLOv10-L and YOLOv10-X experiencing approximately a 12% slowdown in processing speed. These findings indicate that, although our preprocessing method enhances the detection accuracy of deep learning models, it comes at the cost of processing speed. The transformation of original images into preprocessed ones introduces a time delay, primarily due to the repeated computation of Hessian eigenvalues required by the HFV filter across different parameter settings and an execute time during image fusion. Moreover, the increased latency observed when processing preprocessed images, as compared to raw images, is primarily attributable to the increased computational load. Specifically, after the HFV filtering and image fusion steps, the complexity of the regions in the resulting images, derived from the fusion of the original and enhanced images, increases. This additional complexity requires extra processing time by the deep learning network, ultimately contributing to the increased prediction latency. Despite these delays, the method's capacity to markedly improve detection accuracy suggests its potential to effectively address the trade-off between real-time processing speed and diagnostic precision, a well-known challenge in clinical applications. Applying this preprocessing technique to optimized networks, such as RT-DETR R101 and YOLOv10-X, which have already undergone substantial computational reductions, holds potential for real-time diagnostic applications. These findings provide confidence that, with further optimization, our method could be feasibly integrated into clinical workflows, aiding in the accurate and timely diagnosis of coronary artery disease.

Additionally, to thoroughly assess our the efficacy of our approach from various imaging perspectives and to determine the optimal angle for analyzing coronary artery stenosis, we performed an in-depth analysis for each angle within the test dataset. This comprehensive review included segmenting the dataset and evaluating the performance of the top-performing YOLOv10-X model. Specifically, we measured three performance metrics: $AP_{50}(\%)$ for the raw images, and both $AP_{50}(\%)$ and $AP_{val}(\%)$ for the preprocessed images. The detailed results of these assessments are presented in Table 5:

Table 5. Performance of YOLOv10-X Model on Different Imaging Angles.

Imaging Angle	APval (%)	AP_{50}(%)	
	Preprocessed	Original	Preprocessed
LCA zero	55.8	85.0	90.5
LCA LAO	55.8	83.3	87.8
LCA RAO	54.0	83.9	88.3
RCA zero	51.3	81.1	85.2
RCA LAO	49.2	78.8	80.1
RCA RAO	51.7	80.7	84.6

These results indicate that the YOLOv10-X model consistently outperformed on preprocessed images compared to raw images across all imaging angles. Notably, the Imaging Angle LCA zero achieved the highest $AP_{50}(\%)$ on preprocessed data at 90.5 and the highest $AP_{val}(\%)$ at 55.8, suggesting that this angle may be the most suitable for coronary artery stenosis analysis.

4. Discussion

In this study, we investigated the advantages of employing a general HFV filter for enhancing vascular contrast and integrating image fusion to boost the precision of deep-learning-based stenosis detection in coronary angiography images. We also examined whether preprocessing the images would affect the latency of image processing. Furthermore, we assessed the impact of imaging angles on the efficiency of detecting coronary artery stenosis. The study involved training and evaluating seven deep learning models on both preprocessed and raw images. Compared to our previous work [16], our method demonstrates higher accuracy and a more comprehensive analysis of imaging angles, while [16] analyzed the effect of the preprocessing method by testing earlier versions of YOLO and R-FCN, we achieved better detection performance by using more advanced models such as YOLOv10 and RT-DETR. The increased annotations and more complex images have improved the robustness of our method. Furthermore, we tested real-time detection rather than limiting the analysis to image evaluation. In addition, our detailed analysis of different imaging angles provides valuable insights for clinical applications, which was not addressed in [16]. Our findings suggest that preprocessing methods incorporating HFV filtering and image fusion can boost the precision of deep learning models when analyzing intricate coronary angiography images, all while maintaining manageable training complexity. Nonetheless, it is crucial to acknowledge that HFV-filtered images might generate pseudo-vascular structures or inadequately enhance true vessels, which could result in misclassifications and false positives during both the training and detection phases. These results emphasize the importance of thoroughly assessing the scenarios in which the HFV filter can be optimally utilized for preprocessing. Therefore, it is crucial to ascertain whether the enhancement in visual quality compromises the accuracy of the images. This assessment lays the groundwork for further research in image processing.

The performance of the training model is highly influenced by the number of relevant features present in the images. To enhance the model's ability to identify stenosis features in coronary angiography images, we utilized image fusion with HFV filtering to better highlight vascular features, especially those related to stenosis in smaller vessels. This technique specifically tackled the challenge of feature loss after vascular enhancement and mitigated the issue of edge enhancement for small features induced by the filter. Our experimental results show that this approach significantly improves the detection efficiency of branch vessel stenosis in complex coronary angiography images. By enhancing vascular features through image fusion, we not only preserve the essential characteristics of the vessels but also reduce the noise and artifacts introduced by HFV filtering. Our research also sought to explore the potential effects of the proposed technique on feature learning. We meticulously and thoroughly assessed the enhancement in $AP_{50}(\%)$ achieved by our method, while also addressing dataset-related concerns such as class imbalance and the influence of dataset size on our findings. The outcomes reveal that neural networks exhibited superior performance when applied to preprocessed images as opposed to raw images.

Moreover, our study conducted a detailed examination of the impact of various imaging angles on the precision of detecting coronary artery stenosis. The findings from our experiments highlighted a significant observation: the accuracy of stenosis detection is markedly influenced by the imaging angle employed. Specifically, our study indicated that the detection outcomes for the three imaging angles associated with the Left Coronary Artery exhibited higher accuracy compared to those for the Right Coronary Artery. Remarkably, the $AP_{50}(\%)$ value peaked at the LCA zero angle. This notable discrepancy in detection accuracy between the two arterial segments points to an intriguing avenue for further scholarly exploration. This implies that future research aimed at improving the efficiency of coronary artery stenosis detection should consider the potential benefits of certain imaging angles. The enhanced accuracy observed at specific angles, especially for the LCA, highlights the crucial role of imaging angle in improving diagnostic accuracy.

Our study has several limitations that are worth discussing. These limitations involve various aspects of our research methods and dataset, each contributing to a more comprehensive understanding of the inherent constraints in our analysis. First, our dataset primarily includes typical angles used in coronary angiography. This selection is designed to imitate real-world clinical data collection scenarios but introduces specific challenges. Notably, coronary angiography images often feature intricate backgrounds and stenosis that is difficult to identify, which constrain the accuracy of deep learning models. The inclusion of these challenging images emphasizes the clinical and real-world variations faced in practice, indicating a need for additional research to enhance the model's robustness in such conditions. Second, despite the necessity of extracting key frames from coronary angiography video streams in our method, this process has inherent constraints. These challenges are especially pronounced when addressing branch vessels. The patient demographic for coronary angiography predominantly consists of elderly individuals, many of whom have surgical artifacts that often obscure the vessels. Furthermore, the dynamic movement of coronary blood flow makes it exceedingly difficult to acquire key frames that comprehensively portray the aorta and its branches. Consequently, this factor contributes to the relatively limited number of images available in our dataset. Third, although we have meticulously accounted for branch vessel stenosis, numerous instances still go unnoticed and unmarked. This oversight limits the model's proficiency in accurately detecting these branch vessel stenoses and including them in the output. This emphasizes an important area for future research, which could concentrate on improving the model's ability to precisely identify branch vessel stenosis in coronary angiography. Fourth, our experiment faces an issue with the uneven distribution of the dataset. This is primarily due to the presence of overlapping blood vessels in the three imaging angles of the RCA, making it challenging to find suitable images for marking and observing the stenosis locations. In the future, we aim to address the dataset imbalance issue in this experiment by increasing the dataset size and supplementing as many RCA images as possible. Fifth, during the preprocessing stage, we did not deliberately account for variations in image attributes such as brightness. This might have had some impact on the experimental results. We will consider these issues in our future experiments.

These challenges highlight the urgent need for ongoing research to overcome these barriers and enhance our methodology. By focusing on resolving these issues, we can progress toward establishing a more reliable and clinically viable system for detecting coronary artery stenosis. Additionally, the challenges associated with obtaining comprehensive and representative key frames, as well as the complexities of annotating branch vessel stenosis, point to the need for more advanced techniques and larger, more diverse datasets. Future research could benefit from incorporating advanced image processing techniques, such as more sophisticated filtering and segmentation methods, as well as leveraging larger datasets with a wider range of clinical scenarios.

5. Conclusions

Overall, the implementation of the HFV filter in coronary angiography has notably enhanced the clarity of images, emphasizing vascular details while minimizing noise in complicated imaging contexts. The image fusion technique has compensated for the feature loss encountered during the vascular enhancement phase. Experimental outcomes revealed that compared with the unprocessed images, training deep learning models on fusion images can generate an accuracy improvement of about 5% under the premise of less speed loss. Looking forward, it is crucial to increase both the volume and diversity of the dataset, particularly addressing any potential imbalances. Additionally, further development and refinement of existing networks are necessary to improve their ability to recognize stenotic features in complex coronary angiography images.

Author Contributions: Conceptualization, Y.L. and H.S.; Methodology, Y.L. and H.S.; Software, Y.L.; Validation, Y.L., T.Y., and Y.H.; Formal analysis, Y.L.; Investigation, Y.L.; Resources, H.S.; Data curation, Y.H.; Writing—original draft, Y.L.; Writing—review and editing, T.Y.; Visualization, Y.L.; Supervision, H.S.; Project administration, H.S.; Funding acquisition, Y.L. All authors have read and agreed to the published version of the manuscript.

Funding: This research was funded by JST, the establishment of university fellowships towards the creation of science technology innovation, Grant Number JPMJFS2101.

Institutional Review Board Statement: The study involving human participants was reviewed and approved by the Clinical Research Administration Center at Hokkaido University Hospital.

Informed Consent Statement: Informed consent was not obtained for this study, as it was a retrospective study. Accordingly, it is published on the institution's website (https://www.huhp.hokudai.ac.jp/date/rinsho-johokokai/etc_ika/ [accessed on 30 July 2024]) as an opt-out for information disclosure.

Data Availability Statement: The datasets generated and/or analyzed during the current study are available from the corresponding author upon reasonable request.

Conflicts of Interest: The authors declare that they have no competing interests that could influence the conduct or presentation of the work described in this manuscript.

Abbreviations

The following abbreviations are used in this manuscript:

CAD	Coronary artery disease
ICA	Invasive coronary angiography
CNNs	Convolutional neural networks
FFR	Fractional flow reserve
HFV	Hessian-based frangi vesselness
RCA	Right coronary artery
LCA	Left coronary artery
LAO	Left anterior oblique
RAO	Right coronary artery
IHS	Intensity–hue–saturation
RGB	Red–green–blue

R-FCN	Region-based fully convolutional networks
R-CNN	Region-based convolutional neural networks
FCN	Fully convolutional networks
RPN	Region proposal network
ResNet	Residual network
RoIs	Regions of interest
YOLO	You Only Look Once
NMS	Non-maximum suppression
VFL	Varifocal Loss
CIOU	Complete-IoU
DFL	Deep feature loss
PGI	Programmable gradient information
GELAN	General efficient layer aggregation network
TAL	Task alignment learning
RT-DETR	Real-Time Detection Transformer
DETR	Detection Transformer
AP	Average precision
TP	True positive
mAP	Mean average precision
IoU	Intersection over union

References

1. Cacciatore, S.; Spadafora, L.; Bernardi, M.; Galli, M.; Betti, M.; Perone, F.; Nicolaio, G.; Marzetti, E.; Martone, A.M.; Landi, F.; et al. Management of coronary artery disease in older adults: Recent advances and gaps in evidence. *J. Clin. Med.* **2023**, *12*, 523 [CrossRef] [PubMed]
2. Ullah, M.; Wahab, A.; Khan, S.U.; Zaman, U.; ur Rehman, K.; Hamayun, S.; Naeem, M.; Ali, H.; Riaz, T.; Saeed, S.; et al. Stent as a novel technology for coronary artery disease and their clinical manifestation. *Curr. Probl. Cardiol.* **2023**, *48*, 101415. [CrossRef] [PubMed]
3. Maurovich-Horvat, P.; Bosserdt, M.; Kofoed, K.F.; Rieckmann, N.; Benedek, T.; Donnelly, P.; Rodriguez-Palomares, J.; Erglis, A.; Štěchovský, C.; Šakalyte, G.; et al. CT or invasive coronary angiography in stable chest pain. *N. Engl. J. Med.* **2022**, *386*, 1591–160 [PubMed]
4. Schuijf, J.D.; Matheson, M.B.; Ostovaneh, M.R.; Arbab-Zadeh, A.; Kofoed, K.F.; Scholte, A.J.; Dewey, M.; Steveson, C.; Rochitte, C.E.; Yoshioka, K.; et al. Ischemia and no obstructive stenosis (INOCA) at CT angiography, CT myocardial perfusion, invasive coronary angiography, and SPECT: The CORE320 study. *Radiology* **2020**, *294*, 61–73. [CrossRef] [PubMed]
5. Zhang, H.; Mu, L.; Hu, S.; Nallamothu, B.K.; Lansky, A.J.; Xu, B.; Bouras, G.; Cohen, D.J.; Spertus, J.A.; Masoudi, F.A.; et a Comparison of physician visual assessment with quantitative coronary angiography in assessment of stenosis severity in China *JAMA Intern. Med.* **2018**, *178*, 239–247. [CrossRef]
6. Pang, K.; Ai, D.; Fang, H.; Fan, J.; Song, H.; Yang, J. Stenosis-DetNet: Sequence consistency-based stenosis detection for X-ray coronary angiography. *Comput. Med. Imaging Graph.* **2021**, *89*, 101900. [CrossRef]
7. Labrecque Langlais, É.; Corbin, D.; Tastet, O.; Hayek, A.; Doolub, G.; Mrad, S.; Tardif, J.C.; Tanguay, J.F.; Marquis-Gravel, G. Tison, G.H.; et al. Evaluation of stenoses using AI video models applied to coronary angiography. *NPJ Digit. Med.* **2024**, *7*, 138 [CrossRef]
8. Danilov, V.V.; Klyshnikov, K.Y.; Gerget, O.M.; Kutikhin, A.G.; Ganyukov, V.I.; Frangi, A.F.; Ovcharenko, E.A. Real-time coronary artery stenosis detection based on modern neural networks. *Sci. Rep.* **2021**, *11*, 7582. [CrossRef]
9. Rodrigues, D.L.; Menezes, M.N.; Pinto, F.J.; Oliveira, A.L. Automated detection of coronary artery stenosis in X-ray angiography using deep neural networks. *arXiv* **2021**, arXiv:2103.02969.
10. Arefinia, F.; Aria, M.; Rabiei, R.; Hosseini, A.; Ghaemian, A.; Roshanpoor, A. Non-invasive fractional flow reserve estimation using deep learning on intermediate left anterior descending coronary artery lesion angiography images. *Sci. Rep.* **2024**, *14*, 1818 [CrossRef]
11. Ovalle-Magallanes, E.; Avina-Cervantes, J.G.; Cruz-Aceves, I.; Ruiz-Pinales, J. Hybrid classical–quantum Convolutional Neural Network for stenosis detection in X-ray coronary angiography. *Expert Syst. Appl.* **2022**, *189*, 116112. [CrossRef]
12. Frangi, A.F.; Niessen, W.J.; Vincken, K.L.; Viergever, M.A. Multiscale vessel enhancement filtering. In Proceedings of the Medical Image Computing and Computer-Assisted Intervention—MICCAI'98: First International Conference, Cambridge, MA, USA 11–13 October 1998; Proceedings 1; Springer: Berlin, Germany, 1998; pp. 130–137.
13. Bi, R.; Dinish, U.; Goh, C.C.; Imai, T.; Moothanchery, M.; Li, X.; Kim, J.Y.; Jeon, S.; Pu, Y.; Kim, C.; et al. In vivo label-free functional photoacoustic monitoring of ischemic reperfusion. *J. Biophotonics* **2019**, *12*, e201800454. [CrossRef] [PubMed]
14. Huang, M.; Feng, C.; Zhao, D. An Improved Method of Blood Vessel Enhancement Based on Hessian Matrix. In Proceedings of the Fourth International Symposium on Image Computing and Digital Medicine, Shenyang, China, 5–7 December 2020; pp. 197–200.

. Orlova, A.; Sirotkina, M.; Smolina, E.; Elagin, V.; Kovalchuk, A.; Turchin, I.; Subochev, P. Raster-scan optoacoustic angiography of blood vessel development in colon cancer models. *Photoacoustics* **2019**, *13*, 25–32. [CrossRef] [PubMed]

. Li, Y.; Yoshimura, T.; Horima, Y.; Sugimori, H. A preprocessing method for coronary artery stenosis detection based on deep learning. *Algorithms* **2024**, *17*, 119. [CrossRef]

7. Wang, S.; Li, B.; Zhou, S. A segmentation method of coronary angiograms based on multi-scale filtering and region-growing. In Proceedings of the 2012 International Conference on Biomedical Engineering and Biotechnology, Macau, Macao, 28–30 May 2012; IEEE: Piscataway, NJ, USA, 2012; pp. 678–681.

8. Zhu, X.; Cheng, Z.; Wang, S.; Chen, X.; Lu, G. Coronary angiography image segmentation based on PSPNet. *Comput. Methods Programs Biomed.* **2021**, *200*, 105897. [CrossRef]

9. Zreik, M.; Van Hamersvelt, R.W.; Wolterink, J.M.; Leiner, T.; Viergever, M.A.; Išgum, I. A recurrent CNN for automatic detection and classification of coronary artery plaque and stenosis in coronary CT angiography. *IEEE Trans. Med. Imaging* **2018**, *38*, 1588–1598. [CrossRef]

0. Ovalle-Magallanes, E.; Avina-Cervantes, J.G.; Cruz-Aceves, I.; Ruiz-Pinales, J. Transfer learning for stenosis detection in X-ray coronary angiography. *Mathematics* **2020**, *8*, 1510. [CrossRef]

1. Avram, R.; Olgin, J.E.; Ahmed, Z.; Verreault-Julien, L.; Wan, A.; Barrios, J.; Abreau, S.; Wan, D.; Gonzalez, J.E.; Tardif, J.C.; et al. CathAI: Fully automated coronary angiography interpretation and stenosis estimation. *NPJ Digit. Med.* **2023**, *6*, 142. [CrossRef]

2. Isavand Rahmani, A.; Akbari, H.; Saraf Esmaili, S. Retinal blood vessel segmentation using gabor filter and morphological reconstruction. *Signal Process. Renew. Energy* **2020**, *4*, 77–88.

3. Qian, Y.; Wang, Z.; Chen, L.; Huang, Z. Vascular enhancement with structure preservation from noisy X-ray angiogram images by employing non-local Hessian-based filter. *Optik* **2021**, *232*, 166523. [CrossRef]

4. Chen, X.; Jiang, J.; Zhang, X. Automatic 3D coronary artery segmentation based on local region active contour model. *J. Thorac. Dis.* **2024**, *16*, 2563. [CrossRef] [PubMed]

5. Banerjee, R.; Ghose, A.; Mandana, K.M. A hybrid CNN-LSTM architecture for detection of coronary artery disease from ECG. In Proceedings of the 2020 International Joint Conference on Neural Networks (IJCNN), Glasgow, UK, 19–24 July 2020; IEEE: Piscataway, NJ, USA, 2020; pp. 1–8.

6. Wu, Y.; Qi, S.; Wang, M.; Zhao, S.; Pang, H.; Xu, J.; Bai, L.; Ren, H. Transformer-based 3D U-Net for pulmonary vessel segmentation and artery-vein separation from CT images. *Med. Biol. Eng. Comput.* **2023**, *61*, 2649–2663. [CrossRef] [PubMed]

7. Wang, G.; Zhou, P.; Gao, H.; Qin, Z.; Wang, S.; Sun, J.; Yu, H. Coronary vessel segmentation in coronary angiography with a multi-scale U-shaped transformer incorporating boundary aggregation and topology preservation. *Phys. Med. Biol.* **2024**, *69*, 025012. [CrossRef]

8. Wang, Q.; Xu, L.; Wang, L.; Yang, X.; Sun, Y.; Yang, B.; Greenwald, S.E. Automatic coronary artery segmentation of CCTA images using UNet with a local contextual transformer. *Front. Physiol.* **2023**, *14*, 1138257. [CrossRef] [PubMed]

9. Dai, J.; Li, Y.; He, K.; Sun, J. R-fcn: Object detection via region-based fully convolutional networks. *Adv. Neural Inf. Process. Syst.* **2016**, *29*.

0. Diwan, T.; Anirudh, G.; Tembhurne, J.V. Object detection using YOLO: Challenges, architectural successors, datasets and applications. *Multimed. Tools Appl.* **2023**, *82*, 9243–9275. [CrossRef] [PubMed]

1. Terven, J.; Córdova-Esparza, D.M.; Romero-González, J.A. A comprehensive review of yolo architectures in computer vision: From yolov1 to yolov8 and yolo-nas. *Mach. Learn. Knowl. Extr.* **2023**, *5*, 1680–1716. [CrossRef]

2. Wang, C.Y.; Yeh, I.H.; Liao, H.Y.M. YOLOv9: Learning What You Want to Learn Using Programmable Gradient Information. *arXiv* **2024**, arXiv:2402.13616.

3. Wang, A.; Chen, H.; Liu, L.; Chen, K.; Lin, Z.; Han, J.; Ding, G. Yolov10: Real-time end-to-end object detection. *arXiv* **2024**, arXiv:2405.14458.

4. Zhao, Y.; Lv, W.; Xu, S.; Wei, J.; Wang, G.; Dang, Q.; Liu, Y.; Chen, J. Detrs beat yolos on real-time object detection. In Proceedings of the IEEE/CVF Conference on Computer Vision and Pattern Recognition, Seattle, MA, USA, 17–21 June 2024; pp. 16965–16974.

5. Carion, N.; Massa, F.; Synnaeve, G.; Usunier, N.; Kirillov, A.; Zagoruyko, S. End-to-end object detection with transformers. In Proceedings of the European Conference on Computer Vision, Online, 23–28 August 2020; Springer: Berlin, Germany, 2020; pp. 213–229.

electronics

MDPI

Article

A Generative Approach for Document Enhancement with Smal Unpaired Data

Mohammad Shahab Uddin [1], Wael Khallouli [2], Andres Sousa-Poza [2], Samuel Kovacic [2] and Jiang Li [1,*]

[1] Department of Electrical and Computer Engineering, Old Dominion University, Norfolk, VA 23529, USA; muddi003@odu.edu

[2] Department of Engineering Management & Systems Engineering, Old Dominion University, Norfolk, VA 23529, USA; wkhallou@odu.edu (W.K.); asousapo@odu.edu (A.S.-P.); skovacic@odu.edu (S.K.)

* Correspondence: jli@odu.edu

Abstract: Shipbuilding drawings, crafted manually before the digital era, are vital for historical reference and technical insight. However, their digital versions, stored as scanned PDFs, often contain significant noise, making them unsuitable for use in modern CAD software like AutoCAD. Traditional denoising techniques struggle with the diverse and intense noise found in these documents, which also does not adhere to standard noise models. In this paper, we propose an innovative generative approach tailored for document enhancement, particularly focusing on shipbuilding drawings. For a small, unpaired dataset of clean and noisy shipbuilding drawing documents, we first learn to generate the noise in the dataset based on a CycleGAN model. We then generate multiple paired clean–noisy image pairs using the clean images in the dataset. Finally, we train a Pix2Pix GAN model with these generated image pairs to enhance shipbuilding drawings. Through empirical evaluation on a small Military Sealift Command (MSC) dataset, we demonstrated the superiority of our method in mitigating noise and preserving essential details, offering an effective solution for the restoration and utilization of historical shipbuilding drawings in contemporary digital environments.

Keywords: document enhancement; generative adversarial network; denoising; OCR; noise modeling

1. Introduction

Shipbuilding, one of the oldest industries known to humanity, traditionally relied on detailed drawings to guide construction processes before the advent of digital technology. Historically, these drawings were created by hand, making them not only invaluable for their technical accuracy but also as pieces of maritime heritage. However, with the rise of digital technologies, the shift from manual drafting to digital documents has become necessary, introducing several challenges, especially in the preservation and use of old drawings.

Scanned PDF documents, which serve as digital representations of these historical drawings, often suffer from inherent imperfections such as noise and artifacts introduced during the scanning process. These imperfections, compounded by the heavy and heterogeneous nature of the noise, render the documents unsuitable for seamless integration into modern computer-aided design (CAD) platforms like AutoCAD [1]. Traditional denoising methods, designed to mitigate noise in images adhering to well-defined noise models, prove ineffective when confronted with the complex noise structures present in scanned shipbuilding drawings [2–4].

The analysis of the noisy document images reveals that the noise is distinctly different from standard types like Gaussian and salt-and-pepper noise. In Figure 1, noisy image samples from the document show that the noise exhibits characteristics such as streaks, lines, or concentrated imperfections, unlike the random variations typical of Gaussian and salt-and-pepper noise. This suggests that the noise in Military Sealift Command (MSC) documents may stem from scanner artifacts, printer defects, or issues with the original document. Histogram analysis (Figure 1) further supports this distinction: the original noisy image's histogram is skewed towards higher intensity values, unlike the more spread-out Gaussian noise or the distinct spikes of salt-and-pepper noise. These visual and statistical differences confirm that the noise in our document images is unique and does not follow common noise models.

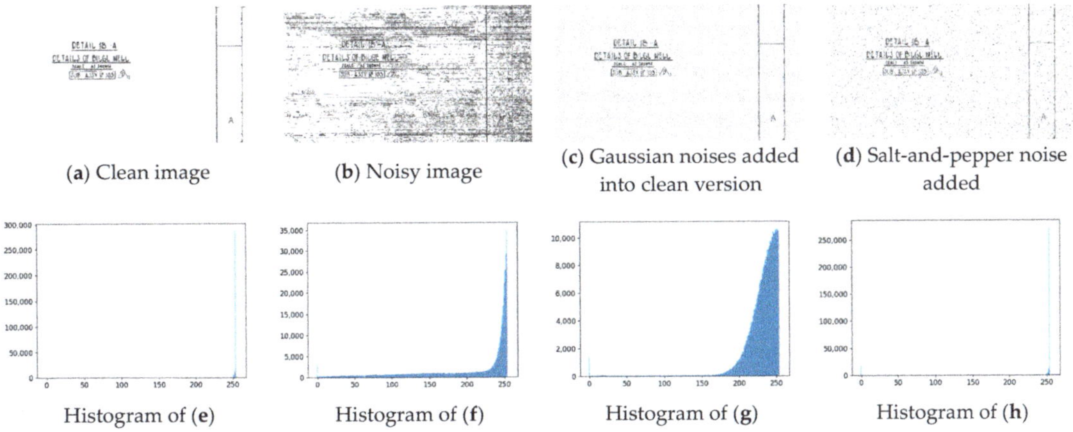

Figure 1. Comparison of different noises. The clean version of the MSC document image shown in (**a**) was obtained by manually removing the noise in (**b**). We created the noisy images (**c**,**d**) from the clean image using gaussian noise and salt-and-pepper noise. We excluded the histogram for pixels of value "255" for better visualization in (**e**–**h**).

To address these challenges, we developed a specialized document enhancement strategy designed specifically for shipbuilding drawings stored as scanned PDF files. Initially, for a small dataset of clean and noisy shipbuilding drawings that were not paired, we trained a CycleGAN model [5] to simulate the noise patterns found in these documents. Subsequently, we created pairs of clean and noisy images from the clean samples in the dataset using the trained CycleGAN model. We then proceeded to train a Pix2Pix GAN model [6] using these image pairs to improve the quality of the shipbuilding drawings. Our method's effectiveness was validated on a dataset from MSC, where it proved superior in reducing noise and retaining crucial details as compared to state-of-the-art methods.

2. Related Work

In this paper, we focus on document noise removal with the goal of preserving critical elements such as text, labels, and architectural details and eliminating scanning noise that cannot be modelled as common noise models such as Gaussian or salt-and-pepper noise. Regular image denoising is outside the scope of this paper. Our objective was to improve the readability and clarity of these documents without losing essential information. Document noise removal methods can be categorized into three groups: (1) traditional techniques that rely on basic image processing algorithms, (2) discriminative methods that employ machine learning models to classify and filter noise, and (3) generative approaches that use generative artificial intelligence (GAI) models to reconstruct clean images from noisy ones. Each of these methodologies offers unique advantages and challenges, which we summarize to highlight their contributions to the field of document image enhancement.

Traditional document denoising methods. Earlier work for document enhancement included global binarization, aiming to find a single threshold value for the entire document to eliminate those noise pixels, and local binarization, utilizing a dynamic threshold value for each pixel to classify image pixels into foreground (black) or background (white) [7,8]. Although thresholding methods continue to evolve, such as the global threshold selection method based on fuzzy expert systems (FESs) that enhance image contrast and use a pixel-counting algorithm for threshold adjustment [9], they are sensitive to document condition and often fail to clean highly degraded images [10]. To address this challenge, energy-based methods were introduced, such as maximizing ink presence with an energy function while minimizing the degraded background [11] and using mathematical morphology to estimate background from the degraded image [12]. However, these handcrafted image processing algorithms often yielded unsatisfactory results.

Discriminative methods. Recently, discriminative deep learning has been introduced for document denoising. In [13], a 2D long short-term memory (LSTM) network was used to determine whether something belonged to text or background noise based on a sequence of its neighboring pixels. A vision-transformer-based encoder–decoder architecture was proposed in [14] to perform document enhancement through similar discriminative analysis for each pixel. However, a significant drawback of discriminative approaches is their dependency on paired datasets comprising noisy and clean images for effective training. Acquiring such paired datasets can be challenging, particularly for historical or rare documents, which limits the scalability and applicability of discriminative techniques for document denoising. This dependency often necessitates extensive manual annotation, which is both time-consuming and resource-intensive, constraining the practical implementation of discriminative models for real-world scenarios.

Generative methods. The realm of image denoising continues to evolve with the introduction of generative models like generative adversarial networks (GANs) [15] and diffusion models [16], and these can be grouped as those requiring paired noisy–clean data for training [17–19], not requiring [20–22], or hybrid [23]. Those generative methods requiring paired datasets for training typically employ the conditional GAN (cGAN) network [24] to learn a transformation function from noisy image domain to clean image domain, and the denoising task is converted as domain conversion. Recently, a diffusion-based framework [25] was proposed for document enhancement and it can be categorized in this group. The main drawback of these methods is that they require large, paired datasets to achieve competitive performance, which are not always possible in practice. For those approaches not requiring paired datasets for training, they typically employ the CycleGAN model to convert noisy image as clean image and vice versa under unsupervised learning with the guidance of the cycle-consistent GAN loss [5]. Therefore, they only require non-paired clean and noisy images for training. However, the performance of these approaches is degraded and not always satisfactory. The representative hybrid method [23] combines the unpaired learning capabilities of CycleGAN [5] with the paired learning advantages of Pix2Pix GAN [6] to enhance document images. This model still needs a paired image dataset for training, and it does not perform well when the available paired dataset is small like our situation.

In this paper, to address the challenges of the hybrid model for document enhancement, we propose novel loss functions to improve the training efficiency of the CycleGAN model. Additionally, we utilized multiple versions of the trained CycleGAN model to generate paired clean and noisy images for supervised training of a Pix2Pix GAN model to remove scanning noise from MSC documents.

3. Proposed Method

The overall architecture of the proposed model is shown in Figure 2. It builds upon CycleGAN and Pix2Pix GAN architectures and includes three stages of learning for document image denoising. In the first stage, we train a modified CycleGAN model to learn the noise model using unpaired clean and noisy images. CycleGAN consists of two generators, G and F, and two discriminators, D_1 and D_2. Generator G converts clean images to noisy ones, while F does the opposite, and D_1 and D_2 perform adversarial learning in noisy and clean domains, respectively. During training, different versions of generator G are saved. In the second stage, we use the saved versions of G to generate different noisy images for each clean image in the dataset for data augmentation. These augmented data are paired clean–noisy images. Finally, we train a Pix2Pix GAN model with the paired augmented dataset for effective denoising. Additionally, we propose novel loss functions to modify the CycleGAN training, including gradient loss and noise loss. After training, the trained Pix2Pix GAN model is used for denoising.

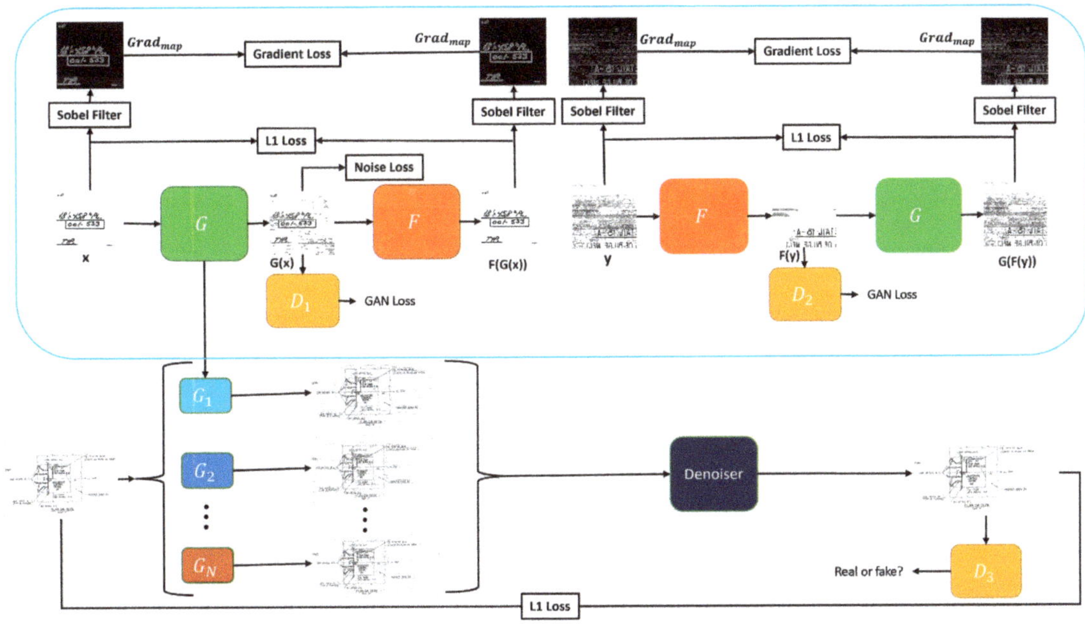

Figure 2. Overview of the proposed method. Blue boundary area shows our modified CycleGAN consisting of two generators, G and F, and two discriminators, D_1 and D_2. G generates noisy images from clean inputs while F reconstructs clean images from noisy ones. The model is trained using a combination of L1 loss, gradient loss, noise loss, and GAN loss. Discriminators D_1 and D_2 are employed to differentiate between real and generated noisy images, as well as real and generated clean images, respectively. The lower part is the data augmentation process using G from the modified CycleGAN and the training of the Pix2Pix GAN model.

3.1. Modified CycleGAN for Noise Model Learning

We begin by training a modified CycleGAN (upper part in Figure 2) with a collection of unpaired clean and noisy document images. This CycleGAN architecture consists of two generators (G and F) and two discriminators (D_1 and D_2). Generator G transforms clean images into noisy versions, mimicking the observed noise patterns in our dataset. Conversely, generator F aims to recover clean images from noisy inputs. We used the ResNet [26] architecture with nine residual blocks for the generators proposed in CycleGAN, implementing patch-based architecture for our discriminators as proposed in [27].

The training process employs a combination of L1 loss to ensure pixel-level similarity between input and recovered clean images, and a gradient loss to encourage realistic noise patterns generated by G. During training, D_1 differentiates between real noisy images and those generated by G, while D_2 distinguishes real clean images from F's outputs. We trained this part following the implementation of the CycleGAN with the GAN loss [6,15],

$$L_{GAN} = L_{GAN\_G}(G, D_1, X, Y) + L_{GAN\_F}(F, D_2, Y, X)$$

where *X*, *Y* are the domains of the clean and noisy images respectively. We also used the L1 loss between original unpaired clean and noisy images (*x*, *y*) and reconstructed images (*F*(*G*(*x*), *G*(*F*(*y*)) as proposed in [5],

$$L_{L1Loss} = |F(G(x)) - x|_1 + |G(F(y)) - y|_1$$

We found that there is a positive correlation between noise level and gradient magnitude. For example, a noisy image has a larger gradient magnitude than its clean version, as shown in Figure 3. We proposed a novel gradient loss to encourage the generators to focus on the noise during training since our goal is to learn the noise model for paired data augmentation. The gradient loss is calculated using the Sobel filter to extract gradient magnitudes from images. While this approach uses gradient magnitude like the existing image processing methods [28–32], we calculated the gradient loss focusing on the noises. Our focus was on its integration with other loss functions to enhance the overall performance during training the modified CycleGAN. The key difference lies in how we combine the gradient loss with other loss functions to optimize both perceptual quality and structural preservation, rather than relying on a single aspect of image quality. The combination of gradient loss with other losses in our framework contributes to the improved performance demonstrated in our results.

$$L_{Gradient\_Loss} = |Grad(F(G(x))) - Grad(x)|_1 + |Grad(G(F(y))) - Grad(y)|_1$$

	Noisy	Clean
Image	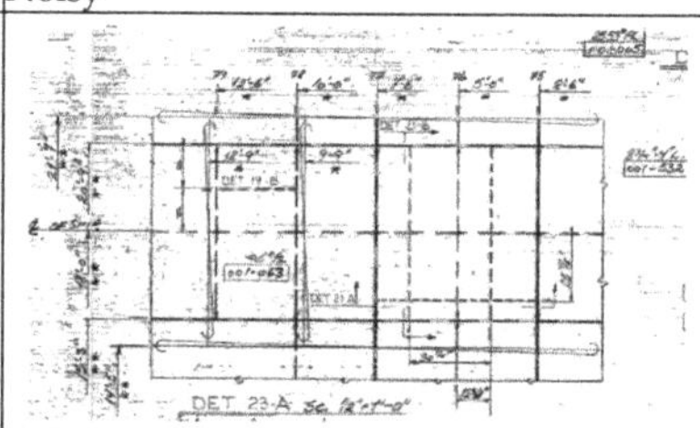	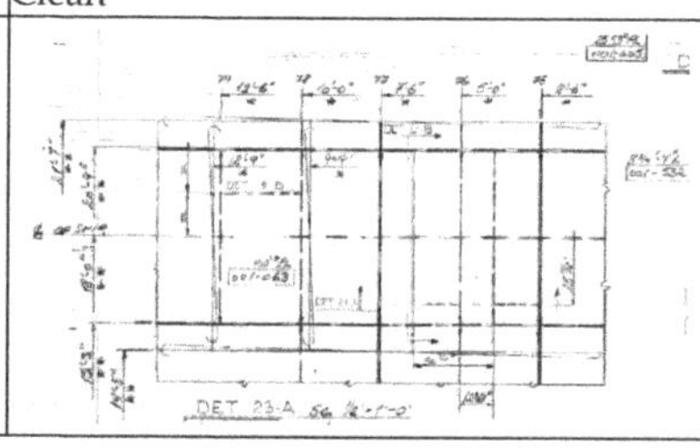
Gradient along x and y direction using Sobel operator	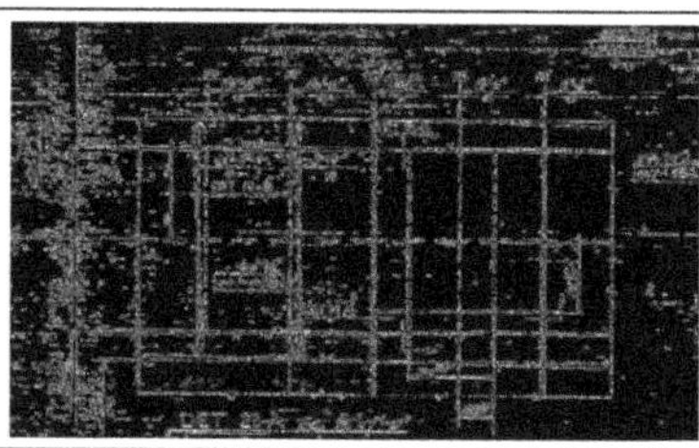	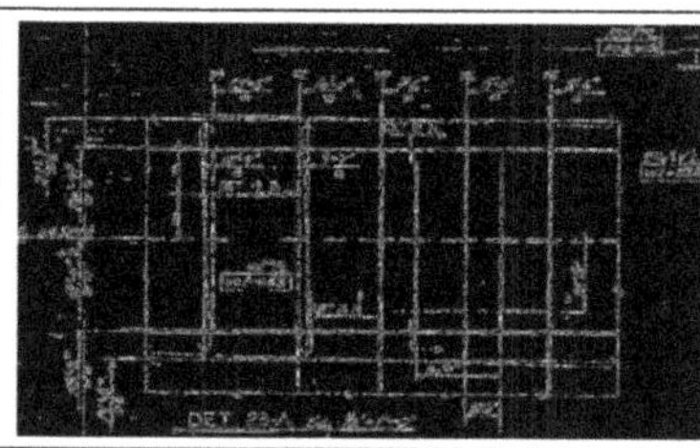
Gradient Magnitude	19.56	9.28

Figure 3. Positive correlation between gradient magnitude and noise level.

Here,

$$Grad(.) = \frac{1}{N}\sum_{N} Grad_{map}(p,q)$$

$$Grad_{map}(p,q) = \sqrt{G_{x-axis}(p,q) + G_{y-axis}(p,q)}$$

(*p*,*q*) is the location of a pixel in the gradient maps G_{x-axis} and G_{y-axis} generated by the Sobel filter from an image along the *x*-axis and *y*-axis, respectively. $Grad_{map}(p,q)$ represents gradient magnitude at (*p*,*q*) pixel location. N represents the number of pixels with gradient magnitude below the threshold. We considered only the gradient magnitudes below a certain threshold. This threshold is chosen to distinguish between noise and edges (where high gradients typically represent edges). During our experiments, we set 200 as the threshold value. So, $Grad(.)$ is the average of these low gradient magnitudes of an image.

As generator G is responsible for generating a noised version of a clean image, we impose a noise loss on the output of G. We calculated noise loss as the gradient magnitude of the output image,

$$L_{Noise_{loss}} = -Grad(G(x))$$

and the overall loss function for the modified CycleGAN model is

$$L_{m_{CycleGAN}} = L_{GAN} + \alpha_1 * L_{L1Loss} + \alpha_2 * L_{Gradient_{Loss}} + \alpha_3 * L_{Noise_{loss}}$$

where α_1, α_2, α_3 are hyperparameters combining the difference loss functions.

3.2. Paired Clean–Noisy Image Generation for Data Augmentation

To capture the variability of document noise, we checkpoint the model G at multiple stages during training, resulting in a collection of models G_ensemble = $\{G_1, G_2, ..., G_{20}\}$. Each G within the ensemble captures the noise characteristics at a specific point in training. After the training of the CycleGAN model, we utilize the G_ensemble to generate a diverse set of noisy variations for each clean image x in X as X_noise = $\{G_1(x), G_2(x), ..., G_N(x)\}$, which are then used in the subsequent Pix2Pix GAN training.

3.3. Training of Pix2Pix GAN for Denoising

The final stage employs a Pix2Pix GAN architecture as a denoiser trained on the newly created paired dataset of clean and noisy images generated in stage 2. This Pix2Pix GAN utilizes a single generator denoiser that maps noisy document images to their clean counterparts. A discriminator (D_3) guides the training process by distinguishing between real clean images and those produced by the denoiser. The architecture of the denoiser is similar to the architecture of G and F. Also, all the discriminators in our model have the same architecture of ResNet.

The GAN loss used for training D_3 is

$$L_{cGAN}(Denoiser, D_3) = \mathbb{E}_{x,y}[logD_3(x)] + \mathbb{E}_x[\log(1 - D_3(Denoiser(x\_noise))]$$

We also used L1 loss between target and output from the denoiser:

$$L_{L1\_loss\_denoiser} = \mathbb{E}_{x,G(x)}[|x - Denoiser(x_{noise})|_1]$$

and the overall loss for training the Pix2Pix GAN is

$$L_{second_{step}} = L_{cGAN}(Denoiser, D_3) + \beta * L_{L1_{loss_{denoiser}}}$$

where β is a hyperparameter combing the two loss functions.

3.4. Evaluation Metrics

Natural image quality evaluator (NIQE): NIQE [33] is a no-reference image quality assessment metric that measures the statistical naturalness of an image. It does so by comparing the visual characteristics of the denoised image to a model of natural images. Unlike traditional metrics that require a reference image for comparison, NIQE operates independently, making it ideal for evaluating referenceless denoised images. It provides a quantitative score that reflects the degree of distortion or unnaturalness in an image, helping to ensure that the denoising process maintains the intrinsic properties of natural scenes.

Ma score: The Ma score [34] is designed for evaluating the quality of super-resolved images without requiring reference images. To calculate the Ma score for an image, we need to extract three groups of statistical features: local frequency features, global frequency features, and spatial features. These features encompass the distribution of discrete cosine transform coefficients, wavelet coefficients, and the spatial discontinuity properties of pixel intensity. Ma score utilizes three regression forests to independently model each group of features. The outputs from these forests are then combined linearly to estimate the final perceptual quality score. Ma score demonstrates a strong correlation with subjective evaluations of visual quality in super-resolved images, providing an effective metric for assessing image enhancement results [35].

Perceptual Index (PI): PI [36] is a comprehensive metric used to evaluate the quality of denoised images without ground truth. It combines the NIQE and the Ma scores, offering a unified measure of perceived image quality. By integrating both objective and subjective assessments, PI provides a robust indicator of how natural and visually pleasing an image appears. This makes it particularly useful in scenarios where human visual perception is a critical factor in judging image quality, ensuring that denoised images meet the expected standards of visual appeal,

$$PI = \frac{1}{2}((10 - Ma) + NIQE)$$

Character error rate (CER): CER is an evaluation metric commonly used in optical character recognition (OCR) tasks, which can also be applied to denoised images. It measures the percentage of characters in the denoised image that are incorrectly recognized by an OCR system. This metric is crucial for assessing the functional quality of denoised images, especially in applications where text readability is important. A lower CER indicates better preservation of text information, signifying that the denoising process has effectively maintained the legibility of characters within the image.

$$CER = \frac{\text{Total number of substitutions} + \text{Total number of insertions} + \text{Total number of deletions}}{Total\ number\ of\ characters\ in\ ground\ truth}$$

Word error rate (WER): WER is another OCR-based metric used to evaluate the quality of denoised images by measuring the accuracy of word recognition. It calculates the percentage of words that are incorrectly transcribed by an OCR system. Similar to CER, WER is essential for determining how well the denoising process preserves the readability of text in images. A lower WER means that more words are correctly recognized, indicating higher functional fidelity of the denoised image. This metric is particularly valuable in contexts where the accuracy of text extraction is critical, such as document scanning and archival applications.

$$WER = \frac{\text{Total number of substitutions} + \text{Total number of insertions} + \text{Total number of deletions}}{Total\ number\ of\ words\ in\ ground\ truth}$$

4. Experiment Setup

4.1. Dataset

The main challenge in training our models was the limited data availability. We had seven documents from MSC with just one document containing noise in specific areas. Six documents had 12 pages in total and the remaining document had 9 pages with noises at some specific locations. We created a dataset of 16 noisy and 117 clean images cropped from these documents for training and testing. Since we had only one document with noises in some locations, we cropped 16 noisy images from it. For training, we utilized 10 noisy and 67 clean images. Figure 4 shows examples of clean and noisy samples from the training set. Using this unpaired dataset, we trained the modified CycleGAN. We then employed the modified CycleGAN to generate 80 noisy images for each of the remaining 50 clean images of the dataset, resulting in a total of 4000 noisy–clean pairs. We used these pairs to train the Pix2Pix GAN model-based denoiser for denoising. Finally, the remaining 6 noisy images were used to test the denoiser.

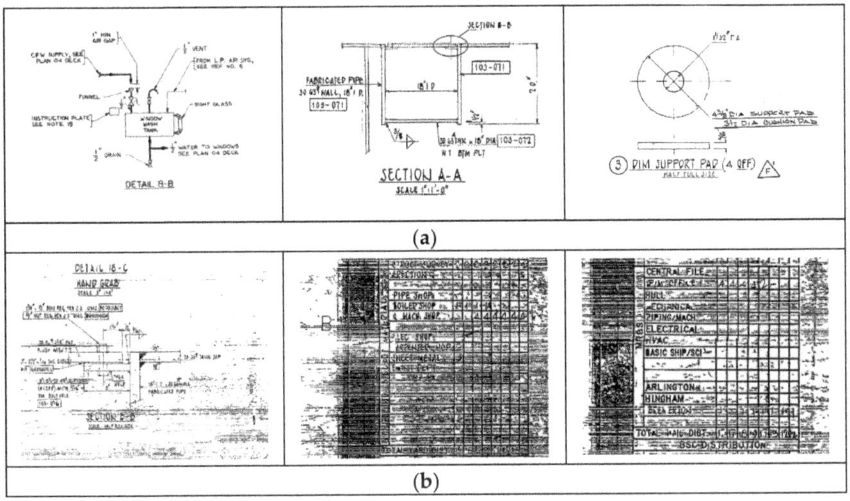

Figure 4. Image samples from training dataset. (**a**) Clean samples from training dataset; (**b**) noisy samples from training dataset.

4.2. Competing Methods

In our study, we compared our proposed method with three other prominent approaches for document noise removal: the CycleGAN model [5], the Otsu method [7], Sauvola's method [8], and a hybrid method [23] combining CycleGAN and Pix2Pix GAN.

CycleGAN [5] is an unsupervised learning approach that aims to learn mappings between two domains without paired examples. In the context of document noise removal, CycleGAN is used to transform noisy document images into clean ones and verse versa. In our proposed method, the basic CycleGAN model is also utilized in the first step to convert noisy images to clean ones.

The Otsu method [7] is a traditional image processing technique used for global binarization. It works by calculating a single global threshold value that minimizes the intra-class variance between the foreground and background pixels. This method is computationally efficient and straightforward to implement. However, its main drawback lies in its sensitivity to document conditions. For highly degraded or unevenly illuminated documents, the Otsu method often fails to accurately distinguish between text and noise, leading to significant loss of information and poor denoising performance. Its reliance on a single global threshold makes it unsuitable for complex noise patterns that vary across the document.

Sauvola's method [8] is an effective local thresholding technique for images with non-uniform backgrounds, particularly in text recognition applications. Rather than computing a single global threshold for the entire image, this approach calculates multiple thresholds for each pixel. These thresholds are determined using specific formulas that consider the mean and standard deviation within a local neighborhood, defined by a window centered on the pixel.

The hybrid method, mentioned in [23], combines CycleGAN and Pix2Pix GAN. In this approach, CycleGAN is first used to generate synthetic paired datasets from unpaired noisy and clean images. Each clean image just generates one clean–noisy image pair. Our proposed method builds on the hybrid approach, including CycleGAN and Pix2Pix GAN, by introducing novel loss functions and the generation of multiple clean–noisy image pairs for denoising.

4.3. Implementation Details

We trained our model in two stages. We first trained the generators G and F for 800 epochs using a constant learning rate of 0.008 and the Adam optimizer. We trained the modified CycleGAN following the training steps mentioned in the original CycleGAN paper [16]. After this training phase, we obtained multiple versions of G, which were subsequently used to generate multiple noisy versions of clean images. In the second stage, we trained the Pix2Pix GAN model with those generated image pairs for 500 epochs with a learning rate of 0.0002. During each training iteration, we used randomly cropped patches of size 256 $\times$ 256. We implemented our proposed model using the PyTorch framework [37] and performed the experiments on an Nvidia V100 GPU.

5. Results

5.1. Results of Noisy Data Generation

The trained generator G successfully created 80 distinct synthetic noisy images for each of the 50 clean images collected from the MSC document. Figure 5 shows seven noisy images generated for one clean image, where each noisy image has different noise characteristics.

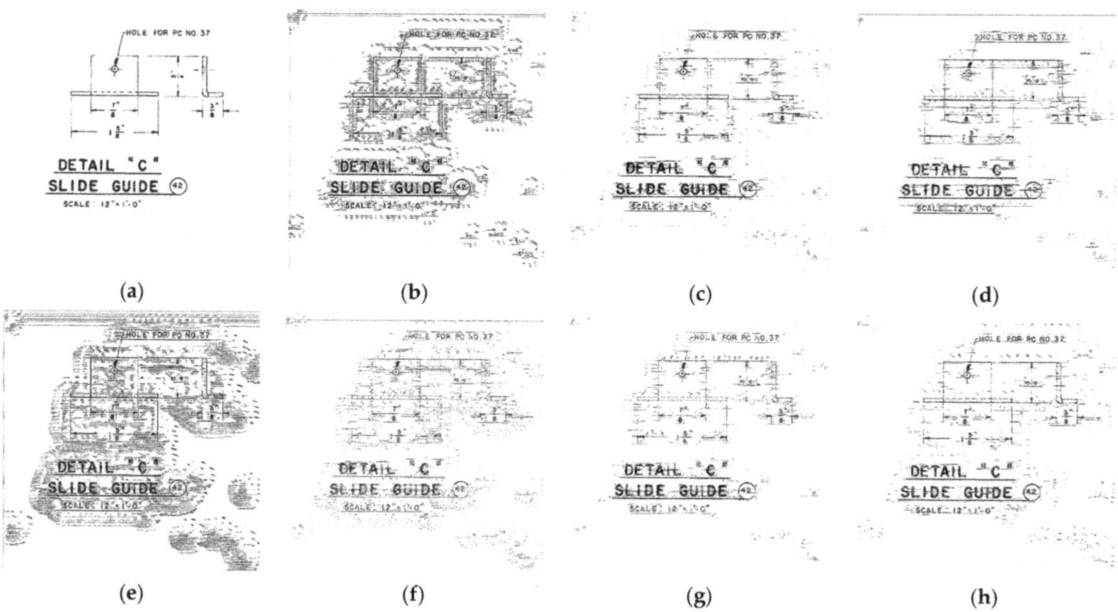

Figure 5. Synthetic noisy images. (**a**) Clean image. (**b–h**) Generated noisy images.

5.2. Visual Inspection of Denoised Images

Figure 6 shows four denoised images by the proposed method. It is evident that the denoised images exhibit remarkable improvements in visual clarity and text legibility. The enhanced documents demonstrate a notable reduction in noise levels, resulting in sharper text and clearer visual elements compared to their noisy counterparts. These qualitative observations highlight the efficacy of the proposed approach in achieving high-quality denoising results.

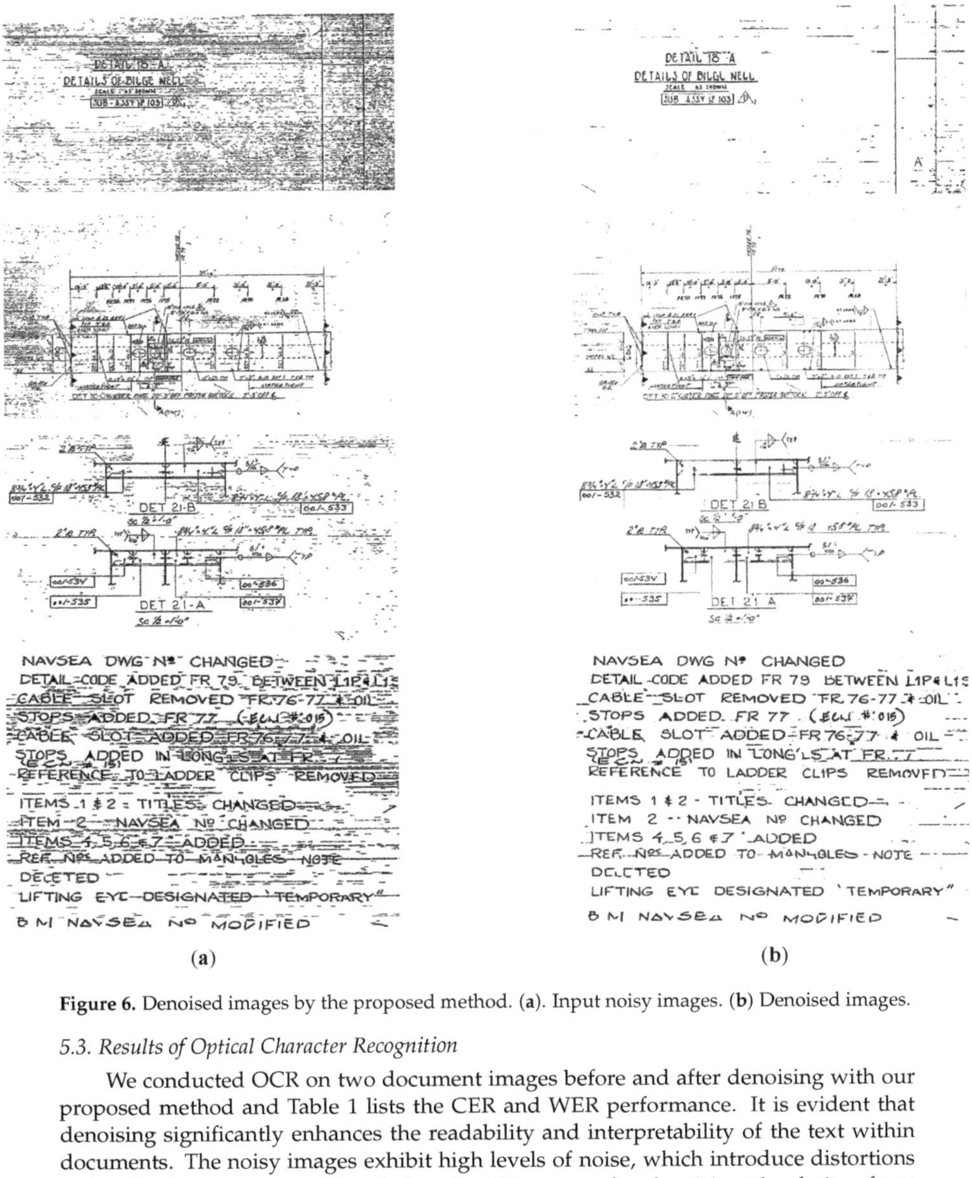

(a) (b)

Figure 6. Denoised images by the proposed method. (**a**). Input noisy images. (**b**) Denoised images.

5.3. Results of Optical Character Recognition

We conducted OCR on two document images before and after denoising with our proposed method and Table 1 lists the CER and WER performance. It is evident that denoising significantly enhances the readability and interpretability of the text within documents. The noisy images exhibit high levels of noise, which introduce distortions and make character recognition challenging. However, after denoising, the clarity of text is noticeably improved, with characters becoming more distinguishable and coherent. Quantitatively, the denoised images consistently demonstrate lower CER and WER values compared to their noisy counterparts, indicating improved accuracy in character and word recognition tasks. Overall, these findings emphasize the significant benefits of denoising in improving the performance of OCR systems.

Table 1. Effects of denoising on CER and WER. Our proposed method can remove the noise, keeping the text-related information intact.

Noisy	Clean
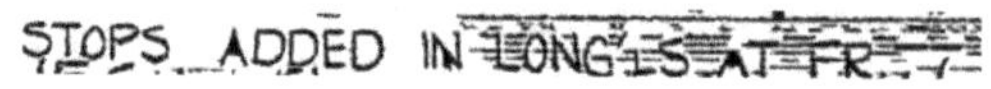	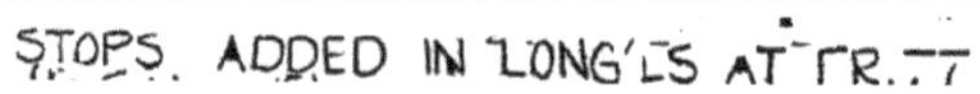
Ground Truth: STOPS ADDED IN LONG'LS AT FR 77 Prediction: STOPS ADDED IN LONG'S AT FR. CER: 12.9% WER: 42.9%	Ground Truth: STOPS ADDED IN LONG'LS AT FR 77 Prediction: STOPS ADDED IN LONG'LS AT FR IT CER: 9.7% WER: 28.6%

Ground Truth: LIFTING EYE DESIGNATED 'TEMPORARY" Prediction: LIFTING EYE DESIGNATED TEMPORARY" CER: 5.6% WER: 25.00%	Ground Truth: LIFTING EYE DESIGNATED 'TEMPORARY" Prediction: LIFTING EYE DESIGNATED 'TEMPORARY" CER: 0.0% WER: 0.0%

5.4. Results of Comparative Study

We applied the proposed method and other competing models to enhance document images and Figure 7 shows two example denoised images. Visual inspection of the different denoised images reveals that our proposed approach consistently produced denoised documents with sharper text and clearer visual elements compared to other models. In contrast, documents processed by methods such as CycleGAN, CycleGAN + Pix2Pix, Otsu, and Sauvola's method show varying degrees of residual noise, blurriness, and distortion, leading to reduced readability and visual clarity. Table 2 lists the four performance metrics of the four competing methods on the testing dataset. Our model consistently outperformed all the competing methods. With the lowest PI score, our model ensures superior perceptual image quality, maintaining fidelity and natural appearance in denoised documents. Additionally, its lower NIQE score indicates enhanced image quality compared to alternative approaches. Furthermore, it achieved the lowest CER and WER values, signifying superior accuracy in character and word recognition tasks.

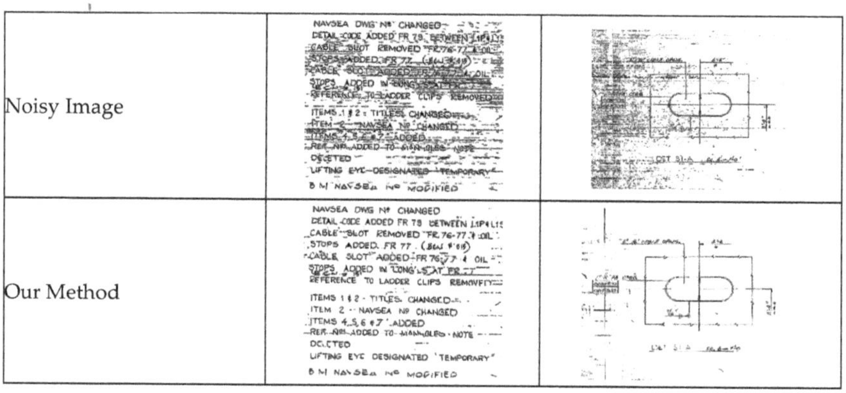

Figure 7. *Cont.*

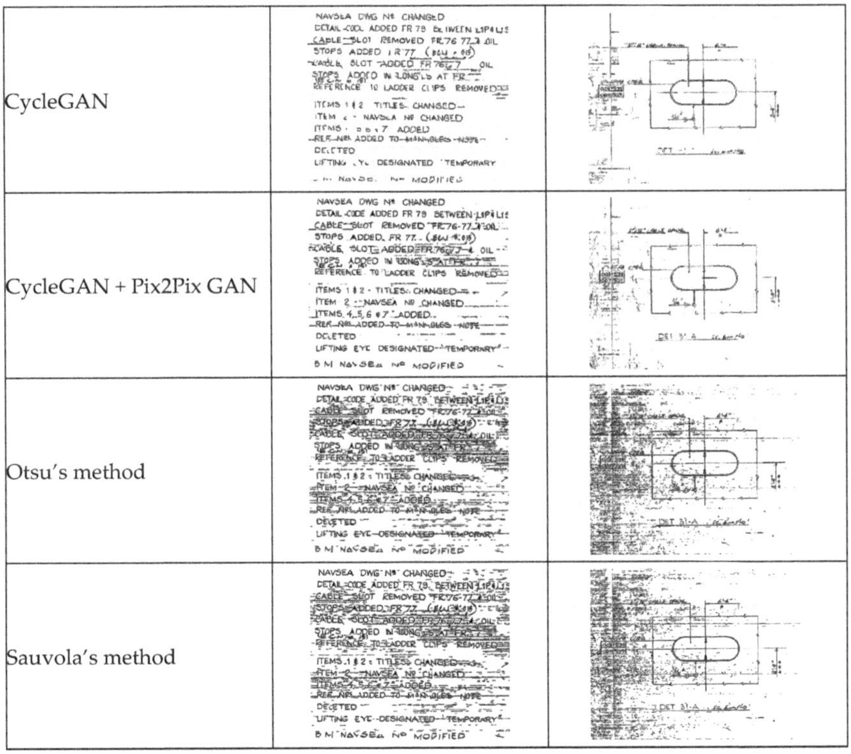

Figure 7. Denoising outputs from different methods. Our proposed method removed most of the noise without removing original structures and texts.

Table 2. Quantitative comparison.

	PI Score	NIQE	Ma Score	CER	WER
EnsembleDoc	6.92	10.77	6.93	0.1176	0.4327
CycleGAN	10.33	18.02	7.36	0.3492	0.7851
CycleGAN + Pix2Pix	7.49	11.64	6.66	0.1405	0.5506
Otsu's method	13.40	23.48	6.68	0.1673	0.5205
Sauvola's method	13.35	23.36	6.65	0.205	0.672
Noisy	8.10	13.01	6.81	0.1287	0.4789

5.5. Results of Ablation Study

Our proposed approach consists of several components including CycleGAN, two novel loss functions, Pix2Pix GAN, and ensemble data augmentation. In this ablation study, we investigated the contribution of each component in the ablation study and the results are listed in Table 3. The results showed that the ensemble augmentation is an important component and significantly improved the performance of the proposed model. Figure 8 shows some intermediate results obtained in the ablation study, and the ensemble data augmentation component improved the denoising results significantly.

Table 3. Performance of ablation study.

CycleGAN	Loss Functions	Pix2Pix GAN	Ensemble Augmentation	PI	NIQE	CER (%)	WER (%)
✓				10.33	18.02	34.92	78.51
✓		✓		7.49	11.64	14.05	55.06
✓	✓			8.44	13.85	27.66	57.41
✓	✓	✓		8.10	12.88	11.44	44.94
✓	✓	✓	✓	6.92	10.77	11.76	43.27

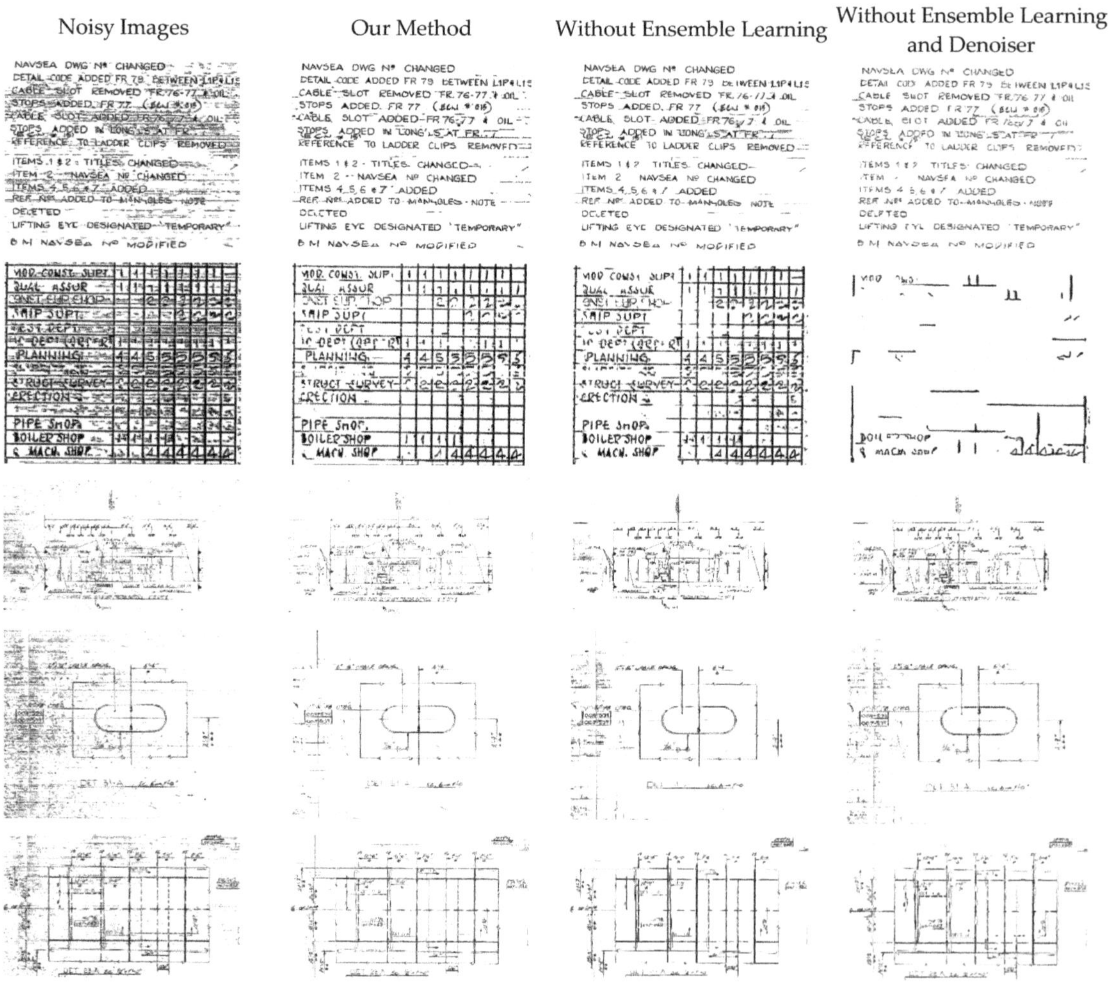

Figure 8. Results of ablation study of the proposed approach.

6. Discussion

The proposed approach combines the unpaired learning capabilities of CycleGAN with the paired learning strengths of Pix2Pix GAN using ensemble data augmentation. We compared the proposed model with a traditional document denoising algorithm, Otsu, a generative approach, CycleGAN, and a hybrid method, CycleGAN + Pix2Pix GAN, for document noise removal. CycleGAN relies solely on small unpaired data and performed poorly, with a PI Score of 10.33, NIQE of 18.02, Ma Score of 7.36, CER of 0.3492, and WER of 0.7851. The hybrid method showed improvements in denoising performance with a PI Score of 7.49, NIQE of 11.64, Ma Score of 6.66, CER of 0.1405, and WER of 0.5506. It was still worse than the proposed method due to the limited pairs of images generated for denoising. Otsu failed to remove the scanning noise in our document images, resulting in a PI Score of 13.40, NIQE of 23.48, Ma Score of 6.68, CER of 0.1673, and WER of 0.5205. Our proposed method achieved the best performance except for the Ma score.

The ensemble data augmentation strategy in the proposed model harnessed the collective knowledge of multiple noise models, leading to more robust and reliable denoising outcomes. For example, the PI score reduced from 7.49 to 6.92, NIQE reduced from 11.64 to 10.77, CER reduced from 0.1405 to 0.1176, and WER reduced from 0.5506 to 0.4327, as shown in Table 2. In practice, obtaining paired clean and noisy images is typically challenging, especially in our application, where historical or rare documents are involved. The proposed ensemble data augmentation technique is an innovative way to generate large-sized paired datasets for learning.

The proposed loss function also improved the denoising performance over the CycleGAN model alone as shown in the ablation study results shown in Table 2. For example, PI improved from 10.33 to 8.44, NIQE from 18.02 to 13.85, CER from 34.92% to 27.66%, and WER from 78.51% to 57.41%, with the new loss function being added for training. Visual inspection also demonstrated crisper text and improved overall visual clarity with the loss function.

Our study has limitations. First, the proposed model still requires unpaired image data for training, which may not always be available in sufficient quantities. Additionally, while our novel loss functions and data generation strategies improve training efficiency, there is still room for enhancing the model's adaptability to extremely diverse noise patterns and document conditions. Future work will focus on further refining the model, exploring more sophisticated generative architectures, and developing techniques to minimize the dependency on unpaired datasets, aiming for more robust and generalizable document noise removal solutions.

7. Conclusions

We proposed a generative AI model to remove scanning noise in engineering documents. The proposed model consists of two steps. In the first step, the CycleGAN model was utilized to train a set of models to convert clean images to different versions of noisy images using a set of unpaired clean and noisy images for training. In the second step, the generated image pairs were used to train a Pix2Pix GAN for noise removal. Additionally, a new loss function was developed to increase the performance of the model. Experimental results on engineering documents collected by MSC demonstrated remarkable performance in effectively suppressing noise while preserving crucial document details. These findings highlighted the potential of our proposed method to significantly improve document processing tasks, making it a valuable tool for various applications requiring high-quality document images.

Author Contributions: Conceptualization, J.L., A.S.-P. and S.K.; methodology, M.S.U. and J.L.; software, M.S.U. and W.K.; validation, M.S.U., J.L. and W.K.; formal analysis, M.S.U., J.L. and W.K.; investigation, M.S.U., J.L., W.K. and S.K.; resources, S.K. and A.S.-P.; data curation, M.S.U. and J.L.; writing—original draft preparation, M.S.U.; writing—review and editing, M.S.U. and J.L.; visualization, M.S.U. and J.L.; supervision, A.S.-P., S.K. and J.L.; project administration, S.K. and J.L.; funding acquisition, S.K. All authors have read and agreed to the published version of the manuscript.

Funding: This research is based upon work supported, in whole or in part, by the U.S. Navy's Military Sealift Command through CACI under sub-contract P000143798-3, project 500481-003.

Data Availability Statement: Data is publicly unavailable due to privacy restrictions.

Conflicts of Interest: The authors declare no conflict of interest.

References

1. *AutoCAD*, version 2022; Autodesk: San Rafael, CA, USA, 2022.
2. Khallouli, W.; Pamie-George, R.; Kovacic, S.; Sousa-Poza, A.; Canan, M.; Li, J. Leveraging Transfer Learning and GAN Models f OCR from Engineering Documents. In Proceedings of the 2022 IEEE World AI IoT Congress (AIIoT), Seattle, WA, USA, 6–9 Ju 2022; pp. 15–21. [CrossRef]
3. Uddin, M.S.; Pamie-George, R.; Wilkins, D.; Sousa-Poza, A.; Canan, M.; Kovacic, S.; Li, J. Ship Deck Segmentation in Engineerin Document Using Generative Adversarial Networks. In Proceedings of the 2022 IEEE World AI IoT Congress (AIIoT), Seattle, W USA, 6–9 June 2022; pp. 207–212. [CrossRef]
4. Sadri, N.; Desir, J.; Khallouli, W.; Uddin, M.S.; Kovacic, S.; Sousa-Poza, A.; Cannan, M.; Li, J. Image Enhancement for Improve OCR and Deck Segmentation in Shipbuilding Document Images. In Proceedings of the 2022 IEEE 13th Annual Ubiquitou Computing, Electronics & Mobile Communication Conference (UEMCON), New York, NY, USA, 26–29 October 2022; pp. 45–5
5. Zhu, J.Y.; Park, T.; Isola, P.; Efros, A.A. Unpaired image-to-image translation using cycle-consistent adversarial network In Proceedings of the 2017 IEEE International Conference on Computer Vision (ICCV), Venice, Italy, 22–29 October 201 pp. 2223–2232.
6. Isola, P.; Zhu, J.Y.; Zhou, T.; Efros, A.A. Image-to-image translation with conditional adversarial networks. In Proceedings of th 2017 IEEE Conference on Computer Vision and Pattern Recognition (CVPR), Honolulu, HI, USA, 21–26 July 2017; pp. 1125–113
7. Otsu, N. A threshold selection method from gray-level histograms. *IEEE Trans. SMC* **1979**, *9*, 62–66. [CrossRef]
8. Sauvola, J.; Pietikäinen, M. Adaptive document image binarization. *Pattern Recognit.* **2000**, *33*, 225–236. [CrossRef]
9. Annabestani, M.; Saadatmand-Tarzjan, M. A new threshold selection method based on fuzzy expert systems for separating te from the background of document images. *Iran. J. Sci. Technol. Trans. Electr. Eng.* **2019**, *43*, 219–231. [CrossRef]
10. Pratikakis, I.; Zagori, K.; Kaddas, P.; Gatos, B. ICFHR 2018 competition on handwritten document image binarization (H-DIBC 2018). In Proceedings of the 2018 16th International Conference on Frontiers in Handwriting Recognition (ICFHR), Niagara Fall NY, USA, 5–8 August 2018; pp. 489–493. [CrossRef]
11. Hedjam, R.; Cheriet, M.; Kalacska, M. Constrained energy maximization and self-referencing method for invisible ink detectio from multispectral historical document images. In Proceedings of the 2014 22nd International Conference on Pattern Recognitio (ICPR), Stockholm, Sweden, 24–28 August 2014; pp. 3026–3031.
12. Xiong, W.; Jia, X.; Xu, J.; Xiong, Z.; Liu, M.; Wang, J. Historical document image binarization using background estimation an energy minimization. In Proceedings of the 2018 24th International Conference on Pattern Recognition (ICPR), Beijing, Chin 20–24 August 2018; pp. 3716–3721.
13. Afzal, M.Z.; Pastor-Pellicer, J.; Shafait, F.; Breuel, T.M.; Dengel, A.; Liwicki, M. Document image binarization using lstm A sequence learning approach. In Proceedings of the 3rd International Workshop on Historical Document Imaging an Processing, Gammarth, Tunisia, 22 August 2015; pp. 79–84.
14. Souibgui, M.A.; Biswas, S.; Jemni, S.K.; Kessentini, Y.; Fornés, A.; Lladós, J.; Pal, U. Docentr: An end-to-end document imag enhancement transformer. In Proceedings of the 2022 26th International Conference on Pattern Recognition (ICPR), Montréa QC, Canada, 21–25 August 2022; pp. 1699–1705.
15. Goodfellow, I.; Pouget-Abadie, J.; Mirza, M.; Xu, B.; Warde-Farley, D.; Ozair, S.; Courville, A.; Bengio, Y. Generative adversaria nets. In *Advances in Neural Information Processing Systems;* Ghahramani, Z., Welling, M., Cortes, C., Lawrence, N.D., Weinberge K.Q., Eds.; Curran Associates, Inc.: Red Hook, NY, USA, 2014; pp. 2672–2680.
16. Croitoru, F.A.; Hondru, V.; Ionescu, R.T.; Shah, M. Diffusion models in vision: A survey. *IEEE Trans. Pattern Anal. Mach. Intel* **2023**, *45*, 10850–10869. [CrossRef] [PubMed]
17. Souibgui, M.A.; Kessentini, Y. De-gan: A conditional generative adversarial network for document enhancement. *IEEE Trans Pattern Anal. Mach. Intell.* **2020**, *44*, 1180–1191. [CrossRef] [PubMed]
18. Zhao, J.; Shi, C.; Jia, F.; Wang, Y.; Xiao, B. Document image binarization with cascaded generators of conditional generativ adversarial networks. *Pattern Recognit.* **2019**, *96*, 106968. [CrossRef]
19. Dang, Q.-V.; Lee, G.-S. Document image binarization with stroke boundary feature guided network. *IEEE Access* **2021**, *9* 36924–36936. [CrossRef]
20. Bhunia, A.K.; Bhunia, A.K.; Sain, A.; Roy, P.P. Improving document binarization via adversarial noise-texture augmentation In Proceedings of the 2019 IEEE International Conference on Image Processing (ICIP), Taipei, Taiwan, 22–25 September 2019 pp. 2721–2725.
21. Tamrin, M.O.; Ech-Cherif, M.E.-A.; Cheriet, M. A two-stage unsupervised deep learning framework for degradation remova in ancient documents. In *Pattern Recognition. ICPR International Workshops and Challenges, Proceedings of the ICPR Internationa Workshops and Challenges, Virtual, 10–15 January 2021*; Springer International Publishing: Berlin/Heidelberg, Germany, 2021 pp. 292–303.
22. Sharma, M.; Verma, A.; Vig, L. Learning to clean: A GAN perspective. In *Computer Vision—ACCV 2018, Proceedings of the 14th Asian Conference on Computer Vision (ACCV), Perth, Australia, 2–6 December 2018*; Springer: Berlin/Heidelberg, Germany, 2019 pp. 174–185. [CrossRef]

. Dutta, B.; Root, K.; Ullmann, I.; Wagner, F.; Mayr, M.; Seuret, M.; Thies, M.; Stromer, D.; Christlein, V.; Schür, J.; et al. Deep learning for terahertz image denoising in nondestructive historical document analysis. *Sci. Rep.* **2022**, *12*, 22554. [CrossRef] [PubMed]

. Mirza, M.; Osindero, S. Conditional generative adversarial nets. *arXiv* **2014**, arXiv:1411.1784.

. Yang, Z.; Liu, B.; Xiong, Y.; Yi, L.; Wu, G.; Tang, X.; Liu, Z.; Zhou, J.; Zhang, X. DocDiff: Document enhancement via residual diffusion models. In Proceedings of the 31st ACM International Conference on Multimedia, Ottawa, ON, Canada, 29 October–3 November 2023; pp. 2795–2806.

. He, K.; Zhang, X.; Ren, S.; Sun, J. Deep residual learning for image recognition. In Proceedings of the IEEE Conference on Computer Vision and Pattern Recognition (CVPR), Las Vegas, NV, USA, 27–30 June 2016; pp. 770–778.

7. Radford, A.; Metz, L.; Chintala, S. Unsupervised Representation Learning with Deep Convolutional Generative Adversarial Networks. *arXiv* **2015**, arXiv:1511.06434.

3. Yan, Q.; Xu, Y.; Yang, X.; Nguyen, T.Q. Single image superresolution based on gradient profile sharpness. *IEEE Trans. Image Process.* **2015**, *24*, 3187–3202. [PubMed]

). Liu, L.; Hua, Y.; Zhao, Q.; Huang, H.; Bovik, A.C. Blind image quality assessment by relative gradient statistics and adaboosting neural network. *Signal Process. Image Commun.* **2016**, *40*, 1–5. [CrossRef]

0. Zhu, J.; Wang, N. Image quality assessment by visual gradient similarity. *IEEE Trans. Image Process.* **2011**, *21*, 919–933. [PubMed]

1. Zhang, B.; Sander, P.V.; Bermak, A. Gradient magnitude similarity deviation on multiple scales for color image quality assessment. In Proceedings of the 2017 IEEE International Conference on Acoustics, Speech and Signal Processing (ICASSP), New Orleans, LA, USA, 5–9 March 2017; pp. 1253–1257.

2. Xue, W.; Zhang, L.; Mou, X.; Bovik, A.C. Gradient magnitude similarity deviation: A highly efficient perceptual image quality index. *IEEE Trans. Image Process.* **2013**, *23*, 684–695. [CrossRef] [PubMed]

3. Mittal, A.; Soundararajan, R.; Bovik, A.C. Making a "completely blind" image quality analyzer. *IEEE Signal Process. Lett.* **2012**, *20*, 209–212. [CrossRef]

4. Ma, C.; Yang, C.-Y.; Yang, X.; Yang, M.-H. Learning a no-reference quality metric for single-image super-resolution. *Comput. Vis. Image Underst.* **2017**, *158*, 1–16. [CrossRef]

5. Chen, H.; He, X.; Qing, L.; Wu, Y.; Ren, C.; Sheriff, R.E.; Zhu, C. Real-world single image super-resolution: A brief review. *Inf. Fusion* **2022**, *79*, 124–145. [CrossRef]

6. Blau, Y.; Mechrez, R.; Timofe, R.; Michaeli, T.; Zelnik-Manor, L. The 2018 PIRM challenge on perceptual image super-resolution. In *Computer Vision—ECCV 2018 Workshops, Proceedings of the European Conference on Computer Vision (ECCV), Munich, Germany, 8–14 September 2018*; Springer: Berlin/Heidelberg, Germany, 2019.

7. Paszke, A.; Gross, S.; Massa, F.; Lerer, A.; Bradbury, J.; Chanan, G.; Killeen, T.; Lin, Z.; Gimelshein, N.; Antiga, L.; et al. Pytorch: An imperative style, high-performance deep learning library. In Proceedings of the Advances in Neural Information Processing Processing Systems 32 (NeurIPS 2019), Vancouver, BC, Canada, 8–14 December 2019.

electronics

MDPI

Article

Temporally Coherent Video Cartoonization for Animation Scenery Generation

Gustavo Rayo and Ruben Tous *

Department of Computer Architecture, Universitat Politecnica de Catalunya, 08034 Barcelona, Spain; gustavo.enrique.rayo@estudiantat.upc.edu
* Correspondence: ruben.tous@upc.edu; Tel.: +34-934054044

Abstract: The automatic transformation of short background videos from real scenarios into other forms with a visually pleasing style, like those used in cartoons, holds application in various domains. These include animated films, video games, advertisements, and many other areas that involve visual content creation. A method or tool that can perform this task would inspire, facilitate, and streamline the work of artists and people who produce this type of content. This work proposes a method that integrates multiple components to translate short background videos into other forms that contain a particular style. We apply a fine-tuned latent diffusion model with an image-to-image setting, conditioned with the image edges (computed with holistically nested edge detection) and CLIP-generated prompts to translate the keyframes from a source video, ensuring content preservation. To maintain temporal coherence, the keyframes are translated into grids and the style is interpolated with an example-based style propagation algorithm. We quantitatively assess the content preservation and temporal coherence using CLIP-based metrics over a new dataset of 20 videos translated into three distinct styles.

Keywords: diffusion probabilistic models; deep learning; animation; generative models; video stylization; video cartoonization; video translation; computer graphics

1. Introduction

There is a constant demand for the creation of new and visually captivating content in terms of images and videos. Cartoon-based videos have been an effective means of communication and entertainment, not only for children but also for people of all ages. However, the creative process has traditionally relied on the skill and creativity of artists, requiring a great deal of manual work. One common task where artists have to invest a significant amount of time is in the creation of assets such as animated backgrounds, which are usually inspired by real scenarios to provide a sense of realism and infuse cultural and geographical context. Their application extends beyond animated films; they could also be used in other areas, such as video games, advertisements, and even educational content.

Recent advances in Artificial Intelligence (AI) have revealed the possibility of automating this process to some extent. The latest progress in conditional generative models offers a promising approach to addressing this issue. Generative models such as GANs have produced impressive results in different tasks, such as style transfer [1], image-to-image translation [2,3], and even in video-to-video translation [4,5]. However, GANs are difficult to train and struggle to capture the full data distribution [6]. More recently, diffusion models [7] have gained popularity and can also be used in many tasks similar to GANs.

Motivated by the demand for tools in visual content creation and the great capabilities demonstrated by diffusion models in image generation, in this work, we extend the use of text-to-image diffusion models for video cartoonization. Concretely, we apply a fine-tuned Stable Diffusion [8] model with an image-to-image setting, conditioned with the image edges (computed with holistically nested edge detection [9]) and CLIP-generated [10] prompts to translate the keyframes from a source video, ensuring content preservation. To maintain temporal coherence, the keyframes are translated into grids and the style is interpolated with the example-based style propagation algorithm from [11] (see Figure 1 for an example). The experiments on a new video dataset demonstrate the effectiveness of the method and the capability of producing temporally coherent videos while maintaining the semantic information. Our contributions include the following:

- A zero-shot method capable of translating short videos into clips with a specified style.
- A new video dataset of backgrounds without people with different camera movements and various landscapes for reproducibility and benchmarking purposes. It is available in the project repository (https://github.com/gustavorayo/video-to-cartoon (accessed on 26 July 2024)).
- A fine-tuned model with the style of Ryo Takemasa, a Japanese illustrator, that can be used to generate images in his style or integrated with other methods that use text-to-image diffusion models. The model is accessible at Huggingface: https://huggingface.co/gustavorayo/ryo-takemasa-v1 (accessed on 26 July 2024).

Figure 1. Frames from source videos and translated videos using the proposed method, featuring the three selected styles: Ryo Takemasa, Studio Ghibli, and Van Gogh. The original frames are shown on the left and top of each style, while the corresponding translated frames are displayed on the right and bottom.

2. Related Work

The general objective of video stylization is to apply a (typically artistic) style to a (typically live action) video while preserving its underlying structure and semantics. There are different variants of this problem, leading to different research lines. The style can be derived from a single independent image (style transfer), propagated from some hand-stylized frames (style propagation), specified through text prompts, or learned from a corpus of images. Here, we focus on the latter approach, which intersects with broader research topics like image-to-image translation, video-to-video translation (also known as translation-based video synthesis), and video editing. The recent success of generative models in image synthesis has established them as the foundational technique for the majority of the methods in the field. The first generative methods to achieve satisfactory results in transforming photos of real-world scenes into cartoon-style images were based on conditional generative adversarial networks, such as CartoonGAN [3], AnimeGAN [12], and the work presented in [13]. Recently, these methods have been outperformed by those based on diffusion models. Pure image-to-image translation methods using diffusion models, like SR3 [14] and Palette [15], operate in a supervised setup, which requires ground truth pairs of images (original and target), making them suitable for tasks like super-resolution or colorization but not for artistic stylization. Therefore, text-to-image diffusion models (e.g., Stable Diffusion [8,16]) are adapted for image-to-image translation using techniques such as SDEdit [17] or ControlNet [18].

2.1. Text-to-Video with Diffusion Models

Most of the video generation methods that use diffusion models are conditioned on text (text-to-video), where a description is provided and the model generates the video based on it. Due to the complexity of training a model to generate videos, many approaches used previously pre-trained text-to-image models with some modifications to enforce temporal consistency.

AnimateDiff [19] and Text2Video-Zero [20] are two recent methods capable of generating videos in some style based on a text description. AnimateDiff [19] extends the personalized text-to-image (T2I) diffusion models based on Stable Diffusion (SD) [8] and converts them into an animation generator. It uses a motion modeling module that is inserted between the pre-trained image layers of a base T2I model and is trained with video clips. During training, the weights of the base T2I models are frozen and only the weights of the module are updated. During inference, the trained module can be used with T2I models fine-tuned with techniques such as DreamBooth or LoRA. This flexibility enables generating animated images with a specific style based on just a text description. Text2Video-Zero [20] exploits the synthesis power of Stable Diffusion (SD) to generate videos. Text2Video-Zero requires as an input a text description and an integer m representing the number of frames. To keep the global scene consistent, the method enriches the latent codes of the generated frames with motion dynamics and implements a cross-frame attention mechanism to preserve the appearance and identity of the foreground object.

While diffusion models have become the de facto approach for generating high-resolution images and videos from natural language inputs, their significant computational costs and long sampling times have driven research into more efficient training methods and faster sampling techniques. One promising path includes Rectified Flow Models [21], a recent generative model formulation. These models create a transport map between two distributions using an ordinary differential equation (ODE), which can be faster to simulate compared to the probability flow ODE in diffusion models. Rectified Flow Models have recently been successfully applied to high-resolution text-to-image synthesis in [16].

Although text-to-video approaches can produce videos with a specific style, they cannot be used in situations requiring specific content and controlled movements. In such cases, it becomes necessary to use a reference video that can be transformed into another video with a new style.

2.2. Video Editing with Diffusion Models

An alternative way to transform a video into a cartoon is by using approaches for video editions. While these models are typically used for making local changes like modifying the attributes of an object, some of them, such as Pix2Video [22], Tune-A-Video [23], and Vid2vid-zero [24], enable global editions including style changes. Consequently, this facilitates the transformation of a video into a cartoon.

Pix2Video [22] takes a sequence of frames of a video clip and generates a new set of images that reflect an edit denoted by a target text. It is built on a Stable Diffusion model conditioned on depth. Pix2Video injects the features obtained from the first frame (anchor frame) and the previous frame by manipulating the self-attention module of the U-Net [25] network. The previous frame preserves the appearance changes and the anchor frame avoids the forgetting behavior on longer sequences. Additionally, to improve the temporal stability, during the first 25 denoising steps, they use noise correction so that the previous and current frames are as similar as possible.

Tune-A-Video [23] extends and fine-tunes Stable Diffusion with a single video to learn the motions of the video. Then, at inference, it can generate novel videos that represent the edits in text prompts, including changes in the style. The modifications involve changing the 2D convolution layers in the U-Net [25] for pseudo-3D convolution layers and extending the spatial self-attention mechanism to the spatial temporal domain. It uses a sparse version of a causal attention mechanism, where the attention matrix is computed using the latent features of the current frame, previous frame, and first frame. This method has the disadvantage of requiring tuning the model for every video.

Vid2vid-zero [24] requires a sequence of frames and two texts, one with the description of the video and the other with the description of the desired video. Vid2vid-zero first inverses each frame in the input video to obtain the latent noise and null-text embedding and then generates the edited video under cross-attention guidance. For temporal modeling, the pre-trained self-attention in the original U-Net [25] blocks is replaced with cross-frame attention that shares the same weights. Aside from the specific changes in the video, this method can also translate a video into a new style by specifying it in the target prompt.

2.3. Video-to-Video Translation

Alternatives for the direct translation of videos into another style are also available. A recent method is Rerender a video [26], a zero-shot text-guided video-to-video translation that divides the translation process into two parts. In the first part, an adapted diffusion model is used to translate the keyframes into a new style, and then, in the second part, the keyframes are propagated to the rest of the frames.

For keyframe translation, Rerender a video replaces the self-attention layers of the U-Net [25] with cross-frame attention layers. The Key K and Value V of the attention are generated using the first and previous frames. Additionally, to constrain the cross-frame to the local shape and texture consistency, optical flow is used to warp and fuse the latent features in the initial steps. In the middle steps, the previous frames are warped and encoded back to the latent space for fusion. Finally, in the late steps, adaptative instance normalization (AdaIN) is applied to keep the color style coherent throughout all the keyframes. In the second part, a patch-based frame interpolation algorithm is employed that uses color, positional, edge, and temporal guidance for dense correspondence prediction. This model yields good results but comes with a high computational cost, requiring over 24 GB of vRAM.

Another alternative for transforming a video into a cartoon is by using tools such as TemporalKit [27]. TemporalKit serves as an extension for the Stable Diffusion web UI, a browser interface that enables image generation or translation through base Stable Diffusion (SD) or personalized models. This extension adds a new tab to the UI, where users can upload a video and specify the parameters to form a grid image with keyframes. By using the capabilities of Stable Diffusion web UI, users can translate the grid image. The resulting image along with the frames of the video are used by TemporalKit to prepare a folder structure ready to be used by EbSynth Beta, a tool that uses example-based video stylization to propagate the style to the rest of the frames. The disadvantage of TemporalKit is that the process is mostly manual and the translation of the keyframes depends on the knowledge of the user.

3. Methods

Our approach involves a two-stage process. Initially, we select specific keyframes from the source video and translate them into a distinct style during the first stage. The subsequent stage involves propagating the style to the rest of frames using the algorithm from [11]. The method pipeline is illustrated in Figure 2 and described in more detail in the following subsections.

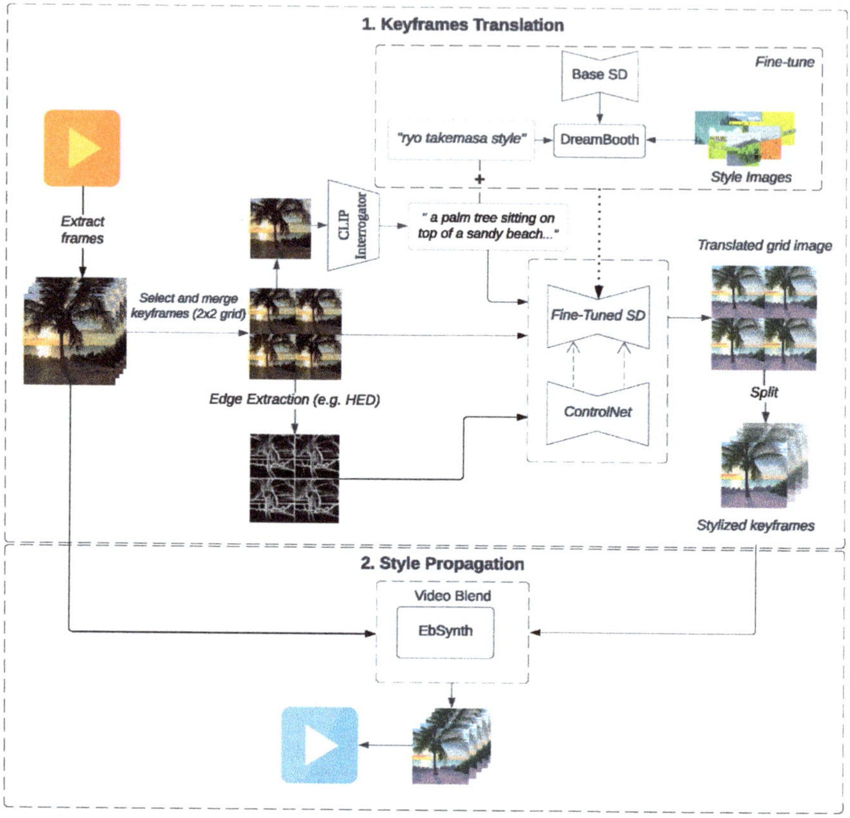

Figure 2. Method pipeline. The process is divided into two main stages: keyframe translation and style propagation executed sequentially as a pipeline. They are represented in dashed boxes as well as their respective subprocesses. In the first stage, four keyframes are selected from the video and combined into a single grid image, which is used for edge extraction. One of the keyframes is used to extract a description using CLIP Interrogator [28]. The resulting description is used to form the final prompt by combining it with the keywords that identify the style in the fine-tuned model (the "+" symbol represents the text concatenation). This prompt, along with the edge map and the grid image, are passed to a subprocess to generate a translated grid image. This subprocess integrates the fine-tuned version of Stable Diffusion (SD) with ControlNet, which conditions the image generation as indicated by the dashed arrows. The resulting translated image is then separated to form the stylized keyframes, which are used in the second stage. In the style propagation stage, the stylized keyframes serve as a reference to propagate the style to the original video frames using EbSynth [11]. The resulting stylized frames are used to create the final cartoonized video. In this figure, solid arrows represent the main flow of data through the process. The dotted arrow indicates that the fine-tuned SD results from the fine-tuning subprocess.

3.1. *Keyframe Translation*

The keyframe translation requires a fine-tuned Stable Diffusion model with the desired style. The model must be fine-tuned with Dreambooth [29], a fine-tuning approach that implants the style and an identifier into a base Stable Diffusion model. Dreambooth is a common approach, and we can find fine-tuned models with different styles on platforms like HuggingFace or Civitai.

Once we have a fine-tuned Stable Diffusion model with the desired style, we can proceed with the frame translation. Stable Diffusion enables image generation guided by text (text-to-image) or based on an image (image-to-image). In our case, we want to keep the structure of the frames and change only the style, so we condition the generation on the source frame using image-to-image translation.

The method begins by extracting the frames from the video and translating keyframes into frames with the intended style. A naive approach could be to translate every keyframe using only the identifier of the style in the fine-tuned model. However, this would lead to significant differences in the translated frames. To mitigate this problem and make the process automatic, we employ a more advanced approach. First, we extract the description of one of the keyframes using CLIP Interrogator, a prompt engineering tool that combines CLIP and BLIP [30] to optimize text prompts that match a given image. The identifier and description are then concatenated and used as a prompt in the fine-tuned version of Stable Diffusion.

Translating the frames independently produces noticeable differences between the frames because the model is not aware of the information in the previous and future frames. To mitigate this problem, other methods such as Pix2Video [22] manipulate the self-attention module of the U-Net network to use features from an anchor frame (first) and previous frame. In our case, we follow a different approach. We select four keyframes within an interval and combine those frames in a grid (2×2) to form a single image in the same way as TemporalKit [27]. The interval is calculated by dividing the total number of frames by three and rounding down to the nearest integer. More frames can be used to form the grid, which may be necessary in videos with large motion to achieve better results, but it requires more computing resources. Using a grid will ensure that the resulting frames are consistent and contain the general features present in the video. The grid size dictates how many frames need to be generated by the generative model versus the style propagation algorithm. Due to the constraints of style propagation, the grid size also sets the maximum video length that can be processed. A larger grid enables the processing of longer videos or videos with rapid structural changes that surpass the abilities of style propagation.

For better preservation of the structure, we add additional conditions using ControlNet [18]. ControlNet allows different conditions for controlling the generation or translation of images (e.g., human pose, segmentation maps, and edges). In our case, the videos consist of landscapes without people, so we use conditions based on edges, which effectively captures the shapes and boundaries. Conditions based on human pose would be more appropriate in clips featuring people. Two common alternatives are Canny edges and HED edges. While either alternative could be used, we selected HED edges for our implementation. The edges are extracted from the grid image.

The grid image, the edges, and the prompt are provided to the fine-tuned model, which produces a stylized image with the same dimensions as the original image. The resulting image is then separated to obtain stylized keyframes. These keyframes are then used to propagate the style to the rest of the frames in the next stage.

3.2. Style Propagation

To make the process faster and improve the temporal coherence, our method uses EbSynth [11], an example-based method for video stylization with a focus on preserving the visual quality of the style, reflecting structural changes and maintaining temporal coherence. It does not rely on neural networks. Instead, it uses an implementation of a non-parametric texture synthesis algorithm.

EbSynth could be used to propagate the style to multiple frames using only a single reference keyframe (basic stylization), but it also enables a more advanced stylization requiring some guidance channels (edge, temporal, and positions) for better style propagation. These guidance channels must be generated separately and provided as arguments. For this reason, we compute the guidance channels following the approach of [26].

The advanced stylization is performed in sequences using a forward pass and a backward pass. A sequence corresponds to the frames between two stylized keyframes. In the forward pass, three guiding channels (G_{temp}, G_{edge}, and G_{pos}) are generated as described in [11] and the style is propagated to the frames in the sequence using the starting keyframe. In the backward pass, different guiding channels are generated and the style is propagated using the keyframe from the end of the sequence. This process produces two separate stylized sequences. Then, each corresponding frame from these sequences is blended to produce the final stylized frames. With 4 keyframes, the process has to be performed three times. The final step is to transform the stylized frames into the new video.

4. Datasets and Style Models

We use two datasets: one composed of images for fine-tuning Stable Diffusion with a custom style and a second dataset consisting of videos to evaluate the results of the method. For fine-tuning Stable Diffusion, we use 100 squared images of 512 pixels containing the Ryo Takemasa style. The video dataset consists of 20 videos extracted from Pexels (https://www.pexels.com/ (accessed on 26 July 2024)). The original dimensions of the videos are 950 × 540 pixels and vary in duration, ranging from 7 s for the shortest to 60 s for the longest. The video dataset is publicly available in the project repository. The videos encompass various camera movements and contain a variety of landscapes, including forests, mountains, roads, buildings, and more. For the experiments, we use only 90 frames center cropped to 512 pixels.

In relation to the style models, we use three distinct ones, each incorporating a different style. We fine-tune one based on the style of Ryo Takemasa, an illustrator based in Nagano, Japan. This model requires the token "ryo takemasa style" in the prompt to generate or translate images in this style. The other two models incorporate the styles of Ghibli Studio and Van Gogh. Both were available at HuggingFace. Ghibli Studio is a Japanese animation studio based in Koganei, Tokio. The model was trained on images from modern anime feature films and needs the token "ghibli style" in the prompts. The model with Van Gogh style was trained with screenshots from the movie Loving Vincent. It requires the token "lvngvncnt" in the prompt.

5. Experimental Setup

For the experiments, we use two environments: one for fine-tuning a Stable Diffusion model with the Ryo Takemasa style and the other for video cartoonization. The first consists of a server equipped with an NVIDIA T4 GPU with 15 GB of vRAM. We employ the Diffusers [31] library to fine-tune stable-diffusion-v1-5 using the DreamBooth technique. We fine-tune the U-Net [25] using 10,000 training steps and a learning rate of 2×10^{-6}. The text encoder is trained for 450 steps with the same learning rate of 2×10^{-6}.

The second environment consists of a a server equipped with an NVIDIA V100 GPU with 16 GB of vRAM. Our code implementation is based on PyTorch [32], and the primary library used is Diffusers [31]. This library contains state-of-the-art diffusion pipelines for generating images, audio, and even 3D structures of molecules. In particular, we use three pipelines: StableDiffusionImg2ImgPipeline for text-guided image-to-image generation, StableDiffusionControlNetPipeline for text-to-image generation using Stable Diffusion with ControlNet guidance, and StableDiffusionControlNetImg2ImgPipeline for image-to-image generation using Stable Diffusion with ControlNet guidance. The final results are generated using StableDiffusionControlNetImg2ImgPipeline (Amazon, Seattle, WA, USA) and the other two for additional experiments.

For automatically extracting the description of a frame, we use CLIP Interrogator [28]. The clip model used was "ViT-L-14/openai" and the blip "blip-large". Huggingface served as the main repository for storing the fine-tuned models. Models with Ghibli and Van

Gogh styles were already available on that platform, and we upload the new model with the Ryo Takemasa style.

6. Metrics

Evaluating a method quantitatively for video cartoonization is a challenging task. A good evaluation should include metrics for style fidelity, content preservation, and temporal coherence. However, there is a lack of metrics to evaluate all these characteristics. Image generative models have been evaluated using Fréchet Inception Distance (FID), a metric that measures the quality and diversity of the generated images. It compares the distribution of generated images with the distribution of real images. This metric has been extended to evaluate diffusion models for videos with Fréchet Video Distance (FVD), which additionally measures the temporal coherence. These metrics have the inconvenience that they do not measure style and content preservation. Furthermore, they require a large sample size, usually greater than 50k [33], making them unfeasible for this work.

The lack of robust metrics has led other works to base the evaluation on user studies [34,35]. For example, Rerender a Video [26], one of the most similar works to our approach, uses a user study with 23 participants to compare the results with other methods. Relying on users has the drawback of leading to subjective human evaluation and might incorporate user biases.

Other approaches [22,23,36,37] incorporate CLIP-based metrics to evaluate some aspects of the models. Following their approach, we use CLIP to assess the temporal coherence and content preservation. The temporal coherence metric consists of computing the cosine similarity between the CLIP embedding of consecutive frames and then computing the average to obtain the final result. The content preservation metric is similar; we use the CLIP embedding of the frames from the source and stylized video and compute the cosine similarity between the embedding of each pair of frames, and then we average the result.

Regarding style fidelity, we encountered challenges in finding feasible metrics. Consequently, we opted to perform a visual analysis and leave this aspect for future work.

7. Results

The method is applied to the 20 videos in the dataset using the three selected styles: Ghibli, Ryo Takemasa, and Van Gogh. The resulting videos are available at https://drive.google.com/file/d/1ErpojLlR_ipJCUxY02rLnpYi1cqSx4ET/view?usp=drive_link (accessed on 26 July 2024). The file contains two folders: one named "1_final_results" with the final results. The second folder, "2_extra", contains two subfolders with additional experiments. One named "naive" employs basic image-to-image translation and basic style propagation. The other is an improvement that uses ControlNet conditions and basic style propagation.

7.1. Style Fidelity and Content Preservation Results

In Figure 3, we can appreciate some frames of two translated videos in each style. As we can see from that figure, the style in the resulting frames is noticeable, and the high perceptual quality is evident. Additionally, the elements are simplified with clearer object boundaries and consistent across the subsequent frames. Another important characteristic is the coherence of the elements across the different frames. In some cases, the shapes are transformed to match the style, as we can see with the trees in the first row (Ryo Takemasa style), but still recognizable for a human. Despite the simplification, subtle elements such as object shadows or light reflection in the water are preserved, as observed in the second row (Ryo Takemasa style).

Figure 3. Qualitative results. In the first column, we show the first frame from four videos. The other four frames were extracted from the corresponding translated videos.

The simplification can be also observed in the videos using the Ghibli style. For example, in the frames of the third row, the shape of the smoke has been transformed into a shape similar to a drawing. The texture of the ground from the frames in the third and fourth rows is constant, only changing between the element boundaries. The results for the Van Gogh style (last two rows) also show good style fidelity and that the content of the video is preserved and recognizable even in cases where the elements are transformed to match the style, as in the forest of the fifth row. It is worth noting that the method produces good results even in cases where certain elements are not present in all the frames. For example, in the last row, the train is initially absent in the first frames but then appears in the following frames, as in the original video.

In addition to the visual results, we measure the content preservation using CLIP-based metrics, following related works [22,23,36]. We use the CLIP embedding of the frames from the source and stylized video and compute the cosine similarity between the embedding of each pair of frames, and then we average the result.

The quantitative results for the content preservation are summarized in Table 1. The results show varying values between the videos. In the Ryo Takamasa style, for example, the video with the highest value has a 0.94 average CLIP cosine similarity between the original frames and the translated frames, while the lowest value is 0.69. Figure 4 shows the frames for these two cases. In the worst case, we can see that the shape of the trees is simplified and the color is changed to match the style. However, the general content is still recognizable. The difference in content preservation is present in the other two styles as well.

Table 1. Content preservation results. Average CLIP cosine similarity between original frames and translated frames. The bold numbers are the highest values, and the underlined numbers are the lowest values for each column. In the last column, we show the total average for each style next to the overall minimum value.

Video Identifier	Ryo Takemasa	Ghibli	Van Gogh
01	0.8586	0.8993	0.9401
02	<u>0.6905</u>	0.8118	0.7492
03	0.8852	**0.9510**	0.9221
04	0.7673	0.8334	0.7602
05	0.7434	0.8233	0.8754
06	0.8839	0.8494	0.8884
07	0.8063	0.8639	0.8090
08	0.7845	0.8815	0.9083
09	0.7806	<u>0.7731</u>	0.7688
10	0.8508	0.8440	0.8667
11	0.8112	0.8262	0.8408
12	0.8467	0.8976	0.7792
13	0.7314	0.8182	0.7511
14	0.9118	0.9200	0.8990
15	0.7733	0.8441	0.8553
16	**0.9367**	0.9288	0.8986
17	0.8027	0.8016	0.8994
18	0.8835	0.9215	<u>0.7072</u>
19	0.8235	0.8568	0.8022
20	0.8573	0.9366	**0.9416**
Avg.	0.8215	0.8641	0.8431

Figure 4. Content preservation. Best and worst cases for Ryo Takemasa style.

7.2. Temporal Coherence Results

Temporal coherence is a fundamental property in videos, and we aim to produce videos that have this property. The temporal coherence metric consists of computing the cosine similarity between the CLIP embedding of consecutive frames and then computing the average to obtain the final result. The results are reported for all the videos in Table 2. The results reveal excellent temporal coherence in the resulting videos. The overall average CLIP cosine similarity for all the styles is 0.99. As a reference, [22] reported 0.976 average temporal coherence using the same metric. The high level of coherence is consistent across every video of the dataset in all the styles, with minimum average values no lower than 0.98.

Table 2. Temporal coherence. Average CLIP cosine similarity between embedding of consecutive frames for 20 videos in the three styles. The underlined numbers are the lowest values for each column.

Video Identifier	Ryo Takemasa	Ghibli	Van Gogh
01	0.9949	0.9963	0.9982
02	0.9928	0.9947	0.9957
03	0.9912	0.9904	0.9885
04	0.9930	0.9947	0.9952
05	0.9919	0.9943	0.9956
06	0.9876	0.9872	0.9868
07	<u>0.9862</u>	<u>0.9841</u>	<u>0.9859</u>
08	0.9922	0.9954	0.9962
09	0.9925	0.9930	0.9979
10	0.9949	0.9918	0.9917
11	0.9968	0.9973	0.9984
12	0.9953	0.9954	0.9957
13	0.9940	0.9942	0.9935
14	0.9923	0.9945	0.9948
15	0.9950	0.9905	0.9968
16	0.9975	0.9972	0.9982
17	0.9979	0.9947	0.9963
18	0.9960	0.9961	0.9956
19	0.9976	0.9971	0.9945
20	0.9929	0.9952	0.9965
Avg.	0.9936	0.9937	0.9946

7.3. Ablation Study

When conducting image-to-image translation with Stable Diffusion, one of the most important parameters is the denoising strength. It controls how much Gaussian noise is added to the reference image before proceeding with the synthesis process. It is important to find the right amount of noise that enables stylization without destroying the image (Appendix A includes examples of image-to-image translation with different denoising strength). The denoising strength can be increased as more conditions are added. However, the fidelity of the style can be affected by the conditions. In Figure 5, we can see the effects and how using a description and ControlNet improves the preservation of the content of the original image (Appendices B–F include examples of image-to-image translation with different conditions and parameterizations).

These conditions also have a great impact on temporal coherence. In Figure 6, we show how these conditions increase the similarity in consecutive frames. For simplicity and better representation, in this graph, we use a basic stylization, propagating the style using only the reference keyframe and without additional guiding channels. In Figure 7, we show the temporal coherence results using a basic stylization versus the advanced stylization, where the style is propagated in sequences based on two keyframes and using additional guiding channels. In the advanced stylization, we can notice a great improvement in the temporal coherence, removing the differences between the frames based on different keyframes, even though there is a small reduction in the similarity between the frames based on the same keyframes.

Generating frames independently has the drawback that the model is not aware of the content of previous and future frames, generating different details in each frame and losing consistency. To address this issue, a more effective approach involves merging all the source keyframes into a single image, translating the combined image, and then splitting it back into individual keyframes. Figure 8 shows the CLIP cosine similarity between consecutive frames using this method compared to the similarity achieved when generating the frames independently.

Figure 5. Ablation study: We present variations in translated images under different conditions with progressively increasing denoising strengths. The initial row illustrates outcomes achieved through image-to-image translation using only the style identifier. The second row shows the results when including a description extracted automatically, while the third row showcases outcomes with the additional inclusion of edge conditions using ControlNet.

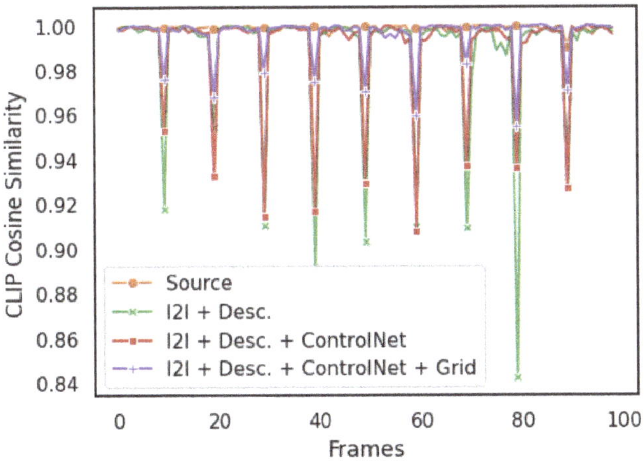

Figure 6. Temporal coherence for a video translated with different conditions. The temporal coherence improves as more conditions are added, especially when translating the frames using grid images.

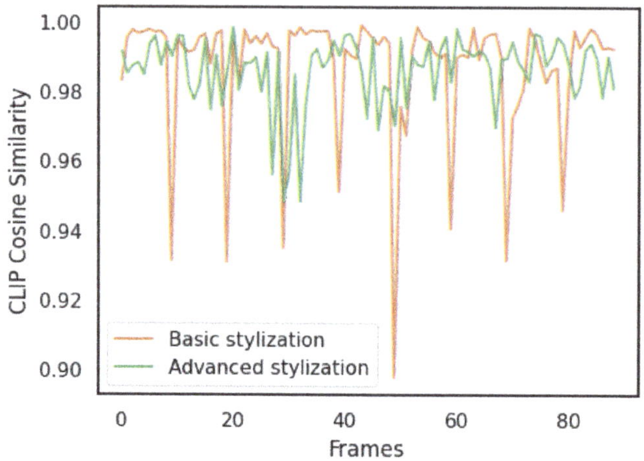

Figure 7. Temporal coherence for basic and advanced stylization. The basic stylization produces clear differences in the stylized frames based on different keyframes, while the advanced stylization improves the temporal coherence.

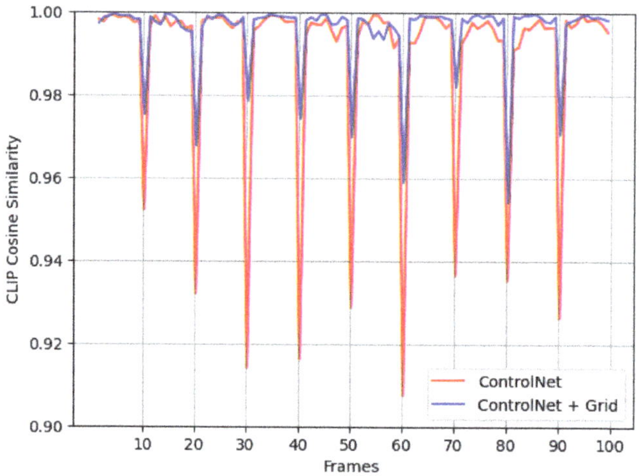

Figure 8. Temporal coherence difference between generating frames independently (red line) vs. generating them using grid images (blue line).

8. Conclusions

This research aimed to develop and apply diffusion models, alongside supplementary tools and techniques, to transform short videos of backgrounds or landscapes into temporally coherent cartoons. This goal was achieved through the creation of an innovative method integrating multiple algorithms, primarily [8,11], enabling the automatic stylization of the short videos or video segments.

A new video dataset has been created and made public for reproducibility and benchmarking purposes. The quantitative and qualitative evaluation demonstrated great capabilities for translating short videos using only the reference video and the specified style, resulting in outstanding temporal coherence. The ablation study underscored the importance of employing multiple conditions and the use of the image grid to enhance the coherence and content preservation. However, it is worth noting that the inclusion of more conditions comes at the expense of reducing the fidelity of the style. It should be noted that all the videos underwent translation using a uniform configuration, implying that superior results could be achieved through customized configurations for individual videos. Furthermore, the introduction of a new dataset and a new fine-tuned model with the Ryo Takemasa style enabled us to evaluate the viability and effectiveness of the proposed method with a custom artistic style that differs from those used during the training of the base generative model. Despite the visual abstraction of the style and the limited dataset of only 100 images, the method demonstrates solid style fidelity, structure preservation, and temporal consistency, highlighting its promising potential for applying custom styles.

Author Contributions: Conceptualization, G.R. and R.T.; methodology, G.R. and R.T.; software, G.R.; resources, G.R. and R.T.; data curation, G.R. and R.T.; writing—original draft preparation, G.R. and R.T.; writing—review and editing, G.R. and R.T.; supervision, R.T. All authors have read and agreed to the published version of the manuscript.

Funding: This work is partially supported by the Spanish Ministry of Science and Innovation under contract PID2019-107255GB, and by the SGR programme 2021-SGR-00478 of the Catalan Government.

Data Availability Statement: The dataset and the code are publicly available at https://github.com/gustavorayo/video-to-cartoon (accessed on 26 July 2024).

Conflicts of Interest: The authors declare no conflicts of interest.

Abbreviations

The following abbreviations are used in this manuscript:

BLIP	Bootstrapping Language–Image Pre-training
CLIP	Contrastive Language–Image Pre-Training
GAN	Generative Adversarial Networks
HED	Holistically Nested Edge Detection
SD	Stable Diffusion
T2I	Text-to-Image

Appendix A. Image-to-Image Translation

Examples of image-to-image translation to three styles with increasing denoising strength. Parameters: prompt= style keywords, denoising strength= from 0.2 to 0.7, inference steps = 25, and guidance scale = 7.

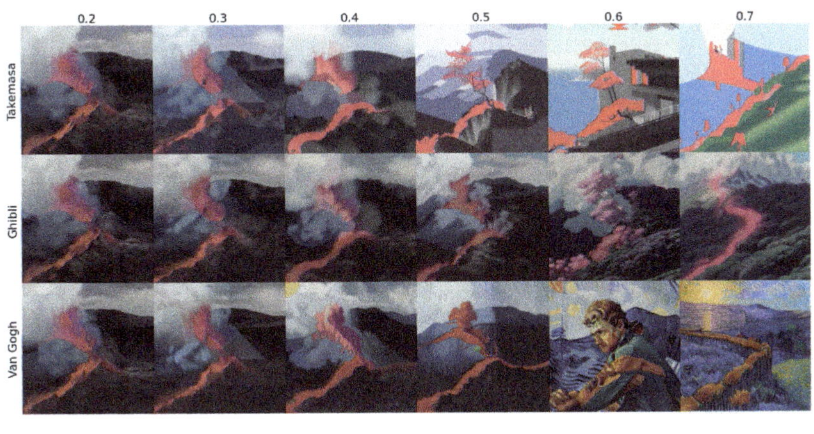

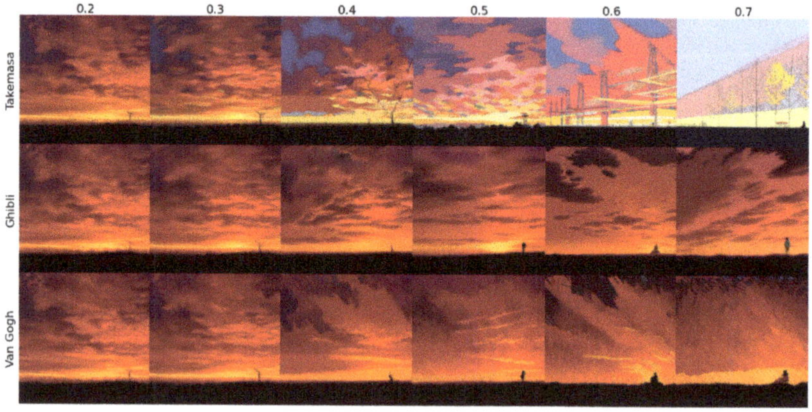

Appendix B. Image-to-Image Translation with Content Description

Examples of image-to-image translation to three styles with increasing denoising strength and a description of the image content. Parameters: prompt = style keywords + description extracted using CLIP Interrogator, denoising strength = from 0.2 to 0.7, inference steps = 25, and guidance scale = 7.

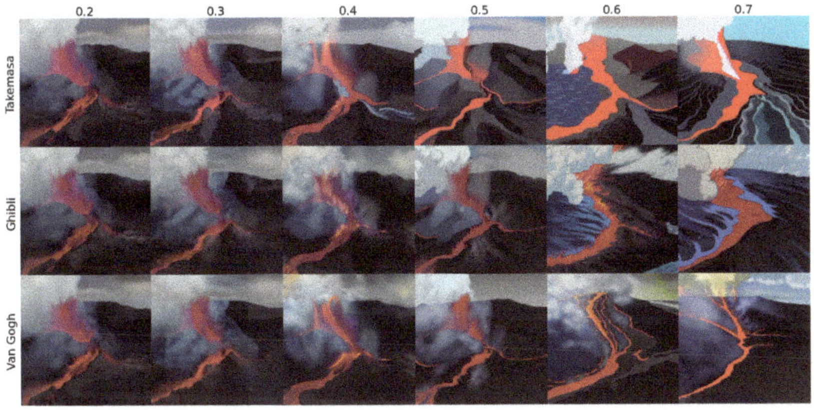
0.2
0.3
0.4
0.5
0.6
0.7
Takemasa
Ghibli
Van Gogh

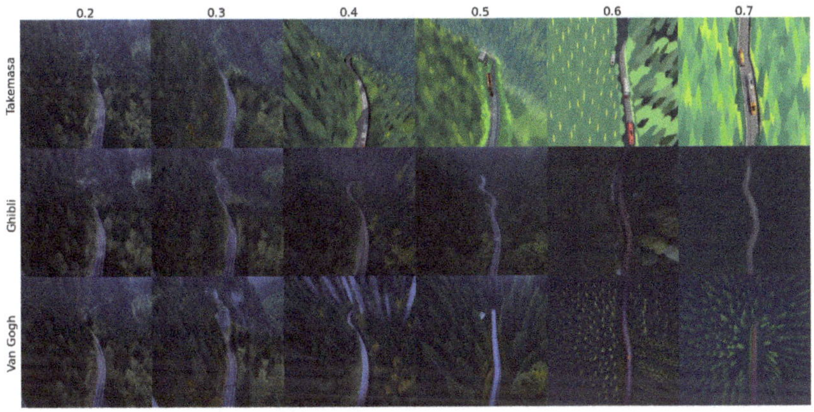
0.2
0.3
0.4
0.5
0.6
0.7
Takemasa
Ghibli
Van Gogh

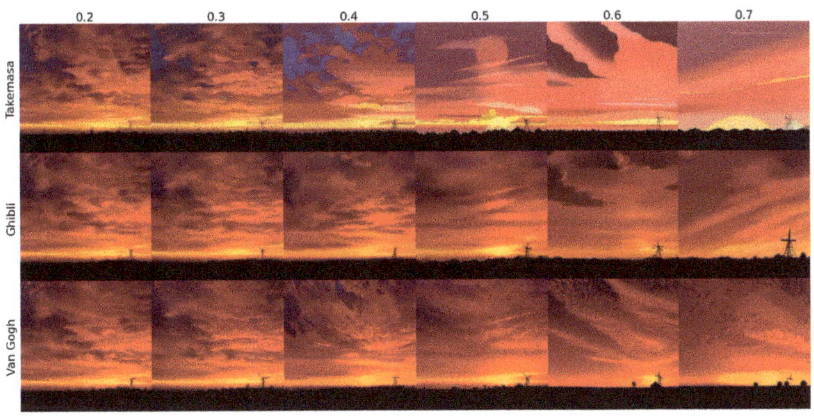
0.2
0.3
0.4
0.5
0.6
0.7
Takemasa
Ghibli
Van Gogh

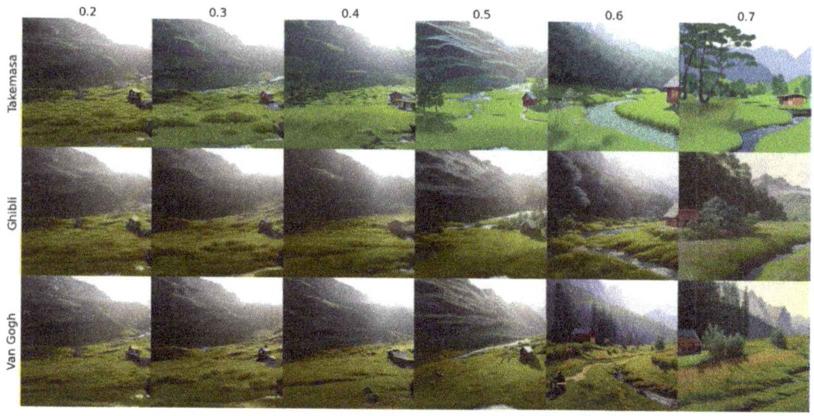

Appendix C. Text-to-Image with ControlNet Conditions

Examples of image generation guided by text and ControlNet conditions using the following parameters: prompt = style keywords or keywords plus description extracted using CLIP Interrogator, inference steps = 25, and guidance scale = 7.5.

Appendix D. Image-to-Image Translation with ControlNet Conditions

Examples of image-to-image translation with various conditioning parameters for three different styles. Parameters: prompt = style keywords or keywords plus description extracted using CLIP Interrogator, denoising strength = from 0.2 to 0.7, ControlNet conditions = HED or Canny edges, inference steps = 25, and guidance scale = 7.5.

Appendix D.1. Ryo Takemasa Style

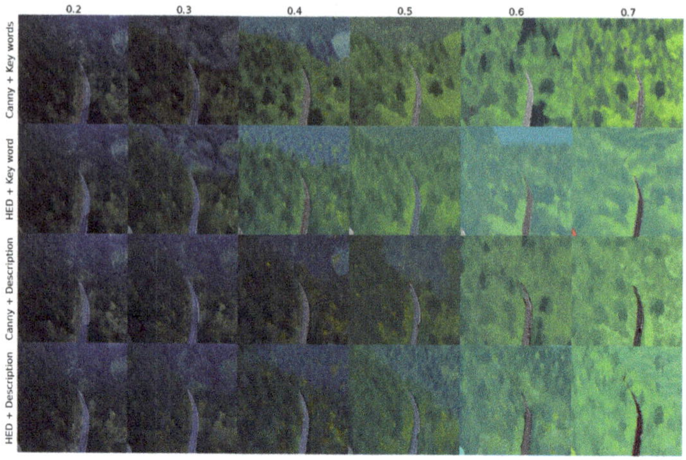

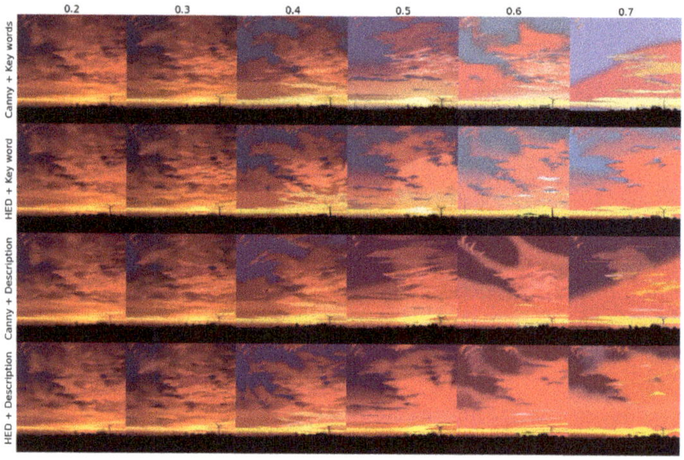

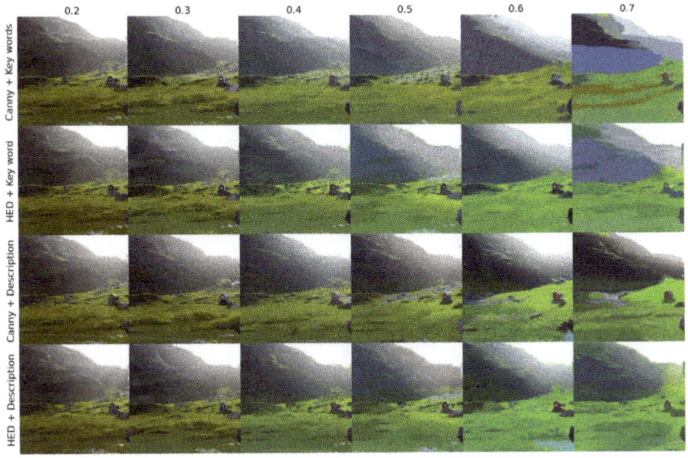

Appendix D.2. Ghibli Style

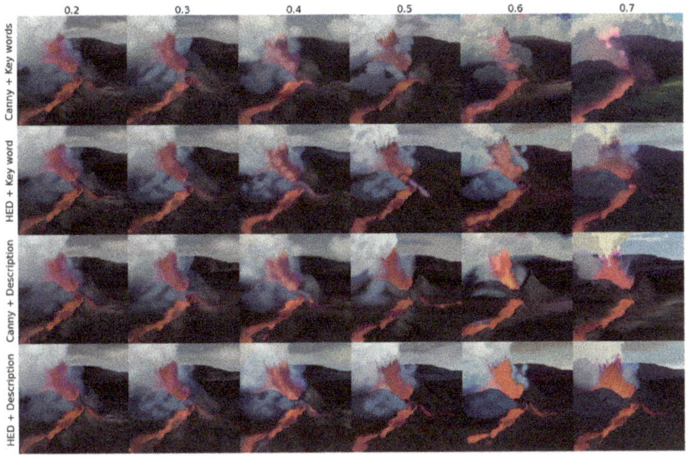

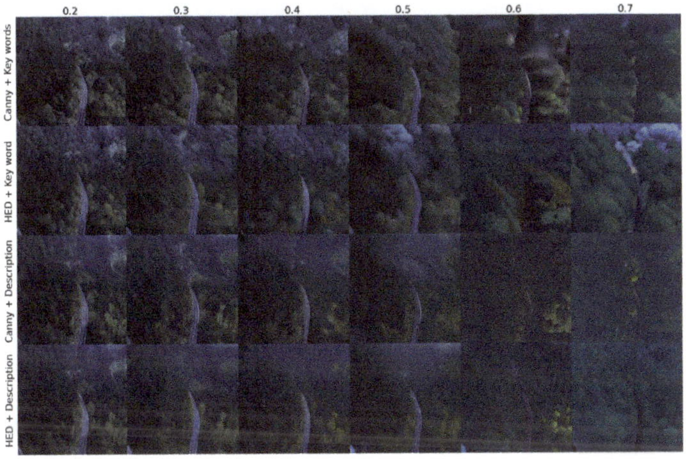

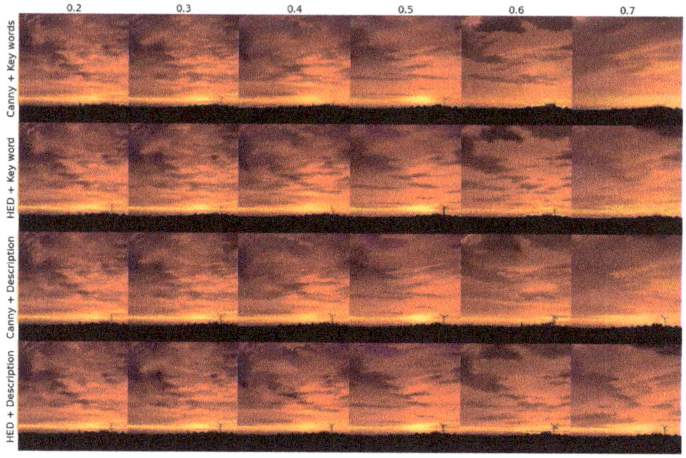
0.2
0.3
0.4
0.5
0.6
0.7
Canny + Key words
HED + Key word
Canny + Description
HED + Description

0.2
0.3
0.4
0.5
0.6
0.7
Canny + Key words
HED + Key word
Canny + Description
HED + Description

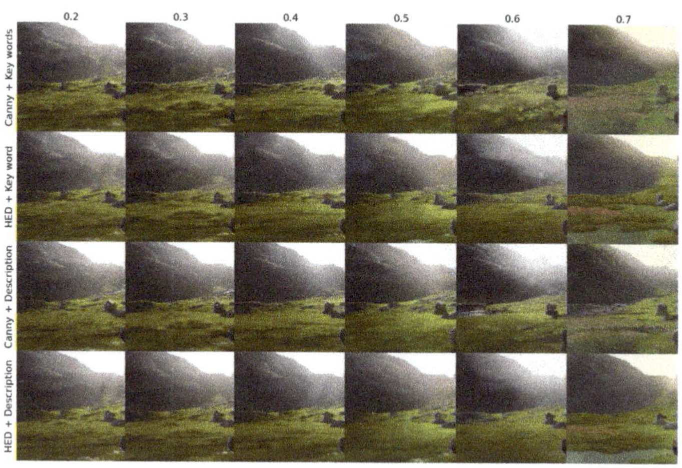
0.2
0.3
0.4
0.5
0.6
0.7
Canny + Key words
HED + Key word
Canny + Description
HED + Description

Appendix D.3. Van Gogh Style

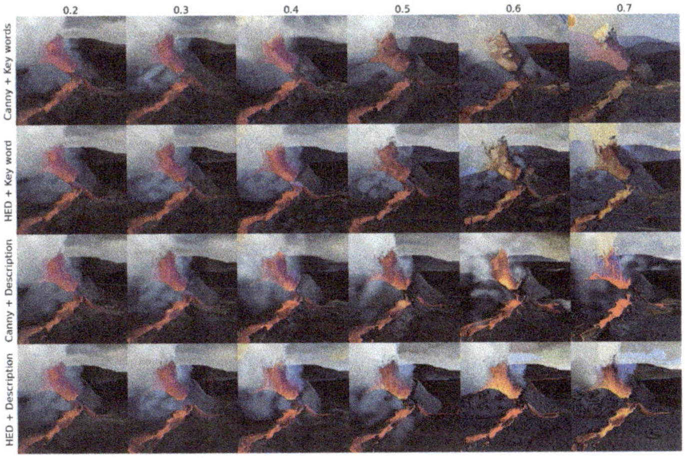

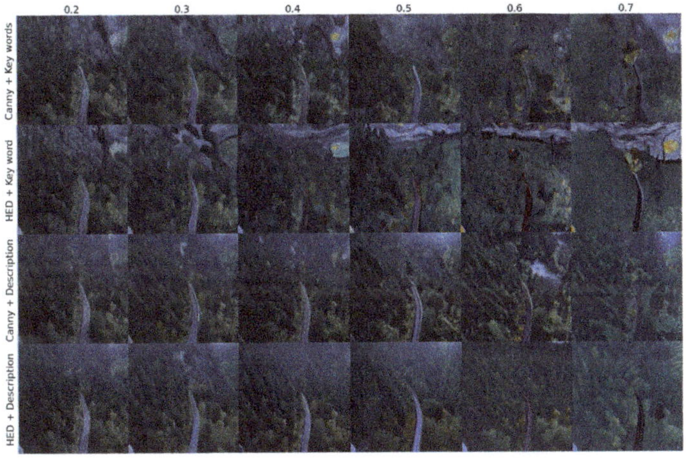

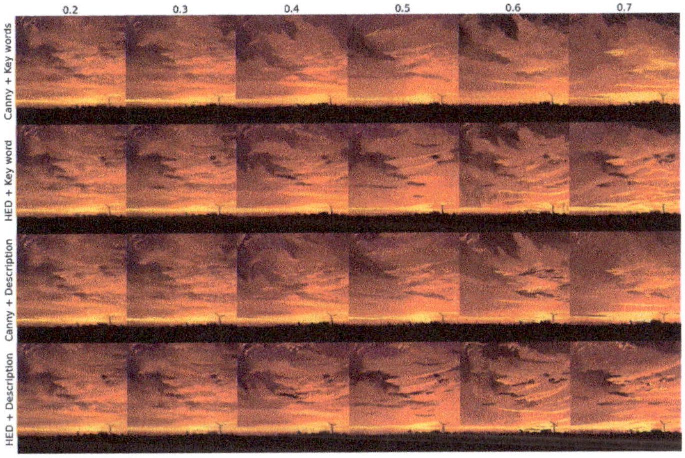

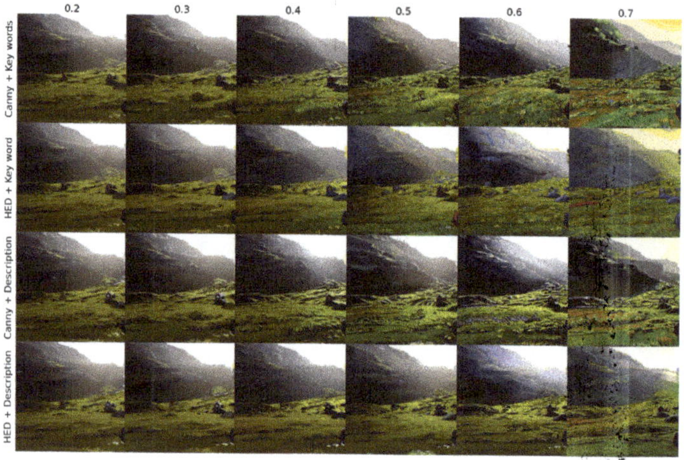

Appendix E. Image-to-Image Translation with Conditions on Weight

Parameters: prompt = style keywords or keywords plus description extracted using CLIP Interrogator, denoising strength = 0.6, ControlNet conditions = HED or Canny edges, inference steps = 25, guidance scale = 7, and condition weight = from 0.3 to 0.9.

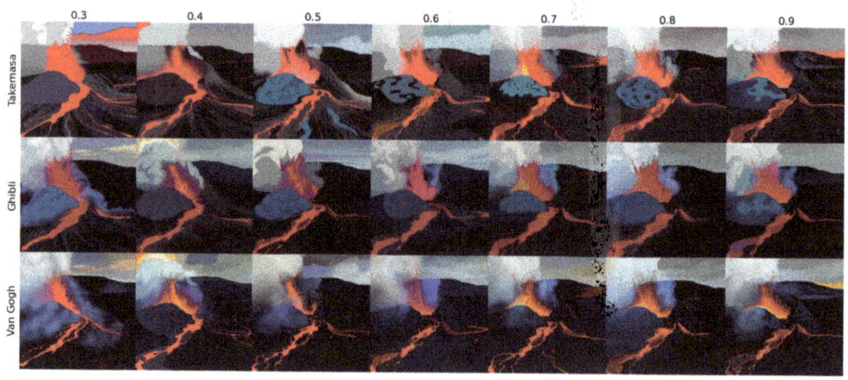

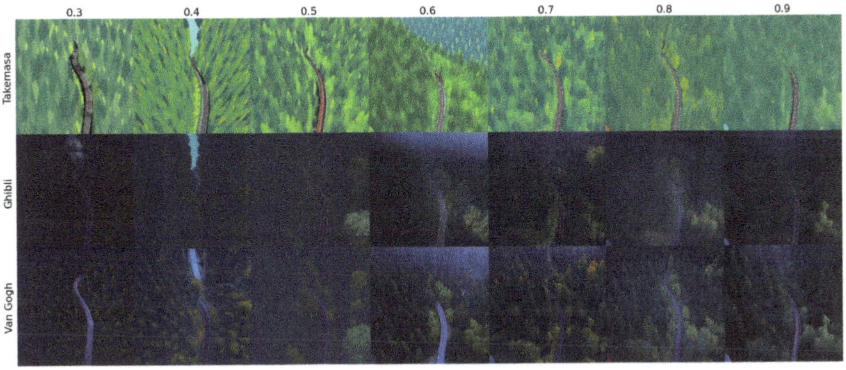

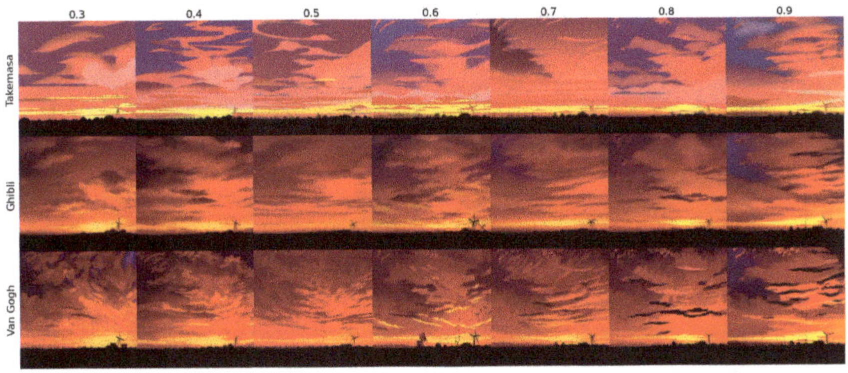

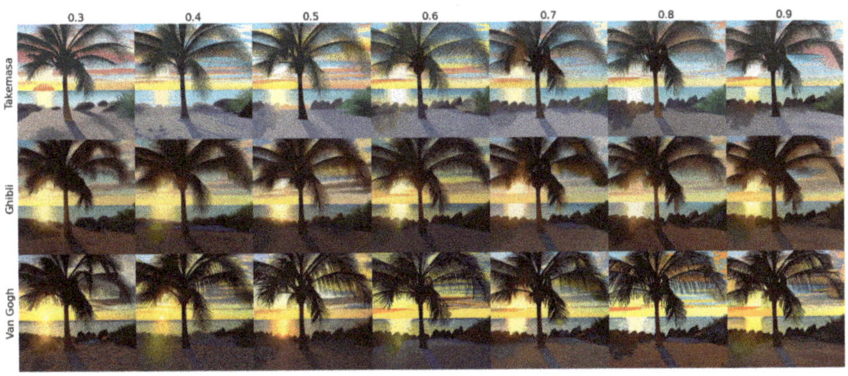

Appendix F. Image-to-Image Translation with Conditions on Limited Steps

Examples of image-to-image translation with ControlNet conditions applied on increasing percentages of denoising steps. Parameters: prompt = style keywords plus description extracted using CLIP Interrogator, denoising strength = 0.6, ControlNet conditions = HED or Canny edges, inference steps = 25, guidance scale = 7, condition weight = 0.7, and condition guidance end = from 0.3 to 0.8.

0.3
0.4
0.5
0.6
0.7
0.8
Takemasa
Ghibli
Van Gogh

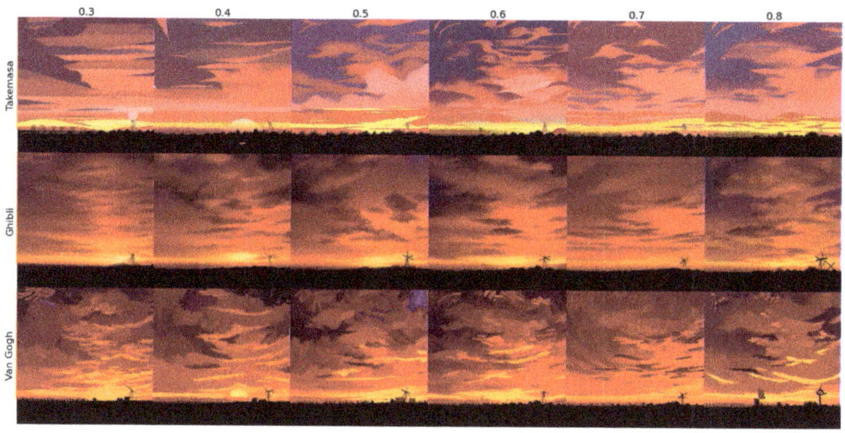
0.3
0.4
0.5
0.6
0.7
0.8
Takemasa
Ghibli
Van Gogh

0.3
0.4
0.5
0.6
0.7
0.8
Takemasa
Ghibli
Van Gogh

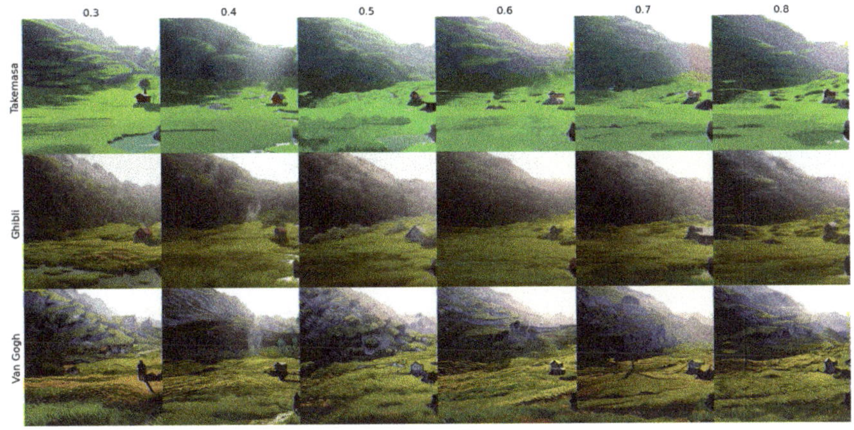

References

1. Karras, T.; Laine, S.; Aila, T. A style-based generator architecture for generative adversarial networks. In Proceedings of the IEEE/CVF Conference on Computer Vision and Pattern Recognition, Long Beach, CA, USA, 15–20 June 2019; pp. 4401–4410.
2. Zhu, J.Y.; Park, T.; Isola, P.; Efros, A.A. Unpaired image-to-image translation using cycle-consistent adversarial networks. In Proceedings of the IEEE International conference on COMPUTER Vision, Venice, Italy, 22–29 October 2017; pp. 2223–2232.
3. Chen, Y.; Lai, Y.K.; Liu, Y.J. Cartoongan: Generative adversarial networks for photo cartoonization. In Proceedings of the IEEE Conference on Computer Vision and Pattern Recognition, Salt Lake City, UT, USA, 18–23 June 2018; pp. 9465–9474.
4. Chen, Y.; Pan, Y.; Yao, T.; Tian, X.; Mei, T. Mocycle-gan: Unpaired video-to-video translation. In Proceedings of the 27th ACM International Conference on Multimedia, Nice, France, 21–25 October 2019; pp. 647–655.
5. Yang, S.; Jiang, L.; Liu, Z.; Loy, C.C. Vtoonify: Controllable high-resolution portrait video style transfer. *ACM Trans. Graph. (TOG)* **2022**, *41*, 203. [CrossRef]
6. Dhariwal, P.; Nichol, A. Diffusion models beat gans on image synthesis. *Adv. Neural Inf. Process. Syst.* **2021**, *34*, 8780–8794.
7. Ho, J.; Jain, A.; Abbeel, P. Denoising diffusion probabilistic models. *Adv. Neural Inf. Process. Syst.* **2020**, *33*, 6840–6851.
8. Rombach, R.; Blattmann, A.; Lorenz, D.; Esser, P.; Ommer, B. High-resolution image synthesis with latent diffusion models. In Proceedings of the IEEE/CVF Conference on Computer Vision and Pattern Recognition, New Orleans, LA, USA, 18–24 June 2022; pp. 10684–10695.
9. Xie, S.; Tu, Z. Holistically-Nested Edge Detection. *Int. J. Comput. Vision* **2017**, *125*, 3–18. [CrossRef]
10. Radford, A.; Kim, J.W.; Hallacy, C.; Ramesh, A.; Goh, G.; Agarwal, S.; Sastry, G.; Askell, A.; Mishkin, P.; Clark, J.; et al. Learning Transferable Visual Models From Natural Language Supervision. In Proceedings of the 38th International Conference on Machine Learning, ICML 2021, Virtual Event, 18–24 July 2021; Volume 139, pp. 8748–8763.
11. Jamriška, O.; Sochorová, Š.; Texler, O.; Lukáč, M.; Fišer, J.; Lu, J.; Shechtman, E.; Sŷkora, D. Stylizing video by example. *ACM Trans. Graph. (TOG)* **2019**, *38*, 107. [CrossRef]
12. Chen, J.; Liu, G.; Chen, X. AnimeGAN: A Novel Lightweight GAN for Photo Animation. In *Artificial Intelligence Algorithms and Applications*; Springer: Singapore, 2020; pp. 242–256. [CrossRef]
13. Liu, Z.; Li, L.; Jiang, H.; Jin, X.; Tu, D.; Wang, S.; Zha, Z. Unsupervised Coherent Video Cartoonization with Perceptual Motion Consistency. *arXiv* **2022**, arXiv:2204.00795. [CrossRef]
14. Saharia, C.; Ho, J.; Chan, W.; Salimans, T.; Fleet, D.J.; Norouzi, M. Image super-resolution via iterative refinement. *arXiv* **2021**, arXiv:2104.07636.
15. Saharia, C.; Chan, W.; Chang, H.; Lee, C.; Ho, J.; Salimans, T.; Fleet, D.; Norouzi, M. Palette: Image-to-Image Diffusion Models. In Proceedings of the ACM SIGGRAPH 2022 Conference Proceedings, New York, NY, USA, 7–11 August 2022; SIGGRAPH'22. [CrossRef]
16. Esser, P.; Kulal, S.; Blattmann, A.; Entezari, R.; Muller, J.; Saini, H.; Levi, Y.; Lorenz, D.; Sauer, A.; Boesel, F.; et al. Scaling Rectified Flow Transformers for High-Resolution Image Synthesis. *arXiv* **2024**, arXiv:2403.03206.
17. Meng, C.; He, Y.; Song, Y.; Song, J.; Wu, J.; Zhu, J.Y.; Ermon, S. SDEdit: Guided Image Synthesis and Editing with Stochastic Differential Equations. *arXiv* **2022**, arXiv:2108.01073.
18. Zhang, L.; Rao, A.; Agrawala, M. Adding conditional control to text-to-image diffusion models. In Proceedings of the IEEE/CVF International Conference on Computer Vision, Paris, France, 2–3 October 2023; pp. 3836–3847.
19. Guo, Y.; Yang, C.; Rao, A.; Wang, Y.; Qiao, Y.; Lin, D.; Dai, B. Animatediff: Animate your personalized text-to-image diffusion models without specific tuning. *arXiv* **2023**, arXiv:2307.04725.
20. Khachatryan, L.; Movsisyan, A.; Tadevosyan, V.; Henschel, R.; Wang, Z.; Navasardyan, S.; Shi, H. Text2Video-Zero: Text-to-Image Diffusion Models are Zero-Shot Video Generators. *arXiv* **2023**, arXiv:2303.13439.

21. Liu, X.; Gong, C.; Liu, Q. Flow Straight and Fast: Learning to Generate and Transfer Data with Rectified Flow. In Proceedings of the The Eleventh International Conference on Learning Representations, ICLR 2023, Kigali, Rwanda, 1–5 May 2023.
22. Ceylan, D.; Huang, C.H.P.; Mitra, N.J. Pix2video: Video editing using image diffusion. *arXiv* **2023**, arXiv:2303.12688.
23. Wu, J.Z.; Ge, Y.; Wang, X.; Lei, S.W.; Gu, Y.; Shi, Y.; Hsu, W.; Shan, Y.; Qie, X.; Shou, M.Z. Tune-a-video: One-shot tuning of image diffusion models for text-to-video generation. In Proceedings of the IEEE/CVF International Conference on Computer Vision, Paris, France, 2–6 October 2023; pp. 7623–7633.
24. Wang, W.; Xie, K.; Liu, Z.; Chen, H.; Cao, Y.; Wang, X.; Shen, C. Zero-shot video editing using off-the-shelf image diffusion models. *arXiv* **2023**, arXiv:2303.17599.
25. Ronneberger, O.; Fischer, P.; Brox, T. Convolutional networks for biomedical image segmentation. In Proceedings of the Medical Image Computing and Computer-Assisted Intervention–MICCAI 2015 Conference Proceedings, Singapore, 18 September 202
26. Yang, S.; Zhou, Y.; Liu, Z.; Loy, C.C. Rerender A Video: Zero-Shot Text-Guided Video-to-Video Translation. *arXiv* **202**, arXiv:2306.07954.
27. Rowles, C. CiaraStrawberry/TemporalKit: An All in One Solution for Adding Temporal Stability to a Stable Diffusion Rende via an Automatic1111 Extension. 2023. Available online: https://github.com/CiaraStrawberry/TemporalKit (accessed on 12 April 2023).
28. Face, H. Clip Interrogator: Prompt Engineering Tool That Combines OpenAI's CLIP and Salesforce's BLIP to Optimize Tex Prompts to Match a Given Image. 2024. Available online: https://github.com/pharmapsychotic/clip-interrogator (accessed on 2 August 2024).
29. Ruiz, N.; Li, Y.; Jampani, V.; Pritch, Y.; Rubinstein, M.; Aberman, K. Dreambooth: Fine tuning text-to-image diffusion models fo subject-driven generation. In Proceedings of the IEEE/CVF Conference on Computer Vision and Pattern Recognition, Vancouve BC, Canada, 17–24 June 2023; pp. 22500–22510.
30. Li, J.; Li, D.; Xiong, C.; Hoi, S. Blip: Bootstrapping language-image pre-training for unified vision-language understanding and generation. In Proceedings of the International Conference on Machine Learning, PMLR, Baltimore, MD, USA, 17–23 July 2022 pp. 12888–12900.
31. von Platen, P.; Patil, S.; Lozhkov, A.; Cuenca, P.; Lambert, N.; Rasul, K.; Davaadorj, M.; Nair, D.; Paul, S.; Berman, W.; et a Diffusers: State-of-the-Art Diffusion Models. 2022. Available online: https://github.com/huggingface/diffusers (accessed on 2 August 2024).
32. Paszke, A.; Gross, S.; Massa, F.; Lerer, A.; Bradbury, J.; Chanan, G.; Killeen, T.; Lin, Z.; Gimelshein, N.; Antiga, L.; et al. PyTorch An Imperative Style, High-Performance Deep Learning Library. In *Advances in Neural Information Processing Systems 32*; Curran Associates, Inc.: New York, NY, USA, 2019; pp. 8024–8035.
33. Borji, A. Pros and cons of GAN evaluation measures: New developments. *Comput. Vis. Image Underst.* **2022**, *215*, 103329 [CrossRef]
34. Yang, S.; Jiang, L.; Liu, Z.; Loy, C.C. Pastiche master: Exemplar-based high-resolution portrait style transfer. In Proceedings of the IEEE/CVF Conference on Computer Vision and Pattern Recognition, New Orleans, LA, USA, 18–24 June 2022; pp. 7693–7702.
35. Zhang, Y.; Huang, N.; Tang, F.; Huang, H.; Ma, C.; Dong, W.; Xu, C. Inversion-based creativity transfer with diffusion models. *arXiv* **2022**, arXiv:2211.13203.
36. Huang, N.; Zhang, Y.; Dong, W. Style-A-Video: Agile Diffusion for Arbitrary Text-based Video Style Transfer. *arXiv* **2023**, arXiv:2305.05464.
37. Qi, C.; Cun, X.; Zhang, Y.; Lei, C.; Wang, X.; Shan, Y.; Chen, Q. FateZero: Fusing Attentions for Zero-shot Text-based Video Editing. *arXiv* **2023**, arXiv:2303.09535.

MDPI AG
Grosspeteranlage 5
4052 Basel
Switzerland
Tel.: +41 61 683 77 34

Electronics Editorial Office
E-mail: electronics@mdpi.com
www.mdpi.com/journal/electronics

www.ingramcontent.com/pod-product-compliance
Lightning Source LLC
Chambersburg PA
CBHW061819210926
51850CB00006B/749